THE PURE WORD

An Unparalleled New Testament
From the Original Greek

of

OUR LORD AND SAVIOUR

JESUS CHRIST

Translation Based on the Knowledge that
Every Word of God is Pure

ONE PATH PUBLISHING

ISBN: 978-0-9995517-0-7

Library of Congress Control Number: 2016931346

Published by
One Path Publishing, LLC
www.OnePathPublishing.com

Printed in China

Preface

The Pure Word

The Pure Word breathes new life and a deeper understanding into your study of God's Word by presenting a New Testament translation that contains the intended depths of scriptural meaning based on the original Greek. Never before has such a pure and genuine English translation been completed and this unprecedented version of the New Testament is an invaluable tool for pastors, theologians, or Bible students that can be studied purely on its own or alongside your favorite version of the Bible.

Why Is The Pure Word Translation Necessary?

Most Biblical scholars agree that all existing English Bible translations contain errors due to various cultural interpretations that resulted from the complexities associated with translating the Greek language into English. As a result, many verses lose the native depth and meaning that the scriptures originally contained which can lead to misunderstanding and division within the Body of Christ.

In fact, many are familiar with church pastors utilizing the practice of hermeneutics (the academic methodology of interpreting text) to decipher and discuss the original Greek meaning rather than relying purely on the available English. For many pastors and Bible students, the use of hermeneutics clarifies crucial points made throughout the New Testament; however, this practice of cross-referencing the original Greek is complex and time-consuming. For each word in the New Testament to be accurately retranslated using this process, it would require a lifetime to complete. As a result, a New Testament translation using this practice of monadic hermeneutics (an accurate single definitive meaning) has never been genuinely completed, until now. *The Pure Word* is the world's first English translation that presents more of the original depth, meaning, and understanding that one would receive if read from the native language during the first century.

The Pure Word Translation Process

The process started with the original inerrant and infallible Greek Scriptures as determined by the King James scholars in 1611. They gathered all 5,309 surviving manuscripts and separated the 2% counterfeit texts. Approximately 98% of the manuscripts were exact copies of each other and only those were used by the scholars in the authorized translation. After the new translation was received by King James, the resulting Greek text became known collectively as the *Textus Receptus* or the Received Text.

We also know that all scripture is inspired by God (2 Tim 3:16), and every Word of God is pure (Psalms 12:6-7; Prov. 30:5). Since each word is pure (without mixture), it stands to reason that God is not ambiguous or indecisive regarding the meaning of His message. As a result, each word has a single specific meaning that is not open to personal interpretation nor shared by another word. Translating the Scriptures in this manner generates a pure monadic translation that presents an unambiguous and clear meaning of the original

Greek that prevents personal interjection, opinion or cultural influence.

The Pure Word translation process took every occurrence of each of the 5,624 Greek root words making up the Gospels and determined the single pure meaning that was originally defined for those words; creating a new concordance with unprecedented accuracy. The "context" of each root word was determined by the entire New Testament as the single meaning of each word had to fit precisely into each and every instance in which that word was used. This step took over twenty years to complete.

The next step in the process was to apply the parsings of the original Greek words one at a time to their direct English counterpart to show the precise meaning intended for each individual word. To parse a word means to analyze it into component morphemes. Morphemes are the smallest units in a language that link a form with a meaning or function. Parsing is generally done on complex languages such as Greek and Latin. Parsing is a complex process, but it breaks down to understanding the simple function and application of individual words which include the tense, aspect, voice, number, mood, cases, gender, person, and periphrastic forms of the words.

Of the 140,745 Greek words comprising the 7,956 New Testament verses, there were over 115,000 words whose parsings had to be applied to their English counterpart. Some Greek word forms do not have parsings (such as conjunctions). As the parsing of each word is applied you can see how Greek elegantly links together the words in a phrase to form a single thought without any inconsistencies. The entire process took over twenty-two years.

Changes in Word Definitions Over Time Have Also Been Corrected

Many of our English words no longer have the same meaning that they had when the KJV scholars used them over 400 years ago. These English words have been updated to match the originally intended meaning of the Greek words. One of the many changes is in the definition of the Greek word πιστευω (strong #4100) which the KJV scholars correctly stated as "Believe". In the 16th century, that word had a completely different meaning than it does today. Back then it meant to "Commit to" or "dedicate your life to" or even "give your life for". It was an action verb in which you had to back up your "belief" with your life. Therefore, when the King James scholars used the word "believeth" in John 3:16:

> "For God so loved the world, that he gave his only begotten Son, that whosoever <u>believeth</u> in him should not perish, but have everlasting life." (KJV)

They understood that they were saying that an individual must "commit their very lives to Christ". *The Pure Word* shows the original meaning of πιστευω by using today's understood concept of "Committing":

> "Because, God has Loved in such a manner the satan's world, so that He Gave His Son, the Only Begotten Risen Christ, in order that whoever is Continuously by his choice <u>Committing</u> for the Result and Purpose of Him, should not perish, but definitely should, by his choice, be Continuously Having Eternal Life." (TPW)

Verse Formatting and use of Capitalization

The translation process produces text that does not always follow grammatically correct English rules as matching English words sometimes don't exist which match the complex Greek parsing; however, to retain the purest meaning possible, the raw translation in English is shown. If we were to go further to massage the English to make it completely conform to today's grammatical rules, we could potentially alter the original intended meaning.

Nouns, pronouns, and verbs which pertain to God's Attributes and Characteristics, or God's Works, Works of the Holy Spirit in us, or Works of Angels (as opposed to works of man) have also been capitalized to further clarify the original Greek meaning to the reader. Using Matthew 10:39 as an example:

> "He that found his soul shall lose it, and he that loses his Living-Soul for the cause of Me shall Find It." (TPW)

Notice the clear distinction between the uncapitalized soul (living for oneself) and the capitalized Living-Soul (serving Christ). The translation brings out more depth of understanding from the original Greek within this verse and all verses.

Understand the Full Meaning of the Gospels as Written over 2,000 Years Ago

The Pure Word is a non-denominational New Testament translation that recognizes the common pitfalls of English, prior translation methods, language, and word definition changes over time, and the mistakes made by previous translators. Nearly every English translation available today strips out much of the original meaning to condense and simplify the text. This loss of meaning that we find in most English translations is often the root of misunderstood doctrines; creating division amongst Christians.

Every word of the original Greek has been retranslated into English through this monadic process while also incorporating the original Greek parsings to their English counterpart presents an unambiguous and clear meaning of the original Greek. *The Pure Word*, by the very nature of the translation process, provides God's clear message throughout all the New Testament scriptures without inconsistency.

By reimplementing the full and original Greek meaning of each word with their parsing as it was understood during the first century, *The Pure Word* is recognized as the most accurate Greek to English translation of the New Testament in the world and is a Biblical resource that every Christian should have.

> "You must be Diligent by your choice, to Stand before God yourself Approved, a worker not ashamed, Straight Cutting the Word of Truth"
> 2 Tim 2:15, TPW

The New Testament

The New Testament

The Gospel According to
Matthew

Genealogy of Jesus through Joseph's line

1 Book of (Sinless) Flesh Nature of Jesus Christ (John 1:41), son of David, son of Abraham. (John 1:13)

2 Abraham has born Isaac; and then Isaac has born Jacob; and then Jacob has born Judas and his brothers.

3 And then Judas has born Phares and Zara out from within Thamar; and then Phares has born Esrom; and then Esrom has born Aram;

4 And then Aram has born Aminadab; and then Aminadab has born Naasson; and then Naason has born Salmon;

5 And then Salmon has born Boaz out from within the Rachab; and then Boaz has born Obed out from within Ruth; and then Obed has born Jessie;

6 And then Jessie has born David his king: and then king David has born Solomon out from within her of Urias;

7 And then Solomon has born Roboam; and then Roboam has born Abia; and then Abia has born Asa;

8 And then Asa has born Josaphat; and then Josaphat has born Joram; and then Joram has born Ozias;

9 And then Ozias has born Joatham; and then Joatham has born Achaz; and then Achaz has born Ezekias;

10 And then Ezekias has born Manasses; and then Manasses has born Amon; and then Amon has born Josias;

11 And then Josias has born Jechonias and his brothers in the time of the carrying away to Babylon;

12 And then after the carrying away to Babylon, Jechonias has born Salathiel; and Salathiel has born Zorobabel;

13 And then Zorobabel has born Abiud; and then Abiud has born Eliakim; and then Eliakim has born Azor;

14 And then Azor has born Sadok; and then Sadok has born Achim; and then Achim has born Eliud;

15 And then Eliud has born Eleazar; and then Eleazar has born Matthan; and then Matthan has born Jacob;

16 And then Jacob has born Joseph, husband of Mary, of whom acted upon by Another from within has born Jesus, Who is being Called Christ.

17 Therefore, all the generations from Abraham until after David fourteen generations, and from David until after the carrying away to Babylon fourteen generations; and from the carrying away to Babylon until after Christ fourteen generations.

Conception of Jesus by Holy Spirit

18 And then a Supernatural Birth of Jesus Christ, for Mary His mother was made espoused to Joseph, before they came together, she was found with Child having in womb, out From The Holy Spirit.

19 And then Joseph, her husband, being Righteous and was not willing to put her to public shame, intended to secretly dismiss her away,

20 And while he has been made pondering these things. Behold an Angel of the Lord in a dream Appeared to him Saying, Joseph, son of David fear not to Take Along Mary your wife, because within her is Made Born by the Holy Spirit.

21 And then she shall give Birth to a Son and shall Call His Name Jesus, because He shall Save His Own People from their sin natures and sins.

22 And then all of this was Now Becoming, that it should be Made Fulfilled that Spirit Spoken by the Lord, through His Prophet Saying:

23 Behold, the virgin shall have in womb

with Child, and she shall Give Birth to a Son and shall Call His Name Emmanuel, which is being Interpreted, God with us. (Isa 7:14)

24 And then Joseph made aroused from natural sleep he did as the Angel of the Lord before Commanded to him, and took along his wife.

25 And he definitely knew her not until after when she gave birth to her Firstborn Son, and called His Name Jesus.

Wise men come from the east

2 And then Jesus was Born in Bethlehem of Judaea in days of Herod the king. Behold mystical wise men from the east came up into Jerusalem.

2 Saying, Wherein is the King of the Jews given birth, because we have Spiritually Discerned His Star in the east, and we have come to worship Him?

3 And when Herod the king heard, he was made troubled and all Jerusalem with him.

4 And he gathered together all the chief priests and scribes of the people. He was inquiring from them wherein the Christ is being Born.

5 And then they spoke to him, In Bethlehem of Judea because so it is now written through the Prophet,

6 And you Bethlehem, in the area of Judah, you are absolutely not the least in the governors of Judah, because out from you shall come out Who is Esteemed. He shall Shepherd My people, Israel. (Micah 5:2)

7 Then Herod secretly called the mystical wise men, inquired from them exactly the time the Star appeared.

8 He sent them to Bethlehem and spoke, Going you must inquire exactly in regard to the Little Child, and then as soon as you should have found, you must tell me so that I also should be coming to worship Him.

9 And then having heard the king they went, and Behold, that Star which they had discerned in the east was going before them, until after it came and stood over where the Little Child was.

10 And when they Spiritually Discerned the Star, they rejoiced with exceedingly great Joy.

11 And when they came into the house, they found the Little Child with Mary His mother, and having fallen down they Worshiped Him, and they opened their treasures having offered gifts to Him: gold, and frankincense, and myrrh.

12 And made warned as according to a dream not to return again to Herod, they withdrew through another of same kind way of travel into their land.

Angel Warns Joseph in a Dream

13 And when they withdrew, Behold an Angel of (the) Lord is Appearing in a dream Saying to Joseph, Be made raising up, must take along the Little Child and His mother and flee into Egypt and you must be there until after whenever I speak to you, because Herod is expecting to be seeking the Little Child to destroy Him.

14 And then he rose up, took along the Little Child and His mother at night and withdrew into Egypt.

15 And He was there until after the demise of Herod, in order that should be made Fulfilled which was Spirit Spoken by the Lord through the Prophet Saying, Out from within Egypt I have called My Son. (Hosea 11:1)

16 Then Herod discerned that he was made mocked by the mystical wise men, and he was made exceeding extremely anger, he sent out and intentionally killed all male children in Bethlehem, and in all the districts thereof, from two years old and down below, according to this time he had exactly inquired from the mystical wise men.

17 Then was Fulfilled that made Spirit Speaking by Jeremiah the Prophet Saying,

18 A voice in Rama was heard wailing, and weeping, and many sorrowing. Rachel

is weeping for her children and would definitely not be encouraged for they were not. (Jer 31:15)

Angel Tells Joseph to Return to Israel

19 And when Herod deceased. Behold, an Angel of the Lord Appeared in a dream to Joseph in Egypt,

20 Saying, Be made raised up. You must take along the Little Child and His mother and go into the area of Israel, because they who are seeking the Living-Soul of the Little Child are now rotting dead bodies.

21 And then he rose up, took along the Little Child and His mother, and came into the area of Israel.

22 And then when he heard that Archelaus was ruling in Judaea in place of Herod his father, he was made afraid to go there, and being made warned in a dream, he withdrew into parts of Galilee.

23 He came and dwelt by his choice in a city called Nazareth, so that Spirit Spoken through the Prophets should be made Fulfilled, for He shall be made called a Nazarene.

John the Baptist

3 And then in those days, John the Baptist is coming up preaching in the desolate wilderness of Judaea.

2 And saying, You must be Repenting by your choice because the Kingdom Rule of Heaven is now approaching near.

3 Because this is he, Spirit Spoken by His Prophet, Esaias, a Voice Loudly Pleading in the desolate wilderness saying, You must prepare The Way of the Lord, make His Paths Straight. (Isa 40:3)

4 And John, himself was having his clothing from camel hair, and a leather girdle about his waist, and his nourishment was locusts and wild honey.

5 Then Jerusalem and all Judaea and all surrounding region of the Jordan went out to him.

6 And were being baptized in the Jordan by him, acknowledging their sin natures and sins.

7 And then he Spiritually Discerned many Pharisees and Sadducees coming with the intent of immersion of themselves. He spoke to them, Oh product of vipers, who has forewarned you, to flee away from the expecting Wrath for Justice?

8 Then you must Finalize Fruits Worthy of Repentance,

9 And think not to be saying inside yourselves, We are having father Abraham, yet I say to you in that God is able out from these stones to raise up children to Abraham.

10 And already also the ax is being laid to the root of all trees, therefore a tree not producing God-Work Fruit is being made cut down and cast into the fire.

11 I am certainly immersing you in water into Repentance. And then after me is coming a Stronger than I am, of whom I am definitely not sufficient to bear His shoes. He shall Immerse you in the Holy Spirit and with fire.

12 Whose fan in His Hand, and He shall thoroughly cleanse His floor, and shall Gather Together His Wheat into the barn, and then shall fully burn the chaff with unquenchable fire.

Jesus Baptized

13 Then Jesus is Coming Up away from Galilee to the Jordon to John, to be immersed by him.

14 Then John restrained Him, saying, I have need to be Immersed by You, and You Come to me?

15 Jesus Answered and Spoke to him, For now you must be concerned because in such a manner it is appropriate for us to Fulfill all Righteousness. Then he gave being concerned to Him.

16 And he immersed Jesus. He Ascended immediately from the water, and Behold the Heavenlies Opened to Him, and He Spiritually Discerned the Spirit of God

Came Down like as a dove, and He Came Upon Him,

17 And Behold, a Voice out from within Heaven Says, This is My Son the Beloved, in Whom I am Pleased. (Isa. 42:1; Ps 2:7)

Jesus Tempted

4 Then Jesus was made Led up into the desolate wilderness by the Spirit to be tempted by the devil.

2 And He fasted forty days and forty nights, afterward He hungered.

3 The tempter came near to Him and spoke, If You are the Son of God You must speak that these stones should become bread.

4 And then He Answered, He Spoke, It is now made Written, man shall definitely not Live by bread alone, but definitely by every Specific Word Going Out through the Mouth of God. (Deut 8:3)

5 Then the devil took along Him into the Holy City, and stood Him upon the pinnacle of the Temple area.

6 And he says to Him, If You are the Son of God You must cast Yourself down below, because it is written that His Angels shall be God Commanded concerning You, and in the place of hands they shall take You up, for fear that You might stumble Your Foot against a stone. (Ps 91:11-12)

7 Jesus again Stated to him, It is now made Written, you shall definitely not spiritually test the Lord your God. (Deut 6:16)

8 Again the devil took along Him into an extremely high mountain, showed Him all the kingdoms of the satan's world and their glory.

9 And says to Him, I will give all these things to You, if You should fall down to worship me. (Deut 6:13)

10 Then Jesus Says to him, You must go away, Oh satan. Because it is now made Written, you shall Worship the Lord your God, and shall be Devoted to Him alone.

11 Then the devil dismissed Him, and Behold, Angels came near and were Serving to Him.

John the Baptist imprisoned

12 And when Jesus Heard that John was delivered up, He withdrew into Galilee.

13 He left Nazareth and came to dwell in Capernaum on the sea coast, among districts of Zabulon and Nephthalim,

14 That the Spirit Spoken through Esaias the Prophet should be made Fulfilled, Saying,

15 The area of Zabulon and the area of Nephthalim, the way of the sea, the other side of the Jordon, Galilee of the Gentiles.

16 The people sitting in darkness discern a Great Light, and to them sitting in the land and shadow of death, Light has Risen to them. (Isa 9:1-2)

Jesus Starts Preaching; Calls Four Disciples

17 From then Jesus began Preaching and Saying, You must Repent by your choice, because the Kingdom Rule of the Heavenlies is now approaching near.

18 And when Jesus was walking near the Sea of Galilee, He Spiritually Discerned two brothers: Simon called Peter, and Andrew his brother casting a throw net into the sea because they were fishermen.

19 And He Called to them. You must Come now After Me, and I Will make you fishermen of men.

20 Then immediately they dismissed the nets and followed Him.

21 And having gone farther ahead from that place, He Spiritually Discerned others of same kind, two brothers: James of Zebedee and John his brother in a ship with Zebedee their father mending their nets, and He Called them.

22 And then they immediately followed Him, parted from the ship and their father.

Preaching and Healing Spreads

23 And Jesus was going about to all of Galilee Teaching in their synagogues, and Preaching the Gospel of the Kingdom Rule, and Healing all sickness and all disease among the people.

24 And the fame of Him went out to all

of Syria, and they offered to Him everyone having evil work afflicted, being made constrained by many diverse sicknesses and torturing torments, and those being demonized, and those being insane, and those paralytic, and He Healed them.

25 And large multitudes of people followed with Him from Galilee, and Decapolis, and Jerusalem, and Judaea, and the other side of the Jordon.

Sermon on the Mount

5 And when He Spiritually Discerned this multitude of people. He Ascended into the mountain and Himself Sat Down. His disciples came near to Him.

2 And He Opened His Mouth Teaching them, Saying,

3 Spiritually Blessed, the poor in Spirit for theirs is the Kingdom Rule of the Heavenlies.

4 Spiritually Blessed, they that are mourning for they shall certainly be made comforted.

5 Spiritually Blessed, the Meek for they shall certainly Inherit the earth.

6 Spiritually Blessed, they that are hungering and thirsting for Righteousness for they shall be made filled.

7 Spiritually Blessed, the Merciful for they themselves shall receive Mercy.

8 Spiritually Blessed, the Purified in heart for they shall Spiritually See God.

9 Spiritually Blessed, the Peacemakers for they shall be called the Sons of God.

10 Spiritually Blessed, those that are made persecuted for the cause of Righteousness, for theirs is the Kingdom Rule of the Heavenlies.

11 Spiritually Blessed, you are when they might scold to shame and might persecute you, and might speak all evil words against you, lying against My Cause.

12 You must rejoice and you must be exceedingly glad for your large Reward in the Heavenlies, because in such a manner they persecuted the Prophets before you.

13 You yourselves are the Salt Flavoring of the earth. And then if the Salt Flavoring might have been made foolish, with what shall it be actually salted? Further, it is capable for nothing, except it be cast outside and trampled down by men.

14 Yourselves are the Light of the satan's world. A city set upon a mountain definitely cannot be hid.

15 Neither be burning a candle and positioning it under a bushel, but definitely upon the candlestick, and brightly shining to all in the house.

16 So you must brightly shine your Light in such a manner before men so that they Discern your God-Works, Works by God, and they might Attribute Glory (Spiritual Perfection) to your Father in the Heavenlies.

Not Come to Destroy, but to Fulfill

17 For you might not suppose that I Come to tear down either the Law or the Prophets. I Come definitely not to tear down but definitely to Fulfill.

18 Because Truly, I am saying to you. Until after whenever Heaven and earth should pass away, that one jot or one tittle should have never ever passed away from the Law, until after all things whatever should come to pass.

19 Whoever therefore, should remove one of these least Commandments and shall teach so, this man shall be called the least in the Kingdom Rule of the Heavenlies, but whoever should do and teach them shall be called great in the Kingdom Rule of the Heavenlies.

20 For I am Saying to you, that except your Righteousness should much more abound in amount than of the scribes and the Pharisees, you should never ever enter into the Kingdom Rule of the Heavenlies.

21 For having heard the Spirit Spoken made to them from old times, that you definitely shall not murder, and whoever might murder shall be guilty in the Final Judgment.

22 But I say to you that all being angry with his brother, without reason, shall be found guilty in the Final Judgment. And then whoever might speak to his brother, Raca, shall be found guilty with the council. But whoever speaks fool, shall be found guilty of hell fire.

23 Therefore, whenever you are offering your gift upon the alter, so there also yourself might remember that your brother is having something against you;

24 You must dismiss your gift there before the alter, and first of all you must be going away, you must be made reconciled with your brother, and then must come offering your gift.

25 You must be bargaining with your adversary quickly while you in the way with him, for fear that your adversary might deliver you up to the judge, and the judge delivers you up to the officer, and you shall be cast into prison.

26 Truly, I am saying to you, you should never ever come out from that place, until after you should repay the last farthing. (Roman Kodrantes)

Jesus Addresses issue of adultery

27 You have heard that made Spirit Spoken to them of old times, You shall definitely not commit adultery. (Ex 20:14; Deut 5:18)

28 And then, I am saying to you, for all whoever that sees a woman to evilly desire for himself, already has committed adultery himself inside his heart.

29 But if your right eye is offending you, you must set it free, and you must cast from you, because it is expedient to you that one of your members should be destroyed, but that not your whole body be made cast into hell.

30 And if your right hand offends, you must cut it off and you must cast it from you, because it is necessary to you that one member of you might be destroyed, and not your whole body should be made cast into hell.

Jesus Addresses issue of divorce

31 And then the Spirit Spoke, For whoever might dismiss away his wife, he must give her a writing of divorcement. (Deut 24:1)

32 But I am Saying to you that whoever might divorce his wife without a communication of fornication is causing her to commit adultery, and whoever might marry her being now made divorced, is committing adultery.

Jesus Addresses issue of oaths

33 Again, you have heard Spirit Speaking by them in old times, that you definitely shall not swear under oath, but you shall yield your oaths to the Lord. (Lev 19:12; Num 30:2)

34 But I am Saying to you, absolutely swear not, neither by Heaven, for that is the Throne of God,

35 Neither by the earth for that is a Footstool for His Feet, nor by Jerusalem, that is the City of the Great King. (Isa 66:1; Ps 48:2)

36 Neither should you swear in your head, for definitely you are not able to make one hair white or black.

37 But your Spiritual Communication must be, emphatically Yes, Yes; definitely No, No. And then more in excess of these, must be out from evil.

Resist not evil and Love your enemies

38 For you have heard it made Spirit Spoken, An eye for an eye and a tooth for a tooth. (Ex 21:24; Lev 24:20; Deut 19:21)

39 But I am Saying to you, not to stand against evil, but definitely whoever will actually slap you with the palm of his hand to your right cheek, you must also turn to him the other of the same kind.

40 And also, he that is willing to have you judged and to take your coat, you must dismiss also your clothes to him.

41 And whoever will compel you one mile, you must move with him two.

42 You must give to him asking you, and

him who willing to borrow from you, you should not turn away.

43 You have heard that, It is Spirit Spoken to be Loving your neighbor, and to be hating your enemy.

44 But I am Saying to you, you must be Continuously Loving your enemies, you must be Blessing them who are cursing you, you must be doing God-Working to them who are hating you, and you must be Continuously Praying in behalf of those despitefully insulting you, and persecuting you.

45 So that you should become Sons of your Father in the Heavenlies, for His sun rises upon the evils and the God-Goods, and rains upon the Righteous and also unrighteous.

46 Because whenever you might love those who are loving you, what reward are you having? So do definitely not the tax collectors the same thing?

47 And whenever you should greet your brothers only, what are you doing more in excess? Definitely, do not the tax collectors in such a manner also?

48 Therefore, yourselves shall be Perfect as your Father, Who in the Heavenlies, is Perfect.

Offerings to God Must be Private

6 You must take heed, you Do not your alms before men to be seen by them, so after that you are definitely not having a Reward with your Father in the Heavenlies.

2 Therefore when you might give alms, you should not sound before you as the hypocrite actors do in the synagogues and in the street lanes, so that they might have been made glorified by men. Truly, I am saying to you, they are having their reward.

3 But when you are giving alms, you must not know what your left hand is doing from your right hand.

4 So that your alms should be in secret and your Father Spiritually Sees in secret. He Himself shall Repay you in that Openly Manifest.

When we Pray (The Lord's Prayer)

5 And when to be Praying you shall definitely not as the hypocrite actors be affectionately loving in synagogues, and might be Praying standing in the street corners, so that whenever they might appear to men. Truly, I am saying to you, that they are having their reward.

6 But when you must Pray, you must enter into your private room and shut your door, you should be Praying to your Father in secret, and your Father, Who is Spiritually Seeing in secret, shall pay you by Openly Manifest.

7 And when Praying you should not vainly repeat, as the heathen, because they think that in their much speaking they shall be made spiritually heard.

8 Therefore, you should not be likened to them, because your Father is Spiritually Discerning that you have need before you ask Him.

9 Yourselves must be Praying, therefore, in such a manner, Our Father, Who is in Heaven, You must Make Holy Your Name.

10 You must make Your Kingdom Rule come. You must make Your Will become as in Heaven, also upon earth.

11 You must give us this day our daily bread,

12 And by Your choice You must Remove from Memory (forgive) to us our debts, as also we are Removing from Memory (forgiving) our debtors.

13 And You should not bring us into temptation, but You definitely must rescue us from evil. For Yours is the Kingdom Rule, and Miracle Power, and Glory Forever. Amen.

14 Because if you should Remove from Memory (forgive) their spiritual death offenses to men, your Heavenly Father shall also Remove from Memory (forgive) yours,

15 But if you not Remove from Memory (forgive) to men their spiritual death offenses, neither shall your Father Remove from Memory (forgive) your spiritual death offenses.

When you Fast

16 And then when you should be fasting, you must not become as the hypocrite actors, sad in countenances, for they disfigure their faces so that they might appear to men to be fasting. Truly, I am saying to you that they have their reward.

17 But you, when fasting, must anoint your head, and you must wash your face,

18 So that you should not be made to appear to men to be fasting, but definitely to your Father in secret, and your Father, Who Spiritually Sees in secret, shall pay to you by Openly Manifest.

Don't Store Treasures on Earth

19 You must not store up for yourselves treasures upon the earth whereto moth and rust corrupts and whereto thieves break through and steal.

20 But you must be storing up for yourselves treasures in Heaven, whereto neither moth nor rust corrupts and whereto definitely no thief breaks through neither steals,

21 Because whereto your treasure is there shall be your heart also.

Your Eye Should be Single

22 The Spiritual Light of the body is the Eye. Therefore, if your Eye should be single, your whole body shall be Full of Light.

23 But whenever your eye might be evil, your whole body shall be full of darkness. If, therefore, the light in you is darkness, how much that darkness?

First Seek the Kingdom of God

24 No man is able to be bond serving two lords; because either he will hate one and love another of a different kind, or shall uphold one and despise another of a different kind. You are definitely not able to Bondserve God and extreme desire to amass wealth.

25 Because of this, I am Saying to you, You must take no thought for your soul, what you might eat or what you might drink, neither for your body, what you might put on. Is definitely not your soul greater than nourishment and the body than clothing?

26 For you must look upon the birds of heaven because definitely they sow not, neither reap, neither gather together into barns, and your Heavenly Father nourishes them. Are yourselves definitely not much more excellent in value to them?

27 And then, who of you taking thought can be added one cubit more stature of age to him?

28 And in regard to clothing why must you take thought? You must admire the lilies of the field how they are growing, definitely not laboring, nor spinning.

29 But I am Saying to you, that not Solomon in all his Glory was clothed as one of these.

30 And then, if the grass of the field today is, and tomorrow is being cast into the oven, is definitely not God in such a manner arraying much more many of you? Oh, of little Faith.

31 Therefore, you should take no thought, saying, What should we eat, or what should we drink, or how should we be clothed?

32 Because all these things the Gentiles seek after; yet your Heavenly Father Spiritually Discerns that you have lack of all these things.

33 But seek first of all the Kingdom Rule of God and His Righteousness, and all these things shall be added more to you.

34 Therefore, you should not take thought for the result of tomorrow, because tomorrow will take thought of itself. Adequate for the day the maliciousness thereof.

Judge Not or You Will be Judged

7 You must not possibly be judging, that you should possibly not be made judged.

2 Because, in what judgment you are judging, you shall actually be made Judged. Also, by that amount of measure you are measuring, it shall actually be made

Measured back to you.

3   And then why are you seeing the speck in the eye of your brother, but definitely not considering the beam in your eye?

4   Or how shall you Spirit Say to your brother, Let (me) be concerned that I should cast out the speck away from your eye. And yet Behold the beam in your own eye.

5   Hypocrite actor, first of all, you must cast out the beam from within your own eye, and then you shall see clearly to cast out the speck from within the eye of your brother.

6   You should not Give the Holy to the dogs (unholy people). Neither should you cast your pearls before pigs (abominable), for fear that they might be trampled down by their feet, and made turned around, they might tear you.

7   You must Ask and it shall be Given to you. You must Seek and you shall Find. You must Knock and it shall be made Open to you.

8   Because all those Asking are Receiving, and he Seeking is Finding, and he Knocking it shall be made Open.

9   Or what man is there of you if ever his son should ask bread, will not hand him a stone?

10   Also, if ever he should ask a fish, shall not hand to him a serpent?

11   Therefore, if yourselves being evil, discern to be giving physical God-Good gifts to your children, how much more your Father, Who is in the Heavenlies, shall be Giving God-Goods to them who are by their choice Asking?

Do What You Wish Done to You

12   Therefore, all things whatever that you should be willing that men should do to you, also in such a manner yourselves must be Finalizing to them, because this is the Law and the Prophets.

Enter the Narrow and Troubled Way

13   You must enter through the narrow Gateway, for wide the gateway and broad the way leading away into damnation, and many are they who are themselves entering through it.

14   For narrow the Gateway, and The Way of Travel is now being made troubled, which is that leading away to Life, and few are they who find it.

Separated by our Good or bad Fruit

15   And then you must beware, separate from the false prophets who come to you in sheep's clothing, but inside they are extortioner wolves,

16   From their fruits you shall Fully Know them. Are they possibly collecting grapes from thorns or figs from briars?

17   In such a manner every God-Good Tree finalizes God-Work Fruits, but the corrupt tree finalizes evil fruits.

18   A God-Good Tree is definitely not able to Finalize evil fruits, neither a corrupt tree to Finalize God-Work Fruits.

19   Every tree produces not God-Work Fruit is made cut off, and is made cast into fire.

20   So then from their fruits you shall Fully Know them.

Even miracles are possible by evil men

21   Definitely not everyone saying to me, Lord, Lord, shall enter into the Kingdom Rule of the Heavenlies, but definitely he that is doing the Will of My Father in the Heavenlies.

22   Many will spirit say to Me in That Day, Lord, Lord, Have we definitely not prophesied in Your Name (Lord, Phil 2:9-11), and in Your Name cast out demons, and in Your Name performed many miracle (dunamis) powers?

23   And then I will Confess to them that I never knew you. You must depart fully from Me, you who are yourselves working lawlessness. (Ps 6:8; 1 John 3:4)

The Good Foundation

24   Therefore, everyone who is Hearing

My Words and is Doing Them, I will liken to a very wise man who is building his house upon the Huge Rock.

25 And the rain came down, and the floods came, and the winds blew, and they fell down against that house, and it definitely has not fallen down because a Grounded Foundation had been made upon the Huge Rock.

26 And everyone Hearing these Words of Mine and not doing them shall be likened to a foolish man, who built his house on the sand.

27 And the rain came down, and the floods came, and the winds blew, and beat upon that house, and it fell down, and the collapse of it was great.

28 And it came to pass when Jesus finished His Words, these multitudes of people were made amazed by His Teaching,

29 Because He was Teaching them as having Authority, and definitely not as the scribes.

Heals leper and Casts Out demons

8 And when He Came Down from the mountain, large multitudes of people followed Him.

2 Behold, a leper came Worshiping Him saying, Lord, If You should will, You can cleanse me.

3 And Jesus stretched out His Hand to touch him, Saying, I Will, you must be Cleansed. And immediately his leprosy was Cleansed.

4 And Jesus Said to him, You must Behold Attentively, you Speak to no man, but definitely you must go away, must show yourself to the priest, and must offer the gift which Moses before Commanded for a Testimony to them.

5 And when Jesus entered into Capernaum, a centurion came near to Him, beseeching Him,

6 And saying, Lord, my male servant is now being made prostrate, paralytic, being severely tormented in my house.

7 And Jesus Said to him, I have come to heal him.

8 And the centurion answering stated, Lord, I am definitely not sufficient that You should enter under my roof, but definitely You only must Speak a Word, and my male servant shall be made cured.

9 Because also I a man am under authority, having under myself soldiers, and I say to this one you must go and he goes, and another of the same kind, I say you must be coming, and he comes, and to my slave you must do this, and he does.

10 When Jesus heard this He marveled, and Spoke to those following, Truly, I Say to you, neither in Israel have I found so much Faith.

11 And then I Say to you, That many from east and west shall now come and be made to sit down with Abraham and Isaac and Jacob in the Kingdom Rule of the Heavenlies,

12 But the sons of the kingdom rule shall be made cast out into outer darkness (Matt 22:13). There shall be weeping and gnashing of teeth.

13 And Jesus Spoke to the centurion, You must go away, and as you have by your choice Committed, it must occur to you. And his male servant was healed in the same hour.

14 And Jesus having come into the house of Peter, He Spiritually Saw his mother in law, being made prostrate also having a fever.

15 And He Touched her hand, and Dismissed the fever from her, and she rose up, and was serving them.

16 And then evening having come, they offered to Him many demonized, and He Cast Out the spirits by a Spiritual Word, and He Healed all those having evil work afflicted,

17 So that it should be Fulfilled, that was made Spirit Spoken through Esaias the Prophet Saying, He Himself took our infirmities and bore our sicknesses. (Isa 53:4)

Follow Jesus Regardless

18 And after Jesus Spiritually Discerned large multitudes of people about Him, He Commanded to go to the other side.

19 One scribe came near and spoke to Him, Teacher, I will follow You wherever You are going.

20 And Jesus Says to him, Foxes have homes in holes, and also birds of the heaven nests, but the Son of Man has definitely not wherein He might lower down His head.

21 And then another of a different kind of His disciples spoke to Him, Lord You must permit me first of all to go, and bury my father.

22 But Jesus Spoke to him, You must follow Me, and you must dismiss the dead to bury their own dead.

Jesus Rebukes the wind and waves

23 And boarded after Him, His disciples followed Him into the ship.

24 Behold, a great earthquake occurred in the Sea, so that by great violent waves the ship was being made covered, but He Himself was Sleeping.

25 And His disciples came near, and awoke Him saying, Lord, we are being destroyed. You must Save us.

26 And He Said to them, Why are you, of little Faith, terrified? Then He Raised Up, Rebuked the winds and the Sea, and it became a great calm.

27 But the men marveled saying, What manner is this, that even the winds and the sea obey Him?

Demons Released into swine

28 And when He Came unto the other side, to the land of the Gergesenes, out from the sepulchers two demonized meet with Him, coming out extremely violent so that any are not capable to pass forth through that way.

29 Behold, they cried out saying, Why us with you, Jesus Son of God? Have You Come being here to torment us before the Special Time?

30 And then far off from them was a herd of many pigs feeding.

31 But the demons beseeched Him saying, If You cast us out, You must permit us to go into the herd of pigs.

32 And He Spoke to them, Come Out, you must Go Away, and they went into the herd of pigs. And, Behold, the whole herd of pigs ran violently upon the steep decline into the Sea and died in the waters.

33 And then those feeding fled, and went into the city, and told everything to them of those being demonized.

34 And, Behold, the whole city came out for the purpose of meeting together with Jesus, and discerning, beseeched that He should depart away from their districts.

Heals a bedridden man

9 And He boarded into a ship, past over, and came into His own city.

2 And Behold they offered to Him a paralytic being made prostrate in a bed, and Jesus Spiritually Saw their Faith, spoke to the paralytic, Child, You must be encouraged. Your sins are now being Removed from Memory (Forgiven) from you.

3 And Behold, certain of the scribes spoke inside of themselves, He is blaspheming.

4 And Jesus Spiritually Discerning their inner thoughts, He Spoke, Why are certain of yourselves pondering evil in your hearts?

5 Because which is easier to speak, I am now Removing from Memory (Forgiving) your sins, Or to speak, you must Raise up for yourself and you must by your choice walk.

6 And then, that you might Know that I, the Son of Man, am having Authority upon the earth to be Removing from Memory (Forgive) sin natures and sins, He then Says to the paralytic, Raise up, you must take up your bed and you must go

away into your dwelling.

7 And rising up, he went to his dwelling.

8 And when the multitudes of people saw, they marveled and Attributed Glory to God, Who Gave such Authority to men.

9 And passing on, Jesus Spiritually Saw from that place a man called Matthew sitting at the desk for paying taxes, and Says to him, You must by your choice be following Me, and having arison, he by his choice followed Him.

10 And it came to pass, He was sitting as at eating in the house, and Behold many tax collectors and sinners having come, were sitting to eat with Jesus and His disciples.

11 The Pharisees saw and then spoke to his disciples, Why then is your Master eating with the tax collectors and sinners?

12 And then Jesus heard, He Spoke, Those being not needful are having definitely no need of a physician being capable, but definitely those who have evil work afflicted.

13 But you must go learn, why I am willing Mercy and definitely not sacrifice, because I came not to Outwardly Call (Gospel) the Righteous, but definitely sinners to Repentance.

Why Jesus' Disciples did not Fast

14 Then John's disciples come near to Him saying, Why then are we and the Pharisees fasting very much, but Your disciples are definitely not fasting?

15 And Jesus Spoke to them, Neither can the sons of the bride chamber be mourning, in regard of as long as the bridegroom is with them? But a day shall come when the bridegroom should be made taken from them, and then they shall fast.

16 And then no man lays a new piece of cloth to old clothes, because taking away the fullness of it separating away from the clothes, and the division becomes worse.

17 Neither cast new wine into old bottles, so that the bottles are not made torn, and the wine made pouring out and the bottles shall be destroyed, but definitely cast new wine into new bottles and both are made preserved.

Ruler's dead daughter Raised

18 He Uttered these things to them, Behold, one ruler came to Worship Him saying, That my daughter for now has been deceased, but definitely come. You must lay Your Hand on her, and she shall live.

19 Jesus rose up and also His disciples and followed Him.

20 And behold, a woman with a bleeding disease twelve years, came near behind, touched the border of His clothes.

21 Because she was saying in herself, if ever I only touched His clothes, I will be made Healed.

22 But Jesus Turned Back, and Spiritually Saw her. He Spoke, You must be encouraged daughter, your Faith Healed you. And the woman was made Healed from that hour.

23 And Jesus came into the house of the ruler, and saw the pipers, and the multitude of people making noise.

24 He Said to them, You must withdraw because the young woman has definitely not died, but definitely is sleeping. And they laughed Him to scorn.

25 But when He cast out the multitude of people, He entered, held to retain her hand, and the young woman rose up.

26 And the fame of Him came out into that whole earth.

Blind Receive sight

27 When Jesus passed on from that place, two blind followed Him, crying out and saying, You must be having Mercy on us Son of David.

28 And when He came into the house, the blind came near to Him, and Jesus Said to them, You must be Committed how I am able to do this. They said to Him, Lord, Emphatically Yes!

29 Then He Touched their eyes, saying,

According to your Faith, it must come to pass for you.

30 And their eyes Opened and Jesus Seriously Commanded them saying, You must Behold Attentively, no man must know.

31 But they, themselves, having departed, commonly reported Him in that whole earth.

Dumb man's demon was Cast Out

32 And when they departing, Behold, they offered to Him a deaf man, being demonized.

33 So also the demon was made cast out, the deaf uttered, and the multitudes of people marveled saying, It never appeared in such a manner in Israel.

34 But the Pharisees were saying, He was casting out the demons by the ruler of the demons.

35 And Jesus went about the cities and all the villages Teaching in their synagogues, and Preaching the Gospel of the Kingdom Rule, and Healing all sickness and all disease among the people.

Harvest is Large but few Workers

36 But Spiritually Discerning the multitudes of people, he had Compassion for them, for they were discouraged and thrown down like as sheep having no Shepherd.

37 Then Saying to His disciples, Certainly the Harvest is large but the workers few.

38 Therefore, you must Pray Earnestly to the Lord of the Harvest, so that He might Send Away workers into His Harvest.

The 12 Apostles are Sent Out

10 And He Invited His twelve disciples, He Gave them Authority so that morally impure spirits be Cast Out by them, and to Heal all sickness and all disease.

2 And then the names of the twelve apostles are these: first Simon, who is called Peter, and Andrew his brother; James who of Zebedee, and John his brother,

3 Philip and Bartholomew, Thomas and Matthew the tax collector, James of Alpheus, and Lebbaeus made surnamed Thaddaeus,

4 Simon the Canaanite, and Judas Iscariot who also delivered up Him in betrayal.

Instructions to the 12 Apostles

5 These twelve Jesus Sent Out, having Given Command to them Saying, Go not into the way of the Gentiles, and enter not into a city of the Samaritans,

6 But you must be Going instead to the now perishing sheep of House of Israel.

7 And then you must be going Preaching Saying that the Kingdom Rule of the Heavenlies is approaching near.

8 You must Heal those being sick, you must Cleanse lepers, you must Raise Up dead, you must Cast Out demons. Freely you have Received, Freely you must Give.

9 Neither possess not gold, neither silver, nor brass coin into your belts.

10 Not wallet for money or pouch for food for the purpose of The Way, neither two coats, nor shoes, nor staffs, because the worker is worthy of his nourishment.

11 Into then whatever city or village you enter, you must inquire who in it is Worthy. You must continue there also until after whenever you should come out.

12 And when you enter into the house, you must greet it.

13 And, certainly, if ever the house is Worthy, the Peace of you, must come upon it; and if not worthy, your Peace must turn back to yourselves.

14 And if those who might have not received you, neither might have heard your Word, come out of that house or that city. You must shake off the dust of your feet.

15 Truly, I am Saying to you, In the Day of Final Judgment, it shall be more tolerable with the area of Sodom and Gomorrah than that city.

Apostles Told what to Expect

16 Behold, I Send you out as sheep in midst of wolves. Therefore, you must become very wise as serpents, and harmless as doves.

17 But beware of men, because they shall deliver you up into councils, and inside their synagogues they shall scourge you.

18 And for the cause of Me, you shall be led to governors and also to kings, for the Purpose of a Testimony to them, and to the Gentiles.

19 But when they might deliver you up, take no thought how or what you should Utter because it shall be Given to you in that same hour, what you shall Utter.

20 Because yourselves are definitely not uttering, but definitely the Spirit of your Father, Who is Uttering in you.

21 And then brother shall deliver up brother into death, and father child, and children shall stand up to parents, and shall put them to death.

22 And you shall be hated by all because of My Name, but having endured for the Purpose of that End, you shall be made Saved.

23 But when they might persecute you in this city, you must flee into another of the same kind. For I say to you, you should never ever have finally finished the cities of Israel, until after whenever the Son of Man should come.

Your Conduct under God

24 A Disciple is definitely not more above his Master, neither a Bondslave more above his Lord.

25 Adequate that disciple that should be as his Master, and the Bondslave as his Lord. If they have called the householder dung god (beelzebub, satan), how much more his household?

26 You should fear them not, therefore, because nothing is now being covered that shall not be made revealed, and the secret that is definitely not made known.

27 What I am Saying to you in the dark, you must Speak in the Light, and what you are Hearing in your ear, you must Preach upon the housetops.

28 And you must not be made afraid of those that kill the body, and they are not able to kill the soul, but instead be made to fear Him much more able to destroy both soul and body in hell.

29 Are definitely not two sparrows selling for a farthing (Roman Assarius), and one of them shall not fall down to the earth, apart from Your Father?

30 But then the hairs of your head, they are all numbered.

31 Therefore, you must not fear. Are yourselves not much more excellent in value to sparrows?

32 Therefore, all who shall Confess by Me before men, I also will Confess with him before My Father in the Heavenlies.

33 But whoever might have disclaimed Me before men, him I also will disclaim, before My Father in the Heavenlies.

Came not to Bring Peace but a Sword

34 You might suppose not that I Came to cast Peace upon the earth. I came definitely not to cast Peace, but definitely a Sword.

35 Because I am Come to set a man in opposition against his father, and a daughter against her mother, and a daughter in law against her mother in law;

36 And a man's enemies, those of his own household. (Micah 7:6)

37 He having affectionately love for dad or mother more above Me is definitely not worthy of Me, and he having affectionately love for son or daughter more above Me is definitely not worthy of Me.

38 And he that is not taking his cross and following after Me, is definitely not worthy of Me.

39 He that found his soul shall lose it, and he that loses his Living-Soul for the cause of Me shall Find It.

How men Receive Reward

40 He that is receiving you is receiving Me, and he that is receiving Me is receiving Him that Sent Me Out.

41 He that is receiving a Prophet in the name of a Prophet is taking a Prophet's Reward. And he who receives a Righteous, in the name of a Righteous, will receive a Righteous Reward.

42 And if whoever should give to one of the least of these to drink only a cold cup, in the name of a disciple, Truly, I Say to you he should never ever lose his Reward.

John in prison Inquired of Jesus

11 And it came to pass, when Jesus had finally finished, He Appointed twelve of His disciples to depart from that place, to be teaching and preaching in their cities.

2 And when John heard inside of the jail, the Works by God by Christ, he sent two of his disciples.

3 He spoke to Him, You, are You the One to come, or do we watch for another of a different kind?

4 Jesus Answered and Spoke to them. You must go tell John what you are Hearing and Spiritually Seeing,

5 Blind receiving Sight, and crippled Walking, lepers Cleansed, and deaf Hearing, dead Raised Up, and poor are having the Gospel Preached.

6 And Spiritually Blessed is whoever never ever might be offended in Me.

7 And when these went, Jesus began to Say to the multitudes of people in regard to John. What came out you to see in the desolate wilderness, a reed shaking by the wind?

8 But definitely what came you out to Spiritually See? A man being arrayed in appealing soft clothes? Behold, those that are wearing appealing softs, they are in the homes of kings.

9 But definitely what came you out to Spiritually See, a Prophet? Emphatically Yes. I am Saying to you and more abundant, a Prophet,

10 Because this is he in regard to whom it is now Written, Behold, I Send Out My Messenger before Your Face, who shall make ready Your Way of Travel before You. (Mal 3:1)

11 Truly, I Say to you, among born naturally of women, definitely no one is now raised up greater than John the Baptist. But Least in the Kingdom Rule of the Heavenlies is Greater than he.

12 And then since the days of John the Baptist for up to now, the Kingdom Rule of Heaven is being pressed, and the forceful are catching it up,

13 Because all the Prophets, and the Law prophesied up to John.

14 And if you will receive it, he is Elias, expected to come.

15 He that is having ears to Hear, you must be Hearing.

16 But what shall I liken to this generation? It is like older children sitting in a marketplace, and calling out to their fellows,

17 And saying, we have piped to you and you have definitely not danced, lamented to you and you have definitely not bewailed.

18 Because John came neither eating nor drinking, and you are saying he has a demon.

19 The Son of Man came eating and drinking, and you are saying, Behold, a gluttonous man and wine drinker, a friend of tax collectors and of sinners. And Wisdom has been Made Righteous from her children.

20 Then He began to Scold sharply those cities, wherein occurred His most excellent Miracle Powers, because they definitely repented not.

21 Woe to you, Chorazin. Woe to you, Bethsaida. For if the Miracle Powers had occurred herein in Tyre and Sidon, which occurred in yourselves, they would have repented long ago in sackcloth and ashes.

22 But I Say to you, it shall be more tolerable for Tyre and Sidon, in the Day of Final Judgment, than for you.

23 And you, Capernaum, which is made exalted up to heaven, shall be made thrust down to hades, for if the Miracle Powers that had occurred in you had occurred in Sodom, it would abide even until this day. (Isa 14:13-15)

24 But I Say to you, that it shall be more tolerable for the area of Sodom in the Final Judgment Day than you.

Revealed to Babes

25 In that Special Time, Jesus Answered. He Spoke, I acknowledge You, Father, Lord of Heaven and of earth, for You Concealed these things from wise and prudent, and Revealed them to infants.

26 Emphatically, Yes, Father, for in such a manner, God-Good Intentions were before You.

27 All things have been Delivered Up by My Father to Me; and no man Fully Knows the Son, except the Father; neither any man Fully Knows the Father, except the Son, and whoever the Son might Intend to Reveal.

Take His Yoke Upon you

28 You must Come now to Me, all that are laboring and are made heavy laden, I also will be Refreshing you.

29 You must take up My Yoke to yourselves, and you must Learn from Me, for I am Meek and Humble in Heart, and you will find a Resting Place for your Living Souls. (Jer 6:16)

30 Because My Yoke (is) Kind, and My Burden is Light.

On Sabbath Jesus Heals dried up hand

12 In this Special Time, Jesus went on the Sabbath through the grain field. And when His disciples hungered, they also began to pluck heads of grain, and were eating.

2 But when the Pharisees saw, they spoke to Him, Behold your disciples are doing, what is definitely not Lawful to do in the Sabbath.

3 But He Spoke to them, Have you definitely not read what David did when he hungered and they with him?

4 How he entered into the House of God, and ate the Bread of Purpose (Shewbread), which was definitely not Lawful for him to have eaten, neither for them with him, except for the priests alone.

5 Or have you definitely not read in the Law, that on the Sabbath the priests in the Temple area are desecrating the Sabbath, and they are guiltless?

6 But, I Say to you, Now is here the Greater than this Temple area.

7 But if you had known why I am preferring Mercy and definitely not sacrifice, you would definitely not have Finally Judged Condemned the guiltless, (Hos 6:6)

8 Because the Son of Man is Lord also of the Sabbath.

9 And having departed from that place, He came into their synagogue.

10 And Behold, a man was there having a dried up hand. And they, that they might accuse him, questioned Him saying, Is it lawful to heal on the Sabbaths?

11 And He Spoke to them, What man of you that shall have one sheep, and if this might fall into a ditch on the Sabbath, shall he definitely not, hold to retain it, and shall raise it up?

12 Therefore, how much is man different in value to a sheep? So that it is Lawful on the Sabbaths to do God-Working.

13 Then He Says to the man, You must stretch out your hand. And he stretched out, and it was restored healthy as the other of the same kind.

14 And then the Pharisees came out and took counsel against Him, so that they might depart to destroy Him.

Isaiah's Prophecy Fulfilled in Jesus

15 But Jesus Knew it, and withdrew from

that place, and large multitudes of people followed Him, and He Healed them all.

16 And He Rebuked them that they do not make Him Openly Manifest.

17 So that it might be Fulfilled which was Spirit Spoken through Esaias the Prophet saying,

18 Behold My Male Servant, Whom I have Chosen for Myself, My Beloved, in whom My Soul is Pleased. I will Position My Spirit with Him, and He shall tell the Final Judgment upon all nations.

19 He shall definitely not be hot tempered, neither cry, neither shall any be hearing His Voice in the streets.

20 A bruised reed, He shall definitely not break to pieces, and a smoking linen shall He definitely not extinguish, until after whenever He might cast out to the Final Judgment, for the Result and Purpose of Victory.

21 And in His Name Gentiles shall expect. (Isa 42:1-4)

A House against itself cannot stand

22 Then they offered a demonized blind and deaf for Him to be healed, so that the blind and deaf also uttered and saw.

23 And all the multitudes of people were astonished and were saying, Is He possibly the Son of David?

24 But the Pharisees heard. They spoke, This man definitely casts not out demons, except by the dung god (beelzebub, satan), ruler of the demons.

25 But now Jesus Spiritually Discerning their inner thoughts Spoke to them, Every kingdom rule fully divided against itself is being brought to desolation. Every city and house fully divided against itself shall definitely not stand.

26 And if satan be casting out satan with himself fully divided, how therefore shall his kingdom rule stand?

27 And if I by dung god am casting out the demons, in whom are your sons casting out? By this they themselves shall be judges of you.

28 But if I am Casting Out the demons by the Holy Spirit, then the Kingdom Rule of God has been Attained among you.

29 Or how can anybody have entered into the strong man's house, and wrecked his vessels, except he first of all bound the strong man, and then wrecked his house?

30 He that is not with Me is against Me, and he not gathering together with Me is dispersed.

31 Because of this I Say to you, all sin nature and sin and blasphemy by man shall be made Removed from Memory (forgiven), but blasphemy of the Spirit shall definitely not be made Removed from Memory (forgiven) to men.

32 And whoever might have spoken a spiritual word against the Son of Man, it shall be made Removed from Memory (forgiven) to him, but whoever might speak against the Holy Spirit, it definitely shall not be made Removed from Memory (forgiven) to him, neither in this Age nor in that expecting.

A Tree is Known by its Fruit

33 Either make the Tree God-Work, and His Fruit God-Work, or make the tree corrupt and its fruit corrupt, because the tree is being made known by the fruit.

34 Oh product of vipers, how are you being evil able to utter God-Goods? Because out from the abundance of the heart the mouth utters.

35 A God-Good man out from within the God-Good treasure of his heart casts out God-Good, and the evil man out from within the evil treasure casts out evil.

36 But I Say to you that every idle word that if man might have uttered, he shall repay in regard to his word in Final Judgment Day.

37 Because out from your Spiritual Words, you shall be Made Righteous; and out from your words, you shall be Finally Judged Condemned.

Sign of Jonah's Three Days and Nights

38 Then answered certain scribes and Pharisees saying, Teacher, We are desiring to discern a Spiritual Miracle Sign from you.

39 Then He Answered and Spoke to them. An evil and adulteress generation seeks after a Miracle Sign, and definitely no Miracle Sign shall be given to it, except the Miracle Sign of the Prophet Jonas.

40 Because as Jonas was in the belly of the whale three days and three nights, in such a manner shall the Son of Man be in the heart of the earth, three days and three nights. (Jonah 1:17)

41 Ninevite men shall arise in the Final Judgment with this generation, and shall condemn it to death, because they repented at the preaching of Jonas, and, Behold, here a Greater than Jonas.

42 The Queen of the South shall rise up in the Final Judgment with this generation, and condemn it to death, because she came out from the ends of the earth to hear the wisdom of Solomon, and Behold, a Greater here than Solomon.

43 And then when the morally impure spirit might came out from the man, passing through dry places seeking a resting place, and definitely not finding;

44 Then he said, I will turn back into my home, from where I came out, and came finding it empty, swept and adorned,

45 Then it goes and takes along with itself seven other ones of a different kind spirits, more evil than itself, entered dwelling there; and being the last of that man shall be worse than the first. In such a manner shall this generation be more evil.

The True Kin of Jesus Do the Fathers' Will

46 Further, when He was Uttering to a multitudes of people, Behold, His mother and His brothers had stood outside seeking to utter to Him.

47 And then one spoke to Him, Behold, Your mother and Your brothers are now standing outside seeking to utter to You.

48 But then He Answering, Spoke, Speaking to him, Who is My Mother, and who are My Brothers?

49 He stretched out His hand to His disciples and Spoke, Behold, My Mother and My Brothers.

50 Because whoever should be doing the Will of My Father in the Heavenlies, he is being My Brother and Sister and Mother.

Parable of the Sower

13 And then in the same day, Jesus departed from the house, He was sitting near to the sea.

2 And large multitudes of people gathered together to Him, so that He boarded and was sitting in a ship. And all the multitude of people stood upon the shore.

3 And He Uttered to them in many parables saying, Behold, a Sower came out to Sow,

4 And in Sowing It, some certainly fell down by the side of The Way of Travel, and birds came and devoured them.

5 But nevertheless, some of the same kinds fell down upon the stony ground whereto definitely having not very much Earth, and immediately started growing because of having no Earth depth,

6 For when the sun has risen and has made scorched also because of not having root, it dried up.

7 But then others of same kind fell down among thorns, and the thorns ascended and fully choked them.

8 But then others of same kind having fallen down upon the God-Work Earth, and indeed Giving Fruit, some a hundred, and some sixty, and some thirty.

9 Who is having ears to Hear you must be Hearing.

Jesus uses Parables to Hide Meaning

10 The disciples came near and spoke to Him. Why then are You Uttering to them in parables?

11 And Answering, He Spoke to them, Because it is now made Given to you to Know the Mysteries of the Kingdom Rule of the Heavenlies, but to them definitely not being given.

12 Because whoever Has shall be Given, and shall abound in amount to him, but whoever definitely has not, then it shall have been made taken away from him.

13 Therefore, I am Uttering this to them in parables because seeing they definitely See not, and hearing they definitely Hear not, neither do they Understand.

14 And it is made satisfying in regard to them in the Prophecy of Esaias Saying, To the hearing you shall hear but you most definitely not Understand, and seeing you shall see and should never ever Spiritually See.

15 Because the heart of this people has hardened, and their ears dull to hear, and their eyes closed, for fear that to Discern with their eyes; and might Hear with their ears, and might Understand with their heart, then they should be Converted and I will Cure them. (Isa 6:9-10)

16 But Spiritually Blessed your eyes for they are Spiritually Seeing, and your ears for they are definitely Hearing.

17 Because, Truly, I Say to you, that many Prophets and Righteous have desired to Discern what you See, and have definitely not seen, and also Hear what you Hear and definitely not heard.

Parable of the Sower Explained

18 Therefore, yourselves must hear the parable of that Sower.

19 All Hearing the Word of the Kingdom Rule and not Understanding, the evil one comes and catches up what is Sown within the heart. This is that Sowed near to The Way of Travel.

20 But Sown in the stony ground is he Hearing the Word, and immediately with Joy Receives it.

21 Then having definitely no root in himself, but definitely is for a time. He is made immediately offended when affliction and persecution has occurred because of the Word.

22 And then Sown among thorns is he Hearing the Spiritual Word, but the cares of this Age and the deceitfulness of riches, choke the Spiritual Word, and it becomes unfruitful.

23 But he made Sown with intent to God-Work Earth is he who Hears and Understands the Spiritual Word, so now then Bears Fruit, and indeed some a hundred, and some sixty, and some thirty.

Seven other Parables

24 Another of the same kind parable He Put Forth to them Saying, The Kingdom Rule of the Heavenlies is made likened to a man who Sowed God-Work Seed in his field.

25 But while the men were sleeping, their enemy came, and sowed tares among the midst of the Wheat, then he went.

26 And then when the grass budded forth and the Fruit appeared, then appeared also the tares.

27 Then came near the slaves to the master of the house. They spoke to him, Lord, have you definitely not Sown in your field God-Work Seed? From what, therefore, is it having tares?

28 And then he stated to them, A man, an enemy, did this. But the slaves spoke to him, Are you Willing, therefore, that we should go to collect them?

29 But he stated, Definitely collect not the tares, for fear that you might Root up the Wheat together with them.

30 You must concern for both to be growing together until the Harvest. And in that Special Time of the Harvest, Spirit Say to the Reapers, you must collect first of all the tares and you must Bind them in bundles to fully burn them, and you must then Gather Together the Wheat into My barn.

31 Another parable of the same kind He

put forth saying, The Kingdom Rule of the Heavenlies is like a grain of mustard seed that a man has received to Sow in his field, 32 Which is indeed the smallest of all seeds, but when it might have been made to grow, it is a great herb, and is becoming a tree so that birds of heaven came and are lodging in its branches.

33 Another parable of the same kind, He uttered to them, The Kingdom Rule of the Heavenlies is like leaven that a woman has taken to hide away in three dry meal measures of flour, until after where the whole had been leavened.

34 All these things Jesus Uttered in parables to the multitudes of people, and without a parable He was definitely not Uttering to them.

35 So that it might be Fulfilled, Spirit Spoken through the Prophet Saying, I will Open My mouth, I will pronounce in parables that being made hidden from the Conception of the satan's world. (Ps 78:2)

36 Then Jesus dismissed the multitudes of people and came into the house, and the disciples came near to Him saying, You must explain specifically to us the parable of the tares in the field.

37 Then He Answered and Spoke to them, He that is Sowing the God-Work Seed is the Son of Man.

38 Then the field is the satan's world, and the God-Work Seed are His Sons of the Kingdom Rule, but the tares are the sons of the evil one,

39 And the enemy that sowed them is the devil, and the Harvest is definitely being the Final End of the satan's world within this Age, and Angels are the Reapers.

40 As then the tares are being collected and are fully burning in fire. In such a manner it shall be in the Final End of the satan's world within this Age.

41 The Son of Man shall Send Out His Angels, and shall Collect out from His Kingdom Rule all offenses (occasions for stumbling to sin), and those doing lawlessness.

42 And He shall Cast them into the fiery furnace; there shall be weeping and gnashing of teeth.

43 Then the Righteous shall shine forth as the sun, in the Kingdom Rule of their Father. Who has ears to Hear, he must be Hearing.

44 Again, the Kingdom Rule of the Heavenlies is like a treasure made hiding in the field which a man had hid, yet finding only Joy to himself, he goes away and sells everything, as much as he has, and buys that field.

45 Again, the Kingdom Rule of the Heavenlies is like a merchant man seeking God-Work pearls,

46 Who found one much more costly pearl; he went, selling in the market all, as much as he had, and bought it.

47 Again, the Kingdom Rule of the Heavenlies is like a seine net cast into the sea, and gathered together from out of every kind;

48 That when it was made fully filled, they rowed back to the shore, and sat down to collect the God-Works into containers, and then cast outside the corrupt.

49 In such a manner it shall be in the Final End of the satan's world of this Age. The Angels shall come out and shall separate the evil out from the midst of the Righteous,

50 And cast them into the fiery furnace. There shall be weeping and gnashing of teeth.

51 Jesus Says to them, Have you understood all these things? They say to Him, Emphatically Yes, Lord.

52 And then He Spoke to them, Because of this every scribe discipled into the Kingdom Rule of the Heavenlies is like a man, a master of the house, who casts out, from within his treasure, the Old for the New of different kind.

Rejected in Nazareth, His Hometown

53 And when it came to pass Jesus had finally fulfilled these parables, He

Removed Himself from that place.

54 And having come into his own country, He Taught them in their synagogue, so
that they were amazed at Him and saying,
From where this Wisdom and Miracle
Powers?

55 Is this man not the carpenter's son? Is
definitely not His mother called Mary, and
His brothers James and Joses and Simon
and Jude?

56 And His sisters, are they definitely not
all with us? From where, therefore, This
One all these things?

57 And they were offended with Him. But
Jesus Spoke to them, A Prophet is definitely
not without honor, except in his own country, and inside his own house.

58 And He could definitely not do many
Miracle Powers there because of their no
Commitment.

John the Baptist is beheaded

14 In that Special Time Herod, the
tetrarch, heard of Jesus.

2 And spoke to his male servants, This
man is John the Baptist himself. He has
been made risen up from the dead; and
because of this, Miracle Powers are being
accomplished in Him.

3 Because Herod held to retain John,
bound and put him in prison because of
Herodias, the wife of Philip, his brother.

4 Because John said to him, It is definitely not Lawful for you to have her.

5 He was willing to kill him, but feared
the multitude of people, because they had
him as a Prophet.

6 And when the birthday of Herod is
being acted upon, the daughter of Herodias danced in the midst and pleased Herod.

7 From where, he confessed, with an
oath, to give to her whatever she asked.

8 And then, instructed before by her
mother, she stated, Give to me here the
head of John the Baptist on a platter.

9 But the king was grieved, because of
the oath he had commanded to give even

while sitting to eat.

10 And sent to have John beheaded in the
prison.

11 And his head was brought on a platter,
and given to the young woman, and she
brought to her mother.

12 And his disciples came near, took up
the body and buried it, and came to tell
Jesus.

13 And having heard, Jesus withdrew
from that place in a ship into a desolate
wilderness to a private place. And when
having heard, the multitudes of people
followed Him on foot from the cities.

14 And Jesus came out to Spiritually See
a large multitude of people, and had
Compassion for them, and He Healed their
sickly.

Five Thousand Fed with Five Loaves

15 And when it was evening, his disciples
came near to Him saying, This place is a
desolate wilderness. And also the hour has
already passed away. You must dismiss
away the multitude of people that they
go into the villages might buy themselves
food.

16 But Jesus Spoke to them, They have
definitely no need to go. Yourselves must
Give them to eat.

17 And then they said to Him, We are
definitely not having here except five
loaves and two fish.

18 And then He spoke, You must bring
them here to Me.

19 And He Commanded the multitudes
of people to be made to sit down upon the
grass, and took the five loaves and two fish,
Looked Up to Heaven, Blessed, and Broke
to Give the bread to the disciples, and then
the disciples to the multitude of people.

20 And they all ate and were filled, and
they took up the abounding in amount of
the fragments twelve hand baskets full.

21 And those that were eating were about
five thousand men, besides women and
little children.

Jesus Walks on a stormy sea

22 And immediately, Jesus compelled the disciples to board into the ship, and go before Him to the other side, while He should dismiss away the multitudes of people.

23 And having dismissed away the multitudes of people, He ascended into the mountain privately to Pray. And when it became evening, He was there alone.

24 But the ship, already in the midst of the sea, was being tormented by the great violent waves because the wind was being contrary.

25 And in the fourth watch of the night, Jesus went toward them Walking on the sea.

26 And the disciples Spiritually Saw Him Walking upon the sea. They were made troubled, saying that it is a ghostly sight, and cried out from fear.

27 But immediately, Jesus Uttered to them Saying, You must be encouraged, I AM, you must not fear.

28 Then Peter answered Him, he spoke, Lord, if You are, You must Command me to come to You on the water.

29 And He Spoke, You must come. And Peter came down from the ship. He Walked on the water to come to Jesus.

30 But when he saw the mighty wind he feared, and beginning to sink he cried out, calling, Lord, You must Save me.

31 And immediately, Jesus stretched out His Hand and took hold of him Saying to him, Oh, you of little Faith, for what purpose have you doubted?

32 And they boarded into the ship. The wind ceased blowing.

33 When inside the ship, they came and Worshiped Him saying, Of Truth, You are the Son of God.

Touching Jesus' Garment and Healed

34 And having passed over, they came into the area of Gennesaret.

35 And when the men of that place Fully Knew Him, they sent out to the whole surrounding region, and offered to Him everyone having evil work afflicted.

36 And besought Him that they might only touch the border of His clothes, and as many as touched were physically saved.

Vain worship, traditions of men

15 Then came near to Jesus those scribes and Pharisees from Jerusalem saying,

2 Why then do your disciples violate the tradition of the elders, because they definitely do not ceremonially wash their hands when they might be eating bread?

3 Then He Answered and Spoke to them, Why then do yourselves violate the Commandment of God because of your tradition?

4 Because God Commanded saying, You must Honor your father and mother, and those speaking evil things of father or mother must decease to death.

5 But yourselves are saying that whoever might speak to his father or mother, A gift by whatever you might have profited out from me.

6 And most might never ever be honoring his father or his mother, for you have annulled the Commandment of your God because of your tradition.

7 Oh hypocrite actors, God-Working Prophesied in Esaias in regard to you, saying,

8 This people approach near to Me with their mouth, and honor me with lips, but is having their heart far away from Me.

9 And then worthlessly they are revering Me, teaching for doctrines, precepts of men. (Isa 29:13)

10 He invited the multitude of people and Spoke to them. You must Hear by your choice and you must by your choice Understand.

11 Definitely not that which enters into the mouth makes unholy the man, but definitely what goes out from the mouth. This makes unholy the man.

12 Then His disciples came near to Him, they spoke to Him, Are You Spiritually Discerning that the Pharisees were offended to hear Your Word?

13 He Answered and then Spoke, Every plant that My Heavenly Father definitely did not plant shall be rooted up.

14 You must dismiss them, they are blind guides of the blind, and then if wherever the blind might be guiding the blind, both shall fall down into a ditch.

15 And then Peter answered, spoke to Him. You must explain specifically to us this parable.

16 And Jesus Spoke, Are you yourselves also, up to now, without Understanding?

17 Do you not yet comprehend that all things that come into the mouth, find a place into the belly, and are made cast out into the sewer?

18 But that which goes out from the mouth, comes out from within the heart, and it makes unholy the man.

19 Because out from within the heart, comes out evil thoughts, murders, adulteries, fornication, thefts, false testimonies, blasphemies.

20 These are the things which are making unholy a man, but to eat with unwashed hands definitely is not making unholy the man.

Even the dogs eat the crumbs

21 And having come out from that place, Jesus withdrew into the parts of Tyre and Sidon.

22 And, Behold, a Canaanite woman from those districts came out, screamed to Him saying, You must Have Mercy on me, Oh Lord, Oh Son of David, my evil work afflicted daughter is demonized.

23 But He Answered definitely not a Word to her; and His disciples came near and earnestly requested of Him saying, You must dismiss her away for she is crying out behind us.

24 He Answered and then Spoke, I am definitely not Sent Out, except to the lost sheep of the House of Israel.

25 Then she came to worship Him saying, Oh Lord, You must help me.

26 But He Answered and Spoke, It is definitely not a God-Work to take bread of the children and cast it down to puppy dogs.

27 Then she spoke, Emphatically Yes, Oh Lord, yet the puppy dogs are eating from the crumbs which are falling down from the table of their master.

28 Then Jesus Answered, He Spoke to her. Oh, woman great is your Faith, it must come to pass to you as you will. And the daughter from that hour was cured.

Many people Healed

29 Jesus departed from that place and came near to the sea of Galilee, and ascended upon a mountain, He was sitting there.

30 And large multitudes of people came near to Him, having with themselves crippled, blind, deaf, lame and many other ones of different kinds, and threw down themselves near to His Feet, and Jesus Healed them.

31 So that the multitudes of people marveled, seeing, deaf uttering, lame healthy, crippled walking, and blind seeing, and they Attributed Glory to the God of Israel.

Four Thousand Fed with Seven Loaves

32 Then Jesus invited His disciples, Spoke, I have compassion on the multitude of people, for they are remaining steadfast with Me already three days, and yet who are definitely not having that they might eat. And I will definitely not dismiss them away without food, for fear that they might be discouraged in the way of travel.

33 And His disciples said to Him, From where, in the wilderness with us, so much bread so that to fill so large a multitude of people?

34 And Jesus Says to them, How many loaves have you? And then they spoke,

seven, and a few little fish.

35 And He Commanded the multitudes of peoples to sit down on the earth.

36 And He took the seven loaves and the fish, Gave Thanks, Broke, and Gave to His disciples, and then disciples to the multitude of people.

37 And they all ate and were made filled, also they took up the abounding in amount of the fragments, seven large hamper size baskets full.

38 And those eating were four thousand men, besides woman and little children.

39 And He dismissed away the multitudes of people, boarded into the ship, and came into the districts of Magdala.

Evil doctrine is compared to leaven

16 The Pharisees also with Sadducees came near to question, and trying Him, to show as example to them a Miracle Sign out of Heaven.

2 He answered and spoke to them, When it becomes evening you say pleasant weather because the heaven is being red.

3 Also, early in the morning it is bad weather this day, because the heaven being red and gloomy. Hypocrite actors, certainly you know judging the face of heaven differences, but the Miracle Signs of Special Times you are definitely not able.

4 An adulterous and more evil generation seeks after a Miracle Sign, and a Miracle Sign will definitely not be given to it, except the Miracle Sign of Jonas the Prophet. And having left them, He went.

5 And His disciples came into the other side, having forgotten to take loaves.

6 Then Jesus Spoke to them, So also Behold Attentively, Give Attention to the leaven of the Pharisees and Sadducees.

7 And then they were reasoning among themselves, saying, Because we definitely took no loaves.

8 And Jesus knew, then Spoke to them, Why do you reason among yourselves of little Faith, because you definitely took no loaves?

9 Are you not yet comprehending, neither remembering the five loaves to the five thousand, and how many hand baskets did you take?

10 Nor the seven loaves to the four thousand, and how many large hamper size baskets did you receive?

11 How do you definitely not comprehend this? I Spoke definitely not in regard of bread to you. Be Giving Attention to the leaven of the Pharisees and Sadducees.

12 They then understood that He Spoke definitely to not take heed to the leaven of bread, but definitely of the teaching of the Pharisees and Sadducees.

Peter's Confession that Jesus is Christ

13 When Jesus came into the parts of Caesarea Philippi, He earnestly requested of his disciples Saying, Whom are men saying, I, the Son of Man to be?

14 And they spoke, Some certainly John the Baptist, then others of the same kind, some Elias, and other ones of a different kind say Jeremiah, or one of the Prophets.

15 He Says to them, Yourselves and whom are you saying I am?

16 Simon Peter Answered and Spoke, You, You are the Christ, the Son of the Living God.

17 Jesus Answered and Spoke to him, Spiritually Blessed are you Simon Barjona, for sinful flesh nature and blood has definitely not revealed to you, but Definitely My Father in the Heavenlies.

18 And I, also I Say to you that you are Peter (petros, small rock), but upon this Huge Rock (petra) I will Build My Assembly, and the gateways of hades shall definitely not triumph against Me.

19 And I will Give to you the Keys of the Kingdom Rule of the Heavenlies, and whatever you shall Bind upon earth shall be made Bound in the Heavenlies, and whatever you might Remove upon the earth shall be made Removed in the Heavenlies.

20 Then He Ordered His disciples that no man might speak that He is Jesus, the Christ.

Jesus rebukes Peter

21 From then began Jesus to Show to His disciples that He must Himself go into Jerusalem, and suffer very much from the elders and chief priests and scribes, and be killed, and Rise Up after the third day.

22 And Peter took Him to self and began to rebuke Him saying, Oh Lord, be by Grace to You, this shall most definitely not be to You.

23 He was made turning around and then Spoke to Peter, You must Move Behind Me, satan, you are an offense to Me, because you definitely regard of value not the things of God, but definitely the things of men.

24 Then Jesus Spoke to His disciples, If any man is Continuously by his choice Willing to Come After Me, he Must by his choice Deny himself, and he Must by his choice Take Up his cross, and he Must Continuously by his choice be Following Me. [Choose you this day whom you will serve, Joshua 24:15]

25 Because whoever that might be willing to save his soul shall destroy it; and he Whoever might Destroy his Living soul for the Cause of Me, shall Find It.

26 Because what does it profit a man, if ever he gain all of the satan's world but might be made to suffer loss of his soul, or what shall a man give in exchange for his soul?

27 Because the Son of Man is Expected to Come in the Glory of His Father with His Angels, and then Pay to every person according to his Deed. (Ps 62:12)

28 Truly, I am Saying to you, There are some now standing here, who should never ever taste death whenever, until after they should Spiritually See the Son of Man coming in His Kingdom Rule.

The Transfiguration

17 And after six days Jesus Took Along Peter, and James, and John his brother, and He bore them up in a high mountain privately for His Own.

2 And was Transfigured before them, and His Face Brightly Shined as the sun, and His clothes became White as Light.

3 And Behold, Moses and Elias Spiritually Appeared to them Talking Together with Him.

4 And Peter answered and spoke to Jesus, Oh Lord, It is a God-Work for us being here. If you are willing, we might make here three Tabernacles one for You, one for Moses, and one for Elias.

5 Uttering to Him further, Behold, a Cloud Full of Light overshadowed them, and Behold, a Voice from out of the Cloud Said, This is My Beloved Son in Whom I am Pleased, you must Hear Him. (Ps 2:7)

6 Also, the disciples heard, having fallen down on their face, and feared exceedingly.

7 And Jesus came near and Touched them. And also He Spoke, You must be made to Raise up and you must not be afraid.

8 When they lifted up their eyes, they saw no man except Jesus Alone.

9 And coming down from the mountain, Jesus, God Commanded them Saying, Speak to absolutely no man this vision, until after wherein the Son of Man Arises out from the Dead.

10 And His disciples questioned Him saying, Why, therefore, are the scribes saying that this Elias must come first of all?

11 And Jesus Spoke to Answer them, Certainly, Elias came first of all and shall restore all things,

12 But I Say that Elias has come already, and that they definitely did not Fully Know him, but definitely did with him whatever they willed. Also In the same manner, the Son of Man is expected to suffer by them.

13 Then the disciples understood this was Spoken to them concerning John the Baptist.

Disciples' uncommitment limits them

14 And they came to the multitude of people. A man came near to Him, kneeling to Him and saying,

15 Oh Lord, You must Have Mercy on my son, for he is insane, and evil work afflicted suffering often because he is falling down into the fire, and often into the water.

16 And I offered him to your disciples, and they were definitely not able to heal him.

17 Jesus Answered and Spoke, Oh faithless generation, and made perverted. Up to how long a time will I be with you? Up to how long a time will I Continue Enduring you? You must bring him here to Me.

18 And Jesus Rebuked him, and the demon came out from him, and the dependent child was made healed from the same hour.

19 Then the disciples came near to Jesus, they spoke to Him privately, Why then were we definitely not able to cast it out?

20 And Jesus Spoke to them, Because of your Uncommitment, Truly because I Say if you should have Faith, as a grain of mustard seed, you shall Spirit Say to this mountain, you must depart from here to there and it shall depart from, and nothing shall be impossible to you.

21 But this kind does definitely not go out except by Prayer and Fasting.

22 And when each returned themselves in Galilee, Jesus Spoke to them. The Son of Man is Expecting to be delivered up in betrayal into hands of men,

23 And they shall kill Him, and after the third day He shall Rise Up. And they were grieved exceedingly.

Jesus pays Temple tribute to not offend

24 And when they came into Capernaum, they that were taking the yearly Temple tribute, came near to Peter and spoke, Does definitely not your Teacher finally fulfill the yearly Temple tribute?

25 He said, Emphatically yes. And when he entered into the house, Jesus prevented him Saying, Simon, what do you think? Of whom are the kings of the earth taking habit of custom or tribute, from their own sons or from those of other men?

26 Peter said to Him, From those of other men. Jesus Stated to him, So then their sons are free.

27 That we might not offend them, go into the Sea, you must cast a hook, and you must take up the first of all of the ascending fish. Open its mouth. You shall find the piece of money. You must take that to Give them for Me and you.

Enter Heaven Only as Children

18 In that hour the disciples of Jesus came near saying, So then, Who is greatest among us in the Kingdom Rule of the Heavenlies?

2 Jesus Invited a little child, and stood him in the midst of them.

3 And He Spoke, Truly, I Say to you, unless you should have been made Turned Around, and you should become as these little children, you should never ever enter into the Kingdom Rule of the Heavenlies.

4 Therefore, whoever should have Humbled himself, as this same little child, is greatest in the Kingdom Rule of the Heavenlies.

5 And whoever should have received such one little child in My Name, is receiving Me.

Do not offend children

6 But whoever might have offended one of the least of these, who are Committing for the result of Me, it is being necessary for him, that he should have made hanged a donkey grinding millstone to his neck, and he be should be sunk in the Open depths of the sea.

7 Woe to the satan's world from necessity of offenses. It is because of the offenses to come, but Woe to that man through whom the offense comes.

8 Then if your hand or your foot offends

you, you must cut it off, and you must cast it from you. It is a God-Work for you to enter into Life crippled or lame, than having two hands or two feet, to be made cast into eternal fire.

9 And if your eye is offending you by your choice, you must set it free and you must cast it by your choice away from you. It is a God-Work for you to enter by your choice with one eye into Life, than having two eyes being cast into the fiery hell.

10 You must Behold Attentively, you should not despise by your choice one of these little ones, because I am Saying to you, that in the Heavenlies by their Angels always see the Face of My Father, Who is in the Heavenlies.

Jesus Came to Save the lost
11 Because the Son of Man has by His choice come to Save that which is now lost.

12 What think you? If it might come to pass a certain man has a hundred sheep, and one might wander out from them, shall he definitely not dismiss the ninety nine, having been made to go in the mountains, seeking the one which is made wandering?

13 And if he might come to pass to find it, Truly, I Say to you, that he rejoices in regard of him much more than with the ninety nine, which were not made wandered.

14 In such a manner, it is definitely not the Will of your Father in the Heavenlies, that one of these little ones should be lost.

15 And if ever your brother might have sinned to you, you must lead away and you must convince him of sin, between you and him alone. If he should have Heard you, you have gained your Brother,

16 But if he might not Hear you, you must take along with you one or two more, that in regard of the mouth of two or three witnesses every specific word might stand. (Deut 19:15)

17 And if he might Refuse to hear them, you must Speak to the Assembly, but if he might refuse to hear the Assembly, then he must be to you as a heathen and a tax collector.

18 Truly I Say to you, whatever you might Bind on earth, shall be now Bound in Heaven; also whatever you might Remove upon the earth, shall be now Removed in Heaven.

19 Again, I Say to you, that if ever two of you agree together upon earth concerning anything whatever, if they might ask, it shall come to pass for them from My Father in the Heavenlies.

20 Because where there are two or three gathered together in My Name, there am I in the midst of them.

Forgive Seventy Times Seven Times
21 Then Peter having come near to Him spoke, Oh Lord, How often shall my brother sin toward me, and I will Remove from Memory (forgive) for him, until after seven times?

22 Jesus Says to him, I am definitely not Saying to you until after seven times, but definitely until after seventy times seven.

23 Because this Kingdom Rule of the Heavenlies is likened to a man, a king, who will take total account, with the Spiritual Word of his Bondslaves.

24 And when he began to take total account, one debtor of ten thousand talents was offered to him.

25 But he is not having it to repay, the lord commanded him and his wife and children also all alike to be sold in the market to repay also as much as he was having.

26 The slave, therefore, fell down and was worshiping him, saying, Oh Lord, you must be Longsuffering to me and I will repay all to you.

27 Then the lord had compassion on that same slave, dismissed away his indebtedness, and removed from memory (forgave) him.

28 But that same slave came out, found his one fellow slave that was indebted to

him a hundred pennies, and he held to retain strangling him, saying, You must pay then whatever that you are indebted to me.

29 Therefore, that fellow slave of his, fell down at his feet beseeching him saying, You must be Longsuffering to me, and I will repay you all.

30 But he would definitely not, but definitely having gone, cast him into prison until after he might repaid the things where he was indebted.

31 When his fellow slaves spiritually saw what had come to pass, they grieved exceedingly, and came to make clear to their Lord, all that had come to pass.

32 Then his lord invited him, saying to him, evil slave, I dismissed all those debts due from you, in fact you beseeched me.

33 Must you definitely be required to also Have Mercy on your fellow slave, in such a manner as I also Had Mercy on you?

34 And his lord was angry, delivered him up to the tormentors, until after when He might repay all that is indebted to him.

35 Also, in such a manner, My Heavenly Father shall Finalize for you, unless every person might Remove from Memory (forgive) from your hearts his brother for his spiritual death offenses.

Jesus tested about divorce

19 And it came to pass, when Jesus had Finally Fulfilled these Spiritual Communications, He Removed Himself from Galilee, and came into the districts of Judaea, on the other side of Jordan.

2 And large multitudes of people followed Him, and He healed them there.

3 Also the Pharisees came near to Him, tempting Him, and saying to Him. If it is lawful for a man to divorce his wife for any reason?

4 Then Answering He Spoke to them, Have you definitely not read how He Created from the beginning? He Created them male and female.

5 And Spoke, For this cause a man shall Leave father and mother and shall Cling to his wife, and the two shall be in one flesh nature. (Gen 1:27; 2:24)

6 So that no more are they two, but definitely one flesh nature. Whom, therefore, God Joined Together, man must not be separating.

7 They say to Him, Why, therefore, did God Command Moses to give a scroll writing of divorcement, and to divorce her?

8 He Says to them, Moses, because for your hardness of heart permitted you to divorce your wife, but from the beginning it is definitely not occurring in such a manner.

9 And I Say to you, that whoever divorced his wife, except for fornication, and married another is committing adultery, and who marries a divorced is committing adultery.

10 His disciples say to Him, If, in this manner, this is being the reason of the man with the woman, it is definitely not essential to marry.

11 Then He Spoke to them, Definitely not all are finding a place for this Spiritual Word, but definitely to whom it is being made Given,

12 Because there are eunuchs, who are born from mother's womb, and in such a manner there are eunuchs, who have been eunuchs made by men, and there are eunuchs who have made themselves eunuchs, because of the Kingdom Rule of Heavenlies. He that is able to be accommodating, he must accommodate.

Must Have Concern for children

13 Then they offered to Him little children, that He might lay His Hands on them and Pray, but the disciples rebuked them.

14 But Jesus Spoke, You must have concern for the little children, and you must not forbid them to come to Me, because of such is the Kingdom Rule of the Heavenlies.

15 Also, He Laid His Hands on them, and went from that place.

Difficult for rich to Enter Heaven

16 Behold, one came near and spoke to Him, Oh God-Good Teacher, Oh God-Good, what might I Do by my choice, in order that I might continuously by my choice be having Eternal Life?

17 Then He Spoke to him, Why call Me God-Good? No one God-Good, except One, that is God. But if you are continuously by your choice willing to enter into Life, you must by your choice keep the Commandments.

18 Then he says, Which? Jesus Spoke, You shall definitely not murder. You shall definitely not commit adultery. You shall definitely not steal. You shall definitely not bear false witness.

19 Honor your father and your mother, and God-Love your neighbor as yourself. (Ex 20:12-16; Deut 5:16-20)

20 The young man says to Him, To all these things I have maintained for myself from my youth. What further do I lack?

21 Jesus Stated to him, If you shall be Perfect, you must be going away, you must sell your material goods, and you must give to the poor, and you will have treasure in Heaven. But you must Come Forward. You must continuously by your choice be Following Me.

22 But when the young man heard this Spiritual Communication, he went grieving, because he was having many acquired possessions.

23 Then Jesus Spoke to His disciples, Truly, I Say to you, that the rich shall hardly enter into Kingdom Rule of the Heavenlies.

24 And again I Say to you, It is easier for a camel to pass through an eye hole of a needle, than the rich to enter into the Kingdom Rule of God.

Many first shall be Last, and last First

25 When His disciples heard Him, they were exceedingly amazed, saying, So then, who can be Saved?

26 And Jesus looked upon them, and Spoke, With man this is impossible, but with God, He is being Exceedingly Able to all.

27 Then answered Peter. He spoke to Him. Behold, we have parted from all, also to follow You. So then, what shall be to us?

28 And Jesus Spoke to them, Truly, I am Saying to you, that yourselves who follow Me in this Regeneration, when the Son of Man should have Sat Down upon His Throne of Glory, yourselves shall Sit Down also on Twelve Thrones to be Judging the Twelve Tribes of Israel.

29 And everyone who has dismissed houses, or brothers, or sisters, or father, or mother, or wife, or children, or fields for the cause of My Name shall take a hundredfold, and shall by your choice Inherit Eternal Life.

30 But many first shall be Last, and the last, First.

Vineyard workers all receive same pay

20 Because the Kingdom Rule of the Heavenlies is like a man, a householder, who came out early in the morning to hire together workers into his vineyard.

2　And when he agreed together with the workers for a penny daily, he sent them out into his vineyard.

3　And he came out about the third hour to Spiritually See others of same kind now standing idle in the marketplace.

4　He spoke to them also, Yourselves must go away also into the vineyard, and I will Give to you whatever might be Righteous. And then they went.

5　Then he came out again about sixth and ninth hour doing in like manner.

6　Then about the eleventh hour he came out and found others of same kind standing idle, and he called to them, Why are you now standing here idle the whole day?

7　They say to him, Because no man has hired us. He says to them, Yourselves also you must go away into the vineyard, and whatever might be Righteous you will receive.

8　When evening came to pass the lord of the vineyard said to his manager, You must call the workers and you must pay their reward, to begin from those last up to those first.

9　And they came about the eleventh hour, they received each a penny.

10　When the first came, they suppose that they would receive much more, but they themselves received only a penny.

11　When they received, they murmured against the householder.

12　Saying, that the last worked one hour, and made equal to us who bore the heavy burden and burning heat of the day.

13　Then he answered one of them, he spoke, Oh fellow, I am definitely not hurting you. Did you not agreed together with me for a penny?

14　You must take up yours and you must go away, I am willing also to Give this to the last in the same manner as also to you.

15　Is it definitely not lawful for me to do what I will with my own? Is the eye of you evil, in the event that I am God-Good?

16　In such a manner shall the last be First, and the first be Last, because many are Inwardly Called (Born Again), but few Elect (foreseen in Heaven). (Matt 22:14)

Jesus Tells about His Crucifixion

17　And Jesus Ascending into Jerusalem, He took along His Own twelve disciples in the way of travel, and as privately Spoke to them.

18　Behold, we are ascending into Jerusalem, and the Son of Man shall be delivered up in betrayal to the chief priests and scribes, and they shall Him condemn to death.

19　And they shall deliver Him up to the Gentiles for to mock, and scourge, and to crucify, and He shall Arise after the third day.

Mother seeks elevation for sons

20　Then the mother of the sons of Zebedee came near to Him with her sons, Worshiping and asking a certain thing alongside of Him.

21　Then He Spoke to her. What do you desire to say to me? You must speak that these two sons of mine should sit down, one by the Right Hand of You, and also one by the Left Hand in Your Kingdom Rule.

22　Jesus Answered and Spoke, You are definitely not now Spiritually Discerning what you are asking. Are you able to Drink My Cup that I expect to Drink, and the Immersion in which I am made Immersed to be Baptized? They say to Him, We are able.

23　And He Says to them, Certainly you shall Drink of My Cup, and the Immersion that I am Immersed, you shall be Baptized, but to sit down by My Right Hand and by My Left Hand is definitely not Mine to Give, but definitely it is now being Prepared for those by My Father.

24　The ten heard, and were very displeased in regard to the two brothers.

25　But Jesus Invited them and Spoke. You are now Spiritually Discerning that the Gentile ruler's lord over them, also exercise their great authority.

26　But it shall definitely not be, in such a manner, among yourselves, but definitely those, whoever might be great among yourselves, he must come to pass to be your servant.

27　And whoever must be First among yourselves, he should strongly desire to be your Bondslave.

28　As the Son of Man definitely did not come to be served, but definitely to serve, and to Give His (Sinless) Flesh Nature of Himself, a Removal Provided (for all our sinful flesh natures) for many.

29　And when they were going out from Jericho, a large multitude of people followed Him.

Two blind men are Healed

30　And, Behold, two blind sitting near to the way of travel, heard that Jesus was passing on, cried out saying, Oh Lord, Son of David, You must Have Mercy on us.

31 And then the multitude of people rebuked them, that they might hold speaking, but they were crying out exceedingly more, saying, Oh Lord, Son of David, You must Have Mercy on us.

32 Jesus Stood, and Called for them, and Spoke. What might you have Me do to you?

33 They called to Him. Oh Lord, that our eyes might be made Opened.

34 Then Jesus had Compassion, He Touched their eyes, and immediately the eyes of them by their choice received sight, and they by their choice followed Him.

Triumphal Entry into Jerusalem

21 And when they approached near to Jerusalem and came into Bethphage to the Mount of Olives, then Jesus Sent Out two disciples,

2 Saying to them, You must go into the village before you, and immediately find a donkey now being bound, and a colt with her. You must remove to lead to Me.

3 And if any might Speak to you, Spirit Say to the certain one, Because the Lord is having immediate need of them. Then he shall send them out.

4 Then all of this came to pass that it should be Fulfilled, Spirit Spoken through the Prophet, Saying,

5 You must speak to the daughter of Sion, Behold, your King is coming to you, Meek and now entering in on a donkey even a colt, the son of a female donkey. (Isa 62:11; Zech 9:9)

6 And the disciples went and did just as Jesus before Commanded them.

7 They lead the donkey and the colt, and laid upon them their clothes, and they sat Him upon them.

8 Then the most multitude of people lay out their clothes in the way of travel, and others of the same kind were trimming branches from the trees, and were them

laying out upon the way of travel.

9 And this multitude of people went before Him and followed crying out, saying, Hosanna to the Son of David, Blessed is He Coming in the Name of the Lord, Hosanna in the Highest. (Ps 118:25-26)

10 He Himself entered into Jerusalem, and all the city shook saying, Who is He?

11 The multitudes of people then called, This is Jesus, the Prophet from Nazareth of Galilee.

Jesus Cleanses Temple money market

12 And Jesus Entered into the Temple area of God, and Cast Out all those selling and buying in the Temple area, and He Turned Over the tables of the money changers, and the seats of those selling doves.

13 And Said to them, It is Written, My Home shall be called a Home of Prayer; but yourselves have made it a den of robbers. (Isa 56:7; Jer 7:11)

14 And the blind and crippled came near to Him in the Temple area, and He Healed them.

15 When the chief priests and the scribes spiritually discerned the wondrous things done, and the dependent children crying out inside the Temple area, and calling Hosanna to the Son of David, they were very displeased.

16 And they spoke to Him. Are you hearing what they are saying? Then Jesus Says to them, Emphatically Yes, have you never read that out from a mouth of infants and the nursing you Make Completed Praise? (Ps 8:2)

Fig tree is Cursed

17 And He left them, came out outside the city into Bethany and camped there.

18 Then early morning He Proceeded Out into the city. He was Hungry.

19 And He Spiritually Discerned one fig tree in the way of travel. He came to it and found nothing upon it except only leaves. And He Said to it, No longer should occur

fruit from you, Forever. And the fig tree instantly dried up.

20 The disciples Spiritually Saw, and marveled saying, How instantly the fig tree dried up.

21 Jesus Answered and Spoke to them, Truly, I am Saying to you, whoever should by his choice have Faith and should be made to not doubt, definitely not only this of the fig tree shall be done, but definitely if to this mountain you should speak, You must be made taken away, and you must be made cast into the sea. It shall come to pass.

22 And all things, whatever you should ask in Prayer Committing, you shall receive.

Jesus' Authority is questioned

23 When He came to the Temple area, the chief priests and the elders of the people came near for His Teaching. They are saying, In what Authority are You doing these things, and who gave You this Authority?

24 Then Jesus Answered. He Spoke to them. I, also, I shall earnestly request of you one Spiritual Word, which if ever you might speak to Me, I also will Spirit Say to you, In what Authority I am doing these things.

25 The immersion of John, from what was it, from Heaven or out from man? Then they reasoned with themselves saying, If we might speak from Heaven, He will Spirit Say to us, Why then, therefore, did you definitely not Commit to Him?

26 But if we might Speak from man, we fear the multitude of people, because all have John as a Prophet.

27 And they answered Jesus. They spoke. We definitely cannot discern to state about him. So this I say to you, neither by what Authority I am doing these things.

Publicans and harlots enter before them

28 But what do you think to yourselves? A man had two children, and he came near to the first, spoke Oh child, you must go away this day, you must be working in my vineyard.

29 Then he answered, spoke, I will definitely not, but afterward, he regretted, he went.

30 And he came near to the second, he spoke in like manner, and he answered and spoke, Oh lord, I (go), and he did not go.

31 Which out from the two did his father's will? They say, To him, the first. Jesus Says to them, Truly, I Say to you, that the tax collectors and the harlots go before you into the Kingdom Rule of God.

32 Because John came to you in Way of Righteousness and you definitely Committed not to him. But the tax collectors and the harlots Committed to him. And when you Spiritually Discerned, you definitely have not afterward regretted and Committed to him.

Kingdom of God taken from them

33 Hear another parable of the same kind. A man, who was a certain householder, planted a vineyard and placed a hedge about it, and dug a wine press inside of it and built a tower, and sharecropped to his husbandmen and journeyed away.

34 And when the special time approached near for fruit, he sent out his slaves to the husbandmen, to receive his fruit.

35 And the husbandmen took his slaves, then certainly beat one, and killed one, and stoned another.

36 Again, he sent out other slaves of the same kind, greater than the first, and they treated them in like manner.

37 Then afterward, he sent out his son to them, saying they shall respect my son.

38 But when the husbandmen spiritually discerned the son, they spoke among themselves, This is the heir, you must come now, we should kill him, and we might hold fast his inheritance.

39 They took and killed and cast him out, outside the vineyard,

40 When, therefore, the lord of the vineyard should come, What shall he do to those husbandmen?

41 They say, he will destroy those evil work afflicted evil workers, and he shall share crop the vineyard to other husbandmen of same kind, who shall yield to him the fruits in the Special Times of them.

42 Jesus Says to them. Have you never read in the Scriptures, that Stone which the builders disapproved, the Same became for the Head of the Corner? It has Occurred from the Lord and is marvelous in our Eyes. (Ps 118:22-23)

43 Because of this, I Say to you that the Kingdom Rule of God shall be taken away from you, and shall be Given to Gentiles, Bringing Forth His Fruit.

44 And the one who has fallen down upon this Stone, he shall be Made Broken. But upon whomever it should have fallen down, it shall grind him to powder.

45 And the chief priests and the Pharisees heard the parable of them, and knew what it is saying in regard to them.

46 They seeking to hold to retain Him, but they feared the multitudes of people, for after that they were having Him as a Prophet.

Righteous Clothing needed for Wedding

22 And Jesus Answered again, Spoke to them in a parable, Saying,

2 The Kingdom Rule of the Heavenlies is likened to a man, a king, who planned Marriages for His Son (Body of Christ).

3 And He Sent Out His Bondslaves to call those being Called Outwardly (Gospel) to the Marriages, and they definitely would not come.

4 Again, He Sent Out other Bondslaves of the same kinds saying, You must speak, calling, Behold my dinner. I have prepared my bull and slew the fatling. And now all things ready, you must come now into the Weddings.

5 But they neglecting, one actually went into his own field, and another into his marketing.

6 Then the others retaining His Bondslaves, they violently treated and killed.

7 When the king heard, he was angry, and sent His armies to destroy those deliberate murderers, and burned up their city.

8 Then He Said to his Bondslaves, Certainly, the wedding is ready, but they who are now being made called were definitely not worthy.

9 Therefore, you must go upon the highways, the ways of travel, and as many as you might find; you must call into the marriages.

10 Those Bondslaves came out into the ways of travel, gathering together all, as many as found both evil and also God-Good, and filled the Wedding sitting as at eating.

11 When the King entered to see those sitting as at eating, he Spiritually Saw a man there who definitely had not put on for himself the Wedding clothing.

12 And he says to him, Oh fellow, how have you entered here having no Wedding clothing? Then there was silence.

13 Then the King spoke to the servants, Bind his feet and hands, you must take away, and you must cast him out into outer darkness. There shall be weeping and gnashing of teeth.

14 Because many are Inwardly Called (Born Again), but few Elect (foreseen in Heaven, Rom 9:11). (Matt 20:16)

Give Caesar his due; and to God, His

15 Then the Pharisees went to take counsel, so that they might entrap Him in Spiritual Communication.

16 And they sent out to Him their disciples with the Herodians saying, Oh Teacher, we Discern that You are True and are teaching The Way of God in Truth, and You are definitely not caring to man, because You are definitely not Seeing to the presence of men.

17 Therefore, You must speak to us, What is Your Thinking? Is it lawful to give tribute to Caesar or definitely not?

18 But Jesus knew their evil action. He Spoke, Oh hypocrite actors, why are you trying Me?

19 You must show as example to Me on the tribute payment. Then they offered a penny to Him.

20 And He Said to them, Whose this image and superscription?

21 They said to Him, Caesar's. Then He Said to them, Therefore, you must pay unto Caesar to Caesar, and then unto God to God.

22 When they heard, they marveled, and parting from Him, they went.

Resurrection question

23 In that same day, the Sadducees, who say there is being not a Resurrection, came near to Him and they questioned Him.

24 Saying, Oh Teacher, Moses spoke if ever anyone might die not having children, his brother shall levirate marry his wife, and shall raise seed to his brother. (Deut 25:5)

25 Then there were with us seven brothers, and the first married and deceased having no seed, dismissed his wife to his brother.

26 Likewise also the second, and the third until after the seventh.

27 Then afterward, the wife of all also died.

28 Therefore, in the Resurrection of the seven whose wife shall she be, because all had her?

29 Jesus Answered and Spoke to them, You must continuously be made deceived, not now Spiritually Discerning the Scriptures, neither the Miracle Power of God.

30 Because in the Resurrection, they are neither marrying nor are being made given in marriage, but definitely they are as Angels of God in Heaven.

31 But in regard of the Resurrection of the dead, have you definitely not read, that Spirit Spoken to you by God, Saying,

32 I AM, the God of Abraham and the God of Isaac and the God of Jacob! God is definitely not the God of the dead, but definitely the God of the Living. (Ex 3:6)

33 And the multitudes of people heard. They were made amazed at His Teaching.

Which is Greatest Commandment?

34 When the Pharisees heard that He had silenced the Sadducees, they gathered together with Him.

35 And one, a lawyer, questioned at Him, trying Him and saying,

36 Oh Teacher, which (is the) great Commandment in the Law?

37 Then Jesus Spoke to him, You shall God-Love the Lord your God inside your whole heart, and inside your whole soul, and inside your whole intellect. (Deut 6:5)

38 This is first and the Great Commandment.

39 And second like to it, God-Love your neighbor as yourself. (Lev 19:18)

40 Inside these two Commandments, hangs the whole Law and the Prophets.

Christ is Whose Son?

41 While the Pharisees were now gathered together, Jesus questioned them,

42 Saying, What do you think in regard to the Christ? Whose Son is He? They said, He is of David.

43 He says to them, How, therefore, David in Spirit called Him Lord, saying,

44 The Lord to My Lord Spoke, You must Sit at My Right Hand until after ever I should Put Your enemies whoever at the Footstool of Your Feet? (Ps 110:1)

45 If, therefore, David calls Him Lord, How is He his Son?

46 And no man was able to answer His Spiritual Communication, neither did any dare, from that day, to question Him anymore.

Condemns scribes and Pharisees

23 Then Jesus Uttered to the multitudes of people and to His disciples,

2 Saying, The scribes and Pharisees sat down upon Moses' seat.

3 All, therefore, whatever, as much as they might have spoken to you, you must be keeping and to Hold as Sacred, but instead you must not do according to their man works, for you must do what they say, but definitely they do not.

4 For they are tying up weighty burdens and grievously borne, and are laying them upon men's shoulders, and they are definitely not willing to move them with their finger.

5 But to all their man works they do to be made seen by men, while they enlarge their phylacteries and magnify the borders of their robes.

6 And also they are affectionately loving the chief room in the suppers, and the chief seats in the synagogues,

7 And the salutations in the marketplaces, and being made called Rabbi, Rabbi, by the men.

8 But yourselves are not to be made called Rabbi, because One is your Master Teacher, Christ, and then all you, yourselves, are Brothers.

9 And you should call no one your Father upon the earth, because One is your Father, Who (is) in the Heavenlies.

10 Nor should you be made called Master Teacher, because One is your Master Teacher, the Christ.

11 But the greatest of you shall be your servant.

12 And whoever shall exalt himself shall be made Humbled, and whoever shall Humble himself shall be made exalted.

13 Woe then to you, Oh scribes and, Oh Pharisees, Oh hypocrite actors, for you are shutting the Kingdom Rule of the Heavenlies before men, because yourselves are definitely not entering, neither admitting those entering to enter.

14 Woe to you, Oh scribes and, Oh Pharisees, Oh hypocrite actors, for you are devouring widows' houses, and in pretense make extended Prayers. Because of this you shall receive more abundant condemnation.

15 Woe to you, Oh scribes and, Oh Pharisees, Oh hypocrite actors, for you go about sea and dry land to make one proselyte, and when it comes to pass, you make him double a son of hell than you.

16 Woe to you, Oh blind guides which say, whoever might swear by the Temple it is nothing; but whoever might swear by the gold of the Temple, he is indebted.

17 Oh foolish and, Oh blind, because which is greater, the gold or the Temple that Makes Holy the gold?

18 And, whoever might swear by the altar, it is nothing. Whoever swears by the gift upon it, he is indebted.

19 Oh foolish and, Oh blind, because which great, the gift, or the altar that Makes Holy the gift?

20 Therefore who has sworn by the altar, swears by it, and by all things upon it.

21 And who swears by the Temple, is swearing by it, and by Him Dwelling in it.

22 And he that swears by Heaven is swearing by the Throne of God, and by Him Sitting upon it.

23 Woe to you, Oh scribes and, Oh Pharisees, Oh hypocrite actors, for you tithe mint, and anise, and cumin, and you dismiss the burdensome things of Law, Final Judgment, and the Mercy and the Faith. These things were required to do, not dismissing the others also.

24 Oh blind guides, you are straining at a gnat and then completely swallowing a camel.

25 Woe to you, Oh scribes and, Oh Pharisees, Oh hypocrite actors, for you cleanse the outward of the cup and platter, but inside from within you are being full of extortion, and lack of control.

26 Oh Blind Pharisee: you must Cleanse first of all that inside within the cup and the platter, in order that the outside of them should become Purified also.

27 Woe to you, Oh scribes and, Oh Pharisees, Oh hypocrite actors, for you resemble whitened tombs which certainly appear beautiful outward, but inside you are full of dead bones, and of all moral impurity.

28 Also, in such a manner, outward yourselves certainly appear Righteous to men, but inside you are full of role-playing hypocrisy and lawlessness.

29 Woe to you, Oh scribes and, Oh Pharisees, Oh hypocrite actors, because you built the tombs of the Prophets, and adorn the sepulchers of the Righteous,

30 And you are saying, if we were in the days of our fathers, we would definitely not ever be their companions in the blood of the Prophets.

31 So that you give witness to yourselves, that you are sons of those who murdered the Prophets.

32 Also, yourselves must fully fill the amount of measure of your fathers.

33 Oh serpents, Oh products of vipers, how should you flee from the Final Judgment of hell?

34 Because of this, Behold, I Send Out to you Prophets, and wise and scribes, and from them you shall kill, and crucify, and from them you shall scourge in your synagogues, and shall persecute from city to city.

35 So that upon you should come all the Righteous blood poured out upon the earth, from the blood of Righteous Abel, until after the blood of Zacharias the son of Barachias, whom you murdered between the Temple Sanctuary and the altar.

36 Truly, I Say to you, all these things shall now come on this generation.

Jesus Mourns over Jerusalem

37 Oh Jerusalem, Oh Jerusalem, you that are killing the Prophets, and casting stones on those being now made Sent Out to you. How often would I have Gathered All Together your children, in this manner a hen gathers all together her chickens under her wings, and you definitely would not?

38 Behold, your home, a desolate wilderness, is being made dismissed. (Jer 22:5)

39 Because I am Saying to you, never ever should you spiritually discern Me since from now, until after you should whenever speak by your choice, Blessed is He Coming in the Name of the Lord. (Ps 118:26)

Events at End of this Age

24 And Jesus went departing from the Temple area, then His disciples came near to show to Him as example the buildings of the Temple area.

2 And Jesus Spoke to them, Are you definitely not Spiritually Seeing all these things? Truly, I Say to you, never ever should dismiss here a stone upon a stone that shall definitely not be made torn down.

3 And Sitting Himself upon the Mountain of Olivet, the disciples came near to Him to be privately saying, You must speak to us, When shall these things be, and what the Miracle Sign of Your coming and the Final End of the satan's world?

4 Jesus Answered and Spoke to them, You must See that no man might by your choice deceive you.

5 Because many shall come in My Name, saying, I AM, the Christ, and many shall by their choice be deceived.

6 Then you shall expect to be hearing wars, and hearing rumors of wars, you must be Beholding Attentively, that you are not being made frightened, because all things must come to pass, but definitely it is not yet the End.

7 Because nation shall raise up against nation, and kingdom rule against kingdom rule, and there shall be famines and pestilences and earthquakes, according to places.

8 When all these things, the beginning

of travails.

9   Then they shall deliver you up to affliction, and they shall kill you, and yourselves shall be made hated by all the nations because of My Name.

10   Also then many shall be offended, and deliver one another up, and hate one another.

11   And many false prophets shall rise up and deceive many.

12   And because of lawlessness being multiplied, the God-Love of many shall become made cold.

13   But he that Endures to his End he shall be Made Saved.

14   And this Gospel of the Kingdom Rule shall be Preached in the whole inhabited earth, for a Testimony to all nations, and then the End shall Now Come.

Flight when Holy Place abomination

15   He that is reading must be comprehending. When, therefore, yourselves should have Spiritually Discerned the abomination of desolation standing in the Holy Place, Spirit Spoken through Daniel the Prophet, (Daniel 9:27)

16   Then them in Judaea, you must flee to the mountains.

17   He upon the housetop must not come down to take up anything out from his house.

18   And he in the field, he must not turn back after to take away his clothes.

19   And Woe to them when having womb with child, and to those nursing in those days.

20   But you must be Praying that your flight might not come to pass during winter, nor in a Sabbath.

Great Tribulation shall come

21   Because then shall be Great Tribulation (affliction), such as definitely not come to pass from beginning of the satan's world until after now, neither should never ever came to pass.

22   And except those days be made shortened, there be definitely not any sinful flesh nature made Saved whatever, but because of the Elect those days shall be made shortened.

23   Then if any man might speak to you, You must behold, here Christ, or here; yourselves should not commit.

24   Because false christs and false prophets shall rise up, and shall give great Miracle Signs and Wonders, so that to deceive, if possible, even the Elect.

25   Behold, I am foretelling to you,

26   Therefore, whatever, they might speak to you, You must behold, he is in the desolate wilderness, you should not come out. You must behold, in the private room, you should not commit.

27   Because as the lightning comes out from the east and appears to the west, in such a manner shall be the Coming of the Son of Man.

28   Because whereto the Dead Body might be, there the Eagles shall be made gathered together.

Christ Returns & Elect are Gathered

29   And immediately after the Tribulation of those days, the sun shall be darkened, and the moon shall definitely not give its shining, and the stars shall fall down from Heaven, and the Miracle Powers of the Heavenlies shall be shaken.

30   And then shall Appear a Miracle Sign of the Son of Man in the Heaven, and then all the tribes of the earth shall bewail, and they shall see the Son of Man Coming Upon the Clouds of Heaven with Miracle Power and very much Glory. (Dan 7:13)

31   And He shall Send Out His Angels with a Great Trumpet Sound, and shall Gather All Together His Elect out from the four winds, from the farthest parts of the Heavenlies to the farthest parts of them. (1 Cor 15:52; 1 Thess 4:16)

This generation sees all this

32 Then learn the parable of the fig tree, when already its branch might become tender, and the leaves should bud out, you know that summer near.

33 And in such a manner, when yourselves should see all these things, Know that it is near at the doors.

34 Truly, I say to you, This generation should never ever pass away, until after all these things whatever should come to pass.

35 Heaven and earth shall pass away, but My Words should never ever Pass Away.

No man knows the day nor the hour

36 And in regard to that Day and hour, no man Spiritually Discerns, neither the Angels of the Heavenlies, except My Father alone.

37 But as the days of Noah, in such a manner, shall be also the Coming of the Son of Man.

38 Because as it was in the days before the flood of Noah, they were enjoying eating and drinking and marrying and given in marriage, until that day Noah entered into the Ark.

39 And definitely not knowing until after the flood of Noah Came, and took away all things. In such a manner shall be also the Coming of the Son of Man.

40 Then shall be two in the field, one is Taken Along and one made parted from.

41 Two women grinding in the mill, one made Taken Along and one made parted from.

42 You must Watch, therefore, for you definitely cannot now discern, what hour your Lord is Coming.

43 But Know this, that if the householder had Spiritually Discerned which watch the thief is coming, he would have watched whenever, and definitely not allowed that one to break through his house.

44 And because of this, yourselves must become Ready, for in an hour as you think definitely not, the Son of Man is Coming.

Who is the Faithful and Wise Servant?

45 So then, who is the Faithful and very wise Bondslave, whom his Lord has made ruler over his Household Health to give them Nourishment in a Special Time?

46 Spiritually Blessed that Bondslave, whom his Lord having Come, shall find doing in such a manner.

47 Truly, I say to you, that He shall make him ruler over all his material goods,

48 And if whenever the evil work slave then might speak in his heart, my lord is delaying to come,

49 And might have begun to strike his fellow slaves, and to eat and to drink with those being drunk,

50 The Lord of that slave shall now come in a day, when he is definitely not watching for, and in an hour which he is definitely not knowing,

51 And he shall cut him up severely, and shall position his part with the hypocrite actors. There shall be weeping and gnashing of teeth.

Parable of ten virgins

25 Then shall the Kingdom Rule of the Heavenlies be likened to ten Virgins, who took their Lamps, came out to a Meeting of the Bridegroom.

2 And five of them were very Wise, and the other five foolish.

3 When the foolish took their Lamps themselves, they took definitely no Oil with themselves.

4 But the very Wise took Oil in their containers with their Lamps.

5 When the Bridegroom is delaying, every person is slumbering and sleeping.

6 Then it was now coming to pass, screaming in the middle of night, Behold, the Bridegroom is Coming. You must be coming out to His Meeting.

7 Then all those Virgins rose up, and trimmed their Lamps.

8 And the foolish spoke to the very Wise, You must give us out from your Oil, because

our Lamps are being extinguished.

9   But the very Wise answered saying, for fear that It might definitely not be sufficient to us, then you must go to them selling, and you must buy much more for yourselves.

10   And when they went to buy, the Bridegroom Came, and those Ready Entered with Him into the Wedding, and the Door was Shut.

11   Afterward, when the other Virgins also were coming, saying, Lord, Lord, You must Open to us!

12   But He Answered and Spoke, Truly, I Say to you, I definitely not now Spiritually Discern you.

13   You must be Watching, therefore, because you definitely are not Discerning the Day, neither the Hour, in which the Son of Man is Coming.

Parable of talents

14   Because, as a man is journeying away, he called his own bondslaves, and delivered up to them his material goods.

15   And then he gave certainly to one five talents, and to one two, and to another one, to everyone according to his miracle power, and immediately he journeyed away.

16   Then who had received five talents went to work, and in thereby to make another five talents of the same kind.

17   And in like manner to whom two he gained himself also another two of same kind,

18   But he that received one, went to dig in the earth, and to conceal the piece of silver of his lord.

19   Then after very much time the lord of those bondslaves comes, and is taking total account with his words.

20   And he that received five talents came near, offered other five talents of the same kind saying, Oh lord, five talents you delivered up to me, behold, I but definitely gained five talents over them.

21   And his lord stated to him, Well, oh good and, oh faithful, oh bondslave, you have been faithful with a few, I will make you over very much, you must enter into the joy of your lord.

22   Another that had received the two talents came near, spoke, Oh lord, two talents you delivered up to me, behold, others of same kind, I have gained two talents over them.

23   His lord stated to him, Well done, oh good and, oh faithful, oh bondslave, you were faithful with a little; I will make you over very much, you must enter into the joy of your lord.

24   Then he who had received the one talent came near and spoke, Oh lord, I knew you that you are a hard man, reaping whereto you have definitely not sown, and gathering together where from you definitely have not scattered.

25   I was afraid, and went to hide your talent in the earth, behold I have your one.

26   His lord answered and spoke to him, Oh evil and, oh lazy, oh bondslave; you have known that I reap whereto I have definitely not sown, and gather together where from I have definitely not scattered,

27   Therefore, you ought to have cast my piece of silver to the exchanger, and I having come earned for myself whatever mine, united with interest.

28   You must therefore, take away from him the talent, and you must give to him having ten talents.

29   Because to him having, at all times, you shall be giving and abounding in amount, but from him not having, also that he is having shall be taken away from him.

30   And you must cast out the unprofitable bondslave into the outer darkness. There shall be weeping and gnashing of teeth.

Judgment, People of All Nations

31   And when the Son of Man should come in His Glory, and all His Holy Angels with Him, then He shall Sit Down upon His Throne of Glory.

32 And before Him all the nations shall be made gathered together, and He shall Separate them from one another, as the Shepherd Separates His Sheep from the kid goats.

33 And He shall certainly Stand the Sheep by His Right Hand, but the goats by the left hand.

34 Then the King shall Spirit Say to those at His Right Hand, You must Come now, those being Now Blessed by My Father, you Must Inherit the Kingdom Rule, prepared for You from the Conception of the satan's world.

35 Because I was hungry and you Gave to Me to eat, thirsty and you Gave Me to drink, a stranger and you Gathered Me Together.

36 Naked and you Clothed Me. I was sick and you Visited Me. I was in prison and you Came to Me.

37 Then shall the Righteous answer Him saying, Oh Lord, when did we Spiritually Discern You being hungry and we nourished, or thirsting and we gave to drink?

38 And when have we Spiritually Discerned You a stranger or naked, and then we gathered together and we clothed?

39 And when did we see You weak, or in prison, and we came to You?

40 And the King answered Spirit Saying to them, Truly, I am Saying to you with as much as done to one of these least of My Brothers, you have done to Me.

41 Then He Spirit Says, and to those at the left hand, You must go from Me, you are now being made cursed into the Fire Eternal, prepared for the devil and his angels.

42 Because I was hungry and you gave Me definitely not to eat, thirsted and you gave Me definitely no drink.

43 I was a stranger and you definitely did not gather together to Me, naked and you did definitely not clothe Me, weak and in prison and you did definitely not visit Me.

44 Then they shall answer Him and say to Him, Oh Lord, when did we see You hungering and thirsting, or a stranger, or naked, or weak, or in prison, and definitely not served You?

45 Then He Answered Saying to them, Truly, I Say to you, as much as you did it not to one of the least of these, you did it not to Me.

46 And these shall go into Eternal torment, but the Righteous into Life Eternal.

Plan to kill Jesus

26 And it came to pass, when Jesus Finally Fulfilled all these Spiritual Communications, He Spoke to His disciples.

2 You discern that after two days the Passover is coming to pass, and the Son of Man is being delivered up in betrayal for being made crucified.

3 Then being gathered together, the chief priests and the scribes and the elders of the people, into the palace of the High Priest, who was called Caiaphas.

4 And counseled that Jesus might be held to retain, by a subtle half-truth (deceit) and might be killed.

5 And they were saying, not possibly in the Feast, that a tumult by the people might not occur.

Jesus Anointed for His Burial

6 And then, it occurred that Jesus was in Bethany in Simon, the leper's house,

7 A woman, having an alabaster container of expensive ointment, came near to Him sitting as at eating, and poured it upon His Head.

8 When His disciples saw, they were very displeased saying, For what purpose this squander?

9 Because this ointment was able to be sold in the market for very much, and given to the poor.

10 When Jesus knew this He Spoke to them. Why are you offering labor to concern yourselves with this woman? For she has worked a Work by God, God-Work, for the Purpose and Result of Me.

11 Because you always are having the poor with you, but Me you are definitely not always having.

12 Because she poured this ointment upon my Body, she did this to prepare burial for Me.

13 Truly, I am Saying to you, whereto wherever this Gospel might be preached in all the satan's world, it shall be uttered, and what she has done for a memorial of her.

Judas went to chief priests

14 Then went one of the twelve called Judas Iscariot to the chief priests;

15 He spoke. What will you give me, also I, I will deliver Him up in betrayal to you? And then they brought to him thirty pieces of silver. (Zech 11:12)

16 And from then, he sought opportunity in order that he might deliver Him up in betrayal.

The Last Supper

17 Then for the First Day of the Feast of Unleavened Bread, the disciples came near to Jesus saying to Him, Wherein should it be prepared for You to eat the Passover?

18 And He Spoke, You must go away into the city to such a man and you must speak to him, The Master Says My Special Time is near to you. I am Finalizing the Passover with My disciples.

19 And the disciples did as Jesus instructed to them, and prepared the Passover.

20 When evening came to pass, He sat as at eating with the twelve.

21 And eating with them, He Spoke, Truly, I Say to you that one, out from yourselves, shall deliver Me up in betrayal.

22 And they began sorrowing exceedingly; every one of them, saying to Him, Is it possibly I, Oh Lord?

23 He Answered and Spoke, He that hand dipped with Me in the dish, the same hand shall deliver Me up.

24 Certainly, the Son of Man is going away, just as it is made Written in regard to Him. But Woe to that man through whom the Son of Man is being made delivered up in betrayal. It was God-Work if that man had definitely not been made born.

25 Then Judas, who delivered Him up in betrayal, answered, spoke, Oh Rabbi, Is it possibly I? He Said to him, You have spoken.

26 When they were eating, Jesus received to take the loaves, and Blessed, and Broke, and was Giving to the disciples, and Spoke, You must Take, you must Eat. This is My Body.

27 And He took the Cup, Gave Thanks and Gave to them saying, You must all Drink of it.

28 Because this is My Blood of the New of a different kind Covenant, being Poured Out, in regard to many, for Removal of sins natures and sins.

29 But I Say to you that I should never ever be Drinking from out of this product of the vine from now, by any means, until after that Day when I will Drink it with you, a New of a different kind, inside the Kingdom Rule of My Father.

30 They sang a hymn, and came out to the Mount of Olives.

Peter Told of his future denial

31 Then Says Jesus to them, Yourselves all shall be made offended in Me in this night, because it is now made Written, For I will strike mortally the Shepherd, and the Safe Flock of Sheep shall be made scattered. (Zech 13:7)

32 But after I Raise Up, I will go before you into Galilee.

33 Then Peter answered and spoke to Him, Although also all shall be made offended in You, I will never be made offended.

34 Jesus stated to him, Truly, I say to you that in this night, before the cock crows, you shall deny Me three times.

35 Peter said to Him, Though if I might die with You, I will definitely not deny You. Also likewise spoke all the disciples.

Garden of Gethsemane

36 Then Jesus came with them into a space of land called Gethsemane, and He Said to the disciples, You must Sit Down in this place until after, where I should go to Pray there.

37 And He took along Peter and the two sons of Zebedee. They began to grieve and be very sleepy.

38 Then He Says to them, My Living-Soul is very sorrowful up to death, you must abide here, and you must be Watching with Me.

39 And He went forward a little while, fell down on His Face, Praying and Saying, My Father if it is possible, You must Pass Away this Cup from Me, but definitely not as I Will, but definitely as You Will.

40 And He came to the disciples and found them sleeping, and Said, Peter, in this manner are you definitely not capable to Watch one hour with Me?

41 You must Watch and you must Pray that you might not enter into temptation. Certainly, the spirit willing, but the sinful flesh nature weak.

42 Again, for a second time He went to Pray Saying, My Father, If this Cup is definitely not able to Pass Away from Me, unless I should Drink it, Your Will must come to pass.

43 He came and found them sleeping again, because their eyes were heavy.

44 And He Dismissed Himself going again to Pray for the third time, Speaking the same Words.

45 Then He came to His disciples and Said to them, And now be sleeping and be refreshed. Behold, we are now approaching near to the hour, and the Son of Man is being made delivered up in betrayal into the hands of sinners.

46 You must Raise Up. Behold, I might be moving along. he is now approaching near to deliver Me up in betrayal.

Jesus Arrest by Judas' betrayal

47 And while He was Uttering to them, Behold, Judas, one of the twelve, came and with him a large multitude of people with swords and wooden staves from the chief priests and elders of the people.

48 And he that is delivering Him up in betrayal gave a miracle sign to them, saying to whomever I might have kissed, He it is you must hold Him to retain.

49 Immediately he came near to Jesus and spoke, You must rejoice, Oh Rabbi. And he kissed Him.

50 Then Jesus Spoke to him, Oh, Fellow, against whom are you present? Then they came near to lay hands upon Jesus, and they held to retain Him.

51 And you must behold, one with Jesus stretched out a hand to withdraw his sword, and struck hard a slave of the High Priest, took away his ear.

52 Then Jesus Called to him, You must turn away your sword into its place, because all of them, who take a sword, shall be destroyed by a sword.

53 Are you thinking that I am for now definitely not able to beseech My Father, and He will Stand with Me with many more than twelve legions of angels?

54 How then should the Scriptures be made Fulfilled? Because this in such a manner must come to pass.

55 In that same hour Jesus Spoke to the multitudes of people, Have you come out as to a robber with swords and wooden staves, to physically take Me? I was sitting Myself daily Teaching to you in the Temple area, and you definitely did not hold to retain Me.

56 But all this comes now to pass that the Scriptures and the Prophets should be made Fulfilled. Then all the disciples parted from Him to flee.

Jesus Before the High Priest

57 And they held to retain Jesus, and lead

Him away to Caiaphas, the High Priest, whereto the scribes and elders had been made gathered together.

58 But Peter was following Him at a distance up to the High Priest's palace, and he entered, and was sitting within with the under servants to see the end.

59 Then the chief priests and elders and the whole council, all were seeking false testimony against Jesus, so that they might put Him to Death.

60 But they found definitely none, yet many false witnesses coming near, afterward definitely not finding, then two bearing false witnesses came near.

61 They spoke. He was Stating, I am able to tear down God's Temple, and in three days build it.

62 The High Priest arose and spoke to Him. Are You answering nothing? What of You is this witnessing against?

63 Then Jesus was holding speech. The High Priest answered and spoke to Him. I adjure you by the Living God that you might speak to us, if You, You are the Christ, the Son of God.

64 Jesus Said to him, You have spoken, but I Say to you, since from now you shall see the Spiritual Appearance of the Son of Man Sitting at the Right Hand of Miracle Power, and Coming Upon the Clouds of Heaven. (Ps 110:1; Dan 7:13)

65 Then the High Priest tore apart his clothes saying, For He has blasphemed. What further need are we having witnesses? Behold, now you have heard His blasphemy.

66 What think you? They answered and spoke, He is found guilty of death.

67 Then they spit on His Face, and beat and slapped Him with the palms of their hands.

68 Saying, you must prophesy to us, You Christ. Who is he that harmfully struck You?

Peter denies Jesus three times

69 Then, Peter was sitting outside in the palace, and one maid servant came near to him saying, You also were with Jesus of Galilee.

70 But he disclaimed before every person saying, I am definitely not now Spiritually Discerning what you are continuously saying.

71 And when he came out before the gate, another of same kind maidservant discerning him said, Also he was there with Jesus, the Nazarene.

72 And again he disclaimed, with an oath, that he definitely was not now discerning the man.

73 Then after a little while they standing now came near to him, and spoke to Peter, Of Truth, you also are of them, because the evidence of your speech confirms.

74 Then he began to utter curses and swearing, that I am definitely not discerning the man. Immediately a cock crowed.

75 And Peter himself remembered the Specific Word of Jesus, Spirit Saying to him, Before a cock crowed, you will deny Me three times. He came outside and wept bitterly.

Taken Before Pontius Pilate

27 When it became early morning, all the chief priests and elders and people took counsel against Jesus, so that He be put to Death.

2 They bound, and Him lead away, and Him delivered up to Pontius Pilate, the governor.

Judas returns silver and hangs himself

3 Then Judas spiritually knowing that he had delivered Him up in betrayal for being condemned to death, now regretting, turned away the thirty pieces of silver to the chief priests and elders.

4 Saying, I have sinned, delivering up in betrayal Innocent Blood. And they spoke,

What to us? You shall see.

5   And he threw down the pieces of silver, inside the Temple. He withdrew, and having gone, he hanged himself.

6   Then the chief priests took the pieces of silver and spoke, It is definitely not lawful to cast them into the gift collection, in fact that it is price of Blood.

7   They took counsel, and bought out from them the potter's field, for the purpose of burying strangers.

8   For this reason, they called the field, that Field of Blood, up to this day.

9   Then was Fulfilled that made Spirit Spoken through Jeremiah the Prophet saying, And they took the thirty pieces of silver, which price He is now being made valued, valued from sons of Israel.

10 And they gave them for the potter's field by reason, the Lord had instructed me. (Zech 11:12-13)

Jesus to Die, Barabbas to be released

11 And Jesus stood before the governor, and the governor questioned Him saying, You, Are You the King of the Jews? And Jesus Stated to him, You are Saying.

12 And when He was made accused by them, the chief priests and the elders, He answered nothing.

13 Then Pilate said to Him, Are you definitely not hearing how much they are witnessing against You?

14 And He had definitely not answered him, neither to one specific word, so that the governor is extremely marveling.

15 According then at a Feast having had a customary practice, the governor set at liberty to the multitude of people, one prisoner, whom they would.

16 And they were having then a notable prisoner called Barabbas.

17 Therefore, they being now gathered together, Pilate spoke to them, Whom are you willing to might have dismissed away to you, Barabbas or Jesus, called Christ?

18 Because he had known that because of envy, they delivered Him up in betrayal.

19 When he is sitting upon his judgment seat, his wife sent out to him saying, Not anything by you to that Righteous Man for I have suffered very much this day according to a dream because of Him.

20 But the chief priests and the elders had persuaded the multitudes of people that they should ask Barabbas, and should destroy Jesus.

21 The governor answered and spoke to them, Who, of these two, are you willing I should set at liberty away to you? Then they spoke, Barabbas.

22 Pilate says to them, What, therefore, shall I do with Jesus called the Christ? They all say to him, You must crucify Him.

23 And the governor stated, Why? Because what evil work did He do? Then they were crying out excessively saying, He must be made crucified.

24 When Pilate knew that he is profiting nothing, but definitely much more tumult was coming to pass, he took water to wash off his hands against the multitude of people, saying, Yourselves shall spiritually see that I am innocent from the Blood of this Righteous One.

25 All the people answered and spoke, His Blood be on us and on our children.

26 Then he dismissed away to them Barabbas, and when he had lashed Jesus, he delivered up that He should be made crucified.

27 Then the soldiers of the governor took along Jesus into the judgment hall. All the band gathered together against Him.

28 They unclothed Him, and placed a scarlet military robe upon Him.

29 And they braided a victor's wreath from thorns. It was laid on His Head, and a reed in His Right Hand, and they kneeled before Him to mock Him saying, You must rejoice, King of the Jews.

30 And they spit on Him. They took the reed and were striking upon His head.

31 And when they had mocked Him, they

unclothed the military robe from Him, and put on Him His clothes, and Him lead away to crucify Him.

Crucifixion of Jesus

32 And they came out to find a Cyrenian man, Simon by name. They compelled him that he take up His cross.

33 And they came into a place called Golgotha, which is called skull place.

34 They gave Him vinegar to drink, being made mixed with bile. He tasted and definitely would not drink.

35 And they crucified Him, divided to themselves His clothes, casting lot that should be made Fulfilled which was Spirit Spoken by the Prophet. They divided My clothes for themselves, and cast lot upon My raiment. (Ps 22:18)

36 And sitting, they were keeping Him there.

37 And placed it over His Head, His accusation made written, THIS IS JESUS KING OF THE JEWS.

38 Then they were crucifying two robbers together with Him, one by the Right Hand, and one by the Left Hand.

39 And those passing by were blaspheming Him, wagging their heads.

40 And saying, You are tearing down the Temple, and within three days it is being built. If you are the Son of God, You must Save yourself. You must come down from the cross.

41 Then likewise, also the chief priests with the scribes and elders mocking Him saying,

42 He Saved others of the same kind, Himself He definitely cannot Save. If He is King of Israel, He must come down now from the cross, and we shall commit to Him.

43 He is now giving confidence to God. He must rescue Him now if He is strongly desiring Him, because He spoke that He is the Son of God.

44 And then the robbers also with Him, having been made crucified together with Him, themselves were scolding Him to shame.

45 Then from the sixth hour (12:00 noon), darkness came to pass on the whole earth, until after the ninth hour (3:00 PM).

46 And about the ninth hour (3:00 PM), Jesus Shouted Out a Great Voice Calling, Eli, Eli, lama sabachthani? This is, My God, My God, Why have You within Me left? (Ps 22:1-24; Ps 69:16-20).

47 And some of them, now standing there that heard said, He is calling for Elias.

48 And immediately one ran out and he took a vinegar filled sponge, and also placed it on a reed, and was giving him to drink. (Ps 69:21)

49 Then the rest said, You must be discerning to see if Elias might be coming to Save Him.

Jesus Dismisses His Spirit

50 Then Jesus again Cried Out with a Great Voice. He Dismissed His Spirit.

51 And behold the Veil of the Temple Sanctuary was split into two, from the top until after down below, and the earth shook, and huge rocks split.

52 And the sepulchers have been made Opened, and many bodies of Saints being now made asleep, have been made Risen Up,

53 And came out from within their sepulchers after His Rising Up, entered into the Holy City, and were made known plainly to many.

54 When the centurion and those with him keeping Jesus, discerned the earthquake and what came to pass, they exceedingly feared saying, Of Truth, He was God's Son.

55 And many women, who followed Jesus from Galilee, serving Him, were perceiving there at a distance,

56 Among whom were Mary Magdalene, and Mary, the mother of James and Joses, and the mother of Zebedee's sons.

Burial of Jesus

57 When evening came to pass, a rich man came from Arimathaea named Joseph, who was also himself discipled to Jesus.

58 He came near to Pilate, asked the Body of Jesus. Then Pilate commanded the Body to be made yielded.

59 And Joseph took the Body, wrapped It in pure linen cloth.

60 And positioned it inside his sepulcher, a New of a different kind, that was chiseled in a huge rock. He rolled a great stone to the door of the sepulcher, and went.

61 But there were Mary Magdalene and the other Mary of the same kind sitting before the tomb.

Guards placed at the tomb

62 Then the next day, which is after the Preparation Day, the chief priests and the Pharisees gathered together to Pilate.

63 Saying, Lord, Yourself has been made to remember what that living deceiver spoke further. I am made Rising Up after three days.

64 Command, therefore, to make certain the tomb, until after the third day, for fear that his disciples might come during the night might steal Him, and might speak to the people, He has been made Risen Up from the Dead, and it shall be the last deception worse than the first.

65 Then Pilate stated to them, Have a sentry, you must be leading away, you must make certain as you are now discerning.

66 They went and made certain the tomb, sealed the stone with the sentry.

Jesus Rises from Dead on Sunday

28 After the end of the Sabbaths, the day is beginning to dawn into first day of the week, came Mary Magdalene and the other Mary of the same kind to see the tomb.

2 And you must behold, a great earthquake occurred for the Angel of the Lord Came Down out from Heaven, Came near and Moved Back the stone away from the door, Sat upon it.

3 Moreover, His countenance was as Lightning and His clothing White like as snow.

4 And from fear of Him, those keepers shook, and became like as dead.

5 The Angel Answered and Spoke to the women, Yourselves must not fear because I Know you are seeking Jesus, Who has been now made crucified.

6 He is definitely not here, because He has Risen Up, just as He Spoke. You must come now. You must See the place whereto the Lord was Laying.

7 And quickly Go. You must speak to His disciples, that He has Risen Up from the Dead and Behold He is going before you into Galilee. There you shall see the Spiritual Appearance of Him. Behold, I have Spoken to you.

8 And quickly they came out from the sepulcher, with fear and great Joy. They ran to tell His disciples.

9 Then as they were going to tell His disciples, Also Behold, Jesus Meet them Saying, You must rejoice. And then they came near to hold to retain His Feet, and they Worshiped Him.

10 Then Jesus Said to them, You must be not Fearing, you must go away, tell My Brethren that they should go into Galilee, there also they shall see the Spiritual Appearance of Me.

Guards tell chief priests

11 When they were going, Behold, some of the sentry came into the city to tell the chief priests all that occurred.

12 They were made gathered together, with the elders and counsel, and also took pieces of silver sufficient to give to the soldiers,

13 Saying, You speak that His disciples came during night, stole Him during our resting asleep.

14 And if ever the governor might hear of this, we will persuade him, and shall be making you secure.
15 Then they took the pieces of silver, did as they were taught. And this was made a communication of them commonly reported with Jews until this day.

The Eleven Meet Jesus in Galilee

16 Then the eleven disciples went into Galilee, into the mountain where Jesus had assigned for them.
17 And they Spiritually Saw Him, and Worshiped Him, but some had doubts.

The Great Commission

18 Jesus came near and Uttered to them Saying, All Authority in Heaven and upon the earth has been Given to Me.
19 Go, therefore. You must disciple all the nations, immersing them in the Name of the Father, and of the Son, and of the Holy Spirit.
20 Teaching them to keep all things whatever I, God Commanded to you, and Behold, I am with you all until after That Day before the Final End of the satan's world of this Age. Amen.

The Gospel According to

Mark

John the Baptist

1 The beginning of the Gospel of Jesus Christ, the Son of God.
2 As now made written in the Prophets, Behold, I am Sending out My Messenger before Your Presence, who will make ready Your Way before You.
3 A Voice is Loudly Pleading in the desolate wilderness, You must Prepare The Way of the Lord. You must Make His Paths Straight. (Mal 3:1; Isa 40:3)
4 It came to pass, John was immersing in the desolate wilderness, also preaching immersion of Repentance after Removal of sin natures and sins.
5 And all the land of Judaea and Jerusalem went out to him, and all were being immersed in the Jordon River by him, acknowledging their sin natures and sins to him.
6 And John was dressed with camel's hair, and a leather belt about his waist, and ate locusts and wild honey.
7 And was Preaching Saying, There is Coming after me One Mightier than I, that I am definitely not sufficient to stooping to remove the leather shoestrings of His shoes.
8 I have certainly immersed you in water, but He shall Immerse you in the Holy Spirit.

Baptism of Jesus

9 And it came to pass in those days, Jesus came from Nazareth of Galilee, and was immersed by John into the Jordan.
10 And immediately ascending away from the water, He Spiritually Saw the heavens being made split, and the Spirit like as a dove Came Down Upon Him.
11 And there occurred a Voice out from the Heavenlies, You are My Beloved Son in Whom I have been Pleased. (Ps 2:7; Isa 42:1)

Tempted in the wilderness 40 days

12 And immediately, the Spirit Sent Him Away into the desolate wilderness.

13 And He was there in the desert forty days, made tempted by the satan, and was with the wild beasts, and the Angels were Serving Him.

Jesus Calls Four fishermen

14 Then after John was Made Delivered Up, Jesus Came into Galilee, Preaching the Gospel of the Kingdom Rule of God.

15 And Saying, The Special Time is now being made Fulfilled. The Kingdom Rule of God is now approaching near, you must be Continuously Repenting by your choice, and you must be Continuously Committing by your choice upon the Good News (Gospel). (1 Cor 15:1-4)

16 Then walking near the Sea of Galilee, He Spiritually Saw Simon and Andrew his brother, casting throw nets in the sea because they were fishermen.

17 And Jesus Spoke to them, You must Come Now After Me, and I will Make You by your choice to Become Fishermen of men.

18 And Immediately they by their choice dismissed their nets. They by their choice followed Him.

19 And having gone a little farther ahead from that place, He Spiritually Saw James, the son of Zebedee, and John, his brother, and they were in the ship mending their nets.

20 And immediately, He Called them, and they dismissed their father Zebedee, in the ship with the rented servants. They went after Him.

Casts Out demon on the Sabbath

21 And they came into Capernaum, and immediately on the Sabbath He entered into the synagogue to teach.

22 And they were amazed at His Teaching, because He was Teaching to them as having Authority, and definitely not the same as the scribes.

23 And there was in their synagogue a man with a morally impure spirit, and he cried loudly,

24 Saying, Let us alone. And why have You, Jesus of Nazareth, come to destroy us? I am now spiritually seeing You, Who You are, the Holy One of God.

25 And Jesus Rebuked him Saying, You must be Silenced, and you must Come Out from within him.

26 And the morally impure spirit convulsed him, cried out with a great voice, and came out from within him.

27 And all awed, so that they were discussing to themselves, saying, Who is this? What (is) His New of a different kind Teaching? Because according to His Authority even the morally impure spirits are instantly Commanded, and they are Obeying Him.

28 Then immediately, came out the fame of Him into all the surrounding region of Galilee.

Heals Peter's mother-in-law

29 And immediately, from within the synagogue, they came out to come into the house of Simon and Andrew, with James and John.

30 And Simon's mother in law was lying having a fever, and immediately they are saying to Him about her.

31 He Came near, Held to retain her hand, and she rose up, and immediately the fever Parted from her, and she was serving them.

32 Then it became evening. When the sun set, they brought to Him all the evil work afflicted and having those being demonized.

33 And all the city was being gathered all together at the door.

34 And He Healed many evil work afflicted having many diverse sicknesses and He Cast Out many demons, and definitely Did Not Dismiss the demons to utter because He Spiritually Knew them.

Preaching to Towns of Galilee

35 And early in the morning extremely before day, He arose, and came out to go into a desolate wilderness place, and He was Praying there also.

36 And Simon and they with him searched after Him.

37 And they found Him, saying to Him, All seek after You.

38 And He Says to them, I should be Leading into the demonized towns that there also I should Preach. For this yet, I am Now Coming Out.

39 And He was Preaching in their synagogues in all of Galilee, and Casting Out demons.

Jesus Heals a leper

40 And a leper came to Him, beseeching Him, and kneeling to Him, and said to Him, that if You might be willing, You are able to cleanse me.

41 And Jesus Had Compassion, stretched out His Hand and Touched him, Saying to him, I will, you must be Cleansed.

42 He Spoke to him, and immediately it Went Away from him, and the leprosy was Cleansed.

43 And having Seriously Commanded him, immediately sent him away.

44 And Saying to him, You must Behold Attentively, speak to no man anything, but definitely you must be going away. You must show yourself to the priest, and you must offer in regard to your purification that Moses before Commanded for the Purpose of a Testimony to them.

45 But He came out, began to Preach very much, and was commonly Reporting the Spiritual Word, so that no longer was He to be able to openly enter into a city, but definitely He was outside in desolate wilderness places, and they were coming to Him from every quarter.

Jesus Heals a paralytic

2 And again, He entered into Capernaum, and after days, it was heard that He was in a home.

2 And immediately many gathered together, so that no longer finding a place neither to the door, and He was Uttering the Word to them.

3 And they came to Him bringing a paralytic, made taken up by four.

4 And not able to get near to Him, because of the multitude of people, they unroofed the roof whereto He was, and removed it to let down the mattress, upon which the paralytic was laying.

5 When Jesus Spiritually Saw their Faith, He Said to the paralytic, Child, your sins are made Forgiven to you.

6 But there were some of the scribes sitting there, and they reasoned in their hearts,

7 Why is He uttering so? This is blasphemy. Who is able to Remove from Memory (forgive) sins except One, God?

8 And immediately, Jesus Fully Knew in His Spirit that they reasoned, in such a manner among themselves. He Spoke to them. Why are you reasoning these things in your hearts?

9 Whether is it easier to speak to the paralytic, Your sins are now being Removed from Memory (forgiven) for you, or to speak, You must Raise Up for yourself, and you Must Take Up by your choice your mattress, and you Must Continuously by your choice Walk?

10 But that you may Spiritually Discern that the Son of Man has Authority to Remove from Memory (forgive) sins upon the earth, He Says to the paralytic,

11 I Say to you, you Must Raise Up for yourself, and you Must by your choice Take Up your mattress, and Go Away by your choice into your home.

12 And immediately, he Rose Up, and Took Up the mattress, Came Out before their sight, so that all were astonished and Attributed Glory (Spiritual Perfection) to God, saying that never have we Spiritually Seen in such a manner.

Called Levi to Follow Him

13 And He came out again, near to the sea, and all the multitude of people was coming to Him, and He was Teaching them.

14 And passing on He saw Levi, the son of Alpheus, sitting at the desk for paying taxes, and Said to him, You must Follow Me, and he arose to follow Him.

Jesus Eats with publicans and sinners

15 And it came to pass, in his house, among them sitting down to eat, many tax collectors and sinners were sitting to eat with Jesus also for many were his Disciples and Followed Him.

16 And the scribes and Pharisees saw Him eating with the tax collectors and sinners, saying to His Disciples, Why even with tax collectors and sinners is He eating and drinking?

17 And Jesus Heard, Saying to them, They that are capable have definitely no need of a physician, but definitely the evil work afflicted have. I come definitely not to Outwardly Call (Gospel) the Righteous, but definitely sinners to Repentance.

Why Disciples don't Fast

18 Also the disciples of John and those of the Pharisees used to be fasting, and also they come to say to Him, Why then do the disciples of John and those of the Pharisees fast, but your Disciples definitely do not fast?

19 And Jesus Spoke to them, The Sons of the Bride Chamber are not able to fast, while when the Bridegroom is with them. As long as they themselves have time with the Bridegroom, they definitely cannot fast.

20 But days shall come, when the Bridegroom should be made taken from them, then they shall fast among them in those days.

21 Also no one sews a piece of new cloth on old clothes, otherwise then the new of a different kind that fullness is taking away from the old, and the division becomes worse.

22 And no man casts new wine into old bottles, in the event that the new wine is tearing the bottles, and the wine is made to pour out, and the bottles shall be destroyed. But definitely new wine must be put into new bottles.

Sabbath was Made for man

23 And it came to pass, He was passing by through the grain fields in the Sabbath, and His disciples began in the way of travel, plucking the heads of grain.

24 And the Pharisees said to Him, Behold, why are you doing in the Sabbath, that which is definitely not Lawful?

25 And He was Saying to them, Have you never read what David did when had need, and he was hungry, and those with him?

26 How he entered into the Dwelling of God, in the place of Abiathar, the chief priest, and ate the loaves of the Bread of Purpose (Shewbread), and also gave to those being with him, that definitely is not lawful to eat except by the priests.

27 And He Said to them, The Sabbath Came for man, definitely not man for the Sabbath.

28 So that, the Son of Man is Lord also of the Sabbath.

Jesus Heals on the Sabbath

3 And He entered again into the synagogue, and there was a man having a withered hand.

2   And they observed Him, if He would Heal on the Sabbath, that they might accuse Him.

3   And He Said to the man, who had the made withered hand, You must Raise up for yourself in the midst.

4   And He Said to them, Is it Lawful to do Good on the Sabbath, or to do evil, to Heal a soul, or to kill? But they held speech.

5   And He Looked around them with Wrath for Justice, being Grieved over the

blindness of their heart, Saying to the man, You Must Stretch Out your hand. And he Stretched Out his hand and it was Restored Healthy as the other of the same kind.

6   And the Pharisees immediately came out with the Herodians, taking counsel against Him, so that He might be destroyed.

Heals many and Demons fall to His Feet

7   And Jesus withdrew with his disciples to the sea and a large multitude of different people from Galilee, and from Judaea followed Him by their choice.

8   And from Jerusalem, and from Idumaea, and the other side of Jordan, and about Tyre and Sidon, a large multitude of different people heard as much as He was Doing, came to Him.

9   And He Spoke to His Disciples, that a small boat might continue there, because that multitude of people should not be troubling Him.

10 Because He Healed many, so that many fell upon Him as were having a severe suffering in order that they might touch Him.

11 And the morally impure spirits, when they saw with perception, fell down before Him, and cried out, calling this, You, You are the Son of God.

12 And He Rebuked the many with them, that they should not finalize Him Openly Manifest.

Jesus Chooses His Apostles

13 And He ascended into the mountain, and invited whom He would to Himself, and they went to Him.

14 And He Appointed Twelve in order that they should be with Him, and in order that He should Send Them Out to be Preaching,

15 And to have Authority to Heal sicknesses and to Cast Out the demons.

16 And He Surnamed to Simon, the name Peter.

17 And James the son of Zebedee, and John, the brother of James. And He added a Surname to them, named Boanerges, that is to say is sons of thunder.

18 And Andrew, and Philip, and Bartholomew, and Matthew, and Thomas, and James,

19 And Judas Iscariot, who also delivered Him up in betrayal, and they came into a home.

20 And again the multitude of people came together, so that they were not able for them neither to eat bread.

21 And hearing from one, they have come out to retain Him, because they were saying that He is beside Himself.

Whoever blasphemes the Holy Spirit

22 And the scribes, who came down from Jerusalem, were saying that by the dung god (beelzebub, satan), the ruler of those demons, are the demons being cast out.

23 And inviting them, He was Saying in a parable to them. How can satan cast out satan?

24 And if ever a kingdom rule should be made fully divided against itself, that kingdom rule is definitely not able to stand.

25 And if ever a house should be made fully divided against itself, that house shall definitely not be able to stand.

26 And if the satan raised against himself, and he fully divides, he definitely cannot stand, but definitely has an end.

27 Definitely no man is able to enter into a stronger man's house to wreck the vessels, unless he first of all binds the stronger, and then shall wreck his house.

28 Truly, I Say to you for at all times sinful acts shall be made Removed from Memory (forgiven) to the sons of men, and blasphemies, as many as, whoever might blaspheme,

29 But he whoever might blaspheme the Holy Spirit is having definitely no Removal (of sins) Forever, but definitely he is guilty for Eternal Final Judgment.

30 Because they were saying, He has a morally impure spirit,

The True Kin of Jesus Do the Fathers' Will
31 Therefore, came His brothers and His mother, and standing outside, sent out to Him, calling for Him.
32 And the multitude of people was sitting down about Him, and they spoke to Him, You must behold Your mother and Your brothers are outside seeking You.
33 And He Answered them Saying, Who is My Mother or My Brothers?
34 And He looked around about them sitting down around Him, Saying, Behold, My Mother and My Brothers.
35 Because whoever has Done the Will of God, the same is My Brother and My Sister and Mother.

The Means to Understand Parables
4 And He began again to Teach, near to the sea and made gathered together to Himself, a large multitude of people, so that He boarded into a ship, to be sitting upon the sea, and all the multitude of people were upon the earth by the sea.
2 And He Taught them in many parables, and was Saying to them in His Teaching,
3 You must be Hearing, Behold, there came out The One Sowing to Sow.
4 And it came to pass in His Sowing, some certainly fell down near to The Way of Travel, and the birds of heaven came and devoured it.
5 And other of the same kind fell down on the stony ground, whereto definitely not having very much Earth, and immediately it started growing, because of having no depth of Earth.
6 When the sun had risen, It has been made scorched, so because it was having no root, it was made dried up.
7 And other of the same kind fell down into the thorns, and the thorns ascended, and choked it, and it gave definitely no Fruit.

8 And other of the same kind fell down into the God-Work Earth, and was giving Fruit, ascending and growing, and bringing some thirty, and some sixty, and some hundred.
9 And He was Saying to them, He who are having ears to Hear, he must be Hearing.
10 And when He became separate with the twelve with him, they earnestly requested of Him about this parable.
11 And He was Saying to them, To you it is now being made Given to Know the Mystery of the Kingdom Rule of God, but to those outside it always occurs in parables.
12 That seeing they might see by their choice, and might not Spiritually See by their choice, and hearing they might hear by their choice, and might not Understand by their choice, for fear that they might be Converted by their choice, and their sinful acts might be Made Dismissed to them. (Isa 6:9-10)
13 And He Says to them, Are you definitely not now Knowing this parable, and how will you Know all the parables?
14 The Sower is Sowing the Word.
15 Then those are they, near to The Way of Travel, whereto the Spiritual Word is being Sown, and when they should Hear, immediately comes the satan, and takes away the Spiritual Word that is being made Sown within their hearts.
16 And these are they likewise being made Sown on the stony ground. Who when they should have Heard the Word, immediately they are by their choice Receiving It with Joy,
17 But are having definitely no root in themselves, but definitely then for a time they are Following. It came to pass, during affliction or persecution because of the Spiritual Word, immediately they are being offended.
18 And these are they which were being Sown among the thorns. These are they who are Hearing the Word,

19 And the cares of this Age, and the deceitfulness of riches, and with the other evil desires concerning others, coming in choking the Spiritual Word, and then It becomes unfruitful.

20 And these are they having been made Sown upon God-Work Earth, who are Hearing the Spiritual Word, and are Accepting for themselves, and are Bearing Fruit, one thirty, and one sixty, and one a hundred.

He that Has, More shall be Given

21 And He Said to them, Is a candle coming that it might possibly be positioned under a bushel or under a bed? Definitely not, that it should be made placed in a candlestick.

22 Because definitely not anything that is secret, that should not be made Manifested, neither became kept secret but it should definitely come Openly Manifest.

23 If any certain man has ears to Hear, he must be by his choice Hearing.

24 And He Called to them, You must Spiritually See what you must be Hearing. By what amount of measure you measure, it shall be made measured to you, and to those Hearing shall be made Added more to you.

25 Because whoever might be Having, to him shall ever be made Given. And who is definitely not Having, what he has shall be taken away from him.

Kingdom of God likened to growing seed

26 And He was Saying, In such a manner, is the Kingdom Rule of God, as if ever a man Casts out Sowing Seed upon the earth,

27 And should sleep and might raise up night and day. And the Sowing Seed might be Budding Forth and might be made Growing Up, in such a manner, as he does definitely not now Spiritually Know.

28 Because of itself the earth bears fruit; first of all the grass, following that a head of grain, following that full wheat among the head of grain.

29 But when the Fruit might be Delivered Up, immediately He Sends Out the Sickle, because the Harvest is Standing. (Joel 3:13)

30 And He Said, What might have been likened to the Kingdom Rule of God? In what parable might it be realized?

31 As a grain of mustard seed, which when sown upon the earth, is of all the smallest seed upon the earth.

32 And when sown it ascends, and becomes surely the greatest of the herbs, and makes great branches so that birds of heaven are able to lodge under the shadow of it.

Jesus uses Parables to Hide Meaning

33 And many such parables He was Uttering to them Spiritual Communication, just as they were being able to Hear.

34 But without a parable He Uttered definitely not to them. And privately, He explained all things to His disciples.

Jesus Calms the sea

35 And in the same day evening came to pass. He Said to them, We should pass through to the other side.

36 And they dismissed the multitude of people. They took along Him as He was in the ship. And then other small boats of same kind were with Him.

37 And there become a great wind storm, and great violent waves were laying into the ship, so that it was already made full.

38 And He was in the stern of the boat with a pillow, Sleeping. And they aroused Him and said to Him, Oh Master, Do you definitely not care that we are perishing?

39 And He was made aroused, Rebuked the wind, and Spoke to the sea. You must be Calm. You must be Still. And the wind Ceased blowing, and it became a great Calm.

40 And He Spoke to them, Why are you so terrified? How have you definitely no Faith?

41 And they had fear, great fear, and said to one another, So then Who is this, that the wind and sea are obeying Him?

Demonic Healed person worships Jesus

5 And they came to the other side of the sea, into the land of the Gadarenes.
2 When He came out from the same ship, immediately, a man with a morally impure spirit, out from the sepulchers, met Him,
3 Who had his housing among the sepulchers, and no man was able to chain, nor bind him.
4 Because he has been bound often, with shackles and chains, and he pulls apart the chains by himself, and breaking into pieces the shackles, and no man was capable to tame him.
5 And always, through night and day, he was in the mountains, and in the places of the dead, crying out and scratching himself with stones.
6 But he Spiritually Discerned Jesus, from at a distance. He ran and worshiped Him.
7 He cried out with a great voice and he spoke, Why to me now with You, Oh Jesus, Oh Son of the Most High God? I urge you, God, that You might not torment me.
8 Yet He Said to it, Morally impure spirit, You must Come Out from within the man.
9 And He Questioned it, What name for you? And it answered, saying, my name is legion, for we are being many.
10 And it beseeched Him very much, that He might not send them out, outside the land.
11 There was then at the mountain a great herd of pigs feeding.
12 And all demons beseeched Him saying, You must send us into the pigs that we might enter into them.
13 And immediately Jesus Permitted them, and the morally impure spirits came out, entered into the pigs, and the herd ran violently upon the steep decline into the sea, even as there were two thousand then strangled in the sea.
14 And they that feed the pigs fled, and declared in the city and in the fields, and they came out to spiritually see what is now occurring.
15 And they were coming to Jesus, and were seeing the demonized who had the legion, sitting, and now made wearing clothes, and being logically minded, and they were made afraid.
16 And they that saw, recited this, how it occurred to the demonized, and in regard to the pigs.
17 And they began to entreat Him to go from their districts.
18 And having boarded Himself into the ship. The one, having been demonized, was beseeching Him that he might be with Him.
19 Then Jesus definitely Dismissed him not, but definitely Said to him, You must Go Away to your home, to yours, and Declare to them whatever the Lord Has Done to you, and Had Mercy on you.
20 And he went, and began to preach in the Decapolis, as much as Jesus had done to him, and all men were marveling.

Jesus Heals a woman's bleeding

21 And Jesus Passed Over in the ship again, into the other side. A large multitude of people had gathered together to Him, and He was near to the sea.
22 And you must behold, there came one of the rulers of the synagogue named Jarius, and he Spiritually Discerned Him, fell down at His Feet.
23 And he very much beseeched Him, saying that My little daughter is near death, that having come, you might lay Your Hands on her, so that she might be Healed and live.
24 And He Went with him, and a large multitude of people followed Him, and thronged Him.
25 And a certain woman being with

bleeding blood twelve years,

26 Also long suffered very much by many physicians, and spent everything from herself and instead profited nothing; but definitely after was coming to worse.

27 Hearing about Jesus, she came with the multitude of people, then touched the backside of His robe,

28 Yet she said, For if I might touch His clothes, I shall be made Healed.

29 And immediately the fountain of her blood was dried up, and she knew in her body that she was now made Cured from the severe suffering.

30 And immediately Jesus Fully Knew in Himself that out from within Him Miracle Power had come out. He turned about among the multitude of people. He Called, Who touched My clothes?

31 And His disciples said to Him, You Spiritually See the multitude of people thronging You and You Say, Who touched Me?

32 And He Looked around to Spiritually See who did this thing.

33 And the woman made fearing and trembling, Spiritually Knowing what had occurred in her, came and fell down before Him, and spoke to Him all the Truth.

34 Then He Spoke to her, Oh daughter, Your Faith has now Healed you, you must go away in Peace and you must be healthy from your severe suffering.

Synagogue ruler's dead daughter Raised

35 While He still is Uttering, they were coming for the ruler of the synagogue, saying, That your daughter has died. Why still bother the Master?

36 Then Jesus immediately Heard the communication he was Uttering, Saying to the ruler of the synagogue. You must not be fearing for yourself, you must only by your choice be Committing.

37 And He definitely was not concerned for anyone to follow together with Him, except Peter, and James, and John the brother of James.

38 And He came into the home of the ruler of the synagogue, and seeing with perception the tumult and weeping and very much clamoring,

39 And having entered, He Said to them, Why are you making noise and weeping? The little child is definitely not dead but definitely is sleeping.

40 And they laughed Him to scorn, but when He had Sent All Away, He Took along the father of the little child and the mother, and those with Him, and came in whereto the little child was lying.

41 And He Held to Retain the hand of the little child, He Said to her, Talitha cumi, which is made interpreted, Young woman, I Say to you, you must Raise Up for yourself.

42 And immediately the young woman raised by her choice and was walking because she was of twelve years, and they were astonished with great ecstasy.

43 And He Ordered them very much, that not any should know this, and He Spoke to give to her to eat.

Rejected in Nazareth, His Hometown

6 And He Came Out from that place and Came into His own country, and His disciples followed Him.

2 And on a Sabbath having occurred, He Began in the synagogue to Teach, and many hearing were made amazed saying, From where This One these things? And what Wisdom has been made given to Him, that such Miracle Powers also occurring through His Hands?

3 Is He definitely not the carpenter the son of Mary, and brother of James, and Joses, and Jude, and Simon? And His sisters, are they not here with us? And they were offended by Him.

4 But Jesus Said to them, A Prophet is definitely not without honor, except in his own country, and among his kinsmen, and in his own house.

5 And He was definitely not able to do a

Miracle Power there, except Healed, Laying His Hands on a few sickly.

6   And He Marveled because of their no Commitment, and He Went about their villages around, Teaching.

Jesus Sends Out Apostles Two by Two

7   And He Invited the twelve and began them, to Send Out two by two. Also He Gave to them Authority over morally impure spirits.

8   And He Gave Command to them that they should take up nothing for way of travel except a staff only, no wallet for money, no bread, no brass coins in their belt.

9   But definitely being made feet covered with sandals, and not put on for yourself two coats.

10   And He Said to them, Whereto if you might enter into a house you must continue there, until after whenever you might come out from that place.

11   And as many as ever receive you not, neither hear you, go out from that place, shake off the dirt under your feet for a Testimony to them. Truly, I Say to you, it shall be more tolerable for Sodom and Gomorrah in the Day of Final Judgment, than for that city.

12   They departed and were Preaching that they should be Repenting.

13   And they Cast Out many demons, and were Anointing with oil and were Healing many sickly.

John the Baptist is beheaded

14   And king Herod heard of Him, because His Name became Openly Manifest, and it was said that John the baptizer has made risen up from the dead, also because this was being the Miracle Powers accomplished in him.

15   Others of the same kinds were saying that it is Elias. And others of the same kinds were saying that He is a Prophet, or as One of the Prophets.

16   When Herod heard, he spoke. This John whom I beheaded, he is him made risen up from the dead.

17   Because Herod himself sent out, held to retain John, and bound him in prison for Herodias, the wife of Philip his brother, for he had married her.

18   Because John said to Herod that is was definitely not lawful for you to have the wife of your brother.

19   And Herodias was conflicted with him, and strongly desired him to be killed, but she definitely could not.

20   And because Herod feared John, spiritually knowing this Righteous and Holy man, and was preserving him, and having heard him, also was participating hearing him very much with pleasure.

21   And when it became a day in time of need, Herod made his birthday supper with his great men, and the chief captains, and those chiefs of Galilee.

22   And this daughter of Herodias entered and danced and pleased Herod and those sitting to eat. The king spoke to the young woman, You must ask me whatever you will, and I will give to you.

23   And he swore to her that whatever you might ask me I will give to you up to half of my kingdom.

24   And coming out she spoke to her mother, What shall I ask? And she spoke, The head of John the Baptist.

25   And she entered immediately with diligence to the king, she asked saying, I will that you should speedily give to me on a platter the head of John the Baptist.

26   And the king became very sorrowful because of the oath, also with those sitting to eat, he willed definitely not to reject her.

27   Immediately, the king sending out for the executioner, instantly commanded to bring the head of him, and going he beheaded him in the prison.

28   And brought his head on a platter, and gave it to the young woman, and the young woman gave it to her mother.

29 And his disciples heard this, came and took up his dead body, and laid it down in a sepulcher.

The Apostles Return

30 And the Apostles gathered together with Jesus and told Him all things, both as much as they Did, and what they Taught.

31 And He Spoke to them, You must come now, yourselves in privacy to a desolate wilderness place, you must be refreshing a little, because there were many coming and going away, and they were not having leisure time to eat.

32 And they went to a desert place by the ship for own privacy.

33 And the multitudes of people saw them going away, and many fully knew them, and many ran together there on foot from every city, and went forward to them, and came together with Him.

Five Thousand Fed with Five Loaves

34 Jesus Came Out and Spiritually Saw a large multitude of people, and had Compassion on them, for they were as sheep not having a shepherd, and He began to Teach them very much. (Num 27:17; Ezek 34:5)

35 And already many an hour has come to pass, and His disciples came near to Him saying then, This place is a desolate wilderness, and already many an hour,

36 You must dismiss them away that they go into the fields around and villages. They should buy themselves bread. Why? Because they definitely might have not to eat.

37 He Answered and Spoke to them. You yourselves must Give them to eat. And they said to Him, Should we go to buy loaves of two hundred pennies, and should give to them to eat?

38 Then He Said to them, How many loaves have you? You must Go Away and you Must See. And Knowing they said five and two fish.

39 And He instantly Commanded them all to be made to sit down by groups, in the green grass by groups.

40 And they sat down, rows by hundreds, and rows by fifties.

41 And He Took the five loaves and two fish, and He Looked Up to Heaven, Blessed, and Broke Pieces of the loaves, and Gave to His disciples that they should put forth to them, and the two fish, all fully divided.

42 And all ate and were made filled.

43 And they took up fragments, twelve hand baskets full also of the fish.

44 And those who ate the loaves were about five thousand men.

Jesus Walks on the wavy sea

45 And immediately, He Compelled His disciples to board into the ship, and go before to the other side to Bethsaida, while He might Dismiss away the multitude of people.

46 And having Said goodbye to them, He Went into the mountain to Pray.

47 And evening occurred, the ship was in the middle of the sea, and He alone upon the earth.

48 And He Spiritually Saw them tormented in the rowing, because the wind was contrary to them, and about fourth watch of the night He comes to them Walking upon the sea, and would have passed forth by them.

49 But they Spiritually Saw Him Walking upon the sea, thought it is being a ghostly sight, and cried loudly.

50 Because they all Spiritually Saw Him, and were made troubled, and immediately He Uttered with them and Said to them, You Must Be Encouraged. I AM. You Must Not Be Afraid.

51 And He Ascended to them into the ship, and the wind ceased blowing, and they were within themselves extremely astonished, and were marveling at more in excess,

52 Because they understood definitely not about what the loaves were, because their heart is now being made hardened.

Many are Healed in Gennesaret

53 And they having passed over, they came upon the area Gennesaret and drew closer.

54 And they came out from the ship. Immediately, they Fully Knew Him.

55 They ran through all the surrounding region. Then they began having the evil work afflicted on mattresses, carrying about whereto they heard that He is there.

56 And whereto ever He Was Passing into villages, or cities, or country sides, in the marketplaces, they laid down those being sick, and beseeching Him that if they might touch the border of His clothes, and whoever had touched Him was made Healed.

We are to Reject man-made traditions

7 And the Pharisees were made gathering together with Him, and certain of the scribes came from Jerusalem,

2 And seeing some of His disciples eating bread with unclean hands, that is with unwashed, they found fault.

3 Because the Pharisees and all the Jews are definitely not eating unless they should ceremonially wash their hands with scrubbing, holding to retain the tradition of the elders.

4 And from the marketplace, they definitely are not eating unless they should be hand washed, and many others are of same kind they have each taken, retaining washing baptisms of cups and pots and brass vessels and beds.

5 After that the Pharisees and the scribes questioned Him. Why then are your disciples definitely not walking according to the tradition of the elders; but definitely are eating bread with unwashed hands?

6 He Answered and Spoke to them, This Esaias, God-Working, Prophesied in regard to you hypocrite actors, As it is made written, This people honors Me with lips, but their heart is already far away from Me.

7 Then you worthlessly revere Me, teaching for doctrines the precepts of men. (Isa 29:13)

8 Because you dismiss the Commandment of God, holding to retain the tradition of men, washing baptisms of pots and cups, and also such many similar others you do, of the same kind.

9 And Said to them, You are rejecting the God-Working Commandment of God, that you might keep your tradition.

10 Because Moses spoke, You must Honor your father and your mother, and who speaks evil things of father or mother, you must be deceasing by death. (Ex 21:17; Deut 5:16)

11 But yourselves say, if any man might have spoken to the father or the mother, Corban, that is to say, it is a gift, if by whatever you might have made profited of me,

12 But you dismiss him to not be any more doing for his father or for his mother,

13 Annulling the Word of God by your tradition, which you have delivered up, and many similar such you are doing by your own choice.

14 And when He Invited all the multitude of people, He Was Saying to them, You must be Hearing Me, everyone, and you must be Understanding by your choice.

15 There is nothing outward of man coming into him that is able to make him unholy, but definitely what goes out from him, that is making the man unholy by his choice.

16 If any man has ears to hear, he must by his choice hear.

17 And when He entered into a home from the multitude of people, His disciples were questioning Him in regard to the parable.

18 And He Said to them, Are you so Without Understanding also? Are yourselves definitely not comprehending that anything outward, that passes into a man, is definitely not able to make him unholy?

19 Because it definitely not comes into his

heart but definitely into the belly, and into the sewer, always cleansing going out by the food.

20 Moreover He Was Saying, That which goes out from within man, that makes unholy the man.

21 Because inside, out from within the heart of man, goes out evil work thoughts, adultery, fornication, and murder,

22 Thefts, greediness, evil actions, subtle half-truth (deceit), extreme irregular immorality, an evil eye, blasphemy, great pride, unthinking foolishness.

23 All these things evil inside, go out and make unholy the man.

Dogs eat the children's crumbs

24 He Arose from that place and Went into the borders of Tyre and Sidon, and Entered into a house definitely no one would know, but He was definitely not able to be hid.

25 For a woman heard, whose her little daughter was having a morally impure spirit, she coming to Him fell down before His Feet.

26 Moreover, the woman was a Greek Syrophenician woman by kindred, and earnestly requested of Him that the demon might be cast out from within her daughter.

27 But Jesus Spoke to her, You must dismiss first of all the children to be filled, because it is definitely not God-Work to take the bread of the children, and cast it down to the puppy dogs.

28 But she answered and said to Him, Emphatically Yes, Lord, and yet the puppy dogs under the table eat from the crumbs of the little children.

29 And He Spoke to her, Because of this Spiritual Word, you must go away, the demon is now come out from within your daughter.

30 And she went into her home, found the demon departed, and her daughter is made prostrate on the bed.

Deaf and dumb man Healed

31 And again, He Came Out from within the district of Tyre and Sidon to come to the sea of Galilee, to the midst of the districts of Decapolis.

32 And they brought to Him a deaf speech impediment, and beseeched Him that He might lay His Hand on him.

33 And Fully Received him, from the multitude of people to own privacy, Put His Fingers into his ears, Made Spittle, and Touched his tongue.

34 And He Looked Up into Heaven, He Groaned and Said to him, Ephphatha, that is to say, You must be made Opened in Newness of Spirit.

35 And immediately his hearing has been made Opened in Newness of Spirit, and the bond of his tongue has been made Removed, and he was uttering correctly.

36 And He Ordered them that they should speak to no one whatever. He was ordering them, but they preached much more abundantly.

37 And they were being made superabundantly amazed saying, He has done all things God-Working, and the deaf are made to hear and the dumb to utter.

Four Thousand Fed with Seven Loaves

8 In those days, the multitude of people was very large, and had nothing that they might eat. Jesus Invited His disciples Saying to them,

2 I have compassion on the multitude of people that already remained steadfast with Me three days and have definitely not when they might eat.

3 And if ever I might dismiss them away without food to their homes, they shall be made discouraged in any way of travel, because they are now coming at a distance.

4 And His disciples answered Him, From where shall anyone be able to fill these with bread here in the wilderness?

5 And He Questioned them, How many loaves have you? And they spoke, Seven.

6   And He Gave Command to the multitude of people, yourselves to sit down upon the earth. And taking the seven loaves, He Gave Thanks, Broke, and was Giving to His disciples, that they should put forth. And they put forth to the multitude of people.
7   And they had a few little fish, and He Blessed, Spoke and put forth to them.
8   Then they ate, and were filled, and also they took up an abundance, seven large hamper size baskets of fragments.
9   And they that had eaten were as four thousand. And He dismissed them away.
10   And immediately He boarded into the ship with His disciples, came into the coast of Dalmanutha.

Pharisees seek a Sign

11   And the Pharisees came out and began to discuss with Him, trying Him, seeking from Him a Miracle Sign from Heaven.
12   And He Sighed deeply in His Spirit Saying, Why is this generation seeking after a Miracle Sign? Truly, I am saying to you, if a Miracle Sign shall be given to this generation?
13   And parting from them, and boarding again into the ship, He went to the other side.

Leaven is doctrines of Pharisees

14   And the disciples had forgotten to take bread, but they were definitely not having in the ship except with themselves one loaf.
15   And He ordered them Saying, You must Behold Attentively. You must Spiritually See of the leaven of the Pharisees, and of the leaven of Herod.
16   And they were reasoning with one another saying, Because we have definitely not loaves.
17   And Jesus knowing them Said to them, Why are you reasoning about the loaves? Are you definitely not yet comprehending, neither Understanding, still you are having now your heart made hardened.
18   Having eyes you are definitely not seeing, and having ears you are definitely not hearing, and you are definitely not remembering. (Jer 5:21)
19   When I broke the five loaves for the five thousand, how many hand baskets full of fragments did you take up? They said to Him, twelve.
20   And when the seven for the Purpose of the four thousand, how many large hamper size baskets you took up then? And they spoke, Seven.
21   And He Said to them, How are you definitely not Understanding?

Jesus Heals blind man

22   And He came to Bethsaida, and they are bringing to Him a blind, and they are beseeching Him that He might Touch him.
23   And He took hold of the hand of the blind, him led out, outside the village, and made spittle upon his eyelids, laid His Hands on him, questioning if he was seeing anything.
24   And looked up saying, I am seeing men same as trees walking.
25   Again, following that, He laid on his hands to his eyes, and made him to look up, and he had been restored, and looked upon all things clearly.
26   And He Sent him Out into his home, saying You should neither enter into the village, nor you should speak to anybody in the village.

Peter Confesses "You are the Christ"

27   And Jesus and His disciples departed for the villages of Caesarea Philippi, and in the way of travel He questioned His disciples saying to them, Who are men saying that I am being?
28   And they answered, John the Baptist, and others of the same kind, Elias, but others of the same kind, one of the Prophets.
29   And He Said to them, But who are yourselves saying that I am? Then Peter answered saying to Him, You, You are the Christ!
30   And He rebuked them, that they say nothing about Him.

Jesus Speaks of His Death; Rebukes Peter

31 And He began to teach them, that the Son of Man must suffer very much, and be disapproved by the elders and chief priests and scribes, and be made killed and Arise after three days.

32 And with boldness, He Uttered that Spiritual Communication. Peter took Him to himself and began to rebuke Him.

33 When He turned about and Spiritually Saw His disciples, He rebuked Peter sharply Saying, You must move back of Me, satan. For you have definitely no regard of value of the things of God, but definitely the things of man.

Jesus Warns All who Follow Him

34 And when He invited the multitude of people united with His disciples, He Spoke to them. Whoever shall be coming after Me must deny himself, and he must take up his cross, and must be following Me.

35 Because that whoever might be willing to Save his soul shall lose it, but whoever should lose his Living-Soul for the cause of Me and the Gospel, the same shall Save it.

36 Because what shall it profit a man if ever he might gain all of the satan's world, but he should suffer loss of his own soul?

37 Or what shall a man give in exchange for his soul?

38 Because whoever might be ashamed of Me and My Words in this adulterous and sinful generation, also of him the Son of Man shall be ashamed, when He should come in the Glory of His Father with His Holy Angels.

The Transfiguration

9 And He Said to them, Truly, I Say to you, that there are some standing here who, definitely should never ever taste of death, until after they should ever Spiritually See the Kingdom Rule of God come in Miracle Power.

2 And after six days, Jesus, takes along Peter and James and John, and He Bears them up into a high mountain, according to own privacy alone, and He was made Transfigured before them.

3 And His clothes became shining extremely white as snow, such as definitely not a bleach upon earth able to whiten.

4 And they Spiritually Saw Elias together with Moses, and they were talking together with Jesus.

5 And Peter answered saying, Jesus, Oh Rabbi, a God-Work is our being here, and we should make three Tabernacles, You one, and Moses one, and Elias one.

6 Because he had definitely not Spiritually Known what he might have uttered, because they were very fearful.

7 And there Occurred a Cloud Overshadowing them, and a Voice came out from within the Cloud Saying, This is My Son, the Beloved, you must be Hearing Him. (Ps 2:7)

8 And abruptly, looking around, they Spiritually Discerned definitely not anymore any man, but definitely Jesus alone with themselves.

9 But themselves coming down from the mountain, He Ordered that they should not recite the things having Spiritually Discerned, except when the Son of Man has Risen out from the Dead.

10 And they held to retain this Spiritual Communication with themselves, discussing Who is the One Arising out from dead.

11 And they questioned Him saying, Why are the scribes saying that Elias must come first of all?

12 And He having Answered Spoke to them, Elias certainly has first come of all to Restore all things, and how is it now made written of the Son of Man, that He should suffer very much, and should be made despised?

13 But definitely I Say to you even that Elias has now come. They have done to him as much as they were willing, just as it is made written in regard to him.

All is Possible to him that Commits

14 And coming to the disciples, He Spiritually Saw the large multitude of people about them, and scribes discussing with them.

15 And immediately all the multitude of people seeing Him, and being greatly awed they also were running forward greeting Him.

16 And He Questioned the scribes. What are you discussing among yourselves?

17 One within the multitude of people answered and spoke, Oh Teacher, I brought my son having a dumb spirit to You.

18 And whereto it might apprehend him, it tears him, and he foams at the mouth, and gnashes his teeth, and withers away. And I spoke to your disciples that they might cast it out and they definitely have not been capable.

19 He Answered and Said to him, Oh faithless generation, to how long a time shall I be with you? To how long a time shall I Continue Enduring of you? You must bring him to Me.

20 And they brought him to Him, and seeing him, immediately the spirit convulsed him, and he fell down upon the earth wallowing, foaming at the mouth.

21 And He Questioned his father, How long a time as this is it occurring to him? And he spoke, Since childhood.

22 And often casts him also into the fire and into water, that it might destroy him, but definitely if any man is able he must help us. Have compassion on us.

23 Then Jesus Spoke to him, If you are able to Commit, all things possible to him Committing by his choice.

24 And immediately the father of the little child cried out with tears calling, Oh Lord, I am Committing, you must help my Uncommitment.

25 When Jesus saw the multitude of people that came running together, He Rebuked to the morally impure spirit, Saying to this dumb also deaf spirit, I, I instantly Command, you must come out from within him, and no longer should you enter into him.

26 And crying out then very much convulsing him, it came out, and he became like as dead, so that many said that he died.

27 But Jesus Took Hold to Retain his hand, Raised him up, and he arose.

28 And He Entered Himself into a home His disciples as private questioned Him. Why were we definitely not able to cast it out?

29 And He Spoke to them, With this kind nothing can come out, except by Prayer and Fasting.

Jesus Speaks of His Death

30 When coming out from that place, they were passing by through Galilee, and were definitely not willing that anyone might know.

31 Because He was Teaching his disciples and was Saying to them, The Son of Man is being made delivered up in betrayal into the hands of men, and they shall kill Him, and being made killed, He shall Arise after the third day.

32 But they were not Understanding the Specific Word, and feared to question Him.

The First is Servant of All

33 And He came into Capernaum, and it came to pass in the house He Questioned them. What in the way of travel were you reasoning with yourselves?

34 But they were holding their speech with one another, because they disputed in their way of travel who (might be the) greatest.

35 He Sat Down and Called for the twelve and Said to them. If any man wills to be first he shall above all be the last and above all a servant.

36 He took a little child and stood him in the midst of them, and took him into His arms, Spoke to them.

37 Whoever might receive one of such

little children in My Name, is receiving Me. And whoever receives Me is definitely not receiving Me, but definitely Him that Sent Me Out.

38 And John answered Him saying, Oh Teacher, we saw one casting out demons in Your Name, who is definitely not following us, and we forbid him, because he was definitely not following us.

39 But Jesus Spoke, You should definitely not forbid him, because any man that is doing Miracle Power in My Name, then shall he be able to quickly speak evil things of Me?

40 Because he that is definitely not against you is in behalf of you.

41 Because whoever should give you to drink a cup of water in My Name, because you are of Christ; Truly, I say to you he should never ever lose his Reward.

You MUST Resist all temptation

42 And whoever might offend one of these littlest that are Committing to Me, it is much more a God-Work if a stone of a mill, encompasses about his neck, and he is made cast into the sea.

43 And if your hand offends you, you must cut it away, it is a God-Work to you to enter into Life lame, than having two hands, to go into hell into the fire unquenchable,

44 Whereto their worm is definitely not pausing, and the fire is definitely not made extinguished.

45 And if your foot offends you, you must cut it away. It is a God-Work for you to enter into this Life crippled, than having two feet to be cast down into hell, into the fire unquenchable,

46 Whereto their worm is definitely not pausing and the fire is definitely not made extinguished.

47 And if your eye offends you, you must cast it out. A God-Work to you is one eye, to enter into the Kingdom Rule of God, than having two eyes to be made cast into fiery hell,

48 Whereto their worm is definitely not pausing and the fire is definitely not extinguished.

49 Because everyone shall be made salted with fire, and every sacrifice shall be made salted with salt.

50 God-Work Salt Flavoring, but if ever the Salt Flavoring might become Saltiness lost, with what shall it be seasoned? You must have Salt Flavoring within yourselves, and you must be in Peace with one another.

Jesus Addresses issue of divorce

10 He Arose after there to come into the districts of Judaea through the other side of the Jordan, and the multitudes of people going together again to Him, and as had been customary practice, again He is Teaching them.

2 And the Pharisees come near to question Him, trying Him, if it is lawful for a man to divorce a wife?

3 He Answered and Spoke to them. Moses God Commanded what to you?

4 And they spoke, Moses permitted a scroll of writing of divorcement written, and to divorce. (Deut 24:1)

5 Jesus Answered and Spoke to them, With your hardness of heart, he wrote to you this Commandment.

6 But from the beginning of Creation, God made them male and female. (Gen 1:27)

7 For this cause man shall leave his father and mother, and he shall be made to cling to his wife,

8 And they two shall be in one flesh nature, so that no more are they two, but definitely one flesh nature. (Gen 2:24)

9 What, therefore, God joined together, man must not be separating.

10 And in the house, His disciples again questioned Him in regard to the same.

11 And He Said to them, Whoever might divorce his wife and might marry another commits adultery against her.

12 And if ever a wife might divorce her husband and might married another, she is committing adultery.

Only as a Little Child Enter Heaven

13 And they offered Him little children, that He might touch them, then the disciples were rebuking to those offering.

14 When Jesus Saw this, He was Very Displeased, and Spoke to them, You Must Be Concerned for the little children, and you Must not forbid them to come to Me, because of such is the Kingdom Rule of God.

15 Truly, I Say to you, that except you should receive the Kingdom Rule of God as a little child, you should never ever enter in yourself.

16 And He took them into His arms, and positioning His Hands on them, He Blessed them.

Hard for the rich to Enter Heaven

17 And He Going Out into the way of travel, one ran forward and kneeled to Him, questioning Him, Oh God-Good Master, what should I Do that I might Inherit Eternal Life?

18 And Jesus Spoke to him, Why are you calling me God-Good? Definitely no one God-Good except One, God.

19 You Know the Commandments. Should not commit adultery. Should not murder. Should not steal. Should not bear false witness. Should not defraud. You must Honor your father and mother. (Ex 20:12-16)

20 And He answered and spoke to Him, Oh Master, these things in every way, I have maintained from my youth.

21 Jesus Looked upon him, and God Loved him, and Spoke to him. One is lacking to you. You must go away, you must sell as much as you have, and you must give to the poor, and you shall have Treasure in Heaven. Also you must have Come Forward, Taking Up your cross, and you must be continuously by your choice Following Me.

22 Then he was gloomy with that Spiritual Communication. He went grieving, because he was having many acquired possessions.

23 And Jesus Looked around Saying to His disciples, How hardly, shall those that are having riches enter into the Kingdom Rule of God.

24 And the disciples were made awed over His Spiritual Communication. But Jesus Answering Again Said to them, Children, how difficult it is persuading them with riches to Enter into the Kingdom Rule of God.

25 It is easier for a camel to enter through the opening of a needle, than a rich (man) to Enter into the Kingdom Rule of God.

26 Then they were excessively amazed, and saying to themselves, Who is able to be Saved?

27 And Jesus Looked upon them Saying, With man definitely impossible, but definitely not with God, because in All Ways with God, He is Exceedingly Able.

Many first shall be Last, and last First

28 And Peter began to say to Him, Behold, we Dismissed All Things and Followed You.

29 Jesus Answered and Spoke, Truly, I Say to you. There is no man who has dismissed house, or brother, or sister, or father, or mother, or wife, or children, or fields for the cause of Me and the Gospel,

30 Except he receives an hundredfold now in this Special Season with persecutions to houses and brothers and sisters, and to mothers and children and fields, and in this coming Age, Life Eternal.

31 But many first shall be Last, and the last First.

Jesus Foretells His Death and Rising

32 And they were in the way of travel ascending into Jerusalem, and Jesus was

Going Before them, and they were awed, and they being afraid were following. He took along again the twelve, and began to Say to them what to be expecting to happen to Him.

33 Saying, Behold, for we are Ascending into Jerusalem, and the Son of Man shall be made delivered up in betrayal to the chief priests and the scribes, and they shall condemn Him to death, and they shall deliver up Him to the Gentiles.

34 And they shall mock Him, and scourge Him, and spit on Him, and kill Him; and after the third day He shall Arise.

James & John ask for Right & Left Hand

35 And going closer to Him, James and John, the sons of Zebedee, saying, Oh Master, we desire that if whatever we might ask, You should do for us.

36 And He Spoke to them, What would you have Me to do for you?

37 And they spoke to Him, Give to us that we should sit down one by Your Right hand, and one by Your Left Hand, in Your Glory.

38 But Jesus Spoke to them, You are definitely not Spiritually Knowing what you are asking for yourselves. Are you able to Drink the Cup that I am Drinking, and the Immersion that I am being made Immersed, Baptized?

39 And they spoke, We are able to be. And Jesus Spoke to them. Certainly the Cup that I am Drinking, you will Drink, and the Baptism that I am being made Immersed, you shall be made Immersed,

40 But to Sit Down by My Right Hand and My Left Hand it is definitely not Mine to Give, but definitely to whom it is made prepared.

41 The ten heard and began to be very displeased in regard to James and John.

42 But Jesus invited them Saying to them, You Spiritually Know that those thinking to reign over Gentiles, being lords over them, and the great of them exercise their authority,

43 But it shall definitely not be so among yourselves, but definitely whoever should be willing to become great among you, shall be servant of you.

44 And whoever might will of yourselves to be chief shall above all be a Bondslave.

45 Because the Son of Man came definitely not to be served, but definitely to serve, and to Give His (Sinless) Flesh Nature, a Removal Provided (for all our sinful flesh natures) for many.

Bartimaeus Receives sight

46 And they were coming into Jericho, and He was going out Himself, and His disciples, and a sufficient multitude of people from Jericho. Blind Bartimaeus, son of Timaeus, was sitting near to the way of travel, begging.

47 He when heard that it was Jesus the Nazarene, he began to cry out and to say, Oh Jesus, Son of David, You must Have Mercy on me.

48 And many rebuked him, that he might be calm, and instead he was crying out very much, Oh Son of David, You must Have Mercy on me.

49 Jesus Stood and Spoke to him to be made called for. And they called for the blind man saying to him, You must be encouraged, you must raise for yourself, He is calling for you.

50 Then he cast aside his clothes, and raised to come to Jesus.

51 Jesus Answered to him Saying, What are you strongly desiring I should do to you? And the blind spoke to Him, Oh Robboni, that I might receive sight.

52 Then Jesus Spoke to him, You must be moving, your Faith has Healed you. And immediately by his choice he Received Sight, and was following Jesus in The Way of Travel.

Triumphal Entry into Jerusalem

11 And when they approached near to Jerusalem at Bethany and Bethphage to the Mount of Olives, He Sent Out two of His disciples.

2 And Said to them, You Must Go Away into the village nearby you, and immediately coming into it you shall find a colt bound, that no man has sat down upon. Remove him. You Must Lead him.

3 And if any man might speak to you, Why are you doing this? You must Speak that the Lord Himself is having need, and immediately he shall send him out here.

4 Then they went and found the colt bound at the outside door at the fork in the road, and removed him.

5 And some of them standing there said to them, Why are you removing the colt?

6 And they spoke to them just as Jesus God Commanded, and they dismissed themselves.

7 And they led the colt to Jesus, and laid their clothes on him, and He Sat Down upon him.

8 And many laid out their clothes in the same way of travel, then flattened branches trimmed from trees, and were laying them out into the way of travel.

9 And they that went before, and they that followed cried out, calling, Hosanna, Blessed now is He coming in the Name of the Lord.

10 Now made Blessed is the coming Kingdom Rule of our father David in the Name of the Lord, Hosanna in the Highest. (Ps 118:25-26)

11 And Jesus Entered into Jerusalem, and into the Temple area, and Looked Around at all things, and being the evening hour already, He came out into Bethany with the twelve.

Curses fig tree with leaves but no fruit

12 And on the next day, they came out from Bethany. He was hungry.

13 And He Saw a fig tree at a distance, having leaves. So then He came, allowing that he shall find something upon it, and coming upon it, He found definitely nothing except leaves, for it was definitely not the special time for figs.

14 Jesus Answered and Spoke to it, No longer, not ever possible to eat any fruit from you in this Age. And His disciples heard Him.

Temple Cleansed from den of thieves

15 And they came into Jerusalem, and Jesus Entered into the Temple area. He began to Cast Out the sellers and buyers in the Temple area, and Turned Over the tables of the money changers and the seats of the dove sellers.

16 And would definitely not be concerned that any vessel be different in value through the Temple area.

17 And He was Teaching Saying to them, Is it definitely not written that My Home shall be called a Home of Prayer by all the nations? But yourselves have made it a den of robbers. (Isa 56:7; Jer 7:11)

18 And the scribes and the chief priests heard it, and they sought how they shall destroy Him, for they feared Him, because all the multitude of people were made amazed at His Teaching.

19 And when the end of day occurred, they went out, outside of the city.

Praying, Must Commit to Receive, Faith

20 And early in the morning they were passing by, Spiritually Discerned the fig tree, now being dried up from the root.

21 And Peter, being made in remembrance, called to Him, Oh Rabbi, Behold, that cursed fig tree is now dried up.

22 And Jesus Answered Saying to them, You must be having Faith of God,

23 Because, Truly, I am Saying to you, That whoever you should have spoken to this mountain, You must be made taken away and you must be cast into the sea, and should not have doubted in his heart,

but definitely should have Committed about what he is saying is coming to pass, it shall be to him whatever he should have spoken.

24 Because I am Saying this to you, In all things whatever you are Praying, asking, you must be Committing what you are receiving, and it shall be to you.

25 And when you should be standing fast, Praying, you must by your choice Remove from Memory (forgive) if you have anything against anyone, that your Father in Heaven might to you Remove from Memory (forgive) your spiritual death offenses.

26 But if yourselves are definitely not Removing from Memory (forgive), neither shall your Father Who is in the Heavenlies Remove from Memory (forgive) the spiritual death offenses of you.

Questioned: "By what authority?"

27 And they were coming again into Jerusalem and walking in the Temple area, there came to Him the chief priests and the scribes and the elders.

28 And they said to Him, By what Authority do You these things, and who gave to You this Authority, that You should do these things?

29 Then Jesus Answered, Spoke to them, I also, I will question you one Spiritual Communication, and you must Answer Me, and I will Spirit Say to you by what Authority I am doing these things.

30 The immersion of John, was it out from Heaven, or out from man? You must Answer Me.

31 And they accounted with themselves, saying if ever we should speak out from Heaven, He shall Spirit Say, Why then, therefore, are you definitely not Committed to Him?

32 But definitely if ever we spoke, out from man, they were fearing all the people, because they were having John that he was in fact a Prophet.

33 And they answering said to Jesus, We are definitely not spiritually knowing, and Jesus Answering Said to them, Neither am I Saying to you by what Authority I am Doing these things.

The wicked husbandmen Judged

12 And He began to say to them in parables, A man planted a vineyard, and placed a hedge about it, and dug a wine vat, and built a tower, and sharecropped it to husbandmen, and he journeyed away.

2 And in the special season, he sent out a slave to the husbandmen, that from the husbandmen he might take from the fruit of the vineyard.

3 Then they took him, beat, and they sent out empty.

4 And again he sent out to them another slave of same kind. They also casting stones, wounded to the head, treated shamefully, and sent out.

5 And again he sent out another of the same kind, and him they killed, and actually many others of same kind, they are beating and are killing.

6 Having still one son, his beloved, and he sent him out last to them, saying that they shall respect my son.

7 But those husbandmen, spoke with themselves, that this is the heir. You must come now, we should be killing him, and the inheritance shall be ours.

8 And they took him, killed, and cast out, outside the vineyard.

9 What, therefore, shall the lord of the vineyard do? He shall come and shall destroy the husbandmen, and give the vineyard to others of same kind.

10 Neither have you read this Scripture? The Stone which the builders disapproved, This has become at Head of the Corner.

11 This came to pass from the Lord, and it was marvelous in our eyes. (Ps 118:22-23)

12 And they sought to hold to retain Him because they knew that He spoke the

parable to them, but they feared the multitude of people, so dismissing themselves, they went.

Give Caesar his due; and to God, His

13 And they were sending forward to Him certain of the Pharisees and the Herodians, that they might trap Him in a Spiritual Communication.
14 And When they came, they say to Him, Oh Master, we Spiritually Discern that You are True, because you definitely look not at the presence of men, and from man it is definitely not caring to You, but definitely upon Truth, teaching The Way of God. Is it lawful to give Caesar tribute or definitely not?
15 Should we give or might we not give? Then Spiritually Knowing their role playing hypocrisy, He Spoke to them. Why do you try Me? Bring to me a penny that I should Spiritually Discern.
16 Then they brought, and He Said to them, Now either whose image or superscription of him? Then they spoke to Him, Caesar's.
17 And Jesus Answered, He Spoke to them. You must yield the things of Caesar to Caesar, and the things of God to God. And they marveled in The Way of Him.

No marriage In Heaven

18 And the Sadducees were coming to Him, who say a Resurrection is not being possible, and they questioned Him saying,
19 Oh Master, Moses wrote to us that if one brother might die, and might leave a wife, and no children might part from, that his brother might take his wife, and might raise seed to his brother. (Deut 25:5)
20 Therefore, there were seven brothers and the first took a wife, dies, and definitely no seed departed from.
21 And the second took her and died, and neither his seed parted from, and the third in like manner,
22 And the seventh took her and definitely no seed parted from, and also last of all, the woman died.
23 In the Resurrection, therefore, when they should arise, whose wife shall she be of them, because the seven had her for a wife.
24 Jesus Answered, and Spoke to them, Are you definitely not being made deceiving because of this? You are not Spiritually Discerning the Scriptures, neither the Miracle Power of God.
25 Because when they should arise from dead neither are they marrying, nor given in marriage, but definitely they are as Angels in the Heavenlies.
26 And then, in regard to the dead that are made Rising Up, have you definitely not read in the Book of Moses, as in the place of the Bush, God Spoke to Him Saying, I, the God of Abraham, and the God of Isaac, and the God of Jacob. (Ex 3:6)
27 He is definitely not the God of dead, but definitely God of the Living. Therefore, yourselves are made deceiving many.

The Greatest Commandment

28 And one of the scribes coming near, heard Him discussing Spiritually Discerning how that He answered God-Working. He questioned Him, Which is the First Commandment of all?
29 And Jesus Answered him, The First Commandment of all, Israel you must Hear, the Lord our God is One Lord.
30 And You shall God-Love the Lord your God out from all of your heart, and out from all of your soul, and out from all your intellect, and out from all of your strength (Deut 6:4-5). This is the First Commandment.
31 And Second like it, God-Love your neighbor as yourself. Definitely no other of the same kind Commandment is greater than these.
32 And the scribe spoke to Him, Oh Master, You spoke God-Working in regard of Truth, for God is One, and there is definitely not

another of the same kind but Him.

33 And to God-Love Him out from your whole Heart, and out from your whole Understanding, and out from your whole Soul, and out from your whole Strength, and your God Loving your neighbor as yourself is greater than all your burnt offerings and your sacrifices. (Lev 19:18)

34 And when Jesus Spiritually Discerned him that he prudently answered, He Spoke to him, You are definitely not far off from the Kingdom Rule of God. And definitely, he was no more daring to question Him.

Christ is Whose Son?

35 Jesus Answered and Said, Teaching inside the Temple area, How say the scribes that Christ is the Son of David?

36 Because David himself spoke by the Holy Spirit, The Lord Spoke to My Lord, You must Sit at My Right Side until after whenever I should Position Your enemies a Footstool for Your Feet. (Ps 110:1)

37 Therefore, David himself called Him Lord, and from where is He, His son? And a large multitude of people were hearing Him with pleasure.

Greater Judgment to scribes

38 And He Said of them in His Teaching, You must Spiritually See of the scribes, who prefer to walk in long robes, and salutations in the marketplaces,

39 And chief seats in the synagogues, and chief rooms in the suppers.

40 They devour the houses of the widows, and pretense long praying. These shall receive more abundant judgment.

41 And Jesus Sat Down nearby to the treasury, to perceive how the multitude of people cast brass coins into the treasury, and many rich were casting very much.

42 And one poor widow came to cast two mites, which is a farthing (Roman Kodrantes).

43 And He invited His disciples, Saying to them, Truly I Say to you, that this poor widow herself casts greater than all have cast into the treasury.

44 Because everyone cast from their abounding in amount, but she out from her poverty cast whatever, all that she was having, all of her livelihood.

End Times; when and what Signs

13 And He Going Out from the Temple area, one of His disciples said to Him, Oh Master, behold, what manner of stones, and what manner of building.

2 Jesus Answered and Spoke to him, Are you Spiritually Seeing these great buildings? Never ever should a stone upon a stone have been made dismissed, which should have never ever been made torn down?

3 And Himself Sitting at the Mount of Olives nearby to the Temple area, Peter and James and John and Andrew were questioning Him in private.

4 You must Speak to us, when shall these things be, and what Miracle Sign should be expected when all these things to be made finished?

5 And then Jesus Answered them, He began Saying: You must be Spiritually Seeing that no one should deceive you.

6 Because many shall come in My Name, saying that I AM, and shall deceive many.

7 And then when you hear wars and rumors of wars, you must not be frightened, because it must come to pass, but definitely, not yet the End.

8 Because nation will be made to rise up against nation, and kingdom rule against kingdom rule, and there shall be earthquakes upon places, and shall be famines, and these disturbances beginnings of travail.

9 But yourselves, you must Spiritually See yourselves, because they shall deliver up you to councils, and you shall be beaten in synagogues. And you shall stand before governors and kings for My Cause, for a Testimony against them.

10 And the Gospel must first of all be made preached in all the nations.

Should you be arrested

11 But when they might lead, delivering you up, you must not take thought before what you should Utter, neither must you meditate, but definitely whatever He should make Given to you in that hour, This you must Utter, because you yourselves are definitely not Uttering, but definitely the Holy Spirit.

12 And then brother shall deliver up brother to death, and father a child, and children shall stand up against parents and shall put them to death.

13 And you shall be hated by all because of My Name, but he that endures to the End, he shall be Saved.

Flee when Abomination made known

14 But when you should Spiritually Discern the abomination of desolation, that Spirit Spoken by Daniel the Prophet, standing whereto he ought definitely not. He that reads must be comprehending, then those inside Judaea must flee into the mountains, (Dan 11:31; 12:11)

15 And then those upon the housetop must not come down into the house, neither to enter to take away anything out from within his house.

16 And him that is being in the field, must not turn back to take away his clothes.

17 But Woe to them wherein having womb with child, and to them nursing in those days,

18 And you must be Praying that your flight not occur in winter.

Great Tribulation shall come

19 Because there shall be days of affliction that such as has definitely not occurred since the beginning of Creation which our God Created up to now, and never ever should be.

20 And except the Lord shortened those days, all sinful flesh nature would definitely not ever be Saved, but definitely because of the Elect whom He has Chosen, those days have been shortened.

21 And then if anyone might speak to you, behold, here the Christ, or behold there, you should not commit.

22 Because false Christ's and false prophets shall be made to rise up, and shall give miracle signs and wonders, to be seducing by deception, if possible, even the Elect.

23 Then yourselves must Spiritually be Seeing, Behold, I am now Foretelling you all things.

Christ Returns & Elect are Gathered

24 But definitely in those days, after that Tribulation, the sun shall be made darkened, and the moon shall definitely not give her shining.

25 And the stars of Heaven shall be falling away, and the Miracle powers in the Heavenlies shall be shaken.

26 And then they shall see the Spiritual Appearance of the Son of Man, coming inside the Clouds, with Miracle Power and very much Glory. (Dan 7:13)

27 And then He shall Send Out His Angels, and shall Gather All Together His Elect out from the four winds, away from farthest part of earth, up to farthest part of Heaven.

No man knows the day nor the hour

28 For now you must learn the parable from the fig tree. When her branch became already tender and is budding out the leaves, be knowing that the summer is near.

29 And so when yourselves should be Spiritually Discerning these things occurring, you must be Knowing that it is near at the doors.

30 Truly, I am Saying to you, that never ever should this generation pass away, not until all these things come to pass,

31 Heaven and earth shall pass away, but My Spiritual Communications should never ever pass away.

32 But in regard of that day and of that hour, definitely no man is now Spiritually Discerning, neither the Angels in Heaven, nor the Son, except the Father.

Watch and Pray

33 You must be Spiritually Seeing. You must be alert and you must be Praying, because you are definitely not Spiritually Discerning, when this Special Time is.

34 As a man traveling far, dismissed his house and gave to Bondslaves his authority, and to every man for his Work of God, and God Commanded that he should be Watching with the Porter.

35 Therefore, you must be Watching, definitely not now Spiritually Discerning, yet when is the Lord of the house coming, either end of day, or midnight, or cock crowing, or early in the morning?

36 If coming unexpectedly, He might find you sleeping.

37 And what I Say to you, I Say to all, You must be Watching!

Chief Priests plot to kill Jesus

14 And then after two days was the Passover (Nisan 14) and Feast of Unleavened Bread (starting Nisan 15-22). And the chief priests and scribes were seeking how, in subtle half truths (deceit), to hold to retain that they might kill Him.

2 But they were saying, Not in the Feast (Feast of Unleavened Bread, following the Preparation Day), for fear that a tumult shall be of the people.

Jesus Anointed for His Burial

3 And even as He, Himself was in Bethany, in the house of Simon the leper, He was sitting down to eat, a woman came to Him having an alabaster container of very valuable ointment of spikenard plant and broke into pieces the alabaster container of the spikenard plant, poured it herself upon His Head.

4 And then certain ones were very displeased within themselves, and said, For what purpose is being her squander of the ointment?

5 For she was able to sell in the market for over three hundred pennies, and be given to the poor. Now she was groaning.

6 And then Jesus Spoke, You must dismiss her. Why are you offering labor concern to her? She has worked a Work by God, God-Work, for the Purpose and Result of Me.

7 For you are always having the poor with yourselves, and when you might be willing, you are able to do well to them, but you are definitely not always having Me.

8 She did what she had taken before to dedicate my Body for Burial.

9 Truly, I Say to you, whereto whenever this Gospel might be preached in all the satan's world, and Who she having Finalized, shall be Uttered for a Memorial to her.

Judas Iscariot plans betrayal

10 And Judas Iscariot, one of the twelve, went to the chief priests, in order that he might deliver up in betrayal of Him to them.

11 And then having heard, they rejoiced, and promised to give to him pieces of silver, and sought how he might deliver up Him conveniently.

The Last Supper

12 And the First Day (starts at sunset) of Unleavened Bread, when the Passover was killed as sacrifice, His disciples called to Him, Wherein shall you be going to prepare that You should eat the Passover?

13 And He Sent Out two of His disciples and Says to them, You must go away to the city and a man bearing a pitcher of water shall meet you. You must follow him.

14 And whereto when he should enter, you must speak to the householder, That the Master is Saying, Wherein is the guestroom whereto I should eat the Passover with My disciples?

15 And he shall show you a great upper

room made laid out there; you must have prepared ready for us.

16 And His disciples departed, and came to the city, and found just as He had spoken to them, and they prepared the Passover.

17 And then it being of evening, He Came with the twelve.

18 And while they themselves were sitting as at eating, Jesus Spoke, Truly, I am Saying to you, that one out from yourselves who is eating with Me, shall deliver Me up in betrayal.

19 And then they began to be grieving, and saying to Him one by one, Who possibly me? And another of the same kind, Who possibly me?

20 And then He Answered, Spoke to them, He is one of the twelve, that is for himself hand dipping with Me in the dish.

21 The Son of Man certainly goes away, just as now written in regard about Him. But Woe to that man through whom the Son of Man is being delivered up in betrayal. It would be God-Work for him if that man was definitely not born.

22 And even as they are continuously eating, Jesus Himself took Bread, Blessed, Broke, and Gave to them, and Spoke, You must take by your choice to Eat. This is My Body,

23 And He took by His choice the Cup, Gave Thanks, Gave to them, and they by their choice all drank of it.

24 And He Spoke to them. This is My Blood which is of the New of a different kind of Covenant which is made Pouring Out to many.

25 Truly, I am Saying to you, that I should never ever Drink from the product of the vine, until after that Day then when I should be Drinking a New of a different kind in the Kingdom Rule of God.

Foretells of Peter's denial of Him

26 And they sang a hymn; they came out to the Mount of Olives.

27 And Jesus Says to them, All shall be made offended in Me in this Special Night, for it is now Written, I the Shepherd will be struck mortally, and the sheep shall also be made to scatter. (Zech 13:7)

28 But definitely after I am made Risen Up, I will Go Before you into Galilee.

29 But Peter was stating to Him, Also, if all shall be made offended, but definitely not I.

30 And Jesus Says to him, Truly I Say to you that this day in this night, before the cock crows twice, you shall deny Me three times.

31 But he said instead more in excess, for If ever I must die together with You, I will definitely not, never, deny You. Then in like manner also all were saying.

Jesus Prays in Gethsemane

32 And they came to that space of land named Gethsemane, and He Said to His disciples, You must Sit Down here while I should Pray.

33 And He took along Peter and James and John with Him, and they began to be greatly awed and to be very sleepy.

34 And Said to them, My soul is very sorrowful up to death. You must continue here, and you must Watch.

35 And went forward a little while, fell down upon the earth, and Prayed that if it is possible this hour might pass away from Him.

36 And He Said, Abba, Father, all things possible with You. Withdraw away this Cup from Me. But definitely not what I Will but definitely what You.

37 And He is came to find them sleeping, and said to Peter, Simon are you sleeping? Are you definitely not capable to Watch one hour?

38 You must Watch and you must Pray that you might not enter into temptation. Certainly, The spirit is willing, but the sinful flesh nature weak.

39 And again, He went to Pray, speaking the same Words.

40 And He returned again to find them sleeping because their eyes were made

heavy, and had definitely no Spiritual Discerning how they might answer Him.

41 And He comes the third time and Says to them, And now sleep, and be refreshed. It is already come the hour. Behold, the Son of Man is being delivered up in betrayal into the hands of sinners.

42 You must raise up. We should move along. Behold, he who is delivering Me up in betrayal is now approaching near.

Arrest of Jesus

43 And immediately, He still Uttering to them, Judas came up, being one of the twelve, and with him a large multitude of people with swords and wooden staves, along with the chief priests and the scribes and the elders.

44 And he that delivered Him up in betrayal gave a token to them, saying that Whoever I should kiss is Him you must hold to retain, and you must lead away securely.

45 And having come, immediately came near to Him saying, Oh Rabbi, Oh Rabbi, and kissed Him.

46 Then they laid their hands upon Him, and held to retain Him.

47 Then one man present drew out a sword, struck harmfully a slave of the High Priest, and took away his ear.

48 And Jesus Answered, Spoke to them, Are you come out as against a robber, with swords and wooden staves, to physically take Me?

49 I was among you each day in the Temple area teaching, and you definitely did not retain Me, but definitely that the Scriptures should be Fully Filled.

50 And they all parted from Him, fled.

51 And one certain young man was following him, being made clothed with a linen cloth upon a naked (body), and the young men held to retain him.

52 And then he left the linen cloth. He fled away from them naked.

Taken before the High Priest

53 And they lead away Jesus to the High Priest, and with him coming together all the chief priests and the elders and the scribes.

54 And Peter followed Him away at a distance, to within the palace of the High Priest, and he was sitting with the under servants, and warming himself within the light of the fire.

55 Then the chief priests and the whole council were seeking testimony against Jesus for putting Him to death, yet they were definitely not finding,

56 Because many were bearing false witness against Him, and the given testimony definitely was not equal.

57 And there arose certain ones bearing false witness against Him, saying,

58 That we heard Him saying this, I will tear down this Temple made with hands, and through three days I will build another of same kind made without hand.

59 But neither was their given testimony in such a manner of themselves equal.

60 And the High Priest arose in the midst, questioned Jesus saying, Are You definitely not answering anything? What are they witnessing against You?

61 Then He was holding speech, and answered nothing. Again the High Priest was questioning Him, and said to Him, You, are You the Christ, the Son of the Most Blessed Worthy of all Spiritual Perfection?

62 And Then Jesus Spoke, I AM, and you will Spiritually See the Son of Man Sitting at the Right Hand of the Miracle Power, and Coming with the Clouds of Heaven. (Ps 110 1; Dan 7:13)

63 Then the High Priest tore apart his coat saying, What need we have of further witnesses?

64 You have heard the blasphemy. How does this appear to you? And everyone condemned Him to death, being found guilty of death.

65 And some began to spit on Him, and

blindfolded His Face, and beat Him, and called to Him, You must Prophesy. and the officers with slaps with palms of hands, were prostrating Him.

Peter denies Jesus three times

66 Then being in the palace down below, one of the maid servants of the High Priest came,

67 And she spiritually discerned Peter warming himself, looked upon him and said to Peter, You also were with this Jesus of Nazareth.

68 But He disclaimed saying, I definitely Spiritually Discern not, nor am I aware of what you are saying. And he came away outside into the vestibule, and a cock crowed.

69 And a maid servant spiritually discerning Him again, began to say to them standing, that he is of them.

70 And then again, he was disclaiming, and after a little while again those standing said to Peter, Of Truth, you are of them, also because you're Galilaean and your speech is similar.

71 But he began to swear, and to bind under a curse that he definitely is not now knowing this man, whom yourselves are saying.

72 And at a second cock crow, Peter also was made in remembrance the Specific Word that Jesus Spoke to him. Before that cock crows twice, you will Deny Me three times, and He lay weeping.

Pontius Pilate questions Jesus

15 And Immediately, for early in the morning the chief priests with the elders and scribes consolidated the counsel, and the whole council bound Jesus. He was carried away, and was delivered up to Pilate.

2 And Pilate questioned Him, You, Are You the King of the Jews? Then He Answered, He Spoke to him, You are saying.

3 And the chief priests themselves were themselves very much accusing Him, but He definitely answered no man.

4 Then Pilate questioned Him again saying, Are you definitely not answering anything? Behold, how much they are witnessing against You.

5 But Jesus answered not anything anymore, so that Pilate marveled.

Chief priests moved the people

6 Then at the Feast, He set at liberty one prisoner to them, whomever they ask.

7 And then there was one called Barabbas who did murder in the dissension, now made bound with whoever made insurrection with him.

8 And the multitude of people shouting out began continuously to ask (to Pilate), Just as he used to be doing for them?

9 But Pilate answered them saying, Are you willing I should set at liberty to you the King of the Jews?

10 Because he was knowing that the chief priests delivered Him up because of envy.

11 But the chief priests agitated the multitude of people much more, in order that he might set at liberty Barabbas to them.

12 And when Pilate answered again, he spoke to them, What, therefore, prefer you that I do to whom you are calling King of the Jews?

13 And then again, they cried out, You must crucify Him!

14 Then Pilate said to them, Why, because what evil work has He done? And then they earnestly cried out, You must crucify Him!

Pilate delivered Jesus to be Crucified

15 So Pilate intended, sufficient to the multitude of people, to decide to set at liberty to them Barabbas, and delivered up Jesus to lashing in order that He be made crucified.

16 Then the soldiers lead Him away, within the palace, that is to say is the Judgment Hall, and there calling together the whole band.

17 And they put on Him purple clothes,

and placed upon Him a braided thorny victor's wreath.

18 And began greeting Him, You must rejoice, Oh King of the Jews.

19 And they struck His head with a reed, and spit on Him, and positioned their knees to worship Him.

Crucifixion of Jesus

20 And when they had mocked Him, they unclothed the purple clothes, and put on Himself His own clothes, and they led Him out in order that they should crucify Him.

21 And they compelled one Simon, a Cyrenian, passing on, coming away from the countryside, the father of Alexander and Rufus, in order that he should take up His cross.

22 And they brought Him to Golgotha, the place that is being interpreted, Place of a skull.

23 And they were giving Him to drink, wine mixed with myrrh, but He definitely took not.

24 And they crucified Him, dividing His clothes, casting lot upon them, who should take away what. (Ps 22:18)

25 And when it was the third hour (9:00 AM), then they crucified Him.

26 And the superscription of His accusation was inscribed, THE KING OF THE JEWS.

27 And united with Him were crucified two robbers, one by the Right Side and one by the Left Side of Him.

28 And the Scripture was made Fulfilled, which Says, And He was made Accounted with the lawless. (Isa 53:12)

29 And they that were passing by were blaspheming Him, wagging their heads at Him and saying, Ah, You that shall tear down the Temple, and build within three days.

30 You must save Yourself, and You must come down from the cross.

31 And likewise also, the chief priests were mocking with one to another with the scribes saying, He Saved others of the same kind, Himself He is definitely not able to Save.

32 Christ, the King of Israel, you must come down now from the cross, in order that we might Spiritually Discern and might Commit. And those crucified together with Him scolded Him to shame.

33 And when it became the sixth hour (12:00 noon), darkness came to pass upon the whole earth, up to the ninth hour.

34 And at the ninth hour (3:00 PM) Jesus loudly pleaded with a Great Voice Saying, Eloi, Eloi, lama sabachthani? which is being made interpreted, My God, My God, for what Purpose have You within Me left? (Ps 22:1-24; Ps 69:16-20)

35 And some of those now standing heard, saying, behold, He is calling for Elias.

36 Then one ran and made full a sponge of vinegar and also placed it upon a reed giving Him drink, saying, You must be concerned for, if we might spiritually discern Elias coming to take You down. (Ps 69:21-29)

Veil of the Temple is Split in Two

37 And then Jesus Himself Dismissed with a Great Voice, Forcefully Exhaled the Holy Spirit.

38 And the Veil of the Temple Sanctuary split into two, from the top to until after down below.

Guard, He Truly was the Son of God

39 And the centurion Spiritually Discerning is now standing by beside Him when in such a manner He had Crying Out, Forcefully Exhaled the Holy Spirit. He spoke, Of Truth, This Man was the Son of God.

40 There were also women away at a distance seeing with perception, among whom were Mary the Magdalene, and Mary the mother of James the less and of Joses, and also Salome.

41 Also when He was in Galilee, they

followed Him and served Him. Also many others of the same kind came up with Him to Jerusalem.

Burial Before the High Sabbath
42 And already it became evening, in fact that is to say it was the Preparation Day [Nisan 14 when priests sacrificed the lambs in the Temple], being the day before the Sabbath. [The First Day of Feast of Unleavened Bread, a High Holy Day]
43 Joseph from Arimathaea, an honorable counselor, who also himself was looking for the Kingdom Rule of God, dared come to enter to Pilate and asked for the Body of Jesus.
44 And then Pilate marveled that already He was now a corpse, and he invited the centurion to question him if he died long ago.
45 And when he knew from the centurion, he bestowed the Body to Joseph.
46 And he bought a linen cloth, and took Him down to enwrap with the linen cloth, and arranged Him within a sepulcher, which was now made chiseling out from a huge rock, and rolled a stone against the door of the sepulcher.
47 And Mary the Magdalene, and Mary of Joses were seeing with perception, wherein He was made positioned.

Jesus Rises Sunday, first day of week
16 And when the weekly Sabbath time past, Mary the Magdalene, and Mary of James, and Salome bought spices coming in order that they should anoint Him.
2 And extremely early in the morning of the first day of the week, they came to the sepulcher at the rising of the sun.
3 And they were saying to themselves, Who will move back for us the stone out from the door of the sepulcher?

Angel Told women that He Arose
4 And they looked up and saw that stone was made moved back, for it was exceedingly great.
5 And having entered into the sepulcher, they Spiritually Discerned a young man Sitting by the Right Side, being Made Clothed in a White Long Robe and they were made greatly awed.
6 And then He Said to them, You must not be made greatly awed. You seek Jesus of Nazareth, Who is now made crucified. He has been made Risen Up. He is definitely not here. Behold, the place whereto they laid Him down.
7 But definitely go away, speak to His disciples and Peter that He is going before you into Galilee. There you shall see Him, the Spiritual Appearance, just as He Spoke to you.
8 They came out quickly, and fled away from the sepulcher, now having trembling themselves, and also ecstasy, and they spoke definitely not anything to any man because they feared.

Jesus Appears to His Disciples
9 And when He had Arisen early in the morning, on the first of the week, He first of all Appeared to Mary of Magdalene, from whom He had Cast Out seven demons.
10 That she being mourning and weeping, went to tell them that had been with Him.
11 And also they heard that He is Living and had been seen by her. They had not Committed.
12 And then after these things, two from them are going walking in the countryside. He made Manifested in another Spiritual form of a different kind.
13 And also they went to tell the others. They neither Committed to them.

Sends His Disciples Into the world
14 Afterward, He was made Manifest to the eleven themselves sitting as at eating, and Scolded Sharply the Uncommitment of them, and hardness of heart, for they

Committed definitely not to those who saw Him, now made Risen Up.

15 And He Spoke to them, Be made Going into all the satan's world. You must Preach the Gospel to every creature.

16 He who has by his choice Committed and has been made Immersed shall be made Saved, and then having by his choice Uncommitted, he shall be made condemned to death.

17 And these Miracle Signs shall Follow Along those that have by their choice Committed in My Name: they shall by their choice Cast Out demons; they shall by their choice Utter in New of a different kind Tongues;

18 They shall Take Up serpents; if they might Drink any deadly thing, it shall definitely not harm to them; they shall Lay Hands on the sickly, and they shall have God-Working.

Christ Ascends to Heaven

19 Certainly, therefore, after the Lord had Uttered to them, He was Received Up into Heaven, and Sat Down at the Right Side of God. (Ps 110:1)

20 And they came away to Preach everywhere, the Lord Working Together with them, and the Word was established by following after with Miracle Signs. Amen.

The Gospel According to

Luke

Luke Declares Reason for his Epistle

1 Forasmuch as many presume to narrate a recitation, in regard to being now fully persuaded among us in matters.

2 Just as eyewitnesses and under servants delivered up to us from the beginning, those things of the Spiritual Word came to pass.

3 I thought, also I, now following along from the beginning all things exactly in order, to write to you, most noble Theophilus.

4 That you should Fully Know, in regard to the things you have been made informed by the Safety of the Word.

Gabriel Sent to Zacharias

5 It came to pass in the days of Herod the king, a certain priest of Judaea named Zacharias, from the priestly course of Abia, and his wife, out of the daughters of Aaron, and her name, Elisabeth,

6 And they were both Righteous in the Presence of God, going in all the Commandments and Righteous Actions of the Lord, Blameless.

7 And there was definitely not any child to them, according as Elisabeth was barren and they were both now well stricken in days.

8 Then it came to pass, in his acting as priest in the priestly order, of his priestly course, seen of God,

9 According to the custom of the Levitical priesthood, he cast lot to burn incense, to enter into the Temple Sanctuary of the Lord.

10 And the whole multitude of different people were Praying outside during the short time of incense.

11 Then he saw the Spiritual Appearance in Him, an Angel of the Lord, now standing by the right sides of the altar of incense.

12 And it troubled Zacharias to Spiritually Discern and fear fell upon him.

13 But the Angel Spoke to him, You must not for yourself fear, Oh Zacharias, since your supplication has been made Spiritually Heard, and of your wife, Elisabeth, shall be born a son to you, and you shall call his name John.

14 And he shall be Joy to you, and also with many shall be made exceeding Joy, rejoicing in regard to his Supernatural Birth.

15 Because he shall be Great in the Presence of the Lord, and he should never ever drink wine or intoxicating drink, and he shall be Filled of the Holy Spirit even from his mother's womb.

16 And many of the sons of Israel, shall he Turn Back to their Lord God.

17 And he shall Go Forward in the Presence of Him in Spirit and Miracle Power of Elias, to Turn Back the hearts of fathers to children, and the disobedient by the Intelligence of the Righteous, to be Preparing a people Made Ready for the Lord.
(Mal 4:5-6)

18 And Zacharias spoke to the Angel, How shall I Know according to this? Because I am an old man, and my wife is now well stricken in her days?

19 And the Angel Answered. He Spoke to him. I am Gabriel that is now Standing in the Presence of God, and was Sent Out to Utter to you, and have Proclaimed these things to you.

20 And, Behold, you shall be unable to speak, and not be able to utter until that day these things come to pass, for wherein you have definitely not Committed to my Spiritual Communications, which shall be made Fully Fulfilled in the Special Time of them.

21 And the people were watching for Zacharias, and were marveling with what was delaying him inside the Temple Sanctuary.

22 And when he came out, he was definitely not able to utter to them, and they Fully Knew that he Beheld Attentively a visitation in the Temple Sanctuary, and he was motioning to them, and was continuously constantly dumb.

23 And it came to pass as the days of his Service to God were made filled, he went to his home.

24 And after those days, his wife Elisabeth conceived, and she secluded herself five months, saying,

25 This the Lord has now done to me in such a manner, in these days in which He Took Note to take away my rejection among men.

Gabriel Sent to Mary, a Virgin

26 And in the sixth month the Angel Gabriel was Sent Out by God to a city of Galilee, which named Nazareth.

27 To a virgin made espoused to a man, one named Joseph from the House of David, and the name of the virgin, Mary.

28 And Entered the Angel to her, He Spoke, You, Made Highly Favored, Must be Rejoicing Now. The Lord is with you; you are now made Blessed among women.

29 And when she Spiritually Discerned, she was made agitated by the Spiritual Communication of Him, and was reasoning what manner should be this Salutation.

30 And His Angel Spoke to Mary, You must not be making yourself fearing, because you have Found Grace with God.

31 And Behold, you Shall Conceive in your womb With a Child, and you Shall Give Birth to a Son, and you Shall Call His Name Jesus.

32 He Shall Be Great, and He Shall Be Called Son of Most High, and the Lord God shall Give to Him the Throne of His father David.

33 And He Shall Reign Over the House of Jacob Forever, and of His Kingdom Rule There Shall Be Definitely No End.

34 Then spoke Mary to the Angel, How shall this be, in fact that I am knowing definitely no man?

35 The Angel Was Made Answered and Spoke to her. For this reason, The Holy Spirit shall Come Upon you, and Miracle Power of the Most High will Overshadow you. And He Who is Holy Is Being Made Born Out From Within you, He Shall Be Made Called The Son of God.

36 And Behold Elisabeth, your kinsmen, she has also conceived a son in her old age, and she being called barren is in her sixth month.

37 For With God Every Single Word Is Definitely Not Impossible.

38 And Mary spoke, Behold, The Handmaiden of the Lord. It has come to pass beyond my dreams To Me According To Your Word. And the Angel Went From her.

Mary Visits Elisabeth in Sixth Month

39 And Mary arose in those days, went into the hill country with diligence, into a city of Judah.

40 And entered into the home of Zacharias and greeted Elizabeth.

41 And it came to pass as Elizabeth heard the salutation of Mary, the babe Leaped for Joy in her womb, and Elisabeth was Filled with the Holy Spirit.

42 And she spoke out with a great voice and spoke, Bless you among women, and Bless the Fruit of your womb.

43 And from what this to me, that The Mother Of My Lord should Come to me?

44 Behold, because as the voice of your salutation occurred in my ears, the babe in my womb Leaped in exceeding Joy.

45 And she, Spiritually Blessed, Committed that she shall be Perfection for those things Now Made Uttered about her from the Lord.

Mary Gives Praise to God

46 And Mary spoke, My soul is Magnifying the Lord.

47 And My Spirit Exceedingly Glad in The Way of God, my Savior.

48 For He has Regarded to the lowliness of His handmaiden. Behold, because from now all the generations shall call me Blessed. (I Sam 1:11)

49 For He Has Done Great Works to me, that Mighty Work and Holy the Name of Him.

50 And His Mercy to generations of generations that are Fearing Him. (Ps 103:17)

51 He Established Dominion with His Mighty Arm, Scattered the proud in intellect of their heart.

52 He has Taken Down mighty authority, even from thrones. He has Exalted the Humble.

53 Those being hungry, He has Filled Up with God-Good, and those being rich, He has Sent Forth empty.

54 He Himself has Remembered Mercy. He has Supported Israel, His Dependent child.

55 Just as He Uttered to our fathers, to Abraham, and to His Seed for the Purpose of the Present Age.

56 And Mary continued with her about three months, and returned to her home.

Elisabeth Gives Birth to John the Baptist

57 Now Elisabeth's time was filled, and she delivered her borne son.

58 And her neighbors and the kinsman heard how the Lord was magnifying His Mercy with her, and they were rejoicing together with her.

59 And it came to pass in the eighth day, they came to circumcise the little child and called him Zacharias, after the name of his father.

60 His mother answered and spoke, Definitely not, but definitely he shall be called John.

61 And they spoke to her, For none is among your relatives who calls himself this name.

62 And then they made signs to his father, Whatever shall you be calling him?

63 And he asked a writing table to write, He said, John is his name, and everyone marveled.

64 And instantly his mouth and his tongue were made Open, and he was Uttering Blessings to God.

65 And fear occurred among all alike dwelling near them, and in all the hill country above Judea, all these words were made rumored.

66 And all these things heard were put in their hearts, saying, So then Who shall this little child be? And the Hand of the Lord was With him.

Zacharias Prophecies

67 And his father Zacharias was made Filled of the Holy Spirit and Prophesied Saying,

68 Most Blessed Worthy of all Spiritual Perfection, Lord God of Israel, for He Himself has Visited and Finalized Removal to Heaven for His People.

69 And He has Raised Up a Horn of Salvation to us in the Home of His male servant David.

70 Just as He Uttered through the mouth of His Holy Prophets, for the present Age.

71 Saved from our enemies and every way from the hand of those hating us.

72 To Finalize Mercy with our fathers, and to yourself Remember His Holy Covenant,

73 An Oath which He Promised to our father Abraham.

74 That He has Given to us without fear, from the hand of our enemies, having been made Rescued to be Devoting to Him,

75 In State of Holiness and Righteousness, in the Presence of Him, All The Days of our Life.

76 And you, little child, shall be called a Prophet of the Most High, because you shall Precede before the Lord's Presence to Prepare His Way of Travel, (Mal 3:1)

77 To Give Knowledge of Salvation to His people by the Removal of their sin natures and sins.

78 Because of Compassion of our God's Mercy by which our Dayspring Shall Visit us from on High.

79 To Fully Appear to those sitting in darkness and shadow of death, to Direct our feet into The Way of Peace. (Isa 9:2)

80 And then the little child grew, and was made strong in Spirit, and was in the desolate wilderness, until after the Day of his Showing to Israel.

Time of Jesus' Birth

2 And it came to pass in those days that a decree came out from Caesar Augustus, to record all of the inhabited earth.

2 This first taxing registration occurred during Cyrenius, governing of Syria.

3 And all went to be made recorded, everyone to their own city.

4 And then Joseph ascended away from Galilee out from the city of Nazareth into Judaea to the city of David, which is called Bethlehem, because he was being from House and family of David,

5 To be recorded with Mary his espoused wife, being great with Child.

6 And it came to pass with them being there, the days were made filled for her to give birth.

7 And she gave birth to her Firstborn Son, and wrapped Him in swaddling clothes, and laid Him in the manger, since there was definitely no place for them in the inn.

Lord's Angel Spoke to shepherds

8 And shepherds were in the land near them, camping and maintaining watch at night over their safe flock.

9 Behold, an Angel of the Lord Stood Ready to them, and the Glory of the Lord

Shone Around About them, and they feared a great fear.

10 And the Angel Spoke to them, Behold, you must not fear because God-Good News is Proclaimed to you, which shall be a Great Joy to all people.

11 For being Made Delivered to you, this day in the city of David, a Savior, Who is Christ the Lord.

12 And this, a Miracle Sign to you, you will find a Babe wrapped in swaddling clothes lying in a manger.

13 And unexpectantly, occurred united with the Angel, a Multitude of Different Heavenly Host Praising God and Saying,

14 Glory to God in the Highest, and upon earth, Peace, God-Good Intentions within men.

15 And it occurred, as the Angels went away from them into Heaven, the shepherd men were speaking to one another, So now we should pass to Bethlehem, and should see This Word come to pass, which the Lord has Made Supernaturally Known to us.

Shepherds Came with Haste

16 And came hurried, and also located both Mary and Joseph, and the Babe laying in the manger.

17 And when Spiritually Discerning, they widely proclaimed about the Word Uttered to them about this Little Child.

18 And all that heard marveled about those things, uttered by the shepherds to them.

19 But Mary was preserving all these words, deliberating these things in her heart.

20 And the shepherds turned back, Attributing Glory and praising God for all the things heard and seen, just as Uttered to them.

Jesus at Temple on the Eighth Day

21 And when eight days have been made filled, they circumcised the Little Child, and called His Name JESUS, called by the Angel before He was conceived in the womb.

22 And when the days of her purification have been made filled according to the Law of Moses (Lev 12:1-8), they brought Him up into Jerusalem to present Him to the Lord.

23 Just as written in the Law of the Lord, that every male that is Opening in Newness of Spirit a womb shall be called Holy to the Lord. (Ex 13:2)

24 And to give a sacrifice according to what the Spirit Says in the Law of the Lord, a pair of turtledoves or two young pigeons. (Lev 12:8)

Simeon Praises and Blessed Him

25 And Behold, a man was in Jerusalem, who (was) named Simeon, and the same man was Righteous and Reverent, Looking for the Consolation of Israel, and the Holy Spirit was Inside him.

26 And he was Now Made Warned, as by the Holy Spirit, that he Spiritually See no death before he Spiritually should See the Lord's Christ.

27 And he Came by the Spirit into the Temple area, and when the parents conveyed the Little Child Jesus in to do for Him, according to the procedure of the Law for Him.

28 Then he Received Him into his arms, and Blessed God, and Spoke,

29 Now Dismiss Away Your Bondslave in Peace, Oh Lord, according to Your Word.

30 For my Eyes have Spiritually Seen Your Salvation,

31 Which You have Prepared before the presence of all the people,

32 A Light to Revelation of Gentiles, and Glory of your people Israel.

33 And Joseph and His mother were marveling at the Uttering about Him.

34 And Simeon blessed Him and Spoke to Mary, His mother, Behold, He is Set for Collapse and Resurrection of many in

Israel, and for a Miracle Sign being made spoken against.

35 And then a long broad two-edged Sword shall pass through your own soul, so that whatever thoughts from many hearts, should be Made Revealed.

Anna also Praises and Blesses

36 And there was Anna, Prophetess, a daughter of Phanuel, from tribe of Aser, she was now well stricken in many days, having lived with a husband seven years from her virginity.

37 And she as eighty four years a widow, wherein definitely not being departed away from the Temple area, she was Being Devoted night and day to fastings and supplications.

38 And she herself being present was giving praise in that hour to the Lord, and was Uttering in regard to Him for all Looking in Jerusalem for Removal to Heaven.

Immediately Return to Nazareth

39 And, as Finally Fulfilled all things, according to the Law of the Lord, they returned into Galilee, to their city, Nazareth.

40 And then the Little Child grew and was Made Strong in Spirit, Fully Filled of Wisdom, and Grace of God was Inside Him.

At Twelve Yrs Old Jesus Goes to Passover

41 And His parents went to Jerusalem every year to the Feast of Passover.

42 And when He became twelve years, they ascended to Jerusalem, according to the custom of the Feast.

Jesus Tarried in Jerusalem

43 And they returning therein, fulfilled the days. The dependent Child Jesus endured them in Jerusalem, and Joseph and His mother knew definitely not.

44 But they supposed Him to be among the company. They came a day's journey, and searched for Him among the kinsmen, and among the acquaintances.

45 And they found Him not. They returned to Jerusalem, seeking Him.

46 And it came to pass after three days, they found Him within the Temple area, Sitting Himself in the midst of the teachers, and Hearing them, and Questioning them.

47 And all that heard Him were astonished at the Understanding and the Answers of Him,

48 As they Spiritually Discerned Him, and were amazed at Him. His mother spoke. Child, why Did You Do So to us? You must in such a manner Behold, your father, also I, grievously sorrowing were seeking You.

49 And He Spoke to them, For where have you sought Me? Had you definitely not Spiritually Discerned that being Me, I must be among those Things of My Father?

50 And they understood definitely not the Word that He Uttered to them.

51 And He Came Down with them, and Came to Nazareth, and was being Subject to them, and His mother carefully kept all these Words in her heart.

52 And Jesus was Developing in Wisdom and stature of age and Grace with God and man. (I Sam 2:26)

John the Baptist Starts Preaching

3 Now in fifteenth year of the reign of Tiberius Caesar, of Pontius Pilate governing Judaea, and of Herod Tetrarch of Galilee, and Philip his brother being tetrarch of Ituraea and land of Trachonitis, and of Lysanias being tetrarch of Abilene,

2 In the time of High Priests, Annas and Caiaphas, the Word of God occurred to John, the son of Zacharias, within the desolate wilderness.

3 And he came into all the surrounding region of the Jordon preaching immersion, after Repentance for Removal of sin natures and sins.

4 As it is Now Written in Book, of the

Words of Esaias the Prophet Saying, A voice of One Loudly Pleading in the desolate wilderness, You Must Prepare The Way of the Lord. Make His Paths Straight.

5 Every valley shall be fully filled, and every mountain and hill shall be brought low, and the crooked shall be into straight, and the roughs into smooth Ways of Travel.

6 And Spiritually See all sinful flesh nature shall see the Salvation of God. (Isa 40:35)

7 Therefore, he said to the multitudes of people that went out to be immersed by him, O product of vipers, who forewarned you to flee from the expecting Wrath for Justice?

8 You must bring forth, therefore, Fruit Worthy of Repentance, and you should not begin to say within yourselves, We have our father Abraham; because I am saying to you that God is able from these stones to raise up children to Abraham.

9 And now, already, the ax is being laid to the root of the trees. Therefore, every tree not bearing God-Work Fruit is being continuously cut off, and is being continuously cast into the fire.

10 And the multitudes of people questioned him saying, Then what shall we do?

11 And then, he said to them, He that has two coats you must impart to him having none, and him having food, you must give likewise.

12 Then came also tax collectors to be immersed and spoke to Him, Oh Master, what shall we do?

13 And then he spoke to them, You are to exact no greater against a person than is now made appointed to you.

14 And then also warriors questioned him saying, What shall we do? And he spoke to them, You must not intimidate any with force, neither take by false accusation, and you must be made content with your wages.

15 And then the people were watching for, and were all reasoning in their hearts in regard to John, for fear that he might be the Christ.

16 John answered saying to all, I certainly immerse you in water, but One Mightier than I is Coming. I am definitely not at all sufficient to remove the leather shoestrings of His shoes. He Himself shall Baptize you in the Holy Spirit and Fire,

17 Whose fan is in His Hand, and He shall Thoroughly Cleanse His floor, and shall Gather Together the Wheat into His barn, but the chaff He shall Fully Burn with Unquenchable Fire.

18 Therefore, actually, he was Entreating many other ones of a different kind. He was Proclaiming the Gospel to the people.

19 But when Herod, the tetrarch, was exposed as sin by him in regard to Herodias, the wife of Philip his brother, and about all those evils Herod did,

20 He added also more to this. And after everything, he shut John up in prison.

When Jesus was Immersed

21 Then it came to pass when all the people were made immersed, and Jesus was Made Immersed and Praying, the Heaven Made Opened.

22 And the Holy Spirit Came Down, in Bodily Appearance, like as a Dove upon Him, and a Voice out from Heaven was Saying, You, You are My Beloved Son, in You I am Pleased. (Isa 42:1; Ps 2:7)

Genealogy of Jesus

23 And Jesus Himself was about thirty years, beginning being as supposed a son of Joseph of Heli,

24 Of the Matthat, of the Levi, of the Melchi, of the Janna, of the Joseph,

25 Of the Mattathias, of the Amos, of the Naum, of the Esli, of the Nagge,

26 Of the Maath, of the Mattathias, of the Semei, of the Joseph, of the Judah,

27 Of the Joanna, of the Rhesa, of the Zorobabel, of the Salathiel, of the Neri,

28 Of the Melchi, of the Addi, of the

84

Cosam, of the Elmodam, of the Er,
29 Of the Joses, of the Eliezer, of the Jorim, of the Mathat, of the Levi,
30 Of the Simeon, of the Judah, of the Joseph, of the Jonan, of the Eliakim,
31 Of the Meleas, of the Menan, of the Mattatha, of the Nathan, of the David,
32 Of the Jesse, of the Obed, of the Boaz, of the Salmon, of the Naasson,
33 Of the Aminadab, of the Aram, of the Esrom, of the Phares, of the Judah,
34 Of the Jacob, of the Isaac, of the Abraham, of the Thara, of the Nachor,
35 Of the Saruch, of the Ragau, of the Phalec, of the Heber, of the Sala,
36 Of the Cainan, of the Arphaxad, of the Sem, of the Noah, of the Noah, of the Lamech,
37 Of the Mathusaia, of the Enoch, of the Jared, of the Maleleel, of the Cainan,
38 Of the Enos, of the Seth, of the Adam, of the God.

Jesus Tempted Forty Days

4 And Jesus, Full of the Holy Spirit, returned from the Jordan, and was Led in the Spirit into the desolate wilderness.
2 Being tried by the devil forty days and now made finished, and definitely not eaten anything in those same days, He was afterward hungered.
3 And the devil spoke to Him. If You are the Son of God, You must speak to this stone, that it should become bread.
4 And Jesus Answered to him Saying, It is Written, that man shall definitely not Live by bread alone, but definitely by Every Word of God. (Deut 8:3)
5 And the devil led Him up into a high mountain, showed Him all the kingdom rules of the inhabited earth in an instant of time.
6 And the devil spoke to Him, All this authority I will give to You, and the glory of them, for it is now made delivered up to me, and then to whoever I will give it.
7 If You, therefore, might worship in the presence of me, all shall be Yours.
8 Jesus Made Answered and Spoke to him, You must go away back of Me, satan, because it is made Written, you shall Worship the Lord your God, and to Him Alone you shall be Devoted. (Deut 6:13)
9 And he moved along Him to Jerusalem, and stood Him upon a pinnacle of the Temple area, and spoke to Him, If you are the Son of God, you must cast Yourself from here down below.
10 Because it is now made written, For he shall god command his angels concerning you, to guard you.
11 And in their hands they shall you take up, for fear that you stumble your foot against a stone.
12 And Jesus Answered, He Spoke to him. This the Spirit Says now, you shall definitely not spiritually test the Lord, your God. (Deut 6:16)
13 And the devil finished every temptation, he departed away from Him until a Special Time.
14 And Jesus Returned, in the Miracle Power of the Spirit, into Galilee, and fame about Him came out before all of the surrounding region.
15 He was Teaching in their synagogues, and He was Attributed Glory (Spiritual Perfection) by all.

Jesus in Nazareth on the Sabbath

16 And He Came to Nazareth where He was nourished, and Entered into the synagogue according to His having had a customary practice in the Sabbath day, and He Arose to Read.
17 And He was handed a scroll of Esaias the Prophet, and He unrolled the scroll, found the place where it was Written,
18 The Spirit of the Lord is With Me, for the Cause of Spirit Anointing Me, to Proclaim the Gospel to the poor. He is now Sending Out Me to Cure the heart, now made brokenhearted, to Preach Removal to the captives, and Recovering of Sight to

the blind, to Send Out with Removal those now being made shackled (by sin nature and sins),

19 To Preach the Accepted Year of the Lord. (Isa 61:1-2)

20 And He Rolled Up the scroll, Yielded Back to the officer, Sat Down, and likewise every eye within the synagogue was attentively looking at Him.

21 And He began to Say to them, For this Day, this Scripture is now made Fulfilled within your ears.

22 And all gave witness to Him, and marveled at the Spiritual Communications of Grace to be going out His Mouth, and they were saying. Is definitely not this the son of Joseph?

23 And He Spoke to them, You shall all Spirit Say to Me this parable. Physician you must heal yourself. Whatever we have heard occurred in Capernaum, you must also do here within your country.

24 And He Spoke, Truly, I Say to you, That definitely no Prophet is accepted in His own country.

25 But I am Saying to you in regard of Truth, many widows were in Israel in the days of Elias, when he made Shut the heaven for three years and six months, as a great famine occurred upon the whole earth.

26 And to none was Elias himself Sent except to Sarepta of Sidon, to a widow women.

27 And many lepers were within Israel in the time of Eliseus the Prophet, and none of them was made Cleansed, except Naaman the Syrian.

All filled with anger to kill Him

28 And all in the synagogue hearing these things were made filled with anger.

29 And arose, casted Him out, outside the city, and moved Him along, up to the brow of the mountain whereon that the city itself had been built, for the purpose to push Him off.

30 But He Passed Through, Going through in the midst of them.

In Capernaum Many are Healed

31 And Descended to Capernaum, city of Galilee, and was Teaching them within the Sabbath.

32 And they were amazed at His Teaching, because the Spiritual Communication of Him was with Authority.

33 And in the synagogue was a man having a morally impure demon spirit, and with a great voice crying loudly.

34 And saying, Let us alone! Why now You, Oh Jesus of Nazareth? Have you come to destroy us? I spiritually discern You. You are that Holy One of God.

35 And Jesus Rebuked him Saying, You must be made Silent and you must Come Out from within him, and the demon threw him down in the midst, Came Out from him, not harming him.

36 And they became filled with amazement over everything, and were talking together to one another saying, What a Spiritual Communication of Him, for with Authority and Miracle Power He Instantly Commands to the morally impure spirits, and they come out.

37 And the roaring sound about Him went out into every place of the surrounding region.

Went to Simon's house

38 Then He Raised, out from the synagogue, to Enter into the house of Simon, and the mother in law of Simon was made constrained by a great fever, and they earnestly requested of Him for her.

39 And He Stood over her, Rebuked the fever, and it parted from her instantly, and she rose to serve them.

Healed All and Cast Out devils

40 When the sun was setting, everyone, as many as were being weak, having many diverse sicknesses, they led them to Him,

and He Laid Hands on every one of them, He Healed them.

41 And also demons came out from many, crying out and saying that, You, You are the Christ, the Son of God, and He Rebuked them. He definitely did not allow them to be uttering because they had Spiritually Discerned Him to be the Christ.

42 And when it became day, He Came Out to go into a desolate wilderness place, and the multitudes of people were seeking Him, and came up to Him, and were holding Him to not be going away from them.

43 And then He Spoke to them, For I must Proclaim also the Kingdom Rule of God in other cities of a different kind, because for this I am now being made Sent Out.

44 And He was Preaching in the synagogues of Galilee.

On Sea of Galilee, Fish Catch

5 And then it came to pass, in that the multitude of people was pressing upon Him to hear the Spiritual Communication of God, and He was now Standing near the Lake of Gennesaret.

2 And He Saw two ships standing alongside of the lake, and the fishermen turned out from them, rinsed their nets.

3 And He Boarded in one of the ships which was that of Simon's, earnestly requested of him to Proceed Out away from the area a little, He Sat Down and was Teaching the multitude of people out from the ship.

4 And as He ceased Uttering, He spoke to Simon, You must Proceed Out into the depths and you must Let Down your nets for a haul.

5 And Simon answered, he spoke to Him, Oh Master, through all of the night we have labored, and have taken nothing, nevertheless, at Your Word, I will let down the net.

6 And having done this, they enclosed a large multitude of different fish, and their net tore apart.

7 And signaled to their partners in the other ship of a different kind to come to physically help them. And they came and filled both ships, so that they were sinking.

Seeing This, they Forsook All for Jesus

8 When Simon Peter Spiritually Discerned, He fell down before Jesus knees saying, You must depart away from me, for I am a sinful man, Oh Lord.

9 Because he fully beheld filled with amazement, and all those united with him, at the haul of fish that they had physically taken.

10 Then likewise also James and John, sons of Zebedee, who were companions with Simon. And Jesus Spoke to Simon, You must not be fearing, since now you shall be Pulling in men.

11 And having brought their ships down upon the earth, they dismissed all, to follow Him.

Jesus Heals a leper

12 And it came to pass, while He is being in one of the cities, and Behold a man full of leprosy, so now he discerning Jesus, he Prayed earnestly falling down on his face saying Oh Lord if You should Will, You are able to cleanse me.

13 And He Put Forth His Hand, Touched him, Spoke. I Will, you must be Made Cleansed, and immediately the leprosy Went From him.

14 And He Gave Command to him, Speak to no man, but definitely you must go to show yourself to the priest, and you must offer for your purification, just as Moses before Commanded, for a Testimony to them.

15 But so much more the Word about Him passed about, and many multitudes of people were coming together to hear, and to be healed by Him from their infirmities.

Forgave sins and Healed a palsied

16 And He was going aside in the desolate

wilderness now to Pray.

17 And it came to pass, in one day as He was Teaching that Pharisees and doctors of the Law were sitting there. They were then coming out from every village of Galilee, and Judea, and Jerusalem. As also Miracle Power of the Lord was for the Curing of them.

18 And Behold, men were bringing in a man on a bed that was palsied, and they sought to bring him in, and position him in the Presence of Him.

19 And they found no means of which to bring him through the multitude of people. They ascended to the housetop, lowered him united with the couch through the tiling into the midst before Jesus.

20 And He Discerned their Faith. He Spoke to him, Man, your sins are Removed from Memory (forgiven) to you.

21 And the scribes and the Pharisees began reasoning saying, Who is this Who Utters blasphemies? Who can Remove from Memory (forgive) sins, except God alone?

22 But Jesus Fully Knew their thoughts. He Answering, Spoke to them. What are you reasoning in your hearts?

23 What is easier to speak? He Removes from Memory (Forgive) your sins, or else speak, You must for yourself raise up and you must by your choice walk?

24 But that you should Discern that the Son of Man has Authority upon the earth to be Removing from Memory (forgive) sins, He Spoke to the palsied man, I Say to you, you must for yourself be Raising Up, and Take Up your couch by your choice. You must be Going by your choice to your home.

25 And instantly, he rose in the presence of them, took up what he was laying upon, went to his home, Attributing Glory to God.

26 And ecstasy took all, and they were Attributing Glory to God, and filled with fear, saying that they discerned extraordinary things this day.

Called Levi to Follow Him

27 And after these things, He Came Out, and saw a tax collector named Levi sitting at the desk for paying taxes, and He Spoke to Him. You must Follow Me!

28 And he rose to leave all. He followed Him.

29 And Levi made a great reception in his own house, and there was a multitude of people, of many tax collectors and others, of the same kind with them that were sitting down to eat.

Scribes and Pharisee murmur

30 And the scribes themselves and Pharisees were murmuring to His disciples saying, Why then do you eat and drink with tax collectors and sinners?

31 And Jesus Answering Spoke to them, Those being healthy are having definitely no need of a physician, but definitely those having an evil work afflicted.

32 I am now definitely not Come to Outwardly Call (Gospel) the Righteous, but definitely sinners to Repentance.

33 And they spoke to Him, Why then are the disciples of John fasting more often, and make supplications, and likewise the disciples of the Pharisees, but Yours eat and drink?

34 And He Spoke to them, Are you not able to make the sons of the bride chamber to fast when the bridegroom is with them?

35 But the days shall come, when the Bridegroom should have been taken away from them; then they shall fast in those days.

36 And He Said also a parable to them, For no one Lays a piece of New of a different kind raiment upon old raiment, and if otherwise the New of a different kind then Splits the old. It is definitely not agreeing together with the piece from the New of a different kind.

37 And no man Casts new wine into old bottles, if otherwise, the new wine shall Tear the bottles, and thereby Pour Out, and

the bottles shall be destroyed.

38 But definitely, new wine must be Put into New bottles, and both are made preserved.

39 And having drunk old (wine), no one immediately prefers new of the same kind because he says, The old is Kind.

Sabbath issues arise with Pharisees

6 And it came to pass in the second Sabbath, they journey through the grain field, and His disciples were plucking the heads of grain, and they were eating, rubbing apart with their hands.

2 And some of the Pharisees spoke to them, Why are you doing what is definitely not Lawful to do in the Sabbath?

3 And Jesus Answering them Spoke, Have you neither read, what David did as when he himself was hungry, also those with him?

4 As he entered into the Dwelling of God, and took the Bread of Purpose (Shewbread), and ate, and gave also to them with him, which is definitely not Lawful to eat, except the priest alone.

5 And He Said to them, For the Son of Man is Lord also of the Sabbath.

6 And also it came to pass in another of a different kind Sabbath, He entered into their synagogue and was teaching, and there was a man whose right hand was withered.

7 And the scribes and Pharisees were observing Him, if He shall heal in the Sabbath, in order that they find an accusation of Him.

8 But He Discerned their thoughts of Him, and Spoke to the man having a withered hand, You must Raise Up for yourself, and you must Stand by your choice in the midst. And he rose to stand.

9 Then Jesus Spoke to them, I will Question you, what is Lawful for the Sabbath, to do God-Good or to do evil, to make Healthy the soul, or to destroy?

10 And looking around at them all, He

Spoke to the man. You must by your choice Stretch Out your hand. And he did so, and his hand was made Restored, healthy as the other of the same kind.

11 And they were filled with irrationality, and rumored among themselves, whatever they beyond their dreams could do to Jesus.

Jesus Appoints the Apostles

12 And it came to pass in those days, He Came Out into the mountain to Pray, and was continuing all night in Prayer of God.

13 And when it became day, He Called Out His disciples, then He Chose from them Twelve, whom also He named Apostles.

14 Simon, whom He also Named Peter and Andrew his brother, James and John, Philip and Bartholomew,

15 Matthew and Thomas, James son of Alpheus, and the Simon being called Zelotes,

16 Judas, James, and Judas Iscariot who also became a traitor.

17 And He Came Down with them, and a multitude of people of His disciples, and Stood in a plain place, and a large multitude of different people from all of Judaea, and Jerusalem, and of the sea coast of Tyre and Sidon came to hear Him, and be cured from their sicknesses,

18 And those being vexed by morally impure spirits, and they were being Healed.

19 And the whole multitude of people was seeking to touch Him, for Miracle Power Came Out from Him, and was Curing everyone.

The Beatitudes

20 And He Lifted Up His Eyes upon His disciples Saying, Spiritually Blessed the poor, for yours is the Kingdom Rule of God.

21 Spiritually Blessed those being continuously hungry now, for they shall be made Filled. Spiritually Blessed those by their choice continuously weeping now, for they shall by their choice Laugh.

22 Spiritually Blessed are you when men

might by their choice hate you, and when they might separate by their choice and might by their choice scold you sharply, and might by their choice cast your name out as evil against the cause of the Son of Man.

23 You must Rejoice in That Day and you must leap for Joy. Behold, because of your large Reward in Heaven, for in like manner did their fathers to the Prophets.

24 But Woe to you, the rich, for you have already your consolation.

25 Woe to you, those now being made filled up, for you shall be hungry. Woe to you that laugh now, for you shall mourn and weep.

26 Woe to you when all men might have spoken God-Working of you, because in like manner did their fathers to the false prophets.

Love your enemies

27 But definitely I say to you who are hearing, you must be Loving your enemies. You must do God-Working to those who hate you.

28 You must be Blessing them cursing you. You must be Praying in behalf of them despitefully insulting you.

29 To him who strikes you upon your cheek, you must by your choice offer concerning the other of the same kind, and him who takes away your clothes, you should not forbid your coat also.

30 And you must always be Giving to those who are asking, and also of him who is taking your belongings away, you must not demand.

31 And just as you are preferring that men do to you, also yourselves must be doing to them likewise.

32 And if you are loving them who are loving you, what Grace are you having? Because sinners also love those who love them.

33 And if you are Doing God-Good to them who are Doing God-Good to you, what Grace is it? Because the sinners also

do that to themselves.

34 And if you might lend to whom you might be expecting to fully receive, what Grace is it? Because sinners also lend to sinners, in order that they might fully receive equal.

35 But you must God-Love your enemies, and you must Do God-Good, and you must lend expecting nothing from, and your Reward will be large, and you will be Sons of the Most High, for He is Kind to the unthankful and evil.

36 Therefore, you must become Merciful, just as also your Father is Merciful.

Issues of Judging others

37 And you must not by your choice be Continuously Judging, that also you should never ever be made Judged. Also you must by your choice Continuously not be Finally Judging Condemned, that also you should never ever be Made Finally Judged Condemned. You must by your choice continuously Remove from Memory (forgive), that also you shall be Made Removed from Memory (forgiven).

38 You be Continuously Giving and it will be made Given to you, a God-Work Measure, being made Pressed Down, and being made Shaken, and shall be made Running Over. These shall Give into your bosom, because the amount of measure you are measuring to them, it shall be made Measured Back to you.

39 And He Spoke a parable to them, Can possibly a blind be guiding a blind? Definitely not, both shall fall down into a ditch.

40 Definitely the disciple is not above his Master. But he, that is now being Made Complete, shall be Whole as his Master.

41 And why Spiritually See to the speck in your brother's eye, but definitely not consider the beam in your own eye?

42 Neither how are you able to say to your brother, Oh brother, you must be concerned to Cast Out the speck in your eye, then definitely not yourself be Spiritually

Seeing the beam in your eye? Oh hypocrite actor, you must first of all Cast Out the beam from your eye, and then you will clearly See to Cast Out the speck in your brother's eye.

Fruit Describes the tree

43 Because a God-Work Tree is definitely not bringing forth corrupt fruit, neither a corrupt tree brings forth God-Work Fruit.
44 For every tree is made known from its own fruit, because out from thorns they definitely are not collecting figs, neither out from a bush are they gathering grapes.
45 A God-Good man out from the God-Good treasure of his heart is bringing forth God-Good, and the evil man out from the evil treasure of his heart is bringing forth the evil. Because out from the abundance of the heart, his mouth is uttering.

House with a Rock Foundation

46 And why are you calling Me, Oh Lord, Oh Lord, and do definitely not what I am saying?
47 Whoever is Coming to Me, and Hearing My Spiritual Communications, and Doing them, I will Give you Forewarning what he is like.
48 He is like a man who is building a house, that dug and also digging deep, laid down a Foundation upon the Huge Rock. And when a flood tide occurred, the flood tore against that house, and it was definitely not shaken. It prevailed because it had a Grounded Foundation upon the Huge Rock.
49 But he that heard and does not is like a man building a house upon the earth without a foundation, that a flood tore against, and immediately it fell down, and came to pass the ruin of that house great.

Centurion' servant Healed

7 In fact, when He Fulfilled all His Words in the hearing of the people, He entered into Capernaum.

2 And a certain centurion's slave, who was more honorable to him, was having an evil work afflicted, expected to decease,
3 And when He heard about Jesus, he sent out elders of the Jews to Him, earnestly requesting of Him, so that having come, He might physically save His slave.
4 And when they came up to Jesus, they entreated Him promptly saying, That he is Worthy for whom He shall offer this concern,
5 Because he is Loving our nation, and he built for us a synagogue.
6 Then Jesus went with them, and having already definitely not far off from the house, the centurion sent friends to Him, saying to Him, Oh Lord, you must definitely not bother, because I am definitely not sufficient that You might enter under my roof.
7 For this reason I neither thought worthy of myself to come to You. but definitely You must speak a Word, and my male servant shall now be made whole.
8 Because I also am a man under authority, and I am made assigning soldiers under myself, and to this one I say you must go, and he is going, and to another of the same kind, you must be coming and he is coming, and to my slave you must do this and he does.
9 When Jesus Heard these things He Marveled at him, and He turned to that multitude of people following Him to Speak, Saying, I have not found so much Faith, no, not in Israel.
10 And those sent, returned into the home to find the sick slave to be Healthy.

A funeral of a widow's son

11 And it came to pass in the next day, He went into a city called Nain, and His disciples and also a sufficiently large multitude of people went together with Him.
12 As when He now approached near to the city gateway, then Behold, they were made carrying out a rotting dead body, the

only born son of his mother and she was a widow, and a sufficiently many multitude of people of the city were united with her.

13 And the Lord Spiritually Discerned her, had Compassion for her, and Spoke to her, You must not be weeping.

14 And He came near to Touch the bier, and they bearing stood, and He Spoke Saying, Oh young man, I Say to you, you must Rise Up.

15 And he that was dead sat up, and began to be uttering, and He gave him to his mother.

16 And then a fear took all, and they Attributed Glory to God, saying that a great Prophet is now being risen up among us, and that God has visited His people.

17 And the Word of Him came out among all Judaea in regard to Him, and within the whole surrounding region.

John the Baptist questions Jesus

18 And the disciples of John told him about all these things.

19 And John sent a certain two of his disciples to invite Jesus, saying, You, Are You He that is coming, or are we watching for another of same kind?

20 And when the men came up to Him, they spoke, John the Baptist is now sending us out to You saying, You, Are You He that is coming or are we watching for another of the same kind?

21 And then in the same hour, He Healed many from sicknesses, and severe suffering, and evil spirits and freely gave to many blind to see.

22 Then Jesus Answered to them, He Spoke, You must go Tell John what you Spiritually Discerned and heard, how the blind received sight, crippled walking, lepers being made clean, deaf hearing, dead bodies risen up, poor having the Gospel proclaimed. (Isa 35:5-6; 61:1)

23 And Spiritually Blessed is he, who is not made offended by Me.

24 And when the messengers of John went, He began to Say to the multitudes of people about John. What came out you into the desolate wilderness to see, a reed made shaken by the wind?

25 But definitely what you came out to see, a man being made arrayed in appealing soft raiment? Behold, they are in the courts of kings in glorious raiment, and existing indulgently.

26 But definitely what are you coming out to see? A Prophet, Emphatically Yes, I say to you, and more in excess a Prophet.

27 This is he about whom it is now made written, Behold, I am Sending Out My Messenger before Your Presence, who shall make ready Your Way of Travel, before You. (Mal 3:1)

28 Because I am Saying to you, Among those born naturally of women, there is definitely no greater Prophet than John the Baptist. But Least in the Kingdom Rule of God is greater than he.

29 And all the people, and the tax collectors who heard, Made their God Righteous, being made Immersed with immersion of John.

30 But the Pharisees and the lawyers rejected the Counsel of God for themselves. None were made immersed by him.

31 And the Lord Spoke, Therefore, who shall be likened to the men of this generation? And to what are they like?

32 They are like little children sitting in a marketplace, and calling out one to another, and saying, We have piped to you and you have definitely not danced, lamented to you and you have definitely not wept.

33 Because John the Baptist came neither eating bread nor drinking wine, and you are saying he has a demon.

34 The Son of Man is now come eating and drinking, and you are saying, Behold, a gluttonous man and a wine drinker, a friend of tax collectors and sinners.

35 And Wisdom is Made Righteous from all her children.

Jesus' feet Anointed by a woman

36 And one of the Pharisees was earnestly requesting of Him that He might eat with Him, and He entered into the house of the Pharisee. He was made to sit down.

37 And, Behold, a woman of the city, who has been a sinner, Fully Knew that He was sitting as at eating in the house of the Pharisee, earned to herself an alabaster container of ointment.

38 And stood near His Feet behind Him weeping, began to wet His Feet with tears, and wiped them with the hairs of her head, and kissed His Feet, and anointed them with ointment.

39 And when the Pharisee, who called Him discerned her, he spoke within himself saying, If He were a Prophet, He would have Known this one, who and what manner of woman who touches Him, for she is a sinner.

40 Jesus Answered and Spoke to him, Oh Simon, I have something to Speak to you. And he states, You must speak, Oh Master.

A Parable on Love and the woman

41 There was a certain creditor, two debtors. One was indebted five hundred penny and another of a different kind, fifty.

42 And when having nothing of themselves to pay, he freely forgave both. You must speak to Me, who, therefore, of them shall love him the greater?

43 Simon answered and spoke, I suppose that to whom he freely forgave the greater. And He spoke to him, You have judged correctly.

44 And He turned to the woman, stating to Simon, See this woman? I entered into your house. You gave me definitely no water for My Feet, but she has wetted My Feet with her tears, and wiped with the hairs of her head.

45 You definitely gave Me no kiss, but she from when I entered, she has definitely not discontinued to be kissing My Feet.

46 My Head with oil you definitely anointed not, but she anointed My Feet with ointment.

47 Which for this cause I am Saying to you, her sins that were many are now made Removed from Memory (forgiven), for she God-Loved much, and to whom little is Removed from Memory (forgiven), he is God-Loving little.

48 And He Spoke to her, Your sins are now Made Removed from Memory (forgiven).

49 And those sitting to eat began to say within themselves, Who is He that is even Removing from Memory (forgiving) sins?

50 And He Spoke to the woman, The Faith of you is now by your choice Continuously Saving you; you must go in Peace.

Preaches in the cities and villages

8 Therein in order so it came to pass that He was going through to city and village, preaching and proclaiming the Kingdom Rule of God, and the twelve united with Him,

2 Also certain women, who were now healed from evil spirits and infirmities: Mary called Magdalene, from whom seven demons had come out,

3 And Joanna, wife of Chuza, manager of Herod, and Susanna, and many other ones of a different kind who were serving Him from their material goods.

Parable of a sower

4 And when a large multitude met together with Him from within every city, He Spoke through a parable.

5 A Sower came out to be Sowing His Sowing Seed, and with His Sowing, some certainly fell down near The Way of Travel, and have been made trampled down, and the birds of heaven devoured it.

6 And other one of a different kind fell down upon rock, and having sprang up withered away because of not having moisture.

7 And another one of a different kind fell down among the midst of the thorns,

and with the thorns made springing up together, they fully choked it.

8   And another one of a different kind fell down upon the God-Good Earth, and made Sprang up yielding Fruit a hundredfold. He was calling for these things Saying, He who has ears to Hear, he must be Hearing.

9   And His disciples questioned Him saying, What might this parable be beyond dreams?

10 And then He Spoke, To you it is made Given to Know the Mysteries of the Kingdom Rule of God, but to others in parables, that seeing they might not see, and hearing they might not understand. (Isa 6:9)

11 Now the parable is this. The Sowing Seed is the Spiritual Communication (Word) of God.

12 And those near The Way of Travel are those Hearing, following that comes the devil, and definitely takes away the Word from their heart, in order that they may not be Saved (through) Committing.

13 And those upon this Rock when they might have Heard with Joy, they are receiving the Spiritual Word, but they are definitely not having root for this definite Special Time Committing, and they are definitely departing away when in the special time of temptation.

14 And then those who fell down into the thorns, these are being those who Heard, and by cares and riches and sensual desires of their natural life are going to be made choking, and definitely not progressing to the end.

15 But those in the God-Work Earth, they are these who in a God-Work Heart, and by God-Good, having Heard the Spiritual Word are holding fast and bearing Fruit by Endurance.

Parable of a candle

16 Having lit a candle none covers it with a vessel or puts it under a bed; but definitely, he places it in a candlestick that they coming in should see the Light.

17 Because it is definitely not secret, that is definitely not openly manifest; neither shall it become kept secret, that shall definitely not be made known, and should come openly manifest.

18 Therefore, You must Continuously Spiritually Look how you are hearing, because whoever should have, to him it shall be given. And whoever that should not be having, even what he thinks he has, shall be taken away from him.

Who are Jesus' Kin?

19 Then came up to Him, His mother and His brothers, and they were definitely not able to possibly reach Him because of the multitude of people.

20 And it was told to him saying, Your mother and Your brothers are now standing outside, strongly desiring to see You.

21 He Answered and Spoke to them, My Mother and My Brothers are those who are by their choice Continuously Hearing My Spiritual Word of God, and are by their choice continuously Doing It.

Calms a storm, Asks about their Faith

22 Now one day came to pass, when also He boarded into a ship with His disciples, and Spoke to them, We should pass through to the other side of the lake, and they launched forth.

23 When they were sailing He fell asleep, and a wind storm came down upon the lake, and were made filled fully, and they were being endangered.

24 And they came near to arouse Him saying, Oh Master, Oh Master, we are perishing. Then He Raised Up, Rebuked the wind and the wave of the water, and they ceased and became calm.

25 And He Spoke to them, Wherein is your Faith? They were made afraid, and they marveled saying to one another, So then, Who is He that even the winds and water are instantly Commanded, and are obeying Him?

Jesus Casts Out a legion of demons

26 And they came ashore in the land of the Gadarenes, which is opposite of Galilee.

27 And when He came out upon the earth, He was met with a certain man out from the city, who was having demons from a sufficiently long time, and definitely not attired with clothes, definitely not abiding in a house, but definitely within the place of the dead.

28 When he discerned Jesus, he cried loudly and fell down before Him, and spoke in a great voice, Why me with You, Jesus, Son of God Most High? I Pray earnestly of You, not to torment me.

29 For He Gave Command to the morally impure spirit to come out away from the man, because many times it had seized him, so he was made bound with chains, maintained in shackles, and tearing apart the bonds, he was made driven by the demon into the desolate wilderness.

30 And Jesus questioned it saying, What is your name? And then it spoke, Legion, for many demons had entered into him.

31 Then they beseeched Him that He might not instantly Command them to go into the bottomless pit.

32 And there was a herd of sufficiently many pigs made feeding in the mountain, and they were beseeching Him that He should permit them to enter into them, and He Permitted them.

33 Then the demons came away from the man, entered into the pigs, and the herd ran violently upon the steep decline into the lake, and drowned.

34 When those feeding them discerned what was now made to occur, then they fled to go tell to the city, and to the countryside.

35 Then they came out to discern what occurred, and came to Jesus, and found the man from whom the demons had departed wearing clothes, and being logically minded sitting near the feet of Jesus, and they were made afraid.

36 And then they who Spiritually Discerned told them how he, who was demonized, was made Healthy.

37 Then all the multitude of the different surrounding region of the Gadarenes, because they were made constrained by great fear, earnestly requesting of Him to go, and He returned, boarding into the ship.

38 And the man, himself, since then the demons had come out, not being united with Him, was Praying earnestly, but Jesus dismissed away him Saying,

39 You must return to your home, and you must recite what God did to you. And he went about all the city preaching what Jesus did to him.

40 And it came to pass, that when Jesus Returned, the multitude of people gladly received Him, because they all were watching for Him.

Heals a women's bleeding

41 And, Behold, there came a man named Jairus, the ruler of the existing synagogue, and he fell down near Jesus's feet. He was entreating Him to enter into his home.

42 Because his only born daughter, as was twelve years, now she was dying inside. But as He was going away, the multitudes of people were crowding Him.

43 And a woman, being with bleeding of blood for twelve years, who paid out to physicians her whole livelihood, definitely not at all availed to be healed by none,

44 Came near behind to touch the border of His robe, and instantly, the bleeding of her blood was brought into health.

45 And then Jesus Spoke, Who touched Me? When all disclaimed, then Peter spoke, also those with Him, Oh Master, the multitudes of people constrains and presses You, and You are saying, Who touched Me?

46 So Jesus Spoke, Somebody touched Me, because I know a Miracle Power came out away from Me.

47 And when the woman discerned that she was definitely not being hidden, she came trembling and fell down before Him. She told to Him, in the presence of all the people, why then the reason she touched Him, and she was as instantly Cured.

48 And then He Spoke to her, Daughter you must be Encouraged, the Faith of you now Healed you. You must go in Peace.

Jairus' daughter Raised from the dead

49 While He yet was Uttering came a certain one, to the ruler of the synagogue, saying to him, Because your daughter is now a corpse, you must not bother the Master.

50 But when Jesus Heard, He Answered to him Saying, You must not be fearing, only you must be Continuously Committing, and she shall be made Healthy.

51 And when He entered into the house, He definitely dismissed, no one to enter except Peter and James and John, and the father and the mother of the dependent daughter.

52 And all were weeping and bewailing for her, but He Spoke. You must not weep; she has definitely not died, but definitely is sleeping.

53 And they laughed Him to scorn; now discerning that she died.

54 And He Sent Away everyone outside, and held to retain her hand and Called for Saying, Maid, you must for yourself be Raising Up.

55 And her spirit Turned Back, and she Raised instantly, and He appointed to give to her to eat.

56 And her parents were astonished, and He Gave to them a Command to speak to no one what had now occurred.

Sent Out the twelve

9 Then He called together His twelve disciples to Give them Miracle power and Authority over all the demons, and to be healing sicknesses.

2 And He Sent Out them to preach the Kingdom Rule of God, and to Cure the sick.

3 And He Spoke to them, You must not take up anything in your journey, neither a staff, nor a wallet for money, nor pouch for food or bread, nor pieces of silver, nor having two coats each.

4 And whatever house you should enter into, then you must continue there, and you must depart from that place.

5 And whoever that might not receive you, whenever you come away from that city, then you must shake off the dust from your feet, for a Testimony against them.

6 And then they departed, passing through to the villages, Preaching the Gospel, and Healing everywhere.

Herod hears of Jesus

7 Then Herod, the tetrarch, heard all that occurred by Him, so was puzzled because some were made saying that John is risen up from the dead,

8 And by some that Elias has been made to appear, and others of the same kind that one Prophet of the old times arose.

9 And Herod spoke, John I have beheaded, but Who is He that I am hearing such about? And he sought to discern Him.

Five Thousand Fed with Five Loaves

10 The Apostles returned, and recited to Him whatever they did. And He going aside, took them along for their private desolate wilderness place, of a city called Bethsaida.

11 And when the multitudes of people knew, they followed Him and He received them, Uttering to them about the Kingdom Rule of God, and was Curing those having need of household health.

12 And when the day began to lower down, and the twelve came near to speak to Him. You must dismiss away the multitude of people, that they go into the villages and the countrysides around that they might find housing and groceries, for we are being here in a desolate wilderness place.

13 But He Spoke to them, Yourselves must Give them to eat. But they spoke, There are definitely not greater to us than five loaves and two fish, unless if possibly we might go to buy food for all this people,

14 Because they were about five thousand men. So He Spoke to His disciples, You must make them sit to eat, groups by fifties.

15 And they did so, and all by their choice made to sit down.

16 Then He took the five loaves, and the two fish, Looked Up to the Heaven, He Blessed, and He Broke Pieces, and Gave to the disciples to be put forth to the multitude of people.

17 And they ate and were all made full, and twelve hand baskets of fragments abounding in amount to them, were taken up.

18 And it came to pass, When He was being separate, Praying, together with His disciples, that He questioned them Saying, Whom are the multitudes of people saying I am?

19 And they answering spoke, John the Baptist, and others of same kind, Elias, and others of same kind, that certain Prophet of old arose.

Peter's Great Statement

20 And He Spoke to them, But whom say yourselves, Me to be? Peter answered and spoke, The Christ of God.

21 And He Rebuked them. He Gave Command to speak this to no one.

22 For He Spoke, The Son of Man must suffer very much, and be disapproved of the elders and chief priests and scribes, and be killed, and after the third day be Risen Up.

Costs of Discipleship

23 And He Said to everyone, If anyone is willing by his choice to come after Me, he must by his choice deny himself, and must by his choice take up his cross daily, and must by his choice be Continuously Following Me.

24 Because whoever might be willing to save his soul shall by his choice lose it, and whoever should Lose his Living-Soul for Me, he shall Save It.

25 Because what is a man-made profiting, gaining all of the satan's world, but destroying himself by his choice or made suffering loss?

26 Because whoever might be by his choice ashamed of Me and My Spiritual Communications to him, the Son of Man shall by His Choice be ashamed when He should come in His Glory and of His Father and of His Holy Angels.

27 But I am Saying to you Of Truth, there are some standing here, who should never ever taste of death, until after they should Spiritually See the Kingdom Rule of God.

The Transfiguration

28 And it came to pass about eight days after these Spiritual Words, He took along Peter and John and James to ascend upon a mountain to Pray.

29 And it occurred while He Prayed, the Appearance of His Person, another One of a different kind, and His Raiment is glittering White.

30 And Behold, Two Men were Talking Together with Him, who were Moses and Elias.

31 Who Spiritually Appeared in Glory Saying that His Leaving was Expected to be Fulfilled in Jerusalem.

32 But Peter and those united with him were made heavy in natural sleep; they fully awoke and Spiritually Saw the Glory of Him, and the two Men now Standing United with Him.

33 And it came to pass, when They disappeared away from Him, Peter spoke to Jesus, Oh Master, a God-Work is our being here, and we might finalize three Tabernacles, one for You, and one for Moses, and one for Elias, not discerning what he was saying.

34 And when he said these things, there occurred a Cloud, and overshadowed them, and they feared within to enter then into that Cloud.

35 And a Voice Occurred Out from the cloud Saying, This is My Son, the Beloved, you must by your choice be Hearing Him. (Ps 2:7; Deut 18:15)

36 And when that Voice ended, Jesus was found alone. And they kept silence, and told nothing in those days, nothing that they Beheld Attentively.

Discipleship Learning

37 And it came to pass that in the next day, they descending from the mountain, He encountered a large multitude of people toward Him.

38 And Behold, a man of the multitude of people, shouted out saying, Oh Master, I Pray Earnestly of You. You must have regard to my son, for being mine only born.

39 And You must behold, a spirit takes him, and he unexpectantly is crying out, and it convulses him associated with foams, bruising him, and resisting to depart fully away from him.

40 And I Prayed earnestly of your disciples in order that they might be casting it out, and they definitely could not.

41 And Answering, Jesus Spoke, Oh faithless and being made perverted generation, up to how long a time shall I be with you, and Continue Enduring you? You must draw near here your son.

42 And even coming near of Him, the demon tore him, and convulsed him to the ground. And Jesus Rebuked the morally impure spirit, and Cured the dependent child, and yielded him back to his father.

43 And they were made amazed by all the Mighty Power of God, and all marveled about all things whatever that Jesus Did. He Spoke to His disciples,

44 You yourselves must put into your ears these Spiritual Words, because the Son of Man is Expecting by His Choice to be made delivered up in betrayal into the hands of men.

45 But they understood not this Word, as it is being made veiled away from them, that none might grasp it, and they were fearing to earnestly request of Him about this Word.

46 Then entered a thought among them, Whoever should be beyond their dreams greatest of them?

47 And Jesus now Spiritually Discerning the thought of their heart, took hold of a little child, stood him with Himself.

48 And He Spoke to them, Whoever should receive this little child in the Name of Me, is receiving Me, even as whoever should Receive Me is Receiving Him that Sent Me Out, because he is existing least among you all, he shall be great. (John 13:12-17)

49 And John answered and spoke, Oh Master, we discerned one casting out the demons in Your Name, and we forbid him, for he is definitely not following with us.

50 And Jesus Spoke to him, You must not forbid one, because he is definitely not against us who is in behalf of us.

51 And it came to pass, to be Made Fulfilling the days for His Ascension, that He Firmly Established His Face to be going toward Jerusalem.

52 And He Sent Out messengers before His Person, and going they entered into a village of Samaritans, so that they prepare for Him.

53 And they definitely received Him not, for His Face was to go to Jerusalem.

54 And when His disciples James and John Discerned, they spoke, Oh Lord, should we speak fire come down from the heaven and consume them, as also Elias did? (2 Kings 1:10-12)

55 But He Turned, and Rebuked them and Spoke, You definitely Spiritually Discern not such a spirit as you are yourselves,

56 Because the Son of man came definitely not to destroy men's souls, but definitely to

Save, and they went into another village of a different kind.

Discipleship Tests

57 And it occurred when they went, in the way of travel, a certain man spoke to Him, Oh Lord, I will follow You whereto ever You should be going.

58 And Jesus Spoke to him, Foxes have a homes in holes, and birds of heaven nests, but the Son of Man, definitely has not wherein He should be lowering down His Head.

59 And He Spoke to another of a different kind, You must Follow Me, and he spoke, Oh Lord, You must permit me to go first of all to bury my father.

60 But Jesus Spoke to him, You must Dismiss the dead to bury their dead, but you must Go Announce the Kingdom Rule of God.

61 And then another of a different kind also spoke, Oh Lord, I will follow you, but first of all You must permit me to say good-bye to those in my home.

62 And Jesus Spoke to him, No man having laid his hand upon a plow, and is after Spiritually Looking back, is fit for the Kingdom Rule of God.

The Seventy are Sent

10 And after these things, the Lord indicated also other seventy of a different kind, and Sent them Out each by two's before His Face, into every city and place where He expected Himself to be coming.

2 Therefore, He was Saying to them, The Harvest certainly large, but workers few. You must Pray Earnestly, therefore, to the Lord of the Harvest, so that He should be sending away workers into His Harvest.

3 You must go away. You must behold, I am Sending you Out as innocent lambs in the midst of wolves.

4 You must bear neither money purse, neither a wallet for money or pouch for food, nor shoes, and you should greet no man upon the way of travel.

5 And into whatever house which you should enter, first of all you must say, Peace to this home.

6 And if certainly the Son of Peace should be there, your Peace shall keep a hold upon it; and if not, He shall return again to you.

7 And in the same house you must continue eating, and drinking from them, because the worker is Worthy of his reward. You must not depart out from house to house.

8 And into whatever city you might now enter, and they might receive you, you must eat what they put forth to you.

9 And you must heal the weak among it, and you must say to them, The Kingdom Rule of God is now Approaching near to you.

10 But into whatever city whenever you should enter, you must speak, and they should not receive you, coming out into the streets of it, you must speak.

11 Even the dust of your city, which was made joined to us from your city, we are wiping you off. But you must be knowing this, that the Kingdom Rule of God is now approaching with intent to you,

12 But I Say to you, it shall be more tolerable for the Sodoms in That Day, than for this city.

13 Woe to you Chorazin, Woe to you Bethsaida, for if in Tyre and Sidon, though long ago, occurred the Miracle Powers that came to pass in you, they would have repented with sackcloth, and sat in ashes.

14 But it shall be more tolerable for Tyre and Sidon in the Final Judgment than for you.

15 And you Capernaum, you exalted up to Heaven, shall be made thrust down to hades. (Isa 14:13-15)

16 He that is hearing you is hearing Me, and he that rejects you, rejects Me, and he that rejects Me, rejects the One Who Sent Me Out.

The Seventy Return

17 And the seventy returned with Joy saying, Oh Lord, even the demons were made subject to us in Your Name.

18 And He Spoke to them, I was perceiving the satan, as lightning by its choice having fallen down out from Heaven.

19 Behold, I am Giving you Authority to Tread Down upon serpents and scorpions, and upon all the miracle power of the enemy, and definitely he shall never ever hurt you.

20 But in this yourselves must rejoice, because not that the spirits are made subject to you; but instead you must be rejoicing that your names are Made Written in Heaven.

21 In that hour Jesus was Exceedingly Glad in Spirit, and Spoke, I Acknowledge You, Oh Father, Oh Lord of Heaven and the earth, for You have Concealed these things from wise and prudent, and Revealed them to infants. Emphatically Yes, Father, in this manner It Became a God-Good Intention Before You.

22 All things are Delivered up to Me by My Father, and none is Knowing Who the Son is except the Father, and Who the Father is except the Son, and to Whomever the Son should be Intending to Reveal.

23 And made turning to His disciples, He Spoke in privacy. Spiritually Blessed, the eyes that Spiritually See what you are Spiritually Seeing,

24 Because I Say to you, that many Prophets and kings have strongly desired to Spiritually Discern what yourselves Spiritually See, and definitely not Spiritually Discerned and to Hear what you are Hearing, and have by their choice definitely not Heard.

How to Inherit Eternal Life

25 And Behold, a certain lawyer arose spiritually testing Him and saying, Oh Master, what shall I Do to Inherit Eternal Life?

26 Then He Spoke to him, What is Made Written in the Law? How are you now reading?

27 And then he answering Spoke, You shall by your choice God-Love the Lord your God out from your whole heart, and out from your whole soul, and out from all your strength, and out from your whole intellect, and your neighbor as yourself. (Deut 6:5; Lev 19:18)

28 So He Spoke to him. You have answered correctly. You must do this and you shall Live.

Story of the Good Samaritan

29 But he, willing to be Made Righteous himself, spoke to Jesus. And who is my neighbor?

30 Then Jesus undertook to Speak, A certain man came down away from Jerusalem into Jericho, and there fell among robbers, that also unclothed him, laid on wounds, and went, dismissing him nearly acquiring death.

31 And then by chance a certain priest came down in that way of travel, and when he discerned him, he passed by on other side.

32 And it came to pass then likewise also a Levite came by the place, discerned, and passed by on other side.

33 But a certain Samaritan was traveling, came to him, Spiritually Discerned, and had compassion to him.

34 And he came near, pressure bound his wounds, applying oil and wine, sat him upon his own animal, and led it to an inn, and took care of him.

35 And upon the next daylight day he came out, casted out two pennies, to give to the innkeeper, and spoke to him, You must take care of him, and anything whatever you might spend more, I will repay to you when I come again.

36 Which, therefore, of these three, are you thinking, now became a neighbor to him who fell into the robbers?

37 And he spoke, He who showed Mercy with him. Therefore, Spoke Jesus to him, You Must Be Going, and you, you Must Be Doing likewise.

Sisters Mary and Martha

38 Now it came to pass, among those going to Him, that He entered into a village, and a certain woman, named Martha, humbly received Him into her home.

39 And there was this sister called Mary, who also sat nearby the Feet of Jesus to hear His Word.

40 But Martha was made occupied about very much serving, standing ready, and spoke, Oh Lord, for you are definitely not caring how my sister left me alone to be serving? You must speak, therefore, to her for me that she should aid me.

41 And Jesus answered, and spoke to her, Oh Martha, Oh Martha, You are taking thought, and made disturbed about very much,

42 But one is needful, Mary then has herself Chosen the God-Good portion, which shall definitely not be made taken away from her.

Lessons to Followers

11 And it came to pass, when He was being in a certain place Praying, as He ceased one of His disciples spoke to Him, Oh Lord, you must teach us to Pray just as also John taught his disciples.

2 And He Spoke to them, When you should be Praying, you must be continuously saying, Our Father in Heaven, You must Make Holy Your Name. You must make Your Kingdom Rule come. You must make Your Will occur in Heaven, and upon the earth.

3 You must give to us our daily bread according to the day.

4 And You must Remove from Memory (forgive) our sin natures and sins to us, because we also are Continuously Removing from Memory (forgiving) everyone indebted to us. And You should not bring us into temptation, but definitely You must Rescue us from evil.

5 And He Spoke to them, Who of you shall have a friend, and shall go to him at midnight, and might speak to him, Oh friend, loan me three loaves.

6 Because a friend of mine came up from a journey to me, and I have definitely not to put forth for him.

7 He also might speak inside to answer, You must not be offering concern of labor to me, already the door is shut, and my little children they are with me in their bed. I am definitely not able to raise to give to you.

8 I Say to you, although he has definitely not raised by his choice so he shall give to him though being his friend, yet because of his begging, he has raised up giving to him as much as he is having lack.

9 And also I Say to you, You must Ask and it shall be Given to you, you must Seek and you shall Find, you must Knock and it shall be Opened to you.

10 Because everyone that asks Receives, and he that seeks Finds, and to he that knocks it shall be Opened.

11 And when a son shall ask bread of you, a dad, shall he not hand him a stone? And if a fish, shall he not hand in place of a fish a serpent to him? (Matt 23:9-12)

12 Or if ever he might ask an egg, shall he not hand him a scorpion?

13 If yourselves, therefore, evil existing, discern to give God-Good physical gifts to your children; how much more your Father from Heaven shall Give the Holy Spirit to you asking Him?

A divided kingdom or house can't stand

14 And He was casting out a demon, and it was dumb. And it came to pass when the demon came out, the dumb uttered. so the multitude of people marveled.

15 But certain ones of them spoke, He cast out the demons by the dung god (satan), the ruler of the demons.

16 And other ones of a different kind trying, sought from Him a Miracle Sign out from Heaven.

17 But He Discerning their motives Spoke to them, Every kingdom rule divided against itself is brought to desolation, and a home (divided) against home falls down.

18 And if satan also be made divided against himself, how shall his kingdom be made to stand? Because you say, I cast out the demons by the dung god (satan),

19 And if I by the dung god (satan) cast out the demons, by whom are your sons casting out? Because of this, they shall be your judges.

20 But if I by a Finger of God Cast Out the demons, so then the Kingdom Rule of God has attained among you.

21 When a strong man fully made armed might maintain his own enclosure, his material goods are in peace.

22 But as soon as a mightier came upon him, moreover might overcame him, and he takes away all the armor of him upon which he had confidence, so then he distributed his spoils.

23 He that is not being with Me is against Me, and he that gathers together not with Me is dispersed.

24 When the morally impure spirit should come out from a man, it passes through dry places seeking a resting place, and not finding, says, I will return into my home from where I came out.

25 And when it came, was finding it swept and adorned.

26 Then it went and received along seven other ones of different kinds of spirits more evil than itself, and entering in it dwells there, and it came to pass the last of that man worse than the first.

27 And it came to pass with Him saying these things, a certain woman lifted up a voice out from the multitude of people, spoke to Him. Spiritually Blessed the womb that bore you and breasts that nursed.

28 But He Spoke, Rather, Spiritually Blessed are they that are Hearing the Word of God, and Maintaining It.

This is an evil generation

29 And when the multitudes of people were thickly crowded, He began to Say, This is an evil generation, it is seeking after a Miracle Sign and there shall be definitely no Miracle Sign given to it except the Miracle Sign of the Prophet Jonas.

30 Because just as Jonas became a Miracle Sign to the Ninevites, so shall be also the Son of Man to this generation.

31 The queen of the south will rise up in the Final Judgment with the men of this generation, and she shall condemn to death them, because she came out, from the ends of the earth, to hear the Wisdom of Solomon, and Behold, a Greater than Solomon here.

32 The men of Nineveh will arise up in the Final Judgment with this generation and they shall condemn it to death, because they Repented at the Preaching of Jonas, and Behold, a Greater than Jonas here.

33 No man, when he has lit a candle, puts in a secret place, neither under a bushel, but definitely upon a candlestick that they coming in might see shining.

34 The Spiritual Light of the body is the Eye. Therefore, when your Eye might be Single, then your whole body is Full of Light, but as soon as it might be evil, then your body full of darkness.

35 You must Take Heed, therefore, that the Light within you is not darkness.

36 Therefore, if all of your Body Full of Light, having not one part full of darkness, all shall be Full of Light, as when the candle with lighting might give lighting, it should by your choice Enlighten you.

Woe scribes, Pharisees, and lawyers

37 And within the Uttering, a certain Pharisee was earnestly requesting of Him so that he might dine with him, and then

He entered to sit down.

38 And when the Pharisee spiritually discerned, he marveled that He did definitely not first of all make hand washing before dinner.

39 And the Lord Spoke to the Pharisee, Now you yourselves are cleansing the outward of the cup and the platter, while inside yourselves are being full of extortion and evil action.

40 Oh mentally unwise, definitely wash not the outward but also wash the inside.

41 But you must Give alms of what you have, and Behold, all is Purified to you.

42 But definitely Woe to you, Pharisees, for you tithe mint and rue and all herbs, but now you are passing away the Final Judgment and the God-Love of God. These things were required to be done, also not to dismiss the other.

43 Woe to you, Pharisees, for you love the chief seat in the synagogues, and the salutations in the marketplaces.

44 Woe to you, scribes and Pharisees, hypocrite actors, for you are as uncertain graves, which men walk upon definitely not Spiritually Discerning.

45 Then answered one of the lawyers saying to Him, Oh Master, Are you saying to us these things, violently treating us also?

46 And then He Spoke, Woe to you also you lawyers, for you are heavily loading men with grievously borne burdens, and yourselves are definitely not lifting one of your fingers to the burdens.

47 Woe to you, because you build the sepulchers of the Prophets, and your fathers killed them.

48 So then you give witness, even give consent to the man works of your fathers, since they certainly killed them, and then yourselves build their sepulchers.

49 Because of this also, the Wisdom of God Spoke, I will Send Out among them Prophets and Apostles, and out from them, they shall kill and also persecute.

50 That the blood of all the Prophets, which was poured out from the Conception of the satan's world, should be made required from this generation.

51 From the blood of Abel until after the blood of Zacharias, which perished between the altar and the House of God. Emphatically Yes! I Say to you, it shall be made required from this generation.

52 Woe to you, lawyers, for you have taken away the Key of Knowledge. You have definitely not entered yourselves, and forbid others to be entering.

53 And when Saying these things to them, the scribes and the Pharisees began to be severely conflicting with Him, and to be provoking Him to Speak about much more,

54 Lying in wait for Him and seeking to snatch something out from His Mouth in order to accuse Him.

Whom to Fear

12 Among those gathered all together, thousands, a multitude of people, so that they began to be trampling down one another, He began to Say to His disciples, that first of all, You must be taking heed to yourselves away from the leaven of the Pharisees, which is role playing hypocrisy.

2 For there is nothing that is now made concealed altogether, which definitely shall not be made revealed, or a secret that definitely shall not be made known.

3 For whatever has been spoken in dark, shall be made heard in the Light, and whatever has been uttered, within the ear in the private room, shall be made preached upon the housetops.

4 And then I Say to you My friends, that you should not be afraid of them who kill the body, for then after these things have nothing more in excess thing to do,

5 But I will forewarn you, whom you should fear. You must Fear Him, after He kills you, has Authority to hurl you down

to hell. Emphatically Yes, I Say to you, You must Fear Him.

6   Are definitely not five sparrows sold for two Roman assarius, and definitely not one of them is forgotten in the Presence of God?

7   But definitely even the very hairs of your head are all numbered. Therefore, you must not fear. You are excellent in value to many sparrows.

8   For I Say to you, that all whoever might Confess in Me before men, also the Son of Man shall Confess in them before the Angels of God.

9   But he that accepts no responsibility to Me in the presence of man, I Will Deny in the Presence of the Angels of God.

10   And any who shall spirit say a spiritual communication toward the Son of Man, it shall be Removed from Memory (Forgiven) for him, but blaspheming about the Holy Spirit shall definitely not be Removed from Memory (Forgiven).

11   And when they might be offering you over to the synagogues and rulers and authorities, You must be taking no thought how or what you should respond or what you should speak.

12   Because the Holy Spirit Shall Teach you in that same hour what you Ought to Speak.

Parable of rich man

13   And one with him out from the multitude of people spoke, Oh Master, you must speak to my brother, to fully divide with me the inheritance.

14   And then He Spoke to him, Oh man, who made Me a justice giver or divider over you?

15   And He Spoke to them, You must Behold Attentively, and you must maintain away from greediness, since any man's Life is definitely not in his abounding in amount of his material goods.

16   And then He Spoke a parable to them Saying, The land of a certain rich man yielded much.

17   And he was reasoning with himself saying, What should I do since I have definitely not wherein to gather together my fruits?

18   And finally he spoke this, I will take down my barns, and build greater, and gather together there all my products, and my God-Goods.

19   And I will spirit say to my soul, soul you have many God-Goods. You are laying up for many years. You must by your choice be refreshing, eat, drink, and be made merry.

20   But God Spoke to him, You mentally unwise, this night your soul is being demanded from you. Then whose shall it be for whom you have prepared?

21   So is this one storing up for himself, and not being rich for the Purpose of God?

Know that your needs are Taken Care Of

22   And then He Spoke to His disciples, I am Saying this to yourselves, You must not take thought to your soul, what you might eat, neither for your body, what you might put on.

23   The soul is greater than nourishment and the body than clothing.

24   You must consider the ravens, how they are definitely not Sowing, neither are they Reaping, where is definitely no private room, neither a barn, and our God nourishes them. How much more are yourselves different in value than a bird?

25   And who of all your cares can add one cubit more to his stature of age?

26   Therefore, if you are neither able in the least, why are you taking thought for the remaining?

27   You must consider the lilies how they grow, definitely not labor nor spin, and so I Say to you, neither Solomon in all his glory was clothed as one of these.

28   If then that God is so arraying the grass being this day in the field, and tomorrow is made cast in an oven, how much more you, Oh of little Faith?

29 And yourselves must not seek what you might eat, neither what you might drink, also you must not be of a doubtful mind,

30 Because all these things the nations of the satan's world seek after, and your Father discerns that you have lack for these things.

Seek Only the Kingdom of God

31 But you must be seeking the Kingdom Rule of God, and all these things shall be made added more to you.

32 You must fear not little Flock, for your Father is Pleased to Give to you the Kingdom Rule.

33 Yourselves must by your choice sell your material goods and yourselves must by your choice give alms. Yourselves must finalize money purses for yourselves being not made old. A treasure in Heavenlies fails not, whereto a thief is definitely not approaching near, nor a moth materially destroying,

34 Because whereto your treasure is, there shall be your heart also.

35 You must be made Clothing About your waist and your Spiritual Lamps be made Burning.

36 And so yourselves like to men looking for their Lord. When He shall be Removed for the Wedding, in order that Coming and Knocking, we should immediately Open to Him.

37 Spiritually Blessed those Bondslaves, that the Lord shall find Watching when He has come. Truly I am saying to you that He shall for Himself be Clothed About, He shall also be made Sitting them down, and having Passed Forth He shall be Serving to them,

38 And if He might Come in the second watch, or might Come in the third watch, and might find so. They are Spiritually Blessed, those same Bondslaves.

39 And this you must be Knowing, that if the householder had Spiritually Discerned what hour the thief is Coming, he would have watched and whenever definitely not have dismissed that he has made to break through his dwelling.

40 So yourselves, you must be making ready, therefore, for the hour you are definitely not thinking, the Son of Man is Coming.

A Faithful or unfaithful servant

41 Then Peter spoke to Him, Oh Lord, was this parable said to us, or also to all?

42 And the Lord Spoke, So who then is that Faithful and very Wise Steward, whom his Lord shall make among His Household Help, to Give in a Special Time, his portion of Meat?

43 Spiritually Blessed, that Bondslave that when His Lord has Come, shall Find him in such a manner doing.

44 Of Truth, I am Saying to you, that He shall Make him Ruler over all His Material Goods.

45 But if that Bondslave then might spoke in his heart, My Lord delays His coming, and might begin to be striking his male servants and maid servants, and also eats and drinks, even being made a drunkard,

46 Then the Lord of that Bondslave shall now come in a day and in an hour he is definitely not watching for, when he is definitely not knowing, and shall cut him up severely, and lay down his part with the faithless.

47 And then that Bondslave who knew the Will of the Lord Himself, and prepared not, neither obeyed to His Will, shall be made to very much beating.

48 But he that knew not, then did that worthy of stripes, shall be beaten little of all. For to whomever very much has been given, very much shall be sought from him, and to whom very much has been put forth, more in excess they shall ask of him.

Came Not for Peace but Separation

49 I have come to Cast Fire upon the earth, and that I Strongly Desire whether I already have made a Fire started.

50 For now I have a Baptism, to be Made Baptized, and how I am Made Constrained until after when it should be Made Finally Fulfilled.

51 You are thinking that I have become near to Give Peace upon the earth, but definitely not; I am Saying to you but definitely instead Separation.

52 Because from now there shall be five in one home, now made divided, three against two, and two against three.

53 A father shall be made divided against son, and a son against father, mother against daughter, and daughter against mother, mother in law against her daughter in law, and daughter in law against her mother in law. (Mic 7:6)

54 And then He was Saying also to the multitudes of people, When you might discern a cloud rising from west, immediately you say a shower is coming, and so it comes to pass.

55 And when a south is blowing, you say there shall be a burning heat, and it comes to pass.

56 You hypocrite actors, you can be discerning now to Prove in Truth the face of the heaven, and of the earth. But how are you definitely not Proving in Truth this Special Season?

57 And yet, why even for yourselves, are you definitely not judging the Righteous?

58 Because as you are going away with your adversary to a ruler, in the way of travel you must give gain from diligence to deliver away from him, for fear that he might haul you to the judge, and the judge deliver you up to the guard, and the guard might cast you into prison.

59 I Say to you, You might never ever come out from that place, until after when you should have repaid the last mite.

Except you Repent, you will perish

13 And there were present, some among them, telling that special time to Him about those, being Galileans, whose blood Pilate had mixed with their sacrifices.

2 When Jesus Answered, He Spoke to them, Do you think that those Galileans, sinners above all the Galilaeans, because they ended suffering such?

3 I Say to you, definitely not, but definitely except you should Repent, you should all yourselves perish in like manner.

4 Or those eighteen upon whom also the tower in Siloam fell down and therein killed them, Are you thinking that these debtors to be more than all the men dwelling inside of Jerusalem?

5 I Say to you, definitely not, but definitely, except you should Repent of all things, you will likewise destroy yourselves.

A tree without Fruit is to be cut down

6 And then He was Saying this parable, A certain one was having now made planted a fig tree in his vineyard, and he came seeking fruit and found in it definitely not.

7 And then he spoke to the vine dresser, Behold, I am coming three years seeking fruit in this fig tree, and definitely not finding. Cut it down. So why is it destroying the earth?

8 And he answered, saying to him, Oh Lord, you must dismiss it also this year, until I might dig about it and cast dung,

9 If indeed, it might Finalize Fruit as expected, but if not you shall cut it down.

10 And when He was Teaching in one of the synagogues in the Sabbath,

Heals a women on the Sabbath

11 And Behold, a woman was having a spirit of infirmity eighteen years, and also was bowed together in the extreme, and not able to straighten up.

12 And when Jesus Spiritually Discerned her, He Called Out and Spoke to her. Woman, your infirmity is now Made Dismissed Away.

13 And He Laid His hands on her, and instantly she was made upright, and she

Attributed Glory to God.

14 And then the ruler of the synagogue answered, being very displeased since Jesus healed on the Sabbath, saying to the multitude of people, There are herein six days, that He must work in them. You must come to be healed then and not on the Sabbath day.

15 The Lord, therefore, Answered him, and Spoke, Oh hypocrite actor, are definitely not every one of you on the Sabbath removing his ox or donkey away from the manger, and it lead away to water?

16 And she is a daughter of Abraham which the satan had bound eighteen years, Behold, also definitely ought she not to be made Removed away from this bond, on this day of the Sabbath?

17 And when He is Saying these things, all those being adverse to Him were made shamed, and then all the multitude of people were rejoicing, in The Way of all the Spiritual Perfection occurring by Him.

Kingdom like a mustard seed

18 Then He was Saying, What is like the Kingdom Rule of God, and what shall it be likened to?

19 It is like a grain of mustard seed, which a man took, casted into his own garden, and it grew and it became into a great tree, so then the birds of the heaven lodged among the branches of it.

Kingdom like leaven

20 And again He Spoke, To what shall I liken to the Kingdom Rule of God?

21 It is like leaven which a woman has taken to hide away in three dry meal measures of flour, until after when all of it was made leavened.

22 And He was journeying through to cities and villages and did teaching and journeying toward Jerusalem.

The last are First, and the first Last

23 And then a certain one spoke to Him,

Oh Lord, are there few that are being made Saved? Then He Spoke to them.

24 You must Strive to Enter in through the Narrow Gateway, for many, I Say to you, shall seek to enter and definitely shall definitely not be capable.

25 Since whenever the Householder might have Risen Up, and then might Shut the Door Closed, and then you might begin to stand outside and knock at the door, saying, Oh lord, Oh lord, you must open to us, and answering, He shall Spirit Say to you, I definitely am not Spiritually Discerning you, from where you are.

26 Then shall you begin to say, We have eaten and drank in the Presence of You, and You have taught in our streets.

27 But He shall Spirit Say to you, I am definitely not Spiritually Discerning you from where you are. You must Depart away from Me, all you workers of unrighteousness.

28 There shall be weeping and gnashing of teeth, when you should have Spiritually Seen Abraham, and Isaac, and Jacob, and all the Prophets in the Kingdom Rule of God, and you are made cast out outside.

29 And they shall now Come away from east and west, and away from north and south, and shall be Made Sitting down in the Kingdom Rule of God.

30 And Spiritually you must behold, they that whoever are last shall be First, and they that whoever are first shall be Last.

Jesus Mourns over Jerusalem

31 Among them the same day came near certain Pharisees saying to Him, You must come away and you must go from here, for Herod shall kill You.

32 So then He Spoke to them, Go and you must speak to this fox, Behold, I am Casting Out demons, and Performing Cures this day and tomorrow, and I am being Made Perfected after the third day.

33 But I must then be having to be going this day, and also tomorrow, since definitely there cannot be The Prophet to

perish outside Jerusalem.

34 Oh Jerusalem, Oh Jerusalem, that kills the Prophets, and stones them Sent Out to you. How often I would have Gathered your children All Together, even as in the manner a hen her brood under her wings, and you definitely would not.

35 You must behold, your home is dismissed to you desolate. And Truly then, I Say to you, that you might never ever Spiritually Discern Me until after This One should Now Come when you should speak, Blessed, He that is Coming in the Name of the Lord. (Jer 22:5; Ps 118:26)

Is it Lawful to Heal on the Sabbath?

14 And it came to pass, He came into a certain home to eat bread on Sabbath among the rulers of the Pharisees, and they were observing Him.

2 And Behold, a certain man was before Him with massive edema.

3 And Jesus was Made to Answer, He spoke to the lawyers and Pharisees Saying, Whether is it lawful to be healing on the Sabbath?

4 And then they remained quiet. So then He took Hold, Cured, and Dismissed him away,

5 And Answered to them. He Spoke, Who of you, in the day of the Sabbath, also definitely shall not immediately draw up his donkey or ox that falls into a deep pit?

6 And they were definitely not capable to reply to these things against Him.

Jesus Teaches Humility

7 And then, He was Saying to them, being made called a parable, how giving heed to the chief rooms they were choosing, Saying to them,

8 When you might be made called by someone to weddings, you should not sit in the chief room, for fear that someone more honorable than you, should be called by him,

9 And coming to you, he will say bidding to you, You must give this one place. And then you might begin with shame, to hold the last place.

10 But when you might be called, go, you must sit down in the last place, that when you are now being called, he might come and he should speak, Oh friend, you must ascend up higher, then it shall be honor to you in the presence of those sitting to eat with you.

11 For anyone who exalts himself shall be Humbled, but he who is Humbling himself shall be made Exalted.

12 Then He Said also to him that called him, When you might make a dinner or supper, you must not possibly be calling for those your friends, or your brothers, or your kinsman, or your rich adjoining neighbors, for fear that they also might invite you again, and might become a payback to you.

13 But definitely when you should make a reception you must call poor, limping, crippled, blind.

14 And you shall be Spiritually Blessed, for they definitely are not having to repay you, because you shall be Made Repaid in the Resurrection of the Righteous.

Don't avoid the Wedding Feast

15 And when one of them, that was sitting to eat, heard these things, he spoke to Him, Spiritually Blessed, whoever shall eat bread in the Kingdom Rule of God?

16 Then He Spoke to him, A certain man made a great supper and called many.

17 And he sent his Bondslave to him at the hour of the supper to speak, being now made calling to them, You must be coming forward now, already all things are ready.

18 And they all began as one to all refuse. The first spoke to him, I have bought a field, and have necessity to come out now to see it. I earnestly request of you, you must have me now made excused.

19 And another of a different kind spoke, I bought five pair of oxen, and them I am

going to prove in truth. I earnestly request you must have me now excused.

20 And another of a different kind spoke, I have married a wife, and because of this I am definitely not able to come.

21 So then that Bondslave came up then to tell his Lord these things. Then, being made angry the Master of the House spoke to his Bondslave, You must depart rapidly into the streets and lanes of the city and you must conduct in here the poor, and limping, and crippled, and blind.

22 And the Bondslave spoke, Oh Lord, it has now occurred, as instantly Commanded, and there is yet place.

23 And the Lord spoke to the Bondslave. You must depart into the ways of travel, and hedges, and you must compel to enter that my home should be made full,

24 For I am saying to you, that none of those men that were called shall taste of My Supper.

A Disciple Must Forsake all

25 And there went together to Him large multitudes of people, and He turned to Speak to them.

26 If any man is coming by his choice to Me, and is definitely not continuously by his choice hating (love less) his own dad and his mother, and his wife and his children, and his brothers and his sisters, and even yet also his own soul, he is definitely by his choice not able to be My disciple.

27 And whoever is definitely not continuously by his choice bearing his cross, and continuously by his choice coming after Me is definitely not continuously by his choice able to be My Disciple.

28 Because who of you is willing to build a tower, definitely not first of all to sit down to continuously count the cost before continuously having the intent to physically finish?

29 For fear that in order to lay down his foundation, and not be continuously capable to finally complete, everyone seeing

with perception might begin to be mocking at him,

30 Saying that this man began to continuously build, but was definitely not capable to finally complete.

31 Or what king going to study another king of a different kind for war, first of all shall definitely not have sat down to consult, whether he is capable with ten thousand to meet another with twenty thousand coming against him?

32 In the event that while he is not yet far away, an ambassador message has been sent out earnestly requesting for peace.

33 So, therefore, whoever, of yourselves, that is definitely not saying goodbye to all his own material goods is continuously being definitely not able to be My disciple.

34 Salt Flavoring is God-Work, but if the Salt Flavoring should be made foolish, with what shall it be made seasoned.

35 It is neither fit for the earth nor for dung. It is cast outside. He who is having by his choice Ears to Hear, he must by his choice be Continuously Hearing.

Scribes and Pharisees complain

15 Then all the tax collectors were approaching near to Him, and the sinners to hear Him.

2 And the Pharisees and the scribes grumbled, saying how He is looking for sinners and eats with them.

Parable of a lost sheep

3 And He Spoke to them this parable saying,

4 What man of you, having a hundred sheep, and lost one of them, Is definitely not leaving the ninety nine in the desolate wilderness, and goes with intent to find the lost until after he might find it?

5 And when he has found, he places it over his own shoulders, rejoicing.

6 And when he came home, therein he called together his friends, and adjoining neighbors, saying to them, You must rejoice

together with me, for I found my sheep that was lost.

7   I Say to you that in the same manner, Joy shall be in Heaven for one sinner Repenting than over ninety nine Righteous who have definitely no need for Repentance.

Parable of a lost coin

8   Or what woman having ten pieces of silver, if she might lose one piece of silver, is definitely not lighting a lamp, and sweeping the house, and carefully seeking until after she might find?

9   And when she has found, she calls together her friends, and the adjoining neighbors, saying You must rejoice together with me, for I found the piece of silver that was lost.

10   In same manner I say to you, Joy occurs, in the Presence of the Angels of God, after one sinner is Repenting.

Parable of the prodigal son

11   And then He Spoke; A certain man was having two sons.

12   And the younger of them spoke to his father, Oh father you must give that part laying of financial substance to me. And he dispensed to them the livelihood.

13   And definitely after not many days, the younger son gathered together all things, journeyed away into a distant land, and there with riotous living scattered his financial substance.

14   And when he spent all, a mighty famine occurred in that land, and he began to be made lacking.

15   And then he went, then joined one of the citizens of that land, and he sent him into his fields to be feeding pigs.

16   And he was desiring to make full his belly from the husks that the pigs were eating, and not anything was given to him.

17   And when he came to himself, he spoke, How many wage earning servants of my father, are abounding in amount of bread, and I am myself perishing in famine.

18   Arising, I will go to my father and spirit say to him, Father, I have sinned to Heaven and in the presence of you,

19   And am no more worthy to be called your son. You must make me as one of your wage earning servants.

20   So then he arose, came to his father himself, but even far off his father having Discerned him, and Having Compassion and having ran, fell upon his neck and kissed him.

21   And the son spoke to him, Oh father, I have sinned to the Heaven, and in the presence of you, and am no more worthy to be called your son.

22   But the father spoke to his slaves. You must bring out the chief long robe first, and you must dress him with it, and you must give a finger ring for his hand, and shoes on his feet.

23   And bring the fattened calf, you must slay and then eat, we should be made merry.

24   For this my son was dead, and Lived Again, and was lost, and Made Found. And they began to be made merry.

25   Now his elder son was in the field, and as coming approached near to the house, heard music and dancing.

26   And he invited one of the male servants, then inquired, what these things might be beyond my dreams?

27   And then he spoke to him, For your brother is now come, and your father slayed the fattened calf, for he is being healthy, fully received.

28   And he was made angry, and definitely not willing to enter. Therefore, his father came out entreating him.

29   And he answered, spoke to the father, Behold, so many years I am bondserving you, and never passed away a commandment of you, and you never gave a kid goat that I might make merry with my friends.

30   And when your son came, he who

devoured your livelihood with harlots, you slayed for him the fattened calf.

31 And then He spoke to him, Oh child you are always with me, also everything of mine is yours.

32 We must be Rejoicing and also being made merry, for your brother, he was dead and Lives Again, and was being lost, and has been Made Found.

A bad steward, worldly wise

16 And He was Saying also to his disciples, A certain man was rich that was having a steward, and the same was reported to him as scattering his material goods.

2 And he called for him to speak to him, What is this I am hearing about you? You must pay back the account of your stewardship, because you can definitely not further be a steward.

3 Then the steward spoke within himself, What might I do since my lord is taking away my stewardship from me? I am definitely not capable to dig. I am disgraced to ask by begging.

4 I know what I will do, that when I should be completely removed of the stewardship, that they might receive me into their homes.

5 So inviting every one of the debtors to his lord, he was saying to the first, How much are you indebted to my lord?

6 And he spoke. A hundred bath measures of oil. And he spoke to him. You must receive your writings and sit down rapidly, you must write fifty.

7 After that he spoke to another of a different kind, How much then are you indebted? And he spoke, hundred cor-measures of wheat, and he said to him, You must receive your writings and you must write in eighty.

8 And the lord fully praised the steward of the unrighteousness, since he did wisely, for the sons of this age among this generation are very wise, more than the sons of the Light themselves.

9 Also I am Saying to you, You must make to yourselves friends of the savings of money of unrighteousness, that when yourselves might fail, they might receive you until the Eternal Habitations of God.

10 He, Faithful in the least is also Faithful in very much, and he unrighteous in the least is also unrighteous in very much.

11 Therefore, if not Faithful in the unrighteous savings of money, who shall be Committing to you the True (Riches)?

12 And if you be definitely not Faithful with that another man's, who shall give to you yours?

13 No household servant can bondserve to two masters, because either he shall hate another one of a different kind, and shall love the other one of a different kind; or shall uphold one, and shall despise the other of a different kind. You are definitely not able to Bondserve God and the savings of money.

Covetous Pharisees criticize Him

14 And the Pharisees heard all these things also, but existing covetous, they also were deriding Him.

15 And He Spoke to them, You are yourselves making righteous yourselves in the presence of man, but God Knows your hearts, for that high among men, is an abomination in the Presence of God.

16 Both the Law and the Prophets until after John, since from then the Kingdom Rule of God is Made Proclaimed, and every man is pressing into It.

17 Then it is easier for the Heaven and the earth to pass away, than one tittle of the Law to fall down.

18 Whoever puts away his wife and marries another of a different kind commits adultery. Also whoever is now made divorced from a husband is committing adultery, marrying.

A Rich man and Lazarus his servant

19 And there was a certain rich man being arrayed in purple clothes, and wearing fine linen, and being made merry every day, sumptuously.

20 And there was a certain beggar named Lazarus, who had been made prostrate at his gate, full of sores.

21 Then but definitely desiring to be filled from the crumbs falling down from the table of the rich, while the dogs were coming to lick his sores.

22 And it came to pass the beggar died, and he to be made carried away by the Angels into the bosom of Abraham, and then also the rich man died and was made buried.

23 And in hades he lifted up his eyes, existing in torturing torments, beholding attentively Abraham at a distance and Lazarus in his bosom.

24 And he called for father Abraham to speak, You must have mercy on me, and you might send Lazarus that he might dip the tip of his finger in water and might cool my tongue, for I am grievously sorrowing in this flame.

25 But Abraham spoke, Oh child, you must yourself remember that you fully received your God-Goods in your life, and Lazarus, likewise the evil works, but now this one is made comforting, and you grievously sorrowing.

26 And so then in all these things, between us and yourselves a great chasm firmly established, so that those willing to come through from here to you should not be able, neither those from that place to us should pass over.

27 Then he spoke, Father, therefore, I earnestly request, that you might send him to the home of my father,

28 Because, I have five brothers, so that he might testify to them, so that they not come into this place of torturing torments.

29 Abraham says to him, They are having Moses, and the Prophets. They must Hear them.

30 And he spoke, Definitely not, father Abraham, but definitely if any from dead might go to them, they shall Repent.

31 And he spoke, if they definitely not hear Moses and the Prophets, neither shall they be persuaded if any should arise out from the dead.

Rebuke and Forgive a Brother

17 Then He Spoke to the Disciples, It is not impossible that offenses come. But Woe through whom it is coming.

2 It is preferable for him, that a grinding donkey millstone is encompassing about his neck, and He be thrown down into the sea, than that he might offend one of the least of these.

3 You must Take Heed to yourselves, that if your brother might sin toward you, you must rebuke him, and if ever he might Repent, you must Remove from Memory (forgive) to him.

4 And if ever he sins seven times a day to you, and seven times a day might turn back to you saying, I Repent, you shall Remove from Memory (forgive) him.

If have Faith as a mustard seed

5 And the Apostles spoke to the Lord, You must add more to our Faith.

6 And the Lord Spoke. If you were having Faith as a grain of mustard seed, saying, That this sycamore must be made Rooted up, and must be made Planted in the sea, then that one Obeys you.

Expected to do your duty

7 But who of you are having a slave plowing, or shepherding, when he entered from the field, shall spirit say, immediately, pass forth, you must sit yourself down.

8 But definitely not. You will spirit say to him, you must prepare that I might dine, and clothe about to serve me until after I might eat and drink, and after these

things, you shall eat and drink.

9   Is he having thankful for grace to this slave, because he did what was made appointed to him? I think definitely not.

10   So also yourselves, when you might have done all things made appointed to you, you must be saying, For we are being unprofitable Bondslaves, since we were indebted to do whatever is now being done.

One of the ten lepers thanked Jesus

11   And it it came to pass, in Himself going to Jerusalem, that He was passing through in midst of Samaria and Galilee.

12   And as He was entering into a certain village, ten men lepers who stood afar off met Him.

13   And they took up a voice saying, Oh Jesus, Oh Master, You must Have Mercy on us.

14   And He Discerned. He Spoke to them. Be Going, you must Show as example, yourselves to the priests, and it came to pass in the going away, they were made Cleansed.

15   And one of them, himself, discerned why he was cured. He returned with a great voice, Attributing Glory to God.

16   And he fell down upon his face near the Feet of Him, Giving Thanks to Him, and he was a Samaritan.

17   And then Answering, Jesus Spoke, Have definitely not been made cleansed, but wherein the nine?

18   They were definitely not found, returning to Attribute Glory to God, except this hybrid Jew.

19   And He Spoke to him, Rise, you must be going, your Faith is now Saving you.

Kingdom Rule of God is Within you

20   And then He was made questioned by the Pharisees, When is coming the Kingdom Rule of God? He Answered them and Spoke, The Kingdom Rule of God is definitely not coming with observation.

21   Neither shall they Spirit Say, You must behold here, or must behold there, because the Kingdom Rule of God is Within you.

When Christ Returns for His Own

22   And then He Spoke to His Disciples, When the days will come, you shall desire to Spiritually See one of the days of the Son of Man, and definitely not Spiritually See (it).

23   And they shall spirit say to you, behold here, or behold there. You should not go, neither should you follow closely.

24   Because as the Lightning, that is Glowing from under Heaven already Brightly Shining from under Heaven, in such a manner shall also be the Son of Man in His Day.

25   But first of all He must Himself suffer very much, and be disapproved away from this generation.

26   And just as it occurred in the days of Noah, also so shall it be in the days of the Son of Man.

27   They were eating, drinking, marrying, given in marriage, until that day Noah entered into the Ark, and the flood of Noah came, and they were all destroyed.

28   Likewise also as it occurred in the days of Lot. They were eating, drinking, buying, selling, planting, building.

29   But that day Lot came out from Sodom, it rained fire and brimstone from heaven, and destroyed all.

30   According to like manner shall it be in The Day the Son of Man is made revealed.

31   In that same day, he who shall be upon the housetop, and his belongings in the house; he must not come down to take away them; and he in the field, likewise, he must not turn back after therein.

32   You must remember Lot's wife.

33   When whoever should seek to save his life shall lose it, and if whoever should Lose it, shall Preserve his Life.

34   I Say to you this, in that night, shall be two in one bed, and one shall be Taken Along, and the other one of a different kind shall be made parted from.

35 Two shall be at grinding, one of them shall be Taken Along, and the other one of a different kind shall be made parted from. 36 Two shall be in the field, the one shall be Taken Along and the other of a different kind parted from.

37 And they answered saying to Him, Wherein, Lord? And He Spoke, Whereto the Body, there gather together the Eagles.

Always be Praying and not be weary

18 And He was Saying a parable to them, that you must always be Praying, and not be weary.

2 Saying, one judge was in a certain city, and was not Fearing God, and was not respecting man.

3 And there was a widow in that city, and she was coming to him saying, You must avenge me from my adversary.

4 And he would definitely not over time, but after he spoke these things within himself, Although now I am definitely not Fearing God, and definitely not respecting man,

5 Yet because this widow offers concern to labor me, I will avenge her, that her habit of coming might not subdue me.

6 And the Lord Spoke, You must be hearing what the judge, of the unrighteousness, is saying.

7 And shall God definitely not bring any Vengeance for His Elect, which Loudly Plead to Him day and night, while He is suffering long with them?

8 I Say to you that He will bring His Vengeance against them swiftly, but when the Son of Man comes, shall He then find Faith upon the earth?

Parable of Pharisee and publican

9 And also He Spoke this parable also to anybody who is now being persuaded in themselves that they are Righteous, and were despising the others.

10 Two men ascended into the Temple area to pray, the one a Pharisee, and the other one of a different kind, a tax collector.

11 The Pharisee stood, prayed to himself these things, God I give thanks, to you, that I am definitely not as other men: extortioners, unrighteous, adulterers, or even as this tax collector.

12 I fast twice during the week. I am tithing all, as much as I possess.

13 And the tax collector, standing at a distance, would definitely not lift up his eyes to the Heaven, but definitely was striking at his chest saying, God you must be merciful to me, the sinner.

14 I Say to you, that before that man came down to his home he is Made Righteous. For everyone that is exalting himself shall be made Humbled, also he humbling himself shall be made Exalted.

Must Receive Him as a little child

15 And then they were also offering babes to Him that He might touch them, but when the disciples discerned, they rebuked them.

16 Jesus invited them and Spoke, You must have concern for the little children to come to Me, and you must not forbid them because of such is the Kingdom Rule of God.

17 Truly I am Saying to you, that unless a person should Receive the Kingdom Rule of God as a little child, that person must never ever enter therein himself.

A rich ruler having possessions

18 And a certain ruler questioned Him saying, Oh Good master, What must I do to inherit eternal life?

19 And Jesus Spoke to him, Why are you saying to Me, Good? None Good except One, God.

20 You discern the Commandments. You should not commit adultery. You should not murder. You should not steal. You should not bear false witness. You must honor your father and your mother. (Ex 20:12-16)

21 And he spoke, These things I have, in every way maintained from my youth.

22 Now when Jesus heard these things, He Spoke to him, Yet one thing you need. You must sell all as much as you are having, and must distribute to the poor, and you shall have Treasure in Heaven, and you must Come Forward and you must Follow Me.

23 And when he heard these things, he became very sorrowful, because he was exceedingly rich.

24 And when Jesus Spiritually Discerned him becoming very sorrowful, He Spoke, How hardly, those that have riches, to be entering into the Kingdom Rule of God.

25 Because it is easier for a camel to enter through a needle opening, than for the rich to enter the Kingdom Rule of God.

26 And when they that heard spoke, Who then can be made Saved?

27 So He Spoke, Those things impossible with man are being Possible with God.

Giving all for Christ's Purposes

28 Then Peter spoke, Behold, I have dismissed all things and we have followed You.

29 And then, He Spoke to them, Truly, I am Continuously Saying to you, that none that has parted from house, or parents, or brothers, or wife, or children for the cause of the Kingdom Rule of God,

30 Who shall never ever Fully Receive exceedingly more, in this Special Time, and in the Age to come, Eternal Life.

Jesus Foretells of His Death

31 Then He took along the twelve to Speak to them, Behold, we are ascending to Jerusalem, and all things now made Written, through the Prophets about the Son of Man, shall be made Finally Fulfilled.

32 Because He shall be delivered up in betraying to the Gentiles, and shall be made mocked, and shall be made violently treated, and shall be made spit on,

33 And scourged, they shall kill Him, and after the third day He shall Arise.

34 And they, definitely, understood none of these, and this Specific Word was made hid from them, and also they were definitely not knowing the sayings made.

Faith Made man's blindness Healed

35 And it came to pass, in His approach near to Jericho, a blind man was sitting, along side of the way of travel, begging.

36 And then hearing the multitude of people journeying through, he inquired what beyond his dreams this might be.

37 And they told him, that Jesus of Nazareth was passing forth.

38 And he loudly pleaded saying, Oh Jesus, Oh son of David, You must have mercy on me.

39 And those going before were rebuking him, that he should hold his speech, and so he cried out very much, much more, Oh Son of David You must have mercy on me.

40 Then Jesus Stood and Commanded he be led to Him, and when he approached near, then He Questioned him.

41 Saying, What are you willing I might do to you? And he spoke, Oh Lord, that I might receive sight.

42 And Jesus Spoke to him, You must receive sight, your Faith is now Healing you.

43 And instantly, he received sight, and was following Him, Attributing Glory to God, and all the people spiritually discerned to give Praise to God.

Zacchaeus Commits to Jesus

19 And Jesus entered passing through Jericho.

2 And there, Behold, a man called by the name of Zacchaeus, and he was chief of tax collectors, and he was rich.

3 And he was seeking to see Jesus, who He is, and definitely not able from the multitude of people, since his stature of age was short.

4 And he outran before to ascend on a sycamore tree, in order that he might discern Him, for He was then expected to pass by.

5   And as Jesus came to the place, He Looked Up and discerned him and Spoke to him, Zacchaeus, hurry, you must come down because this day I must continue in your home.
6   And he hurried to come down, and humbly received Him, rejoicing.
7   And when all discerned, they were grumbling, saying, Why has He entered to be housed with a sinful man?
8   And Zacchaeus stood to speak to the Lord, You must behold, Oh Lord, the half of the material goods I am giving to the poor, and in the event that I have of anyone anything taken by false accusation, I will pay back fourfold.
9   And Jesus Spoke to him, Since this day Salvation has occurred to this home, also according as also he is being a Son of Abraham.
10 Because the Son of Man has come to Seek, and to Save, that which is now lost.

Parable on rule of having
11 And then hearing these things of them, He added more to Speak a parable, because He was being near Jerusalem, and thinking themselves, they are expecting that instantly, the Kingdom Rule of God is to be discovered.
12 He Spoke, therefore, A certain man, more noble, went into a distant land to take for himself a kingdom rule, and to return.
13 And calling his ten Bondslaves, he gave to them ten pounds of money, and spoke to them, You must profit in business up to I come.
14 But it's citizens hated Him, and sent out an ambassador message back to Him saying, They would definitely not be willing to have Him Reign over us.
15 And when it came to pass when he came again, having received His Kingdom, then He spoke, to call for these Bondslaves to him to whom He gave the pieces of silver, in order that he might know who gained what through business.

16 Then came up the first saying, Lord your pound of money further gained ten pounds of money.
17 And he spoke to him, Well done, Oh God-Good Bondslave for in the least you have become Faithful, you must be having authority over ten cities.
18 And the second came saying, Oh Lord, your pound of money brought five pounds of money.
19 And He spoke also to this one, Also of you, you must be over five cities.
20 And another of a different kind, came saying, Oh Lord, behold your pound of money, I was having reserving in a napkin.
21 Because I was fearing you, for you are an austere man, definitely not taking up what you laid down, and are reaping where you definitely not sowed.
22 And He Says to him, Out from your mouth I will Judge you. Oh you evil slave. You; had discerned that I am an austere man, taking up what has definitely not been laid down, and reaping where I have definitely not sown.
23 Why then also have you definitely not given my exchange money to the bank, and to exact itself whatever united with interest when I came?
24 And He spoke to them standing, you must take away from him the pound of money, and you must give to him having the ten pounds of money.
25 And they spoke to Him, Oh Lord, he is having ten pounds of money.
26 Because I Say to yourselves, That all that are having shall be made given, and from him having not, even that he is having, shall be taken away, separated from him.
27 But those, My enemies, that would not I Reign over them, you must lead here and you must execute before Me.

Ascending to Jerusalem
28 And when He was going He Spoke these things, before ascending into Jerusalem.

29 And it came to pass, as He approached near to Bethphage and Bethany to the Mount, made calling Olives, He Sent Out two of his Disciples,

30 Saying, You must go away to the nearby village, in which coming into you will find a colt is now bound upon which, not at any time, a man has sat down. Removing, you must lead him.

31 And if any man earnestly requests of you, Why then are you removing so, You should Spirit Say to him that the Lord Himself has need of him.

32 Then those Sent Out, went and found just as He Spoke.

33 And as they were removing the colt, its masters spoke to them. For why are you removing the colt?

34 And they spoke. The Lord is having need of him.

35 And they led him to Jesus, and tossed their garments upon the colt, and they sat Jesus on (them).

36 And as He was going, they were spreading their clothes underneath Him in the way of travel.

37 And when He was approaching near to it, already at the descent of the Mount of Olives, all the multitude of different disciples began to rejoice, praising God with a great voice for all those discerned Miracle Powers.

38 Saying, Blessed the Coming King in the Name of the Lord, Peace in Heaven and Glory in the Most High. (Ps 118:26)

39 And some of the Pharisees from the multitude of people spoke to Him, Oh Master, you must rebuke your Disciples.

40 And Answering He Spoke to them, I Say to you that if they should hold their speech, the stones shall cry out.

Jesus Weeps Over Jerusalem

41 Then as He approached near, He Spiritually Discerned the city. He Wept over it.

42 Saying, If you had known the things now within your Peace, in this your day,

even you, even yet, but now it is made hid away from your eyes.

43 There shall now come days upon you. And your enemies shall clothe a trench about you, and fully surround you, and they shall constrain you from all around.

44 And they shall demolish you, and also your children within you. And they among you shall definitely have no concern for a stone upon a stone, for having definitely not known this Special Time of your Oversight.

Made My House a den of thieves

45 And then entering into the Temple area, He began Casting Out the sellers therein, and he that is buying.

46 Saying to them, It is now Made Written that My Home is a Home of Prayer, but yourselves have made it a den of robbers. (Isa 56:7; Jer 7:11)

Chief priests plot to kill Jesus

47 And as He was Teaching daily in the Temple area when then the chief priests and scribes and chiefs of the people were seeking to destroy Him,

48 And were definitely not finding what they might do, because all the people were attentive to hearing Him.

Chief priests question His Authority

20 And it came to pass, in one of those days, He was Teaching to the people in the Temple area, and Preaching the Gospel. The chief priests and the scribes being present with the elders,

2 And spoke to Him saying, You must speak to us, by what Authority Do You Do these things? Who is He that Gave You this Authority?

3 He Answered and Spoke to them. Also I Earnestly Request of you one Word, and you must speak to Me.

4 The baptism of John, was it out from Heaven, or out from man?

5 Then they reasoned together among

themselves saying, For if we might speak out from Heaven, He shall Spirit Say, Why then, therefore, have you definitely not committed to him?

6   But if we might speak, Out from man. All the people will stone us to death, because they are now made reassured John is being a Prophet.

7   And they answered, they are not now discerning from where.

8   Then Jesus Spoke to them, Neither am I Saying to you with what Authority I Do these things.

Parable of the wicked husbandmen

9   Then began He to Say to the people this parable. A certain man planted a vineyard, and share cropped it to husbandmen and journeyed away, a sufficiently long time.

10   And in the special season, he sent out a bondslave to the husbandmen, that they should give to him, from the fruit of the vineyard; but the husbandmen beat him, him sent forth empty.

11   And again added more, he sent another bondslave of a different kind, and they also then beat, dishonored, and so also him sent forth empty.

12   And yet he added more, to send a third, and then also they wounding him sent away.

13   Then spoke the lord of the vineyard, What should I do? I will send my son, the beloved, maybe discerning, they shall be made respecting him.

14   But, when the husbandmen discerned him, they were reasoning to themselves saying, This man is the heir, we should come now to kill him that the inheritance might become to us.

15   So they cast out, to kill him outside the vineyard. What, therefore, shall the hord of the vineyard do to them?

16   He shall come and destroy these husbandmen, and give the vineyard to others of same kind. And when they heard, they spoke, Never ever has it come to pass.

17   He looked upon them, and Spoke, What, therefore, is now Written? This Stone, which builders disapproved, the Same has become at the Head of the Corner. (Ps 118:22)

18   Whoever falls down upon that Stone shall be Made Broken. But whoever It might fall down upon, It shall grind him to powder.

Method to bring Jesus to Death

19   And in the same hour, the chief priests and the scribes sought to lay hands upon Him, because now they knew that He Spoke this parable to them, but they feared the people.

20   They observed and sent out spies, themselves pretending to be righteous, that they might take hold of His Words for to deliver up Him to the rulers, and the authority of the governor.

21   And they questioned Him saying, Oh Master, we spiritually discern that you are saying and teaching correctly, and definitely not receiving a person, but definitely in truth you are teaching The Way of God.

22   Is it lawful for us to give to Caesar tribute, or definitely not?

23   But He considered their craftiness. He Spoke to them, Why are you trying Me?

24   You must show as example to Me a penny. Whose image and superscription is it having? They answered and spoke, Caesar's.

25   And then He Spoke to them, You must pay accordingly, to Caesar what of Caesar, and to God the things of God.

26   They were definitely not capable to take hold of His Words before the sight of the people, now marveling at His Answer and they kept silence.

Sadducees question Resurrection

27   Then some of the Sadducees, which are against being a Resurrection, came near to question Him.

28   Saying, Oh Master, Moses wrote to us, If any man's brother might die having a

wife, and he should die childless, that his brother should take his wife and should raise seed to his brother.

29 Therefore, there were seven brothers, and the first took a wife, died childless,

30 And the second took the wife, and he died childless.

31 And the third, took her in like manner, and then also the seventh, and left definitely no children and died.

32 Afterward, likewise the woman died also.

33 Therefore, in the Resurrection, whose wife of them is she becoming, because seven had her to wife?

34 And Jesus Answering Spoke to them, The sons, of this Age, are marrying and are being given in marriages.

35 And those Counted Worthy to acquire the same of this Age, and of the Resurrection from the dead, neither are marrying, nor giving in marriages.

36 Because neither more to die because they are Able like Angels, and they are Sons of God, being Sons of the Resurrection. (Ex 3:6)

37 And when the dead are made Rising Up. Also Moses disclosed in the place of the Bush, as saying the Lord the God of Abraham, and the God of Isaac, and the God of Jacob.

38 For He is definitely not the God of the dead, but definitely, of the Living, because all things are Living through Him.

Christ is Whose Son?

39 Then some of the scribes answering, spoke, Oh Master, You have Spoken God-Working.

40 And after that none were daring to be questioning Him anymore.

41 Then He Spoke to them, How are they saying, Christ is being the Son of David?

42 When David himself is saying in the Book of Psalms, The LORD (Jehovah) Spoke to My Lord, You must Sit at My Right Side,

43 Whenever, while I should Have Positioned Your enemies, a Footstool for Your Feet. (Ps 110:1)

44 David, therefore, calls Him Lord, so how is He his Son?

45 Then everyone of the people heard Him Speak to His Disciples.

Beware of the evil scribes

46 You must beware of the scribes, which strongly desire to walk with long robes, and have affectionately love for salutations in the marketplace, and chief seats in the synagogues, and chief rooms in the suppers,

47 Which devour widow's houses, and pretense long Praying. They shall receive more in excess condemnation.

Poor widow Gave more than all

21 And then He looked up, He Spiritually Discerned the rich casting their gifts into the treasury.

2 And He Discerned also a certain starved widow casting there two mites.

3 And He Spoke, Of Truth, I am Saying to you, that this poor widow cast much more than all.

4 Because all these, from their abounding in amount to themselves, cast in for the gifts of God, but she from her lacking, cast all the livelihood which she was having.

Disciples Questioned about future

5 And as some were saying about the Temple area, how adorned with God-Work stones and gift offerings, He Spoke,

6 These things which you are seeing with perception, the days shall come in which a stone shall definitely be parted from a stone, which shall definitely be made torn down.

7 And they questioned Him saying, Oh Master, therefore, when shall these things be, and what shall be the Miracle Sign should be expecting when these things occur?

8　And He Spoke, You must Spiritually See, that you should not be made deceived, because many shall come in My Name saying, That, I AM, and the Special Time is now approaching near. Therefore, you should not go after them.

9　But when you might hear, wars and disorders, you should not be made terrified, because these things must come to pass first of all, but definitely, being definitely not immediately the End.

10　Then He Said to them, Nation shall rise up against nation and kingdom rule against kingdom rule.

11　And also great earthquakes in places, and famines, and pestilences, and also there shall be frightening sights, and shall be even great Miracle Signs of Heaven,

Endurance Possess your souls

12　But before all these, they shall lay their hands upon you, and they shall persecute, delivering up in the synagogues, and into prisons, leading to kings and governors for the cause of My Name.

13　And it shall turn out to you for a Testimony.

14　Therefore, you must settle yourselves in your hearts, not to plan to respond,

15　Because I Will Give you a Mouth and Wisdom, that all those being adverse to you shall definitely not be able to speak against, or stand against.

16　And yourselves shall be delivered up even by parents, and brothers, and kinsmen, and also friends of yourselves, and they shall put to death.

17　And you shall be hated by all, because of My Name.

18　But the hair of your head should never ever be destroyed.

19　In your Endurance you must Possess your souls.

Jerusalem surrounded by enemies

20　And when, you might Discern, Jerusalem being surrounded by encamping armies, then you should Know that the desolation of it is now approaching near.

21　Then those in Judaea, you must be fleeing into the mountains, and those in the midst of it, you must depart out, and those in the lands you must not enter into it.

22　For these are days of vengeance, there these things are having been made Fulfilled which are now written.

23　But Woe to them therein having womb with child, and to them that are nursing in those days, because there shall be great necessity in the earth, and evil wrath against this people.

24　And they shall fall down by the mouth of the sword, and shall be lead captive into all nations. And Jerusalem shall be made treaded down by the nations, until the Special Times of the Gentiles should have been made Fulfilled.

Miracle Signs in sky

25　And there shall be Miracle Signs in the sun, and moon, and stars, and upon the earth anguish of nations with perplexity, with sea and high wave sounding.

26　Men are losing breathing from fear, and from expectation of them coming upon the inhabited earth, because the powers of the heavenlies shall be made shaken.

Christ Returns in the Clouds

27　And then, they shall look upon the Spiritual Appearance of the Son of Man Coming upon a Cloud with Miracle Power, and very much Glory.

28　And when these begin to come to pass, you must straighten up and you must lift up your heads, since your Separation Removal is approaching near.

Fulfilled in this generation

29　And He Spoke a parable to them, You must discern the fig tree, and all the trees.

30　When they should shoot forward

already, you are Spiritually Seeing for yourselves, knowing that already summer is near.

31 So also yourselves, when you should discern these things occurring, you must Know that the Kingdom Rule of God is near.

32 Truly, I say to you, this generation should never ever pass away, until after whenever all things should come to pass.

33 Heaven and earth shall pass away, but My Words shall most never ever pass away.

Pray always to be Worthy

34 Then you must take heed to yourselves, for fear that it might make your hearts heavy in indulgence, and drunkenness, and cares of this existence, and that sudden Day should Stand Ready against you,

35 Because as a snare it shall come upon all that reside upon the face of all the earth. (Isa 24:17)

36 Therefore, you must be alert in all Special Times, Praying earnestly that you should be Counted Worthy to escape all these things expected to occur, and stand before the Son of Man.

37 And then, in the day He was Teaching in the Temple area, and at night He departed to camp in the mountain, called Mount of Olives.

38 And all the people came early in the morning to hear Him in the Temple area.

Unleavened Bread was Passover

22 For now the Feast of Unleavened Bread (Nisan 15-22), is being made called the Passover (Nisan 14, now made an idiom by the people through centuries), it was approaching near.

Chief priests talk with Judas Iscariot

2 And the chief priests and the scribes were seeking how they might intentionally kill Him, yet they were fearing the people.

3 And then entered satan into Judas, surnamed Iscariot, being of the number of the twelve.

4 So he went to talk together with the chief priests and the captains, about how he might deliver Him up in betrayal.

5 And they rejoiced, and agreed with him to give pieces of silver.

6 And he acknowledged, and sought opportunity to deliver Him up in betrayal to them, with absence of the multitude of people.

The Last Supper

7 And then came the day of Unleavened Bread (used as idiom for Passover, see Luke 22:1), when the Passover must be killed as sacrifice.

8 And then He Sent Out Peter and John Saying, Go, you must prepare for us the Passover that we should Eat.

9 And they spoke to Him, Wherein should we prepare?

10 He Spoke to them, Behold, after you enter into the city, a man bearing a pitcher of water shall encounter you. You must follow him into the house where he is passing into.

11 And you shall Spirit Say to the householder of the house, The Master is Saying to you, Wherein is the guestroom whereto I should eat the Passover with My disciples?

12 And also he will show you a great upper room, now laid out there. You must prepare.

13 They went and found just as He now is Spirit Saying, and prepared the Passover.

14 And when the hour occurred, then His twelve Apostles sat down with Him.

15 Then He Spoke to them. With Desire I have Desired to Eat this Passover with you before I suffer.

16 Because I am Saying to you, that I should never ever eat anymore out from this, until after it is Fulfilled inside the Kingdom Rule of God.

17 And He Received a Cup, Gave Thanks, Spoke. You must Receive this, and you must Divide to yourselves,

18 Because I am Saying to you, that I

should never ever drink from this product of the vine, until after the Kingdom Rule of God should come.

19 He having Given Thanks receiving, He Broke the Bread, and Gave to them Saying, This is My Body being made Given in behalf of you, This you Must Do in Remembrance of Me.

20 And in like manner, the Cup, after they dined, Saying, This Cup is the New of a different kind Covenant in My Blood, that is made Poured Out in your behalf,

21 But Behold, the hand delivering Me up in betrayal, (is) with Me at this table.

22 And indeed, the Son of Man is going according to that now made determined, but Woe to that man through whom I am delivered up in betrayal.

23 And they began to discuss among themselves, so then who might, out from themselves, be expected to practice this.

Jesus Sets the Example of Serving

24 And there also became a dispute among themselves, who of them is thought to be greatest?

25 And He Spoke to them, The kings of the nations have dominion, and they of them having control of them, are made called benefactors.

26 But then yourselves definitely not so, but definitely the greatest among you must become as the younger, and he that is esteemed as he that is serving.

27 Because who is greatest, either he that sits as at eating, or he who serves? Is definitely not he that is sitting as at eating? But, I AM, among the midst of you, as He that is serving.

28 But yourselves you are now continuing constantly with Me in My temptations.

29 I also Grant to you a Kingdom Rule, just as My Father Granted to Me.

30 That you should Eat and you should Drink at My Table in My Kingdom Rule, and Sit Down upon Thrones, Judging the Twelve Tribes of Israel.

Foretells Peter's denial

31 And then the Lord Spoke, Oh Simon, Oh Simon, Behold, the satan insists to sift you as wheat,

32 But I have Prayed Earnestly about you, that your Faith should not fail, also when you have been Converted you must firmly establish your Brethren as in time past.

33 And then he spoke to Him, Oh Lord, I am ready with You, both into prison and into going to death.

34 And then He Spoke, I am Saying to you, Peter, the cock shall definitely not crow this day than before you should three times deny that you are not now Spiritually Discerning Me.

Apostles Given Instructions

35 And He Spoke to them, When I Sent you Out with absence of a money purse, and pouch for food, and shoes, lacked you anything? And they spoke, Nothing.

36 Therefore, He Spoke to them, But definitely Now, he that is having a money purse or a wallet for money or pouch for food take up likewise, and he that is not having, he must sell his garment, and he must buy a sword.

37 Because I Say to you, even this that is Written, must be Finally Fulfilled in Me. And He was made accounted with the lawless, and because the things concerning Me have an End. (Isa 53:12)

38 And then they spoke, Oh Lord, Behold, here two swords, and He Said to them, It Is sufficient.

At Mount of Olives Praying

39 He departed and went out according to custom into the Mount of Olives, and his Disciples also followed Him.

40 And when He has come to the place, He Spoke to them, You must Pray to not enter into temptation.

41 And He was made withdrawn from them, about a stone throw, and positioning His knees was Praying.

42 Saying, Father, if you are intending, you must withdraw this Cup away from Me, but not My Will, but definitely Yours must Come to Pass.

43 And then He was made to see the Spiritual Appearance of an Angel from Heaven strengthening Him.

44 And having now become in agony, He was more earnestly Praying; and His sweat occurred like as Drops of Blood coming down upon the earth.

45 When He Rose from Prayer, and came to His Disciples, He found them made resting asleep from the grief.

46 And He Spoke to them, Why are you sleeping? Raise. You must be Praying that you should not enter into temptation.

Jesus betrayed and arrested

47 And while He yet was Uttering further, you must behold a multitude of people, and he that was called Judas, one of the twelve, went forward of them, and having approached near to Jesus, kissed Him.

48 But Jesus Spoke to him. Oh Judas, are you delivering up in betrayal the Son of Man with a kiss?

49 When those about Him discerned, they spoke to Him. Oh Lord, shall we allowing that strike hard with a sword?

50 And a certain one of them struck hard the slave of the High Priest, and took away his right ear.

51 Jesus Answered and Spoke, You must allow until after this. And He Touched his ear, having Cured him.

52 Then Jesus Spoke to them which came up to Him with the chief priests, and captains, and elders of the Temple area. Are you now coming out as against a robber, with swords and wooden staves?

53 For daily I was with you in the Temple area. You had definitely not stretched out your hands against Me, but definitely this is your hour with the authority of darkness.

Peter denies Jesus three times

54 They then physically took Him, lead, and conducted Him into the home of the High Priest, and Peter followed at a distance.

55 And when they lit a fire in middle of the hall, and they sat together, Peter was sitting in the midst of them.

56 But Behold, a certain maid servant that sitting before the light of fire and alternatively looking to him, spoke, Were you also with Him?

57 And he disclaimed Him, saying, Oh woman, I definitely am not now discerning Him.

58 And after a little measure, another of a different kind discerned him stating, You, are you also of them? And Peter spoke, Oh man, I definitely am not.

59 And having parted about one hour, another one of same certain kind, was confidently affirming also saying, Of truth, he was with Him, also because he is a Galilean.

60 And Peter spoke, Oh man, I am definitely not saying! I am not discerning Him! And instantly while yet he was uttering, the cock crowed.

61 And the Lord Turned, and Looked Upon Peter, to remind Peter of the Spiritual Word of the Lord, as He Spoke to him, Before cock crowed, you will Deny Me three times.

62 Peter came outside and wept bitterly.

63 And the men that constrained Jesus were mocking, beating Him.

64 And when they blindfolded Him, they were striking His Face, and questioning Him saying, You must Prophesy, who is harmfully striking You?

65 And many other ones of a different kind, saying blaspheming to Him.

66 And as it became day, the group of elders of the people, and chief priests, and also scribes gathered together, and Him led up to their council saying,

67 If You, You are the Christ, You must speak to us. And then He Spoke to them, If I should Speak, you might never ever Commit.

68 And if I also earnestly request of, you might never ever answer Me, or you might dismiss Me away.

69 Away from now, the Son of Man shall sit at the Right Hand of the Miracle Power of God. (Ps 110:1)

70 Then all spoke, You, Are You therefore, the Son of God? And then He Stated to them, Yourselves are Saying that, I AM.

71 And they spoke, What further need have we of His Testimony? Because we have heard from His Own Mouth.

Before Pilate and Herod

23 And all the multitude of different ones having arose, lead Him to Pilate.

2 And they began to accuse Him saying, We found Him perverting the nation, and forbidding to be giving tribute to Caesar, saying, Christ Himself is being King.

3 And then Pilate questioned Him saying, You, Are You King of the Jews? And He Answered him Stating, You Are Saying.

4 Then Pilate spoke to the chief priests and the multitudes of people. I am finding no cause with this man.

5 And then they were more insistent saying, that He is agitating the people, teaching against all of Judaea, beginning from Galilee, up to here.

6 When Pilate heard Galilee, He questioned if the man is Galilaean.

7 And fully knowing that He is from the authority of Herod, sent Him again to Herod who also was being in Jerusalem in those days.

8 And when Herod discerned Jesus, he was extremely glad because he was strongly desiring to be content to spiritually discern Him, through hearing very much about Him, and expected to discern some Miracle Sign occurring by Him.

9 Then he questioned Him, in spiritual words sufficiently himself, but then He Answered to him nothing.

10 And the chief priests and the scribes had stood, and strongly accused Him.

11 And Herod, with his armies, despised and mocked Him, clothed Him in bright apparel, sent Him again to Pilate.

12 And in this same day, both Pilate and Herod became friends with one another, because being before some hatred was between them.

Taken Back to Pontius Pilate

13 And then Pilate called together the chief priests, and the rulers, and the people.

14 He spoke to them. You have offered This Man to me as turning away the people, and you must behold, I having examined for judgment in the presence of you, I found no cause in This Man which you are accusing against Him.

15 But definitely neither Herod, because I sent yourselves again to him, and you must behold, nothing worthy of death is practiced by Him.

16 Therefore, having disciplined Him, I will set at liberty.

17 For then having necessity to set at liberty one to them at the Feast,

18 They then cried loudly all at once calling, You must take away Him, and then you must set at liberty to us Barabbas,

19 Who was cast into prison, because of a certain dissension and murder, occurring in the city.

20 Pilate, therefore, again called out, strongly desiring to set Jesus at liberty.

21 But they were shouting, saying, You must crucify. You must crucify Him.

22 And then, He spoke a third time to them, Because what evil work did He? I have found no cause of death in Him. Therefore, I disciplined, I will set Him at liberty.

23 Then they were pressing upon a great voice asking to crucify Him, and the

voices of them, and also the chief priests triumphed.

Delivered Jesus to be Crucified

24 And Pilate gave sentence, the requests of them, to come to pass.

25 And then he dismissed away to them, whom they asked, who because of dissension and murder was cast into prison. And Jesus was delivered up in betrayal, to the will of them.

Crucifixion

26 And as they led Him away, they took hold of one Simon, a Cyrenian, coming from a field. They laid on him the cross, bringing behind Jesus.

27 And then followed Him a large multitude of different people, and woman so also bewailing and lamenting Him.

28 But Jesus Turned to them, Spoke, Oh daughters of Jerusalem you must not weep for Me, but you must weep for yourselves, and for your children.

29 For you must behold, days are coming in which they will Spirit Say, Spiritually Blessed are the barren, and the wombs that definitely not have born, and the breasts that have not nursed.

30 Then will they begin to say to the mountains, you must fall down upon us, and the hills, you must cover us.

31 For if they are doing these things in the sap filled tree, what might occur in the dried up wooden item?

32 And also two other ones of a different kind criminals, who intentionally kill, were led with Him.

33 And when they went to the place called Skull (Golgatha), there they crucified Him and the criminals, actually one by the Right Side, and another by the Left.

34 Then Jesus was Saying, Father, Remove from Memory (forgive) them because they definitely are not Spiritually Discerning what they are doing. And they divided His clothes by casted lot.

35 And the people stood seeing with perception. And the rulers united with them also derided, saying others of the same kind He Saved, He must Save Himself if He is the Christ, the Elect of God.

36 And then also the soldiers were mocking Him, and coming near, offering vinegar to Him.

37 And saying If You, You are the King of the Jews, You must Save Yourself.

38 And also a superscription was then written over Him writings in Greek language, and in Latin, and in Hebrew: He is the KING OF THE JEWS!

39 And one of those criminals hanging, blasphemed Him saying, If You, You are the Christ, You must Save Yourself and us.

40 But the other one of a different kind answered rebuked him saying, Are you not Fearing God, for you are in the same Judgment?

41 And we indeed are Fully Receiving Righteously worthy, because of whatever we practiced, but He has Practiced no wrong.

42 And he said to Jesus, Yourself must remember me, Oh Lord, when You should come in Your Kingdom Rule.

43 And Jesus Spoke to him, Truly, I am Saying to you, This day you shall be with Me in Paradise.

44 And it was about the sixth hour, and darkness occurred over the whole earth, until after the ninth hour.

45 And the sun was darkened, and the Veil of the Temple Sanctuary was split in the middle.

46 After Jesus Called for in a Great Voice, He Spoke, Father, into Your Hands I Put Forth My Spirit. And having Spoken these things, He Forcefully Exhaled the Holy Spirit.

Guard declares Truly He was Righteous

47 Now when the centurion Spiritually Discerned what occurred, he Attributed Glory, saying, This in fact was a Righteous Man.

48 All the multitudes of people were standing together at this spectacle. Seeing with perception what occurred, they struck their chests themselves, and returned.

49 And all His acquaintances, and the women having followed together with Him from Galilee had stood at a distance, beholding attentively these things.

Joseph sought Jesus' Body

50 And behold, there a man named Joseph, a counselor; existing a God-Good man, and Righteous.

51 The same from Arimathaea, a city of the Jews, he is definitely not now agreeable to the counsel and their deed, who also was looking himself for the Kingdom Rule of God.

52 This man came near to Pilate, asking the Body of Jesus.

53 And he took it down, he wrapped it in linen cloth, and positioned it in a place of the dead hewn in stone, where definitely none were never yet laid.

54 And that day was Preparation Day, and the Sabbath began to dawn.

55 And the women following behind also, who were now coming together with Him from Galilee, saw the sepulcher, then as having laid His Body,

56 They returned, and prepared spices and ointments, and indeed remained quiet on the Sabbath, according to the Commandment.

Resurrection on the first day of the week

24 Now upon the first day of the week, very early in the morning, they and also others with them coming to the place of the dead, bringing those spices they prepared.

2 And they found the stone moved back away from the sepulcher.

3 And they entered to find definitely no Body of the Lord Jesus.

4 And it came to pass, they were made puzzled among themselves about this, and Behold, two Men being present with them in Glowing Angel Garments.

5 And becoming afraid of them, they then were lowering down their faces to the earth. They Spoke to them, Why are you seeking the Living among the dead?

6 He is definitely not here, but definitely is Risen Up. Yourself must remember, as He Uttered while yet being among you in Galilee.

7 Saying, The Son of Man must be delivered up in betrayal into the hands of sinful men, and be crucified, and after the third day to Arise.

8 And they themselves remembered His Specific Words.

Disciples thought it was idle gossip

9 And returned from the sepulcher to tell all these things above all to the eleven, and to all the others.

10 Then were Mary Magdalene, and Joanna, and Mary of James, and others with them that were saying to the Apostles these things.

11 And their words appeared in the presence of them like as idle gossip, and they also were not committing to them.

12 Then Peter raised up, and ran to the sepulcher, and stooped down to Spiritually See the linen clothes laying alone, and went marveling to himself what was now occurring.

Jesus on the road to Emmaus

13 And, you must behold, two of them were going within that Day to a village named Emmaus, that has already sixty furlongs away from Jerusalem.

14 And they talked together to themselves about all these things happening.

15 And it occurred, when they were talking to themselves and discussing, that He, Jesus, Approached Near going together with them.

16 But their eyes were not retaining to Fully Know Him.

17 And then He Spoke to them, What words these, which you are exchanging with one to another? And you are walking sad in countenance?

18 And then answered one whose name Cleopas, he spoke to Him, Traveler, are you alone inside of Jerusalem, and have definitely not known what occurred with Him in these days?

19 And He spoke to them, What? And they spoke to Him, Concerning Jesus of Nazareth, who was a Man, a Prophet exceedingly able in Work by God and the Spiritual Word Before the Sight of God, and all the people.

20 So that both the chief priests and also our rulers delivered Him up into judgment of death, and crucified Him.

21 But we were expecting that He is the Expected to Remove Israel. But definitely, yet with all these things this third day, since this Day is moving along when these things have occurred.

22 But definitely, also certain women of us, astonished us, becoming in an early hour to His sepulcher.

23 And when they had not found His Body, they came saying that they had Beheld Attentively a Visitation of an Angel and Saying that He is Living.

24 And certain with us went to the sepulcher, and found in such a manner just as also the women spoke of Him. They were then definitely not Spiritually Seeing.

25 Then He Spoke to them, Oh uncomprehending and slow in heart to Commit to all that the Prophets Uttered.

26 Ought definitely not Christ have suffered these things, and Entered into His Glory?

27 And beginning at Moses, and from all the Prophets, He was interpreting to them, in all the Scriptures, those about Himself.

28 And they approached near to the village where they were going, and He went as though going far further.

29 But they constrained Him saying, You must continue with us, for it is within the evening hour, and the day is lowering down. He Entered and Abode with them.

30 And it came to pass, He was made Sitting to eat with them. He took the Bread, Blessed, Broke, and was handing it to them.

31 Then their Eyes were made Opened in Newness of Spirit, and they Fully Knew Him, but He being Vanished away from them.

32 And they spoke one to another. Were definitely not our heart burning within us, in the way of travel with us, as He was Uttering with us, and as He Opened in Newness of Spirit the Scriptures to us?

33 They arose that same hour, returned into Jerusalem, and found the eleven now made united together, and then united with them.

34 Saying now the Lord has been made Risen Up, and in fact has made Simon see the Spiritual Appearance.

35 And they were imparting how in the way of travel as He was now made known to them in the Breaking of the Bread.

Gave Understanding of the Scriptures

36 And as they were uttering these things to them, Jesus Stood in midst of them and Said to them, Peace to you.

37 But they were made terrified, and becoming afraid thinking they were seeing a Spirit.

38 And He Spoke to them, Why are you troubled, and why then are doubts ascending in your hearts?

39 Behold, My Hands and My Feet, for Myself, I AM. You must handle Me. You must Spiritually Discern, for a Spirit has definitely not (Sinless) Flesh Nature and Bones, just as you see Me have.

40 And when He Spoke this, He showed as an example to them, His Hands and His Feet.

41 And still being Uncommitted themselves for the Joy and marveling, He Spoke to them. Have you any eatable meat in this place?

42 So they handed Him a part of broiled fish, and also of a honeycomb comb.

43 He Took and Ate in the presence of them.

44 And then He Spoke to them. These Spiritual Words that I Uttered to you, while I was yet with you, that all things must be Fulfilled, which is now made Written in the Law of Moses, and in Prophets, and in Psalms concerning Me.

45 Then their mind, He Opened in Newness of Spirit, to be Understanding the Scriptures.

The Great Commission

46 And Spoke to them, It is now made Written in such a manner, and in same manner must the Christ suffer, and Arise Out from the Dead, after the third day.

47 And to preach in His Name, Repentance and Removal of sin natures and sins to all nations, beginning from Jerusalem.

48 And you, yourselves, are Witnesses of these things.

Promise of Holy Spirit Coming

49 And, Behold, I am Sending Out the Promise of My Father to you yourselves, but you must sit down in the city of Jerusalem, where until after you should put on the Miracle Power from on High.

Jesus was Carried Up to Heaven

50 And He Lead Out them, outside already up to Bethany, and He Lifted Up His hands, Blessing them.

51 And it came to pass, while Blessing them, He had parted away from them, and was being borne up into Heaven.

52 And they worshiped Him, returning to Jerusalem with great Joy.

53 And were all unceasingly in the Temple area Praising and Blessing God. Amen.

The Gospel According to

John

In Beginning the Word was God

1 In the Beginning was the Word, and the Word was with God, and the Word was God.

2 The Same was in the Beginning with God.

3 All things were Made by Him, and without Him not one thing was Made.

4 In Him was Life, and the Life was the Light of men.

5 And the Light is Shining in the dark, and definitely the dark Apprehended it not.

Light to Bear Witness to Commit

6 It came to pass, a man was Sent Out From God, whose name, John.

7 He Came for a Testimony in order that he should Bear Record to the Light, that everyone through Him should Commit by their choice.

8 He was definitely not that Light, but definitely that he should Give Witness to the Light,

9 That was the True Light, Who Gives Light to every man coming into the satan's world. (Eph 5:13-14)

10 He was in satan's world, and satan's world was Made by Him. and the satan's world Knew Him definitely not.

The Only Begotten Risen Christ

11 He came to His own, and for the Purpose and Result of His own. By their choice, they definitely each Received Him not.

12 But as many as Received Him to them He Gave Authority to Become Children of God, to them that are continuously by their choice Committing for the Purpose and Result of His Name. (Lord Jesus Christ, Phil 2:9-11)

13 Who was Made Born, definitely not out from blood, neither out from will of sinful flesh nature, neither out from will of man, but definitely Made Born Out From God.

14 And the Word was made (Sinless) Flesh Nature, and Dwelled among us, and we saw His Glory, the Glory as from the Only Begotten Risen Christ of the Father, Full of Grace and Truth.

John Bare Witness of Him

15 John is Bearing Record to Him, and cried out saying, This was He of Whom I spoke. He is Coming after me. He being Before me, Who was Earlier than me,

16 And out from the Fullness of Him, we all have Received, and Grace for Grace, [Grace (God's Method) is Christ Within you (Faith, God's Means; Heb 11:1, Col 1:27), through your Obedience, Doing what you cannot Do.]

17 For the Law was made given through Moses. The Grace and the Truth came through Jesus Christ.

18 No man has Beheld Attentively God at any time. The Only Begotten Risen Christ Son, Who is in the bosom of the Father, He Imparted Him.

19 And this is the Testimony of John, when the Jews sent out priests and Levites, out from Jerusalem, to earnestly request of Him, Who are You?

20 And He confessed, and disclaimed not, but confessed that I am definitely not the Christ.

21 And they earnestly requested of him, Therefore, who? Are you Elias? And he said, I am definitely not. Are you that Prophet? And he answered, definitely not.

22 Therefore, they spoke to him, Who are you that we may give an answer to them that sent us? What do you say concerning yourself?

23 He stated, I, a voice loudly Pleading in the desolate wilderness. Make Straight The Way of Travel of the Lord, just as Esaias the Prophet spoke. (Isa 40:3)

24 And they which were made sent out were of the Pharisees,

25 And they earnestly requested of him, and spoke to him. Why, therefore, do you baptize, if you are definitely not the Christ, neither Elias, nor the Prophet?

26 John answered them, saying, I immerse in water, but now is Standing in the midst of you, Whom yourselves are definitely not now Spiritually Discerning.

27 He it is, Who coming after me, is now being before me, Whose leather shoestrings of His shoes, that I should definitely not be worthy to remove.

28 These things occurred in Bethabara, other side of the Jordon, whereto John was immersing.

29 The next day John is Spiritually Seeing Jesus coming to him, and says, Behold, the Sacrificial Lamb of God, Who is taking away the sin nature and sin of the satan's world.

30 This is He about Whom I spoke. After me is Coming a Man, Who is now occurring Before me, for He was being Earliest to me.

31 Also, I definitely had not Spiritually Discerned Him, but definitely that He should be made Manifest to Israel. Because of this, I have come with immersing in water.

32 But John gave witness, Saying, That I was now Seeing the Spirit Come Down like as a dove from Heaven, and Abode upon Him.

33 Also definitely, I had not Spiritually

Discerned Him, but definitely He that Sent me to immerse in water, the Same Spoke to me. Upon Whom Whoever you should Spiritually Discern the Spirit Coming Down and Abides upon Him, He it is Who is Immersing in the Holy Spirit.

34 Also, I Beheld Attentively, and Bore Record that He is the Son of God.

Andrew and Peter Followed Him

35 Again, the next day, John had stood then with two of his disciples,

36 And Looking upon Jesus Walking was saying, Behold the Sacrificial Lamb of God.

37 And the two disciples heard him Uttering, and followed Jesus.

38 Then Jesus turned and Saw them following. He Said to them, Who are you seeking? And they spoke to Him, Oh Rabbi, saying by interpretation, Oh Master, wherein are You abiding?

39 He Said to them, You must come and you must Discern. They came and Discerned wherein He was abiding, and continued with Him that same day, as it was then the tenth hour.

40 One of the two, who heard John and followed Him, was Andrew, the brother of Simon Peter.

41 He first found his own brother Simon, and said, I have now found the Messiah, Who is being interpreted the Christ.

42 And he lead him to Jesus, and when Jesus Looked upon him, Jesus Spoke. You are Simon, the son of Jonas. You, You shall be called Cephas, by interpretation, Peter.

43 The next day Jesus would depart to Galilee, but finding Philip, then Said to him, You must follow Me.

Philip and Nathanael Followed Him

44 Now Philip was of Bethsaida, the city of Andrew and Peter.

45 Philip found Nathanael and said to him, We are now Finding Jesus, the son of Joseph from Nazareth, Whom Moses Wrote in the Law and the Prophets.

46 And Nathanael spoke to him, Can anything out from Nazareth be God-Good? Philip said to him, You must come and you must Discern.

47 Jesus Discerned Nathanael coming to Him, and Said to him, Behold, an Israelite of Truth, in whom is definitely no subtle half-truth (deceit).

48 Nathanael said to Him, From where are You Knowing me? Jesus Answered, and Spoke to him. Before Philip called for you, I Discerned you were under the fig tree.

49 Nathanael answered, and said to Him, Oh Rabbi, You, You are the Son of God. You, You are King of Israel.

50 Jesus Answered, and Spoke to him. Before I Spoke to you, I Discerned you under the fig tree. Be Committing, you shall see the Spiritual Appearance of greater than these.

51 And He Said to him. Truly, Truly, I am Saying to you, from now you shall See the Spiritual Appearance of Heaven, now being made Opened, and Angels of God Ascending and Coming Down upon the Son of Man. (Gen 28:12)

Cana Wedding

2 And the third day became a wedding in Cana of Galilee, and the mother of Jesus was there.

2 And there also, Jesus was called, and His Disciples to the wedding.

3 And when they lacked wine, the mother of Jesus said to Him, They have definitely no wine.

4 Jesus Said to her. Oh woman, why to Me for you? My Hour is not yet now come.

Beginning of Miracles in Cana

5 His mother said to those servants. Anything, whatever, He might Say to you, you must do.

6 And there were setting six stone carved water pots after the purification

of the Jews, accommodating two or three firkins each.

7   Jesus Said to them, You must make the water pots full of water, and they made them full up to the brim.

8   Then He Said to them, You must draw now and you must bring to the ruler of the feast, and they brought.

9   And as the ruler of the feast tasted the water now Made Wine, and he had definitely not discerned from where it is, but the servants had discerned drawing the water. The ruler of the feast called for the bridegroom.

10 And he said to him, Every man first of all sets out the God-Work wine, and when they might be made drunk, then the younger aged. You until after are keeping the God-Work wine up to for now.

11 This, the beginning of Miracle Signs Jesus Did in Cana of Galilee, and Manifest His Glory, and His disciples Committed, for the Purpose and Result of Him.

12 After this, He came down to Capernaum, He, and His mother, and His brothers, and His Disciples, and they continued there definitely not many days.

Cleanses the Temple

13 And the Jew's Passover was near, and Jesus ascended into Jerusalem.

14 And found in the Temple area those selling oxen, and sheep, and doves, and the changers of money sitting.

15 And He made a whip from ropes. He Cast Out all from the Temple area, and also the sheep, and the oxen, and Poured Out the money changers' collection, and He Overturned the tables.

16 And Spoke to them that were selling doves. You must Take Away these things from here. You must not make My Father's Home a home of trade.

17 And His Disciples themselves remembered that it is now made Written, the God-Good Zeal for Your Home has devoured Me. (Ps 69:9)

Jews ask for a Sign

18 Then, the Jews answered and spoke to Him, what miracle sign are you showing us, that you do these things?

19 Jesus Answered and Spoke to them. You Must Remove this Temple, and in three days I will Raise It Up.

20 Therefore, the Jews spoke, In forty and six years they have made built this Temple, and You shall Raise It Up in three days?

21 But then, He was Saying, in regard to the Temple of His Body.

22 When, therefore, He has Risen Up out from the Dead, His Disciples themselves remembered why this was said to them, and they Committed to the Scripture, and the Spiritual Communication which Jesus Spoke.

23 And as He was in Jerusalem with the Passover, within the Feast many Committed to His Name, seeing with perception His Miracle Signs that He was Doing.

24 But Jesus Himself was definitely not Committing Himself to them, because He Knew everyone.

25 So also then He was having definitely no need that anybody should witness about man, because He was Knowing what was in man.

You Must be Born from Above

3 There was a man of the Pharisees, named Nicodemus. He was a ruler of the Jews.

2   He came to Jesus by night, and spoke to Him, Oh Rabbi, we are Spiritually Discerning that You, a Teacher, is now Coming from God, because no man is able to do these Miracle Signs that You Do, unless God should Be with Him.

3   Jesus Answered and Spoke to him. Truly, Truly, I Say to you, that except anyone should be Made Born from Above, he is definitely not able to Spiritually Discern the Kingdom Rule of God.

4   Nicodemus says to Him, How can an aged man be born? Is he never able to enter

a second time into his mother's womb, and be born?

5   Jesus Answered, Truly, Truly, I Say to you, That except anyone should have been Made Born out from water and of Spirit, he is definitely not able to Enter into the Kingdom Rule of God.

6   That which is made born out from the sinful flesh nature is sinful flesh nature, and that being now Made Born Out From the spirit is Spirit.

7   You must marvel not that I Spoke to you, You must be Made Born from Above.

8   The Spirit is blowing whereto He Wills, and you are Hearing the Voice of Him. But definitely, you are definitely not now Spiritually Discerning from Where He is Coming, or wherein He is Going Away. In such a manner is everyone who is now Made Born Out From the Spirit.

9   Nicodemus answered, and spoke to Him, How can these things be?

10 Jesus Answered, and Spoke to him, You, You are a teacher of Israel, and are not definitely knowing these things?

11 Truly, Truly, I am Saying to you, We are Uttering what We are now Spiritually Discerning. And then We Behold Attentively, We are Bearing Record, and you are definitely not Receiving Our Testimony.

12 If I have Spoken earthly things to you, and you are definitely not Committing (putting yourself under the guidance and orders of another), how, if I should have Spoken to you Heavenly Things, shall you Commit?

13 For no man is now Ascending into Heaven, except He having Come Down out From Heaven, the Son of Man Who was Inside Heaven.

14 And just as Moses elevated up the serpent in the desolate wilderness, in such a manner must the Son of Man be Elevated Up.

15 That whoever is continuously by his choice Committing for Result and Purpose of Him, should not be destroyed, but definitely should have Life Eternal.

For God Loved in such a manner

16 Because, God has Loved in such a manner the satan's world, so that He Gave His Son, the Only Begotten Risen Christ, in order that whoever is Continuously by his choice Committing for the Result and Purpose of Him, should not perish, but definitely should, by his choice, be Continuously Having Eternal Life. [Committing means putting your entire being under the orders of another.]

17 Because God definitely Sent not out His Son into the satan's world that He should Judge the satan's world, but definitely that the satan's world through Him should be Made Saved.

18 He that is by his choice Continuously Committing to Him is definitely not Judged, and he not Committing is now Made Judged already, because he is not now by his choice Committing to the Name of the Only Begotten Risen Christ, the Son of God.

19 And this is the Final Judgment, for the Light is Now Come into the satan's world, and men loved by their choice the darkness much more than the Light, because their man works were evil.

20 Because everyone who practices foul evil is hating the Light, also definitely not coming to the Light, that his man works might not be made exposed as sin.

21 But he that is Doing the Truth is Coming to the Light in order that his Work by God might be Manifest because it is by God Working.

Apostles Baptized in Jordon

22 After these things, Jesus and His Disciples came into the area of Judaea, and there He was staying with them, and was immersing.

23 And John was also immersing in Aenon near to Salim, for there was very much water there, and they were coming up and were being made immersed,

24 Because John was not yet now being made cast into prison.

John Teaches about Jesus

25 Then became a questioning about purification from John's disciples with the Jews.

26 And they came to John, and spoke to him, Rabbi, He that was with you on the other side of Jordan, to whom you are now Bearing Record, behold, He is immersing and everyone is coming to Him.

27 John answered and spoke, A man is definitely not able to receive anything, except it should be now made Given to Him from Heaven.

28 You yourselves are witness to me that I spoke, I am definitely not the Christ, but definitely that I am now being made Sent Out before Him.

29 He that is having the Bride is the Bridegroom, but the friend of the Bridegroom is now Standing and Hearing Him, he must be Rejoicing with Joy, because of the Voice of this Bridegroom. Then this, my Joy, is now Made Fulfilled.

30 Then He must Increase, but I am made decreasing.

31 He that is coming from Above is Over All. He that is out from the earth is of the earth, and utters of the earth, and He that is Coming Out from Heaven is Over All.

32 And what He is now Beholding Attentively and Heard, to This He is giving Witness, and none is Receiving His Testimony.

33 He that has Received His Testimony has Sealed that God is True,

34 Because, Whom God has Sent Out is Uttering the Words of God, because God definitely Gives not the Spirit by an Amount of Measure (to Him).

35 The Father is Loving the Son, and All Things are now Given in His Hand.

36 He that is Continuously by his choice Committing for the Purpose and Result of the Son, is Continuously having by his choice Life Eternal. But instead being continuously disobeying by his choice to the Son, he shall definitely not Spiritually See Life, but definitely the Wrath for Justice of God is definitely continuing by his choice upon himself.

Apostles Baptize more than John

4 As, therefore, the Lord knew that the Pharisees heard, that Jesus is immersing now many more Disciples than John.

2 And though Jesus Himself definitely was not immersing, but definitely His Disciples.

Jacob's well and the Samaria women

3 He parted from Judaea, and went again into Galilee.

4 Then He must be passing through Samaria.

5 Then coming to a city of Samaria called Sychar, a neighbor of a space of land Jacob gave to Joseph, his son,

6 Now Jacob's well was there. Jesus, therefore, is now being labored from the travel. So He was sitting Himself at the well. It was about the sixth hour.

7 A woman of Samaria came to draw water. Jesus Said to her, You must Give Me to drink,

8 For His disciples had gone into that city to buy nourishment.

9 Then the woman said to Him, How is it you, a Jew, are asking from me, a Samaritan woman, to drink, because Jews are definitely not dealing with Samaritans?

10 Jesus Answered and Spoke to her, If you had Spiritually Discerned the God-Gift of God, and Who it is that is Saying to you, You must Give Me to drink, that whatever you asked Him, He would have Given you Living Water.

11 The woman said to Him, Sir, You neither are having means of drawing, and the deep well is deep. From what, therefore, are You having Living Water?

12 Are You, You not greater than our father Jacob who gave us this deep well, and he himself drank from it, and his sons and his cattle?

13 Jesus Answered and Spoke to her,

Whoever drinks from this water shall thirst again.

14 But whoever should Continuously Drink of the Water, that I Shall Give to him, should never ever thirst in this Age. But definitely, the Water that I Shall Give to him, shall become in him a Fountain of Water Springing High into Life Eternal.

15 The woman says to Him, Oh Sir, You must give me this Water that I should thirst not, neither should I be coming to this place to draw.

16 Jesus Says to her. You must be going away. You must call for your husband. Then you must come to this place.

17 The woman answered and spoke, I have definitely no husband. Jesus Said to her, You Spoke God-Working that you have definitely no husband,

18 Because you had five husbands, and now whom you are having is definitely not your husband. This you are now spirit saying True.

19 The woman says to Him, Sir, I perceive that You, You are a Prophet.

20 Our fathers worshiped in this mountain, but yourselves say, that in Jerusalem is whereto the place one must worship.

21 Jesus Said to her, Oh woman, you must Commit to Me, since an hour is coming when neither in this mountain, nor in Jerusalem shall you worship the Father.

22 Yourselves worship what you are definitely not now discerning. We are Spiritually Discerning Whom we Worship, because Salvation is out from the Jews.

23 But definitely the hour is Coming, and Now Is, when the True Worshipers shall Continuously Worship the Father in Spirit and in Truth, and because the Father is seeking such to Worship Him.

God is a Spirit, I AM

24 God, a Spirit, and they Worshiping Him must Continuously Worship in the Spirit, and in Truth. (Ex 3:14-15)

25 The woman says to Him, I spiritually discern that Messiah is coming, Who is called Christ. When He should come, He shall declare all things to us.

26 Jesus Says to her, I AM, Who Utters to you.

27 And at this came His disciples, and they marveled that He was Uttering with the woman. However, none spoke, What are you seeking, or why are You Uttering with her?

28 Therefore, the woman dismissed her water pot and went into the city, and said to the men,

29 Come now, spiritually discern a Man Who spoke to me everything, as much as I did. Is He possibly the Christ?

30 Then they departed from the city, and came to Him.

31 And in between, the disciples were earnestly requesting of Him saying, Oh Rabbi, You must eat.

32 But He Spoke to them, I have Meat to Eat, that yourselves are definitely not Spiritually Discerning.

33 Therefore, the disciples said to one another, Has not any man brought to Him to eat?

34 Jesus Said to them, My Food is that I should be doing the Will of Him that Sent Me, and I should Make Perfect His Work by God.

35 Are definitely are not yourselves saying, Is yet about four months, and then comes the harvest? Behold, I Say to you, you must Lift Up your eyes and you must See the lands that are already White to Harvest.

36 But he that is Reaping receives a Reward, and gathers together Fruit to Life Eternal, that also He Sowing, and he Reaping should be Rejoicing Together.

37 Because upon this the Spiritual Word is True, for another of Same Kind is Sowing, and the another of Same Kind is Reaping.

38 I Sent Out yourselves to Continuously Reap where yourselves are definitely not

now laboring. Others of Same Kind are now laboring also. Yourselves are now entering into their labor.

39 And, out from the same city, many of the Samaritans Committed to Him, because the Spiritual Word of the woman, that gave Witness, He Spoke to me all things, as much as I did.

40 Therefore, as the Samaritans came to Him, they earnestly requested of Him to continue with them, and He continued there two days.

41 And many more Committed because of His Spiritual Communication.

42 And also were saying to the woman, that we are Committing ourselves, no more because of your speech; because we are now Hearing, and Spiritually Discerning that He is Of Truth the Christ, the Savior of the satan's world.

To Cana of Galilee a nobleman

43 Then after two days He departed from that place, and went into Galilee,

44 Yet Jesus Himself Bear Record that a Prophet is definitely having no honor in his own country.

45 Therefore, when He came into Galilee, the Galilaeans received Him, having also beheld attentively all things which He did in Jerusalem in the Feast because also they came to the Feast.

46 So Jesus came again into Cana of Galilee, whereto He turned water to wine, and there was a certain nobleman whose son was sick in Capernaum.

47 When he heard Jesus is now coming out from Judaea into Galilee, he went to Him and earnestly requested of him that He come down and should cure his son, because he was expecting to die.

48 Then Jesus Spoke to him, Except you should discern Miracle Signs and Wonders, you may never ever Commit.

49 The nobleman said to Him, Oh Lord, You must come down before my little child dies.

50 Jesus Says to him, You must go, your son is living. And the man Committed to the Spiritual Words which Jesus Spoke to him, so he went.

51 And already as he is coming down, his slaves met and told him, saying that your dependent son is living.

52 Therefore, he inquired from them in what hour when he had been amended and the fever parted from him. They spoke to him that yesterday at the seventh hour.

53 Therefore, the father knew that in the same hour that Jesus Spoke to him, Your son is Living, so he Committed himself and his whole house.

54 Again coming out from Judaea into Galilee, this the second Miracle Sign Jesus did. (John 2:5-8)

Pool of Bethesda

5 After these things was a Feast of the Jews, and Jesus ascended into Jerusalem.

2 Now there is in Jerusalem a pool having five porches by the sheep market designating in Hebrew script, Bethesda.

3 In them lay sick, a large multitude of different sick, blind, crippled, withered, waiting for the moving of the water.

4 For an Angel was coming down at a Special Time into the pool and Troubled the water. As soon as the first, whoever holding illness took the first step, after the disturbance of the water, was made Healthy.

5 And a certain man was there, while having some infirmity thirty and eight years.

6 Jesus Spiritually Discerned him, and also He Knew that already he was having a long time lying. He Said to him, Would you become healthy?

7 He being sick Answered to Him, Lord, I have definitely not a man, that when the water might have been made Troubled, might cast me into the pool, but, then while I am coming another of the same kind

comes down before me.

8   Jesus Says to him, You must for your-self Raise Up, you must by your choice Take Up your mattress, and you must by your choice Walk.

9   And immediately, the man became Healthy, and Took up his mattress, and was Walking, but that same day was of the Sabbath.

10   Therefore, the Jews said to him being now made Healed, It is definitely not law-ful for you to take up the mattress on the Sabbath.

11   He answered to them, The Same who Made me Healthy Spoke to me, You must Take Up by your choice your mattress and you must by your choice Walk.

12   Therefore, they earnestly requested of him, Who is the man that spoke to you, You must take up your mattress and you must walk?

13   He that was Made Whole, had defi-nitely not discerned Whom He is, because Jesus conveyed Himself Away. A multitude of people were in that place.

14   After these things, Jesus found him in the Temple area, and Spoke to him. Behold, you are now become Healthy. You must not any longer sin, that no worse thing might occur to you.

15   The man went and declared to the Jews, that Jesus is Who made him healthy.

16   And because of this, the Jews persecut-ed Jesus, and were seeking to kill Him, for these things He was doing in the Sabbath.

Jews heard God was His Father

17   But yet, Jesus Answered them, My Father is Working for now, also I am Working.

18   Therefore, because of this the Jews were seeking much more to kill Him, for He definitely not only was removing the Sabbath, but definitely also Saying, His Own Father was God, making Himself Equal to God.

19   Therefore, Jesus Answered, and Spoke to them. Truly, Truly, I am Saying to you, the Son is definitely not able to be Final-izing anything from Himself, except what He should be Spiritually Seeing whatever the Father is Finalizing by His choice, be-cause whatever these things also the Son likewise is Finalizing by His choice.

20   Because the Father is Affectionately God-Loving to the Son, and is Showing Him all things that He is Finalizing, and He shall Show to Him Greater Works by God than these, that yourselves should be marveling.

21   Because as the Father is Raising Up the dead, and Offering Spiritual Life, also so the Son is Offering Spiritual Life, to whom by His choice is strongly desiring.

All Judgment Given to the Son

22   Because as the Father Judges none, but definitely, He is now Giving all Final Judg-ment to His Son.

23   That everyone should be Honoring the Son, just as they are Honoring the Father. He that is not Honoring the Son, is defi-nitely not Honoring the Father that Sent Him.

24   Truly, Truly, I Say to you, He that is Continuously Hearing My Word, and is Continuously Committing to Him that is Sending Me, is Continuously Having Life Eternal, and is not Continuously Coming into Final Judgment, but definitely, is now Continuously Departing out from death, into Eternal Life.

25   Truly, Truly, I am Saying to you, that an hour is Coming, and Now Is, when the dead shall be Hearing the Voice of the Son of God, and they that have Heard shall Live.

26   As, because the Father is Having Life in Himself in such a manner, He Gave also to the Son, to be Having Life in Himself.

27   And has Given Authority to Him to Execute also Final Judgment, since He is the Son of Man.

Kind of Works Determines your future

28 You must marvel not at this, for the hour is Coming, in which all those in the graves shall Hear His Voice.

29 And shall go out, they that have Done God-Goods, into the Resurrection of Life, and then they that were practicing foul evil, into Resurrection of Final Judgment.

30 I can definitely not of Myself do anything. Just as I am Hearing I am Judging, and My Final Judgment is Righteous, for I definitely Seek Not My Will, but definitely the Will Of The Father Who Sent Me.

31 If I should give witness to Myself, My Testimony is definitely not True.

32 There is Another of the Same Kind giving witness of Me, and I Discern that the Testimony that He is Bearing Record about Me, is True.

33 Yourselves sent out to John, and he has Given Witness to the Truth.

34 But I Receive definitely not testimony from men, but definitely, I am Saying these things that yourselves might be made Saved.

35 He was the Spiritual Lamp made Burning and Shining. And yourselves have willed in the Light of him to be exceedingly rejoicing for a short time.

Father Sent Jesus Who Bears Record

36 But I have a greater Testimony than John, because of those Works by God that the Father Gave to Me that I should Fulfill them, His Work by God that I am Finalizing, Bearing Record of Me because the Father is Sending Out Me.

37 And the Father Himself Sent Me, to now be Giving Witness about Me. You are neither Hearing His Voice at any time, nor Beholding Attentively His Appearance.

38 And you definitely are not having His Word Continuing in you, because those yourselves are definitely not Committing to the One Whom He Sent Out.

39 Search the Scriptures, for in them you think yourselves among those Having Eternal Life, but they are They which are Continuously Bearing Record of Me.

40 But you will definitely not Come to Me that you might have Life.

41 I Receive definitely not Glory (Spiritual Perfection) from men.

42 But definitely, I am now Knowing you, that you are definitely not Having the God-Love of God inside yourselves.

43 I am now Coming in the Name of My Father, and you are definitely not Receiving Me. If another of the same kind might come in one's own name, you shall receive him.

44 How are yourselves able to Commit, continuously receiving glory from one to another, and definitely not be Continuously Seeking Glory from God Alone?

45 You must not think that I will accuse you to the Father. There is Moses accusing you, in whom yourselves expect.

46 Because if you were Committing to Moses, you whoever, were Committing to Me because he Wrote of Me.

47 But if you are definitely not Committing to his Writings, how shall you Commit to My Words?

Five Thousand Fed with Five Loaves

6 After these things, Jesus went to the other side of the sea of Galilee of Tiberias.

2 And a large multitude of people followed him, for they were beholding attentively His Miracle Signs, which He was doing upon those being sick.

3 And then Jesus went up into a mountain, and there was sitting with His disciples.

4 And the Passover Feast of the Jews was near.

5 As soon as Jesus Lifted Up His eyes, and Saw that a large multitude of people was coming to Him, He Said to Philip, From where shall we buy bread in order that they should eat?

6 And this, He was Saying to try him,

because He Himself Spiritually Discerned, what He was expecting to do.

7 Phillip answered Him, loaves of two hundred pennies, is definitely not sufficient for them, that everyone of them should take a certain little measure.

8 One of the disciples, Andrew, the brother of Simon Peter, said to Him,

9 There is one lad here that is having five barley loaves and two prepared fish, but definitely, what are these things for so many?

10 And Jesus Spoke, Make the men sit down. And there was very much grass in the place to sit down. Then the men numbered about five thousand.

11 And Jesus Took the loaves, and after He Gave Thanks, He Distributed to the disciples, and the disciples To Them sitting as at eating, and Likewise from the prepared fish, As Much As they were desiring.

12 And as they were Made Filled up, He Said to his disciples, You must gather together the fragments Abounding in amount, that not any one might be lost.

13 Therefore, they gathered together twelve hand baskets made full of fragments, that Abounded in amount to those being now feed from the five loaves of barley.

14 As soon as those men Discerned what Miracle Sign Jesus Did, they said, That He is, Of Truth, that Prophet that is coming into the satan's world.

Jesus Walks on high waves of water

15 Therefore, when Jesus recognized they expected to come and catch Him up, in order that they might make Him king. Again He, Himself alone, withdrew into a mountain.

16 And as evening occurred, His disciples came down to the sea.

17 And they boarded into the ship. They were coming to the other side of the sea to Capernaum, and it became already dark, and Jesus had definitely not come with them.

18 And also the sea was made aroused by a great wind blowing.

19 Therefore, as having now rowed twenty or thirty furlongs, they see Jesus Walking upon the sea, and coming to pass near the ship, and so they are afraid.

20 But He Said to them, I AM, You must not be fearing. (Ex 3:14-15)

21 Therefore, they willingly received Him into the ship, and immediately the ship came to the area at the place they were moving.

Labor not for meats that perish

22 The next day, the multitude of people standing on the other side to the sea, discerning that there was definitely no other of the same kind of small boat there, except possibly that same one wherein his disciples boarded, and that Jesus definitely went not with His disciples into the small boat, but definitely His disciples went alone.

23 Then others of same kind small boats came from Tiberias, near the place whereto they had eaten bread and the Lord had Given Thanks.

24 When therefore, the multitude of people discerned that Jesus definitely is not there, nor His disciples, they themselves also boarded into ships, and came into Capernaum seeking Jesus.

25 And finding Him, on the other side of the sea, they spoke to Him. Oh Rabbi, how long a time are you being here?

26 Jesus Answered them and Spoke, Truly, Truly, I Say to you, you are seeking Me, not that you discerned Miracle Signs, but definitely that to eat from the bread, and be filled.

27 You must work not for the meat, which is continuously perishing, but definitely the Meat which is Continuously Continuing into Life Eternal, which the Son of Man shall Give to you, because the Father God has Sealed Him.

This is the Work of God

28 Then they spoke to Him, What should we continuously by our choice be doing in order that we should be Continuously Working the Works by God of our God?

29 Jesus Answered and Spoke to them. This is the Work by God from God that you should by your choice Commit for the Purpose and Result of Whom He has Sent Out.

30 Therefore they spoke to Him, What Miracle Sign then are You doing so that we should discern and should Commit to You? What are You Working?

I am the Bread of Life

31 Our fathers ate Manna in the desolate wilderness, just as is now made Written, He Gave them Bread from Heaven to eat. (Ps 78:24)

32 Therefore, Jesus Spoke to them, Truly, Truly, I Say to you, Moses definitely is not now giving you the Bread from Heaven, but definitely My Father is Continuously by His choice Giving to you the True Bread from Heaven.

33 Because the Bread of God is He Who is Continuously Coming Down from Heaven, and is Continuously Giving Life within the satan's world.

34 Then they spoke to Him, Oh Lord, you must give to us this Bread always.

35 And Jesus Spoke to them, I AM, the Bread of Life, he that is Continuously Coming to Me by his choice should never ever Hunger, and he that is by his choice Continuously Committing for the Purpose of Me, shall definitely not any more at any time Thirst.

36 But definitely I Spoke to you, that you are now beholding Me attentively, but you are not now by your choice Continuously Committing.

37 All whom the Father is Continuously Giving to Me, he shall by his choice Now Come to Me, and he that is Continuously by his choice Coming to Me should never ever by My Choice be cast out outside.

38 For I am now Coming Down out from within Heaven, in order that definitely I should not Do My Will, but definitely the Will of Him that Sent Me.

39 And this is the Will of the Father Who Sent Me, that all whom He is Now Giving to Me by His Choice, I should lose nothing by My Choice of them, but definitely I will Raise him in the Last Day.

40 And this is the Will of Him that Sent Me, that Anyone by his choice Continuously Perceiving the Son, also Continuously by his choice Committing for the Purpose and Result of Him should be Continuously by his choice Having Life Eternal, and I, I will Raise him in the Last Day.

41 Therefore, the Jews were murmuring about Him, for He Spoke, I AM, the Bread, Who Came Down from Heaven.

42 And they were saying, Is definitely not this Jesus, the son of Joseph, whose father and mother we know? How, therefore, is He Saying that, He is now Coming Down from Heaven?

43 Therefore, Jesus Answered, and Spoke to them. You must not murmur among yourselves.

44 No one is Continuously Able by his choice to Come to Me except the Father, Who Sent Me, should by His choice Have him Drawn Out, and I will Raise him in the Last Day. (John 6:40; 12:32)

45 It is now made Written in the Prophets, And they shall all be Taught of God. Everyone, therefore, that has Heard by his choice and has Learned by his choice from the Father is Continuously Coming to Me.

46 Definitely not that any man has Continuously Beheld Attentively the Father, except He Who is from God. He is now Continuously Beholding Attentively the Father.

47 Truly, Truly, I am Saying to you, He that is Continuously Committing for the Purpose and Result of Me, is by his choice Continuously Having Life Eternal.

48 I AM, the Bread of Life.

49 Your fathers ate Manna in the desolate wilderness and died.

50 This is The Bread, Who is Coming Down from Heaven, that a man should Eat of It, and should not die.

51 I AM, the Living Bread, Who, Came Down from Heaven. If anyone should by his choice Eat of this Bread, he shall by his choice Live Forever. And that Bread that I will Give is My (Sinless) Flesh Nature, that I will Give in behalf of the life of the satan's world.

How can we eat His Flesh?

52 Then the Jews quarreled among themselves saying, How can He Give to us His (Sinless) Flesh Nature to eat?

53 Therefore, Jesus Spoke to them, Truly, Truly, I am Saying to you, except you should eat by your choice the (Sinless) Flesh Nature of the Son of Man, and should drink His Blood, you definitely are not having continuously by your choice Life in yourselves.

54 Whoever is Continuously Enjoying Eating (Sinless) Flesh Nature of Me, and is Continuously Drinking the Blood of Me, is definitely having continuously by his choice Life Eternal, and I will Raise him Up in the Last Day.

55 Because My (Sinless) Flesh Nature Of Truth is Meat, and My Blood Of Truth is Drink.

56 He that is Continuously Enjoying Eating (Sinless) Flesh Nature of Me, and is Continuously Drinking Blood of Me, is Continuously Abiding in Me, also I in him.

57 Just as the Living Father Sent Me Out, also I am Living because of the Father, and he that is Enjoying Eating Me, also he shall Live because of Me.

58 This is that Bread Who has Come Down from Heaven, definitely not just as your fathers ate Manna and died. He that is Continuously Enjoying Eating This Bread Continuously by his choice shall Live Forever.

59 These things He Spoke Teaching in the synagogue in Capernaum.

The flesh profits nothing

60 Many, therefore, of His disciples heard. They spoke, This is a hard Word. Who, of ourselves, is able to hear?

61 And then Jesus Spiritually Discerned in Himself that His disciples murmured about this, He Spoke to them, Is this offending you?

62 If ever then, should you See the Son of Man Ascending whereto He First Was?

63 It is the Holy Spirit that Offers Spiritual Life, the sinful flesh nature is definitely not profiting anything. The Specific Words that I Utter to you is Holy Spirit, and is Life Eternal.

64 But definitely, from yourselves there are them who are definitely not Committing, because from the beginning Jesus had Spiritually Discerned who they are that are not Committing, also the certain one who shall be delivering Him up in betrayal.

65 And He was Saying, Because of this, Spirit Says to you, that no man is able to Come to Me, except Given to him from My Father.

Many Disciples leave

66 From this, many of His disciples thereto went back, and were walking no more with Him.

67 Then Spoke Jesus, therefore, to the twelve, And shall not yourselves be going away?

68 Then Simon Peter answered Him. Oh Lord, to whom shall we go? You have the Words of Life Eternal!

69 And we are now by our choice Committing, and are now by our choice Knowing that You, You are the Christ, the Son of the Living God.

70 Jesus Answered them, Definitely have not I Myself Chosen you twelve, and one of you is a devil.

71 For He was Saying this of Judas of Simon Iscariot, because he was expected to deliver Him up in betrayal, being one of the twelve.

Jews sought to kill Him

7 So then, after these things, Jesus walked in Galilee, because He would definitely no more walk in Jewry (Judaea), for the Jews were seeking to kill Him.

2 And now the Jew's Feast of pitched Tabernacles was near.

3 His brothers, therefore, spoke to Him, You must depart from here and you must go away into Judaea, in order that also Your disciples might see Your Works by God that You are Doing,

4 Because, definitely, no man does anything in secret and also he himself is seeking in being boldness, while You must Manifest Yourself through doing these things to the satan's world.

5 Because, neither were His brothers Committing for the Result and Purpose of Him.

6 Then Jesus Says to them, My Special Time is not yet present, but your Special Time is always ready.

7 The satan's world definitely cannot hate you, but Me it hates, because I give Witness about it that the man works of it is continuously evil.

8 You must ascend, yourselves, to this Feast. I will not yet be ascending to this Feast, for My Special Time is not yet now Made Fulfilled.

9 When He Spoke these things to them He continued in Galilee.

10 But as his brothers ascended, then He also ascended Himself into the Feast, definitely not openly, but definitely as in secret.

11 Then, the Jews sought Him in the Feast, and saying, Wherein is He?

12 And there was very much murmuring by the multitudes of people about Him. Indeed, some were saying that He is God-Good, and others of the same kind were saying, definitely not, but definitely He is deceiving the multitude of people.

13 However, none plainly uttered about Him, because of the fear of the Jews.

Jesus at the Feast of Tabernacles

14 Now, already in the very midst of the Feast, Jesus has ascended into the Temple area and was Teaching.

15 And the Jews marveled saying, How is He now discerning letters, never learning?

16 Jesus Answered them, and Spoke, My Teaching is not Mine, but definitely His that Sent Me.

17 If any man should be willing to be continuously by his choice Doing His Will, he shall Know about the Teaching, whether it is out From God, or I am Uttering of Myself.

18 He, that is uttering away from himself, is seeking his own glory, but He that is Seeking His Glory that Sent Him, He is True, and there is definitely no unrighteousness in Him.

19 Is definitely not Moses now giving to you the Law, and yet none of you are by your choice keeping the Law? Why are you seeking to kill Me?

20 The multitude of people answered and spoke. You are having a demon. Who is seeking to kill You?

21 Jesus Answered and Spoke to them. I have done one Work by God, and everyone is marveling.

22 Moses, because of this, is now giving to you circumcision. This is definitely not from Moses, but definitely from the fathers, and you are circumcising a man upon the Sabbath.

23 If a man upon the Sabbath is receiving circumcision, in order that the Law of Moses should not be removed, why are you being enraged at Me? I Made a whole man Healthy on the Sabbath.

24 You must not judge according to outward appearance, but definitely, you must judge by Righteous Final Judgment.

25 Then were saying some of Jerusalem,

Definitely is not He Whom they are seeking to kill?

26 But behold, He is Uttering with Boldness, and they in fear of Truth are saying nothing to Him. Have the rulers known that He is Truth, the Christ?

27 But definitely we discern Him from where He is, but when Christ is coming, definitely no man is Knowing from where He is.

28 Then, Jesus Cried Out in the Temple area Teaching, and Saying, You are also now by your choice discerning Me also, also you are discerning by your choice from where I am, and that I come definitely not of Myself, but definitely He Who Sent Me is True, whom yourselves are definitely not now discerning.

29 But, I am Knowing Him, for I am From Him and also He Has Sent Me Out.

30 Then, they were seeking to catch Him, but no one laid a hand upon Him, for His Hour had not yet come.

31 And many of the multitude of people Committed to Him, and were saying, That when the Christ Comes, Will He possibly do greater Miracle Signs than these, which This Man has Done?

32 The Pharisees heard the multitude of people murmuring these things about Him, and the Pharisees and the chief priests sent out officers, in order that they might catch Him.

33 Therefore, Jesus Spoke to them. Yet a little time I am with you, and then I am Going Away, to Him Who Sent Me.

34 And you shall seek Me, and not find, and then whereto, I AM, you yourselves, shall definitely not be able to come.

35 Then the Jews spoke among themselves. Wherein is He expecting to go that we shall definitely not find Him? Is He expecting to go to those widely scattered among the forbidden Gentiles, and teaching the Gentiles?

36 What is His Communication that He has Spoken? You shall be Seeking Me, and shall definitely not find, and whereto, I AM, yourselves are not able to come.

37 Then, In that last day of the Great Feast, Jesus had Stood and Cried Out Saying, If ever anyone might Thirst, he must be continuously by his choice Coming to Me, and he must continuously by his choice Drinking.

38 He that is continuously by his choice Committing for the Purpose of Me, just as Scripture has Spoken, Rivers of Living Water will Flow Out from his belly.

39 Now this He Spoke in regard to the Spirit, Whom they that are Committing to Him, were Expected to Receive, because the Holy Spirit was not yet (Given), for Jesus has never yet been made Glorified.

A division of the people

40 Therefore, many of the multitude of people heard these words. They were saying, Of Truth, He is the Prophet.

41 Others of the same kind were saying, He is the Christ. But others of same kinds were saying, Yet is the Christ coming out from Galilee?

42 Have definitely not the Scriptures spoken, that out from the Seed of David, and from Bethlehem, the village whereto was David, that Christ is coming out?

43 Then became a division in the multitude of people, because of Him.

44 And some of them were willing to catch Him, but definitely no one laid their hands on Him.

45 Then came the officers among the chief priests and Pharisees, and they spoke to them. Why then have you definitely not led Him?

46 The officers answered. Never, in such a manner, has a man Uttered as this Man.

47 Then the Pharisees answered to them, Are yourselves not now been made deceived?

48 Have not any of the rulers or of the Pharisees Committed for the Purpose of Him?

49 But definitely this multitude of people, that are not knowing the Law, are cursed.
50 Nicodemus, he that came by night to Him, being one of them, says to them,
51 Our Law is not judging any man unless it hears from him first, and it might know what he does?
52 They made answer, and spoke to him, Possibly are you also out from Galilee? Search and behold, where definitely no Prophet is now made risen up, out from Galilee.
53 And every man went to his own home.

Adulterous woman brought before Him

8 Jesus then went to the Mount of Olives.
2 And early in the morning, He Came Up again into the Temple area, and all the people came to Him, and He Sat Down, Taught them.
3 And the scribes and Pharisees lead a woman to Him, apprehended in adultery, and stood her in the middle.
4 They said to Him, Master, this woman was apprehended committing an adultery act.
5 Now Moses, in the Law, God Commanded us that you are to cast stones at such; therefore, What are you saying?
6 Now this they were saying to try Him, that they might be having to accuse Him. But Jesus stooping down below, was writing with His Finger on the earth, possibly as though further.
7 So as they were continuing with intent earnestly requesting of Him. He straightened up, Spoke to them. He without sin of yourselves, you must cast the first stone at her.
8 And again, He stooped down below, Writing in the earth.
9 And they that heard it, by being Made Convinced of sin by their conscience were departing, one by one, beginning from the elder to the last, and now Jesus was made left alone, while the woman is standing in the midst.
10 When Jesus straightened up, and Saw no one but the woman, He Spoke to her. Woman, wherein are they, those accusers of you? Definitely, has no man condemned you to death?
11 And then, she spoke, No man, Lord. And Jesus Spoke to her, Neither am I Condemning you to death. You must be going, and you must not be sinning any longer.
12 Then Jesus Uttered again to them saying, I AM, the Light of the satan's (rebellers) world. He that is Continuously Following Me, shall definitely not possibly walk in the dark, but definitely shall be Having the Light of Life.
13 Therefore, the Pharisees spoke to Him. You are giving Witness to Yourself; Your Testimony is definitely not True.
14 Jesus Answered, and Spoke to them, Though I give Witness to Myself, My Testimony is True; for I discern from where I Came, and to wherein I Go Away, but yourselves are definitely not now Spiritually Discerning from where I Came, and wherein I am Going Away.

Jesus' Testimony is of God

15 Yourselves, judge according to your sinful flesh nature. I am definitely not Judging any man.
16 And if I should Judge, then My Final Judgment is True; for definitely I am Not Alone, but definitely I and the Father, Sending Me.
17 It is also Written, in your Law, that the Testimony of two men is True.
18 I AM, the Witness about Myself, and the Father Sending Me is Giving Witness about Me.
19 Then, they were saying to Him, Wherein is your Father? Jesus answered, You are neither now Spiritually Discerning Me, nor My Father. If ever you had Spiritually Discerned Me, you would had Spiritually Discerned My Father also.
20 These Words Uttered Jesus in the

treasury, Teaching in the Temple area, and not any man caught Him, for His Hour had not yet Come.

21 Then Spoke Jesus again to them, I Go Away and, you shall seek Me, and you shall die in your sin natures and sins. Whereto I am Going Away, yourselves are definitely not able to Come.

22 Then said the Jews, Will He possibly kill Himself? For he is saying, Whereto I go away, yourselves are definitely not able to come.

23 And He Spoke to them. Yourselves are out from down below. I am Out From Above. You, yourselves, are of this the satan's world. I am Definitely Not of this the satan's world.

24 I Spoke, therefore, to you, that you shall die in your sin natures and sins, because unless you might Commit that, I AM, you shall die in your sin natures and sins.

25 Then they were saying to Him, You, Who are You? And Jesus Spoke to them. This certain thing, since the beginning, I am continuously Uttering to you.

26 I have very much to Utter, and to Judge concerning you, but definitely, He that Sent Me is True. Also, I Say These Things to the satan's world, that I have Heard from Him.

27 They have definitely not recognized, that He was Saying to them, The Father.

28 Then Jesus Spoke to them. When you have Elevated Up the Son of Man, then you will know that, I AM, and from Myself I Do nothing, but definitely, just as My Father has Taught Me, I am Uttering these things.

29 He that Sent Me is With Me, and the Father has not dismissed Me alone. For I Do, always, those things Pleasing to Him.

30 Uttering these things of Himself, many Committed, for Purpose of Him.

The True Disciples

31 Then Jesus was Saying to the Jews that Committed to Him. If you, yourselves, should Continue in My Spiritual Words, you, Of Truth, are My disciples,

32 And you shall Know the Truth, and the Truth shall Make you Free.

33 They answered Him, We are being the Seed of Abraham, and we are not now bondserving, at any time. How are You Saying that you shall be Made Free?

34 Jesus Answered them, Truly, Truly, I am Saying to you, that whoever is continuously by his choice doing sin nature and sin is a slave of sin nature and sin.

35 And moreover, the slave is definitely not continuing in the house forever. The Son is Continuing Forever.

36 If, therefore, the Son might have Made you Free, in fact you shall be Free.

37 I discern that you are Seed of Abraham, but definitely you are seeking to kill Me, for My Spiritual Communications are not finding a place in you.

38 I Utter what I am now Beholding Attentively with My Father, and yourselves are doing, therefore, what you are now beholding attentively from your father.

False children of Abraham

39 They answered, and spoke to Him, Abraham is our father. Jesus Said to them, If you were the children of Abraham, you would have been doing the Works by God of Abraham.

40 But now you are seeking to kill Me, a Man that is now Uttering the Truth to you, which I have Heard from God. This Abraham did not do.

41 Yourselves are doing the man works of your father. Then they spoke to Him. We are, not now, made born from fornication. We are having one father, our God.

42 Jesus Spoke to them. If God were your Father, you would be Loving Me because I have Come Out from God, and I am Now Coming neither of Myself, but definitely Coming Out because He Sent Me.

43 Why then are you not Knowing My speech? You are definitely not even able to Hear My Spiritual Word.

44 Yourselves are out from your father

the devil, and the evil desires of your father you are willing to do. He was a murderer from beginning, and was definitely not standing in the Truth, for there is definitely no Truth in him. When he might be uttering the lie, he is uttering of his own, for he is a liar and the father of it.

45 And then since I am Saying the Truth, you will definitely not be Committing to Me.

46 Which of you are convincing Me of sin nature and sin? And if I am Saying the Truth, why then are yourselves not Committing to Me?

47 He that is of God is Hearing the Words of God. Because of this, yourselves are not Hearing, for you are definitely not of God.

Jews accuse Jesus of having a devil

48 Therefore, answered the Jews and spoke to Him. Are we not God-Working saying that You are a Samaritan, and You are having a demon?

49 Jesus Answered, I am definitely not having a demon. But definitely, I am honoring My Father, and yourselves are dishonoring Me.

50 And I am definitely not seeking My Own Glory. There is One Seeking and Judging.

51 Truly, Truly, I am Saying to you, If any man should Keep My Word, he should Never Ever Perceive death Forever.

52 Then spoke the Jews to Him, Now we know that You have a demon. Abraham died and the Prophets, and You are saying if any might Keep My Word, they should Never Ever Taste of Death Forever.

53 Are You greater than our father Abraham who died, and the Prophets who died? Whom are You making Yourself?

54 Jesus Answered, If I Glorify Myself, My Glory is nothing. My Father is Attributing Glory to Me, of whom yourselves are saying that He is your God.

55 Yet you are not now Knowing Him, but I Spiritually Discern Him. And if I should

speak, that I Spiritually Discern Him not, I shall be like yourselves, a liar. But definitely I Spiritually Discern Him, and Keep His Spiritual Words.

56 Your father Abraham was Exceedingly Glad, that he Spiritually Discerned My Day. And he Spiritually Discerned It, and Rejoiced.

57 Then the Jews spoke to Him, not yet having fifty years and Abraham is now beholding attentively?

58 Jesus spoke to them, Truly, Truly, I Say to you before Abraham was, I AM.

59 Then they took up stones to cast at Him, but Jesus Hid, and Departed from the Temple area Passing Through the midst of them, and so was Passing On.

Blind Man from birth is healed

9 And as He was passing on, He Spiritually Discerned a man blind from natural birth.

2 And His disciples earnestly requested of Him saying, Master, who sinned, this man or his parents that He might be made born blind?

3 Jesus Answered, Neither has this man sinned, nor his parents; but definitely that the Works by God might be made Manifest in him.

4 I must Work the Works by God that Sent Me while it is Day. Night is Coming when no man can Work.

5 When I should Be in the satan's world, I should Be the Light of the satan's world.

6 When He Spoke these things, He made spittle to the ground, and made clay out of the spittle, and He Anointed with clay to the eyes of the blind.

7 And He Spoke to him, You must go away. You must wash yourself in the pool of Siloam (which is by interpretation is made sending out to go). And then he washed himself and came Seeing.

8 Therefore, the adjoining neighbors and those who are seeing him with perception that he was first blind, were saying, Is this

not he that was sitting and begging?

9   Others of same kind were saying, that this is he, and others of the same kind that he is like him, but he was saying, that I am he.

10 Therefore, they were saying to him, How were your eyes made Opened?

11 He Answered and Spoke, A man called Jesus made clay, and anointed my eyes with clay, and spoke to me. You must Go Away to the pool of Siloam and you must Wash yourself. I went and washed myself and received sight.

12 Then they spoke to him, Wherein is He? He said, I am not now discerning.

13 They led him, he who was blind in time past, to the Pharisees,

14 And it was a Sabbath when Jesus Made the clay, and Opened his eyes.

15 Then the Pharisees also again earnestly requested of him how he received sight, so he spoke to them. He laid clay on my eyes, and I washed, and I am seeing.

16 Therefore, some of the Pharisees said, This man is not from God, for He definitely is not keeping the Sabbath. Others of the same kind were saying, How is a sinful man able to make such Miracle Signs? And there was a division among them.

17 They say to the blind again, What are you saying about Him that Opened your eyes? And then He spoke that He is a Prophet.

Jews question blind mans' parents

18 Therefore, while they called for the parents of him that received sight the Jews had definitely not for themselves Committed about him that he was blind, and that he had received sight.

19 And they earnestly requested of them saying, Is he your son, who yourselves now say that was made born blind? How then does he from now see?

20 His parents answered them and spoke, We are discerning that he is our son, and that he was made born blind.

21 But how he is now seeing is not now discerned, or Who Opened his eyes, we are neither not now discerning. He is having stature of age himself. You must earnestly request of him. He will utter for himself.

22 These things his parents spoke, for already they were fearing the Jews, because the Jews had agreed that if anyone should himself confess Christ, he should have to be put out from the synagogue.

23 Because of this his parents spoke, since he is having stature of age, you must earnestly request of him.

Jews question blind man again

24 Therefore, they called a second time for the man that was blind, and spoke to him. Attribute God the Glory. We discern that This Man is a sinner.

25 Therefore, He answered and spoke, that whether He is a sinner I am not now discerning, the One I am now discerning, for I was blind, for now I am seeing.

26 Then they spoke to him again. What did He to you? How has He Opened your eyes?

27 He answered them, I have spoken to you already, and you have not heard. Why will you not hear again, but will yourselves become His disciples?

28 Then they reviled him and spoke. You are His disciple, but we are being disciples of Moses.

29 We are now discerning that God Uttered to Moses, as for Him, we are not now discerning from where He is.

The blind man again answered

30 The man answered and spoke to them. Because in this is a marvel, that you yourselves do not discern from where He is, but He Opened my eyes.

31 Now we Spiritually Discern that God is definitely not Hearing sinners, but definitely if any man should be a Worshipper of God, and should be continuously doing His Will, He is definitely Continuously Hearing This One.

32 From out of the Age, it was not heard that any man Opened eyes of a born blind. 33 If he was not from God, He could not do anything.
34 They answered and spoke to him. You were made born in sins, and you are teaching all of us? And they cast him out, outside.

Lord Jesus Finds the Healed blind man
35 Jesus Heard that they Cast him Out outside, and when He found him He Spoke to him. Are you Committing to the Son of God?
36 He answered then and spoke, Who is He, Lord, that I might Commit to Him?
37 Then Jesus Spoke to him, Now you are now Him Beholding Attentively, and He that also is Uttering with you is He.
38 And he stated, Lord, by my choice I am Continuously Committing, and he Worshiped Him.
39 And Jesus Spoke, For Judgment I came into this the satan's world, that they who are not Spiritually Seeing might Spiritually See, and those who are spiritually seeing might become blind.
40 And the Pharisees who were with them heard these things, and spoke to Him. But are we not being blind also?
41 Jesus Spoke to them, If you were blind, you should not ever have sin, but now you say that you are spiritually seeing, therefore your sin is continuing.

I am the Door of the Sheep
10 Truly, Truly, I say to you, He that is not Entering through the Door into the Sheep Enclosure, but definitely ascends some other way, the same is a thief and a robber.
2 But He that Enters through the Door is Shepherd of the Sheep.
3 To This One the Porter is Continuously Opening, and the sheep are Continuously Hearing His Voice, and He is Continuously Calling His own sheep by name, and is Continuously Leading them out.
4 And when He might Send Away His own sheep, He Goes before them, and the sheep are Continuously Following Him, for they are now continuously Discerning His Voice.
5 And a strange man they should by their choice never ever follow, but definitely will flee from him, for they are now continuously not Spiritually Knowing a strange man's voice.
6 Jesus Spoke this proverb to them, but then they knew definitely not what He was Uttered to them.
7 Then Spoke Jesus to them again, Truly, Truly, I am Saying to you that, I AM, the Door of the sheep.
8 All whoever came before Me, they are thieves and robbers, but definitely the sheep have definitely not heard them.
9 I AM, the Door. If any man should enter through Me, he shall be made Saved, and shall enter and come out, and shall find pasture.
10 The thief is definitely not coming except that he might steal, and might put to death, and might destroy. I have come that they should have Life, and should be having more in excess.

I am the Good Shepherd
11 I AM, the God-Work Shepherd. The God-Work Shepherd is Laying Down His (Sinless) Flesh Nature in behalf of the Sheep.
12 But he that is an hireling, and definitely not being a Shepherd, whose own Sheep they are definitely not, sees the wolf coming and parts from the Sheep, and flees and the wolf catches them up and disperses the Sheep.
13 So the hireling flees for he is a hireling, and is definitely not caring himself about the Sheep.
14 I AM, the God-Work Shepherd, and I Know Mine, and am made Known by Mine.

15 Just as the Father Knows Me, also I am Knowing the Father, and I am Laying Down My (Sinless) Flesh Nature in behalf of the Sheep.

Other Sheep are not of this Fold
16 And other Sheep of the same kind by My choice I am Having, I also by My choice must Lead, who are definitely not out from this Fold. They also Hear My Voice and I must Lead. There shall be One Safe Flock, One Shepherd.
17 For this My Father Loves Me, for by My choice I Lay Down My (Sinless) Flesh Nature, that I should by My choice Take It Again.
18 Definitely no man takes It away from Me, but definitely I Lay It down of Myself. I have Authority to Lay It down, and I Have Authority to Take to Receive It to have it again. This Commandment I have Received from My Father.

Many Jews said he has a devil
19 Therefore, a division again occurred among the Jews because of these Spiritual Words.
20 And then many of them were saying, He is having a demon and He is being insane. Why are we hearing Him?
21 Others of same kind were saying, These things being definitely not words demonized. No demon can be opening blind eyes.

My Sheep hear My Voice and Follow Me
22 And now the Feast of Dedication occurred in Jerusalem, and it was winter.
23 And so Jesus was walking in the Temple area upon Solomon's porch.
24 Then the Jews surrounded Him and were saying to Him, How long a time until after our soul is taken away? If You, You are the Christ, speak to us plainly.
25 Jesus Answered them, I Spoke to you but you are not Committing. The Works by God that I Do in My Father's Name, these things are giving Witness to Me.
26 But definitely yourselves are not Committing, because you are not of My sheep, just as I Spoke to you.
27 My Sheep are Continuously by their choice Hearing My Voice. Also I, I am by My Choice Continuously Recognizing Them, and They are Continuously by their choice Following Me.
28 Also I, I am Continuously by My choice Giving to them Life Eternal, that they should never ever perish Forever, and definitely not one shall himself be caught up out from My Hand.
29 My Father, Who is now Continuously Giving them to Me is Greater than All, and definitely none can be Continuously caught up out from My Father's Hand.

I and My Father are One
30 I and My Father (We) are being One.
31 Then the Jews bore stones again in order that they might stone Him.
32 Jesus Answered them. Many God-Works, Works by God, I have Shown you from My Father. Because of which Work by God of Him, are you stoning Me?
33 The Jews answered Him saying, For God-Work, Work by God, we are definitely not stoning you, but definitely for blasphemy, and that You being a man are making Yourself God.
34 Jesus Answered them, Is it definitely not written in your Law, I spoke, You are gods? (Ps 82:6)
35 If He spoke them gods, to whom the Word of God occurred, and the Scripture cannot be Removed,
36 That the Father Made Holy and Sent Out into the satan's world, yourselves are saying this, You are blaspheming. For I Spoke, I am the Son of God.
37 If I definitely do not the Works by God of My Father, you must not be Committing to Me,
38 But if I Do, though you might not be Committing to Me, you must be Committing

to the Works by God, that you should Recognize, and should have Committed by your choice, that the Father in Me, I also in Him.

39 Therefore, they sought again to catch Him, but He Departed out from their hand.

40 And He went again to the other side of Jordan, into the place whereto was John, when he first of all was immersing, and He continued there.

41 And many came to Him and said, How John certainly did no Miracle Signs, but All Things John Spoke about This One were True.

42 And many Committed to Him there.

Lazareth is sick, Jesus waits two days

11 Now a certain man being sick was Lazarus of Bethany, the village of Mary and Martha her sister.

2 She was that Mary that anointed the Lord with ointment, and then wiped His Feet with her hair, whose brother Lazarus was sick.

3 Therefore, his sisters sent out to Him saying, Lord, behold, whom You are Affectionately God Loving is sick.

4 When Jesus heard, He Spoke. This infirmity is definitely not to death, but definitely in behalf of the Glory of God, in order that the Son of God should be Attributed Glory through him.

5 Now Jesus Loved Martha, and her sister, and Lazarus.

6 As soon as He heard that he is sick, then He actually continued in the place where He was two days.

7 After that He Said this to the disciples, We must move along into Judaea again.

8 His disciples said to Him, Oh Master Teacher, now the Jews are seeking to stone You, and are You moving there again?

9 Jesus was to Answer. Are there definitely not twelve hours in a day? If any man should Walk in this Day, he is definitely not stumbling, for he is Spiritually Seeing the Light of this the satan's world.

10 But if any man might be walking in the night, he stumbles for the Light is definitely not in him.

11 These things He Spoke, and after this Said to them, Lazarus, our friend, is now resting Asleep, but definitely I Go, so that I should Awake him from Sleep.

12 Then spoke the disciples to Him. Oh Lord, if he is now made to sleep, he shall be made healthy.

13 But Jesus had Spirit Said about the death of him then, and they thought he was saying this about resting in natural sleep.

14 Then, therefore, Jesus Spoke to them plainly, Lazarus has died.

15 And I am glad because of you that I was definitely not there, but definitely so that you should be Committed. We should move along to him.

16 Then Thomas, being made called Didymus, spoke to his fellow disciples. We should move along also, that we might die with Him.

I am the Resurrection and the Life

17 Therefore, came Jesus to find him, having already four days in the sepulcher.

18 Now Bethany was near Jerusalem, as fifteen furlongs away.

19 And many, from the Jews, had come before them for Martha and Mary, in order that they might comfort them about their brother.

20 Then as Martha heard that Jesus was coming, she met with Him, but Mary was sitting herself in the home.

21 Then Martha spoke to Jesus. Oh Lord, if You were here, my brother had definitely not ever been a corpse.

22 But definitely even now, I Spiritually Discern that whatever, whenever, You Yourself should ask God, God shall Give to You.

23 Jesus Said to her. Your brother shall himself Arise.

24 Martha says to Him, I am Spiritually Discerning that he shall Arise in the Resurrection, within the Last Day.

25 Jesus Spoke to her, I AM, the Resurrection and the Life, he that is continuously by his choice Committing to Me, though he should die, he shall Live.

26 And whoever is Continuously Living and Continuously Committing for the Purpose of Me should never ever die Forever. Are you Continuously Committing to this?

27 She says to Him, Emphatically Yes, Lord, I myself am now Committing that You, You are the Christ, the Son of God, Who is Come into the satan's world.

28 And when she spoke these things, she went and called for Mary, her sister, secretly speaking, The Master is Present and is calling for you.

29 As she heard that, she is made rising up quickly, and came to Him.

30 Jesus had not yet come in the village, but definitely was in that place whereto Martha meet with Him.

31 As soon as the Jews that were with her in the house, and comforting her, saw that Mary rapidly arose and departed, they followed her, saying that she goes away to the sepulcher that she might weep there.

32 Then as Mary came to whereto Jesus was and saw Him, she fell down at His Feet saying to Him, Oh Lord, If You were here my brother should definitely not ever have died.

Lazarus Raised from the dead

33 Therefore as Jesus Saw her weeping, and the Jews coming together with her weeping, He Groaned in the Spirit, and Troubled Himself.

34 And He Spoke, Wherein is he now laying down? They said to Him, Oh Lord, You must come, and also You must see.

35 Jesus shed tears.

36 Then the Jews were saying; Behold, how He Affectionately Loved him.

37 And some of them spoke, Could definitely not this man, who opening the eyes of the blind, have healed in order that he might not have died?

38 Then Jesus again Groaning in Himself came to the sepulcher, and it was a cave, and a stone was laid upon it.

39 Jesus Said, You must take away the stone. Martha, his sister, said to Him, Oh Lord already he is a rotting dead body, because he has been stinking four days.

40 Jesus Said to Her, Spoke I definitely not to you, that if you should have Committed, you shall Spiritually See the Glory of God?

41 Then they took away the stone where was laying the rotting dead body, and Jesus taking up His eyes Above, and Spoke, Father I Give Thanks to You that You have Heard Me.

42 Now I Know that Always You are Hearing Me, but definitely because of the multitude of people being idle, I Speak that they might Commit, that You Sent Me Out.

43 And when He Spoke these things, He Cried with a Great Voice, Oh Lazarus, Come Forward Outside.

44 And then he that was a rotting dead body Came Out bound hands and feet in grave clothes, and his outward appearance had been made bound about with a napkin. Jesus Said to them, You Must Remove it, and you Must Have Concern for him to move.

45 Then many of the Jews, who came to Mary, and seeing what Jesus did, Committed to Him.

46 But some of them went to the Pharisees, and they spoke to them, what Jesus did.

High Priest plots to kill Jesus

47 Then the Pharisees and chief priests gathered together a council and said what are we to do because This Man is doing many Miracle Signs?

48 If we should have concern for Him in this manner, all shall Commit to Him, and the Romans shall come, and take away both our place and nation.

49 And a certain one of them, Caiaphas,

being a High Priest that same year, the same spoke to them. Yourselves are definitely not discerning anything.

50 Neither are you reasoning that it is essential to us, that One Man should die in behalf of the people, or that the whole nation should not be destroyed.

51 And this spoke he definitely not of himself, but definitely being High Priest that year, he Prophesied that Jesus was expected to Die in behalf of the nation.

52 And definitely not in behalf of that nation only, but definitely in order that He should also gather together the scattered Children of God, into one.

53 Then from that day, they counseled that they should kill Him.

Jesus Walked no more openly

54 Jesus, therefore, further walked definitely not boldly among the Jews, but definitely went from that place into the land near a desolate wilderness, into a city made called Ephraim, and there also He stayed with His disciples.

55 And the Jews Passover was near, and many ascended to Jerusalem, out from the land before the Passover in order that they should purify themselves.

56 Then they sought Jesus, and standing with one another in the Temple area said, How does it seem to you, that He might never ever come to the Feast?

57 Now both the chief priests and the Pharisees had given a commandment, that if any might know wherein He is, he should disclose, so that they might catch Him.

Mary Anoints Jesus for His Burial

12 Then Jesus six days before the Passover came to Bethany, whereto was Lazarus, that was a corpse, who has been risen up from the dead.

2 So they made for Him a supper there, and Martha was serving, and Lazarus was one of them sitting to eat with Him.

3 Then Mary took a pound weight of spikenard plant ointment, of much more costly spikenard plant, to anoint the Feet of Jesus and wiped His Feet with her hair, and the house filled full from the odor of the ointment.

4 Then said one of his disciples, Judas Iscariot of Simon, who is being expected to deliver Him up in betrayal,

5 Why then was this ointment not sold in the market for three hundred pennies, and made given to the poor?

6 But he spoke this definitely not that he was caring for the poor, but definitely himself since he was a thief, and he was also having the bag for money, so was bearing that made put in.

7 Then Jesus Spoke, You must have concern for the purpose and result of her Holding this as Sacred for the Day of My Burial.

8 For the poor you always have with you, but you are definitely not always Having Me.

9 Therefore, a large multitude of people of the Jews knew that He is there, and came definitely not only because of Jesus, but definitely that Lazarus should be seen whom He Raised Up out from dead.

10 But the chief priests consulted, in order that they might be killing Lazarus also,

11 Because many Jews through him were moved, and were Committing to Jesus.

Triumphal Entry into Jerusalem

12 The next day a large multitude of people was coming to the Feast, hearing that Jesus was coming into Jerusalem.

13 They took palm branches of palm trees, and came out for greeting Him, and crying out, Hosanna, Blessed the King of Israel, coming in the Name of the Lord. (Ps 118:25-26)

14 And Jesus, finding a young ass, Sat Down upon him, just as is Made Written.

15 You must not be fearing, daughter of Sion. Behold your King coming, sitting upon a colt of a donkey. (Isa 40:9; Zech 9:9)

16 At first even these things His disciples

had not Recognized, but definitely when Jesus was made Glorified (Raised), then they themselves Remembered, that these things were being Made Written about Him, and they did these things to Him.

17 Therefore, the multitude of people being with Him was bearing record when He Called for Lazarus out from the sepulcher, and Raised Him Up out from the dead.

18 Because of this, the multitude of people also met with Him, for it heard that He had done this Miracle Sign.

19 The Pharisees, therefore, spoke among themselves. Perceive how you are definitely not influencing anything? Behold, the world has gone after Him.

20 Certain Greeks were there, of those ascending, in order that they might worship in the Feast.

21 Therefore, they came near to Philip, who was from Bethsaida of Galilee, and earnestly requested of him saying, Oh Sir, we would see Jesus.

22 Philip comes and says to Andrew, and again Andrew and Philip say to Jesus.

23 Then, Jesus Answers to them Saying, The hour is now coming that the Son of Man should be Made Attributed Glory.

24 Truly, Truly, I Say to you, except a grain of wheat that has fallen down into the earth should die, it continues alone, but if it should die, it is bringing very much Fruit.

25 He affectionately loving his soul shall destroy it. And he Hating his soul in this the satan's world shall Maintain It into Life Eternal.

26 If any man should be Serving Me, he must be Continuously by his choice Following Me. And whereto I AM, there shall My servant be also. And if any man should be Continuously by his choice Serving Me, him My Father shall Honor.

27 Now My Soul is troubled, and What should I Speak to the Father? You must Save Me out from this hour. But definitely for this, I have come for the Purpose and Result of this Hour.

Prince of this world now cast out

28 Father, You must Attribute Glory to Your Name. Then Came a Voice Out from Heaven, I have both Attributed Glory, and I will Attribute Glory Again.

29 The multitude of people, therefore, that standing now and hearing, were saying thunder occurred, others of the same kind were saying an Angel Utters now to Him.

30 Jesus Answered and Spoke, This Voice is now made definitely not because of Me, but definitely for you.

31 Now is Final Judgment of this the satan's world. Now shall the prince of this the satan's world be made cast out, outside.

32 Also I, if I should be made Elevated Up from the earth, I will Draw Out All Men to Myself. (John 6:40,44)

33 Moreover, this He was Saying, signifying what Death He was Expecting to Die.

34 The multitude of people made answer to Him. We heard from the Law that the Christ is Continuing Forever. So how are you saying, The Son of Man must be Elevated Up? Who is this Son of Man?

35 Therefore, Jesus Spoke to them, While yet a little time is the Light with you. You must be Walking while you are having the Light, that the dark should not apprehend you. For he that is walking in the dark is definitely not Spiritually Discerning wherein he is being led away.

36 While you are having the Light, you must be Committing to the Light, in order that the Sons might be of Light. Jesus Uttered these things, and Went to be Hidden Away from them.

37 For He is now Doing so many Miracle Signs before them. They were definitely not Committing to Him,

38 That the Spiritual Communication of Esaias the Prophet should be made Fulfilled which he Spoke, Oh Lord, Who has Committed to the Hearing of us, and to Whom the Mighty Arm of the Lord has been Made Revealed? (Isa 53:1)

39 Because of this they were definitely not

able to be Committing, for Esaias spoke again,

40 He is now blinding their eyes and is now hardening their heart, that they might not Spiritually Discern with their eyes, or might not Comprehend with their heart, that they should be Made Converted, and I will Myself Cure them. (Isa 6:10)

41 These things Spoke Esaias when he Spiritually Discerned His Glory and Uttered about Him.

Jesus Declares He Came to Save world

42 However, even out from the rulers, many then committed to Him. But definitely because of the Pharisees, they were definitely not Confessing, that they should not become put out from the synagogues,

43 Because they loved the glory of man much more than the Glory of God.

44 Jesus Cried Out and also Spoke. He that is Committing to Me, is definitely not Committing to Me, but definitely to the One Sending Me.

45 And he that is Perceiving Me, is Perceiving Him that Sent Me.

46 I am Now Coming a Light into the satan's world, in order that everyone Committing by his choice to Me, should not have continued in the dark.

47 And if any man should have Heard My Words, and should have not Committed, I will definitely not Judge him, because I have definitely not Come that I should Judge the satan's world, but definitely that I might have Saved the satan's world.

48 He that is rejecting Me, and is not Receiving My Words, is having One that is Judging him. The Spiritual Word that I Utter, the same shall Judge him in the Last Day.

49 For I have definitely not Uttered out from Myself, but definitely the Father Who Sent Me. He Gave a Commandment to Me, What I should Speak, and What I should Utter.

50 And I Spiritually Know that His Commandment is Eternal Life. Therefore, I am Uttering just as the Father is Spirit Saying to Me, in that manner I Utter.

The Last Supper (Chapters 13-17)

13 Now before the Feast of the Passover, when Jesus Spiritually now Knows that the Hour is Now Come, that He should Depart from this the satan's world to His Father, Having Loved His Own in the satan's world, He Loved Them to the End.

2 And Supper being ended, already the devil is now being cast into the heart of Judas Iscariot of Simon, in order that he should deliver Him up in betrayal.

3 Jesus Knowing that His Father is Now Giving all things into His Hands, and that He Came Out Away from God, Now is Going Away to God.

Washes Disciples feet, for an Example

4 He is Made to Rise Up at the Supper, and lays down His robes, and taking a towel, wrapped Himself.

5 Following that, He poured water into the basin and began to Wash the Feet of His disciples, and wiped them with the towel, in which He was wrapped.

6 Then He came to Simon Peter, and he then said to Him, Oh Lord, are you then washing my feet?

7 Jesus has been Made to Answer and Spoke to him. What I Do to you, you shall definitely not discern for now, but you shall Recognize These Things Afterward.

8 Peter said to Him, You should never ever wash my feet, forever. Jesus Answered him. If I should not Wash You, you definitely Have No Part with Me.

9 Simon Peter said to Him, Oh Lord, not my feet only, but definitely also my hands and my head.

10 Jesus Said to him. He that is now Made Washed is definitely Having No Need, than to Wash Feet, but definitely he is Purified Whole and you are yourselves

Purified, but definitely not everyone.

11 Because He had Spiritually Discerned, who should deliver Him up in betrayal. Because of this, He Spoke, Definitely not all you are Purified.

12 When, therefore, He Washed their feet, He took His robes and sitting down again, He Spoke to them. Are you Recognizing what I am now Doing to you?

13 Yourselves are calling for Me, Master and Lord, and you are saying God-Working, because I am.

14 If I, therefore, Your Lord and Your Master, have Washed your feet, you yourselves, also are indebted, to be Washing one another's feet.

15 For I have Given you an example, that just as I have Done to you, also yourselves should be doing.

16 Truly, Truly, I am Saying to you, a Bondslave is definitely not greater than his Lord, neither an Apostle greater than He Sending him.

17 If you are Knowing these things, you are Spiritually Blessed if you should do them.

Jesus Foretells of His betrayal

18 I am definitely not saying to all of you, I am now Knowing whom I have Chosen for Myself, but definitely in order that the Scriptures should have been made Fulfilled. He that Enjoyed Eating Bread with Me, lifted up his heel against Me. (Ps 41:9)

19 For by now, I am Saying for you before it has come to pass, that when it should occur, you should have Committed by your choice that, I AM.

20 Truly, Truly, I am Saying to you, whoever receives anybody if I should Send, is receiving Me, and he receiving Me, is receiving Him that has Sent Me.

21 Jesus, made Troubled in Spirit, Spoke these things. Then He Bear Record and Spoke, Truly, Truly, I am Saying to you, that one of you shall deliver Me up in betrayal.

22 Then the disciples were looking at one

to another, perplexed in regard to what He was Saying.

23 Now, there was one of His disciples leaning upon the bosom of Jesus, whom Jesus was Loving.

24 Therefore, Simon Peter was gesturing to inquire whoever this one should be, beyond dreams, about whom He is Saying.

25 And then the same fell upon the chest of Jesus saying to Him, Who is it, Lord?

Gave sop to Judas, Judas left

26 Jesus Answered, The same is he with whom I have hand dipped a biteful. When He having hand dipped a biteful, He gave to Judas Iscariot of Simon.

27 And after the biteful, then entered into the same, the satan. Then Jesus Said to him, Then that which you are doing, you must accomplish it more hastily.

28 Now none, sitting as at eating, knew for what Intent He Spoke this to him.

29 For some were thinking in fact that Judas was having the bag for money, that Jesus was saying to him, you must buy what we have needful for the Feast, or that something should be given to the poor.

30 He then took the biteful, then immediately departed, and it was night.

A New Commandment is Given

31 When therefore, he departed, Jesus Said, Now the Son of Man has been Made Attributed Glory, and God has been Made Attributed Glory In Himself.

32 If God has been made Attributed Glory in Himself, God shall also Attribute Glory to Him in Himself, and shall immediately Attribute Glory to Him.

33 Little Children, yet a little while I am with you, you shall seek Me, and just as I Spoke to the Jews, To whereto that I Go Away yourselves are not able to come, but for now I Say to you,

34 A New of a different kind Commandment I am Giving to you, that you should God-Love one to another, just as I have

Loved you, in order that also yourselves should God-Love one another.

35 By this all shall know that you are My disciples, if you should have God-Love in one to another.

36 Simon Peter said to Him, Oh Lord, wherein are you Going Away? Jesus Answered him. To whereto I am Going Away, you definitely cannot now follow. Afterward, then you shall Follow Me.

37 Peter says to Him, Oh Lord, Why then can I definitely not be following You for now? I will lay down my soul in behalf of you.

Peters' three denials are Foretold

38 Jesus Answered him. Will you lay down your soul in behalf of Me? Truly, Truly, I Say to you, that definitely a cock shall not crow until after when you should have denied me three times.

The Way, the Truth, and the Life

14 Your heart must not be made continuously troubling; you are Continuously Committing to God, and you must be Continuously Committing to Me.

2 In My Father's House there are many Abodes, if not so I would have Spoken to you. I am going to Prepare a Place for you.

3 And if I should Go and I should Prepare a place for you, I am Coming Again, and I will Receive Each of you to Myself, that Whereto, I AM, you should be yourselves also.

4 And to Whereto I am Going Away, you now Spiritually Discern, and The Way you are now Spiritually Discerning.

5 Thomas said to Him, Oh Lord, we are definitely not now Spiritually Discerning Wherein you are Going Away. And how are we able, to now be Spiritually Discerning The Way?

6 Jesus Said to Him, I AM, The Way, and The Truth, and The Life. None, not one, is Coming to the Father except through Me.

7 If you had Known Me, also you had Known My Father, and that from Now you are Knowing Him, and you are Now Beholding Him Attentively.

8 Philip said to Him, Oh Lord, You must Show us the Father, and it is sufficient to us.

9 Jesus Said to him, I am Being so much time with you, and you definitely are not Now Knowing Me, Philip? Behold, he that is Now Beholding Attentively Me, is Now Beholding Attentively the Father. So then, how are you Saying, You must Show us the Father?

10 Are you definitely not Committing that I Inside the Father, and the Father is Inside Me? The Word that I am Uttering to you, I am definitely not Uttering from Myself. But the Father Continuing Inside Me, He is Doing the God-Works.

11 You Must be Committing to Me that I inside the Father and the Father inside Me, but if not, because of My Works by God you Must be Committing to Me.

12 Truly, Truly, I Say to you, he that is Committing to Me, the Works by God that I Do, he shall Do also. And Greater than these shall he Do, because I am Going to My Father.

13 And Whatever anyone ever shall Ask in My Name, this I Will Do, that the Father should Attribute Glory in the Son.

14 If you should Ask anything in My Name, I Will Do It.

The Coming of the Holy Spirit

15 If you should God-Love Me, you must by your choice Keep My Commandments,

16 And I will Earnestly Request of the Father, and He will Give you Another of the same kind Advocate, in order that He should Continue with you Forever,

17 The Spirit of The Truth Whom the satan's world is definitely not able to Receive, because it is not Perceiving Him, neither is Recognizing Him, but yourselves Know Him that is Abiding with you, and shall be Inside you.

18 I will definitely Not Part from yourselves as orphans, I am Coming Within yourselves.

19 Yet a little while and the satan's world perceives Me no more, yet you are Perceiving Me. Because I am Living, yourselves Shall Live also.

20 In That Day you yourselves shall Know that I Inside My Father, and yourselves Inside Me, also I Inside you.

He who Keeps My Commands Loves Me

21 He that is having My Commandments and is Keeping them, the same is he that is Loving Me, and he that is Loving Me shall be Loved by My Father, and I will God-Love Him, and Myself Make Known plainly to him.

22 Judas said to Him, definitely not the Iscariot, Oh Lord, how is it now become, that You Expect Yourself to be Made Known plainly to us, and definitely not to the satan's world?

23 Jesus Answered and Spoke to him. If any man should God-Love Me, He shall Keep My Words, and My Father will God-Love him, and We will Come to Him, and We will Finalize an Abode with him.

24 He that Continuously Loves Me not is definitely not Continuously Keeping My Words, but the Word that you are Continuously Hearing is definitely not Mine, but definitely the Father's that Sent Me.

25 These things I am now Uttering to you, Continuing with you.

Holy Spirit will Teach you All Things

26 And the Advocate, the Holy Spirit, Whom the Father shall Send in My Name, then He shall Teach you All things, and shall Remind you All things, Whatever I have Spoken to you.

27 Peace I am Concerning for you. I am Continuously Giving to you My Peace, definitely not just as the satan's world gives, I am Giving to you. Your heart must not be made troubling. You must neither

be in terror.

28 You have Heard how I Spoke to you, I am Going Away and I am Coming for you. If you God-Love Me, you have been Made Rejoicing that because I have Spoken. I am Going to the Father, because My Father is Greater than I am.

29 And now I am Spirit Saying to you before it Comes to pass, that when it should Occur, you should have by your choice Committed.

30 I will not anymore Utter very much more with you, because the ruler of this the satan's world is coming, and definitely is not having anything of Me.

31 But definitely in order that the satan's world should have Known that I am Loving the Father, and just as the Father God Commanded Me, in this manner I am Finalizing. You must raise up, We should be moving along from here.

I am The Vine

15 I AM, the True Vine, and My Father is the Husbandman.

2 Every small Branch in Me bringing not Fruit, He Takes Away, and anyone that is Bringing Fruit, He is Spiritually Cleansing him, that he should be Bringing much More Fruit.

3 Already yourselves are Purified, because of the Spiritual Word that I am Now Uttering to you.

4 You must have Continued Inside Me, also I Inside you, just as the small branch is not able to bring Fruit from itself, except it should have Continued Inside the Vine, in this manner neither yourselves except you should have Continued Inside Me.

5 I AM, The Vine, yourselves are the small Branches. He that is Continuing In Me, also I Inside him, he is Bringing very Much Fruit, for without Me you are definitely not Able to Finalize anything.

6 If any man might not have Continued Inside Me, he has been Made Casted outside as the small branch, and has been

Made Dried up, and they are gathering together by their choice, also they are Cast into the fire, and it is Made Burning.

7 If you should Continue Inside Me, and My Words should Continue Inside you, if whatever you should by your choice strongly Desire, you shall Ask for yourselves, and it shall Occur for you.

8 In this My Father has been Made Attributed Glory, that you should Bring very Much Fruit, and you should Become My disciples.

9 Just as the Father has Loved Me, also I have Loved you. You must Continue inside My God-Love.

10 If you should Keep My Commandments, you shall Abide in My God-Love, just as I have Kept My Father's Commandments, and Abide in His God-Love.

11 These things I am now Uttering to you, that My Joy Inside you should Continue, and your Joy should be Made Fulfilled.

12 This is My Commandment, that you should Love one another just as I have Loved you.

13 Greater God-Love no man is Having than this, that any man should Lay Down his soul in behalf of his friends.

14 Yourselves are My friends, if you should be Doing whatever I God Command you.

15 I Call you Bondslaves no more, for the Bondslave is definitely not Now Spiritually Discerning what his Lord is Doing, but I am now Spirit Saying Friends, for all things which I have Heard from My Father I have Made Known Supernaturally to you.

16 You yourselves have definitely not chosen Me, but definitely I have Myself Chosen you, and I have Positioned you that yourselves should Go Away, and should Bring Fruit, and that the Fruit of yourselves should be Continuing, that whatever any one should Ask the Father in My Name, He should Give to you.

17 These things are God Commanded to you, that you should God-Love one another.

The satan's world hates you

18 If the satan's world is hating you, you know it is now, first of all hating Me, before you.

19 If you were of the satan's world, the satan's world would affectionately love whoever of its own. But because you are definitely not of the satan's world, but definitely I have for Myself Chosen you out from the satan's world, because of this, the satan's world is hating you.

20 You must remember the Spiritual Word that I have Spoken to you, A Bondslave is definitely not greater than his Lord. If they persecuted Me, they shall also persecute you. If they have Held as Sacred My Spiritual Word, they will Hold as Sacred yours also.

21 But definitely all these things they shall do to you, because of My Name, since they definitely do not discern the One sending Me.

22 Except I have Come and Uttered to them, they were not definitely having sin, but now they are definitely having no pretense for their sin nature and sin.

23 He that is hating Me, also is hating My Father.

24 If I have not Done the Works by God among them which none other of the Same Kind is now doing, they were definitely having no sin, but now they also are beholding attentively Me, and are now hating both Me and My Father.

25 But definitely in order that the Word should have been made Fulfilled, therein made Written in their Law, For they have hated Me without cause. (Ps 69:4)

Holy Spirit will Help Testify of Me

26 But when the Advocate should have Come, Whom I will Send to you from the Father, the Spirit of Truth, Who is Going Out from the Father, He shall be Bearing Record of Me.

27 And yourselves also are Bearing Record, since from the Beginning you are with Me.

Followers Warned of persecution

16 These things I am now Uttering to you, that you should not be made offended.

2   They shall make you to be put out from synagogues, but definitely a short time is coming, that anyone killing you should have thought to be offering worship to God.

3   And these things they shall do to you, because they know definitely not the Father, neither Me.

I Depart, to Send the Holy Spirit

4   But definitely these things I am now Uttering to you, that when that short time should come, you should be remembering yourselves that I Spoke these things to you. And I Spoke definitely not to you at the beginning, because I was with you.

5   But now I am Going Away to Him that Sent Me, and none of you are earnestly requesting of Me, Wherein are You Going Away?

6   But definitely because I am now Uttering these things to you, grief is now Fully Filling your heart.

7   But definitely I am Saying to you the Truth. It is Essential for you that I Should Go, because if I should not Go, the Advocate shall definitely not Come to you, but if I Should Go I will Send Him to you.

8   And when He has Come, He shall Expose as sin the satan's world of sin nature and sin, and of Righteousness, and of Final Judgment.

9   Of sin nature and sin, because certainly they are definitely not Committing to Me.

10 And of Righteousness, because I am Going Away to My Father, and you are not further seeing Me anymore.

11 And of Final Judgment, because the ruler of this the satan's world is Now being Made Judged.

12 I have yet very much to Say to you, but definitely you are definitely not Able to Bear for now.

13 But when He, the Spirit of Truth, should Come, then He shall Guide you into All Truth, because He shall definitely not Utter from Himself, but definitely whatever He might Hear, He shall Utter, and Coming He shall Declare to you.

14 He shall Attribute Glory to Me, for He shall Take of Me, and shall Declare to you.

15 All things that the Father is Having are Mine. Because of this, I Spoke that He shall Take from Me, and He shall Declare to you.

Ask in the Authority of My Name

16 A little while and you are definitely not Seeing Me, and again a little while and you shall for yourself Spiritually See Me, because I Go Away to the Father.

17 Then spoke from among His disciples one to another, What is this that He is Saying to us, A little while and you are definitely not seeing Me with perception, and again a little while, and you shall See the Spiritual Appearance of Me then because I am Going Away to the Father?

18 Therefore, they said, What is this He is Saying, A little while? We are definitely not discerning what He is Uttering.

19 Jesus then knew what they were willing to earnestly request of Him, and Spoke to them. Are you seeking among yourselves, about this that I Spoke? A little while, and you are definitely not seeing Me with perception, and again a little while, and you shall See the Spiritual Appearance of Me.

20 Truly, Truly, I say to you, that you yourselves shall weep and yourselves lament, but the satan's world shall rejoice, and yourselves shall be made to grieve, but definitely your grief shall end in Joy.

21 A woman, when she should be delivering is having grief, because her hour has come, but when the little child should be born, she is not anymore further remembering of the affliction because of the Joy, that a man has been made born into the satan's world.

22 And yourselves, therefore, are certainly having grief now, but I will See you again, and your heart shall Rejoice, and your Joy none is taking away from you.

23 And in that same Day, you shall definitely not earnestly request anything of Me. Truly, Truly, I Say to you that whatever you should Ask the Father in My Name, it shall be Given to you.

24 Up to now, you have definitely not Asked in My Name. You must Ask and you shall Receive, that your Joy should now be Made Fulfilled.

I have Overcome the world

25 These things I am Now Uttering to you in proverbs. The Hour is coming when I shall definitely no more be Uttering further in proverbs to you, but definitely I shall Plainly Declare to you of the Father.

26 By that same day you shall ask for yourselves in My Name, and I am definitely not Saying to you, that I will earnestly request of the Father for you,

27 Because the Father Himself is Affectionately Loving you, for yourselves have Affectionately Loved Me, and you are now Committing, that I Came Out from God.

28 I Came Out from the Father and I Came Into the satan's world. Again, I Part From the satan's world, and I am Going to the Father.

29 His disciples said to Him, Behold, now, You are Uttering plainly, and You are not Saying a proverb.

30 Now we are Knowing that You Spiritually Discern all things, and You definitely need not that any man might be earnestly requesting of You. By this, we are Committing that You Came Out from God.

31 Jesus made Answer to them, From now are you Committing?

32 Spiritually Behold, the Hour is coming even is Now Come, that every man should be made dispersed to his own. Even you might dismiss only from Me, and yet I am definitely not alone, for My Father is With Me.

33 These things I am Now Uttering to you, that in Me you should Have Peace. In the satan's world you shall have affliction, but definitely you Must Be Encouraged. I Have Overcome the satan's world.

The Lord Prays to His Father

17 These things Uttered Jesus, and He Lifted Up His Eyes to Heaven, and Spoke. Father, the Hour is Now Come. You must Attribute Glory to Your Son, in order that Your Son also, should Attribute Glory to You.

2 Just as You have Given Him Authority over all sinful flesh nature, in order that He should Give Life Eternal to whomever that You are Now Giving to Him.

3 And this is Eternal Life, that they should be Knowing You continuously, the Alone True God, and Jesus Christ, Whom You have Sent Out.

4 I have Attributed Glory to You on the earth. I have Made Perfect the Work by God that You are Now Giving Me, in order that I should Finalize.

5 And now, O Father, You must Attribute Glory to Me with Yourself, with the Glory that I was Having With You Before the satan's world which was to be.

I Have Manifest You to men

6 I have Manifested Your Name to the men out from the satan's world that You are Now Giving to Me. They were Yours, and You are Now Giving them to Me, and Your Words they are Now Holding as Sacred.

7 Now they are Knowing that Everything that You are Now Giving to Me is from You.

8 For I am Now Giving to them the Words, that You are Now Giving to Me, and they have Received Them, and they have Known Of Truth that I have Come Out from You, and they have Committed that You have Sent Me Out.

Jesus Prays for His Followers

9 I am Earnestly Requesting for them. I am definitely not Earnestly Requesting for the satan's world, but definitely for whom You are Now Giving to Me, for they are Yours.

10 And all Mine are Yours, and Yours Mine, and I am Being Now Made Attributing Glory Inside them.

11 And I am further no more in the satan's world, but these are in the satan's world, and I am Coming to You Holy Father. You must Keep them in Your Name that You are Now Giving to Me, that they should be One, just as We.

12 When I was with them in the satan's world, I was Keeping them in Your Name. Those You are Now Giving to Me, I have Maintained, and none of them has for himself been destroyed, except the son of the damnation, that the Scriptures should have been Made Fulfilled.

13 And now I am Coming to You, and I am Uttering these things in the satan's world, that they should be Having My Joy Fulfilled in themselves.

The world will hate Jesus' Followers

14 I am Giving them Your Word, and the satan's world has hated them, for they are definitely not of the satan's world, just as I am definitely not of the satan's world.

15 I am definitely not Earnestly Requesting that You take them away out from the satan's world, but definitely that You should Keep them Out From the evil.

16 They are definitely not of the satan's world, just as, I AM, definitely not of the satan's world.

Make them Holy by Your Truth

17 You must Make them Holy by The Truth of You. The Word is the Truth of You. (1 John 5:6)

18 Just as You have Sent Me Out into the satan's world, I also have Sent them Out into the satan's world. (John 20:21)

19 And in behalf of them, I am Making Myself Holy, in order that they also should now be Made Holy Inside Truth. (John 14:6; John 17:11, 21-22)

Pray for them that they Convert

20 Definitely not in regard of these only, that I am continuously Earnestly Requesting but definitely also in regard to those, who shall be Committing for the result and purpose of Me, through their Spiritual Communication.

21 In order that they All should be One, just as You, O Father in Me, also I in You, in order that they should be One in Us also, in order that the satan's world should have Committed that You have Sent Me Out.

22 And My Glory which You are now Giving to Me, I am now Giving to Them; that just as We are being One, They should be One.

That they may all be Perfect

23 I in Them and You in Me, that They should now be Made Perfect in One, in order that the satan's world should be Knowing that You Sent Me Out, and You have God-Loved Them just as You have God-Loved Me.

I Pray that they may Be with Me

24 Father, Whom You are now Giving to Me, I am Willing that Whereto I AM, that They also should be Perceiving My Glory with Me that You have Given to Me, for You have Loved Me before the Conception of the satan's world.

Your Love in them, and I in them

25 Oh Righteous Father, yet the satan's world has definitely not known You, but I have Known You, and These have Known that You have Sent Me Out.

26 And I have Made Known to Them, Your Name, and I will Make Known, in order that the God-Love with which You have God-Loved Me, should be Inside Them, and also I Inside Them.

Our Lord's betrayal and arrest

18 Jesus Spoke these things. He came out with His disciples to other side of Brook Cedron whereto was a garden into which also He entered with His disciples.

2 And Judas, who delivered Him up in betrayal wherein the place that Jesus had often made gathered together there with His disciples.

3 Then Judas also received a band of officers from the chief priests and Pharisees, coming there with lanterns and lamps and weapons.

4 Jesus, therefore, Discerning All things that are coming against Him, came out to Speak with them, Whom are you seeking?

5 They answered Him, Jesus of Nazareth. Jesus Says to them, I AM. And Judas also, who delivered Him up in betrayal, stood with them.

6 As soon as He Spoke to them that, I AM, they thereby went backward and fell down to the ground.

7 Then He Questioned them again. Whom are you seeking? And they spoke, Jesus of Nazareth.

8 Jesus Answered, I have Spoken to you that, I AM. If, therefore, you are seeking Me, you must dismiss these to be going away,

9 That the Spiritual Word should be Fulfilled which He Spoke, For those You are Now Giving to Me, I have definitely not lost anyone of them.

10 Then Simon Peter having a sword drew it out, and harmfully struck a slave of the High Priest and cut away his right ear, and, Malchus, the name for the slave.

11 Then Jesus Spoke to Peter, Put Away your sword into the sheath. The Cup which the Father is Now Giving to Me, shall I never ever Drink It?

12 Then the band, and the chief captain, and officers of the Jews physically took Jesus and bound Him,

13 And lead Him away first of all to Annas, because He was father in law of Caiaphas, who was the High Priest that same year.

14 Now it was Caiaphas who was counseling the Jews, how it is essential One Man be destroyed in behalf of the people. (John 11:49-53)

Peter denies Jesus

15 And Simon Peter was following Jesus, also another disciple of same kind that was an acquaintance with the High Priest, both went with Jesus into the palace of the High Priest.

16 But Peter stood at the door outside. Then came out the other disciple of same kind, who was an acquaintance of the High Priest, and spoke to the door keeper, and conducted in Peter.

17 Then the maid servant, the portress, said to Peter, Are you not also of the disciples of this man? He said, I am definitely not.

18 And the slaves and the officers had stood there making a fire of coals, for it was cold weather, and they were warming themselves with them. Also Peter is now standing warming himself.

High Priest examines Jesus

19 Then the High Priest earnestly requested of Jesus about His disciples, and about His Teaching.

20 Jesus Answered Him, I Uttered plainly to the satan's world. I always Taught in the synagogues, and in the Temple area, whereto always the Jews come together, and in secret I have Uttered nothing.

21 Why are you questioning Me? You must question who are now hearing what I have Uttered to them. Behold, they are now knowing what I Spoke.

22 And when He has Spoken these things, one ot the officers now standing, gave a slap with palm of hand to Jesus, speaking, Are you answering the High Priest in such a manner?

23 Jesus made Answer to him, If I have Uttered an evil work afflicted, you must witness of the evil work, but if God-Working, why are you beating Me?

24 Then Annas sent Him out, bound to Caiaphas, the High Priest.

25 And Simon Peter has been now standing and warming himself. They spoke, therefore, to him. Are not you also of His disciples? He disclaimed Him and spoke. I am definitely not.

26 One of the slaves of the High Priest, being a kinsman whose ear Peter cut away, says Have I definitely not seen you in the garden with Him?

27 Again, then, Peter disclaimed, and immediately, a cock crowed.

Jesus taken to Pilate

28 Then they led Jesus away from Caiaphas to the Judgment Hall, and it was being early morning. But also they would definitely not enter into the Judgment Hall, that they definitely might not be made defiled, but definitely in order that they should eat the Passover.

29 Therefore, Pilate came out and spoke to them, What accusation are you bringing against This Man?

30 They answered and spoke to him, Except He was an evil doer, we would definitely not have ever delivered Him up to you.

31 Then Pilate spoke to them, take Him yourselves and judge Him, according to your Law. The Jews, therefore, spoke to him. It is definitely not lawful for us to kill,

32 In order that the Spiritual Communications of Jesus should be Made Fulfilled, which He Spoke, signifying what Death He was expecting to Die.

33 Then Pilate entered into the Judgment Hall again, and called for Jesus, and spoke to Him. Are you King of the Jews?

34 Jesus Answered him. Are you saying this of yourself, or have others of same kind spoke to you about Me?

35 Pilate answered, Am I possibly a Jew? Your own nation and the chief priests delivered You up to me. What have You done?

36 Jesus Answered, My Kingdom is definitely not of this, the satan's world. If My Kingdom Rule were out from this, the satan's world, My under servants would fight whoever, that I should not be made delivered up to the Jews. But now, instead, My Kingdom Rule is definitely not from here.

37 Pilate, therefore, spoke to Him. Are you a king then? Jesus Answered, You are saying that, I AM, a King? I am Now Made Born also for this. I am Come into this, the satan's world, in order that I should Give Witness to the Truth. Anyone that is with the Truth is Hearing My Voice.

38 Pilate says to Him, What is Truth? And when he spoke this, he came out again to the Jews, and says to them, I am finding no accusation against Him.

39 But a custom is with you, that I might dismiss away one to you in the Passover. Are you intending, therefore, that I might dismiss away to you the King of the Jews?

40 Then they all cried again, saying, Not Him, but definitely Barabbas! Now Barabbas was a robber.

Pilate examines Jesus

19 Then, therefore, Pilate took to receive and then scourged Jesus.

2 And the soldiers braided a crown of thorns, placed it upon His Head, and clothed Him with a purple robe.

3 And were calling, Rejoice King of the Jews! And they were giving Him slaps with palms of hands.

4 Then Pilate came out, outside again, and said to them. Behold, I am leading Him outside to you, that you should know that I am finding, NO accusation against Him.

5 Then came out Jesus outside wearing the thorny crown, and the purple robe, and he says to them, Behold, The Man!

6 When then the chief priests and the

officers discerned Him, they screamed, calling, You must Crucify, Crucify Him. Pilate said take Him yourselves, and you must crucify Him because I definitely find No accusation against Him.

7   The Jews answered him. We have a Law and by our Law He ought to die, because He made Himself the Son of God.

8   When Pilate, therefore, heard this Spiritual Word, he was made much more afraid.

9   And entered again into the Judgment Hall, and said to Jesus, From where are you? But Jesus gave definitely no Answer to him.

10 Then Pilate says to Him, Are You definitely not uttering to me? Are You definitely not discerning that I have authority to crucify You, and authority to have You set at liberty?

11 Jesus Answered. You were having definitely no authority against Me except it is Now Made Given to you from Above. Because of This, he that delivered Me up in betrayal to you has the greater sin.

12 Out from this, Pilate sought to dismiss Him away, but the Jews were crying out saying, If you should dismiss Him away, you are definitely not a friend of Caesar. Any who makes himself a king is against Caesar.

13 As soon as Pilate heard this word, he lead Jesus outside, and he sat down in the judgment seat in a place called Pavement, also Hebrew script, Gabbatha.

14 And it was Preparation Day of the Passover, and about the sixth hour, and he says to the Jews, Behold your King!

15 But they screamed, you must take up, you must take up, you must crucify Him. Pilate said to them. Shall I crucify your King? The chief priests were made to answer, We have definitely no king except Caesar.

Pilate delivers Jesus to be Crucified

16 Then, therefore, he delivered Him up to

them, in order that they take Jesus along, that He should be made crucified, and they led away.

17 And He, bearing His cross, came out into that called place of a skull, which Hebrew script makes called Golgotha.

18 Whereto they crucified Him and with Him two others of same kind, one side, also other side, then Jesus, the middle.

19 And Pilate wrote also a title and put upon the cross, and there was made written, JESUS OF NAZARETH THE KING OF THE JEWS.

20 This title, therefore, read many of the Jews, for the place was near the city, whereto they were made to crucify Jesus. It was made written, Hebrew script, Greek, and Latin.

21 Then, the chief priests said to Pilate, You must not write, the King of the Jews, but definitely that He Spoke, I am King of the Jews.

22 Pilate answered, That which I wrote, I wrote.

23 Then the soldiers when they have crucified Jesus, took His clothes and divided to four parts, to every soldier a part. And the coat was a seamless coat woven from the top through the whole.

24 Then they spoke to one another, We should not split this, but definitely, we should cast lots for it. Then that Scripture should have been made Fulfilled that say, They divided My clothes among themselves, also for my raiment they cast lot (Ps 22:18). Then, indeed, the soldiers did these things.

25 Now alongside to the cross of Jesus had stood His mother, and His mother's sister, Mary of Cleophas, and Mary Magdalene.

26 Jesus, therefore, Discerning His mother, and the disciple standing that He Loved, Said to His mother, Woman, Behold, your Son.

27 Following that, He Said to the disciple, Behold your mother, and from that same hour the disciple took her into his own

home.

28 After this, Jesus Spiritually Discerned that already all things are now being made Finally Fulfilled, that the Scripture should have been Made Perfect. He Said, I Thirst. (Ps 69:21)

29 Then a vessel set full of vinegar, also filling a sponge of vinegar, and placing it upon a hyssop, offered to His Mouth.

30 Then when Jesus received the vinegar, He Spoke. It is now made Finally Fulfilled, and Lowering down His Head, He Delivered Up the Spirit.

Not a Bone of Jesus was broken

31 This is the Jews Preparation Day, therefore, the Body should not continue on the cross by the Sabbath. In fact the Preparation Day was for the Great Day, their Sabbath. They earnestly requested of Pilate that they should break to pieces their legs and they should be made taken away.

32 Then came the soldiers and broke to pieces the legs, indeed of the first, and then the other of same kind crucified together with Him.

33 But for when they came to Jesus they discerned Him as already a corpse. They definitely broke not His Legs to pieces.

34 But definitely one of the soldiers stabbed His Side with a spear, and immediately came out Blood and Water.

35 And He that Beheld Attentively Bear Record, and His Testimony is True. Also, He is Knowing what He Saying is True, in order that yourselves by your choice should be Committed.

36 For these things Came To Pass in order that the Scriptures should be Made Fulfilled. A Bone of Him shall definitely not be made broken into pieces. (Ex 12:46; Ps 34:20)

37 And again another of a different kind Scripture Says, They shall Spiritually Look Upon Whom they have pierced. (Zech 12:10)

Burial in a sepulcher

38 Then after these things, Joseph from Arimathaea, being a disciple of Jesus, but being hidden because of fear of the Jews, earnestly requested of Pilate that he might take away the Body of Jesus, and then Pilate permitted him to come, and take away the Body of Jesus.

39 And there came also Nicodemus, who first of all came to Jesus at night, bringing about a hundred pounds mixture of myrrh and aloes.

40 Then they took the Body of Jesus, and bound Him with linen cloths with the spices, just as is custom of the Jews to prepare burial.

41 Now in the place whereto He had been Made Crucified was a garden, and in the garden a New of a different kind sepulcher, therein that never yet none laid down.

42 Therefore, there they laid down Jesus, because of the Jews Preparation Day, for the sepulcher was near.

Jesus Rises the first day of the week

20 The first day of the week, Mary Magdalene is coming early in the morning being still dark to the sepulcher, and seeing the stone taken away from the sepulcher,

2 So then she runs and comes to Simon Peter and to the other disciple of same kind that Affectionately Loved Jesus, and says to them, They have taken away the Lord out from the sepulcher, and I Spiritually am definitely not Knowing wherein they have put Him.

3 Therefore Peter and the other disciple of the same kind departed, and were coming to the sepulcher.

4 So they were running, the two together, yet the other disciple of same kind outran more hastily than Peter, and came first to the sepulcher.

5 Then, he stooping down, definitely not yet entering, he saw the linen clothes lying,

6 Then comes Simon Peter following

him, and entered into the sepulcher, and perceived the linen clothes lying.

7 And the napkin that was over His Head, wrapped, but definitely lying apart in one place, definitely not with the linen cloths.

8 Then, therefore, entered also the other disciple of same kind who came first to the sepulcher, and he Spiritually Discerned and Committed,

9 For they never yet Spiritually Discerned the Scripture, that He ought to Arise from the Dead.

10 Then the disciples went again to themselves.

Jesus appears to Mary Magdalene

11 But Mary had stood at the sepulcher, weeping outside, then she was weeping as she looked down into the sepulcher.

12 And sees two Angels in White Sitting themselves, one at the head, and one at the feet, whereto used to be laying the Body of Jesus.

13 And then they Say to her, Oh woman, why are you weeping? She Says to them. Because they have taken away my Lord, and I definitely Know not wherein they have laid Him down.

14 And when she spoke these things, she turned around about backward, and sees Jesus now Standing, and definitely knew not that it is Jesus.

15 Jesus Said to her, Woman, Why are you weeping? Whom are you seeking? She, thinking that He is a gardener, said to Him, Oh Sir, if you borne Him, you must speak to me. Wherein have you laid Him down? Also, I will take Him away.

16 Jesus Said to her, Oh Mary, then she turned around, then saying to Him, Oh Rabboni, which is to say, Oh Master.

17 Jesus Said to her, You must not touch me, for I am not yet Ascended to My Father. But you must Go to My Brethren, and you must Speak to them. I am Ascending to My Father, and your Father, and to My God, and to your God.

18 Mary Magdalene Came to Tell the disciples that she has now Seen Attentively the Lord, and these things He Spoke to her.

Jesus appears to the Disciples

19 Then being evening, the same day, the first day of the week, and the doors shut whereto the disciples were gathered together, because of fear of the Jews, Jesus Came and Stood in the very midst, and Said to them, Peace to you.

20 And when He was Speaking this, He Showed them His Hands and His Side, as soon as the disciples Spiritually Saw the Lord they were Made Glad.

21 Then Jesus Spoke to them again, Peace to you, just as My Father is Now Sending Me Out continuously by His Choice, I also, I am continuously Sending you by My choice. (Jn 17:18)

22 When He Spoke this, He Breathed on, and is Saying to them, You must Take to Receive by your choice the Holy Spirit.

23 Any whenever of whose sin natures and sins you should Dismiss by your choice, they are Made Dismissed to them. Any whoever you should Retain by your choice, they are Made Retained.

Thomas Commits to Christ

24 But Thomas, one of the twelve, called Didymus, was definitely not with them when Jesus Came.

25 Then the other disciples of same kind were saying to him, We have Attentively Seen the Lord. But he Spoke to them, Except I should see in His Hands, the print of the nails, and should put my finger in the print of the nails, and put my hand into His Side, I will definitely not Commit.

26 And after eight days again His disciples were inward, and Thomas with them. Then Jesus Came, with the doors shut. He Stood in the midst and Spoke, Peace to you.

27 Then He Said to Thomas, You must bring your finger here, and you must Spiritually Discern My Hands, and you must

bring your hand and put into My Side, and you must be not faithless but definitely Faithful.

28 And Thomas answered and spoke to Him, my Lord and my God!

29 Jesus Said to him, Oh Thomas, Because you are now Continuously Beholding Me Attentively, you are now Continuously Committing. Spiritually Blessed, those that have not Seen, yet have Committed.

30 And then, actually, many other Miracle Signs of same kind did Jesus in the Presence of His disciples, which are definitely not Written in this Book.

31 But these things are made Written that you should by your choice have Committed, that Jesus is the Christ the Son of God, and that Committing by your choice, you should be having by your choice Life in His Name.

Seven Disciples go fishing

21 After these things, Jesus Manifested Himself again, to the disciples at the Sea of Tiberias, and Manifested in such a manner.

2 Together were Simon Peter, and Thomas called Didymus, and Nathanael of Cana in Galilee, and those of Zebedee, and two others of the same kind of His disciples.

3 Simon Peter said to them. I am going away fishing. They said to him, also we are coming with you. They departed and ascended into the ship immediately, and in that night caught nothing.

When morning came Jesus was there

4 But in early morning already occurring, Jesus Stood on the shore. However, the disciples had Spiritually definitely not Known that it is Jesus.

5 Then Jesus Said to them, Little children are you not having any solid meat? They answered to Him, Definitely not at all.

6 And He spoke to them, You must cast the net to the right side part of the ship, and you shall find. Then they cast, and yet not anymore were they capable to draw it out, for the multitude of different fish.

7 So then, that same disciple that Jesus Loved said to Peter, It is the Lord! Simon Peter, as soon as he heard that it is the Lord, he wrapped on himself a fisher's coat because he was naked, and cast himself into the sea.

8 And the other disciples of the same kind came in a small boat, yet were not far off from the area, but definitely as away from two hundred cubits, drawing the net of fish.

9 Then as they disembarked on the earth they physically saw a fire of coals laid, and prepared fish laid upon, and bread.

10 Jesus Said to them, You must bring of the prepared fish, which you now have caught.

11 Simon Peter ascended, and drew out the net full of great fish upon the earth, a hundred fifty three, and being so large, the net definitely had not been made split.

12 Jesus Said to them, You must come now to dine. And none of His disciples were daring to inquire of Him, Who are You? Spiritually Knowing that He is the Lord.

13 Then Jesus comes, and takes the bread and gives to them, and the prepared fish likewise.

14 This is already the third time that Jesus Manifested to His disciples, having made Risen Up out from the Dead.

Simon, Do you Love Me?

15 Then, when they had dined, Jesus Said, Oh Simon Peter, son of Jonas, are you Loving (agapao, pure unselfish love) Me greater than these? He said to Him, Emphatically Yes, Oh Lord, You Spiritually Know that I affectionately love (phileo, brotherly love) You. He Said to him, You must Feed My Lambs.

16 He Said to him, again, the second time, Oh Simon Jonas, are you Loving (agapao) Me? He said to Him, Emphatically Yes, Oh Lord, You Spiritually Know that I

affectionately love (phileo) You. He Said to him, You must Shepherd My Sheep.

17 He Said to him the third time, Oh Simon Peter, do you affectionately love (phileo) Me? Peter was made grieved, because He Spoke to him the third time, Are you affectionately loving (phileo) Me? So then he spoke to Him, Oh Lord, you Spiritually Know all things. You Know that I affectionately love (phileo) You. Jesus Said to him, Feed My Sheep.

18 Truly, Truly, I Say to you, When you were younger, you were girding yourself, and walked wherever you were willing, but when you should have aged old, you shall stretch out your hands, and another shall gird you, and they shall bring you whereto you definitely not prefer.

19 And this He Spoke signifying what Death, he shall by His choice Attribute Glory to God. And having Spoken this, He Said to him, You must Follow Me.

Peter asks about John

20 Then Peter turning back Spiritually Sees the disciple whom Jesus Loved following, who also leaned on His chest in the Supper, and spoke, Lord, who is delivering You up in betrayal?

21 Peter seeing him said to Jesus, Lord, what about him?

22 Jesus Says to him, if he should continue until after I come, what to you? You must Follow Me.

23 Then came out an account to the Brethren, that the same disciple is not dying, yet Jesus Spoke not to him that he is not dying, but definitely, What to you, if I might Will him to continue until after I come?

24 This is the disciple who is Witnessing to These Things, and Writing These Things, and we Spiritually Discern that his Testimony is True.

25 And there is also many other things of same kind, Jesus did, which if they should be made Written, everyone, I assume the satan's world itself has not been accommodating the books written. Amen.

The Acts
of the Apostles

Taught by Christ for 40 days

1 The earlier Spiritual Communication I have actually made of all things, Oh, Theophilus, that Jesus began both to Do and to Teach,

2 God Commanded to the Apostles, whom He had Chosen through the Holy Spirit until that day He was Received Up.

3 To whom also He Presented Himself Living, after He had suffered with many Infallible Proofs, through the forty days He was Spiritually Seen by them, and Saying to them about the Kingdom Rule of God.

Told not to depart from Jerusalem

4 And assembled together with them, He Gave Command to them to not be going forth from Jerusalem, but Definitely being available for the Promise of the Father, which you have Heard of Me,

5 Because John certainly immersed in water, but yourselves shall be made Baptized in the Holy Spirit, definitely not long after these days.

You will Receive Power of the Holy Spirit

6 Indeed, therefore, coming together they questioned Him saying, Oh Lord, if in this time are You Restoring the Kingdom Rule to Israel?

7 And He Spoke to them, It is definitely not for you to Know the times or the Special Seasons, that the Father has Put In His own Authority.

8 But definitely, you shall receive Miracle Power of the Holy Spirit Coming Upon you, and you shall be Witnesses of Me and in Jerusalem, and also in all of Judea, and Samaria, and until after the last parts of the earth.

Jesus Taken Up in a cloud

9 And when He Spoke these things, they saw Him Lifted Up, and a Cloud undertook Him away from their eyes.

10 And as they were attentively looking, He Went into Heaven, and Behold, two Men stood by them in White Apparel,

11 Who also Spoke. Oh men of Galilee, why are you now standing looking upon to Heaven? The same Jesus Whom was Received Up away from you into Heaven, shall so Come in This Manner, that you are Seeing Him going into Heaven.

Stayed in the upper room in Prayer

12 Then they returned into Jerusalem away from the Mount called Olives, which is near Jerusalem, having a Sabbath day's journey.

13 And when they entered they ascending into the upper chamber, where they were tarrying and also Peter, and James, and John, and Andrew, Philip, and Thomas, Bartholomew, and Mathew, James of Alpheus, and Simon the Zelotes, and Judas of James.

14 These all were Continuing with full agreement in Prayer and in Supplication, united with women, and Mary, the mother of Jesus, and united with His brothers.

Selected Matthias by lot

15 And in those days there was mutually a multitude of people's names among them, as a hundred twenty. Peter arising in the midst of the disciples, Spoke.

16 Oh men, Oh Brethren, the Scriptures must be Fulfilled, the same that the Holy Spirit has forewarned through the mouth of David concerning Judas, that became a guide to those that physically took Jesus,

17 Since he was being numbered together with us, and he has secured the lot of his serving.

18 Certainly then, this man possessed a space of land from the reward of unrighteousness, and falling headfirst the middle became burst open, and all His bowels spilled out.

19 And it became known to all that are dwellers in Jerusalem, so that the same space of land be called in their own language Aceldama, that is a space of blood land.

20 Yet it is written in the Book of Psalms, You must let his place in the sheep fold be desolate wilderness. So that not one must be dwelling in it, and his oversight another of a different kind Take to Receive beyond dreams. (Ps 69:25; Ps 109:8)

21 Therefore, it is required of these men coming together with us, in all the time that the Lord Jesus Entered and Came Out among us,

22 Beginning from the immersion of John, until after the day that He was Received Up from us, to become Witness of His Resurrection, United One with us of these things.

23 And they stood two, Joseph called Barsabas, who was surnamed Justus, and Matthias,

24 And they Spoke Praying, Oh Lord, You Know the hearts of all. You must Indicate from these two, which one You would Choose,

25 To receive allotment of this Service of Calling and Apostleship, from which Judas violated, to go to his own place.

26 And they gave their lots, and the lot fell down upon Matthias, and he was made Numbered with the eleven Apostles.

The Promised Holy Spirit Came

2 And when the day of Pentecost was fulfilled, they were all in the same with one accord.

2 And suddenly there became from Heaven, a roaring sound as driving of a turbulent strong wind, and Fully Filled all the dwelling where they were residing.

3 And there Spiritually Appeared to them as Cloven Tongues like as Fire Sitting Down mutually upon everyone there.

4 And they were all Filled with the Holy Spirit, and began to Utter in another of a different kind Tongue, just as the Spirit was Giving them to Sound Forth. (Gift of Tongues: 1 Cor 12:10; 1 Cor 14)

Jews from all the world gathered

5 And there were reverent Jews, men from every nation under Heaven dwelling in Jerusalem.

6 And when this Sound occurred the multitude of different people came together, and were made confused, because they were perceiving everyone, his own language being Uttered by them. (Gift of Interpretation of Tongues: 1 Cor 12:10; 1 Cor 14)

7 And they were all astonished and were marveling, saying to one another, Behold, are definitely not all them that are uttering Galileans?

8 And how are we Hearing every person in our own language, wherein we have been born?

9 Parthians and Medes, and Elamites, and those dwelling in Mesopotamia, and also Judaea, and Cappadocia, in Pontus, and Asia,

10 Phrygia, and also Pamphylia, Egypt, and the parts of Libya about Cyrene, also those newcomers, Romans, and both Jews and proselytes.

11 Cretans, and Arabians, we are Hearing their Uttering, in our Tongues the Great Works by God.

12 And they were astonished and all were puzzled, saying same kind to another of same kind, Beyond Dreams, whatever would this be?

13 And other ones of a different kind are scoffing, saying, These are filled with new wine!

Peter Addressed the large crowd

14 But Peter, standing with the eleven, lifted up his voice, and sounded forth to them, Men of Judea, and ye that dwell in Jerusalem, All This must be Known to you, and you must be giving regard to my Words.

15 Because these are definitely not drunken as yourselves are supposing, because it is the third hour of the day,

16 But definitely this is that now made Spirit Saying through the Prophet Joel.

17 And it shall be in the last days, Says God, I will Pour Out from My Spirit upon anyone with a sinful flesh nature, and your sons and your daughters shall Prophesy, and your young men shall Spiritually See Vision Appearances, and your Elders shall Dream Sleeping Visions.

18 And yet upon My Bondslaves and upon My Handmaidens, in those same days, I will Pour Out from My Spirit, and they shall Prophesy.

19 And I will Give Wonders in the Heaven above, and Miracle Signs upon the earth down below, blood, and fire, and vapor of smoke.

20 The sun shall be made replaced to darkness and then the moon to blood before the great and memorable Day of the Lord to come.

21 And it shall be that anyone, whoever, that should call for himself upon the Name of the Lord, shall be Made Saved. (Joel 2:32)

22 Men of Israel, hear these Spiritual Words, Jesus of Nazareth, a Man made Proved of God among you, by Miracle Powers and Wonders and Miracle Signs, which God did through Him in the midst of you, just as you yourselves Know.

23 Him, by the Determined Counsel and Foreknowledge of God, you have taken, bound, and delivered by lawless hands, intentionally killed, cruelly crucifying,

24 Whom God has Raised, Removing the travail of Death, according as definitely was not possible to hold to retain Him by it.

25 For David is saying about Him, I was before Seeing in the Presence of the Lord through all things, for He is by my Right Hand, that I should not have been made shaken.

26 Because of this, my heart has been made Merry and even yet my tongue Exceedingly Rejoicing, and my sinful flesh nature shall Lodge in Expectation,

27 For You shall definitely not forsake my soul in hades, neither shall You give Your Personally Holy to Spiritually See corruption.

28 You have Made Known Supernaturally to Me The Ways of Life. You shall Fully Fill Me with Gladness with Your Presence. (Ps 16:8 11)

29 Oh men, Oh Brethren, being Lawful to speak with boldness to you about the patriarch David, that so he is deceased and made buried and he is in his place of the dead among us until this day.

30 Therefore, Existing a Prophet and Spiritually Knowing that God Swore to him an Oath, that from the Fruit of His Loins, according to a (Sinless) Flesh Nature, to Raise the Christ to Sit Down upon His Throne. (Ps 132:11)

31 He Uttered about the Resurrection of Christ, foreseeing that the Living-Soul of Him was definitely not made left in hades, nor the (Sinless) Flesh Nature of Him has not Spiritually Seen corruption. (Ps 16:10)

32 God Raised this Jesus of whom we all are being witnesses.

33 Therefore, by the Right Hand of God being Made Exalted, and He also Received the Promise of the Holy Spirit from the Father, Who Poured Out This, that yourselves are now Spiritually Seeing and Hearing,

34 For David had not ascended into the Heavenlies, but he is saying himself. The LORD Spoke to My Lord You Must Sit at My Right Hand,

35 Until after I should Put whomever Your enemies under the Footstool of Your Feet. (Ps 110:1)

Whom ye Crucified, Lord and Christ

36 Therefore, all the House of Israel must know securely, that God has Made this Jesus, Himself Whom yourselves have crucified, both the Lord and Christ.

37 Now when they heard this they were made pricked in their heart, and also spoke to Peter and to the other Apostles. Oh men, Oh Brethren, what shall we do?

Repent for the Removal of your sins

38 Then Peter stated to them, You must Repent, and you must be Made Immersed, every person of you, in the Name of Jesus Christ, after Removal of sin natures and sins and shall Receive the God-Gift of the Holy Spirit.

39 Because the Promise is to you and to your children, and all those in far off, whoever should Invite the Lord our God.

40 And also, with many more Spiritual Words of a different kind, he Emphasized and Encouraged saying, You must be Made Saved from this crooked generation.

41 Then gladly, they were certainly gladly receiving his Spiritual Words, and were Made Immersed. The same day were made added about three thousand souls.

42 And they were Continuing in the Apostles' Teaching and Fellowship, and in Breaking of Bread, and in Prayer.

New Life and Holy Spirit Manifested

43 And very much fear came upon every soul, and many Wonders and also Miracle Signs occurred through the Apostles.

44 And all that were Committing by their choice were with them, also they were having all things common.

45 And were selling in the market their acquired possessions and substances, and were dividing them to all according as whoever was having need.

46 And as also, they continuing daily with one accord in the Temple area, and also at home they were partaking in Breaking Bread with nourishment, exceeding Joy and singleness of heart.

47 Praising God and having Thankfulness for Grace with all the people, and the Lord was adding more Saved to the Assembly daily.

Peter and John Healed a cripple

3 Then Peter and John for themselves were ascending to the Temple area for the ninth hour of Prayer.

2 And a certain man existing being crippled from his mothers' womb, who was borne to be laid down every day at the Temple area door called Beautiful, to ask alms from those passing into the Temple area.

3 Who Spiritually Seeing Peter and John, expecting to go into the Temple area, was earnestly requesting alms.

4 And Peter attentively looked upon him united with John spoke, You must look to us.

5 And then he was giving heed to them, watching for something to receive from them.

6 Then Peter spoke, Pieces of silver and gold exist definitely not with me. But what I am having, this I am giving to you, in the Name of Jesus Christ of Nazareth, you must Raise Up for yourself, and you must Walk by your choice.

7 And catching him by the right hand, he raised up instantly by his choice, and his feet and ankle bones were made strong.

8 And jumping up, he stood, and was walking, and entered united with them into the Temple area, walking, and leaping up, and praising God.

9 And all the people Spiritually Saw him walking and praising God.

10 And also they were fully knowing him, that he was among those that were sitting for alms, in the way of the Beautiful Gateway of the Temple area, and were made filled with amazement and ecstasy over what is now happening to him.

11 But as the crippled made cured is holding to retain Peter and John, all the wondering people ran together to them on the porch called Solomon.

Peter Preached Repentance

12 And when Peter Spiritually Saw, He answered to the people. Oh men of Israel, why are you marveling at this? Or why are you attentively looking as by our own miracle power or godliness we made him to walk?

13 The God of Abraham and Isaac and Jacob, the God of our fathers has Attributed Glory to His Child Jesus, Whom yourselves delivered up and disclaimed Him in the presence of Pilate, the same judging to set Him at liberty.

14 But yourselves disclaimed the Righteous and Holy One, and asked for a man, a deliberate murderer, to be freely forgiven to you.

15 And killed the Lord Author of Life, that God Raised Up from the Dead, whereof we are being Witnesses.

16 And by Faith of His Name, him whom you are seeing and Spiritually Discerning has been Made Strong. His Name and Faith through Him has given to him his complete Health before you all.

17 And now Oh Brethren, I Spiritually Perceive that by ignorance you have acted, as also your rulers,

18 But God Who has Shown Before through the Mouth of all His Prophets, for Christ to suffer in the same manner, He has Fulfilled.

19 Therefore you must Repent and be Converted for blotting out your sin natures and sins, so that whenever the Special Restoring should Come from the Presence of the Lord,

20 And He should Send Jesus Christ, Preached Before to you.

21 Whom, indeed, Must the Heaven Receive until the Time of Restitution of all things that have been God Uttered through the Mouth of all His Holy Prophets for the Age.

22 Because Moses, indeed, Spoke to the fathers, that a Prophet same as me shall the Lord your God shall Raise from your Brethren. Him you shall Hear in all things whatever He should Utter to you. (Deut 18:15-19)

23 And it shall be that all whose soul might not ever Hear This Prophet, the same shall be Made Destroyed out from the people.

24 And then, also, all the Prophets from Samuel and in order, as many as Uttered also have Before Shown these days.

25 You are yourselves, the sons of the Prophets and the Covenant that God granted to our fathers, saying to Abraham, And through your Seed shall all the families of the earth be made to benefit. (Gen 22:18)

26 To you first of all, God Raised His Child Jesus, Sent Him Out to Bless you in turning away every person from your evil actions.

Five thousand Committed to Him

4 And as they were uttering to the people, the priests, and the captain of the Temple area, and also the Sadducees themselves stood ready,

2 Being grieved because of them Teaching the people, and Proclaiming much in Jesus, the Resurrection out from the dead.

3 And they laid hands upon them, and put for keeping until tomorrow, wherein it was because already the evening hour.

4 And many that were hearing the Spiritual Word, Committed, and the number of the men occurred about five thousand.

Peter brought before the High Priest

5 And it came to pass on the next daylight day, to gather them, the rulers and elders and scribes together

6 In Jerusalem, then Annas the High Priest, and Caiaphas, and John, and Alexander, and those who were kindred of the High Priest.

7 And standing them in the midst, they were inquiring by what Miracle Power or in what Name have you done this yourselves?

8 Then Peter, Filled with the Holy Spirit, Spoke to them, Rulers, and people, and

Elders of Israel,

9 While we this day are made examined for judgment about the benefit of the weak man, by Whom he is now made Healthy.

10 Be it known to you all, and to all the people of Israel, that in the Name of Jesus Christ of Nazareth, that yourselves crucified, Whom God Raised Up out from the Dead, he by This One is now standing, in the presence of you, Healthy.

11 This is the Stone, the least esteemed by you the builders, Who became at the Head of the Corner. (Ps 118:22)

12 Also definitely Salvation is not in anyone other, because there is not another name of a different kind, given under Heaven among men by Whom we are required to be made Saved.

Peter commanded not to preach

13 Now perceiving the boldness of Peter and John, and apprehending that they are illiterate and ignorant men, they were marveling but mutually fully knowing them and also that they were United with Jesus.

14 And seeing the man now made healed standing United with them, they were having nothing to speak against.

15 But when they commanded them to go outside of the council, they pondered with one another.

16 Saying, What shall we do with these men? For indeed, because through them, the known Miracle Sign has now occurred, Openly Manifest to all that are dwelling in Jerusalem, and we are definitely not able to disclaim.

17 But definitely, that it not spread to many more among the people, we should threaten them with a threat, to no longer utter about anything in the Name of This Man.

18 And calling them, they gave command to them not to speak intelligibly, nor to Teach at all in the Name of Jesus.

19 Peter and John answered and spoke to them, Whether it is Righteous in the Presence of God to hear much more of you or of God, you must judge,

20 Because we definitely cannot not utter the things that we have Spiritually Discerned and have heard.

21 So further threatening, they set them at liberty, finding nothing how they might punish them, because all the people Attributed Glory (Spiritual Perfection) to God for what is now occurring,

22 Because the man was greater than forty years on whom this Miracle Sign of curing occurred.

Assembly Rejoices

23 And being set at liberty, they came to their own, and told what the chief priests and the elders spoke to them.

24 And when they heard, they took up their Voice to God with one accord and Spoke, Oh Lord, You, the God who made the Heaven, and earth, and sea, and all that in them (Ex 20:11),

25 Who through the mouth of David, your dependent child Spoke, Why do the nations rage and the people imagine delusions?

26 The kings of the earth have stood and the rulers have been made gathered together against Him, against the Lord, and against His Christ. (Ps 2:1-2)

27 Because in Truth they, Herod and mutually Pontius Pilate with the nations and the people of Israel, have been made gathered together against Your Holy Child Jesus, Whom You have Spirit Anointed,

28 To do whatever Your Hand and Your Counsel have Predetermined to Occur.

29 And now, Lord, You must Take Note against their threatening's, and You must Give to Your Bondslaves to Utter all Your Spiritual Words with Boldness,

30 By You stretching out Your Hand to Cure, and Miracle Signs, and Wonders, occurring through the Name of Your Holy Child Jesus.

Had all things in common

31 And when they were made Praying earnestly, the place in which they were made Gathering Together was made to shake, and all were Made Filled with the Holy Spirit, and were Uttering by their choice the Spiritual Word of God with Boldness.

32 And the heart of the multitude of different people was Committed, and their soul as one, and neither was any one saying about his own material goods, but definitely they were being of their own all things common.

33 And the Apostles were yielding back with great Miracle Power, to the Testimony of the Resurrection of the Lord Jesus, and also the Great Grace was upon them all.

34 For neither lacked anyone existing among them, because all the owners of space of lands or existing houses were selling, bringing the prices sold in the market.

35 And they laid them down by the Apostles' feet. And it was made distributed to every person, according as to whomever was having any need.

36 And Joses, who was called Barnabus by the Apostles, is interpreted, Parmenas, the son of consolation, a Cyprus Levite, from the kindred,

37 Existing to himself a field, sold, brought the money, and laid (it) down by the Apostles feet.

Ananias and Sapphira lied, died

5 But a certain man named Ananias, united with Sapphira his wife, sold an acquired possession,

2 And kept back of the price, and his wife also completely understood, and bringing laid down a certain part by the feet of the Apostles.

3 But Peter spoke, Oh Ananias, why then has the satan filled full your heart to lie to the Holy Spirit, and you to keep back from the price of the space of land?

4 You definitely are not Abiding. While it was continuing made sold in the market by your existing authority, why have you designed about this matter in your heart to definitely not lie to man for yourself, but definitely to God?

5 And Ananias hearing these Spiritual Words fell down and gave up the soul and spirit, and great fear occurred upon them hearing all these things.

6 And the younger arose, enwrapped, brought out and buried him.

7 And it became as a space of three hours, then the wife herself entered, not Spiritually Discerning what came to pass.

8 And then Peter made an answer to her, You must speak to me, whether you were made paid so much for the space of land, and she spoke, Emphatically Yes, so much.

9 Then Peter spoke to her, How then was he made to agree together with you to tempt the Spirit of the Lord? Behold, the feet of those that buried your husband, shall also bring you out through the door.

10 Then she instantly fell down by his feet, and gave up the soul and spirit. When the young men entered, they found her dead, so bringing out, they buried with her husband.

11 And great fear came to pass upon all the Assembly, and upon all that were hearing these things.

Apostles put in prison

12 And by the Hands of the Apostles occurred many Miracle Signs and Wonders among the people, and they were all With One Accord in that Porch of Solomon.

13 Also, of the rest none were daring to be made to join to them, but definitely the people were magnifying them.

14 And those Committing were made added much more to the Lord, multitudes of different people, both men and women.

15 So that they brought out the weak upon the streets, and positioned beds and mattresses in order that, if the shadow of Peter overshadowing might be coming

upon anyone of them.

16 Then were coming together also a multitude of different people out of surrounding cities of Jerusalem for bringing weak and made vexed by morally impure spirits, who were all made Healed.

17 Then the High Priest arose and all they with him, being a sect of the Sadducees, they were made filled with evil envy.

18 And laid their hands on the Apostles, and put them in keeping publicly.

19 But the Angel of the Lord in the night, Opened the prison doors, and mutually Leading them Out, Spoke,

20 You must Go Stand and you must Utter in the Temple Area to the people all the Words of this Life.

21 And Hearing That, they entered in the Temple area coming up early in the morning. They were Teaching, but the High Priest and those united with him called together a council. And all the senate of the sons of Israel now sent out to the jail to lead them.

22 But when the officers came up, they definitely found them not in the prison, they each returned and told,

23 Saying that actually they found the jail shut up with all safety, and the guards outside standing before the doors, but opening within, we have not found.

24 Now as the priest and the captain of the Temple area and the chief priests were puzzling about these Spiritual Words, and also they have heard about this, whatever has come to pass beyond dreams,

25 Then one came up to tell them saying that, Behold, the men that you put in the prison are in the Temple area, now standing and Teaching the people.

26 Then the captain went with the officers, lead them, definitely not with violence because they were fearing the people that they might not be made stoned.

27 And leading them to stand within the council, and the Chief Priest now questioned them.

28 Saying, have we definitely not given command to you, by command to not be Teaching in This Name? And behold, you are now filling Jerusalem full with your Teaching, and you are intending to inflict us with the Blood of This Man.

29 Then Peter and the Apostles answered, Spoke, We ought to Listen to God much more than men.

30 The God of our fathers Raised Up Jesus that yourselves violently killed, hanging upon a Tree.

31 Him, God has Exalted Lord Author and Savior, at the Right Hand of Him, to Give Repentance to Israel, and Removal of sin natures and sins.

32 And we are being His Witnesses, by the Words of these things, and also the Holy Spirit, Whom God has Given to them Listening to Him. [God and Him in this verse are referring only to God the Father. The Father resides in Heaven, and we are to only Pray to and obey the Father just as Jesus did on earth. Jesus Prayed only to the Father and did God's Works through His obedience to the Father, as we are to do likewise, with Jesus' Holy Spirit leading us.]

Gamaliel spoke for release

33 This, when they were hearing, they were made cut, and they were consulting to intentionally kill them.

34 Then arose a certain man in the council, a Pharisee named Gamaliel, a doctor of the Law, always of great reputation to the people, commanded to put the Apostles outside some little measure.

35 And also he spoke to them, Oh men of Israel, You must take heed to yourselves, in the way that you are expecting to practice these things upon these men.

36 For before these days arose Theudas, saying to be somebody himself, to whom a number of men, about four hundred clinged, who were intentionally killed, and all that were persuaded by him scattered and came to pass to nothing.

37 After this, arose Judas the Galilean in

the days of taxing registration, and departed away sufficiently many people after
him, he also perished, and all, as many as
were made persuaded by him scattered.

38 And now I say to you, You must depart
away from these men, and you must allow
them, for if this counsel should be out from
man or man work, this shall be made torn
down,

39 But if it is of God, you shall definitely
not be able to it tear down, for fear that you
should be found opposing God.

Apostles released with a warning

40 And they were made persuaded by
him, and invited the Apostles, beat, and
give command not to Utter in the Name of
Jesus, and set them at liberty.

41 They then certainly went from the
presence of the council, Rejoicing that they
had been made Counted Worthy to be
dishonored in behalf of His Name.

42 And also every day in the Temple area
and in a home, they definitely ceased not to
Teach and Proclaim Jesus Christ.

Widow neglected, seven chosen

6 And in those days of multiplying of the
disciples, there became murmuring
from the Greek speaking against the Hebrews, because their widows were missed
in the periodic Serving.

2 Then the twelve, invited the multitude
of different disciples, spoke, It is definitely
not pleasing, our leaving the Spiritual
Word of God, to serve tables.

3 Therefore, Oh Brethren, you must visit
out from you seven men Witnesses, Full of
the Holy Spirit and Wisdom, that we shall
make rulers over this need.

4 But we shall be continually in Prayer,
and the Service (of Calling) of the Spiritual
Word.

Stephen and others chosen

5 And the Spiritual Communication
pleased in the presence of all the multitude
of different people, and they chose for
themselves Stephen a man Full of Faith and
the Holy Spirit, and Philip, and Prochorus,
and Nicanor, and Timon, and Parmenas,
and Nicolaus, a proselyte of Antioch,

6 Whom they stood in the presence of
the Apostles, and then Praying, laid their
Hands on them.

7 And the Word of God Grew, and a great
number of disciples multiplied exceedingly
large in Jerusalem, and also a multitude of
priests were obeying to the Faith.

Lies told against Stephen to quiet him

8 And Stephen Full of Faith and Miracle
Power was doing great Wonders and
Miracle Signs among the people.

9 Then arose certain ones of the synagogue called Libertines, and Cyrenians,
and Alexandrians, and those of Cilicia and
Asia, discussing about Stephen.

10 And they were definitely not capable to
stand against the Wisdom and the Spirit
from Whom he was Uttering.

11 Then they induced men to commit
perjury, saying that they heard him uttering words blasphemous against Moses
and God.

12 And also they stirred together the
people, and the elders, and the scribes, and
they standing ready seized him, and lead to
the council.

13 And also stood false witnesses, saying
this man definitely ceases not blasphemous words, that is uttering against this
Holy Place, and the Law.

14 For we heard him saying that Jesus
of Nazareth Himself shall tear down this
place, and shall change the customs which
Moses delivered up to us.

15 And all those sitting themselves in the
council attentively looked upon him, discerned his face, like as the face of an Angel.

High Priest hears Stephen's Speech

7 Then spoke the High Priest, When
are you having these things in such a

manner?

2　And then he stated, Oh men, Oh Brethren, and Oh fathers, you must hear, the God of Glory Spiritually Appeared to our father Abraham, when he was in Mesopotamia before he dwelt in Charran.

Abraham obeyed God

3　And Spoke to him, You must Come Out from your area, and from your relatives, and you must Come Forward into the area whichever I will Show you. (Gen 12:1)

4　Then He came out from the area of Chaldaeans, after there dwelt in Charran. After his father died, He carried him into the area, in this which yourselves are now dwelling.

5　And He gave to him definitely no inheritance in it, neither a seat of judgment with stool for feet, yet He promised to give to him his possession upon occupying, and to his Seed after him. There being yet definitely no child to him.

6　And God Uttered in this manner that his Seed shall be a foreigner in another area, and they shall become their slaves, so also shall be evil harm for four hundred years. (Gen 15:13; 17:8)

7　And the nation to whomever they should bondserve, I will Judge. I, God have Spoken, for after these things they shall depart, and they shall be devoted to Me, in this place. (Gen 15:14; Ex 3:12)

Covenant of Circumcision

8　And He Gave to him a Covenant of circumcision, and so Isaac was to be born, and circumcised him on the eighth day, as Isaac, then Jacob, and then Jacob's twelve patriarchs.

Jacob's twelve sons; Joseph sold

9　And the patriarchs strongly desiring to envy, traded Joseph into Egypt, but God was with him.

10　And set him free out from every affliction of his, and gave Grace and Wisdom to him before the sight of Pharaoh, king of Egypt, so he made him ruler, being esteemed over Egypt, and all of his House of Pharaoh.

Great draught; Jacob into Egypt

11　Now there came a famine over all the area of Egypt and Canaan, and a great affliction, and yet our fathers found definitely no sustenance.

12　When Jacob heard there was wheat in Egypt, he first of all sent forth our fathers,

13　And at the second (return), Joseph was made known to his brothers, and the kindred of Joseph became openly manifest to the Pharaoh.

14　Then sent out Joseph to summon his father, Jacob, and all his relatives, seventy five souls.

15　And Jacob came down into Egypt, and deceased, he and our fathers.

16　And was made transferred to Sychem, and laid down in the place of the dead that Abraham firmly acquired, with pieces of silver from the sons of Emmor of Sychem.

Jacobs family grew in Egypt

17　But just as the time of the Promise which God swore to Abraham approached near, the people increased and multiplied in Egypt,

18　Until when another King of a different kind arose, that Spiritually knew not Joseph. (Ex 1:8)

19　This man dealt subtly with our kindred. He evil harmed our fathers, to force them to cast out their newborns, thereby to not preserve life.

Moses by Pharaoh's daughter

20　Within this Special Time Moses was born, who was reared three months in the home of his father, and was handsome from God.

21　And when he was imperiled, Pharaoh's daughter received him up, and reared him for her own son.

22 And Moses was disciplined in all wisdom of Egyptians, and was exceedingly able in words and in man works.

23 And as he fulfilled forty years' time, it ascended in this heart to visit his brethren, the sons of Israel.

24 And seeing somebody being hurt, he defended, and taking revenge for the oppressed, he struck mortally the Egyptian.

25 He supposed that his brethren understood him, how that God through his hand would give Salvation to them, but they had definitely not understood.

26 And the next day, he saw them quarreling and brought them together for Peace. He spoke, Men, you are brothers yourselves, Why are you hurting one another?

27 But he that was unjust to his neighbor cast him away, speaking, Who made you a ruler and justice giver over us?

28 Will you not intentionally kill me, in the manner that you intentionally killed the Egyptian yesterday? (Ex 2:14)

29 Then, with this word, Moses fled, and became a foreigner in the area of Midian, where he has born two sons. (Ex 2:13-15)

After 40 years; Burning Bush

30 And having fulfilled forty years in the desolate wilderness of the mountain Sinai, The Angel of the Lord Spiritually Appeared to him within the Flame of a Fiery Bush.

31 When Moses saw, he marveled at the vision, and he came near. And to him behold, the Voice of the Lord came to pass to him,

32 I am the God of your fathers, the God of Abraham, and the God of Isaac, and the God of Jacob (Ex 3:6, 15). Then Moses trembled, becoming definitely not daring to Behold.

33 Then the Lord Spoke to him, You Must Remove the shoes from your feet, because the Place upon the earth in which you are now standing is Holy.

34 I have Seen the sight of the evil treatment of My people in Egypt, and Heard the groaning of them, and I have Come Down to Set them Free, and now you Must Come Forward. I will Send you Forward into Egypt.

35 This Moses that they disclaimed, speaking: Who made you a ruler and justice giver? Him, Whom God Sent Out, a Ruler and Remover by the Hand of the Angel, Who Spiritually Appeared to him in the Bush.

36 He Lead them Out Doing Wonders and Miracle Signs in the area of Egypt, and in the Red Sea, and in the desolate wilderness forty years.

37 This is that Moses, who Spoke to the sons of Israel, A Prophet to you shall the Lord God Raise of you from your Brethren, same as I, Him you shall Hear. (Deut 18:15)

38 This is He that was in the Assembly in the desolate wilderness with the Angel, Who Uttered to him in Mount Sinai, and with our fathers who Received the Living Oracles to Give to us.

39 To Whom our fathers would definitely not become Obedient, but definitely cast away, and turned their hearts to Egypt,

40 Speaking to Aaron, You must make us gods that will precede us, because this Moses that led us out from the area of Egypt, we are definitely not Knowing what is occurring with him. (Ex 32:1)

41 And they made a calf in those same days, and brought up sacrifice to the idol, and were making merry among themselves for the man works of their hands.

42 Then God Turned Around, and delivered them up to be devoted to the host of heaven, just as written in the book of the Prophets, Have you, House of Israel, not offered to Me even as sacrifice slain beasts for forty years in the desolate wilderness?

43 And you received up the tabernacle of moloch, the star of your god remphan, and the models that you made to worship them. Even I will Carry yourselves beyond Babylon.

44 The Tabernacle of Testimony, just

as He appointed for Himself, was for our fathers in the desolate wilderness, Uttering to Moses to make it according to the Model that he had Beheld Attentively,

Joshua Led them into the New Land

45 Which also our fathers that came after conducted in with Jesus occupying the possession of the Gentiles, whom our Father God drove out from the presence of our fathers, until after the days of David,

46 Who found Grace in the Presence of God, so asked to guarantee an earthly Tabernacle for the God of Jacob,

47 But Solomon built for Him the House of God.

48 But definitely the Most High dwells definitely not in temples made with hands, just as the Prophet Says.

49 Heaven My Throne and the earth a Footstool for My Feet. What House of God shall you Build Me, Says the Lord? Or what the Place for My Spiritual Heavenly Rest?

50 Has definitely not My Hand done all these things? (Isa 66:1-2)

51 Oh obstinate and Oh uncircumcised in heart and ears. Yourselves are continuously opposing the Holy Spirit, as your fathers so also yourselves.

52 Who of the Prophets have definitely not your fathers persecuted and killed, who have shown before about the Arrival of the Righteous One? Now yourselves are become traitors and deliberate murderers.

53 You, who have received the Law upon Assignment by Angels, and you have definitely not maintained it (the Lord's Inner Holy Spirit Teachings).

Stephen is martyred

54 When they heard these things they were made cut to their hearts and ground their teeth against him.

55 But he, existing Full of the Holy Spirit, attentively looked into Heaven. He Spiritually Saw the Glory of God, and Jesus now Standing at the Right Side of God.

56 And spoke, Behold, I see the Heaven now made Opened, and the Son of Man Standing at the Right Side of God.

57 Then they cried out with a great voice, constrained their ears, and ran violently with one accord against him.

58 And cast him out outside the city, casting stones, and the witnesses laid aside their clothes near the feet of a male youth called Saul.

59 Even as they were stoning, Stephen was Calling upon and Saying, Oh Lord Jesus, You must Receive my spirit.

60 And positioned on His knees, he cried out with a great voice, Oh Lord, You should not bring to them this sin. And speaking this, he was Made to Rest Asleep.

Saul persecutes the Assemblies

8 And Saul was consenting to his killing, and in the same day occurred a great persecution, and also upon the Assembly in all Jerusalem, and also the Apostles were made scattered widely in the lands of Judea and Samaria.

2 And then reverent men together carried Stephen, and made great lamentation over him.

3 As for Saul he was making havoc of the Assembly and also coming into the homes, dragging both men and women, delivering up into prison.

4 Therefore, they were certainly scattered widely passing throughout, Proclaiming the Word.

Philip Preached in Samaria

5 Then Philip descended to the city of Samaria, Preaching Christ to them.

6 And also the multitudes of people were Taking Heed with Full Agreement to the Sayings made by Philip, with those Hearing them, and also Seeing the Miracle Signs which he Did.

7 For many demonized, many morally impure loudly pleading spirits were coming out with long great sound, and the

palsied and crippled were Made Healed.

8   And there occurred great Joy in that city.

9   But then a certain man, before being in the city using magic, named Simon, and astonished the nation of Samaria, saying himself to be somebody great,

10   That all took heed from small to great, saying, This man is the miracle power of the great god.

11   And they were taking heed to him because by sufficiently long time the magic astonished them,

12   But when they Committed to Philip Preaching the Gospel about the Kingdom Rule of God, and the Name of Jesus Christ, they were Made Immersed, both men and women.

13   For then Simon himself also Committed and was made Immersed. Continuing with Philip he was astonished, both Seeing the Miracle Signs and Miracle Powers Occurring.

14   And when the Apostles in Jerusalem heard that Samaria had Received the Word of God, they Sent Peter and John out to them.

15   When they came down, they Prayed for them that they should Receive the Holy Spirit.

16   For as He was not yet falling upon them, only that they were Made Immersed Existing in the Name of the Lord Jesus.

17   Then they were laying Hands on them, and they were Receiving the Holy Spirit.

18   When Simon saw that through the Laying On of Hands of the Apostles is Made Giving the Holy Spirit, he offered them money,

19   Saying, To I also you must give this authority, that upon whomever I might lay on hands he should Receive the Holy Spirit.

20   But Peter spoke to him, Your exchange money with you should be for damnation. You have supposed that the God-Gift of God is possessed through money.

21   You are neither portion, definitely nor lot in this Word, because your heart is definitely not Straight in the Presence of God.

22   Therefore, you must Repent of this your malicious desire for evil work, and you must Pray Earnestly to God, that so then in the event that He shall Remove from Memory, Forgive, for you the imagining of your heart,

23   For I Behold Attentively you being in the bile of bitterness, and uniting bond of unrighteousness.

24   Simon answered and spoke, You Must Pray earnestly yourselves in Behalf of me to the Lord, so that nothing should come upon me that you are Now Being Spirit Saying.

25   Therefore, indeed Testifying and Uttering the Word of the Lord, they returned to Jerusalem, and also in many villages of the Samaritans they Preached the Gospel.

Philip Preaches to an Ethiopian

26   And an Angel of the Lord Uttered to Philip Saying, You must Raise and yet you Must Go southward, in the way of travel coming down from Jerusalem to Gaza, which is desolate wilderness.

27   And he Arose and Went, and you must Spiritually Beholding an Ethiopian eunuch, who had come to worship in Jerusalem, a man of mighty authority to Candace, queen of the Ethiopians, who was over all of her treasure house.

28   And also he was returning, and sitting in his chariot, reading the Prophet Esaias.

29   Then the Spirit Spoke to Philip, you Must Come near, and you Must be Made Joined to this chariot.

30   Philip ran forward and heard him reading from the Prophet Esaias, and he Spoke, When are you yet Knowing what you are reading?

31   And he spoke, How am I ever able, except someone should guide me? He encouraged Philip to ascend and also to sit down with him.

32   And the passage of the Scripture

being read was, He was Lead as a sheep to the slaughter, and as a dumb Sacrificial Lamb before the sight of His shearer, so He Opened definitely not His Mouth.

33 In His humiliation His Judgment was taken away, and who shall recite His generation? For His Life is made Taken Up from the earth. (Isa 53:7-8)

34 And the eunuch answered to Philip, Speak, I Pray earnestly of you, of whom is the Prophet saying this, of himself or about some other one of a different kind?

35 Then Philip Opened his mouth and began Proclaiming Jesus to him from this Scripture.

36 And as they went upon the way of travel they came to a certain water, and the eunuch stated, You must behold, water. What forbids me to be Made Immersed?

Philip Baptizes Ethiopian eunuch

37 And Philip spoke, If you are Committing Continuously by your choice from within all of your heart, it is Lawful. And he answered speaking, I am Committing Continuously by my choice to Jesus Christ being the Son of God.

38 And he commanded the chariot to stand, and they both came down into the water, both Philip and the eunuch, and he immersed him.

39 And when they ascended out from the water, the Spirit of the Lord Caught Up Philip, and the eunuch saw him definitely not anymore, yet he went on his way of travel Rejoicing.

40 But Philip was found at Azotus, and passing through, he was Preaching the Gospel in all the cities, until after he Came to Caesarea.

Saul Converted on road to Damascus

9 So Saul further breathing out threatening and murder toward the disciples of the Lord, came near to the High Priest.

2 He asked of him epistles to Damascus to the synagogues, so that if he might find anyone being on the way of travel, both men and women, so also they should be lead bound to Jerusalem.

3 And in going, He was being approaching near to Damascus, and unexpectedly a Light from Heaven Shined Around him,

4 And falling down to the earth, he Heard a Voice Saying to him, Oh Saul, Oh Saul, Why are you persecuting Me?

5 And he spoke, Who are You, Oh Lord? And the Lord Spoke, I AM, Jesus that you are persecuting. Hard for you to kick against the pricks?

6 And also he trembling and awing spoke, Oh Lord, What are You Willing me to do? And the Lord to him, You Must Raise and you Must Enter into the city, and I shall Utter to you what you Must Do.

7 And the men who are journeying together with him, stood speechless, hearing actually the sound, but perceived nothing.

8 And then Saul was Made Risen Up from the earth, and when his eyes were opened he saw nothing, and led by hand, they conducted him into Damascus.

9 And he was three days not seeing, and had definitely not eaten, neither drank.

Ananias Sent to Paul

10 And there was a certain disciple in Damascus by the name of Ananias, and to him the Lord Spoke in a vision. And Ananias Spoke, Behold me, Oh Lord.

11 And the Lord to him, Rise, you must go in the street called Straight, and you must seek in the house of Judas, Saul of Tarsus. Behold for he is Praying.

12 And he has Spiritually Discerned in a Vision a man named Ananias, entering and Laying on him a Hand so that he Should Receive Sight.

13 Then Ananias answered, Oh Lord, I am now hearing from many about this man, that he has done evil work to your Saints in Jerusalem.

14 And here he has authority from the chief priests to bind all that are calling

upon Your Name.

15 But the Lord Spoke to him, You Must Go, for he is a Vessel of Election to Me. He is to Bear My Name in the presence of the nations, and to kings' sons and also Israel.

16 Yet, I will Forewarn him, what he Must suffer in behalf of My Name.

Paul Sees, Filled with the Holy Spirit

17 And Ananias went and entered into the house, and Laid his Hands on him. He spoke, Oh Brother Saul, the Lord Jesus Whom you Spiritually Saw in the way of travel that you were coming has Sent me Out, so that you should Receive Sight, and you should be Made Filled with the Holy Spirit.

18 And immediately, there fell off from his eyes like as scales, he Received Sight instantly and Arose, he was made Immersed.

In Damascus Paul Preached Christ

19 And when he received nourishment, he was Strengthened. Then Saul was with the disciples in Damascus certain days.

20 And Immediately he was Preaching Christ in the synagogues, that He is the Son of God.

21 But all that heard were astonished, and were saying, Is this definitely not he that wasted those that are calling upon this Name inside of Jerusalem, and came here for this, in order that he should lead them bound to the chief priests?

22 But Saul, instead was made More Strengthened, confusing the Jews dwelling in Damascus, confirming together that this Man is the Christ.

Paul Escapes to Jerusalem

23 And then as were made fulfilling sufficiently many days, the Jews counseled for themselves to intentionally kill him.

24 But their lying in wait had been Made Known to Saul, and also they were observing the gateways both by day and also by night, so that they might intentionally kill him.

25 Then the disciples took him by night, lowered him by the wall, letting down inside of a large hamper size basket.

26 And when Saul came up into Jerusalem, he attempted to join the disciples, but all were fearing him, not Committing that he is a disciple.

Barnabas Persuaded Apostles

27 But Barnabas took hold, having led him to the Apostles, and he recited to them how in the way of travel he Spiritually Saw the Lord, and that He had Uttered to him, and how in Damascus he Spoke Boldly in the Name of Jesus.

28 And he was with them coming in, and going out inside of Jerusalem.

Brethren Helped him to Tarsus

29 And he is Speaking Boldly in the Name of the Lord Jesus, both Uttering and Discussing with the Greek speaking, but they were presuming to intentionally kill him.

30 When the Brethren Fully Knew, they brought him down to Caesarea, and sent him forth toward Tarsus.

31 Then actually the Assemblies upon all of Judea, and Galilee, and Samaria were having Peace, being made Edified, and they were Multiplied, going in the Fear of the Lord, and in Consolation of the Holy Spirit.

Peter Heals Aeneas; many Saved

32 And it came to pass, Peter passed through every way to descend also to the Saints that dwell in Lydia.

33 And he found there a certain man named Aeneas, who was palsied, lying on a mattress for eight years.

34 And Peter spoke to him, Aeneas, Jesus Christ is Curing you. You Must Raise by your choice and you Must Straighten yourself, and immediately he arose.

35 And all that were dwelling in Lydda and Saron Spiritually Saw him there, Turned About to the Lord.

Peter Raises Tabitha from the dead

36 And in Joppa there was a certain female disciple named Tabitha, which interpreted is called Dorcas. She was full of God-Goods, Works by God, and alms which she was Doing.

37 It came to pass in those days, that she had been sick, died, and they washed and they laid her down in an upper chamber.

38 And in that Lydda was near to Joppa, the disciples heard that Peter was therein. They sent two men out to him, encouraging him to not hesitate to pass through to them.

39 Then Peter Arose and Came Together with them that came up, leading up to the upper chamber, and all the widows were weeping having stood beside her, and they showed as examples, the coats and garments that Dorcas made, being with them.

40 But Peter Sent Away them all outside, positioned his knees, Prayed, and Turned back to the body, Spoke, Oh Tabitha, You Must by your choice Raise, and then she by her choice Opened her eyes and Spiritually Seeing Peter, she Sat Up by her choice.

41 And he Gave a hand to her, Raising her, and Called for the Saints and the widows, Presenting her Living.

42 And it became Known by all in Joppa, and many Committed to the Lord.

43 And it came to pass that he Continued sufficiently many days in Joppa with Simon, a tanner.

Cornelius, a centurion's Vision

10 There was a certain man in Caesarea named Cornelius a centurion of the band called Italian,

2 Devout and Fearing God with all his home, and also gave many alms to the people, and Prayed earnestly with God unceasingly.

3 He Saw in a Vision openly, about the ninth hour of the day, an Angel of God Entering to him and Speaking to him, Oh Cornelius,

4 And attentively looking at Him, he also became afraid. He spoke, What is it Oh Lord? And He Spoke, Your Prayers and your alms have Ascended for a Memorial in the Presence of God.

5 And now you Must Send men to Joppa, and you Must Send for Simon that is called Peter.

6 He guest lodged with a certain Simon, a tanner, whose house is by the sea. He Shall Utter to you what you Ought to Do.

7 Then as the Angel went who Uttered to Cornelius, he called for two of his household servants, and also a continually devout soldier to him.

8 And when he had imparted to them all things, he sent them out to Joppa.

Peter's Vision of unclean meat to eat

9 And the next day they journeyed there, and approached near they ascending to the city. Peter was upon the housetop Praying, about the sixth hour.

10 And he became very hungry and would have eaten food, but being Ready he then Fell Upon this Trance.

11 And perceived Heaven Opening, and a vessel Coming Down to him as a certain great sheet bound at four corners, and lowered upon the earth.

12 Inside of this existing all four footed animals of the earth, and wild beasts, and creeping things, and birds of heaven.

13 And there came a Voice to him, Raise Peter, you Must Slay, and you Must Eat.

14 But Peter spoke, Not so, Oh Lord, for I never have eaten anything made unholy, or morally impure.

15 And the Voice again for the second time to him, What God has Cleansed, you Must Not Make unholy.

16 And this occurred for three times, and again the Vessel was made Received Up into Heaven.

17 Then as Peter puzzled in himself whatever that Vision he should beyond dreams Have Spiritually Discerned, and you must behold, the men sent out from Cornelius

made inquiry at the house of Simon, being Present at the gate.

18 They called for and inquired whether Simon, who was called Peter, guest lodged in this place.

Peter Invited by three men

19 And while Peter pondered about the Vision, the Spirit Spoke to him, Behold, three men are Seeking you.

20 But definitely Arise Up, you must Come Down, and you Must Go with them, judging no differences, since I Sent them Out.

21 Then Peter came down to the men Sent Out from Cornelius to him. He spoke, Behold, I am he whom you Seek. For what reason are you present?

22 And they spoke, Cornelius, the centurion, a Righteous man and Fearing God, and also Bearing Record by all the nation of the Jews, was made Warned as by an Holy Angel to Send for you Into his home, and to Hear Words from you.

23 Then invited them in and guest lodged them, and the next day Peter Departed with them, and some of the Brethren from Joppa came together with him.

To Caesarea to meet Cornelius

24 And the next day they entered into Caesarea, and Cornelius was Watching for them. He Called Together his kinsman and necessary friends.

25 Then as Peter was to enter, Cornelius encountered him, falling down, Worshiped at his feet.

26 But Peter Raised him up, saying, You must Raise, I also myself am a man.

27 And he talked with him, and entered finding many had Come Together.

28 And he also stated to them, You yourselves are aware as it is unlawful for a man, a Jew, to join or come near to another nation. But God has Shown to me to Not Call any man unclean or morally impure.

29 For this Reason, without contradiction, being Sent For, I Came to inquire, therefore, what Spiritual Word you Sent for me.

30 And Cornelius stated, I was Fasting from fourth day until this hour. And I was Praying in my home the ninth hour, and Behold a Man was Standing in the presence of me in Bright Apparel.

31 And He Stated, Oh Cornelius, He has Spiritually Heard your Prayers, and your alms have Made yourself Remembered in the Presence of God.

32 You must Send, therefore, to Joppa and you must Summon Simon who is called Peter. He is guest lodged in the house of Simon the tanner by the sea, who having come up shall Utter to you.

33 Speedily, therefore, I sent for you, and also you have done God-Working to Come Up. Now then we are all present in the Presence of God, to Hear all things being before Commanded to you by God.

Peter first time Preaching to Gentiles

34 Then Peter Opened his mouth to Speak, Of the Truth, I Apprehend for myself that God is definitely No Respecter of a person.

35 But definitely in Every Nation he that is Fearing Him, and is Working Righteousness is Accepted by Him.

36 The Spiritual Word that is Sent Out to the sons of Israel is proclaiming Peace through Jesus Christ. He is Lord of All.

37 Yourselves are now Spiritually Knowing the Word has Come to pass to all of Judaea, having begun from Galilee after the Immersion that John Preached.

38 As God Spirit Anointed Him, Jesus of Nazareth, with the Holy Spirit and Miracle Power, Who, because God was With Him, then passed throughout doing God-Good Work and Curing all those being made oppressed by the devil.

39 And we are being Witnesses of All Things that He Did in this land, and also in Judea, and in Jerusalem, Who was intentionally killed, hanging upon a Tree.

40 Him, God Raised Up after third day,

and Gave Him to Become Openly Manifest, 41 Definitely not to all the people, but definitely to Witnesses Hand Chosen Before by God, to us who Ate with and Drank with Him after He Raised out from the Dead.
42 And He Gave Command to us to Preach to the people and Testify, that it is He that is made Determined by God, the Judge of the Living and the dead.
43 This One, all the Prophets were Witnessing to receive Removal of sin natures and sins through the Name of Him, to everyone that is continuously by his choice Committing to Him.

Holy Spirit Poured Out to Gentiles

44 While yet Peter Uttered these Words, the Holy Spirit Fell Upon all those Hearing the Spiritual Word.
45 Those of the circumcision, the Faithful that Came Together with Peter, were Astonished, because also upon the Gentiles the God-Gift of the Holy Spirit is Poured Out.
46 For they Heard them Uttering with Tongues and Magnifying God. Then answered Peter,
47 Can possibly any man forbid water that these not be Immersed, who also Received the Holy Spirit just as we?
48 And also it was Before Commanded to them to be Immersed in the Name of the Lord. Then they earnestly requested of him to Intend to continue some days.

Peter defends his actions to Apostles

11 And the Apostles and the Brethren that were in Judea, heard that also the Gentiles had received the Spiritual Word of God.
2 And when Peter ascends into Jerusalem, those of the circumcision contended with him.
3 Saying that you have entered to uncircumcised men, and eaten with them.
4 But Peter beginning, was expounding to them in order, saying,

5 I was in the city Joppa Praying, and Spiritually Seeing, in an Ecstasy Vision, a certain vessel Coming Down as a great sheet with four corners being Lowered from Heaven, and coming as far as me.
6 Then I was attentively looking on to behold, and Spiritually Saw the four footed animals upon the earth, and the wild beasts, and creeping things, and the birds of heaven.
7 And I Heard a Voice Saying to me, Raise Peter and you must Slay and you must Eat.
8 But I Spoke, Not so, Oh Lord, for never has entered into my mouth anything made unclean or morally impure.
9 But by a second Voice Answered to me Out from Heaven, What God has Cleansed, you must not make unholy.
10 And this occurred for three times, and again Drew Up all into the Heaven.
11 And Behold, speedily three men being present in the house, therein being made Sent Out to me from Caesarea.
12 And the Spirit Spoke to me, Come Together with them not judging differences for yourself. Moreover those six Brethren came with Me and we entered into the man's home.
13 And also he told us how he had Spiritually Seen an Angel Standing in his home, and Spoke to him, You must Send Out men to Joppa, and you must Send for Simon called Peter,
14 Who shall Utter Words to you by which you shall be Made Saved, and all your home.
15 And when I then was to begin to Utter, the Holy Spirit Fell upon them as upon us in the beginning.
16 Then I myself remembered the Word of the Lord, as He was Saying, John indeed has immersed yourselves in water, but you shall be Made Immersed in the Holy Spirit.
17 If then God Gave to them the same God-Gift as also to us, Committing with Intent to the Lord Jesus Christ. Then who

am I that I was Capable to forbid God?

18 When Hearing these things, they remained quiet, and were Attributing Glory to God, saying, So then also God has Given Repentance to the Gentiles into Life.

Barnabas Sent to Antioch
19 Therefore, actually scattering widely from the affliction that occurred after Stephen, they passed through up to Phenice, and Cyprus, and Antioch Uttering to any the Word allowing that no more only to Jews.
20 And some of them were Cyprus and Cyrenian men, who entering into Antioch, they were Uttering to the Greek speaking, Preaching the Lord Jesus.
21 And the Hand of the Lord was with them, and also a large number Committed, turned about to the Lord.
22 When the Word was made Heard to the ears of the Assembly in Jerusalem about this, and also they sent forth Barnabas to pass through up to Antioch.
23 Who, when coming up, and Spiritually Seeing the Grace of God, he rejoices and was Encouraging all, that with Purpose of heart to Remain Steadfast with the Lord,
24 For he was a God-Good man and Full of the Holy Spirit and Faith, and Added more, a sufficient multitude of people, to the Lord.

Barnabas Departs to Tarsus for Paul
25 Then Barnabas departed to Tarsus searching for Saul.
26 And when he found him, it came to pass he led him to Antioch. And that in a whole year they gathered together with the Assembly, both to Teach a sufficient multitude of people, and also the Christian disciples in Antioch to be warned as first over all.
27 For there in those days descended Prophets from Jerusalem to Antioch.
28 And one of them arose named Agabus, signifying through the Spirit, that a great famine is to be Expected upon all the inhabited earth, which also came to pass in the time of Claudius Caesar.
29 And then, every person of the disciples just as any having ability, determined of themselves to send Service to those Brethren dwelling in Judaea.
30 Which also they did, sending out to the Elders through the Hand of Barnabas and Saul.

Herod kills James, brother of John
12 Then about this special time, Herod the king laid his hands to evil harm any from the Assembly.
2 And intentionally killed James, the brother of John, with a sword.

Herod holds Peter in prison, Passover
3 And so he Spiritually Saw this is pleasing to the Jews, he added more to physically take also Peter. Then these were the Days of Unleavened Bread.
4 And when then catching, he put into prison, delivering up to four quaternions of soldiers to maintain him, intending after the Passover to bring up him to the people. ('Passover' defined idiomatically in Luke 22:1)
5 Indeed, therefore, Peter was made kept in prison, but fervent Prayer was coming to pass by the Assembly to God in behalf of him.

Angel Takes Peter from prison
6 And when Herod expected to bring him before that same night, Peter was sleeping, made bound in chains between two soldiers, and also with two guards before the door keeping the watch.
7 And Behold, an Angel of the Lord Stood Ready, and Light Brightly Shined in the dungeon, and Striking Hard the side of Peter Raised him Up, Saying, You must Raise in haste, and the chains fell from his hands.
8 And also the Angel Spoke to him, You must Clothe About, and you must have Feet being Covered with your sandals, and

so he did. And He Said to him, You must Clothe with your robe, and Follow Me.

9   And he departed following Him, and definitely discerned not that it was True which was occurring through the Angel, then thinking he Spiritually Saw a Vision.

10 Then passing through the first and second prison, they came to the gateway of iron that progresses into the city, which Opened of itself to them. And coming out, they went forward to one street lane and immediately the Angel Departed Away from him.

11 And when Peter became to himself, he Spoke, Now I Spiritually Know Of Truth that the Lord Sent Forth His Angel and Set me Free out from the hand of Herod, and also from all the expectation of the people of the Jews.

Peter goes to brethren

12 And also Completely Understanding, he came to the house of Mary the mother of John, called Mark, where they were sufficiently United Together and Praying.

13 And when Peter knocked at the door of the gate, the maid servant named Rhoda came near to obey.

14 And when she fully knowing the voice of Peter, for joy she definitely opened not the gate, but ran in to tell that Peter stood before the gate.

15 And they spoke to her, You are insane. But she was confidently affirming to have in such a manner, that they were saying, It is His Angel.

16 But Peter was continuing to knock with Intent, and opening, they saw him and were astonished.

17 But he was beckoning to them with a hand to keep silence. He recited to them how the Lord Lead him Out from the prison. He spoke, And you must tell James and the Brethren these things. And departing, he went to another place of a different kind.

18 Now becoming day there was definitely no little commotion among the soldiers.

So then, where was Peter?

19 And when Herod seeking after him, and found him not, he examined for judgment and commanded the guards to be led away. And he descended from Judaea for Caesarea to stay.

Herod eaten by worms

20 And Herod was very displeased with Tyre and Sidon. But with full agreement they presented to him, and persuaded Blastus, the chamberlain of the king, to ask peace, because of their land being nourished by the noblemen.

21 And upon a set day Herod put on royal apparel, and sitting down upon a judgment seat made an oration to them.

22 And the public was shouting, The voice of god and definitely not of a man.

23 And instantly the Angel of the Lord struck him mortally for that he gave definitely not the Glory to God. He gave up the soul and spirit and became eaten of worms.

24 But the Word of God Grew and Multiplied.

Barnabas and Saul took Mark

25 And Barnabas and also Saul returned out from Jerusalem fulfilling their Service (of Calling), and took with them John, called Mark.

First missionary journey of Paul

13 Now there were certain Prophets and Teachers in the Assembly that was in Antioch, and also Barnabas and Simeon called Niger, and Lucius, and also Cyrenian Manaen brought up with Herod the tetrarch, and Saul.

2   While they ministered to the Lord and fasted, the Holy Spirit Spoke, So now you must Separate to Me both Barnabas and Saul for the Work by God wherein I am Inviting them.

3   Then when they had Fasted and Prayed, and Laid Hands on them, they Dismissed away.

Paul, Barnabas, and Mark in Cyprus

4   So they, indeed, were made Sent Forth by the Holy Spirit. They descended into Seleucia from that place, and also then sailed away for Cyprus.

5   And being in Salamis they Proclaimed much the Word of God in the synagogues of the Jews. They then had also, under servant John.

6   And passing through the island as far as Paphos, they found a certain mystical wise man, a false prophet, a Jew, whose name, Barjesus,

7   Which was with the deputy, Sergius Paulus, a prudent man who invited Barnabas and Saul, seeking after to hear the Word of God.

8   But Elymas, the mystical wise man, for so his name is made interpreted, stood against them, seeking to prevent the deputy from the Faith.

9   Then Saul, but now Paul, filled with the Holy Spirit, now attentively looked upon him.

10   And spoke, Oh, full of all subtle half-truth (deceit) and all evil mischief, son of the devil, enemy of all Righteousness, you shall definitely not cease to pervert the Straight Ways of the Lord.

11   And now, Behold, the Hand of the Lord is upon you, and you shall be Blind, not seeing the sun until a Special Time. And instantly a mist fell upon him, and darkness, and seeking by the hands to be led about.

12   Then the deputy seeing what had occurred, Committed, being amazed at the Teaching of the Lord.

From Pamphylia, Mark departed

13   Then moving up from Paphos, those with Paul, came to Perga of Pamphylia, but John departing fully from them returned to Jerusalem.

At Antioch of Pisidia, Paul Spoke

14   But they having passed through from Perga came up to Antioch of Pisidia, and entered into the synagogue on the Sabbath day. They sat down.

15   And after the reading of the Law and the Prophets, the ruler of the synagogue, sent out to them saying, Oh men and Oh Brethren, if you have a word with encouragement for the people, you must be saying.

16   Then Paul arising also beckoned with his hand, he spoke. Oh men, Israelites, and you that are Fearing God, you must Hear.

17   The God of this one people, Israel, chose our fathers, and Exalted the people when traveling as strangers in the area of Egypt, and with a high Mighty Arm Lead them out from there.

18   And then as for forty years' time, he suffered behaviors of them in the desolate wilderness.

19   And when He had Taken Down seven nations in the area of Canaan, He divided by lot their earth to them.

20   And after these things He Gave to them Judges as four hundred and fifty years up to Samuel the Prophet.

21   After there, they asked a king, and God Gave to them Saul the son of Cis, a man of the tribe of Benjamin, for forty years.

22   And when He had Completely Removed him, He Raised Up to them David for a king to them, and being a Witness Spoke. I Found David, of the man Jesse, after My own Heart, that shall do all My Will. (1 Sam 13:14)

23   God of This Seed, according to the Promise, has Raised Up the Savior Jesus to Israel.

24   John Preached Before the personal entrance of Him, Immersion of Repentance, to all the people of Israel.

25   And, as John Fulfilled his course Saying, Who were you surmising me being, I am definitely not He, but definitely behold, there is Coming After me, the One I am definitely not worthy to remove the shoes of His Feet. (John 1:27)

26   Oh men and Oh Brethren, Oh sons of

Abraham's kindred, and who among you are Fearing God? To you He has Sent Out the Spiritual Word of this Salvation,

27 For they who are dwelling in Jerusalem and their rulers are not Understanding of Him and the Voice of the Prophets Fulfilled as they Judging, being read every Sabbath.

28 And finding no reason for death themselves, they asked Pilate to intentionally kill Him.

29 And when they had Finally Fulfilled all things in regard to Him as Made Written, they took down from the Tree, laid down in a sepulcher.

30 But God Raised Him Up from the Dead.

31 Then was Spiritually Seen over many more days by those having come up with Him from Galilee to Jerusalem, who are Witnesses of Him to the people.

32 And we Proclaim to you that with these things, the Promise to the fathers Came to pass.

33 For this, God has also Fulfilled the same to us His Children, Raising Jesus, as also Made Written in the Second Psalm, You, You are My Son, this day I have Born You from Above.

34 And that He Raised Him from the Dead, no longer expected to return to corruption, in such a manner the Spirit is Saying, That I Give to You, the Personally Holy, the Faithful of David. (Isa 55:3)

35 For this reason, and in another of a different kind He Says, Definitely You shall not Give the Personally Holy of You to see corruption. (Ps 16:10)

36 For David, indeed, Served to his own generation by the Counsel of God, has been made to Sleep, and added more to his fathers, and saw corruption.

37 But He Whom God Raised Up, definitely saw no corruption.

38 It must be known, therefore, to you men, Brethren, that by This One, Removal of sin natures and sins is made Proclaimed much to you.

39 And from all these you could definitely not be able in the Law of Moses to be Made Righteous, whereby in This One, all that are by their choice Continuously Committing are continuously being Made Righteous.

40 You must Spiritually See, therefore, that nothing should come upon you that the Spirit is now Made Saying by the Prophets,

41 The Despisers must Spiritually Discern, and must Marvel, and must be made Vanished Away for the Work I am Working in this your day. A Work by God that you might never ever have Committed by your choice, whether anyone should certify to you. (Hab 1:1-5)

42 And setting out from the synagogue of the Jews, the Gentiles were entreating them to utter these Words with them between the weekly Sabbath.

43 And now made removed from the synagogue, many of the Jews and revering proselytes followed Paul and Barnabas, who were Speaking further to them, Persuading them to Continue with Intent in the Grace of God.

Jews contradicting and blaspheme

44 And when coming to the Sabbath, almost all the city was made gathered together, to hear the Spiritual Word of God.

45 But when the Jews discerned the multitudes of people, they were made filled with evil envy and were saying against those things from Paul, contradicting and blaspheming.

Why they Preach to the Gentiles

46 Then Paul and Barnabas spoke boldly. They spoke, It was first of all necessary to be made Uttered the Spiritual Communication of God, but for after that, you are casting it away, and Judging yourselves definitely not worthy of Eternal Life. Behold, we are Turning to the Gentiles.

47 Because in this manner, the Lord God

Command is Now Made to us: I am Now by your choice definitely Positioning You for a Light to the Gentiles, To You being for Salvation up to the uttermost parts of the earth. (Isa 49:6)

48 When the Gentiles Heard, they were Rejoicing, and Attributed Glory by their choice to the Word of the Lord, and they have by their choice Committed, as many as are now Continuously made Assigned to Life Eternal.

49 And the Word of the Lord was Excellent in Value through all the land.

50 But the Jews made hostile the revered and honorable woman, and the chiefest of the city, and stirred up persecution against Paul and Barnabas, and cast them out from their districts.

51 But they shook off the dust of their feet against them. They came into Iconium.

52 And the disciples were Fully Filled of Joy, and with the Holy Spirit.

Paul & Barnabas in Iconium Synagogue

14 And it came to pass in Iconium, as they entered themselves into the synagogue of the Jews and Uttered in such a manner, so that a large multitude of different people, both of the Jews and of Greeks Committed.

2 But the disobedient Jews stirred up, and evil harmed the souls of the Gentiles, against the Brethren.

3 Therefore, actually a sufficiently long time they stayed speaking boldly for the Lord, witnessing to the Spiritual Word of His Grace, and giving Miracle Signs and Wonders occurring through their Hands.

4 But the multitude of different people of the city split, and there were indeed those united with the Jews, and those United with the Apostles.

Escape to Lystra and Derbe

5 But as there became an aim of the Gentiles and also the Jews, united with their rulers, to violently treat and to cast stones at them.

6 They completely understood, fled for refuge into the cities of Lycaonia, Lystra and Derbe, and the surrounding region.

7 There also there they were preaching the Gospel.

Paul Heals a crippled man

8 And in Lystra a certain man who had never walked, crippled from his mother's womb, not empowered in his feet is existing sitting.

9 This man was hearing the Uttering of Paul who attentively looked to him, and Spiritually Discerned that he was having Faith to be Healed.

10 He Spoke with a great voice, You must Raise by your choice upon your Upright Feet. And Leaping up he was Walking.

11 And when the multitudes of people saw what Paul did, they lifted up their Lycaonia voice saying, the gods have come down to us likened to men.

People saw them as gods

12 And also they actually called Barnabas, Jupiter, and Paul, Mercury, for after that he was esteemed in Spiritual Communication.

13 And then the priest of Jupiter was before their city at the gate with bulls, willing to kill as sacrifice, and bringing garlands united with the multitudes of people.

14 When the Apostles, Barnabas and Paul heard, they tore apart their clothes, sprang in toward the multitude of people crying out,

15 And saying, Oh Sirs, why do these things? Also, we are similar passions as you men, preaching the Gospel to you, to Turn Away from these things of self-worship, turn back to the Living God that Created the heaven, and the earth, and the sea, and everything in them.

16 Who in generations past allowed all nations to go their ways,

17 And yet but in fact, He definitely not

dismissed Himself without Witness, and though Doing God-Good, Giving us from Heaven rain showers and Special Seasons, filling up Fruitful Nourishment and Gladness in our hearts.

18 And with these sayings, they with difficulty rested the multitudes of people, that they not kill as sacrifice to them.

Jews stoned Paul and left for dead

19 And then came upon Jews from Antioch and Iconium, and persuading the multitudes of people, and having stoned Paul, dragging outside the city, supposing him to be a rotting dead body.

Returned back through Derbe

20 And when the disciples surrounding him, he arose, entering into the city, and the next day came out with Barnabas into Derbe.

21 Both preaching the Gospel in that same city, and discipling sufficiently many, they returned into Lystra and Iconium and Antioch,

22 Confirming the souls of the disciples, Encouraging to Persevere in the Faith, yet because through very much affliction, we must Enter into the Kingdom Rule of God.

23 And then Praying with Fasting, they hand Chose themselves Elders in the Assembly, put them forth for the Purpose and Result of the Lord, they Committed them.

24 And passing through the Pisidia, they came to Pamphylia.

25 And when they uttered in Perga the Spiritual Words, they came down into Attalia.

Sailed back to Antioch

26 After there, they then sailed away to Antioch, where from they were Delivered up to the Grace of God, for the Work by God which was Fulfilled.

God Opens Door of Faith to Gentiles

27 And when they came up and gathered together the Assembly, they declared all that God had Accomplished among them, and that He Opened the door of Faith to the Gentiles.

28 And there they stayed not a little time with the disciples.

Jews circumcising for salvation

15 And certain men descending from Judaea were teaching the Brethren, that except you should be made circumcised by custom of Moses, you are definitely not able to be Saved.

Sent to Jerusalem to settle a matter

2 And therefore no little dissension occurred, Paul and also Barnabas arguing with them. They assigned Paul and Barnabas and certain others of the same kind from themselves to ascend to the Apostles and Elders in Jerusalem for this question.

3 Then, indeed, with journeying for the Assembly they were passing through Phenice, and Samaria, Certifying the Conversion of the Gentiles, and were causing great Joy to all the Brethren.

4 And when they came up to Jerusalem, they were made gladly received by the Assembly, and the Apostles, and the Elders, and also declaring what God had done among them.

5 But there raised some from the heresy of the Pharisees, saying that they ought to commit to be circumcising themselves, and also to give command to keep the Law of Moses.

The Council in Jerusalem

6 And the Apostles and Elders gathered together to Spiritually Discern, in regard to the Spiritual Word about this.

7 And when became very much arguing, Peter arose, spoke to them. Oh men, Oh Brethren, yourselves are aware of that from the old days God Chose among us that the Gentiles by my mouth heard the Spiritual Word, the Gospel, and Committed.

8   And God Knows the hearts, He Gave Witness to them, Giving them the Holy Spirit, just as Also to us.

9   And Judged No Differences between us and also them, so Cleansing their hearts by Faith.

10 Now, therefore, why tempt God to lay a yoke on the neck of the disciples, that neither we, nor our fathers were capable to bear?

11 But definitely, we are Committing through the Grace of the Lord Jesus Christ, they to be Saved in this Manner also.

12 Then all the multitude of different people kept silence, and were hearing Barnabas and Paul imparting what God accomplished with Miracle Signs and Wonders, among the Gentiles through them.

13 Then after they kept silence, James answering said, Oh men, Oh Brethren, you must Hear me.

14 Simeon imparted just as first of all, God Visited to Take Out from the Gentiles a people for His Name.

15 And to this Agree Together with the Words of the Prophets, just as written,

16 After these things I will Each Return, and Build again the Tabernacle of David that fell down, and the ruins thereof I will Build again, and I will Make it upright.

17 So that the remainder of men which ever inquire after the Lord, and at all times the Gentiles upon whom My Name is Called among them Saying, The Lord is Doing all these things.

18 Known to God are all His Works by God for the Age.

19 For this reason, I Judge to not be harassing since the Gentiles are Turning About to God.

20 But definitely to Write to them to Abstain Away from the defilements of idols, and fornication, and strangled, and blood,

21 For Moses from generations of old is preached in the city, having him to be read every Sabbath in the synagogues.

22 Then it seemed the Apostles and Elders with all of the Assembly Chose from themselves to send men to Antioch with Paul and Barnabas, Judas surnamed Barsabas and Silas, esteemed men among the Brethren.

23 The Apostles and the Elders wrote this thing by their hand. Then to the Brethren at Antioch, and Syria, and Cilicia, the Brethren of the Gentiles, Rejoice!

24 For after we heard that certain ones from us were coming out to trouble you by spiritual words, defeating your souls, saying you to be made circumcising and to be keeping the Law; definitely we Have Not, for ourselves, ordered these things.

25 It seemed to us, becoming with Full Agreement, to Choose men to Send to you United with our Beloved, Barnabas and Paul,

26 Men, Delivering up their souls in behalf of the Name of our Lord Jesus Christ.

27 We are now Sending out, therefore, Judas and Silas to Tell them through Spiritual Communication after the same things.

28 For it Seemed to the Holy Spirit and to us, to not lay much heavier burden to you, but these Necessary Things,

29 To Abstain from meat offered to idols, and blood, and strangled, and fornication. Being carefully Keeping oneself Out From these, you Act Well. Farewell.

Returned to Antioch

30 Indeed therefore, dismissing away they came to Antioch, and Gathering together the multitude of different people, handed the Epistle.

31 And reading, they Rejoiced over the Consolation.

32 And also Judas and Silas, and being Prophets themselves, encouraged by many Words, and Confirmed the Brethren.

33 And after they spent a little time, they Dismissed away from the Brethren with Peace, with Intent to the Apostles.

34 It seemed that Silas Intended to Continue in this place.

35 Paul and also Barnabas were staying in Antioch teaching and preaching the Gospel, the Spiritual Word of the Lord, with also many other ones of different kinds.

Paul and Barnabas disagree over Mark

36 And after some days, Paul spoke to Barnabas, So now turning about, we should Visit our Brethren in every city therein that we have Proclaimed much the Word of the Lord, how they are Having.

37 And Barnabas then consulted to take with him, John, called Mark.

38 But Paul thought worthy departing away from them since separation from Pamphylia, neither to take with him for the Work by God, so they neither came together among themselves.

39 Therefore a provocation occurred, so that to separate away themselves one from another, and also Barnabas took along Mark to sail away to Cyprus.

Paul takes Silas; Starts second journey

40 Then Paul for himself Designating Silas to depart, was Delivered up by the Brethren to the Grace of God.

41 And he passed through Syria and Cilicia, confirming the Assemblies.

At Lystra, Timothy joins Paul and Silas

16 Then he arrived in Derbe and Lystra, and Behold, a certain disciple was there named Timothy, the son of a certain Jewish Faithful woman and a Greek father,

2 Who was made Witnessed by the Brethren in Lystra and Iconium.

3 Him would Paul depart United with him, also he would take to circumcise him because of the Jews, because all being in the same place, they had known his existing father, who himself a Greek.

4 And as they were journeying through the cities, they delivered up to them the Decrees to Maintain, made Judged by the Apostles and the Elders in Jerusalem.

5 Indeed, then the Assemblies were Made Strong in the Faith, and were Abounding in Amount, in number each day.

6 Now passing through Phrygia and the land of Galatia, Made Forbidden by the Holy Spirit to Utter a Spiritual Word within Asia,

7 After coming to Mysia, they were tempted to go to Bithynia, but the Spirit definitely Not Allowed them.

8 And passing forth to Mysia, they came down into Troas.

Paul has Vision to go to Macedonia

9 And Paul Spiritually was Made to See a Vision in the night. A certain Macedonia man was standing encouraging him, and Saying Come through into Macedonia. You Must Help us.

10 And as Spiritually Discerning the vision, we Sought immediately to Depart into Macedonia, Confirming together that the Lord has Invited us to Preach to them.

11 Therefore, launching forth from Troas, we came directly to Samothracia, and also next to Neapolis.

Philippi on Sabbath at riverside

12 And also from that place to Philippi, which is the chief city, a colony, a portion of Macedonia, and we were in this city Staying some days.

13 And also on the Sabbath day we came outside of the city near the river where Prayer is supposed to be, and also sitting down, we Uttered to women Coming together.

Lydia invite to stay at her house

14 And a certain woman named Lydia, a seller of purple of the city Thyatira, who was Revering God, was Hearing this Utterings being Made by Paul. The Lord Opened her heart in Newness of Spirit to Give Attention.

15 And then as she was Immersed and

also her home, she encouraged saying, If you are now Judging me being Faithful to the Lord, enter into my home and you must abide. She constrained us.

Girl with spirit of divination

16 And it came to pass, we went for Prayer. A certain maid servant demonized with a spirit of divination meet us, who by her fortune telling offered very much concern for the gain from diligence offered to her masters.

17 She followed behind Paul and us, crying out saying, These men are Bondslaves of the Most High God who are proclaiming much to us The Way of Salvation.

18 And this she was doing over many days, and Paul having been made Grieving then turned about and he Spoke to the spirit, I am Giving Command to you, in the Name of Jesus Christ Come Out away from her, and it came out from her that hour.

Paul and Silas beaten and imprisoned

19 And when the masters spiritually discerned that it, the expectation of their gain from diligence, came out of her, they took hold of Paul and Silas. They drew out into the marketplace to their rulers.

20 And drawing them near to the magistrates, they spoke, These men, existing Jews, are exceedingly troubling our city.

21 And proclaim many customs, which are definitely not lawful for us to accept neither observe being Romans.

22 And the multitude of people rose up together against them, and the magistrate tore off their clothes, commanding to beat with rods.

23 And also laying many stripes on them, they were cast into prison, giving command to the jailer to securely keep them,

24 Who having received such a command, cast them into the innermost prison, and made certain their feet into wooden stocks.

Philippian jailer and his were Saved

25 And about midnight Paul and Silas were Praying, Singing Hymns to God, and the prisoners intently heard them.

26 And suddenly became a great Earthquake, so that to Shake the Foundations of the jail, and also all the doors Instantly Opened, and all the Bonds Let Loose.

27 And the jailer became waking out of sleep, and Spiritually Discerning the doors of the prison being Opened, drawing out a sword expected to intentionally kill himself, supposing the prisoners to be escaped.

28 But Paul Called for with a great voice, Saying, You must practice no evil work to yourself, because we are all being in this place.

29 Then he asking a light, sprung in and trembling, becoming fallen down before Paul and Silas.

30 And going before them outside stated, Sirs, What must I Do that I should be made Saved?

31 And then they Spoke, You must Commit by your choice with Intent to the Lord Jesus Christ, and you shall be Made Saved, and your Home.

32 And they Uttered to him the Spiritual Word of the Lord, and to All in his house.

33 And he took them along in the same hour of the night, washed their wounds, and were made Immersed, he and all his instantly.

34 And also, Leading them up into his house, he put forth a Table and Exceedingly Rejoiced with all his house now Continuously by their choice Committing to God.

Released from prison

35 And when it became day, the magistrates sent out to the sergeants saying, You must dismiss away those men.

36 And the jailer told these Spiritual Words to Paul, for the magistrates sent out in order that you should dismiss away. Therefore, come out now. You must be

made going in Peace.

37 And then Paul stated to him, Having beaten us publicly, existing Roman men without trial, cast into prison, and now secretly casting us out? Definitely not! Yet but definitely, they must come themselves leading us out.

38 And the sergeants declared this to the magistrates, and hearing these single words, they feared because they are Romans.

39 And they came to encourage them earnestly requesting to depart from the city, then lead them out.

40 And they came out from the prison to enter into Lydia, and Spiritually Discerning, the Brethren Encouraged them and they Departed.

To Thessalonica

17 And then going through to Amphipolis and Apollonia, they came into Thessalonica, whereto there was the synagogue of the Jews.

2 And as having had a customary practice for Paul, he entered with them, and upon three Sabbaths Disputed with them from the Scriptures.

3 Opening in Newness of Spirit, and putting forth that Christ must suffer, and to Arise from the Dead, and that He is the Christ Jesus that I Proclaim much to you.

4 And some of them have been made Persuaded, and associated with Paul, and Silas, and also of revered Greeks a large multitude of different people, and also of the chief woman, definitely not a few.

The Jews were joined to evil men

5 And strongly desiring to envy the disobedient Jews then received to themselves certain evil men of the baser sort, and gathered a crowd making noise in the city, and also standing ready at the house of Jason seeking them to be lead into the public.

6 But not finding them, dragged Jason and also certain brothers to the city rulers, loudly pleading, These men that disturbed the inhabited earth are present in this place also.

7 Whom Jason humbly received, and these practice all things against the decrees of Caesar, saying is being another King of a different kind, Jesus.

8 And they troubled the multitude of people and the city rulers hearing these things.

9 And receiving sufficiently from Jason and the others, they dismissed them away.

Paul and Silas sent out to Berea

10 And the Brethren immediately by night sent forth both Paul and Silas to Berea, who coming up passed into the synagogue of the Jews.

11 And these, which were more noble than those in Thessalonica, who Received the Word with all Readiness of mind, as examining for Judgment the Scriptures daily, whether these Things having been so, beyond dreams.

12 Therefore certainly, many of them also have Committed of the honorable Greek woman and men, definitely not a few.

13 But as Jews of Thessalonica recognized that also in Berea by Paul, he had Made Proclaimed much the Word of God, they came there also, shaking the multitudes of people.

14 And then immediately the Brethren sent forth Paul, going as on the sea, but both Silas and Timothy enduring there.

15 And those conducting Paul lead him up to Athens, and they were setting out taking a Commandment to Silas and Timothy that as they should come urgently to him.

Paul goes to Areopagus in Athens

16 Now while Paul was waiting for them at Athens, his spirit was made Reacting in him, seeing the city was wholly given to idolatry.

17 Therefore, he was certainly Disputing with the Jews in the synagogue and with

they Revering, and Conversing among all in the marketplace daily.

18 And then certain philosophers, of the Epicureans and the Stoics, deliberated with him. Some said, Whatever shall beyond dreams this babbler to be saying? And some think he to be a promoter of strange demons, because he was Proclaiming to them this Jesus and about His Resurrection.

19 And also they took hold of him with intent. They led to the Mars Hill, saying, Can we be knowing what this New of a different kind teaching made uttering from you?

20 Because you are bringing strange things to our hearing. We intend, therefore, to know whatever is being these things you are strongly desiring beyond dreams.

21 Then all the Athenians and strange newcomers of a different kind were having leisure time in nothing other than to say, or to hear a new of a different kind something.

Paul on Mars Hill gives Message

22 Then Paul stood in the midst of Mars Hill stating, Athenian men, I am Perceiving in all things you as too superstitious.

23 For passing through and thinking about your devotions, also I found a commemorative of which had been made inscribed, TO UNKNOWN GOD, of whom, therefore, you are ignorant, showing reverence to Him, I proclaim much to you.

24 God that Created the satan's world and all things in it, He is Existing the Lord of Heaven and earth, definitely not Dwelling in temples having been made with hands.

25 Neither is made healed by hands of men, needing anything further, He Gives life to all and also breath to all.

26 And also has Made from One Blood every nation of men to dwell upon all the face of the earth, having determined the Special Times Appointed Before, and the Bounds of their location.

27 So then if to be seeking the Lord, yet by their choice, handled and found Him by their choice beyond dreams, and though definitely not existing far off from everyone of us.

28 Because in Him we are living and made moving, and we are being also as certain of your poets spirit saying, For also we are being His offspring.

29 Therefore, existing the kindred of God, we ought definitely not to suppose that the Divine Godhead is being liken to gold or silver or graven stone craft from man's imagination.

30 Therefore actually, the times of ignorance God winked at, but now is Continuously Giving Command to all men everywhere to be continuously by their choice to Repent.

31 Since He has Brought the day to reality, in which He is Expecting to Judge the inhabited earth in Righteousness, by That Man in whom He has Determined Faith [Christ in you], Offering concern to everyone, Arising thereof out from the Dead. (Ps 9:8)

32 And when they heard the Resurrection of the dead, some certainly were scoffing, and then spoke, We will hear you again for ourselves about this.

33 So then, Paul departed from the midst of them.

34 And specific men joined to him. They Committed by their choice, among whom also Dionysius the Areopagite, and a woman named Damaris, and others of a different kind with them.

To Corinth; Aquila and Priscilla

18 And after these things Paul being made separated from Athens, came to Corinth.

2 And finding a certain Jew named Aquila of Pontus and his wife Priscilla, recently kindred came from Italy, because Claudius had appointed all Jews to go forth from Rome, he came near to them.

3 And because he being of the same

craft, he continued with them, and he was working with the craft, because they were tent makers.

4 And he was Disputing in the synagogue in every Sabbath, Persuading both Jews and Greeks.

5 And as both Silas and also Timothy descended from Macedonia, Paul was made Constrained in the Spirit, Testifying to the Jews about Christ Jesus.

6 And when they were resisting themselves and blaspheming, he shook off his clothes, he spoke to them, Your blood upon your head. I am Purified from now. I Will for myself Go to the Gentiles.

7 And he departed from that place, came into the house of one by name of Justus, who Revered God, whose house was attached to the synagogue.

8 And Crispus, the ruler of the synagogue, Committed to the Lord united with all of his home, and many of the Corinthians Hearing were Committing, and were made Immersed.

9 Then the Lord Spoke through a Vision in the night to Paul, You must not fear for yourself, but definitely you must Utter, and you should not hold Speaking.

10 Since I am With you, and none shall for himself lay on you to evil harm you, since I am Having Many people in this city.

Paul stayed a year and 6 months

11 And he sat down also for a year and six months, Teaching among them the Spiritual Word of God.

12 When Gallio was deputy of Achaia, the Jews with one accord revolted against Paul, and lead him to the judgment seat,

13 Saying, This man is greatly persuading men to revere God against the Law.

14 And when Paul expecting to Open his mouth, Gallio spoke to the Jews, If then actually it was any hurtful wrong or evil lewdness, Oh, Jews, ever to continue enduring you, according to the Word,

15 But if it is a question about Spiritual Words and names and of your Law, according to your spiritually seeing them, yet I intend to definitely not be judge of these things.

16 And he expelled them away from the judgment seat.

17 And then all the Greeks took hold of Sosthenes, the ruler of the synagogue, striking him before the judgment seat, but Gallio cared not for these things.

Paul, Priscilla and Aquilla to Ephes.

18 And Paul further remaining steadfast sufficient days, he then saying goodbye to the Brethren, sailed away to Syria united with himself Priscilla and Aquila, shearing his head in Cenchrea, because of having a vow.

19 And when they arrived at Ephesus, they also left him in this place, and he entering into the synagogue Disputed with the Jews.

20 And when they earnestly requested of him to continue a greater time alongside of them, he assented definitely not.

Kept the Feast in Jerusalem

21 But definitely saying goodbye to them spoke, I Must by all means again Observe the Feast coming in Jerusalem. But I will return again to you, God Willing. And he launched forth away from Ephesus.

22 And descending into Caesarea, he ascended and greeted the Assembly. He came down to Antioch.

Antioch and through all Galatia

23 And after spending some time he came out, passing through in order the land of Galatia and Phrygia, Confirming all the disciples.

Apollos Taught by Aquila and Priscilla

24 And a certain Jew named Apollos of Alexandria, an eloquent man, arrived in Ephesus with kindred. He was exceedingly able in the Scriptures.

25 He was informed in The Way of the Lord, and was Fervent in the Spirit. He was Uttering and Taught exactly about the Lord, but aware only of the Immersion of John.

26 And also He began to Speak boldly in the synagogue, and when Aquila and Priscilla heard him, they took him to themselves and expounded The Way of God more perfectly to him.

27 And intending himself to pass into Achaia, the Brethren wrote exhorting the disciples to Gladly Receive him, who when he came up he Deliberated very much with them Committed through Grace,

28 Because he Strongly was Persuading the Jews publicly, Showing as Example by the Scriptures that Jesus is the Christ.

Paul Arrives in Ephesus

19 And it came to pass that while Apollos was in Corinth, Paul passed through the upper coasts coming to Ephesus, and finding certain disciples.

Paul Baptizes and Laying of Hands

2 He spoke to them, Have you Received the Holy Spirit after you Committed? And they spoke to him, But definitely, we have not Heard whether there is a Holy Spirit.

3 And also He Spoke to them, To what, then, were you made Immersed? And they spoke, To the immersion of John.

4 Then Paul Spoke, John indeed immersed the immersion of Repentance for a person, saying that they should Commit to Him Coming after him, that is, to Christ Jesus.

5 When they Heard, they were Immersed in the Name of the Lord Jesus.

6 And when Paul Laid his Hands on them, the Holy Spirit Came Upon them, and they were Uttering in Tongues, and also they were Prophesying,

7 And all the men were about twelve.

Spoke in synagogue 3 months

8 Then he entered into the synagogue Speaking boldly over three months, Disputing and Persuading in regard to the Kingdom Rule of God.

Stays at school of Tyrannus 2 years

9 And as some were made hardened and disobedient, speaking evil things of The Way in the presence of the multitude of different people, he Separated from the disciples. He departed away from them, Disputing every day in the school of one Tyrannus.

10 And this occurred over two years, so that all that dwell in Asia heard the Word of the Lord Jesus, both Jews and Greeks.

Special Miracles by Paul

11 And also God was Doing Miracle Powers acquired through the Hands of Paul.

12 Even so that upon those being sick, napkins or aprons Induced from his Touch also were Made to Deliver them from the sicknesses, and also the evil spirits Came Out from them.

13 And then some of the vagabond Jews, exorcists, presumed to name the Name of the Lord Jesus over those demonized with more evil spirits, saying, We urge you by Jesus Whom Paul preaches.

14 And there were some seven sons of the high priest Sceva, a Jew, who did this.

15 And the evil spirit answered, spoke, Jesus I know and Paul I am aware of, but yourselves, who are you?

16 And the man, in whom was the evil spirit, jumped upon them, and overpowered them. It prevailed against them, so that naked and made wounded they escaped from the same home.

17 And this became known to all, both Jews and Gentiles dwelling in Ephesus, and fear fell upon all them, and they were made magnifying the Name of the Lord Jesus.

18 And also many that were now Committing by their choice were coming acknowledging and declaring their deeds.

Books burned and Word grew

19 And sufficiently many of those that practiced curious works were fully burning those necessary books in the presence of everyone. Also they found added together the price of them, even as five thousand pieces of silver.

20 So according to His Dominion, the Spiritual Word of the Lord Grew and Prevailed.

Timothy and Erastus to Greece

21 Now as these things were Made Fulfilled, Paul settled for himself in the Spirit, passing through Macedonia and Achaia, going to Jerusalem, Speaking, Then after I am there, I also Ought to See Rome.

22 And so he sent out into Macedonia two that were Serving him, Timothy and Erastus. He gave Heed for a little time in Asia.

23 And it came to pass according to the Special Time, that definitely no little commotion concerning "The Way",

Silversmith Demetrius riots city

24 Because a man named Demetrius, a silversmith, making silver temples of Diana, was offering for himself concern for definitely not a little gain from diligence to the craftsmen.

25 Also those uniting together with such workers spoke, Oh sirs, are you aware of that out from this is our wealth of due gain from diligence?

26 And you are perceiving and hearing that definitely not only in Ephesus, but definitely almost all of Asia, which this Paul has persuaded to completely remove a sufficient multitude of people saying, that they are definitely not gods, being made by hands.

27 So definitely not only this is endangering particularly us until to come beyond reproof, but definitely also of those of the temple area of the great goddess Diana. For no account to be expected, so also to be taken down, for her mighty power is being revered of all Asia and the inhabited earth.

28 And after they heard they became full of anger and crying out saying, Great Diana of the Ephesians.

29 And the whole city was made filled with confusion, and they also ran violently with one accord to the theater to seize Gaius and Aristarchus of Macedonia, travel companions of Paul.

Paul Held Safe by Brethren

30 And when Paul intended to enter into the public, his disciples were definitely not allowing him.

31 And then certain of the chiefs of Asia, who were friends to him, sent to him and encouraging to not give himself into the theater.

32 Some indeed of same kind were crying out then about others of same kind, because the assembly was made confused, and they had come together definitely not discerning much of any cause.

33 And from out of the multitude of people, Alexander, for the Jews before instructed, was pushing him forward. Alexander then willing to respond to the public beckoned with a hand.

34 But when fully knowing that he is a Jew, they all became as by all with one voice, crying out for two hours, The Great Diana of the Ephesians.

35 And when the town clerk quieted the multitude of people, he stated, You Ephesian men, for what man is not knowing that the Ephesian City is a devoted temple servant to the great goddess Diana, and the image which fell down from Jupiter?

36 Without contradiction are these things, then you must yourselves be quiet, and to exist to practice nothing reactionary,

37 For you have led these men, neither temple robbers, nor blasphemers of your goddess.

38 Therefore, if actually Demetrius and also with his craftsmen have a word against any baser sort, then move along

with the deputies. They must be charging by themselves.

39 But if you seek after anybody concerning another ones of different kind, they shall be made to explain in the lawful assembly.

40 For also, we are endangered to be made charged for no cause for the dissension of this day. We shall definitely not be able to yield an existing account for this gathering.

41 And after speaking these things, he dismissed away the assembly.

Paul to Greece (Macedonia)

20 And after the tumult ceased, Paul invited Greeting to the disciples, then Departed to go into Macedonia.

2 And when passing through the coasts and Encouraging them themselves in many Spiritual Words, he came into Greece,

3 And also he abode three months there being because the Jews laid in wait for him. He was expecting to launch forth into Syria. Advice occurred to return through Macedonia.

4 And then accompanied him as far as Asia, Sopater of Berea, and of the Thessalonians, Aristarchus and Secundas, and Gaias of Derbe, and Timothy, and then of Asia, Tychicus and Trophimus.

5 These going forward, abided for us in Troas.

Sailed from Philippi to Troas

6 And after the days of Unleavened Bread we sailed away from Philippi, and came as far as five days to them in Troas, where we stayed seven days.

7 And upon the first day of the week, the disciples Gathering together to Break Bread. Paul was Preaching, giving Reasonings to them. And also expecting to set out the next day, he Prolonged the Spiritual Communication as far as midnight.

Eutychus fell out of window

8 And there were sufficiently many lamps in the upper chamber, where they were now made gathering together.

9 And with Paul Preaching, with Giving much more Reasonings, a certain male youth named, Eutychus, sitting in a window, slumped down in deep natural sleep. He slumped down by natural sleep, falling down for three stories down below, and taken up dead.

10 And when Paul came down, fell upon him and embracing him, he Spoke. You must not make noise because his soul is inside him.

11 And after that also he ascended and Breaking Bread, and in eating of sufficient food, and also Talking until break of day. In such a manner, he departed.

12 And when they lead the living male child, they were also made definitely not a little encouraged.

Travels to Miletus

13 And then we went forward to the ship, launching forth for Assos, from that place expecting to receive up Paul, for in this manner he was appointed, expecting to be going on foot.

14 And as he deliberated among us at Assos, receiving him up, we came to Mitylene.

15 Next, after there we then sailed away to arrive next to Chios, and another day of a different kind we docked at Samos, and continuing by Trogyllium, we then having made to come into Miletus.

16 For Paul had Judged to bypass Ephesus, so that it should not occur to spend time in Asia. He was hurrying for allowing that it is possible beyond dreams for him to be in Jerusalem the day of Pentecost.

Calls Ephesus Elders and Bids Farewell

17 And then from Miletus he sent to Ephesus, summoned for himself the Elders of the Assembly,

18 And as when they came up to him, he spoke to them. Yourselves are being aware of from the first day that I entered into Asia, how with you I had for myself been at all times,

19 Bondserving the Lord with all humility, and with many tears and temptations that happened to me, with the Jews lying in wait.

20 As I drew back nothing being Essential, not declared to you, and to Teach you publicly, and even in homes,

21 Testifying both to Jews and also Gentiles Repentance toward God and Faith of our Lord Jesus Christ.

22 And now, Behold, I am being Made Bound in the Spirit to go to Jerusalem, Not Spiritually Knowing what among them I will encounter.

23 But there, the Holy Spirit is Testifying in every city Saying, that bonds and afflictions are Abiding to me.

24 But definitely, no Account affects me, neither having my soul more Honorable to myself, as to Fulfill my course with Joy, and to the Service of Calling that I Received by my choice from the Lord Jesus, to Testify to the Gospel of the Grace of God.

25 And now, Behold, all among yourselves whom I pass through preaching the Kingdom Rule of God, I Spiritually Know that yourselves shall not Spiritually See my face anymore.

26 For this reason, I bear witness to you in this Specific Day, that I am Purified from the blood of all,

Take Heed, I have Warned you

27 For I have definitely not drawn back, to Declare to you All the Counsel of God.

28 You must Take Heed, therefore, to yourselves, and to all the Flock, over whom the Holy Spirit has Positioned you Overseers, to Shepherd the Assembly of God, whom He Purchased by His Own Blood,

29 Because I am Now Spiritually Knowing this, that after my Departing burdensome wolves shall enter for themselves among you not sparing the Flock.

30 And out from yourselves, they shall arise for themselves, perverted men uttering by their choice, to withdraw the disciples after them.

31 For this reason, you must Watch, Remembering that for three years, night and day, I definitely Ceased Not with tears to Warn everyone.

Commends them to God

32 And now, Brethren, I am Putting you Forth to God, and to the Word of His Grace, that is able to Build up, and to give you an Inheritance among All who are Now Being Made Holy.

33 I have desired no man's pieces of silver or gold or raiment.

34 And now, you Know yourselves that these hands have Serviced to my needs, and those being with me.

35 I have Forewarned to you all things, how in such a manner Laboring, you ought to Support the weak, and also to Remember the Words of the Lord Jesus, how He Spoke, It is much more Spiritually Blessed to Give than to receive.

36 And Speaking these things, Kneeling his knees, he Prayed United with them All.

37 And they all became Weeping sufficiently long, and Falling upon Paul's neck, were kissing him.

Sorrow, are Told will not see him again

38 Grievously Sorrowing, specifically by the Words that he had Spirit Said that they are not to expect to see his face anymore. And they Journeyed with him to the ship.

Paul goes to Jerusalem by ship

21 And as it came to pass launching forth we withdrew from them, coming directly to Coos, and the next day after into Rhodes, after there into Patara.

2 And finding a ship passing over to Phenicia, entering we launched forth.

3   And discovering Cyprus, so then we left it on the left hand sailing into Syria, and made brought down in Tyre, because the ship was unloading the merchandise thereto.

4   And locating disciples, who through the Spirit Said to Paul not to ascend into Jerusalem. We continued with Intent in this place seven days.

5   And when our days became fully complete, we departed, women and children journeying with us all going to outside the city, and we Knelt the knees upon the shore Praying.

6   And greeting one another we entered into the ship, and they returned to their own homes.

7   And when we finished the course sailing from Tyre, we arrived at Ptolemais, and greeted the Brethren, abiding one day with them.

8   And the next day departed, those with Paul came into Caesarea, and entered in the home of Philip, the evangelist, which was of the seven. We abided with him.

9   And this one was having four virgin daughters, who Prophesied.

Agabus Prophesied of Paul's arrest

10   And we continued with Intent there many more days. A certain Prophet named Agabus, descended from Judea.

11   And when he Came to us, then he took away Paul's belt, and also bound his hands and feet. He spoke, This the Holy Spirit Says, The man whose girdle this is, he in such a manner, the Jews shall bind in Jerusalem, and deliver up into the hands of Gentiles.

12   And then as we heard these things, both we, and the residents there, now beseeched him not to ascend into Jerusalem.

Paul said they were ready to die

13   Then Paul answered, Why do you weep and crush my heart? Because I have been Ready definitely not only to be Bound, but definitely also to Die in Jerusalem, in behalf of the Name of the Lord Jesus.

14   But when he was not persuaded, we remained quiet. We spoke, The Will of the Lord must be Occurring.

15   And after those days, those packing up were ascending into Jerusalem,

16   And then also the disciples from Caesarea coming together with us, leading with them one Mnason from Cyprus, an old disciple with whom we should have been made to guest lodge.

Arrived in Jerusalem to Apostles

17   And when we ended in Jerusalem, the Brethren Received us Gladly.

18   And next Paul had gone with us to James, and also all the Elders Came Up,

19   And Greeting them, Imparting to everyone what God had Done among the Gentiles, through His Service of Calling.

20   And when they Heard, they Attributed Glory to the Lord, and also spoke to him. You see Oh brother, how thousands of Jews there are committing, and all alike existing by their choice zealous for the Law.

Accused of false teachings

21   And they are informed about you, that you teach apostasy away from Moses in all the Jewish nations, saying not to circumcise their children, nor to walk after the customs.

22   What therefore? Because that now you are coming, all the multitude of different people ought to come together. They shall hear.

Paul asked to do a symbolic favor

23   Do, therefore, this that we are saying to you. Four men of us are having a vow upon themselves.

24   These taking along, you must be made purified with them and you must ensure cost in the way of them to shave your head. And they should all know that this is made informing concerning you. For you are not

walking disorderly, but also yourself definitely maintaining the Law.

25 We wrote an Exhortation Judging to not be holding such (holding to Law), except to be Maintaining Themselves from meat offered to idols, and from blood, and from strangled, and from fornication. These in regard to the Gentiles who are now by their choice Continuously Committing.

26 Then Paul received along the men. Having made the day with them was made purified. They had gone into the Temple area announcing the accomplishment of the days of ceremonial purification, up to when the offering had been made offered in behalf of everyone of them.

Jews saw Paul in the temple

27 And when as they were expecting the seven days to finish, the Jews from Asia saw him in the Temple area, uproared all the multitude of people, and laid their hands upon him.

28 Crying out, Oh men, Oh Israel, you must help This is the man that is against the people, and the Law, and this place, and everywhere he teaches all ways further, and also conducted into the Temple area the Gentiles, and making unholy this Holy Place,

29 Because they saw before in the city with him Trophimus the Ephesian, whom they supposed that Paul now conducted into the Temple area.

30 And also the whole city was moved, and all of the people gathered together. And they then took hold of Paul, him drawing out, outside the Temple area, and immediately shut the doors.

31 And seeking to kill him, the news ascended to the chief captain of the band, that all Jerusalem is now made uproared.

Soldiers and centurions intercede

32 He speedily took along soldiers and centurions, ran down to them, and seeing the chief captain and the soldiers, they ceased striking Paul.

33 Then the chief captain approached near, took hold of him and commanded to bind with two chains, and inquired whoever he beyond dreams might be, and what he is doing.

34 Others within the multitude of people of same kind and others of the same kind were loudly pleading one thing, that not being able to know then the certainty of the tumult, he commanded to lead him into the castle.

35 And when he came upon the stairs, who happened to bear him by the soldiers, because of the violence of the multitude of people,

36 For the multitude of different people were following, crying out, You must take away him.

Paul given permission to Speak

37 And also Paul expecting to be made conducted into the castle, he said to the chief captain, Is it lawful then for me to speak something to you? Then he stated, Are you knowing Greek?

38 So then you are definitely not the Egyptian, who before these days disturbed, and lead out to the desolate wilderness four thousand men of assassins.

39 But Paul spoke, I am actually a man being a Jew of Tarsus of Cilicia, definitely not a mean city citizen, Praying Earnestly that you must Permit me to Utter to the people.

40 And permitting to him, Paul Stood upon the stairs, beckoning by hand to the many people and a stillness occurred, he Called out in the Hebrew language Saying,

Paul Defends himself

22 Oh men, Oh Brethren, and Oh fathers, you must Hear now my defense to you.

2 And when they heard that he was calling out in the Hebrew language, they offered concern to much more silence, and he stated,

3 I am certainly a Jewish man born in

Tarsus of Cilicia, yet reared in this city alongside of the feet of Gamaliel, disciplined in the strict manner of the Jewish fathers of the Law, existing zealous for God, just as all you are yourselves this day.
4   I persecuted those of this way to death, as far as tying up and delivering up into prisons, both men and also woman.
5   And as also the High Priest witnessing me, also along with all the group of elders, from them also I received epistles to go also to lead the Brethren, those thereto being now made bound in Damascus, to Jerusalem in order that they should be made terribly punished.

Paul tell of his Conversion
6   And it came to pass that my going and approaching near to Damascus about noon, unexpectedly from the Heaven, a sufficiently long Light shined around about me.
7   And also I fell down upon the ground and Heard a Voice Saying to me, Oh Saul, Oh Saul, why are you persecuting Me?
8   And I answered, Who are You, Oh Lord? And also He Spoke to me, I AM Jesus of Nazareth, Whom you are persecuting.
9   And they that were with me had actually seen the Light, and became afraid, but they heard definitely not the Voice Uttering to me.
10 And I spoke, What should I Do Oh Lord? And the Lord Spoke to me, Raise, you must go into Damascus, there also it shall be Made Uttered to you, about all whatever is made Assigned to you to Do.
11 And as I was definitely not looking upon from the Glory of that same Light, I am made led by hand by those together with me, to come into Damascus.

Tells of Restored Sight and his Baptism
12 And one Ananias, a devout man according to the Law, witnessed by all Jews that are dwelling (there).

13 Coming to me, and Standing ready to Speak to me, Oh Brother Saul you Must Receive Sight. I also myself that same hour Looked up upon him.
14 And he Spoke, The God of our fathers has Hand Chosen you for Himself to Know His Will, and Spiritually See the Righteous (One), and to Hear the Voice of His Mouth.
15 For you shall be a Witness for Him to All men of what you are Seeing Attentively and have Heard.
16 And now what are you expecting? Raise, you must be Immersed for yourself. Also you Must Wash Away for yourself your sin nature and sins, Calling Upon the Name of the Lord.

How Lord Sent him to the Gentiles
17 And it came to pass, I returned to Jerusalem, and while I was Praying in the Temple area, I Became in a Trance.
18 And I Spiritually Saw Him Saying to me, You Must Hurry and you Must Come Out in Haste out from Jerusalem, since they shall definitely not accept your Testimony about Me.
19 Also I spoke, Oh Lord, they are aware that I was imprisoning and beating in the synagogues them that are Committing to You.
20 And when the blood of Stephen, Your martyr, was shed, I also was being present and consenting to his killing, and maintaining the clothes of them intentionally killing him.
21 And He Spoke to me, You Must Go, for I will Send you forth to far off Gentiles.

Then Jews uproared against him
22 And they were hearing his Spiritual Word until this, then lifted up their voice saying, You must take away such from the earth, because it is definitely not proper for him to live.
23 And they screamed and threw down their clothes, and cast dust into the air.

Captain takes Paul into castle

24 The chief captain commanded him to be made lead into the castle. He spoke to examine him by severe suffering, in order that they should fully know why was shouted in such a manner an accusation of him.

Paul asks "I am Roman and no trial?"

25 And as they fastened him with leather shoestrings, Paul spoke to the standing centurion. Is it lawful then for you to whip without trial, if the man a Roman?

26 And when the centurion heard, he came near to tell the chief captain saying, You must behold attentively, what you are expecting to do, for this man is a Roman.

27 Then the chief captain came near and spoke to him, You must say to me if you are a Roman? And then, he stated, Emphatically Yes.

28 And also the chief captain answered, With a large sum I possessed this citizenship. And Paul stated, But I was born so.

29 Then immediately they departed away from him, who were expected to examine him, and then the chief captain was afraid, fully knowing that he is a Roman, and because he had bound him.

30 But instead the next day, intending to know with certainty what they from the Jews accused, he removed him from the bonds, and commanded the chief priests and all of their council to come themselves, and brought down Paul to stand before them.

Paul before council with soldiers

23 And Paul attentively looking at the council spoke, Oh men, Oh Brethren, I prevailed in all God-Good conscience to God until this day.

2 And the High Priest, Ananias, instantly commanded those standing by him to strike him in the mouth.

3 Then Paul spoke to him, God is expected to strike you, you whited wall! For you are sitting to judge me according to the Law, and you commanded me to be struck contrary to the Law.

4 And those standing spoke, Are you reviling the High Priest of God?

5 And also Paul stated, I had definitely not Spiritually Discerned, Brethren, that he is a High Priest, for it is made Written, you shall definitely not Spirit Say an evil work afflicted about the ruler of the people.

6 But when Paul recognized that one part was Sadducee and that the other one Pharisees of a different kind, he cried out in the council, Oh men, Oh Brethren, I am a Pharisee, the son of a Pharisee of the Expectation and Resurrection of the dead, I am being made judged.

7 And when he had uttered this, a dissension occurred between the Pharisees and the Sadducees, and the multitude of different people was made split.

8 For, indeed, the Sadducees say there is being no Resurrection, nor Angel, nor Spirit, but the Pharisees are confessing both together.

9 And there occurred a great screaming, and there arose the scribes, those part of the Pharisees, quarreling themselves saying, We find no evil work in this man, for if a Spirit Uttered to him or an Angel, we should not fight against God.

10 And there became a large dissension, the chief captain fearing with sincere apprehension that Paul might have been pulled apart by them, commanded the army to come down, caught him up from the midst of them, and also to lead into the castle.

Lord said, Paul to Testify in Rome

11 And the next night the Lord Standing ready Beside him, Spoke, You Must be Encouraged, Paul, because as you have Testified about Me in Jerusalem, so you Must also be Bearing Record in Rome.

Forty Jews vow to kill Paul

12 And when it became day, certain Jews

gathered themselves bound under a curse, saying neither to eat nor drink until after when they should kill Paul,

13 And there were greater than forty who had made this conspiracy.

14 They who coming near to the chief priests and elders spoke, We have ourselves accursed bound under a curse, to eat no food, definitely not until after we should kill Paul.

15 Now, therefore, yourselves with the council make known plainly to the chief captain, as expecting to have more perfect knowledge about him, so that tomorrow he should be brought down to yourselves. And then after approaching near, we are being ready to intentionally kill him.

Paul's nephew heard of plot

16 And when Paul's sister's son heard about the plot, he came up, entered into the castle and told Paul.

17 Then Paul invited one of the centurions, stating to him, to lead away this male youth to the chief captain, because he has something to tell him.

18 Then indeed he took along him leading to the chief captain, and stated that the prisoner Paul invited him earnestly requesting of me that this male youth be lead to you, having something to utter to you.

Captain told of plot by nephew

19 Then the chief captain took hold of him by hand, and withdrew to his own privacy to inquire, What is this you have to tell me?

20 And He spoke, The Jews have agreed that in earnestly requesting of you, so that tomorrow for the purpose of council, you should bring Paul down, as expecting something more perfect to inquire in regard to him.

21 Therefore, you should not be persuaded by them, for they lie in wait for him, of them greater than forty men, who have themselves bound under a curse to neither eat nor drink until after when they should intentionally kill him, and now they are ready, looking for a promise from you.

22 Then indeed the chief captain dismissed away the male youth, giving command to divulge nothing about these things made known plainly to me.

Soldiers take Paul to Caesarea

23 And he invited two certain ones of the centurions, he spoke, You must prepare two hundred soldiers so that they should be made to go up to Caesarea, and seventy horsemen, and two hundred spearman, away at the third hour of this night.

24 And also to assist with animals in order for Paul to sit on. He should be physically saved for Felix the governor.

25 He wrote an epistle fully beholding to this model,

26 Claudius Lysias to the most noble governor Felix, Rejoice.

27 This man was made physically taken by the Jews, and they are expecting to intentionally kill. I, standing ready with an army to set him free, because having learned he is a Roman,

28 And intending to know why the accusation was charged, I brought him down into their council.

29 Then I found being made charged for questions of their Law, but nothing worthy of death, or having a crime charged to him of bonds.

30 And then it was made disclosed to me that the Jews expecting for the man are laying in wait. I speedily sent to you giving command for the accusers against him to say before you. Farewell.

31 Indeed, therefore, the soldiers according to those made appointed to them, received up Paul, led through the night to Antipatris.

32 And then by the next day, they allowed the horsemen with him to be going to return to the castle.

Governor Felix holds Paul for trial

33 Who, entering into Caesarea, and handing the epistle to the governor, presented also Paul to him.

34 And when the governor had read and questioned from which province he is, and then he inquired that, from Cilicia.

35 Then he was stating, I will formally hear you when your accusers should come up. And also he commanded him to be maintained in the Judgment Hall of Herod.

Paul's accusers present charges

24 And after five days, the High Priest, Ananias, came down with the elders, and a certain orator, Tertullus, who made known plainly against Paul to the governor.

2 And when he was called, Tertullus began to accuse saying, Very much peace is acquired through you, and worthy deeds have occurred to this nation through your provision.

3 We gladly receive most noble Felix at all times and also everywhere, with all thankfulness.

4 But in order that I should not hinder to you much, I entreat you to hear our few words for your clemency.

5 Because we have found this man a pestilence, and a mover of dissension among all the Jews upon the inhabited earth, and also a ringleader of the Nazarene heresy,

6 Who also has tried to desecrate the Temple area, which we held to retain, and there we would be judging according to our Law.

7 But then passed forth the chief captain, Lysias, he lead away out from our hands with very much violence,

8 Commanding his accusers to come to you, who along with you shall be able to examine him for judgment about all, fully knowing these things that we are accusing him.

9 And then the Jews agreed, affirming these things to have been in this manner also.

Paul's Defends charges

10 After that the Governor gestured to him to say, Paul answered, Being aware of out from many years, you are judging the nations, this I am responding cheerfully in regard to myself.

11 That you are able to know, there are definitely not much more than twelve days for me since that I will have ascended worshipping inside of Jerusalem.

12 And they found me neither in the Temple area disputing against anybody, either arousing up a multitude of people, nor in the synagogues, nor in the city.

13 Neither are they able to prove in regard to that they are now accusing me.

14 But this I confess to you that after the way that they are calling heresy, so I am devoted to the God of my Jewish fathers, Committing to all that is now made Written in the Law and the Prophets.

15 Having Expectation toward God, which even they themselves are looking for, a Resurrection to being expected of the dead, both the Righteous and also the unrighteous.

16 And in this I am Minding Myself to have a conscience without offense unceasingly to God and for men.

17 And now after many more years, I have come up bringing much alms and offerings to my nation.

18 Wherein certain ones, Jews from Asia, who found me purifying in the Temple area, definitely not with a multitude of people, neither with tumult,

19 Yet if any certain ones have beyond dreams to accuse against me, those ought to be presenting before you.

20 Or these themselves must speak, if any found in me hurtful wrong in the time I stood before the council.

21 Or in regard to this One Voice, that I cried out standing among them, that about the Resurrection of the dead, I am being made judged by you this day.

22 And when Felix heard these things,

knowing a more perfect regard to "That Way", he deferred them. He spoke, When Lysias the chief captain should come down, we shall have knowledge as yourselves.

Paul kept with liberty and had visitors
23 And also appointing a centurion to keep Paul, both to have rest, and nothing forbidding his own privacy to service or to come near to him.

Felix privately visited Paul
24 And after certain days having come up, Felix with Drusilla, his Jewish wife being present, he sent for Paul and heard him concerning about the Christ of Faith.
25 And as Disputing to him about Righteousness and Self Control and Judgment Being Expecting, Felix became afraid. He answered, You must go currently, but having time, then I being partaking shall summon you,

Felix hoped for bribe money
26 And then with all this, he also expected that money shall be made given to him by Paul, so that he should have removed him for this reason, and he more often was sending for him for talking to him.

After 2 yrs Festus is new Governor
27 But after two years, Porcius Festus received succession in office. Felix was made fulfilled, and also willing to arrange for the Jews a thankfulness, Felix left Paul bound.

Trial by Festus
25 As soon as Festus entered the province, after three days he ascended for Jerusalem from Caesarea.
2 And then the High Priest and the chiefs of the Jews made known plainly to him, against Paul, and entreated him,
3 Asking thankfulness against him, so that he should send for him to Jerusalem, they lying in wait to intentionally kill him upon the way of travel.

4 Actually Festus then answered to keep Paul in Caesarea, and to expect himself therein to go out swiftly.
5 Therefore, he stated, if any man among you is exceedingly able, he must go down with myself, to be accusing this man in wrong,
6 And when he stayed among them greater than ten days, he came down into Caesarea, The next day he sat down upon the judgment seat commanded that Paul be made to move along.
7 And he having come up, the Jews having been shunned, coming down away from Jerusalem brought also many burdensome complaints against Paul that were definitely not capable to be proved.
8 He responded for himself, neither have I sinned any against the Law of the Jews, nor against the Temple area, nor against Caesar,

Festus wanted trial in Jerusalem
9 But Festus willing to arrange a thankfulness to the Jews, answered Paul, You shall have to speak ascending there into Jerusalem about these things to be judged before me.

Paul Appeals to Caesar
10 Then Paul spoke, I am now standing before the judgment seat of Caesar, where I ought to be made judged. I have wronged no Jews as you also very well fully know.
11 Because, If indeed I am wronging, or I have practiced anything worthy of death, I refuse definitely not to die, but if I am not any of the things they accuse me, none is able by them. I am freely appealing to Caesar.
12 Then Festus talked together with the counsel, You are calling to answer to Caesar, to Caesar you shall go.

Festus informs King Agrippa
13 And after some time of days past, King Agrippa and Bernice arrived to Caesarea

to greet Festus.

14 And when as they had stayed there many more days, Festus communicated to the king saying, Yet there is a certain man, Paul, a prisoner that Felix left,

15 About whom, I being in Jerusalem made known plainly, the chief priests and the elders of the Jews are asking just punishment against him.

16 To whom I answered that it is definitely not the custom of Romans to freely give any man to damnation else than before having the presence of accusers placed with the accused, and also receive defense beyond our dreams in regard to the crime charged to him.

17 Therefore, they having come together in this place doing nothing with delay. The next day, I sat down in the judgment seat, commanded the man to move along.

18 I myself was surmising that the accusers introducing the accusation were not bringing that about to reality.

19 And I had certain questions about their own superstition against him, and about a certain Jesus being a corpse, that Paul affirmed to be Living.

20 And I was being perplexed upon questioning about this one. I said, Is he otherwise intending beyond his dreams to go to Jerusalem to be judged there also about these things?

21 But when Paul himself appealed to be kept for the Imperial audience, I commanded him to be kept until after when I should send him to Caesar.

22 Then Agrippa stated to Festus, I intend now to hear the man myself, and he stated, Tomorrow, you shall hear him.

23 Then the next day, Agrippa and Bernice came with very much pomp, and entered into the audience room and also united with the chief captain and men being as principal of the city, and by command of Festus, Paul was made moved along.

24 And Festus states, king Agrippa, and all those present with us, you are seeing this man, about whom all the multitude of different Jews make intercession of me in both Jerusalem and this place, loudly pleading that he must not live any longer.

25 But when I apprehended nothing worthy of death was practiced by him, and that he called upon the Imperial, I judged to send him.

26 Of whom I have definitely not any certainty to write to my lord, for this reason, I have him brought before you, and specifically before you king Agrippa, so that being by examination I should be having something to write,

27 For it seems to me unreasonable to send a prisoner, and not to signify an accusation against him.

Trial by King Agrippa

26 Then Agrippa stated to Paul, You are permitted to say in behalf of yourself. Then Paul responded, stretching out his hand.

2 I Spiritually Blessed esteeming myself, Oh king Agrippa, I expect to respond before you this day about all that I am made charged by the Jews,

3 I Spiritually now discern you are naturally an expert, and also specifically about the Jewish customs and questions. For this reason I Pray Earnestly of you to patiently hear me.

4 Therefore actually my existence since from beginning, recalling all things of the Jews out from youth, to be among my nation in Jerusalem,

5 Foreknowing me from the beginning, if they would witness how according to the strictest sect of our religion, I lived a Pharisee.

6 And now I am standing being made judged, for the Expectation of the Promise to the fathers, occurring from God.

7 To which our Twelve Tribes fervently devoting over night and day, expecting to arrive to this Expectation, I am made

charged Oh king Agrippa by the Jews.

8 Why should it be made judged faithless with you, allowing that God is Raising Up the dead?

9 Therefore, I actually thought myself required to practice very much contrary to the name of Jesus of Nazareth.

10 Which also I did in Jerusalem and receiving authority from the chief priests, I shut up many of His Saints in prison, and also intentionally killing them. I was putting down the voting stone.

11 And in every synagogue I often terribly punished them, compelling to blaspheme, and also excessively mad against them, I persecuted while also in outside cities.

Paul Tells of his Conversion

12 In which also I went to Damascus with authority and authorization from the chief priests.

13 At midday upon the way of travel, I Spiritually, Oh king, saw a Light from Heaven, above the brilliance of the sun Shone around about me and Went with me.

14 And when all of us fell to the earth, I Heard a Voice Uttering to me, and saying in the Hebrew language, Oh Saul, Oh Saul, Why are you persecuting Me? It is hard for you to kick against the pricks.

15 And I spoke, Who are you, Oh Lord? And He Spoke, I am Jesus that you are persecuting.

16 But definitely you must raise, and you must stand upon your feet, for because for this I have Spiritually Appeared to you an under servant, and to you to be Hand Chosen for Myself a Witness, to whom Mutually you have Spiritually Seen, and also to whom I will Spiritually Appear to you,

17 Setting you Free from the people, and from the Gentiles, to whom I am now Sending you Out,

18 To Open their eyes, to Turn About from darkness into the Light, and from the authority of the satan, with Intent to God,

that they Receive Removal of sin natures and sins and Heritage among those Made Holy by Faith of Me.

19 From where, Oh king Agrippa, I was definitely Not Disobedient to the Heavenly Visitation.

20 But definitely first of all in Damascus, and also Jerusalem, and also to all in the land of Judea, and I was Telling to the Gentiles to Repent, and Turn About to God, Practicing Works by God Worthy of Repentance.

21 For these causes the Jews physically took me in the Temple area, attempting to violently kill.

22 Having Acquired Help, therefore, from God until this day, I am Standing the same both Witnessing to the least and also to the great, saying nothing except whatever the Prophets Uttered, and also what Moses Expected to come to pass.

23 Allowing that Christ suffered, Allowing that First out from Resurrection of the Dead, and Expected to Proclaim much Light to the people and to the Gentiles.

24 For while Responding these things himself, Festus stated with a great voice, Oh Paul, you are being insane with the many writings, you are already turning mentally mad.

25 But he stated I am definitely not insane Oh most noble Festus, but definitely Sounding Forth the Words of Truth and Seriousness.

26 Because the king is aware about these things, before whom also I am Uttering Speaking Boldly, for some of these certain things being definitely not hid from him, because I am Persuaded this was definitely not anything made practiced in a corner.

Paul almost Persuades King Agrippa

27 Oh King Agrippa, are you committed to the Prophets? I Spiritually Know that you are committing.

28 Then Agrippa stated to Paul, In a little you are Persuading me to Become a

Christian.

29 And Paul spoke, I Wish Whoever to God, also by few or by many, definitely not only you but definitely also everyone, all who Hear me this day, To Become such manner I Also am, except for these bonds.

30 And when he had spoken these things, the king, and the governor, and also Bernice rose, and they that were sitting with them.

31 And when they had withdrawn, they were uttering to one another saying that, This man has practiced nothing worthy of death or bonds.

Would be free if not appealed to Caesar

32 Then Agrippa stated to Festus, This man could be set at liberty, except that he had not called upon Caesar. (Acts 23:11)

Sent to Rome by ship

27 And when as it was made judged we then sailed away for Italy. They delivered up mutually Paul and also certain other ones, prisoners of a different kind, to a centurion named Julius, of the imperial band.

2 And entering in the ship Adramyttium launching forth to places, expecting to sail to Asia, being with us, Aristarchus, a Macedonian of Thessalonica,

3 And also after another of a different kind, I was brought down at Sidon, and also Julius also kindly treated Paul, permitting him to go with friends to acquire freshening.

4 After there launched forth, sailed past Cyprus, because of the winds being contrary.

5 And also, upon sailing over the open depths to Cilicia and Pamphylia, we descended into Myra of Lycia.

6 There also the centurion found a ship of Alexandria sailing to Italy, he booked us therein himself.

7 Then sailing slowly in sufficient days, also with difficulty passed by Cnidus, the wind not further allowing us, we sailed past Crete by Salmone.

8 And also hardly sailed by it, came to a certain place called Fair Havens, which was near a city, Lasea.

9 For now a sufficiently long time past and it was already dangerous for sailing, Paul was Admonishing because also of fasting already to be passing forth.

Paul Predicts much loss if by sailing

10 And said to them, Oh sirs, I perceive that with trauma and very much damaged loss, definitely not only the cargo and the ship to be expecting sailing, but definitely also our souls.

11 And the centurion was made persuaded by the ship master and the ship owner, instead of that Paul before is made Saying.

12 The harbor is existing but not accommodating to winter in, the many more settled to advise to launch forth after there, if by any means they are able to arrive into Phenice to winter, a harbor of Crete, looking to southwest and to northwest.

13 And when the South wind blew gently, they thought to retain their purpose, taking up, they sailed by close Crete.

Severe storm arose at sea

14 But definitely not long after they cast out against it, a tempestuous wind called, Euroclydon,

15 Then seized the ship and being not able to tack into the wind, we were brought to hand driving.

16 And running past some small island called Clauda with difficulty, we were hardly capable of control, to end with the skiff,

17 While with helps taken up, they were used to be undergirding the ship, and also fearing that unless they fell away into quicksand, they let down the sails so they were made driven.

18 And then we being made violently storm tossed to the next day, they did lighten.

19 And after the third day, they threw

down the tackling of the ship with their own hands.

20 And when neither sun nor star fully appeared in many more days, and also definitely not a little bad weather was now pressing upon expectations, removing away every way for us to be saved.

Angel Told Paul no loss of life

21 And then existing after long abstinence, then Paul stood in the midst of them, he Spoke, Oh Sir, he ought indeed, to have been listening to me, that not to have launched forth away from Crete, and also gained this trauma and damaged loss.

22 And now I am presently Admonishing you to be cheerful because there shall be definitely no loss of soul from you, but of the ship,

23 Because there stood this night by me an Angel of God, of Whose I am and also to Whom I am Devoted.

24 Saying, You must not fear Paul. You Must Stand before Caesar, and Behold, God has freely Given to you All that are sailing with you.

25 Yet, sirs, for this reason, you must be Cheerful for I am Committing to God, that in this manner, it shall be according to the manner, He is made Uttering to me.

26 So He must have us to Fall Away upon a certain island.

About to abandon ship

27 Now as the fourteenth night came to pass, it became different in value for us in the Adria; about middle of the night the sailors themselves surmised to draw near a certain land.

28 And depth sounded found twenty fathoms, and having parted a little measure then again depth sounded, finding fifteen fathoms.

29 And also afraid, fearing that they might fall upon rough places, they threw down four anchors from the stern of the boat, wishing the day to occur.

30 And the sailors seeing to flee out from the ship, then let down the skiff into the sea under pretense, as expecting to put out an anchor from the bow of the ship.

Paul Warns for all to stay on ship

31 Paul spoke to the centurion and the soldiers, Except they continue in the ship, yourselves definitely cannot be saved.

32 Then the soldiers cut away the ropes of the skiff and allowed it to fall away.

Fourteenth day of fasting, they eat

33 And as far as those expecting the day to occur, Paul encouraged all to be partakers of nourishment saying, This day, the fourteenth day, watching for without eating, you are persisting taking nothing.

34 For this reason, I encourage you to take to self, because this existing nourishment for your health, because not a hair from your head shall fall down.

35 And when he had spoken these things and he receiving the bread, he Gave Thanks to God, Breaking in the presence of all, and began to eat.

36 Then it came to pass they all so now cheerfully received to themselves nourishment.

They lighten the ship

37 And we were all in the ship two hundred seventy six souls.

38 And when not hungry for nourishment, they lightened the ship, casting out the wheat into the sea.

All Escaped Safely to land

39 And when it became day, they were definitely not fully knowing the area, but a certain bay was beheld having a shore into which they were consulting if they were able to drive in the ship.

40 And when they remove away the anchors, they were allowing for the sea together with letting loose the bands of the rudder, and lifted up the mainsail to the

blowing, holding into the shore.

41 And falling among at a place where two seas joined, the boat ran aground, and then actually the bow of the ship stuck fast continued unmovable, and the stem of the boat was made removed by the violence of great violent waves.

42 And the soldiers counsel was they should kill the prisoners in order that not any swim out to flee away.

43 But the centurion intending to physically save Paul forbid them this intention, and also commanded those that are able to swim to hurl ahead of with intent to set out to earth.

44 And the rest, some actually on boards, and those on anything from the ship, and in this manner they all became physically saved upon the earth.

On Island of Melita

28 And when physically saved, then they fully knew that it is being made called the island of Melita.

2 While barbarians offer definitely no concern, because having acquired affection to mankind for us, they started a burning fire to receive to themselves all of us because of the rain showers being present, and because of the cold weather.

Paul bitten by snake, but Lives

3 And when Paul had bunched up a multitude of different sticks, and laid on the burning fire a viper came out from the warmth fastened on his hand.

4 And as the barbarians saw the wild beast hanging from his hand, they were saying among one to another, By all means this man is a deliberate murderer, who was physically saved from the sea, justly punished has definitely not been allowed to live.

5 Therefore, actually shaking off the wild beast in the fire, he suffered no evil work.

6 And they were watching for him, with very much intent and they watched for expecting to swell or fall suddenly dead, and perceived nothing wrong upon him, it came to pass they changed their minds saying, he is a god.

7 And in the surrounding place, there existing a space of land for the chief of the island, named Publius, that welcomed, courteously guest lodging us three days.

Paul Heals the father of Publius

8 And it came to pass the father of Publius was made constrained to lie from fever and bloody diarrhea, to whom Paul entered and Prayed, Laying Hands on him, Cured him.

9 As soon as this occurred others were coming near, and those also having infirmities in the island were Made Healed.

10 Who also honored assigned to us with many honors, and bringing up, they laid on before to what was needful.

After three months they sail away

11 So after three months, we launched forth in a ship of Alexandria, wintering in the island, by registry, Castor and Pollux.

12 And bringing down into Syracuse, we continued with Intent three days.

13 From where we wondered about arriving into Rhegium, and after one day became full (sail) to the South (wind), the following day came into Puteoli.

14 Where we found Brethren, made encouraged by them to continue with Intent seven days, and in this manner, we came into Rome.

Brethren Came to Greet Paul

15 After there, the Brethren heard of us, they came out for meeting us as far as Appii Forum and The Three Taverns, Paul who seeing Gave Thanks to God, he took courage.

Paul in Rome, calls chief Jews

16 And when we came to Rome, the centurion delivered up the prisoners to the captain of the guard, but Paul was made

permitted to continue by himself with the soldier maintaining him.

17 And it came to pass after three days Paul called together those being the chief of the Jews, and when they came together, he said to them, Oh men Oh Brethren, I have done nothing contrary to the people, or customs from our Jewish fathers. I was delivered up a prisoner from Jerusalem, into the hands of the Romans,

18 Who examined for judgment, were intending to me set at liberty, because there was no accusation of death to exist in me,

19 But the Jews contradicting, I was made compelled to call upon Caesar, definitely not that I am having any Gentile to accuse.

20 Therefore, for this accusation I have been encouraged by you, Spiritually Knowing and to Speak further, for the cause for the Expectation of Israel, I am encompassed with this chain.

21 And they spoke to him, We neither received writings about you from Judea, nor any brother coming up to tell, or uttered any about evil of you.

22 But we are thinking worthy to hear from you, because of what you are actually regarding of value about this heresy, which is known to us, because everywhere it is spoken against.

Appointed a day to Hear him

23 And when they assigned him a day, there were many more now coming to him to whom he was Expounding in the lodging, emphasizing the Kingdom Rule of God, and also Persuading them about Jesus, both from the Law of Moses, and the Prophets from early in the morning until after the evening hour.

24 And some certainly were made Persuaded from the things said, but some were Uncommitted.

25 And when they were disagreed among themselves they were dismissing away after Paul Spoke one Word for God-Working, The Holy Spirit God-Working Uttered through Esaias the Prophet to our fathers,

26 Saying, You must Go to this people and you must Speak, hearing you shall hear, and most definitely should not Understand, and seeing you shall see, and most definitely should not Spiritually Discern.

27 For the heart of this people has been made hardened, also their ears have dulled hearing, and their eyes have closed, for fear that they might Spiritually Discern with their eyes, and their ears might Hear, and their heart might Understand, and they might be Converted, and I shall make them Whole. (Isa 6:9-10)

Salvation is Also to the Gentiles

28 Therefore, it must be known unto you, that the Salvation of God has been made Sent Out to the Gentiles, and It shall be Heard.

29 And when He had spoken these things, the Jews went having very much arguing among themselves.

Freely Taught two more years

30 Then Paul continued two whole years in his own rented house, and gladly received all that were coming in to him,

31 Preaching the Kingdom Rule of God, and teaching about the Lord Jesus Christ with all boldness, no one forbidding.

The Epistle of Paul the Apostle to the

Romans

Apostle for Obedience of Faith

1 Paul, Bondslave of Jesus Christ, Inwardly Called (Born Again) an Apostle, now being Made Separate for the Gospel of God,

2 Which He has Promised before through His Prophets in the Holy Scriptures.

3 Concerning His Son, was Made Out From the Seed of David relating to flesh nature (by heritage).

4 Made Determined the Son of God with Miracle Power, according to the Spirit of Holiness by Resurrection out from the Dead, Jesus Christ our Lord, (Rom 1:18)

5 By whom we Have Received Grace and Apostleship, for the Purpose of Obedience of Faith, Among All nations in Behalf of His Name. (Rom 16:26)

6 Among whom you are also yourselves Inwardly Called (Born Again) of Jesus Christ.

7 To all that be in Rome, Beloved of God, Inwardly Called (Born Again) Saints, Grace to you and Peace from God our Father, and Lord Jesus Christ.

Your Faith is spoken about

8 First of all, I certainly Give Thanks to my God through Jesus Christ in behalf of all of you, that your Faith is being made Proclaimed much in all the satan's world,

9 Because God is my witness, to Whom I am Devoted in my spirit to the Gospel of His Son, as without ceasing, I make Mention of you.

10 Always in my Prayers, Praying earnestly, if by any means already, a time shall be made to prosper in the Will of God to come to you,

11 Because I greatly desire to see you, that I should Impart to you some Spiritual Spirit Gift to firmly Establish you.

12 And this is encouraged together with you through the mutual Faith one to another in you and also me.

13 Now I would definitely not prefer you to be ignorant Brethren, for often I purposed to come to you, and was forbidden so far to Come Forward that I might have some Fruit also among you, just as also among other Gentiles.

14 I am a Debtor both to Greeks, and also to barbarians, both to the wise, and also the uncomprehending.

15 Also in such a manner yet I am willing to preach the Gospel to you in Rome.

Power of God for Salvation

16 For I am definitely not ashamed of the Gospel of Christ, because it is the Miracle Power of God for Salvation, to all that are Continuously Committing, to the Jew first of all, and also to the Gentile,

Revealed from Faith to Faith

17 Because therein the Righteousness of God Himself is made revealed out from Faith to Faith, just as I am now made writing, For the Righteous shall be Living by Faith. (Hab 2:4)

Wrath of God Revealed

18 Because the Wrath for Justice of God is Made Revealed from Heaven Against All ungodliness and unrighteousness of men, who are holding the Truth in unrighteousness. (Rom 1:4)

19 Since that which is Known of God Is Openly Manifest in them; because God has Manifested it to them,

20 Because His invisible things from Creation of the satan's world are Made Clearly Seen, being Made Comprehended from the Workmanships, and also His Everlasting Miracle Power and also Godhood,

whereto they are Being without excuse.

21 Since they Recognized God, they have definitely not Attributed Glory as to God or Gave Thanks, but definitely were made empty self worships in their thoughts, and their heart without Understanding was made darkened.

22 Affirming to be wise, they were made foolish,

23 And changed the Glory of the Incorruptible God with a Likeness of a corruptible man image, and of birds, and four footed animals, and creeping things.

For this, God Gave Them Up

24 For this reason, God also delivered them up with the evil desires of their hearts for moral impurity to dishonor their bodies among themselves.

25 Who exchanged the Truth of God with the lie, and have reverenced and been devoted to the creature more than the Creating One, that is Most Blessed Worthy of all Spiritual Perfection, Forever, Amen.

26 Because of this, God delivered up them to evil affections of dishonor, and also because their females exchanged the natural sexual use into that against nature.

27 And also likewise, the males parted from the natural sexual use of the female, to be made inflamed in their homosexual lust of one to another, male with male producing indecency, and fully receiving within themselves, this payback required of their deception.

God Gave Them Up to reprobate mind

28 And just as they have definitely not Proved in Truth to be having God in Full Knowledge, God Delivered them Up to a reprobate mind to do that which is not being proper.

29 Being fully filled with all unrighteousness, fornication, evil action, greediness, maliciousness; full of envy, murder, contention, subtle half-truth (deceit), evil behavior, whisperers,

30 Slanderers, haters of God, injurious, proud, boasters, inventors of evil work, willfully disobedience to parents;

31 Without Understanding, Covenant breakers, without natural affection, unalterable, unmerciful.

32 Who having Fully Known the Righteous Action of God, that they who are practicing such are worthy of death, they are not only doing themselves, but definitely also are consenting to practicing the same.

Judgment according to Truth

2 For this reason, you are without excuse, Oh man, because by every way against whom you are judging, you are judging another of a different kind, you are condemning to death yourself, because that Judged, you are practicing yourself.

2 But we are Discerning according to Truth, that the Judgment of God is against them that practice such.

3 And then account this, Oh man, who is judging them who are practicing such, and doing the same, that you shall escape the Judgment of God?

4 Or are you despising the Riches of His Gentleness, and Forbearance, and Longsuffering; not Understanding that the Kindness of God in Leading you to Repentance?

5 But according to your hardness and impenitent heart, you are storing up to yourself Wrath for Justice in the Day of Wrath for Justice and Revelation of the Righteous Judgment of God,

Judges every man by his Deeds

6 Who will pay back to every man according to his Works by God. (Ps 62:12)

7 They, certainly according to Endurance of God-Good Work by God, are seeking Glory, and Honor, and Incorruption, Life Eternal.

8 But for those also actually having confidence out from strife, and being disobeying to the Truth, in unrighteousness, anger

and evil wrath,

9   Affliction and distress, upon every soul of man that produces evil work, both of Jews first of all, and also Gentiles.

God Respects no man's person

10 But Glory and Honor and Peace, to all that are Working God-Good, to Jew first of all, and also to the Gentile.

11 Because there is no respect of persons with God.

12 Because whoever has sinned without Law as lawlessly, shall also be destroyed without Law as lawlessly, and as many as have sinned in Law, shall be Judged by Law.

13 Because definitely not the hearers of the Law are Made Righteous with God, but definitely the Effectual Doers of the Law are Made Righteous.

14 Because when the Gentiles having not the Law, these might do by nature the Law, having not the Law, they are a Law to themselves,

15 Which do exhibit the Work by God of the Law written in their hearts, also giving witness of their conscience, and their reasoning either accusing or proving innocence between themselves,

16 Wherein the Day when God shall Judge the secrets of men, according to my Gospel, by Jesus Christ.

Must Circumcise your Heart in the Spirit

17 Behold, you are continuously made classified Jews, and you are keeping a hold in the Law and you are boasting in God.

18 You are Knowing His Will, and are Proving in Truth and made informed, being excellent in value by the Law.

19 And you are also now being persuaded, being a guide yourself to the blind, a light of them in darkness,

20 An instructor of mentally unwise, a teacher of infants, having a form of Knowledge and of the Truth in the Law.

21 You, therefore, that are teaching other ones of a different kind, are you definitely not teaching yourselves? You, that are preaching no one to steal, are you stealing?

22 He that is saying not to commit adultery, are you committing adultery? Are you abhorring idols? Are you doing sacrilege?

23 Are you those boasting in Law? Through the broken Commandment of the Law, you are dishonoring God.

24 For the name of God is made blasphemed among the Gentiles because of you, just as now wherein made written. (Isa 52:5)

25 Because circumcision indeed is profiting if you should be practicing Law; but if you should be a transgressor of Law, your circumcision is now become uncircumcision.

26 Therefore, if an uncircumcision should maintain the Righteous Actions of the Law, shall definitely not his uncircumcision be made accounted for circumcision?

27 And uncircumcision of nature finally fulfilling the Law shall Judge you, who through learning and circumcision, a transgressor of the Law.

28 Because he is definitely not a Jew among the openly manifest, neither the circumcision in sinful flesh nature among the openly manifest.

29 But the hidden within Jew and circumcision of heart in Spirit, not in learning, whose Full Praise not from men, but from God.

Truth of God Judges all men

3   Therefore, what more in excess of the Jew? Or what advantage of circumcision?

2   Very much in every manner, actually because they have Made Committed first of all to these Oracles of God.

3   Because what if some have Uncommitted, shall not their Uncommitment destroy the Faith of God?

4   Not ever possible, for God must be True, but every man a liar; just as made Written, so that you whoever should be Righteous in your Spiritual Communication, and

you should Overcome when you are made Judged. (Ps 51:4)

5 But if our unrighteousness commends the Righteousness of God, what shall we Spirit Say, that God (is) unrighteous, inducing His Wrath for Justice according to the saying of a man?

6 Not ever possible, otherwise, how shall God Judge the satan's world?

7 Because, if the Truth of God abounds in amount by my falsehood for His Glory, why am I still also made Judged as a sinner?

8 And not blaspheme but just as some state, that just as we are saying, That we might be doing evil works whose condemnation is Just in order that God-Goods should come.

None Righteous in themselves

9 Therefore, then are we being better? Definitely not in any way. We have proven before, because all being under sin nature and sin, both Jews and also Gentiles.

10 For just as it is Made Written that there is definitely none Righteous, not one.

11 There is definitely none that is Understanding. There is definitely none that diligently seek after God. (Ps 14:2)

12 Together every Way they have avoided. They have become useless. Definitely none is doing Gentleness. Definitely not any is, up to One. (Ps 14:3)

13 Their throat is now made an open tomb, with their tongues they have used deceit, poison of asps under their lips, (Ps 5:9; Ps 140:3)

14 Whose mouth, full of cursing and bitterness. (Ps 10:7)

15 Their sharp feet have shed blood.

16 Devastation and misery in their way,

17 And a way of Peace, they definitely know not. (Isa 59:7-8)

18 Definitely is no fear of God before their eyes. (Ps 36:1)

19 But now, we Discern that the Law is Saying, to those within the Law, that every mouth Uttering should have been made stopped, and all the satan's world should become under Judgment before God.

20 Since out from man work of Law, definitely not any sinful flesh nature shall be Made Righteous in the Presence of Him, because through the Law the Full Knowledge of the sin nature and sin.

Righteousness through Faith

21 But just now Righteousness of God without the Law is now being made Manifest, being Made Witnessed by the Law and the Prophets;

22 That Righteousness of God through Faith of Jesus Christ, for all and to all those Committing, because definitely there is no distinction,

23 Because all have sinned and are made lacking the Glory (Spiritual Perfection) of God,

24 Being Made Righteous freely by His Grace, through the Separation Removal in Christ Jesus,

25 Whom God has Purposed for Himself, a Mercy Seat through Faith by His Blood, for the Purpose of Declaration of His Righteousness, because of the passing over of the sinful acts that are past.

26 With a Declaration of His Righteousness in the Forbearance of God, in the Special Time now, wherein He is Righteous, and the One Making Righteous by Faith with Jesus.

27 Therefore, wherein is rejoicing? Is it excluded through which Law of man works? Definitely not, but definitely through the Law of Faith.

28 Therefore, we are accounting, Faith makes a man Made Righteous without man works of Law.

29 Either God only of the Jews, but definitely not also of Gentiles? But emphatically yes, also of Gentiles.

30 Seeing One God, Who shall Make Righteous circumcision of Faith, and uncircumcision by Faith.

31 Therefore, are we destroying Law by

Faith? Not possible ever, but we are definitely bringing to health the Law.

Commitment makes a man Righteous

4 Therefore, what shall we Spirit Say, Abraham our father Found according to sinful flesh nature?

2 Because, if Abraham has been Made Righteous out from man works, he is having happiness, but definitely not before God.

3 Because what is the Scripture Saying? That Abraham Committed to God, and it was made Accounted to him for Righteousness. (Gen 15:6)

4 Now to him that is Working, the Reward is definitely not Accounted According to Grace, but definitely According to Debt.

5 But to him that is not Working, but is Continuously Committing to Him that is Making the ungodly Righteous, His Faith is Accounting for the means of Righteousness.

Faith for Means of Righteousness

6 Even as David also is Saying, the Blessedness of the man to whom God is Continuously Accounting Righteousness without God-Works.

7 Spiritually Blessed, whose lawlessness's have been Made Removed from Memory (forgiven), and whose sin natures and sins were Made Blotted Out.

8 Spiritually Blessed, the man to whom the Lord might never ever Account sin. (Ps 32:1-2)

9 Therefore, this Blessedness upon circumcision, or so also in regard to uncircumcision? Because we are saying that Faith was Made Accounted to Abraham for the means of Righteousness.

10 How, therefore, has it been made accounted being in circumcision, or in uncircumcision? Definitely not in circumcision, but definitely in uncircumcision.

11 And he Received the Miracle Sign of Circumcision, a Seal of the Righteousness of Faith among the uncircumcision, for he is being the father of all those Committing among the uncircumcision for the Purpose that also Righteousness be Accounted to them.

12 And the father of Circumcision to them not of circumcision only, but definitely to them who are walking orderly in the steps of Faith of our father Abraham, while he was yet in uncircumcision,

Law only makes Faith void

13 Because the Promise definitely not through the Law to Abraham or his Seed, as his Heir to be being in the satan's world, but definitely through the Righteousness of Faith.

14 Because if they, heirs out from the Law, Faith is now made empty, and the Promise is now made destroyed.

Permanent Promise by Faith

15 Because the Law produces Wrath for Justice, because when definitely no Law, neither is a broken Commandment.

16 Because of this, in order that out from Faith according to Grace, for there being a permanent Promise to all the Seed, definitely not those out from the Law only, but definitely also out from Faith of Abraham, who is father of us all.

17 For just as is made written, I have positioned you for a father of many nations, (Gen 17:5) to those nearby Committed to God, Who is Offering Spiritual Life to the dead, and calling those things that are not, same as they are.

18 Who by Expectation Committed to Expectation, for the Purpose of becoming himself the father of many nations, according to the Spirit Saying Made, In such a manner your Seed shall be. (Gen 15:5)

19 And being not weak in Faith, he considered definitely not his own body already now being made dead, existing some place about hundred years old, and the dead state of Sarah's womb.

20 For he doubted definitely not after that

Promise of God through uncommitment, but definitely he was made More Strengthened by Faith, Attributing Glory to God.
21 And being made Fully Persuaded that what he is now being Promised, He is Exceedingly Able also to Perform.
22 So for this reason, it was Made Accounted to him for Righteousness. (Gen 15:6)

All through Commitment to Risen Lord
23 For now definitely not made Written because to him only, that it was Accounted to him,
24 But definitely also because for us, to whom it is expecting to be Accounted to us, who are Committing to the Raised Up Jesus our Lord out from the Dead.
25 Who was Delivered Up because of our spiritual death offenses, and was Made Raised Up for us, Making us Righteous.

Made Righteous by Faith
5 Therefore, being Made Righteous out from Faith, we are having Peace with God through our Lord Jesus Christ,
2 Through Whom also we are Now Having Access by Faith into the means of His Grace in which we are now Standing, being Joyful in Expectation of the Glory of God.
3 And definitely not only so, but definitely we also are being Joyful in afflictions, now Spiritually Discerning that the affliction produces Endurance,
4 And the Endurance, Experience, and the Experience, Expectation,
5 And the Expectation is definitely not being confounded, for the God-Love of God is now made Poured Out Inside our hearts, through the Holy Spirit Made Given to us.
6 Because we, still being weak, Christ Died according to an Appointed Time in behalf of the ungodly.
7 For hardly in behalf of a Righteous man shall one die, yet in behalf of a God-Good man, perhaps, some are even daring to die.

8 But God commends His Own God-Love to us, for while we were yet sinners, Christ died in our behalf.
9 Very much more then, being now Made Righteous by His Blood, we shall be made Saved away from the Wrath for Justice through Him.

Much more, Saved by His Life
10 Because if while we were enemies, we were Made Reconciled to God through the Death of His Son, very much more being Made Reconciled, we shall be Made Saved by His Life.
11 Definitely not only so, but definitely being Joyful also in God through our Lord Jesus Christ, by Whom we now have Received the Reconciliation.

Death Passed to all men by Law
12 Through means of this, as by one man sin nature and sin entered into the satan's world, and death through means of the sin nature and sin, so death passed through to all men, whereby all have sinned by their choice.
13 Because until Law, sin nature and sin was in the satan's world, but sin nature and sin was definitely not accounted responsible, being no Law.
14 But definitely death ruled from Adam as far as to Moses, and even over them that have not sinned in the likeness of Adam's broken Commandment, who is a model for Him Expected. (1 Cor 15:45-50)

By Jesus Christ the Gift of Grace
15 But definitely not as the spiritual death offense, in another manner so also the Spirit Gift. If because of the spiritual death offense of one many have Died, instead very much the Grace of God and the God-Gift by the Grace of the One Man, Jesus Christ, has Abounded in Amount for Many,
16 The Gift Given by God, and definitely not as through one sinning. Because actually judgment on one to condemnation

to destruction, and then the Spirit Gift for many spiritual death offenses for the Purpose and Result of Righteous Rule of Practice. (Adam's sin to death vs. Christ's cross to Life; 1 Cor 15:45-47)

Jesus also Gift of Righteousness

17 Because after the spiritual death offense of one, the Death has Reigned through One. Very much more through the Overflowing of Grace, and of the God-Gift of those Receiving Righteousness in Life, they shall be Reigning by the One, Jesus Christ.

18 So then, therefore, as by the spiritual death offense of one (Adam) upon all men for condemnation to destruction, in same manner also through the Righteous Action of One (Jesus) upon all men for Making us Righteous in Life.

19 Because as through the disobeying of the one man, many have been made sinners, in the same manner also through the Obedience of One, many shall be made Righteous.

20 Moreover, Law then entered in that the spiritual death offense should exceed in quantity. When the sin nature and sin exceeded in quantity, the Grace Super Abounded.

21 That as sin nature and sin ruled in death, even so Grace should Rule in Righteousness through Jesus Christ our Lord for Life Eternal.

Freed from Sin

6 What therefore shall we Spirit Say? Shall we by our choice continue with intent to sin nature and sin, that Thankfulness for Grace should be Exceeded in Quantity?

2 That NOT possible ever! How shall we, who have Died by our choice to the sin nature and sin, Live by our choice still with it? (Answer in Rom 7:24-8:2)

3 Instead, are you not Understanding that those made Immersed into Christ Jesus have been Made Immersed into His Death?

4 Therefore, we have been Made Buried through the Immersion with Him into Death in order that as Christ has been Made Risen Up from the Dead through the Glory of the Father, in such a manner also, we should Walk by our choice in Newness of a Different Kind of Life Eternal.

5 Because if we are Now Becoming by our choice Planted Together in the Likeness of His Death, but definitely then we shall also be of His Resurrection.

Our old man Crucified with Him

6 Knowing this, that He has been Made Crucified Together with our old man, that the body of the sin nature and sin should be Made Done Away, that we are no longer by our choice are to bond serve to the sin nature and sin.

7 Because he that Died by his choice is now Made Righteous, away from the sin nature and sin.

8 And if now we have Died United with Christ, we are by our choice Committing that we shall also Live Together with Him.

9 Continuously Spiritually Discerning that Christ has been made Risen Up out from Dead, He Dies by His choice no more. No more by His choice is Death having dominion over Him.

10 Because that He Died, He Died for the sin nature and sin one time (to take them away), but in that He is Continuously Living, He is Living as God.

11 And in such a manner, also yourselves must be accounting yourselves to be actually Dead to the sin nature and sin, then Continuously be Living to God with Christ Jesus our Lord.

12 Therefore, the sin nature and sin must not by your choice be reigning in your mortal body, to obey it in the evil desires thereof.

Yield yourselves to God as Alive

13 Neither must you by your choice present your members instruments of unrighteousness for the sin nature and

sin, but definitely you must be Presenting yourselves to God, as continuously being by your choice Living out from the Dead, and your members Instruments of Righteousness for God.

14 Because your sin nature and sin shall certainly not by your choice have dominion, because you are definitely not under the Law, but definitely under Grace.

15 What, therefore, shall we sin by our choice, because we are definitely not under the Law, but definitely under Grace? That not possible ever to occur!

16 Are you definitely not now Spiritually Discerning that to whom you present yourselves Bondslaves for obedience, you are slaves to whom you are obeying, whether in fact, of sin nature and sin to death, or of Obedience to Righteousness?

Not servants of sin, now Freed

17 But Thankfulness for Grace from God, because you were slaves of sin nature and sin, but you have by your choice Obeyed out from the heart, that Model Made Delivered Up for Teaching.

18 And then being Made Free away from the sin nature and sin, you have been Made Bondslaves for Righteousness.

19 I am saying by manner of man, because of the infirmity of your sinful flesh nature, because you have presented your members as slaves to moral impurity and lawlessness for the result of lawlessness. Now in such a manner, you must have by your choice presented your members Bondslaves for Righteousness for the result of Personal Holiness.

20 Because when you were slaves of sin nature and sin, you were free from Righteousness.

21 Therefore, what fruit were you used to be having then, for which you are now ashamed, because the end of that (is) death.

22 But just now having been Made Free, away from the sin nature and sin, you have now been by your choice Made Bondslaves

to God, having your Fruit for the result of Personal Holiness, the End after that, Life Eternal.

23 Because the wages of sin nature and sin, death; but instead the Spirit Gift of God, Eternal Life inside Christ Jesus our Lord.

Also you are now dead to Law

7 Are you continuously being ignorant, Brethren, because I am uttering Law to these knowing? The Law is continuously having dominion over a man for whatever time he is living.

2 Because a woman living subject to a husband is now made bound by Law. But if ever the husband might die, she is now made loosed from the Law with the husband.

3 Therefore, so then if her husband is living she shall be warned as she might become an adulterous with another man. But if her husband might have died, she is free from the Law, not being herself an adulteress, occurring with another man.

4 So that, my Brethren, then yourselves have been made put to Death in Body from the Law by the Body of Christ, made Risen Up out from the Dead, for the Purpose of you becoming One with Another of a Different Kind, in order that we should bear Fruit by God,

5 Because when we were in the sinful flesh nature, the sufferings of the sins, which through the Law used to be accomplished in our members to bear fruit to death.

6 But just now we have been made loosed from the Law, having Died in what we used to be held, so that we are bondserving in Newness of a Different Kind of Spirit and definitely not in oldness of writings.

Inner sin once killed me by Law

7 What, therefore, shall we Spirit Say? Is the Law sin nature and sin? Not possible ever! But definitely, I have definitely not Known the sin nature and sin except

through the Law, and also because I had definitely not Spiritually Discerned evil desire, except the Law was saying, You shall definitely not evilly desire. (Ex 20:17)

8 But the sin nature and sin having taken occasion through the Commandment produced in me all evil desire, because without Law, sin nature and sin (was) dead.

9 And then I used to be living without Law as in time past, but when the Commandment came sin nature and sin lived again, and I died.

10 And the Commandment for the Purpose of Life, it was made found by me for the Purpose of death,

11 Because sin nature and sin taking occasion by the Commandment deceived me, and through it killed me.

Law is Holy, Righteous, and Good

12 So that actually the Law Holy, and the Commandment Holy, and Righteous, and God-Good.

Law Spiritual, but I sin-natured

13 Is not that, therefore, which is God-Good now become death to me? Not possible ever! But definitely sin nature and sin, in order that it should be made to appear sin nature and sin, produces death through that God-Good to me, that sin nature and sin by the Commandment should become beyond measure sinful.

14 Because we are now Spiritually Discerning that the Law is Continuously Spiritual. But I am continuously carnal sinful flesh nature, being now made sold in the market under the sin nature and sin.

15 Because what I am continuously producing, I do definitely not recognize, because what I am continuously definitely not willing, this I am continuously practicing, but definitely I am continuously hating this that I am continuously doing.

16 If then what I definitely would not be willing to do continuously, this I am continuously asserting to the Law for God-Work.

17 And then just now, no more I am producing it, but definitely the sin nature and sin continuously dwelling in me.

18 Because what I am Spiritually Discerning that is in me, that is definitely no God-Good that is dwelling in my sinful flesh nature, because to be willing is constantly with me, but how to continuously produce God-Work, I am definitely not finding.

19 I am willing to be doing God-Good (received after my New Birth from Above, John 6:29), yet definitely not. But definitely while definitely not willing, I am continuously practicing this evil work.

20 Now then if I am definitely not strongly desiring to continuously do this, I am no more producing this, but definitely the sin nature and sin continuously dwelling inside me.

21 So then, I am finding a law, that I am continuously willing to do the God-Work, but the evil work is constantly with me.

22 For I delight in the Law of God according to the Inward Man (my spirit with Christ Indwelling after Born from Above, 1 Cor 6:17).

23 But I Spiritually See another law of a different kind in my members, continuously warring against the law of my mind, and lead me captive to the law of sin nature and sin which is in my members.

Wretched man; must Bondserve Lord

24 Wretched man that I am, Who shall rescue me out from the body of this death?

25 I Give Thanks to God by Jesus Christ our Lord. So then, therefore, I myself with my mind will actually Continuously Bondserve to the Law of God (in the New Covenant), but with the sinful flesh nature, the law of sin nature and sin.

No condemnation Inside Christ

8 So then, now no condemnation to destruction Inside Christ Jesus, no more continuously by their choice walking

according to the sinful flesh nature, but definitely according to the Spirit.

2   For the Law of the Spirit of Life in Christ Jesus (fixed nature in New Covenant), has made me Free from the Law of sin nature and sin, even death (fixed nature in Old Covenant).

3   Because the impossible of the Law (of Old Covenant), in that it was weak by the sinful flesh nature, God then sent His own Son in the Likeness of sinful flesh nature of sin, and then in regard to sin nature and sin, Condemned to Death the sin nature and sin in His Likeness of sinful flesh nature,

We Fulfill Righteousness of Law

4   That the Righteous Action of the Law should be made Fulfilled in us, who are Continuously Walking by our choice not according to sinful flesh nature, but definitely According to the Spirit.

5   Yet they that are continuously according to sinful flesh nature, are by their choice continuously regarding of value the things of the sinful flesh nature, but they According to the Spirit, the Things of the Spirit.

6   Because the mind of the sinful flesh nature is death, but the Mind of the Spirit, Life and Peace.

7   Since the mind of the sinful flesh nature, enmity toward God, for it is definitely not made subject to the Law of God, because not able to be.

In the flesh you cannot please God

8   So then they that are being in sinful flesh nature are definitely not able to please God.

9   But you, yourselves, definitely are not in sinful flesh nature, but Definitely in the Spirit, if it be so the Spirit of God is Dwelling in you. But if anybody is definitely not having by his choice the Spirit of Christ, he is definitely not of Him.

If Christ Inside you, flesh is dead

10 And if Christ Within you, the body actually dead because of sin nature and sin; but the Spirit, Life because of Righteousness.

11 But if the Spirit of Him that Raised up Jesus out from the Dead, is Dwelling in you, He that Raised Up the Christ out from the Dead, shall be by His Choice Offering Spiritual Life also to our mortal bodies, by Him that is Indwelling your spirit Inside you. (1 Cor 6:17)

12 So then, therefore, Brethren, we are debtors, definitely not to the sinful flesh nature, to be living by your choice according to sinful flesh nature.

13 Because if you are living by your choice according to sinful flesh nature, we are expecting by our choice to die. But if you are continuously by your choice putting to Death in body the deeds of the body, you shall be Living by the Spirit.

14 Because as many as are Continuously Made Led by the Spirit of God, they are Continuously the Sons of God.

15 Because you have definitely not received by your choice the spirit of bondage of evil, again to fear, but definitely you have Received by your choice the Spirit of Adoption, by Whom we are Crying out by our choice, Abba, Father.

Spirit In us, as Children of God

16 The Spirit Himself also, is Continuously giving Witness to our spirit, that we are Being Children of God.

17 And if Children, then Heirs, actually Heirs of God, and Fellow Heirs of Christ, if it be so that we by our choice are Continuously suffering with (Him), in order that we should also be made Glorified Together.

18 Because I am accounting that the sufferings of this now Special Time, definitely not worthy to the Expecting Glory to be Made Revealed in us.

19 Because the earnest Expectation of the Creation is waiting the Revelation of the Sons of God.

20 Because the Creation has been made

subject to self-importance (vanity), definitely not willingly, but definitely because of Him that was Subjected in The Way of Expectation.

21 For also the Creation Itself shall be Made Free from the bondage of evil the Eternal death, for the Purpose and Result of the Liberty of the Children of God's Glory.

22 Because we are Discerning that All Creation is groaning together, and is travailing in pain together until now.

23 And definitely not only (Creation) but definitely Ourselves also Having Firstfruit of the Spirit, even we Ourselves groan within ourselves waiting Adoption (Rom 8:15; John 17:21-23), the Separation Removal of our body.

24 Because we are Made Saved with Expectation, and Expectation that is made seen is definitely not Expectation; because whatever anyone is physically seeing, why is he yet Expecting?

25 But if we are definitely not Spiritually Seeing the things we are Expecting, we are waiting by Endurance.

26 And in like manner, also the Spirit is Aiding us in our infirmities because we are definitely not Discerning how we should Pray in as much as He Must, but definitely the Spirit Himself is Interceding in Behalf of us, with Groanings not being uttered.

27 And then He that is Searching the hearts, is now Discerning what the Mind of the Spirit, when Making Intercession before God in Behalf of Saints.

Conquerors through Christ In us

28 And we are now Spiritually Discerning that all things are Working Together with God-Good to them Loving God, to them who according to Purpose are Inwardly Called (Born Again).

29 About whom He has Foreknown (1 Peter 1:19-20), He then has Predetermined (John 6:40) by His choice Conformed to the Image of His Son, that He is Being the Firstborn among many Brethren.

30 Moreover whom He has by His choice Predetermined them, He also by His choice Outwardly Called (Gospel), and whom He has by His choice Outwardly Called (Gospel), these He has also by His choice Made them Righteous, and whom He has also by His choice Made Righteous, to these He has also by His choice Attributed Glory.

31 What, therefore, shall we Spirit Say to these things? If God in Behalf of us, who against us?

32 Yet, He that definitely Spared Not His own Son, but definitely Delivered Up Him in Behalf of us all, how shall He, United With Him, also definitely not Freely Give to us All things?

33 Who shall charge against God's Elect? God is Making Righteous.

34 Who is condemning to death? Christ Died and also Much More. He has been Made Risen Up, Who is also by the Right Hand of God, Who also is Continuously Making Intercession in behalf of us.

35 Who shall be separating us away from the God-Love of Christ? Affliction, or distress, or persecution, or famine, or nakedness, or peril, or sword?

36 Just as is now Made Written, For the Cause of you, we are made put to death in body the whole day (Mt 16:24; Mk 8:34; Lk 9:23). We are made accounted as sheep of slaughter. (Ps 44:22)

37 But definitely, in all things, we are More Than Conquerors through Him that Loved us,

38 Because I am now Persuaded that neither death, not life, nor Angels, nor rulers, nor miracle powers, nor things now present, nor things expected,

39 Nor high thing, nor depth, nor any other creature of a different kind, shall be made able to separate us away from the God-Love of God, which is in Christ Jesus our Lord.

Who are True Israelites?

9 I am saying Truth by Christ, I am definitely not lying, my conscience also is Giving Witness to me in the Holy Spirit.

2   That I am in great grief and continuous sorrow in my heart,

3   Because I myself used to be wishing to be accursed away from Christ in behalf of my Brethren, my kinsmen according to sinful flesh nature.

4   Who are Israelites, of whom the Adoption, and the Glory, and the Covenants, and the Law Giving, and the Worship, and the Promises.

5   Of whom the fathers, even out from whom is the Christ With (Sinless) Flesh Nature, Who Was In Every Way In The Place of God, thereby Most Blessed Worthy of All Spiritual Perfection, Forever. Amen.

6   And definitely not such as that the Spiritual Word of God is now being definitely no effect, because definitely not all of Israel, the same Israel,

7   For neither are they all children, the seed of Abraham, but definitely in Isaac shall your Seed be made Outwardly Called (Gospel). (Gen 21:12)

8   That is, these children of the sinful flesh nature that are definitely not the Children of God, but definitely the children of the Promise are being accounted for Seed.

9   Because His Spiritual Word of Promise at this Special Time, I will come and Sarah shall have a son. (Gen 18:10)

10   And not only, but definitely when Rebecca having conceived from one, our father Isaac;

The nations being not yet born

11   Because being not at all born, neither practicing any God-Good or evil work in order that the Purpose of God should be Continuing according to Election, definitely not out from man works, but definitely out from The Outward Calling (Gospel, 1 Cor 15:1-4). [Elect (Mark 13:20,22,27; Matt 22:14) according to Foreknowledge (1 Peter 1:1-2,19-20; Acts 2:23). Foreknowledge and foreknown is Seeing the end from the beginning (Isaiah 46:9-10; John 6:40).]

12   It was made Spirit Spoken to her, that the oldest (nation) shall bondserve to the younger aged (nation). (Gen 25:23)

13   Just as Written, Jacob (the nation) I have Loved and Esau (the nation) I have hated. (Mal 1:2-3)

Unrighteousness never with God

14   What, therefore, shall we not Spirit Say? Unrighteousness with God? Not possible ever!

15   Because He said to Moses, I will have Mercy on whomever I should have Mercy, and I will have pity to whomever I should have pity. (Ex 33:19)

16   So then, therefore, definitely not of those willing, neither of those running, but definitely of God Giving Mercy.

17   For the Scripture Says to Pharaoh, Even for you this, I have raised you up, so that I should exhibit in you My Miracle Power, and so that My Name should be made announced in all the earth.

18   So then, therefore, He is having Mercy on whom He is willing, He hardens then whom He prefers. (John 6:40)

19   Will you Spirit Say then to Me, Why is He yet finding fault? Because who is now standing against His Intention?

20   Rather you, Oh man, who are you that is replying against God? Shall that thing Formed not Spirit Say, Why have you Made me Formed in such a manner?

21   Has definitely not the potter of the clay authority out from his same lump, to actually make thee a vessel for Honor and another for dishonor?

22   What if God is willing to exhibit His Wrath for Justice, and make known Supernaturally His Mighty Work, to bring in very much Longsuffering vessels of Wrath for Justice to be making complete for damnation?

23 And that He should make known Supernaturally the Riches of His Glory to vessels of Mercy, who have before prepared for Glory.

24 Even Him Who has Outwardly Called (Gospel) us, definitely not only out from the Jews, but definitely also out from the Gentiles.

25 As also He Says in Hosea, I will Outwardly Call (Gospel) My people, them that are definitely not My people. I am Made Loving to them that are definitely not made Loving.

26 And it shall be in the place where I Spirit Spoke to them. Definitely not My people, there yourselves shall be Made Called, Sons of the Living God. (Hos 2:23)

27 Moreover, Esaias was Crying Out in behalf of Israel, Though the number of the sons of Israel should be as the sands of the sea, a small number shall be made Saved,

28 Because He is Finishing Spiritual Communication and Making Short with Righteousness, for the Lord shall be Finalizing, Now Making Short a Spiritual Communication upon the earth. (Isa 10:22-23)

29 And just as Esaias said before, Except the Lord of Hosts has Left within us a Seed, though we have become as Sodom and as though made likened to Gomorrah.

Righteousness Out From Faith

30 What shall we Spirit Say, The Gentiles who are not following closely after Righteousness, have apprehended Righteousness, even the Righteousness out from Faith?

31 But Israel followed closely the Law of Righteousness, has definitely not attained to the Law of Righteousness.

32 Why then, because definitely not out from Faith, but definitely as out from man works of Law, because they stumbled against the Stumbling Stone, that Precious Stone?

33 Just as it is Now Made Written, Behold, I am Laying Down in Sion a Stone of Stumbling and a Huge Rock of Offense, and all that are by their choice Continuously Committing in The Way of Him shall definitely not be made ashamed. (Isa 28:16)

Man does not possess Righteousness

10 Brethren, indeed the God-Good Intention of My heart and Supplication to God is for Salvation in Behalf of Israel.

2 Because I am a witness to them that they have a God-Good Zeal of God, but definitely not according to Full Knowledge.

3 For they are being ignorant of the Righteousness of God, and seeking by their choice to bring to reality their own righteousness, they have definitely not been, for themselves, subjected to the Righteousness of God.

Righteousness from Committing

4 For Christ, the End of Law for Righteousness, in every way to those that are Continuously Committing.

5 Because Moses Wrote about the Righteousness of the Law, that a man who has by his choice obeyed them shall live by them. (Lev 18:5)

6 But the Righteousness from Faith is saying in this manner, You should not speak in your heart, Who shall ascend into Heaven? Is this Christ to be brought down?

7 Or, Who shall come down into this bottomless pit? Is Christ to be brought up from the Dead?

8 But definitely what is He saying? That Specific Word is near you, in your mouth, and in your heart. This is the Specific Word of Faith that we are preaching. (Deut 9:4-7; 30:11-20)

9 That if you should admit Truth with your mouth, Lord Jesus, and should Commit in your heart that God has Raised Him up out from Dead, you shall be made Saved.

10 Because with the heart he is Made Continuously Committing for Purpose of Righteousness, and with mouth he is Made Continuously Confessing Truth for result of Salvation.

11 For the Scripture Says, Whoever by his choice is Continuously Committing in The Way of Him shall definitely not be made ashamed. (Isa 28:16)

No difference for Jew or Greek

12 For there is definitely no distinction with the Jew and also the Greek, because the same Lord rich to all by all means that Call Upon Him,

13 Because whoever that should Call upon the Name of the Lord shall be Made Saved. (Joel 3:5)

14 How then shall they Call upon to Whom they have definitely not Committed? And how shall they Commit to Whom they have definitely not Heard? And how shall they Hear without Preaching?

15 And how shall they Preach, except they should be made Sent Out, just as it is now made Written, As beautiful the feet of them who are Preaching the Gospel of Peace, Proclaiming the God-Goods. (Isa 52:7)

16 But definitely they have definitely not all Obeyed the Gospel, because Esaias said, Lord, Who have Committed to our Report? (Isa 53:1)

17 So then Faith from Hearing and the Hearing through the Word of God.

18 But definitely I say, Have they never ever Heard? Rather, His Utterance has come out upon all the earth, and their Words to the ends of the inhabited earth. (Ps 19:4)

19 But definitely I say, Has Israel never ever Known? Earlier, Moses said, I will provoke you to jealousy by definitely not a nation, I will anger you by a nation without Understanding. (Deut 32:21)

20 But Esaias was very Bold, and said, I was actually Made Found Inside them that sought Me not. I actually Became Openly Manifest to them that were questioning Me not.

21 But to Israel He Says, All day I have Stretched out My hands to a disobeying and contradicting people. (Isa 65:2)

God not cast away Israel

11 I say then, Has not God cast away His people? Not possible ever! For I, also, am an Israelite from Seed of Abraham, of tribe of Benjamin.

2 God has definitely not cast away His people that He Foreknew. You are definitely not Spiritually Discerning in Elias what the Scriptures are saying as he makes intercession to God against Israel saying, (Ps 94:14)

3 Oh Lord, They have killed your Prophets, and ruined your alters. Also I am left alone, and they are seeking my soul. (1 Kings 19:10)

4 But definitely what Says the Answer of God to him? I Myself have seven thousand men left who have definitely not bowed a knee to Baal.

5 In this manner, therefore, also Now in this Special Time, a remnant according to the Election of Grace, is Now Being Made.

6 And if by Grace, then no more out from man works, otherwise Grace becomes no more Grace. But if out from man works, no more is Grace, otherwise Work by God is not more man work. [Grace (God's Method) is Christ Within you (Faith, God's Means; Heb 11:1, Col 1:27), through your Obedience, Doing what you cannot Do.]

But now God has Blinded Israel

7 What then, Israel has definitely not obtained the things that it is seeking after; but the Election has obtained; and others have been made hardened. [Elect according to Foreknowledge (1 Peter 1:2). Foreknowledge is Seeing the end from the beginning (Isaiah 46:9-10).]

8 Just as it is now Made Written, God had given them a spirit of slumber, eyes that Spiritually See not, and ears that Hear not, until after this Day. (Isa 29:10; Deut 29:4)

9 And David said, Their Table must be Made into a snare and into a trap and into an offense and so for their Payback.

10 They must have their eyes made darkened that they Spiritually See not, and their back must unceasingly be bowed down always. (Ps 69:22-23)

Salvation also to the Gentiles

11 I say then, have they not offended by sin that they should fall down? Not ever possible! But definitely by their spiritual death offense, the Salvation to the Gentiles, thereby from them provoked to jealousy.

12 And if through the spiritual death offense of them, the riches of the satan's world and the riches of the Gentiles the fault of them, how much more the Fullness of them?

13 Because I say to you Gentiles, that I am an Apostle indeed to the Gentiles. I am Attributing Glory to my Service of Calling,

14 If by any means how I might provoke to imitation (which are) of my flesh (Jewish), and might Save some of them.

15 For if the loss of life of them in the satan's world, what Reconciliation Admission except Life out from the dead?

16 For if the Firstfruit Holy, also the Lump, and if the Root Holy, also the Branches.

17 And if some of the Branches are made broken off, and you, being a wild olive tree, has been Made Grafted in among them, then you have become a Partaker of the Root, and the richness of the Olive Tree.

Gentiles Beware, and not boast

18 You must not boast against the Branches. For if you are boasting against, you are definitely not bearing the Root, but definitely the Root you.

19 You shall then Spirit Say, The Branches are broken off that I should be Made Grafted in.

20 God-Working against the Uncommitment, they have been made broken off, but you are Standing by Faith, you must not be high minded. But definitely you must be Continuously Fearing,

21 Because yet if God spared definitely not the natural Branches, Fear that neither shall He spare you.

22 You must behold, therefore, the Gentleness and severity of God, actually severity upon those who fall down, but upon you Gentleness, if you should Continue with Intent in the Gentleness, otherwise also you shall be made cut off.

23 And also, if they should not continue with intent in Uncommitment, they shall be Grafted In, because God is Exceedingly Able to Graft them in again.

24 Because if you have been made Cut Off from the wild olive tree by nature, and Grafted In against nature to a God-Good Olive Tree, how much more according to nature, shall these be made Grafted In to His Own Olive Tree.

Israel Restored at End of the Age

25 Because I would have definitely not desired, Brethren, that you should not be ignorant of this Mystery, with yourselves very Wise. This blindness of part with Israel is now occurring until when the Fullness of the Gentiles enters.

26 And so all Israel shall be make Saved, just as is now Made Written, There shall now Come out from Sion the Rescuer, and He shall turn away ungodliness from Jacob.

27 For this My Covenant with them, when I should Take Away their sin natures and sins. (Isa 59:20-21)

28 Indeed, according to the Gospel, enemies to yourselves, but according to the Election, Beloved, to the Father.

God Calls and Gives Mercy

29 For the Spirit Gifts and the Service of Calling of God, without Repentance.

30 And because also as yourselves in times past have been disobedient to God, but now by the disobedience of these you have been Given Mercy.

31 Even so these now that have disobeyed that through your Mercy they also should be given Mercy.

32 For God included them all in disobedience,

that He should give Mercy to all.

33 Oh the depth of Riches, both of Wisdom and of Knowledge of God. As unsearchable His Judgments and untraceable His Ways.

34 Because who has known the Mind of the Lord, or who became an advisor of Him? (Isa 40:13)

35 Or who first gave to him, then he shall be made repaid?

36 For from Him and through Him and for Him, all things to Him, the Glory Forever. Amen.

Present your bodies a Living Sacrifice

12 Therefore, I beseech you Brethren, by the Sympathies of God, to Present your bodies to God, a Living Holy Sacrifice, well pleasing to God, your Reasonable Word Worship.

2 And you must not conform to this Age, but definitely you must be Made Transfigured, by the Renewing of your mind to a New Kind for you to Prove in Truth, what is that God-Good, and Well Pleasing, and Perfect Will of God.

Measure Faith every man of you

3 Because I am saying through the Grace given me, to everyone that is among you, not to regard self highly above what he ought to regarding of value, but definitely regarding of value to be Logically Minded, as God has Fully Divided a Measure of Faith to every man.

4 For even as we have many members in one Body and all members definitely not having the same Deed.

5 So we are being one large Body inside Christ, and then (every) one members as one of another.

Gifts according to Grace Given

6 Having then differing Spirit Gifts according to the Grace that has been Made Given to us, whether Prophecy, according to the proportion of Faith,

7 Or Service (of Calling) in the Serving, or Teaching in the Doctrine,

8 Or he that Encourages in the encouragement, he that is Imparting in Simplicity of God-Good Intentions, he that is Standing Before to maintain with diligence, he that is Having Mercy on in cheerfulness,

9 God-Love Unfeigned, fully Hating evil, joining in the God-Good.

10 By Brotherly Affection for one to another, Kindly Affectioned, giving preference to honor one to another.

11 Not lazy in Diligence, being Fervent in the Spirit, Bondserving the Lord,

12 Rejoicing in Expectation, enduring affliction, continuing in Prayer,

13 Being Sharing to the need of the Saints, following closely to being Hospitable.

14 You must Bless them that persecute you. You must Bless and you must not curse.

15 To Rejoice with rejoicing, and to Weep with weeping,

16 Regarding of Value yourselves for one to another, but not regarding of value highly, but definitely being unpresuming in yourselves to be Humble. You must not become very wise among yourselves.

Live peaceably with all men

17 Not paying back any evil work for evil work. Providing yourselves God-Work in the presence of all men.

18 If possible those of yourselves being in Peace with all men.

19 Beloved, avenge not yourselves, but definitely you must give place to Wrath for Justice, because it is now made written, the Lord Says, Vengeance mine, I will repay, (Deut 32:35)

20 Therefore, if your enemy might be hungry you must give him food, if he might be thirsting you must give him to drink. Do this, because you shall be loading coals of fire upon his head. (Prov 25:21-22)

21 You must not be made overcome by evil work, but definitely you must Overcome the evil work with God-Good.

Respect Government authority

13 Every soul must be yourselves subjecting to superior authority, because there is definitely no authority except from God. And authorities are now being Made Assigned by God.

2 So that, whoever resists for himself under the authority is now standing against the Assignment of God, and they now for themselves standing against, shall receive condemnation.

3 Because rulers are definitely not a fear of God-Good Works by God, but definitely of the evil works. Will you then not fear the God-Good Authority? But you, having Full Praise from it, Must Obey,

4 Because to you he is a servant of God for God-Good. But if you should do evil work, you must be fearing, because he wears a sword definitely not without reason, because a servant of God is an Avenger of evil doing; for Wrath for Justice upon him that practices the evil work.

5 For this reason, a necessity to be subjected, not only because of the Wrath for Justice, but definitely also because of your conscience.

6 Because by this you are also finally fulfilling tribute, because they are God's servants, thereto they being continuing for this.

7 You must pay back, therefore, all debts due, tribute to whom tribute, habit of custom to whom habit of custom, fear to whom fear, Honor to whom Honor.

God-Love to all

8 You must owe no man anything, except to God-Love one another of a different kind, because he that is Loving another is Fulfilling the Law.

9 For you shall definitely not commit adultery, you shall definitely not murder, you shall definitely not steal, you shall definitely not bear false witness, you shall definitely not evilly desire, and if any other one of a different kind Commandment, it is made briefly comprehended in this Spiritual Commandment, namely, You shall God-Love your neighbor as yourself. (Ex 20:13-15; Lev 19:18)

10 God-Love works no evil work to his neighbor. Therefore, God-Love (is) the Fullness of the Law.

11 And the Spiritually Discerning this Special Time, the hour that we have been made Risen Up already from natural sleep, for now our Salvation is nearer than when we Committed.

12 The night has developed, and the Day is now approaching near. We should put off, therefore, for ourselves the man works of darkness, and we should put on for ourselves the weapons of the Light.

13 We should Walk Honestly as in the day, not in revelings and drunkenness, not bedrooming (illicit sex), and extreme irregular immorality, not contention and evil envy.

Make no provision for the flesh

14 But definitely you must put on the Lord Jesus Christ, and you must make no provision of the sinful flesh nature for doing evil desires.

Receive him that is weak in Faith

14 Him that is being weak in the Faith you must receive for yourselves, but not for distinguishing differences in thoughts.

2 One is certainly committed to eat all things. And another being weak eats herbs.

3 He that is eating must not be despising he that eats not. And he that is not eating must not judge him that is eating, because God has Received him to Himself.

4 Who are you, you judging another man's household servant? To one's own Lord he stands fast or falls down. Because moreover God is Exceedingly Able to have him Stand.

5 One certainly judges a day above another day; some judge another day alike. Every man must be made fully persuaded, in his own mind.

6   He that Regards of value the day Regards of value to the Lord, and none that regards of value the day definitely not Regards of value to the Lord. He that is Eating to the Lord, is Eating Giving Thanks because from God, and he that is not Eating to the Lord, is definitely not eating with Giving thanks to God.

7   For none of us is living to himself and none dies to himself.

8   And also, because whether we should Live, we Live to the Lord. And also whether we might die, we Die to the Lord. Both, therefore, whether we should Live and also whether we should Die, we are Being the Lord's.

9   Because for this Christ both Died, and has Arisen, and has Lived Again that He should Have Dominion both of the dead and the Living.

10 But why are you judging your brother? Or also why are you despising your brother? For we shall all stand before the Judgment Seat of Christ.

11 It is now Made Written, because I am Living Says the Lord, every knee shall Bow to me, and every tongue shall themselves Acknowledge to God. (Isa 49:18; 45:23)

12 So then, therefore, everyone of us shall Give an account of himself to God.

No man should put a stumbling block

13 You should, therefore, not any longer be judging one another, but definitely this you must have judged much more, that none position a stumbling stone or offense to his brother.

14 I Spiritually now discern and I am now made persuaded by the Lord Jesus, that nothing unclean by itself, except to him accounting anything to be unclean, to him, unclean.

15 But if your brother is made grieved because of food, you are not Walking according to God-Love. You must no more destroy him with your food, in behalf of whom Christ Died.

16 Therefore, he must not be made blaspheming the God-Good of yourselves.

God's Kingdom not meat and drink

17 Because the Kingdom Rule of God is definitely not meat and drink, but definitely Righteousness and Peace and Joy in Holy Spirit.

18 For he that in these things is Bond-serving Christ, Well Pleasing to God and approved with men.

19 So then, therefore, we should follow closely the things of Peace and Edification for ourselves.

20 You must not tear down the Work by God for the cause of food. All things, indeed, purified. But definitely, evil work for that man eating with stumbling.

21 God-Work (is) to not eat flesh, neither to drink wine, nor in that wherein your brother stumbles, or is made offending, or is being weak.

Whatever is not of Faith is sin

22 Are you having Faith? Have to yourself in the Presence of God. Spiritually Blessed, he that judges not himself in what he is Proving in Truth,

23 And he that is doubting, is now made condemned to death, if ever he might eat, since definitely not out from Faith, and all whatever definitely not out from Faith is sin nature and sin.

Strong should Bear weakness of weak

15 We that are Exceedingly Able are indebted to bear the weaknesses of those not empowered, and not to please ourselves.

2   Because everyone of us must please his neighbor for his God-Good for Edification.

3   For even Christ Well Pleased Deliberately not Himself, but definitely just as now Made Written, The reproaches of those scolded to shame you, fell upon Me. (Ps 69:9)

4   For whatever was Made Written before, has been Made Written before for Our Doctrine, in order that through Endurance and Encouragement of the Scriptures, we should be Having Expectation.

5   Now the God of Endurance and

Encouragement has Given to you beyond dreams, who to regard of value thereby one to another, according to Christ Jesus.

6   In order that, with full agreement with one mouth, you should Attribute Glory to God, even the Father of our Lord Jesus Christ.

7   For this reason, you must Receive to yourself one to another, just as also Christ Received us to Himself, into the Glory of God.

Christ a Servant to Circumcision

8   Now, I say that Jesus Christ Became a Servant of the Circumcision in Behalf of the God of Truth, to establish the Promises of the fathers.

9   And the Gentiles in Behalf of Mercy, Attribute Glory to God, just as it is Made Written, Because of This I will for Myself Acknowledge You among the Gentiles, and in the Name of You, I will Sing Melody. (Ps 18:49)

10 And again, He is Saying, You must be Made Merry, Oh Gentiles, with His people. (Deut 32:43)

11 And again, Gentiles you Must be Continuously Praising the Lord at all times, and All the people must be Fully Praising Him! (Ps 117:1)

12 And again, Esaias, is Saying, There shall be a Root of Jesse, and He that is Arising is Reigning over nations, in Him shall Gentiles Expect. (Isa 11:10)

13 Now the God of Expectation, Fully Fill you by your choice beyond dreams with All Joy and Peace, by Committing Continuously by your choice with Expectation for the Abounding in amount to you with the Miracle Power of the Holy Spirit.

Paul a Servant to the Gentiles

14 And I myself also I am Made Persuaded about you, My Brethren, that even yourselves are Filled of Goodness, Fully Filled of all Knowledge, Able also to warn one another.

15 More boldly then I Have Written to you, Brethren, from respect as reminding you, because of the Grace that is Given to me by God.

16 That I, Being a Servant for Jesus Christ to the Gentiles, Sacredly Serving the Gospel of God, that the well Acceptable Offering of the Gentiles, should be Made Holy in the Holy Spirit.

17 Therefore, I have Rejoicing in Christ Jesus, to those things with God.

18 Because I definitely dare not utter anything which Christ has definitely not Produced in me, for Obedience of the Gentiles in the Word and Work by God.

19 By Miracle Power of Miracle Signs and Wonders in the Miracle Power of the Spirit of God, so that I from Jerusalem and to around as far as those of Illyricum, I am Fulfilling the Gospel of Christ.

20 In such a manner, then, I am Endeavoring to be Preaching the Gospel, whereto Christ has definitely not been made named, in order that I should not be building upon another man's Foundation,

21 But definitely just as it is Made Written, To whom He was definitely not Made Declared about Himself, they shall Spiritually See, and they that are definitely not Hearing, shall Understand. (Isa 52:15)

Paul wishes to see Rome, way to Spain

22 For this reason also, I was made very much hindered from coming to you.

23 But just now having no place any longer in these parts, and having a great desire for many years to come to you,

24 As if ever I should go into Spain, I am expecting I will come to you, for journeying through to see you, so that to journey with you from there. If first of all, I should be in part made filled up by you.

25 But just now, I am going to Jerusalem to serve to the Saints.

26 For Macedonia and Achaia have been pleased to make a certain contribution for the poor Saints in Jerusalem.

27 Because they are pleased also to be debtors themselves, for if the Gentiles have been partakers with them in their Spiritual (things), they also are indebted to minister to them in their carnal sinful flesh nature (things).

28 Therefore, when I have performed this, I have sealed to them this Fruit, I will go by you into Spain.

29 And I am now Spiritually Discerning that when I am coming to you, I shall come in Fullness of Blessing of the Gospel of Christ.

30 Now I beseech you, Brethren through our Lord Jesus Christ, and through the God-Love of the Spirit, agonize together with me in Prayers to God in behalf of me,

31 That I might be made rescued from the disobedient in Judaea, and that my Serving to Jerusalem might become well accepted to the Saints,

32 That in Joy I should come to you through the Will of God, and should Reenergize you.

33 Now the God of Peace with You All. Amen.

Greetings

16 I commend to you Phoebe our sister, that is a servant of the Assembly that is in Cenchrea.

2 That you look for her, in the Lord, worthily of the Saints, and you should assist her in whatever matter of you she might have lack, and because she has been made a comforter of many, and of me myself also.

3 Greet Priscilla and Aquila my Fellow Laborers in Christ Jesus,

4 Who in behalf of my soul have put in place their own neck, to whom definitely not only I alone Give Thanks, but definitely also all the Assemblies of the Gentiles.

5 Also you must Greet the Assembly in their home. Epaenetus my Beloved who is Firstfruit of Achaia for Christ.

6 You must Greet Mary, who Labored very much for us.

7 You must Greet Andronicus and Junia, my kinsmen, and my fellow prisoners, who are notable among the Apostles, who also Became before me in Christ.

8 You must Greet Amplias, my Beloved in the Lord.

9 You must Greet Urbane, our Fellow Laborer in Christ, and Stachys my Beloved.

10 You must Greet Apelles approved in Christ; you must Greet those of Aristobulus.

11 You must Greet Herodion, my kinsmen, you must great those of Narcissus, who are in the Lord.

12 You must Greet Tryphena and Tryphosa, who labor in the Lord. You must Greet the Beloved Persis, who labored very much in the Lord.

13 You must Greet Rufus, Elect in the Lord, and his mother and mine.

14 You must Greet Asyncritus, Phlegon, Hermas, Patrobas, Hermes, and the Brethren united with them.

15 You must Greet Philologus and Julia, Nereus and his sister, also Olympas and those Saints united with him.

16 You must Greet one another with a Holy kiss. The Assemblies of Christ are Greeting you.

Avoid them with contrary doctrine

17 Now I beseech you, Brethren, Mark them, the oppositions, and those of offenses against the Teaching that yourselves have learned to Follow, and you must Avoid Away from them,

18 For such, bondserve definitely not for our Lord Jesus Christ, but definitely for their own belly, and through kind words and blessing, they are deceiving the hearts of those that are without evil works.

19 Yet your Obedience has become known to all. I rejoice, therefore, in the way of you, but I would prefer you Wiser, certainly being for the God-Good, but harmless for the evil work.

20 And the God of Peace shall bruise the

satan under your feet wherein swiftly. The Grace of our Lord Jesus Christ with you. Amen.

Salute you

21 Timothy my Fellow Laborer, and Lucius, and Jason, and Sosipater, my kinsmen Greet you.

22 I, Tertius, who Wrote this epistle, Greet you in the Lord.

23 Gaius my host and all of the Assembly are Greeting you. Erastus, the chamberlain of the city, and Quartus, the Brother are Greeting you.

24 The Grace of our Lord Jesus Christ with you all. Amen.

Obedience to Faith

25 Now to Him able to firmly Establish you according to my Gospel, and the Preaching of Jesus Christ according to the Revelation of the Mystery, from time Eternal Kept Silent.

26 And also but now is Made Manifest through the Scripture Prophetic Writings, according to the Authority of the Commandment of God, the Eternal God, for the Result of Obedience of Faith, Made Known Supernaturally to all the nations. (Rom 1:5)

27 To alone Wise God through Jesus Christ, the Glory Forever. Amen.

[Written to the Romans from Corinthus, and sent by Phebe of the Assembly at Cenchrea]

The First Epistle of Paul the Apostle to the

Corinthians

Greetings

1 Paul, Inwardly Called (Born Again) an Apostle of Jesus Christ through the Will of God, and Sosthenes, our Brother.

2 To the Assembly of God which is in Corinth, now being Made Holy in Christ Jesus, Inwardly Called (Born Again) Saints, United with all those calling upon the Name of our Lord Jesus Christ, so in every place of theirs and also ours.

3 Grace to you and Peace from God our Father and the Lord Jesus Christ.

I Thank God On Behalf Of you

4 I am Giving Thanks to my God always for you, by the Grace of God, Who was Made Given to you in Christ Jesus.

5 That in everything you have been Made Enriched by Him in all Spiritual Communication and all Knowledge.

6 Just as the Testimony of Christ has been Made Established in you, (Col 1:27)

7 So that you are not made lacking in any Spirit Gift, waiting the Revelation of our Lord Jesus Christ,

8   Who shall also Establish you up to the End, Unaccused in the Day of our Lord Jesus Christ.

9   God Faithful, by Whom you have been Made Outwardly Called (Gospel) for Fellowship of His Son, Jesus Christ our Lord.

You have a problem: divisions

10 Now I beseech you Brethren, by the Name of our Lord Jesus Christ, that you should be Saying All Alike, and there should be no division among you, and then should be Made Complete in the Same Understanding of mind, and in the Same Advice.

11 For it has been Made Evident to Me about you, my Brothers from Chloe, that there are contentions among you.

12 Now I am saying this, that everyone of you is saying, I certainly am of Paul; and I of Apollos; and I of Cephas; and I of Christ.

Christ is not divided

13 Is Christ now made fully divided? Was not Paul made crucified for you? Or were you immersed in the name of Paul?

14 I Give Thanks to God that I definitely immersed none of you, except Crispus and Gaius,

15 That not anybody should have spoken that I have immersed in my name.

16 And I immersed also the home of Stephanas, and now I discern definitely not whether I have immersed any other of the same kind,

17 Because, Christ Sent me Out definitely not to immerse but definitely to Proclaim, not with wisdom of words, that the cross of Christ should not be made empty.

18 For the Spiritual Communication of the cross is, to them that are certainly continuously perishing, mindless foolishness, but to us, who are being Continuously Made Saved, it is the Continuous Miracle Power of God.

19 Because it is now Made Written, I will destroy the wisdom of the wise and will reject the understanding of the prudent.

Wisdom of the world is foolishness

20 Wherein wise, wherein scribe, wherein disputer of this Age? Has God definitely not Made Foolish the wisdom of this the satan's world?

21 Because for after that in the Wisdom of God, the satan's world by wisdom definitely knew not God, it pleased God, by the mindless foolishness of preaching, to Save those that are Continuously Committing.

22 Yet for after that the Jews are asking a Miracle Sign, and the Greeks are seeking wisdom,

Christ is Power and Wisdom

23 But we are preaching Christ now being made Crucified to Jews, certainly an offense, and to Greeks, mindless foolishness,

24 But to them, who Inwardly Called (Born Again), mutually Jews and also Gentiles: Christ, Miracle Power of God, and Wisdom of God.

25 Because the foolish of God, is wiser than men. And the weak of God, is Stronger than men.

26 Because you are Spiritually Seeing your Service of Calling, Brethren, how definitely not many wise with sinful flesh nature, definitely not many exceedingly able, definitely not many more noble,

Foolishness to confound the wise

27 But definitely God has Chosen for Himself the foolish of the satan's world, that He should Confound the wise: And God has Chosen for Himself the weak of the satan's world, that He should Confound the mighty.

28 And the base things of the satan's world, and the things now being made despised, and the things that are not, God Himself has Chosen, in order that He should Destroy those things which are,

No flesh shall glory in His Presence

29 So that all sinful flesh nature should not boast in the Presence of Him.

30 But out from Him, you yourselves are of Christ Jesus, Who of God is made to us Wisdom, and Righteousness, and Personal Holiness with Separation Removal,

31 That just as is now Made Written. He that is boasting, he must be boasting in the Lord.

Faith is of the Power of God

2 Also I come to you, Brethren. I come definitely not with superiority of Spiritual Communication or Wisdom, proclaiming much to you the Testimony of God,

2 Because I judged definitely not to Spiritually Discern anything among you except Jesus Christ, and Him Crucified.

3 And I was with you in infirmity, and in fear, and in very much trembling.

4 And my Spiritual Communication and my Preaching, definitely not in persuasion by manner of man's wisdom, but definitely in Demonstration of the Spirit and Miracle Power.

5 That Faith of yourselves should not be of wisdom of men, but definitely of Miracle Power of God.

Speak Wisdom among Perfect

6 But we utter Wisdom among them Perfect, and definitely not that wisdom of this Age, neither of the rulers of this Age that is being made Destroyed.

7 But definitely we are Uttering the Wisdom of God in a Mystery now Made Concealed, which God by His choice Predetermined before the Ages for our Glory (Spiritual Perfection),

8 Which none of the rulers of this Age knew, because if they knew they would have definitely not ever have crucified the Lord of Glory.

9 But definitely, just as is now Made Written, that eye has definitely not seen, or ear definitely not heard, and to the heart of man has definitely not Ascended to what God has prepared for them Loving Him. (Isa 64:4)

10 But God has Revealed to us by His Spirit, because the Spirit is searching all things, also the Depths of God.

11 Because what men are now spiritually discerning the things of a man, except the spirit of man in him? Even so, the things of God none Spiritually Discerns, except the Spirit of God.

12 Now we have definitely not received the spirit of the satan's world, but definitely the Spirit from God, that we should Spiritually Discern that from God is Freely Given to us,

13 Which also we are Uttering, definitely not taught in words of man's wisdom, but definitely Holy Spirit Taught, by comparing Spiritual to Spiritual.

14 But the natural sensual soulish man receives definitely not the Things of the Spirit of God, because it is mindless foolishness to him, and he is not able to know because they are Spiritually being Made Examined for Judgment,

15 But he that is Spiritual is actually Examining for Judgment of all things, yet he is Made Examined for Judgment by none,

16 Yet who by his choice actually Has Known the Mind of the Lord, who by his choice actually shall Be United Together with Him? But moreover, we are Actually Having the Mind of Christ. (Isa 40:13)

Sinful flesh natures is carnal

3 And I, Brethren, could definitely not utter to you as Spiritual, but definitely as carnal sinful flesh nature, as infants in Christ.

2 I have given to you to drink milk and definitely not food, because you were not yet able, but definitely neither are you now yet able.

3 For you are yet carnal sinful flesh nature, because whereto among you evil zeal, and contention, and oppositions. Are you definitely not carnal sinful flesh nature and walking as man?

4 For when might some say, I am actually

of Paul, and another of a different kind, I of Apollos, Are you definitely not being carnal sinful flesh nature?

We are Servants of God's Work

5 Who then is Paul, and who Apollos? But definitely Servants through whom you have Committed, even as the Lord has Given to every man,

6 I have Planted, Apollos Watered, but definitely God was Giving the Increase.

7 So that neither he that is Planting anything, nor he that Waters, but definitely God is Giving the Increase.

8 Now he that is Planting and he that is Watering are One, and every man shall Receive his own Reward, according to his own Labor.

9 For we are being Fellow Laborers by God, a Caretaker by God. You are a Building by God.

10 According to the Grace of God Made Given to me, as a wise master builder, I am Now Laying Down the Foundation, and another of the same kind is Building Up. But every man must by his choice be Spiritually Seeing how he is Building Up.

Christ is Foundation for building

11 For other Foundation of the same kind can none lay down, than that is Being Laid, Who is Jesus Christ.

12 Now if any man build up upon this Foundation: gold, silver, most precious stones, wood items, grass, stubble,

13 Every man Work by God shall become Openly Manifest, for the Day shall Make Evident, how by Fire it is Made Revealing. And the Fire shall Prove in Truth what kind (of) work is of every man.

14 If any certain man Work by God is Continuing, which he has Built Up, he shall Receive Reward.

15 If any man's man work shall be made fully burned, he shall be made to suffer loss, but he himself shall be Made Saved, but so as through fire.

By Christ we are God's Temple

16 Are you now definitely not Spiritually Discerning that you are a Temple of God, and the Spirit of God is Dwelling Inside yourselves? (Luke 17:20-21)

17 If any man is spiritually corrupting by his choice the Temple of God, God shall Spiritually corrupt him, because the Temple of God is Holy, Which you are yourselves.

18 He must not be deceiving himself. If anyone is thinking to be wise, over yourselves, in this Age, he Must Become a fool, that he should Become Wise,

19 For the wisdom of this the satan's world is mindless foolishness with God. For it is now Made Written, He Outsmarts the wise in their craftiness.

20 And again, The Lord is knowing the thoughts of the wise, that they are self-worship.

21 So that, let no man boast in men, because ALL Above is yours.

22 Whether Paul, or Apollos, or Cephas, or the satan's world, or life, or death, or present, or expecting, All Above is yours.

23 And yourselves Christ's; and Christ God's.

We are Servants and Stewards

4 A man must be in such a manner accounting us as Under Servants of Christ, and Stewards of the Mysteries of God.

2 And moreover, it is sought in Stewards, that finally he should be made found a Faithful man.

3 But with me it is thereby small that I should have been made examined for judgment by you, or by manner of man's day, but definitely I examine for judgment not myself,

4 For I completely understand nothing myself, but definitely I am definitely not Made Righteous in this, and He that is Examining me for Judgment is the Lord.

5 So that you must not judge anybody before the Special Time, until after

whenever the Lord should come, Who also shall Bring to Light the secret things of darkness, and shall Manifest the Counsels of the hearts, and then Full Praise shall be for every man of God.

Do not esteem yourself above others

6   And these things, Brethren, I have transformed for myself and Apollos, because in order that you should have learned by us not to be regarding of value above what is now made written, that no one should be made arrogant in behalf of one against another of a different kind.

7   For who of you is judging differences? Moreover what are you having which you have definitely not taken to receive? Then if you also have taken to receive, why are you boasting as having not taken?

8   Already you are not being hungry. Already you have been rich. You have reigned without us. But yet, I would that you Reigned in order that we might Reign Together with you.

9   For I think that God has proved us the least Apostles, as appointed to death, that we became made a theater to the satan's world, both to Angels, and men.

10   We fools for Christ, but you very wise in Christ. We weak, but yourselves stronger. Yourselves glorious, but we treated without honor.

11   For now, until this hour, yet we are hungry, and might be thirsting, and are being naked, and are made beaten, and are homeless,

12   And laboring, working with our own hands, made reviled we Bless, made persecuted we Continue Enduring,

13   Being made blasphemed, we are encouraging, as garbage of the satan's world. For up to now, we become dirt wiped off all things.

14   I am writing these things definitely not to disrespect you, but definitely as my Beloved children, I am warning.

Take me, Paul, as an Example

15   Because though you might have ten thousand instructors in Christ, but definitely not many fathers, because in Christ Jesus I have yourselves Born from Above, through the Gospel.

16   Therefore, I encourage you, you must become close Followers of me.

17   Because of this I have sent Timothy to you, who is my Beloved child and Faithful in the Lord, who will make you to Remember My Ways, which in Christ, just as everywhere I am Teaching in all Assemblies.

God's Kingdom is not in Word

18   And as now, my not coming to you, some have been made arrogant.

19   And I will come to you rapidly, if the Lord should Will, and I will definitely not recognize the account of those being arrogant, but definitely the Miracle Power.

20   For the Kingdom Rule of God definitely not in Word, but definitely in Miracle Power.

21   What will you? Should I come to you with a staff, or in God-Love, and also the Spirit of Meekness?

Fornication cannot be tolerated

5 Fornication is absolutely being made heard among you, and such fornication that neither is made named among the Gentiles, so that one is having his father's wife.

2   And yourselves, you are now made arrogant, and definitely not having mourned instead, in order that he that has done this man work, should be made put away out from the midst of you.

3   For I certainly, as absent in the body but present in the Spirit, already I am now judging as if present he that in such a manner produces this,

Remove anyone who sins from you

4   In the Name of our Lord Jesus Christ gather together yourselves, and united

with my Spirit in the Miracle Power of our Lord Jesus Christ,

5   To deliver up such to the satan for destruction of the sinful flesh nature, that his spirit should be made Saved in the Day of the Lord Jesus.

6   Your happiness definitely not God-Work. Are you definitely not Spiritually Discerning that the smallest leaven leavens the whole lump?

7   Therefore, Spiritually Cleanse out that old leaven, that you should be a new of the Same Kind Lump just as you are Unleavened Bread. Also because Christ, our Passover, has been made killed as Sacrifice in Behalf Of Us.

8   So that we should feast not with old leaven, neither with leaven of maliciousness and evil action, but definitely with unleavened bread of Sincerity and Truth.

9   I wrote to you in an epistle not to associate with fornicators,

10 Yet then not with all the fornicators of this the satan's world, or the greedy, or extortioners, or idolaters, otherwise so then you ought to come out from the satan's world,

This also applies to any brother

11 But just now, I have written to you not to associate, if any one named a brother (is) either a fornicator, or greedy, or idolater, or reviler, or drunkard, or extortioner, neither to eat with they that are such,

12 Because when I and those outside are judging, yourselves are definitely not Judging those within.

13 But them outside God shall Judge. So also, you put away that evil one out from you. (Deut 17:7)

Saints shall Judge world and Angels

6 Dare any of yourselves having a matter between an other one, to be made judged before the unrighteous, and definitely not before the Saints?

2   Are you definitely not Spiritually

Discerning that the Saints shall certainly Judge the satan's world; and if the satan's world is Being Made Judged by yourselves, are you unworthy, by the least, of Judging by laws for Judging?

3   Are you not now Spiritually Discerning that we shall Judge Angels, how much more yet this existence?

Why no Judgment among yourselves?

4   Then, if you should be having Judging by laws for Judging actually about this existence, sit down with them being least esteemed in the Assembly.

5   In this manner I am saying disrespect to you. Is there definitely not among you a wiser, not one, that shall be Made Able to Judge Differences among the midst of his Brethren?

6   But definitely brother is made judged against brother, and this among the faithless.

7   Therefore already indeed absolutely a fault is among you, when having judgments among yourselves. Why then are you definitely not much more wronged? Why then are you definitely not being made much more defrauded?

8   But definitely you are hurting yourselves, and defrauding, and also these things to Brethren.

Unrighteous will not inherit Heaven

9   Are you definitely not Spiritually Discerning that unrighteous shall not Inherit Kingdom Rule of God? You must not be deceived, neither fornicators, nor idolaters, nor adulterers, nor effeminate, nor sodomites,

10 Nor thieves, nor greedy, nor drunkards, definitely not revilers, definitely not extortioners, they shall definitely not Inherit Kingdom Rule of God.

11 Also these were certain ones, but definitely you have been washed away for yourselves, but definitely you have been Made Holy, but definitely you have been

Made Righteous in the Name of the Lord Jesus, and by the Spirit of our God.

12 All things are lawful for me, but definitely all things are definitely not essential. All things are lawful for me, but I will definitely not be made controlled by anything.

13 Foods for the belly, and the belly for foods; but God shall destroy these things, even them. Now the Body, definitely not for fornication, but definitely for the Lord, and the Lord for the Body.

14 Moreover God has both Raised Up the Lord, and shall Raise us Up by His Miracle Power.

Your bodies are Members of Christ

15 Are you definitely not now Spiritually Discerning that your bodies are Members of Christ? Therefore, are they taken up Members of Christ to might make them become forbidden members of a harlot? Not possible ever!

16 Or are you definitely not now Discerning, that he that is made joined to the harlot is one body? Because He shall be stating, Two is into one sinful flesh nature. (Gen 2:24)

17 But he that is Made Joined to the Lord is One Spirit.

18 Flee fornication. Though all sinful acts whatever might be done outside the body, but the man that is sexually sinning, is sinning upon his own body.

19 Instead, now you Know definitely that your body is a Temple of the Holy Spirit Inside you, Whom you are Having of God, and you are definitely not your own?

20 Because you have been made Bought with a price, so now you must Attribute Glory (Spiritual Perfection) to God in your Body, and in your Spirit, Who is of God.

Avoid fornication by marriage

7 Now in regard to what you have written to me, Not God-Work for a man to be touching of a woman for himself.

2 Nevertheless, because of fornication, every man must be having for himself a wife, and every woman must be having her own husband.

3 The husband must pay back the kind acts owed to the wife and likewise the woman also to the husband.

4 The wife is definitely not controlling her own body, but definitely the husband. Likewise, then also the husband is definitely not controlling his own body, but definitely the wife.

5 Deprive not one another, except whenever something out from consent to a Special Time that you should be giving to fasting and Prayer, and again with Intent that you might be coming together, that the satan might not tempt you because of your lack of control.

6 But I say this by permission, definitely not by authority of Commandment of God.

7 Because I would all men are being as myself, but also definitely every man is Having his own Spirit Gift out From God, that actually one, in such a manner and another in another manner.

8 I say, then, to the unmarried, and the widows. It is God-Work if they should continue, as also I.

9 But if they are not self-controlled, they must marry. Because it is best to marry than to be made burning.

No divorce

10 And to these now marrying, I give Command, definitely not I, but definitely the Lord, A woman is not to be separated away from a husband.

11 But if she is made to be separate, now she must continue to stay unmarried, or she must be made reconciled to the husband. Dismiss not a husband or a wife.

12 But to others I am saying, definitely not the Lord, if any Brother has a wife faithless, and she consents to dwell with him, he must not dismiss her.

13 And a woman who has a husband faithless, and he consents to dwell with her, she must not dismiss him.

14 Because the faithless husband is now being Made Holy by the wife, and the faithless wife by the husband, so then otherwise your children are morally impure, but now they are Holy.

Let uncommitting depart

15 But if the faithless is being separating for himself, you must be made separate. A Brother or a Sister is definitely not being made a bondslave while therein such, for God is now Outwardly Calling (Gospel) us to Peace.

16 Because, Oh wife, what are you now discerning, whether you shall Save the husband, or what are you now discerning, Oh husband, whether you shall Save the wife?

17 Except as God has Fully Divided to every person, as the Lord is now Outward Calling (Gospel) everyone, so he must be Walking, and so I am appointing in all the Assemblies.

Circumcision means nothing

18 Has any been made Outwardly Called (Gospel) made circumcised? You must not become uncircumcised. Has any been made Outwardly Called (Gospel) in uncircumcision? You must not be made circumcised.

19 Circumcision is nothing, and uncircumcision is nothing, but definitely keeping of God's Commandments.

Stay within your Service of Call

20 Every man must be Continuously Continuing in his Service of Calling, in this he has been made Outwardly Called (Gospel).

21 Are you, a slave made Outwardly Called (Gospel)? You must not care, but definitely if you are able to become free, you must use instead.

22 Because, a slave Outwardly Called (Gospel) by the Lord, is the Lord's Freeman. And likewise, a free Outwardly Called (Gospel), is a Bondslave of Christ.

Be not slaves of men

23 You have been made Bought for a Price. You must not become slaves of men.

24 Brethren, in whatever every person has been made Outwardly Called (Gospel), therein this one must Continue with God.

25 And now in regard to virgins, I have definitely no Commandment of God of the Lord. I am giving advice, but yet being Faithful as one Receiving Mercy from the Lord.

26 I suppose; therefore, this existing God-Work because of the present necessity, that this in such a manner is being a God-Work for a man.

Marriage brings trouble in flesh

27 Are you now being made bound by a wife? You must not seek to be loosed. Are you now made removed away from a wife? You must not seek a wife.

28 But also if you should marry, you have definitely not sinned, also if a virgin marry, she has definitely not sinned. Nevertheless, such shall have affliction in the sinful flesh nature, but I am sparing of you.

Being Steadfast is the answer

29 But this I state Brethren, that this Special Time is finally made shortened, and they now having wives as those that might be having none.

30 And they that are weeping as not weeping, and they that are rejoicing as not rejoicing, and they that are buying as not holding.

31 And they that use this the satan's world as not abusing, because the fashion of this the satan's world is passing on.

32 And I would have you without concern. That being unmarried, he of the Lord take thought of how he shall well please the Lord.

33 But he that is married takes thought of the things of the satan's world, how he shall please his wife.

34 There is now made fully divided, the

wife and the virgin. The unmarried takes thought to the things of the Lord, that she should be Holy both in Body and in Spirit. But those married are caring to the things of the satan's world, how to please the husband.

35 And this I say to be necessary to them of your own, definitely not that I lay a noose to you, but definitely to the honorable, and focused on the Lord without distraction.

36 But if any man supposes to be behaving inappropriately with his virgin, if she should be past menopause, or so ought to become, he must do whatever he is strongly desiring. He is definitely not sinning. They must marry.

37 Nevertheless, whoever was standing steadfast in his heart, having no necessity, but has authority over his own will, and is now judging this in his heart that he is keeping his virgin, he is doing God-Working.

38 So that also he that gives (her) in marriage does God-Working, but he that gives not in marriage does best.

39 A wife is now made bound by Law for that time her husband is living, but if her husband should be resting asleep, she is free to whoever she will to be married, only in the Lord.

40 But she is Spiritually Blessed if she should Continue in such a manner, according to my advice. And I think that also, I have the Spirit of God.

Knowledge puffs up, Love builds

8 And now about the meat offered to idols, I discern that we all have Knowledge. Knowledge is being arrogant, but God-Love is being edifying.

2 And if any thinks he is now Spiritually Discerning anything, he is never yet not now Knowing just as he ought to Know.

3 But if any man is Continuously Loving God, he is now Made Knowing by Him.

4 In regard to the meat, therefore, of the meat offered to idols, we Spiritually Discern that an idol (is) nothing in the satan's world, and that not another of a different kind god, except One.

5 Also, because if it be so, they are called gods, whether in heaven or upon the earth, they are many gods and many lords.

Father and Christ only answer

6 But definitely to us One God the Father out from Whom All Things, and we for the Purpose and Result of Him, and One Lord Jesus Christ, by Whom are All Things, and we By Him.

7 But definitely not in everyone this Knowledge, for some with the conscience of the idol, as up to for now are eating meat offered to idols, and their conscience being weak is made unclean.

8 But our food recommends us definitely not to God, for neither if we might have eaten are we abounding in amount, neither if we might eat not are we made lacking.

Let not your Liberty hurt people

9 You must Spiritually See, that fearing that authority of you, this might become a stumbling stone to the weak.

10 Because if a certain one might Spiritually Discern you, who have Knowledge, sit down to eat in a temple of idols, the conscience of him being weak will definitely not be made edified, for result that he is eating meat offered to idols.

11 And by your Knowledge, the weak Brother for whom Christ Died, shall be destroyed,

12 But in that manner, you are sinning toward the Brother, and striking his conscience being weak, you are sinning toward Christ.

13 For the result of this, if food offends my Brother, I should definitely not eat any more flesh for the Age, that I should not offend my Brother.

Paul's Apostleship authority

9 Am I definitely not an Apostle? Am I definitely not free? Have I definitely not Beheld Attentively our Lord Jesus Christ? Are you yourselves definitely not my Work by God in the Lord?

2   If I am definitely not an Apostle to others of same kind, but yet definitely I am to you, because you are yourselves the Seal of my Apostleship in the Lord.

3   My defense to them that examine me for judgment is this.

4   Have we then definitely not Authority to eat or to drink?

5   Have we then definitely not Authority to lead about a sister, a wife, as also other Apostles, and the Brethren of the Lord, and Cephas?

6   Or I alone and Barnabas, we definitely have no Authority to not work.

7   Who is warring for himself for one's own wages? As in time past, who plants a vineyard, and eats not of the fruit of it? Or who shepherds a safe flock, and eats not from the milk of the safe flock?

8   Else I utter these things not according to man. Definitely not, even the Law Says these things.

9   Because it is Made Written in the Law of Moses, You shall definitely not muzzle an oxen treading out the Harvest. Is not the caring of the oxen by God? (Deut 25:4)

10 By all means because of us He Says before for us, because He Has Written, For he that plows ought to be plowing in the way of Expectation, and he that is treading out the Harvest in his Expectation to be partaking in Expectation.

11 Allowing that we have Sown Spiritual to you, Great. Otherwise, shall we reap those things of your carnal sinful flesh nature?

However, authority we don't use

12 If others of same kind are partaking of this authority over you, instead, we have definitely not used from this authority, but definitely we are refraining in order that we should have not given any hindrance to the Gospel of Christ.

13 Are you definitely now not discerning this, that they working in Sacred things, eat out from the Temple area? They that are attending at the altar are being partakers at the altar.

14 In another manner, has the Lord appointed that they, who are proclaiming much the Gospel, to be Living for the Gospel.

15 Moreover, I am not now using these things. Also I have definitely not written these things, in this manner that it should become a God-Work by me. Instead for me to die, else that my happiness should be made empty.

16 For if I should definitely not be Preaching the Gospel, I am not happy, because necessity is laying upon me, and Woe to me if I am not Preaching the Gospel,

My Reward is freely preaching the Gospel

17 Because if I willingly practice this, I have a Reward, where if after my will, I am now made Committed to a Stewardship.

18 What then is my Reward, that I Preach the Gospel without charge? I should set out the Gospel of Christ, for the Purpose that I abuse not my Authority in the Gospel.

Being all to all, that might win some

19 For being free from everyone in all things, I have become by my choice a Bondslave, that I should Gain that More Excellent.

20 And I became to the Jews as a Jew, that I might gain the Jews; to them under the Law as under Law, that I might gain them under the Law.

21 To them lawless as lawless, not being lawless to God but definitely Lawful to Christ, that I might gain the lawless.

22 I became to the weak as weak that I might gain the weak. I am becoming all things that I might by all ways Save someone.

Also to be a Partaker with you

23 And this I Do for the Gospel, that I might become a Partaker with you.
24 Are you definitely not Spiritually Discerning that they who are running in a race actually runs all, and one receives the prize? In this manner you must be running that you should have Apprehended by your choice.

Striving for mastery, temperance

25 And everyone that is striving is Self Controlling All. Therefore then they might actually receive that corruptible victors wreath, but we Incorruptible.
26 I, accordingly, so run, definitely not as uncertainly, in such a manner I am boxing, as definitely not beating the air.
27 But definitely, I Subdue my body, and bring it into Subjection, fearing that I have Preached to others of same kind, I myself should have become a reprobate.

Fathers all drank of Christ

10 Moreover, Brethren, I would definitely not prefer you to be ignorant. How that our fathers were all under the Cloud, and all passed through the Sea,
2 And all have gotten Immersed to Moses in the Cloud, and in the Sea,
3 And all Ate the same Spiritual Food,
4 And all did Drink the same Spiritual Drinking, for they were Drinking out from that Spiritual Huge Rock following, and that Huge Rock was Christ.
5 But definitely God was definitely not pleased with many more of them, because they have been made overthrown in the desolate wilderness. (Num 14:16)

These were examples of sin

6 Now these became made our models for us for the Purpose that being we have not evil desiring of evil works, just as also they themselves desired.
7 Neither become idolaters, just as some of them, as is now made written, The people sat down to eat, and to drink, and arose to play. (Ex 32:6)
8 Neither should we be sexually sinning, just as some of them. And having sexually sinned, they fell down in one day, three thousand. (Ex 32:28)
9 Neither should we spiritually test Christ, just as even some of them have tested, and have been destroyed by the serpents.
10 You must neither murmur, just as also certain of them murmured, and have been destroyed by the destroyer.
11 Now these things all likewise were happening to them for Models Made Written for Warning to us, upon whom the End of the Ages have arrived.

Take heed yourselves, don't sin

12 So that he that is thinking he Stands, must be Spiritually Seeing that he should not fall down.
13 Definitely no temptation is now taking yourselves, except by manner of man. But God (is) Faithful, Who shall definitely not allow yourselves to be made tempted more above what yourselves are Able. He shall definitely Finalize United With the temptation even the Basic Understanding for yourselves to be Able to Undergo. (James 1:13-14)

Be not as them, flee idolatry

14 For result of this, my Beloved, you must Flee Away From idolatry.
15 I say as to very wise, you yourselves must judge by your choice what I state.
16 The Cup of Blessing, of Whom we Bless, is it definitely not of The Fellowship of the Blood of Christ? The Bread of Whom we are Breaking, is it definitely not of The Fellowship of the Body of Christ?
17 For we being many are One Bread, One Body, because we are all being Partaking of that One Bread.
18 You must Spiritually See, Israel according to sinful flesh nature, Are they

definitely not eating sacrifices? Are they companions at the altar?

19 Therefore, what am I stating? That any idol is anything, or that meat offered to idols is anything?

20 But definitely those that are killed as sacrifice, the Gentiles kill as sacrifice to demons, and definitely not to God. And I would definitely not that you companion with demons. (Deut 32:17)

21 You definitely cannot drink the Cup of the Lord, and also the cup of demons. You definitely cannot be partakers of the Table of the Lord, and of the table of demons.

22 Neither are we provoking the Lord to jealousy? Are we being stronger than He?

Do all to the Glory of God

23 All is lawful to me, but all is definitely not essential. All is lawful, but all is definitely not edifying.

24 You must not be seeking your own, but definitely every man the things of the other one of a different kind.

25 Whatever is sold in the meat shop eat, examining for judgment nothing, because of the conscience.

26 Because the earth, the Lord's, and the fullness of it. (Ps 24:1)

27 And if any faithless calls you, and you are willing to go, all that is put forth to you, you must eat examining for judgment nothing, because of conscience.

28 But if any speak to you, This is meat offered to idols, you must eat not, because of he that disclosed and the conscience of him, because the earth is the Lord's, and the fullness thereof. (Ps 24:1)

29 And conscience I say, definitely not your own, but definitely that of the other one of a different kind. Yet why then, is my liberty being made judged by another of same kind conscience?

30 For if I am a partaker by Grace, why am I blasphemed, in behalf of that I am Giving Thanks?

31 Whether, therefore, you eat, or you drink, or whatever you Do, you must always Do for the Glory of God.

32 Being without offense, both to the Jew, and the Gentile, also the Assembly of God.

33 Just as also I, everyone in all things, am pleasing not myself, but definitely seeking the necessary that many might be made Saved.

Be Followers of me, as I Follow Christ

11 You must become close followers of me, just as I also of Christ.

2 Now I fully praise you, Brethren, that in all things you are now yourselves made remembering me, and just as I have delivered up to you the traditions, you are holding fast by your choice.

Ladies' hair meant for covering

3 I desire that you Spiritually Know that the head of every man is the Christ, and head of woman the man, and head of Christ the God.

4 Every man Praying or prophesying having (covering) upon (his) head, is shaming to his Head.

5 And every wife Praying or prophesying with head uncovered is shaming her head, because she is so also herself as one being made shaven.

6 For, if even she must cut for herself her hair, a wife is definitely not made covered. For if it is defilement for a wife to cut her hair or to be made shaved, she must be made covered,

7 For a man actually ought to definitely not be covering his head, while existing the image and Glory of God. And the woman is the Glory of man.

8 For the husband is definitely not from the wife, but definitely the wife from the husband.

9 And because definitely not was a man made created for the woman, but definitely the woman for the man.

10 Because of this, the wife ought to have authority over her head because of Angels.

11 But neither a husband without a wife, nor a wife without a husband in the Lord,
12 For as the wife from the husband, so also the husband through the wife, but all things from God.
13 You must judge by your choice among yourselves. Is it appropriate for a wife to be uncovered Praying to God?
14 Or is not nature itself teaching you, yourselves, that a husband is indeed a dishonor to himself, if he should be having long hair by his choice?
15 But if a wife should have long hair, it is a Glory to her, for her locks of hair is made given to her for a covering.
16 But if anyone thinks to be contentious, we are definitely not ever having by our choice such a custom, neither the Assemblies of God.

Lord's Supper is defiled by some

17 Now this I am giving Command, that I am not fully praising, definitely not Coming Together for the better, but definitely for the less.
18 For first of all, you actually are Coming Together in the Assembly, I am hearing about divisions existing among you, and I am partly committing to some.
19 For there must be heresies also among you, in order that you to be approved, should become openly manifest among yourselves.
20 Then, you Coming Together with yourselves, definitely not to eat the Lord's Supper,
21 Yet every person takes before his own supper by eating, and one is actually being hungry, and another drunk.
22 Yet, unless you have definitely not houses to eat and to drink in? Or are those of the Assembly despising God? And are shaming them not having? What should I speak to you? I should definitely not fully praise you in this.
23 For, I have received along from the Lord, that which also I have delivered up to you, that the Lord Jesus in that same night that He was made delivered up in betrayal, took Bread,
24 And when He Gave Thanks, He Broke, and Spoke, You must Take to Receive by your choice. You must Eat by your choice. This is My Body which is being made Broken in behalf of you. You must Eat This in Remembrance of Me.
25 In like manner also, the Cup after He Supped, He Said. This Cup is the New Covenant of a Different Kind in My Blood. This you must do as often as whenever you should drink by your choice, in Remembrance of Me.
26 Because as often as whenever, you should eat by your choice this Bread, and you should drink by your choice this Cup, you are proclaiming much the Death of the Lord, until where whenever He should come.
27 So that whoever should be eating continuously by his choice this Bread, or should be drinking continuously by his choice this Cup of the Lord disrespectfully, shall be guilty of the Body and Blood of the Lord.
28 But a man himself must be Proving in Truth continuously by his choice, and in such a manner he must eat continuously by his choice of the Bread, and he must drink continuously by his choice of the Cup,
29 For he eating and drinking disrespectfully, is eating and drinking condemnation to himself, not continuously by his choice judging differences in the Lord's Body.
30 By this many among you (are) weak and sickly, and content to be made resting asleep. (Heb 6:3)

Fellowship as One Body

31 Because if we were judging differences yourselves, we would definitely not be made judged whatever.
32 But being made Judged by the Lord, we are made disciplined, in order that we

should not be condemned to death with the satan's world. (2 Tim 2:25)

33 So that my Brethren, Coming Together to eat, you must wait for one another.

34 And if any are hungry, you must eat in home, that you should be Coming Together, not for condemnation. And the rest I will appoint as whenever I might come.

Spiritual Gifts

12 Now in regard to Those Things Spiritual, Brethren, I am definitely not Willing You to be ignorant.

2 You are Spiritually Knowing that you were Gentiles, lead away to dumb idols, as though you were made led.

3 For this reason, I am making known Supernaturally to you that none Uttering by the Spirit of God Says, Jesus accursed. And none is able to Speak, Lord Jesus, except by the Holy Spirit.

4 Now there are differences of Spirit Gifts, but the same Spirit.

Admin and Operation all by Holy Spirit

5 And there are differences of Administrations with the Lord Himself.

6 And there are differences of Operations, but it is the same God, Who accomplishes All in all.

7 But the Manifestation of the Spirit is Made Given to every person, with that which is Being Essential by His Choice.

Nine Gifts and three divisions of Gifts

8 For to one is actually Made Given by the Spirit, a Spiritual Word of Wisdom, and to another of same kind, a Spiritual Word of Knowledge, according to the same Spirit.

9 And to another of a Different kind, Faith, by the same Spirit, and to another of same kind, Spirit Gifts of Healings, by the same Spirit.

10 And to another of same kind, Operations of Miracle Powers, and to another of same kind, Prophesy, and to another of same kind, Distinguishing Differences of spirits/Spirit, and to another of a Different kind, Kinds of Tongues, and to another of same kind, Interpretation of Tongues.

11 Now all these Things are Accomplishing the One and the Same Spirit, Dispensing by His choice, Privately to every person just as He Intends.

One Body and One Holy Spirit

12 Yet even as the Body is One, and having many members, and all the members of that One Body, being many, are One Body, so also the Christ.

13 So because therein we all in One Spirit, we all have been Made Immersed into One Body, whether Jew or Gentile, whether slaves or free, and everyone has been Made Given to Drink for the Purpose and Result of the One Spirit.

14 Because also the Body is Now definitely not one member, but definitely Many.

15 If the foot might speak, Because I am definitely not a hand, I am definitely not of the body. Definitely not by this, is it not out of the Body?

16 And if the ear might speak, because I am definitely not an eye, I am definitely not of the body. Definitely not by this, is it not out of the body?

17 If all of the body an eye, wherein the hearing? If all of hearing, wherein the smelling?

18 But just now, God has for Himself Positioned the members, every One a Person of them in the Body, just as He Has Willed.

Many members and one Body

19 And if All were one member, Wherein the Body?

20 But now actually many members, and one Body.

21 And the eye definitely cannot speak to a hand, I have definitely no need of you, or again, the head to the feet, I have definitely no need of you,

22 But definitely, very much more those

members of the Body, seeming existing weak, are necessary.

23 And those of the Body, we think to be without honor, we are placing honor upon them more in excess, and our unfashionable parts have dignity more in excess.

24 Then our honorables definitely have no need, but definitely God mixed together the Body being made, giving honor more in excess to those lacking,

25 In order that there should be no division in the Body, itself, but definitely that members might take the same thought, in behalf of one another.

26 And whether one member suffers, all the members suffer with him, or one member is made Attributing Glory (Spiritual Perfection), all the members rejoice together.

You in the Body of Christ, parts many

27 Now yourselves you are the Body of Christ, and members out from within particular.

28 And God has actually positioned some in the Assembly, first of all, Apostles, second Prophets, third Teachers, after that Miracle Powers, then Spirit Gifts of Healings, Helps, Directors, kinds of Tongues.

29 Not all Apostles, not all Prophets, not all Teachers, not all Miracle Powers,

30 Not all are having by their choice Spirit Gifts of Healings, not all are Uttering by their choice in Tongues, not all are by their choice Interpreting,

31 But you must be by your choice earnestly desiring the better Spirit Gifts, and yet I show to you by your choice about a more excellent Way.

God-Love is the Greatest Gift

13 Though I Utter with Tongues of men and of Angels, and have not God-Love, I become sounding as a brass coin, or a clamoring cymbal.

2 And though I should be Having Prophecy, and should be Spiritually Discerning all Mysteries, and all Knowledge, and though I should have all Faith so that to Completely Remove mountains, and I should not be having God-Love, I am nothing.

3 And though I should give food from all my material goods, and though I should deliver up my body, that it should be made burned, and I should not be having God-Love, it profits nothing. [Ye must be Born from Above (John 3:3-7; 1 Pet 1:23)]

Characteristics of God-Love

4 God-Love is Longsuffering, is Kind, and God-Love is definitely not strongly desiring to envy, and God-Love definitely is not bragging and definitely is not arrogant,

5 Behaves definitely not inappropriately, seeks definitely not its own, is definitely not made reacting, is definitely not accounting evil work,

6 Is not Rejoicing in unrighteousness, but is Rejoicing Together in the Truth,

7 Refrains all things, Commits to all men, Expects all things, Endures all things.

8 God-Love is never being no effect. Whether Prophecies, then they shall be Made Finished, whether Tongues, they shall Cease, whether Knowledge, it shall be Done Away.

Now we Know in part only

9 Because we Know out from part, and we Prophesy out from part,

10 But when should come that Who (is) Perfect, then that by part shall be Made done away, destroyed.

11 When I was an infant, I used to utter as an infant. I regarded of value as an infant. I was accounting as an infant, but when I became a man, I am doing away with those things of the infant,

12 Because for now we are Spiritually Seeing through a mirror within darkly, but then face to Face. For now I am Knowing by part, but then I will Fully Know, just as also I have been made Fully Known.

13 And just now Continues Faith, Expectation, God-Love, these three things, but the greatest of these, God-Love.

Follow God-Love, desire Gifts

14 You must follow closely God-Love, and strongly desire the things Spiritual, but much more that you should Prophesy.

Tongues Speak not to men

2 Because he that Utters in a Tongue, Utters definitely not to man, but definitely to God. Yet is heard by the Spirit, moreover is Uttering Mysteries.
3 But he that is Prophesying is Uttering Edification to men, and Encouragement, and Comfort.
4 He that is Uttering in Tongue is Edifying himself, but he that is Prophesying is Edifying the Assembly.
5 I will that you all Utter in Tongues, and much more that you should be Prophesying, because greater is he that is Prophesying than he that Utters in Tongues, except it is Interpreted, that the Assembly receives Edification.

Rev., knowledge, prophecy, doctrine

6 Just now, Oh Brethren, even if I should come to you uttering in Tongues, What will I profit you, except I should utter to you either in Revelation, or in Knowledge, or in Prophecy, or in Teaching?
7 Even things lifeless give sound, whether pipe or harp, if distinction of utterance should not be given, how shall it be made known what is piped or harped?
8 For yet if the Trumpet should give an uncertain sound, who shall be ready for war?
9 So also yourselves, except you give an understandable Spiritual Word through the tongue, how shall you be made uttering that which shall be made recognized because you are uttering into the air?
10 Allowing that so many kinds of sounds have been acquired beyond dreams are in the satan's world, and them not without speech.
11 Therefore, if I should not Spiritually Discern the Miracle Power of the voice I will be uttering, a barbarian; and he that utters to me, a barbarian.
12 So in such a manner, you, yourselves, in fact are zealous for Spiritual gifts. You must be seeking that you should abound in amount to the Edification of the Assembly.
13 For result of this, he that is uttering in Tongue must be Praying, that he should Interpret,
14 Because if I should be Praying in a Tongue, my spirit is Praying, but my Understanding of mind is unfruitful.
15 Therefore, how is it, I will Pray with the Spiritual Gift, and also I will Pray with Understanding of mind? I will sing melody with the Spiritual Gift, and also I will sing melody with Understanding of mind.
16 Then if you should bless with the Spiritual gift, how shall he be occupying the place of the unlearned spirit say, Amen, to your thanksgiving, for after that he discerns definitely not what you are saying?

Get Understanding to Teach

17 For you, indeed, are Giving Thanks God-Working, but definitely the other one of a different kind is definitely not made edified.
18 I Give Thanks to God, I am Uttering in Tongues much more than you all.
19 But definitely In the Assembly, I am willing to utter five Spiritual Words, through my Understanding of Mind, that I might also inform others of same kind, than with ten thousand Spiritual Words in a Tongue.
20 Oh Brethren, you must not be a little child in mental faculty, but definitely in malicious desire for evil work you must be infants, and in mental faculty, be Perfect.
21 In the Law it is Made Written, That in other Tongues, and in other lips of a

different kind I will utter to this people, and in such a manner they shall not Spiritually Hear Me, Says the Lord. (Isa 28:11-12)

Tongues a sign to faithless
22 So that the Tongues are for a Miracle Sign, definitely not to the Committing but definitely to the faithless, and Prophecy, definitely not to the faithless but definitely to the Committing.

Prophesying preferred Gift
23 If, therefore, all of the Assembly should Come Together to themselves, and all should be Uttering in Tongues, but unlearned or faithless should enter, shall they not definitely spirit say that you are insane?
24 But if everyone should be Prophesying, and a certain one faithless or unlearned should enter, he is convinced of sin by all, he is made examining for judgment by all means.
25 And in this manner, the secrets of his heart becomes Openly Manifest, and in such a manner, falling down upon his face by his choice, he shall worship God, telling in fact that God is in you.

The order of Gifts to use in meetings
26 How then is it, Oh Brethren? When yourselves should Come Together, every person of yourselves has by his choice a Psalm, has by his choice a Teaching, has by his choice a Tongue, has by his choice a Revelation, has by his choice an Interpretation, it must be occurring always for Edification.
27 Whether anyone utters by his choice in a Tongue, by two or at most three, but each by part, so also one must be by his choice Interpreting.
28 But if there might not be an interpreter, he must keep silence by his choice in the Assembly, and he must by his choice utter to himself and to God.
29 When the Prophets two or three must by their choice utter, then you must judge differences of others of the same subject.
30 If anything should be revealed to another of same kind sitting, the first must by his choice keep silence,
31 Because you are all able by your choice to Prophesy each one, that all might by his choice learn, and all should be made encouraged.
32 And the Spiritual gifts of Prophets are made subject to the Prophets,
33 Because God is definitely not of disorder, but definitely of Peace as in all the Assemblies of the Saints.
34 Your women must keep silence by their choice in the Assemblies, because it is definitely not made permitted to them to utter, but definitely to be for themselves subjected, just as also the Law is saying,
35 And if any to learn, they shall in their own home. They must be questioning the husbands, because it is a defilement for the wives to utter in the Assembly.
36 Either the Spiritual Word of God came out from you, or arrived to you alone?
37 If any man thinks to be a Prophet, or Spiritual, he must be Fully Knowing what I am writing to you, because they are Commandments of the Lord.
38 But if any man is being ignorant by his choice, he must be ignorant by his choice.
39 So that, Oh Brethren, you must strongly desire to Prophesy, but you must not forbid to Utter in Tongues.
40 All things must be occurring Honestly, and according to a priestly order.

Christ's Death, Burial and Resurrection
15 Moreover, Oh Brethren, I am continuously Making Known Supernaturally to you the Gospel, which I Preached to you, which also you have each Received, and in which you are now continuously Standing.
2 Through which also you are being Continuously Made Saved, if you are Continuously Holding by your choice to

that Spiritual Word I Proclaimed to you, except you have Committed by your choice without reason. (without repentance)

3   Because I Delivered up to you, when first that I also by my choice Received, how Christ Died by His Choice in Behalf of our sin natures and sins, According to the Scriptures.

4   And that He was Made Buried, and that He was Made Risen Up after the third day, According to the Scriptures.

Christ Seen by men and Paul last

5   And that He was Spiritually Seen by Cephas, then by the twelve.

6   After that, He was made Spiritually Seen by over five hundred Brethren at one time, wherein many more continuing up to for now, but also some have been made resting asleep.

7   After that He was Spiritually Seen by James, following that by all Apostles.

8   And last of all, as though out from due time, I also was made Spiritually Seeing.

9   Because I, I am the least of the Apostles, that is definitely not sufficient to be called an Apostle, since I persecuted by my choice the Assembly of God.

10 But by the Grace of God, I am what I am, and His Grace in me is definitely not delusional. But definitely, I labored more in excess of them all, definitely not I, but definitely the Grace of God united with me.

11 Therefore, whether I or they in such a manner, we are by our choice preaching, and in such a manner have by our choice Committed.

If Christ Raised not, it is all in vain

12 Now if Christ is made preached that He is now made Risen Up out from the Dead, how say some among you, that there is definitely no Resurrection of the dead?

13 But if there be definitely no Resurrection of the dead, neither is Christ now made Risen Up.

14 And if Christ is definitely not now Risen Up, so then our preaching delusional, and also your faith delusion.

15 So then we are made found false witnesses of God, that by God we witnessed for God, that He Raised Up Christ, if so be Whom He has definitely not Raised Up. So then the dead are definitely not made raised up.

16 Because if the dead are definitely not made raised up, neither is Christ Raised Up.

17 And if Christ has definitely not been Made Raised Up, your faith (is) self-worship. You are yet in your sin natures and sins.

18 So then, they also, who have been sleeping in Christ, have perished.

19 If in this life only, we are being now expecting in Christ only, we are being of all men miserable.

In Adam all die, in Christ all Live

20 But just now Christ is Risen Up out from the dead, being the Firstfruit of them that are now sleeping.

21 For after that through man, the death, then through a Man, the Resurrection of the dead.

22 For as in Adam all die, so now in Christ all shall be made Offered Spiritual Life.

23 But every man in his own order, Christ the Firstfruit, after that those of Christ with His Coming.

24 Following that, the End, when He should Deliver Up the Kingdom Rule to God and Father, when He should destroy all power, and all authority, and miracle power.

25 For He must Reign until whenever He Should put all the enemies under His Feet.

26 The last enemy being destroyed, death.

27 For He has subjected all under His Feet. But when He should Speak, all that is made subjected, evident that He (is) excepted, Who has subjected all things under Him. (Ps 8:6)

28 And when all should have been subjected to Him, also then He the Son shall be made subjected to Him, subjecting All

to Himself, in order that God should be All in All.

29 Then what shall they do, who are made immersed in behalf of the dead, if absolutely the dead definitely Rise Up not? Why then immerse in behalf of the dead?

30 And why are we endangered every hour?

31 As I am dying daily, which I have with our rejoicing in Christ Jesus our Lord.

32 If after men, I fight wild beast in Ephesus, What profit to me, if the dead are definitely not made Rising Up? We should eat and drink, because tomorrow we are dying. (Isa 22:13)

33 You must not be deceived, evil work associates are spiritually corrupting Kind moral rules.

34 You must Righteously arouse from stupor, and not be sinning for lack of Knowledge of God. I am saying, having some disrespect to you.

Sown in death, raised Incorruptible

35 But definitely some shall Spirit Say, How are the dead made Rising Up? And with what body are they coming?

36 You mentally unwise. What you are sowing is definitely not made Offering Spiritual Life, except it should die.

37 And you are sowing definitely not the Body, but definitely you shall become sowing naked grain, whether acquiring wheat beyond dreams, or some other.

38 But God is Giving to it a Body, just as He Wills, and to every person His own Body of the Seeds.

39 All sinful flesh nature, definitely not the same flesh nature, but definitely other of same kind flesh nature, indeed, of man, and another of same kind flesh nature of animals, and another of same kind of fish, and another of same kind of birds.

40 Also Heavenly bodies, and earthly bodies, but definitely another of a different kind, indeed, that Glory of those that are Heavenly, and those other of a different kind of the earthly.

41 Another of the same kind Glory of the sun and another of same kind Glory of the moon, and another of the same kind Glory of the stars, for a star differs in value with a star in Glory.

42 So also the Resurrection of the dead, it is made sown in Eternal death, Raised Up in Incorruption.

43 It is made sown in dishonor, Raised Up in Glory, made sown in infirmity, made Raised Up in Miracle Power.

44 It is made sown a natural sensual soulish body. It is made Raised Up a Spiritual Body. There is a natural soulish body, and there is a Spiritual Body.

45 And so it is now made written, The first man Adam was made for a Living soul, the last Adam for the Spirit Offering Spiritual Life. (Gen 2:7)

46 But definitely first of all definitely not that Spiritual, but definitely the natural sensual soulish, after that the Spiritual.

47 The first man out from the earth, earthy, the second man, the Lord, out from Heaven. (Gen 2:7)

48 Such as the earthy, such also the earthy, and such as the Heavenly, such also the Heavenlies.

49 And just as we have worn the image of the earthy, we shall wear also the image of the Heavenly.

50 Now this I state, Oh Brethren, that the sinful flesh nature and blood definitely cannot Inherit the Kingdom Rule of God; neither Eternal death inherit Incorruption.

I show you a Mystery

51 You must Spiritual behold, I am saying a Mystery to you. We shall actually definitely not all be made to sleep, but we shall all be made changed.

52 In an atom of time, in the twinkling of an eye, when the Last Trumpet yet shall Sound, and the dead shall be made to Rise Up Incorruptible, and we shall be made Changed. (Matt 24:31; 1 Thess 4:16)

53 For this corruptible is required to put on for itself Incorruption, and this mortal to put on for itself Immortality.

54 So when this corruptible shall have put on for itself Incorruption, and this mortal should have put on for itself Immortality, then shall come to pass the Spiritual Word that is now made Written, Death is completely swallowed up in Victory. (Isa 25:8)

55 Wherein the sting of you, Oh death? Wherein the victory of you, Oh hades? (Hos 13:14)

Death sting, sin; Law, its strength

56 Nevertheless, the sting of death is the sin nature and sin, and the power of the sin nature and sin, the Law. (Old Covenant)

57 But Thankful for Grace from God, Who is Giving us the Victory, through our Lord Jesus Christ. (New Covenant)

58 So that, Oh my Beloved Brethren, you must be Steadfast, Immovable, Abounding in Amount in the Work by God of the Lord, always Spiritually Discerning that your labor definitely is not delusional in the Lord.

On first day of week

16 Now concerning the collection for the Saints, as I have appointed to the Assembly of Galatia, so also you must do yourselves.

2 Upon the first day of the week, every person of you among yourselves must be positioning, storing up that whatever anybody should be made prospering, in order that when I should come should occur no collection then.

3 And when I should come up, if whoever you should Prove in Truth through epistles, these shall I send to carry away for your thankfulness to Jerusalem.

4 And if it should be worthy that I also go, they shall go with me.

Paul's plans

5 Now I will come to you when I should pass through Macedonia, because I am passing through Macedonia.

6 And acquiring by you I will continue along, or then I will winter in order that yourselves might journey with me wherever I go.

7 Yet I would definitely not be seeing you for now in the route taken, but I am expecting to continue with Intent a certain time with you, if the Lord should permit.

8 But I will continue with Intent in Ephesus until after Pentecost.

9 A Great Door and Powerful is now opening for me, and many being adversaries.

10 Now if Timothy should come, you must Spiritually See that he should be with you without fear, because he is Working the Work by God of the Lord as I also.

11 Therefore, that not anybody should despise him, but you must journey with him in Peace, that he should come to me, for I am waiting for him with the Brethren.

12 As in regard to Apollos, our Brother, I very much encouraged him that he by all means should come to you with the Brethren, but he has definitely not a will that he should now come, but will come when he should have leisure time.

Watch and Stand Fast in Faith

13 You must Watch by your choice. You must Stand Fast by your choice with the Faith. You must be manly. You must be made strong.

14 All things of yourselves must be with God-Love. (the uniting bond: Col 3:14)

15 Now I am encouraging you, Oh Brethren, you Spiritually Know the house of Stephanas, that it is the Firstfuit of Achaia, and they have assigned themselves for Serving to the Saints.

16 And also yourselves then should be made subjecting to such, laboring, in order that to always be working together with them.

17 Also, I am rejoicing upon the coming of Stephanus and Forunatus and Achaicus,

for they have satisfied that lacking of you.

18 For they have refreshed my Spirit and yours, therefore, you must Fully Know them as such.

19 The Assemblies of Asia are greeting you, Aquila and Priscilla are greeting you very much in the Lord, united with the Assembly in their home.

20 All the Brethren are greeting you. You must greet one another with a Holy kiss.

21 The salutation with my hand, Paul.

Must Love Christ or be Judged

22 If anyone is not Affectionately Loving (phileo) the Lord Jesus Christ, he must be accursed, maran-athata accursed (Divine Judgment Accursed).

23 The Grace of the Lord Jesus Christ with you.

24 My God-Love with all of you in Christ Jesus. Amen.

[The first written to Corinthians from Philippi through Stephanas, and Forunatus, and Achaicus, and Timothy]

The Second Epistle of Paul the Apostle to the

Corinthians

Salutation

1 Paul an Apostle of Jesus Christ through the Will of God, and Timothy our Brother, to the Assembly of God which is in Corinth, with all the Saints who are in all of Achaia.

2 Grace to you and Peace from God our Father and the Lord Jesus Christ.

Paul's sufferings, and gratitude

3 Most Blessed Worthy of all Spiritual Perfection, the God and Father of our Lord Jesus Christ, the Father of Sympathies, and the God of all Encouragement.

4 Who Encourages us in the way with all our affliction, for He is Able to Encourage us in all affliction, through the Encouragement that ourselves are Made Encouraged by God,

5 Because just as the sufferings of Christ Abound in amount in us, in such a manner through Christ it is Abounding in amount and Encouragement for us.

6 And whether we are made troubled for your Encouragement and Salvation, for accomplishing in Endurance of the same sufferings which also we suffer, or made Encouraging for your Encouragement and Salvation, and our Permanent Expectation in behalf of you,

7 Spiritually Knowing that as you are Companions of the sufferings, so also the Consolation.

8 For we would you definitely not be ignorant, Brethren, in behalf of the affliction of us which occurred to us in Asia, that as we had been made beyond measure burdened above our power, so that we have been made despaired even to live.

9 But definitely we in ourselves had the sentence of death, that we should not be having confidence in ourselves but definitely in God, Who is Raising Up the dead,

10 Who Rescued us out from so great a death, and He shall Rescue for those now being Expected, also He shall further Rescue.

11 Also, you are helping together by supplication in behalf of us, in order that out from many persons, the Spirit Gift upon us should have been Made to Give Thanks by many on our behalf.

God has Spirit-anointed Together
12 For our Rejoicing is this, that the Testimony of our conscience, where in Simplicity of God-Good Intentions and Sincerity of God, definitely not in carnal sinful flesh nature wisdom but definitely in the Grace of God, we behave in the satan's world, and abundantly toward you.
13 For we are definitely not writing another of same kind to you, but definitely before what you are reading instead also Fully Knowing, and I expect that you shall Fully Know even up to the End,
14 Just as also you have Fully known us of part, that we are being your Happiness, even as also yourselves ours in the Day of the Lord Jesus.
15 And in this confidence I intending to come to you first, that you should have a second Thankfulness for Grace.
16 And to pass through to you in Macedonia, and again from Macedonia to come to you, and after for to journey with you to Judea.
17 Then this I am consulting, so then I have used not any lightness, neither that consulting according to sinful flesh nature consulting, in order that it should be with me emphatically Yes, Yes, or definitely No, No.
18 But that the Faithful God for our Spiritual Communication to you, definitely not be emphatically Yes and definitely No.
19 Because the Son of God, Jesus Christ, Who in you, through our preaching by me and Silvanus and Timothy, was definitely not being emphatically Yes and definitely No, but definitely in Him being continuously emphatic, Yes.
20 Because that the Promises of God in Him (are) emphatically Yes, and in Him

Truly to the Glory of God through us.
21 And He Who Establishes us with you in Christ, also God has Spirit Anointed us,
22 Who has also Sealed us, and has given the Down Payment of the Spirit in our hearts.
23 Moreover, I call upon God, a Witness upon my soul, that sparing you I have not come more to Corinth,
24 Because we definitely are having no dominion over your Faith, but definitely we are being Fellow Laborers of your Joy, for by Faith you are Now Standing.

With much anguish of heart I wrote you
2 Now I judge this myself, that I not come again to you in grief.
2 For If I am grieving you, then who is he being merry to me, except he being made sorry by me?
3 And I wrote this myself to you, that I should not be having grief coming from yourselves. He was required to rejoice with me, giving confidence to you all, that my Joy is of you all.
4 Because out from very much affliction and anguish of heart I wrote to you with many tears, in order that I should definitely not make sorrow, but definitely that you should Know the God-Love that I am Earnestly having for you.

Freely Forgive those who repent
5 But if any is sorrowing, I am definitely not sorrowing, but definitely from respect in order that I should not owe to you all.
6 Sufficient to such, his complete rebuke, caused by many more.
7 So that on the contrary, instead you have to freely forgive and to comfort, unless how he, the such, should not be made completely swallowed by more abundant grief.
8 For this reason I am encouraging you to Verify God-Love to him.
9 And because for this also I have Written, that I should know the Proof of you,

whether you are Obedient in all things.

10 But to whom you freely Forgive anything then I also, for if I am now freely Forgiving any, then I am now freely Forgiven by you in the Person of Christ,

11 In order that we should not make a gain for the satan, for we are definitely not ignorant of his comprehensions.

12 Moreover, when coming for Troas for the Gospel of Christ, even a Great Door by the Lord was Opened to me.

13 I definitely had no rest in my Spirit, not to find my own Brother Titus, but definitely saying goodbye to them, I came out into Macedonia.

We corrupt not the Word of God

14 Now Thankfulness for Grace from God, Who always is causing us to Triumph in Christ, and Manifests the Savor of His Knowledge through us in every place.

15 For we are being to God a Sweet Savor of Christ, in them that are Made Saved, and in them that are perishing,

16 Actually, to some a Savor of death to Death, and to others a Savor of life to Life. And who sufficient to these things?

17 For I am being definitely not as the many vending the Word of God, but definitely as out from Sincerity, but definitely as out from Before the Presence of God, I am Uttering by Christ.

Made Able Servants of New Covenant

3 Are we beginning again to Commend ourselves? Or that we are not having lack, as certain ones with commendation epistles to you, or commendations from you.

2 Yourselves are our Epistles, Spirit Written in our hearts, Known and Read by all men.

3 Since you are being Made Manifest, an Epistle of Christ, Made Serving by us, Made Spirit Written, definitely not with ink, but definitely by the Spirit of God, Living definitely not in stone carved tablets, but definitely in the fleshy tablets of the heart.

4 And then such Confidence have we through Christ toward God.

5 Definitely not that we are being sufficient to account for ourselves anything as from ourselves, but Definitely our Sufficiency from God,

6 Who also Made Us Able Servants of the New of a Different Kind Covenant, definitely not of the letter but definitely of the Spirit, because the letter is killing, but the Spirit is Offering Spiritual Life.

7 But if the Administration of death in the writings engraved in stones was with Glory, so that the sons of Israel could not attentively look upon the face of Moses, because of the Glory of His face which is made done away,

8 How shall definitely not much more the Administration of the Spirit be in Glory?

If replaced Law was Glory, then more ...

9 For if the Administration of the Sentence Judging Glory to many, much More in amount the Administration of the Righteousness is the Abounding in Glory.

10 Because that not now continuously made Attributing Glory, is now Attributing Glory in This One, for the particular cause of the Excelling in Quality of Glory,

11 Because if that Made Done Away in Glory, very Much More is That Continuing in Glory,

12 Having then such Expectation, we are using very Much boldness.

13 And definitely not, even as Moses was putting a veil over his own face, that the sons of Israel not attentively look upon to the End of that being Made Done Away. (Ex 34:35)

Even now the veil is over their hearts

14 But definitely, their comprehension has been made stony blind, yet until this today the veil over their reading of the Old of Age Covenant Continues, nothing is

made uncovered whatever. It is Certain, Continuously Made Done Away By Christ.
15 But definitely until after this day, at which time they are made reading Moses, the Veil is laying over their heart,

When it should Turn to the Lord?
16 Nevertheless, at which time it should turn back to the Lord, the Veil is made Removed Away.
17 Now the Lord is that Spirit, and Where the Spirit of the Lord, there, Liberty.
18 But we are all now Made an Uncovered Face, Beholding as in a mirror the Glory of the Lord, are Being Made Transfigured to the Same Image from Glory to Glory, even as from the Spirit of the Lord.

Our Gospel is hid to them that are lost
4 Through having This Service (of Calling), just as we have Received Mercy, we are definitely not being weary.
2 But definitely Renouncing the secret things of shame, be not walking in craftiness, neither deceitfully handling the Word of God, but definitely by Manifestation of the Truth, Commending yourselves to every man's conscience in the Presence of God.
3 But if now our Gospel is being made covered, it is now being made covered in them that are lost,
4 In whom the god of this Age has blinded the comprehension of the faithless to not penetrate into them the Illumination of the Gospel of the Glory of Christ, Who is the image of God.

We have this Treasure in earthen vessels
5 For we are preaching definitely not ourselves, but definitely Christ Jesus the Lord, and ourselves your Bondslaves because of Jesus. (John 13:7-13)
6 For God has Spoken a Light to Brightly Shine out from within darkness, that Brightly Shined inside our hearts with the Illumination of the Knowledge of the Glory

(Spiritual Perfection) of God inside the Presence of Jesus Christ. [Heart is your soul (mind, emotion, and will) and your spirit combined with the Holy Spirit (1 Cor 6:17)]
7 But we are having this Treasure within earthen vessels, that the Excellency of the Miracle Power should be of God and not of us.

So death works in us, but Life in Jesus
8 We are made troubled in every way, but definitely not made distressed, perplexed but definitely not being in despair,
9 Persecuted but definitely not forsaken, cast down but definitely not destroyed.
10 Always carrying about in the body the Dead State of the Lord Jesus, that the Life also of Jesus should be made Manifest in our Body,
11 Because we continuously are Living by our choice, already Delivered Up in Death through Jesus, in order that also the Life of Jesus should be made Manifest against our mortal sinful flesh nature.
12 So that actually the Death in us, is for ourselves Accomplishing instead Eternal Life Within yourselves.
13 Even Having the same Spirit of Faith, according to that now made Written, I Committed by my choice for this reason Uttered, and we are Continuously Committing for this reason and Uttering continuously. (Ps 116:10)
14 Spiritually Knowing He that Raised Up the Lord Jesus, shall also by Jesus Raise us Up, and He shall Stand United with you.
15 Yet above all, because of you, that the Grace Exceed in Quantity through your many More Excellent Thankfulness should Abound in Amount to the Glory of God.
16 For this reason we are definitely not weary by our choice, but definitely allowing that yet our outside man is materially destroyed, but definitely the Inside is Made Becoming New day after day.
17 Because a light weight moment of our

affliction is producing Beyond Measure in Excellent Eternal heavy Weight of Glory In us,

18 That not of ourselves looking at that made seen, but definitely Made Looking at that Not Made Seen, because for a time seeing physically, but that Not Made Seen, Eternal.

We have a building from God

5 For we Spiritually Know that if this our earthly house of Personal Tabernacle has been made torn down, we are continuously by our choice having a Building from God, an Eternal House Made Without Hand in the Heavenlies.

2 For also in this we are continuously groaning, greatly desiring to be Clothed Upon with our Body Habitation Dwelling from Within Heaven.

3 Also If so be that having been Dressed (Rev 3:5 and 18), we shall definitely not be made found naked,

4 For we are being in the Personal Tabernacle groaning being burdened, in regard that willing definitely not to be unclothed, but definitely to be Clothed Upon, in order that the mortal should be Made Completely Swallowed by the God Eternal.

We walk by Faith, not by sight

5 For God producing us for this same thing, also Giving to us the Down Payment of the Spirit.

6 Then being Confident Always and Spiritually Knowing that being home in the body, we are being Separated from the Lord,

7 For we are continuously by our choice Walking by Faith, definitely not by sight.

Absent in body, Present with the Lord

8 So we are continuously by our choice Confident and Pleased much more to be Separated from the body and to be Home with the Lord.

9 For this reason now we are Continuously Endeavoring, whether being home or being Separated, to be Well Pleasing to Him.

All is Accomplished through His body

10 For He is Required to Manifest our every way before the Judgment Seat of Christ, that every person should have earned for himself through the body with what has been practiced by his choice, whether God-Good or evil work.

11 Therefore, Spiritually Knowing the Fear of the Lord to be Persuading men, we are now Made Manifesting to God, and I expect also to be Made Manifest in your consciences.

12 For, again, we are definitely not by our choice commending ourselves to you, but definitely are giving occasion to you to be Happy in behalf of us, that we should be having against some that are boasting in presence, and definitely not in heart.

13 For whether we have been Astonished by God, or we are being Logically Minded to you,

If one Died for all, all are dead

14 Yet the God-Love of Christ Constrains us, Judging this, that if One Died in Behalf of all, so then all have by their choice Died.

15 And He Died in Behalf of all, that they who are Living should no longer be living in behalf of themselves, but definitely in Behalf of Him Who Died by His choice and was Made Risen Up.

16 So that we by now, are not now knowing anyone according to sinful flesh nature, how allowing that after also we knew Christ after the flesh, but definitely now Not Anymore Knowing.

In Christ we are New Creations

17 So that if any man with Christ, a New of a Different Kind Creation, old things are Passed Away, Behold, All things are Now Occurring New of a Different Kind.

18 And All Things From God, Who has

Reconciled Us to Himself Through Jesus Christ, and has Given to Us the Service (of Calling) of Reconciliation.

19 For as God Was In Christ, Reconciling the satan's world to Himself, not accounting their spiritual death offenses to them, and Put Inside us the Spiritual Word (Christ Himself) of Reconciliation.

He has Finalized sin for us

20 Then, we are continuously by our choice Ambassadors in Behalf of Christ, as God Beseeching Through Us; we are Praying earnestly in Behalf of Christ. You must be Made Reconciled to God.

21 Because He Who Knew no sin nature and sin, has in Behalf of us Finalized sin nature and sin, in order that we should become Righteousness of God Inside Him.

Now Workers Together with Him

6 We are then Working Together, so Encouraging you to not Receive therein the Grace of God in delusion.

2 For He is Saying, In a Special Time Accepted I Heeded to you, and in the Day of Salvation, I Helped you. Behold now a Well Accepted Spiritual Time. You must now Spiritually Behold the Day of Salvation. (Isa 49:8)

3 Giving no occasion of stumbling in anything, that the Serving (of Calling) has not been made criticized,

4 But definitely in all things Commending ourselves as Servants of God, in very much Endurance, in afflictions, in necessities, in distresses,

5 In stripes, in prisons, in disorders, in labors, in watchings, in fastings,

6 By Pureness, by Knowledge, by Longsuffering, by Gentleness, by the Holy Spirit, by Love Unfeigned,

7 By the Word of Truth, by Miracle Power of God, by the Instruments of Righteousness of the Right hand and of the Left,

8 Through Glory and dishonor, through evil report and Good Report, as deceivers and True,

9 As being made unknown and Made Fully known as dying, and you must Spiritual Behold we Live, as Disciplined, and not put to death in body.

10 As sorrowful continuously, yet Rejoicing as very much poor, yet Enriching as having nothing, yet Holding Fast all things.

Unequally yoked with faithless

11 Our mouth is Open to you, Corinthians, our heart is now made enlarged.

12 You are not made distressed in us, but Distressed in your Compassion.

13 Now your payback as children I am saying, yet yourselves must be made enlarged.

14 You must not be unequally yoked with faithless, for why Companionship for Righteousness then with lawlessness, and why Fellowship for Light with darkness?

15 And what Comradeship for Christ with worthless evil (the satan)? Or what Portion for the Faithful with the faithless?

16 And what Agreement for the Temple of God with idols? For you are yourselves a Living Temple of God, just as God has Spoken, For I will Indwell In them, and I will Walk In them, and I Will Be their God, and they shall Be My People.
(Lev 26:12; Ezek 37:27)

Come out, Separate yourself

17 For this reason, you Must Come Away from the midst of them, and you Must Be Separate, Says the Lord, and you Must Not Touch of morally impure, also I as a result Will Receive You. (Isa 52:11)

18 And you Shall Have a Father to you, and yourselves shall be To Me for Sons and Daughters, Says the Lord Almighty.
(2 Sam 7:8-14)

Complete Holiness of Spirit in fear

7 Having, therefore, these Promises, Beloved, we should be Cleansed Ourselves by our choice from all evilness of sinful flesh nature, and Continuously by

your choice Complete Holiness of Spirit in Fear of God.

2 You must find a Place for us. We have wronged none. We spiritually corrupted none. We have made a gain of none.

3 I am saying, definitely not sentence judging, because I am Foretelling that you are in our hearts for the Purpose to have Died Together, even as to be Living Together.

4 Very much my Boldness toward you. Very much my Rejoicing in behalf of you. I am Fully Filled in Encouragement. I am Super Abounding for myself in Joy, in all our affliction.

5 Also, because of our having come to Macedonia, our sinful flesh nature is now having by our choice no rest, but definitely being made troubled in every way, quarrels outward, fears inside.

6 But definitely we are Encouraged, God Encouraged our low degree, in the Coming of Titus.

7 And definitely not only in his Coming, but definitely also in that Encouragement that has made Comfort to you, declaring to us your Earnest Desire, your Sorrowing, your God-Good Zeal for me, so that I much More Rejoiced.

8 For if also I have grieved you in that epistle, I am definitely not regretting but though I was regretting, because for Spiritually Seeing that this same epistle also grieved you for a short time.

9 Now I am rejoicing, definitely not because you have been made grieved, but definitely that you Sorrowed in Repentance, for you Grieved before God, that in nothing you might have suffered loss of us.

Grief of Repentance before God

10 For the Grief of Repentance before God Produces for Purpose and Result of Salvation, but the grief of the satan's world without Repentance produces death.

11 Yet Spiritually Behold this, who before God has Grieved you, has produced much Diligence in you, but definitely Defense, but definitely Strong Disapproval, but definitely Fear, but definitely Earnest Desire, but definitely God-Good Zeal, but definitely Punishment. In every way you have Commended yourselves to be Pure in this matter.

12 Also, so then, if written to you to definitely not be unjust for the cause, neither having made wrong the cause, but definitely to make Manifest the cause with your Diligence among you, in behalf of us in the Presence of God,

13 Because of this, I am now made Comforted by this consolation of you earnestly, and I have been made Glad much more for the Joy of Titus, because it is making the Spirit of him Refreshed, from all things of you.

14 For if I am now boasting anything in behalf of him to you, I am definitely not made shamed. But definitely as with all in Truth I have Uttered to you, also in such a manner our Rejoicing in Titus, being Truth.

15 And his compassion earnestly for you is in remembrance of all your Obedience, as with Fear and trembling you Received him.

16 I am Rejoicing, therefore, that in all I am Confident in you.

Excel in Giving

8 Moreover, I am making Known Supernaturally to you, Oh Brethren, the Grace of God now Made Given in the Assemblies of Macedonia.

2 How in much Experience of affliction, the overflowing of their Joy, and by the depth of their poverty, they Abounded in Amount in the Riches of their Simplicity of God-Good Intentions.

3 For according to Miracle Power, I am Witnessing even more than Miracle Power of own accord,

4 Praying earnestly with very much Encouragement of us, to receive with us the Grace and the Fellowship of the Serving to

the Saints,

5   And definitely not just as we expected, but definitely Gave Themselves by their choice, first of all to the Lord, and then to us by the Will of God.

6   Wherein, we Encouraged our Titus that just as had begun before, so also He should Perform in you also by your choice, the same Grace. [Grace (God's Method) is Christ Within you (Faith, God's Means; Heb 11:1, Col 1:27), through your Obedience, Doing what you cannot Do.]

7   But definitely as you Abound in Amount in all things, in Faith, and in Spiritual Communication, and in Knowledge, and in Diligence, and from yourselves with God-Love upon us, that also in this the Grace should be Abounding in Amount.

8   I say definitely not according to Commandment of God, but definitely by the Diligence of other ones of a different kind, and that of this yourselves, Proving in Truth, Truthful God-Love.

9   Because you know the Grace of our Lord Jesus Christ that for you He being Rich became poor, that yourselves through His poverty you should be Rich.

10   And in this I give advice, this is expedient for you who not only began, but definitely also to be willing to begin before, since a year ago,

11   Then just now also you must by your choice Perform so that to Finalize. From Readiness of mind to be Willing to have to Perform even as in such a manner,

12   For if there is a readiness of mind being set before, anyone well accepted in as much as if he might be having, definitely not in as much as definitely not having,

13   For definitely not in order that others of same kind rest, and affliction for you, but definitely by equality in this current Special Time for the Abundance of you to those lacking.

14   Also in order that the same Abundance, might become for those of you lacking, so that it might become equality.

15   Just as written, he that has very much not exceeded in quantity, also he of little definitely has no lack.

16   But thankfulness for Grace to God, that is giving the same Diligence, in behalf of you by the heart of Titus.

17   For actually Diligent, he Received Encouragement, but of his own accord he came out to be existing with you.

18   And we have Sent with him the Brother, of whom has the Full Praise in the Gospel, through all of the Assemblies.

19   And not only Hand Chosen by the Assembly, but definitely also our travel companion united with this Grace, the same is made administering by us to the Glory of the same Lord. and your Readiness of mind.

20   Standing Removed to this, not anyone should criticize us in this liberality, which is administered by us,

21   Providing God-Work definitely not only in the Presence of the Lord, but definitely also in the presence of men.

22   And we have sent with them our Brother, that we, being often diligent in very much, have Proved in Truth, and just now very diligently for you being much more in very much confidence,

23   Whether in behalf of Titus, my Companion, also a Fellow Laborer for you, or our Brethren Apostles of the Assemblies, the Glory of Christ,

24   Then a Declaration of your God-Love, and our rejoicing in behalf of you, for you must exhibit them for yourselves, also in the presence of the Assemblies.

God Loves a Cheerful Giver

9   Yet in regard to the Serving to the Saints, actually it is more in excess for me to write to you,

2   Because I Spiritually Discern your Readiness of mind, that I am boasting of you to Macedonia, that Achaia is now made ready from a year ago, also out from you God-Good Zeal is Provoked by your

more excellent choice.

3   So I have Sent the Brethren, that it is our Happiness in behalf of you should not in this respect be made empty. That just as I was saying, you should be made ready,

4   For fear how the Macedonians might come with me, and find you unprepared. We might be made shamed that we should not say, when yourselves rejoicing among this Spiritual Being.

5   Therefore, I esteemed necessary to encourage the Brethren, that they should go forward to you, and they should prepare before, showing before your blessing, being ready for them in such a manner as a Blessing, and not as greediness.

6   But this, he sowing meagerly, also meagerly shall reap, and he Sowing for Blessing, in the Blessing also he shall Reap.

7   Every person just as he estimates in his heart, not that out from grief or out from necessity, because God is Loving a cheerful giver.

8   And God is Exceedingly Able to abound in amount all Grace to you, in order that in every way always having all contentment, you should be abounding in amount in all God-Good, Work by God.

9   Just as It is made Written, He has dispersed, He has Given to the starving. His Righteousness is Continuing Forever.

10   Now He that Fully Furnishes Seed to the Sowing and Bread for meat, Furnishes beyond dreams, and Multiplies beyond dreams, and your Sowing Seed and Growing beyond dreams, the Products of your Righteousness,

11   Being made enriched in all things, for all Simplicity of God-Good Intentions that produces through us, Thanksgiving to God.

12   For the Administration of this Service to God, definitely not only is supplying that lacking of the Saints, but definitely also Abounding in Amount by very much Thanksgiving to God,

13   By the Experience of this Service, Attributing Glory to God, by the subjection of your Profession in the Gospel of Christ, and Simplicity of God-Good Intentions of Fellowship for them, and for all,

14   And by their Supplication for you, greatly desiring you to Excel in Quality by the Grace of God for yourselves.

15   Grace then from God with His Indescribable God-Gift.

Apostle's Authority

10 Now I Paul myself, Encourage you through the Meekness and Clemency of Christ, who in presence actually lowly among you, but being absent I am Confident toward you.

2   But I am Praying Earnestly that not being present, to be Bold with Confidence, to be Accounting to Dare with certain ones, accounting us as walking according to sinful flesh nature.

Walking In the flesh, not by flesh

3   Because Walking while the sinful flesh nature, we are definitely not Warring for ourselves by the sinful flesh nature,

4   Because the Weapons of our Warfare, definitely not carnal sinful flesh nature, but definitely Exceedingly Able through God, to the Pulling Down of strongholds.

5   Taking Down reasonings, and every high thing lifted up against the Knowledge of God, and leading captive All Comprehension to the Obedience of Christ.

6   And having in readiness to Avenge all disobeying, when your Obedience should have been Made Fulfilled.

7   Are you looking at the person? If any man is Persuaded in himself, he must account this to be of Christ. For again just as he himself of Christ, in the same manner also we of Christ.

Though I boast by our Authority

8   And also if now I should boast, yet more abundantly about our Authority, which the Lord has Given to us for Edification, and definitely not for your pulling down, I

will definitely not be made disgraced,

9   That I should not seem as though to make you fearful by Epistles.

10 For his epistles certainly are stating weighty and strong, but coming in his body, weak, and his Spiritual Communication least esteemed.

11 Such must account this, that such as we being absent are being in Spiritual Communication by Epistles, such also in Work by God being present.

12 Because we dare not make ourselves or compare ourselves with some that commend themselves, but definitely they are measuring themselves by themselves, and comparing themselves among themselves, are definitely not Understanding.

13 But we will definitely not boast therein without measure, but definitely according to the Amount of Measure of the Rule of Conduct that God has Fully Divided to us, a measure even to reach as far as you.

14 For as we are neither not stretching beyond our own reach to you, yet, because as far as you have also attained in the Gospel of Christ.

15 Definitely not boastful of things without measure in another man's labor, but having Expectation when your Faith is Made Increasing in you, to be Magnified according to our Rule of Conduct into Overflowing.

16 To preach the Gospel beyond you, definitely not by another man's rule of conduct, boasting in readiness.

17 But he that is boasting, he must be boasting in the Lord,

18 Because he that is commending himself is definitely not he that is approved, but definitely whom the Lord Commends.

Simplicity of God-Good

11 I would you are continuing enduring me a little while in unthinking foolishness, but definitely Continue Enduring with me.

2   I am earnestly desiring for you of God with God-Good Jealousy, because I have espoused you to one Husband, that I have Presented a Pure Virgin to Christ.

3   And I am not fearing as the serpent deceived Eve in his craftiness, in such a manner the Comprehensions of you might be made spiritually corrupt away from the Simplicity of God-Good Intentions in Christ.

4   Because, If actually there comes another preaching of the same kind Jesus that we have definitely not preached, or receiving another of a different kind Spirit that you have not taken to receive, or another Gospel of a different kind that you have definitely not received, you are Continuing Enduring God-Working.

5   For I account I be lacking nothing of the Chiefest Apostles.

6   But if also while unlearned in communication, but definitely not in Knowledge, but definitely in All Things we have made Manifest in Everything for the purpose and result of you.

7   I have Finalized sin nature and sin, humbling myself, in order that yourselves should be Made Exalted, because I have preached the Gospel of God to you without pay.

8   I have robbed others of the same kinds of Assemblies, taking wages, for Service (of Calling) to you.

9   And when I was present with you and lacking, I was definitely not burdensome to none because that lacking to me the Brothers coming from Macedonia have supplied, and in all things I have kept myself from being burdensome to you, and I will Hold as Sacred by my choice.

10 The Truth of Christ is in me. For definitely this rejoicing shall not be made sealed from me in these parts of Achaia.

11 Why then? Because I definitely God-Love you not? God is Knowing.

12 But what I Do, then I Do, that I should cut off an occasion for them strongly desiring an occasion that in their boasting, they should be made found just as also we,

Satan disguised as an Angel of light

13 For such false apostles, deceitful workers, transforming into apostles of Christ.

14 And definitely not a marvel, because the satan (rebeller) himself transforms into an angel of light.

15 Therefore, definitely not great, if also his servants are made transformed as servants of righteousness whose End shall be according to their man works.

Paul's suffering

16 I say again that not anybody should think me being mentally unwise, and then if not thought as mentally unwise you must receive me, that I might be joyful some little while.

17 That which I utter, I am definitely not uttering according to the Lord, but definitely as with an unthinking foolishness, in this Spiritual Being of rejoicing.

18 In fact many are boasting with the sinful flesh nature, I also shall boast.

19 For with pleasure being Very Wise you Continue Enduring with the mentally unwise.

20 For you Continue Enduring, if anyone enslaves you, if anyone devours, if anyone takes, if any man lifts up something for himself, if any man beats you on the face.

21 I say about dishonor, as that we have been weak, in that whoever then any might dare to say in unthinking foolishness, I also am daring.

22 Are they Hebrews? I also. Are they Israelites? I also. Are they Seed of Abraham? I also.

23 Are they servants of Christ? Utter fooling? I more! In behalf of labor earnestly, in wounds above measure, in prisons frequent, in deaths often,

24 By the Jews five times, I received forty save one,

25 Three times beaten with rods, once stoned, three times shipwrecked, a night and a day I have been in the ocean.

26 In travel often, in perils of floods, in perils of robbers, in perils by kindred, in perils by Gentiles, in perils in city, in perils in wilderness, in perils in sea, in perils among false Brethren,

27 In labor and grieving, in watchings often, in famine and thirst, in fastings often, in cold weather and nakedness.

28 Besides those things without, that which upon me daily, the care of all the Assemblies.

29 Who is weak and I am definitely not weak? Who is made offended and I definitely not being made burning?

30 If I must boast, I will boast of the things of my infirmities.

31 The God and Father of our Lord Jesus Christ, Who is Most Blessed Worthy of all Spiritual Perfection Forever, is now Knowing that I am definitely not lying.

32 In Damascus the local ruler under Aretas the king, protected the Damascenes city, strongly desiring to catch me,

33 And through a window, I was made let down in a basket through the wall, and Escaped his hands.

A man Caught Up to Glory

12 So now it is definitely not necessary for me to boast, because I will come to Visitations and Revelations of the Lord.

2 I Spiritually Know a man after fourteen years in Christ, whether in the body I am definitely not Spiritually Discerning, or outside the body I am definitely not Spiritually Discerning. God Spiritually Knows, such was made Caught Up to the Third Heaven.

3 And I Spiritual Know such a man, whether in body or outside the body, I definitely Know not. God Knows.

4 But he was made Caught Up into Paradise, and Heard Unspeakable Words, which is definitely not Lawful for man to Utter.

5 Of such I will boast in behalf of, but definitely not boast of myself, except in my

infirmities.

6 For though I should strongly desire to boast, I will definitely not be mentally unwise, because I will Spirit Say the Truth, but I am forbearing that not any about me should have been accounted above than that physically seen in me, or that any Heard from me.

Given a thorn in the flesh

7 And for my Excellency of the Revelations, in order that I should not exalt myself, I Was Given a disability of the sinful flesh nature, a messenger of the satan (rebeller) that he should command me, in order that I should not be made exalting myself.

8 For this I Beseeched the Lord three times, that it should depart away from me.

My Grace is Sufficient for you

9 And His Spirit Said to me, My Grace is Sufficient for you, because My Miracle Power is Made Perfect in infirmity. Most gladly, therefore, I will instead boast in my infirmities, in order that the Miracle Power of Christ might Rest Upon me by my choice.

10 For this reason I am pleased by my choice in infirmities, in traumas, in necessities, in persecutions, in distresses for Christ, for when I am weak, then I am Exceedingly Able.

Signs of Apostleship

11 I am becoming mentally unwise boasting. Yourselves have compelled me, because I was indebted by you to be Commending, yet to be behind in nothing of the Chiefest Apostles, allowing that also I am nothing.

12 Indeed the Miracle Signs of an Apostle have been Made Produced among you, in all Endurance, in Miracle Signs, and Wonders, and Miracle Powers.

13 For what is it, you were made overcome more than other Assemblies, except that I myself was definitely not burdensome to you? You must freely forgive me this unrighteousness.

I did not burden you, neither Titus

14 Behold the third time I have been ready to come to you, and definitely not be burdensome to you, for I am definitely not seeking yours, but definitely you, for the children ought definitely not to store up for the parents, but definitely the parents for the children.

15 And I will most gladly spend, and will be made spent for your souls, although when Earnestly I am Loving you, the less I am Made Loved.

16 But it must be so, I have definitely not burdened you, but definitely existing crafty, I took you with subtlety.

17 Have I not made a gain from you, by anybody of whom I sent out to you?

18 I have encouraged Titus, and sent together with him a Brother. Has Titus definitely not made a gain of you? Walked we definitely not in the same Spirit, also in the same steps?

Paul hopes they are Repentant

19 Again, are you thinking that we are proving innocence to you? Always, Oh Beloved, Before the Presence of God and in Christ, we Utter Edification in behalf of you.

20 Because I am afraid, fearing coming I might definitely not find you such as also I am preferring to find you, such as you would definitely not be fearing contentions, evil envyings, angers, strifes, slandering, whispering, arrogance, disorders.

21 That not coming again, my God might Humble me among you, and I will mourn many who sinning before, and not repented about their moral impurity, and fornication, and extreme irregular immorality which they have practiced.

Plans third visit, Warns about sin

13 This is the third time I am Coming to you. In the mouth of two or three witnesses every specific word shall Stand. (Deut 19:15)

2 I foretold and told before as being present the second time, and now being absent, I am writing to those sinning before and to all others. If I should come to you again I will definitely not spare.

3 In fact you are seeking a Proof of Christ Uttering in me, while to you He is definitely not weak, but definitely Controlling Inside you.

4 For even though He was made Crucified from infirmity, but definitely is Living by Miracle Power of God, and yet we also are weak in Him, but Live United with Him by Miracle Power of God toward you.

Examine yourselves

5 You must be Trying yourselves whether you are in the Faith. You must Prove in Truth yourselves. Are you definitely Fully Knowing how that Jesus Christ is Inside you, unless you are certain reprobates?

6 But I expect that you shall Know that we are being definitely not reprobates.

7 Now I wish to God that you do not any evil work, definitely not that we should be made to appear Approved, but definitely that yourselves Do God-Work, though we be as reprobates,

8 Because we can do nothing whatever against the Truth, but definitely in Behalf of the Truth.

9 For I am glad when we might be weak and yourselves might be Exceedingly Able, and this also I wish, for your Completion.

10 This because I am absent, I am writing in order that being present, I should not use sharpness according to the Authority which the Lord has given to me for Edification and definitely not for pulling down.

Finally Brethren, be Perfect

11 Finally, Brethren, rejoice, you must be Made Complete. You must be encouraged. Him you must Regard of value. You must be in Peace. God-Love of God and Peace shall be with you.

12 You must Greet one another with a Holy kiss.

Benediction

13 All the Saints Greet you.

14 The Grace of the Lord Jesus Christ, and the God-Love of God, and the Fellowship of the Holy Spirit (be) With You All. Amen.

[The second written to Corinthians from Philippi of Macedonia through Titus and Lucas]

The Epistle of Paul the Apostle to the

Galatians

An Apostle Called by Jesus Christ

1 Paul an Apostle, not of men, neither by man, but definitely through Jesus Christ and God the Father who Raised Him up out from the dead.

2 And all the Brethren with me, to the Assemblies of Galatia.

Sets us Free from this evil age

3 Grace to you and Peace from God the Father, and our Lord Jesus Christ.

4 Who Gave Himself in Behalf of our sin natures and sins, so that He might Set us Free from this present evil age, according to the Will of God and our Father.

5 To Whom the Glory Forever and ever. Amen.

I marvel that you strayed so soon

6 I marvel that you are so rapidly transferred from Him, that Outwardly Called (Gospel) you in the Grace of Christ, to another gospel of a different kind.

7 Which is not another of same kind, except there are some that are troubling you, and would replace the Gospel of Christ.

8 But definitely if we or an Angel from Heaven proclaims to you against the Good News Gospel Proclaimed to you, he must be continuously accursed. (1 Cor 15:1-8)

9 As we are Saying before, also I am Saying from now again, if any man proclaims to you another gospel, than that you have each Received, he must be continuously accursed.

10 Because Do I for now Persuade men or God? Or seek to please men? Yet, if I was more pleasing to men, I definitely would not ever be a Bondslave of Christ.

The Gospel is not from man

11 But I Make Known Supernaturally to you, Brethren, that the Gospel which has been made Preached by me, that it is definitely not according to man.

12 Because neither Have I Received along from man, nor have I been Made Taught, but definitely through Revelation of Jesus Christ.

13 Yet you have heard my behavior as in time past in Judaism, that as beyond measure, I used to be persecuting the Assembly of God, and used to be wasting them,

14 And used to be developed in Judaism, very much above equals in age among my kindred, existing earnestly zealous of traditions of my ancestral fathers.

15 But when it pleased God, who separated me from my mother's womb, and Outwardly Called (Gospel) through His Grace,

16 To reveal His Son in me, in order that I Preach His Gospel in the nations, immediately I conferred not with sinful flesh nature and blood,

17 Neither went I to Jerusalem to those Apostles before me, but definitely went to Arabia, and again returned to Damascus.

18 That after three years, I went to Jerusalem to get acquainted with Peter, and intended to continue with him fifteen days.

19 But another one of a different kind of the Apostles discerned I none, except James, the Brother of the Lord.

20 Now that which I am writing to you, Behold in the Presence of God, that I definitely lie not.

21 After that, I came into the parts of Syria and Cilicia.

22 And was unknown by face unto the Assemblies of Judaea in Christ.

23 Only that they were hearing how he that persecuted us as in time past, now Proclaimed the Faith, that as in time past he was wasting.

24 And they with me Attributed Glory to God.

After 14 years, Barnabas and I return

2 After that through fourteen years, again I ascended to Jerusalem with Barnabas, and also with taking Titus.
2 And according to Revelation I ascended and communicated to them that Gospel of a different kind that I am Preaching among the nations, but privately thinking to them fearing that I might run or have run in delusion,
3 But definitely, Titus a Greek who was with me, was not made compelled to be made circumcised,
4 And then because of the false Brethren secretly entering, who then entered in to spy our liberty that we have in Christ Jesus, that they might enslave us for themselves,
5 To whom we gave place by subjection not for an hour, that the Truth of the Gospel might continue constantly with you,
6 But from them, who were as in time past such a manner thinking they were being somebody, were definitely not excellent in value to me. God receives no man's person, for they who were thinking conferred nothing,

I to the Gentiles, Peter to the Jews

7 But definitely on the contrary, discerning that I am being now Committed to the Gospel of the uncircumcision, just as Peter of the circumcision.
8 For He that accomplished in Peter to Apostleship of the circumcision, accomplished also in me for the Gentiles.
9 And recognizing the Grace made given to me, James and Cephas and John, who are seeming to be pillars, gave the Right Hands of Fellowship to me and Barnabas, that we to the Gentiles, and they to the circumcision.
10 Only that we might be remembering of the poor. That I also have been diligent myself to do this,

But when Peter came, I blamed

11 But when Peter came to Antioch, I stood against to his face, for he was to be now made blamed,
12 Because before certain ones came from James, he was eating with the Gentiles, but when they came, he was drawing back and was separating himself, fearing them of the circumcision,
13 And the other Jews with him acted hypocritically also, so that Barnabas himself also was made misguided by their role playing hypocrisy.
14 But definitely, when I discerned that they are not Walking Honestly to the Truth of the Gospel, I spoke to Peter before all. If you a Jew are living existing like Gentiles, and not as do the Jews, Why are you compelling the Gentiles to do as the Jews?

Man not made Righteous by Law

15 We by nature Jews, and definitely not sinners of the Gentiles,
16 Knowing that a man is not Made Righteous from man works of the Law, except through Faith of Jesus Christ. Even we have Committed into Christ Jesus, in order that we have been Made Righteous by Faith of Christ, and definitely not by man works of Law, since any sinful flesh nature will not be Made Righteous from man works of Law,
17 But if we are Seeking to be Made Righteous in Christ, and when we have been Made Found sinners ourselves, has not Christ become a servant of sin nature? Not possible ever!
18 Because if these things have been torn down I am building again, I am commending myself a transgressor,
19 Because, I with the Law have Died by the Law, that I should Live to God,
20 I am made Crucified together with Christ, nevertheless I am Living, yet not anymore I, Christ is Living inside me. And that which is now living with sinful flesh nature, I am Living by the Faith of the

Son of God Who Loved me, and Delivered up Himself in Behalf of me. [Faith (God's Means) is Christ Within you (Heb 11:1, Col 1:27); His indwelling Mind of Christ in you after a New Birth from Above.]

21 I am not rejecting the Grace of God, because if Righteousness (came) by the Law, so then Christ Died without cause.

Uncomprehending Galatians

3 Oh, uncomprehending Galatians, who has by choice fascinated you, that you are not Made Persuaded by the Truth made written before your eyes? Jesus Christ is now made being Crucified inside you.

2 This only would I learn from you, Received you the Spirit from man works of the Law, or from Hearing of Faith?

3 Are you so uncomprehending? Having Started in the Spirit, are you now continuously performing for yourselves in sinful flesh nature?

4 Have you suffered so much without reason? If so be that without reason?

5 He that by your choice Fully Furnishes you the Spirit and by your choice Accomplishes Miracle Powers among you, then out from man works of Law or out from Hearing of Faith?

By Faith are Children of Abraham

6 Just as Abraham Committed by his choice to God, then he was made accounted Righteousness in Him.

7 So then, you are knowing that they out from Faith, they are sons of Abraham.

8 And then God Foreseeing that out from Faith, He is Making Righteous the nations. The Scriptures preached before the Gospel to Abraham, That All the nations shall be Made Blessed by you, (Gen 12:3)

9 So that they who of Faith are Made Blessed with the Faithful Abraham,

10 Because those out from within man works of Law are under a self curse, for it is now Made Written, Cursed all alike who are not persevering in all ways now being made written in the scroll of the Law to do them. (Deut 27:26)

No man is made Righteous by the Law

11 But because within the Law, he is not Made Righteous with God. Evident that the Righteous Live out from within Faith. (Hab 2:4)

12 And the Law is definitely not out from within Faith. But definitely the man that does them shall be living within them. (Lev 18:5)

13 Christ Purchased Out (from the satan's world) us from the self cursing of the Law, becoming a self cursing in Behalf of us. For It is now Made Written, cursed all that is hanging upon a Tree, (Deut 21:23)

14 That the blessing of Abraham for the nations should Come to pass within Christ Jesus, that the Promise of the Spirit should be Received through Faith.

Promises Made to Seed

15 Brethren, I say according to man, even if a Covenant is now Made Verified, no man rejects or adds.

16 Now to Abraham the Promise was Made Spirit Spoken then about his Seed saying, definitely not even as seeds in regard of many, but definitely as in regard of One, even as your Seed Who is Christ. (Gen 12:7-15; Gen 24:7)

17 And this I say, that the Covenant is now Made Confirmed before by God in Christ. That which after four hundred and thirty years becoming the Law is definitely not annulling to destroy the Promise.

18 For if the Inheritance out from the Law, no more out from the Promise, but God is now freely giving to Abraham through the Promise.

Promise by Faith of Jesus Christ

19 Where then the Law? It is made added more for this Cause of broken Commandments, until when the Seed should come to whom it is now Promised, having been

Appointed through means of Angels within the Hand of a Reconciler.

20 Now a Reconciler is not of one, but God is One.

21 Then the Law against the Promises of God? Not possible ever! Because if a Law had been Made Given, being Able to Offer Spiritual Life in fact, whatever used to be out from Law would be Righteousness. (Gal 3:24, 28-29; Col 1:27-29)

22 But definitely the Scripture has concluded all under sin nature and sin, in order that the Promise out from within Faith of Jesus Christ, should be Made Given to those Committing Continuously by their choice.

23 But before Faith came we were made protected under the Law, being enclosed to Faith Expected to be Made Revealed.

24 So that the Law is now by our choice Become our Schoolmaster for Christ, that we might be Made Righteous out from Faith.

25 But Faith has Come, we are Being no more under a Schoolmaster,

26 Because you are all Sons of God through Faith of Jesus Christ.

27 For as many as have been Made Immersed for the Purpose and Result of Christ have for ourselves Put on Christ.

28 There is no more Jew nor Gentile, there is not slave nor free, there is not male nor female, for you yourselves are One in Christ Jesus.

29 And if yourselves of Christ, so then you are Abraham's Seed, and Heirs according to Promise.

We Receive His Adoption of Sons

4 And now I say that the heir, an infant at that time, is not different in value than a slave. The Master being Above All,

2 But definitely is under Managers and Stewards until the Time Appointed by the Father.

3 And in such a manner, when we were infants we were being made slaves, under the basic elements of the satan's world.

4 But when the Fullness of Time was come, God Sent Forth His Son made of a woman being under the Law,

5 That He should have Purchased Out from under the Law, that we should have Fully Received the Adoption.

6 And because you are Sons, God has Sent Forth the Spirit of His Son into your hearts, Crying Out, Abba, Father.

7 So that you are no more a slave, but definitely a Son, and if a Son then an Heir of God through Christ.

How turned weak and beggarly?

8 But definitely then, actually not Spiritually Discerning God, you bondserved to them that by nature were not gods.

9 But now after that Knowing God, much more Made Known by God, how are you turning back again to the weak and beggarly basic elements, that you are from the beginning strongly desiring to be bondserving again?

10 You observe days and months and special times and specific years.

11 I am afraid for you, fearing that I am now laboring for you without reason.

12 Brethren, I am Praying earnestly for you. You must become as I, since I also as yourselves. You have definitely not hurt me.

13 And you discern that through infirmity of the sinful flesh nature, I preached to you at the first.

14 And my temptation in my sinful flesh nature, you definitely have not despised, neither fully rejected, but definitely you Received me as an Angel of God, as Jesus Christ.

15 Where then, was your blessedness? Because I am witnessing from you how, if possible, you would have given to me your removed eyes.

16 So that am I now being your enemy, Speaking the Truth to you?

17 They are fervently desiring you, definitely not God-Working, but definitely to have excluded you, in order that you might fervently desire them.

18 But God-Work always to be Made Fervently Desiring in God-Work, and not only when I be present with you.

19 My little children, for whom again, I am Travailing in birth until when Christ should be Made Formed in you.

20 So I was preferring to be present with you for now, but to change my voice, for I am perplexed by you.

Allegory of Hagar and Sara

21 You must say to me, you that prefer to be under the Law, are you definitely not hearing the Law?

22 For it is made written that Abraham had two sons, one out from the maid servant, and one out from the free.

23 But definitely he that actually is now made born out from the maid servant according to sinful flesh nature, but he out from the free, through the Promise,

24 Who is being made an allegory, for they are the two Covenants, one actually from Mount Sinai, being born for bondage of evil, who is Hagar.

25 For this Hagar is Mount Sinai in Arabia, and compares to Jerusalem, that now is bondserving with her children.

26 But Jerusalem Above is free, which is mother of us all.

27 Because it is now made written, Oh barren, you must have made merry definitely not giving birth. You must have been tearing, and you must have been loudly pleading definitely not travailing in birth, for many children of the desolate, than instead those having a husband. (Isa 54:1)

28 Now we, Oh Brethren, as Isaac, we are Being Children of Promise.

29 But definitely as then, He that was born according to sinful flesh nature was persecuting him having been made Born according to the Spirit, but also now in this same manner.

30 But definitely, what are the Scriptures saying, You must cast out the maid servant and her son, because the son of the maid servant should not inherit with the son of the free. (Gen 21:10)

31 So then, Brethren, we are being definitely not the children of the maid servant but definitely of the free.

Circumcision profits nothing

5 Therefore, you must be standing fast in the Liberty in which Christ has Made us Free, and you must not be made conflicting again with the yoke bondage of evil.

2 Behold, I Paul say to you, that if you might be made circumcised, Christ shall certainly profit you nothing.

3 For I bear witness again to every man circumcised, that he is a debtor to do the whole Law.

4 You have been made loosed from Christ, who by the Law are being made righteous. You have fallen from Grace,

5 Because we out from Faith through the Spirit are waiting in the Expectation of Righteousness.

6 Because in Christ Jesus neither circumcision is availing anything, nor uncircumcision, but definitely Faith is accomplishing through God-Love.

7 You used to be Running God-Working, who has beaten you back? You are not Made to be Confident in the Truth.

8 This persuasion definitely not from Him that is Outwardly Calling (Gospel) to you.

9 A smallest leaven leavens the whole lump. (If not absolutely Pure and Perfect, 1 Cor 5:6-8)

10 I have confidence in you by the Lord, that you shall not regard of value another of the same kind, but he that is troubling you shall bear his judgment; whoever that one might be.

11 And I, Brethren, if I still preach circumcision (of the Law), why am I still made persecuted, so then is now the offense of the cross made destroyed?

12 I would that they disturbing you shall be now cut away.

13 Because, Oh Brethren, yourselves only have been made Outwardly Called (Gospel) in Liberty, not for occasion to the sinful flesh nature, but definitely through God-Love you must by your choice be Continuously Bondserving one another.

14 Because all the Law is being made Fulfilled in one Word, in this, You shall God-Love your neighbor as yourself. (Lev 19:18)

15 But if you bite and devour one another, you must see that you might not be made consumed by one another.

Walk in the Spirit, not under the Law

16 For this I say, you must Walk in the Spirit, and never ever finally fulfill evil desire of sinful flesh nature.

17 Because the sinful flesh nature is evilly desiring by your choice against the Spirit, and the Spirit against the sinful flesh nature, and these things are adverse one to another, that whatever you might not be willing by your choice, these things you might do by your choice.

18 But if you are being Made Led by the Spirit, you are definitely not under the Law.

19 Now the man works of the sinful flesh nature are openly manifest, which is adultery, fornication, moral impurity, extreme irregular immorality,

20 Idolatry, assistance by evil spirits (via any method including drugs), hatreds, contentions, evil jealousies, angers, strifes, oppositions, heresies,

21 Envyings, murders, drunkennesses, revelings, and the like. These things, that I am telling before to you, just as also I forewarn this, that they who practice such shall definitely not Inherit the Kingdom Rule of God.

The Fruits of the Spirit

22 But the Fruit of the Spirit is God-Love, Joy, Peace, Longsuffering, Gentleness, Goodness, Faith,

23 Meekness, Self Control; against such there is no Law.

24 And they that are of Christ Have Crucified the sinful flesh nature, united with the sufferings and the evil desires.

25 If we Live in the Spirit, we should also Walk Orderly in the Spirit.

26 We should not be desiring praise to self, challenging for ourselves one another, envying by our choice one another.

Be not deceived; what man Sows

6 Brethren, yet if a man should have been taken before in any spiritual death offense, yourselves that are Spiritual must Reinstate such in the Spirit of Meekness. Take heed to yourself, you might not have been made tempted also.

2 You must bear one another's heavy weights, and in such a manner you must Have Satisfied the Law of Christ.

3 For if any man is thinking he is being something, he is nothing. He is mentally misleading himself.

4 But every man must Prove in Truth his own Work by God, and then he shall have happiness in himself alone, and not in another of a different kind.

5 For every man shall bear his own burden.

6 But him that is Made Continuously Informing must be a Sharer of the Word, Continuously Informing in All God-Good things.

7 You must not be made deceived. God is not to be made laughed at, because whatever a man should sow, this also he shall reap.

8 For he that sows for the purpose and result of his own sinful flesh nature, shall reap from the sinful flesh nature Eternal death. But he that Sows for Purpose and Result of the Spirit, shall Reap from the Spirit Eternal Life.

9 For Finalizing God-Work, we should not be wearying for the Special Time, because not being made discouraged, we shall be privately Reaping.

10 Therefore, so then as we are having time, we should be Working the God-Good

to all, specifically then to the Household members of Faith.

11 You Must Discern how Important a letter I have Written to you, with my hand.

12 Those who shall show off in their sinful flesh nature, they would compel you to be made circumcised, only that they might not be made persecuted for the Cross of Christ.

13 For neither they themselves being circumcised maintain the Law, but definitely are desiring you to be made circumcised, in order that they might be joyful in your sinful flesh nature.

14 But it not become possible ever that I am boasting, except in the Cross of our Lord Jesus Christ, by whom the satan's world is now made Crucified to me, also I to the satan's world.

We are a New Creature

15 Because in Christ Jesus, neither circumcision avails anything nor uncircumcision, but definitely a New of a Different Kind Creation.

16 But those who will Walk Orderly with this Rule of Conduct, Peace upon them, and Mercy, and upon the Israel of God.

17 Henceforth, he must not be offering concern to me for labor, because I bear the scars of the Lord Jesus in my body.

18 Brethren, the Grace of our Lord Jesus Christ with your spirit. Amen.

[Written to Galatia from Rome]

The Epistle of Paul the Apostle to the

Ephesians

A Greeting by Paul

1 Paul, Apostle of Jesus Christ, by the Will of God, to the Saints who are being in Ephesus, and to the Faithful in Christ Jesus.

2 Grace to you and Peace, from God our Father, and the Lord Jesus Christ.

All Spiritual Blessings by Christ

3 Most Blessed Worthy of all Spiritual Perfection, the God and Father of our Lord Jesus Christ, Who has Blessed us with all Spiritual Blessing in the Heavenlies in Christ.

4 Just as He actually for Himself has Chosen us inside Himself, before the Conception of the satan's world, for us to be Holy and Faultless Before the Presence of Him by God-Love.

5 Having by His choice Predetermined us for Adoption through Jesus Christ to Himself, according to the God-Good Intention of His Will.

6 To Full Praise of Glory of His Grace, wherein He has Made us Highly Favored among those now being Made God Loving.

7 In Whom we have Separation Removal through His Blood, the Removal of spiritual death offenses, according to the Riches of His Grace.

8 Wherein He has Abounded in amount toward us in all Wisdom and Intelligence.

Made Known to us the Mystery

9 Having Made Known Supernaturally to us the Mystery of His Will, according to His God-Good Intentions which He has Purposed in Himself.

10 For the Stewardship of the Fullness of times, briefly comprehended, that all things are within Christ, both in Heavenlies and those things on the earth.

11 In Him with Whom also we Have Obtained an Inheritance, having Made Predetermined according to the Purpose

of Him, Who is Accomplishing All things, by the Counsel of His Will.

12 For we, to be for the Full Praise of His Glory, who are first continuously by our choice Expecting in Christ.

13 In Whom yourselves have also Heard the Word of Truth, the Gospel of your Salvation, in Whom also after you by your choice have Committed, you were Made Sealed with that Holy Spirit of Promise,

14 Who is the Down Payment of our Inheritance, for the Separation Removal of the Possession, for Full Praise of His Glory.

Spirit of Wisdom and Revelation

15 Because of this, also I have heard about your Faith of the Lord Jesus, and the God-Love for all the Saints,

16 I am not ever ceasing Giving Thanks in behalf of you, making mention of you in my Prayers.

17 That the God of our Lord Jesus Christ, the Father of Glory, should Give to you the Spirit of Wisdom and Revelation in the Full Knowledge of Him.

18 The Eyes of your intellect for your Spiritual Discerning are being Made Enlightened, that He has the Expectation of His Service of Calling, and what the Riches of the Glory of His Inheritance in the Saints.

And Greatness of His Power to us

19 Also what is the Excelling in Quality in Greatness of His Miracle Power to us who are Committing, according to the Effectual Working of the Dominion of His Strength.

20 Which He Accomplished in Christ, Raising Him Up Out from the Dead, and He Sat Down by His Right Hand in the Heavenlies.

21 Far Above any ruler and authority and miracle power and lordship, and every name being named, not only in this Age, but definitely in That Expecting.

22 And has Subjected all things under His Feet, and He has been Given Head above all things to the Assembly,

23 Who is His Body, the Fullness of All Things in every way Being Fulfilled.

We were dead in offenses and sins

2 And yourselves being dead for the spiritual death offenses and the sin natures and sins,

2 Wherein as in time past then you have walked according to the Age with this the satan's world, according to the ruler of the authority of the air, the spirit that now is continuously accomplishing in the sons of disobedience.

3 Among whom, also, we all have behaved in time past by the evil desires of our sinful flesh nature, fulfilling the will of the sinful flesh nature and of the intellects, and were by nature children of evil wrath, same as others.

But God-Love Quickened us

4 But God being Rich in Mercy, because of His very much God-Love, with which He Loved us,

5 Even when we were dead in spiritual death offenses, He has Quickened Together with Christ. You are now being Made Saved by Grace. [Grace (God's Method) is Christ Within you (Faith, God's Means; Heb 11:1, Col 1:27), through your Obedience, Doing what you cannot Do.]

6 And has Raised (Us) Up Together, then Sit (Us) Together in the Heavenlies in Christ Jesus.

7 That in the Ages to come upon (us), He should exhibit the Excelling in Quality the Riches of His Grace in Gentleness to us in Christ Jesus.

8 For by Grace you are now being made Saved through Faith, and This definitely not out from yourselves, the Gift of God (Himself in you),

9 Definitely not out from man works, in order that not any man might boast.

God-Good Works of God

10 For We are Being His Workmanship, Being Made Created in Christ Jesus in The Way of God-Good Works by God, Which God before Prepared, that we should Walk In Them.

Gentiles and Jews now United

11 For this reason, yourselves must remember that yourselves, as in time past, Gentiles in the sinful flesh nature, called uncircumcision by them called circumcision, made with hands in sinful flesh nature.

12 That in that time you were without Christ, being made aliens of the citizenship of Israel, and strangers of the Covenants of Promise, having no expectation, and without God in the satan's world.

13 But just now in Christ Jesus, yourselves who as in time past were far off, have become Near by the Blood of Christ.

14 For He is our Peace, Who has Made Both One, and has Removed the Middle Wall of partition.

Abolished in His flesh, all enmity

15 Having Destroyed in His (Sinless) Flesh Nature the enmity of the Law of the Commandments with Ordinances, that He should create the two in One New of a Different Kind Man in Himself, Finalizing Peace.

16 That He should Fully Reconcile Both Together in One Body to God, by the cross, having Killed the Enmity in Himself.

17 And Coming, He Proclaimed Peace to you far off and near.

Foundation of Apostles and Prophets

18 That through Him, we Both Together are having Access by One Spirit to the Father.

19 So then, therefore you are no more strangers and foreigners, but definitely Fellow Citizens of the Saints and Household Members of God.

20 Built up, on the Foundation of the Apostles and Prophets of Jesus Christ

Himself, Being the Chief Corner Stone,

21 In Whom all the Building is being Made Tightly Joined Together, Growing into a Holy Temple in the Lord.

You are a Habitation of God

22 In Whom also yourselves are being Made Built Together for a Habitation of God in the Spirit.

Revelation Made Known to me

3 For this cause I Paul, the prisoner of Christ Jesus, in Behalf of you, the Gentiles,

2 If so be that you have heard of the Stewardship of the Grace of God, which is Given to me for you.

3 How according to Revelation, He has Made Known to me the Mystery, just as I wrote before a little therein.

The Mystery of Christ

4 To those able to read, to Comprehend my Understanding in the Mystery of Christ.

5 Which in another of different kind generations, it has not been Made Known Supernaturally to sons of man, as now Made Revealed by His Holy Apostles and Prophets by the Spirit.

6 The Gentiles to be Fellow Heirs and even of the same Body, and Partners Together of His Promise by Christ in the Gospel.

7 In Which I have Become a Servant, according to the God-Gift of the Grace of God Given to me, according to the Effectual Working of His Miracle Power.

Fellowship of the Mystery

8 To me, who am less than least of all the Saints, Given His Grace to Preach the Gospel among the Gentiles, the Unsearchable Riches of Christ.

9 And to Enlighten all about the Fellowship of the Mystery, that has been made Concealed from the Age by God, Who has Created all things by Jesus Christ.

10 In order that now the manifold Wisdom

of God might be Made Known from the Beginning, even by the Partakers of Authority of the Heavenlies in the Assembly.

11 According to Purpose of the Age, which has been Finalized in Christ Jesus our Lord.

12 In Whom we Have Boldness and Access in Confidence with the Faith by Him.

13 For this reason I am Asking not to be wearied, in these my afflictions in Behalf of you, which is your Glory.

Miracle-Power for Inner Man

14 For this That Cause I bow my knees to the Father of our Lord Jesus Christ.

15 Out from Whom the Whole Family in Heavenlies and upon earth is Made Named.

16 That He might Give to you, according to the Riches of His Glory, to be Made Strong with Miracle Power through His Spirit, for the Purpose of the Inner Man.

Christ in your hearts by Faith

17 That Christ Dwell by Faith in your hearts now being Made Rooted in God-Love and being Made a Grounded Foundation. (1 Cor 3:10-13)

18 In order that yourselves should have by your choice been Enabled to Apprehend, United with all the Saints, what the Width and Length and Depth and Height,

19 And Mutually to Know God-Love, the Excelling in Quality of the Knowledge of Christ, that you might be made Fully Filled in all the Fullness of God.

20 And now to Him More Able Above All, to Accomplish More in Excess than of what we ask or comprehend, according to the Miracle Power Accomplishing Inside us.

21 To Him the Glory in the Assembly by Christ Jesus, for all the generations of the Age of the Ages. Amen.

Only One Body and One Spirit

4 I, therefore, the prisoner in the Lord, am Encouraging you to Walk Worthily of the Service of Calling in which you have been Made Outwardly Called (Gospel),

2 With all Humility, and Meekness with Longsuffering, Continuing Enduring one to another in God-Love.

3 Being diligent to Keeping the Unity of the Spirit in the Uniting Bond of Peace.

4 There is One Body and One Spirit, just as also you have been Made Outwardly Called (Gospel), in One Expectation of your Service of Calling.

5 One Lord, One Faith, One Immersion.

6 One God and Father Over All, Who is Above All, and Through All, and In You All. [All refers to those Saints and Faithful in Christ Jesus, to whom this is written, Eph 1:1]

Each Given a Measure of God-Gifts

7 And by One, every person of us have been made Given the Grace, according to the Amount of Measure of the God-Gift by Christ.

8 For this reason, it Says, Ascending to On High, He Captured Captivity, and Gave Spiritual Gifts to men. (Ps 68:18)

9 And He that is Ascended, What is He, except He that also first of all Came Down into the lower parts of the earth?

10 He that Came Down, He is also He that Ascended Far Above All Heavenlies that He might Fully Fill All things.

11 And He indeed Gave some Apostles and some Prophets and some Evangelists and some Shepherds, and also Teachers.

12 For the Perfecting of the Saints, for the Work by God in Service (of Calling), for the Edification of the Body of Christ,

13 Until we All Achieve to the Unity of Faith, and the Full Knowledge of the Son of God, to the Perfect Man, to a measure of Stature of age of the Fullness of Christ.

Speak Truth in Love

14 That we no longer should be infants, tossing back and forth, and made carrying about with every wind of doctrine, by the trickery of men in craftiness, with their method of deception.

15 But Speaking by our choice the Truth in God-Love, we should by our choice Grow into Him in All things, Who is the Head, the Christ.

16 From Whom the Whole Body Tightly Joined Together, and made Confirming Together, through the Supply of every ligament according to the Effectual Working of One in the amount of Measure to Every particular Person, Making the Growth of the Body, Building of Itself in God-Love.

Walk not as other Gentiles walk

17 This I say, therefore, and bear witness in the Lord, You no longer walk, just as after other Gentiles walk, in self importance of their understanding of mind.

18 With their intellect being now made darkened, being now made alienated of the Life of God, through the ignorance that is in them, because of the blindness of their heart,

19 Who being now past feeling have delivered up themselves to extreme irregular immorality, for gain from diligence of moral impurity, every way by greediness.

Put off the old man, be in the Spirit

20 But yourselves have definitely not, in such a manner, Learned Christ.

21 If so be that you have Heard Him, and have been Made Taught by Him, just as Truth is in Jesus.

22 To Put Off yourselves with the former behavior the old man, which is made spiritually corrupt, according to the evil desires of deceitfulness,

23 And to be Made Renewing in the Spirit of Understanding of your mind.

24 And to Put On the New Man of a Different Kind, that by God has been Made Created in Righteousness, and State of Holiness of Truth.

25 For this reason, Putting Away lying, every man must Utter Truth with his neighbor, for we are Being members one of another.

26 When you must be made angry, you must not sin. You must not allow the sun to go down upon the provoked anger of you.

27 Neither must you be giving place to the devil.

28 He that is stealing, you must no longer steal, instead, as you must now labor, working with his hands something God-Good, in order that he might be having to impart to him that has need.

29 Not any corrupt spiritual communication must go out from your mouth, but definitely if any God-Good to Edification of the needful, that it might give Grace to those hearing.

30 And you must not grieve the Holy Spirit of God, in Whom you have been Made Sealed for the Day of Separation Removal.

31 You must take away from yourselves all bitterness, and anger, and evil wrath, and screaming, and blasphemy, united with all malicious desire for evil work.

32 And you must be Kind to one another, tenderhearted, freely forgiving to our own, just as also God by Christ Freely Forgave us.

Let no man deceive you

5 Therefore, you must be Close Followers of God, as Beloved children.

2 And Walk in God-Love just as also Christ has Loved us and Delivered Up Himself in Behalf of us, an Offering and Sacrifice to God for odor of sweet Savor.

3 But fornication, and all moral impurity, or greediness, neither let it be named among you, just as is appropriate for Saints.

4 Nor filthy obscenity, no mindless talking, or jesting that are definitely not being appropriate, but definitely instead Thankfulness.

5 Yet this you must be now knowing, that every fornicator, or morally impure, or greedy who is an idolater, definitely has no Inheritance in the Kingdom Rule of Christ or God.

6 You must let no man deceivingly seduce you with delusional spiritual words, because through these things is coming

the Wrath for Justice of God upon the sons of disobedience.

Fruit of the Spirit is our Light

7 You must not be, therefore, partners together with them.

8 Because you were darkness in time past, but now Light in the Lord, you must be Walking as Children of Light.

9 Because the Fruit of the Spirit, in all Goodness and Righteousness and Truth,

10 Proving in Truth what is Well Pleasing to the Lord.

11 And you must not be participating in the unfruitful man works of darkness, but instead you Must then Expose as sin.

12 Because the private occurrings by them are morally shameful, even to say.

13 But all things are being Made Exposed as sin by the Light, all things are Made Manifested because the Light is Making Manifest.

14 For this reason He Says, You must be Risen Up you that are natural sleeping, even as you Must Have Arisen out from the dead, and Christ shall Give Light to you.

Walk Wise, Understand His Will

15 You must be Spiritually Seeing then how exactly you are Walking, not as unwise but definitely as Wise.

16 Purchasing Out from the satan's world the Special Time, for the days are evil.

17 Because of this you must become not mentally unwise, but definitely Understand about the Will of the Lord.

18 And be not made drunken with wine in having some partying, but definitely you must be Made Fully Filled with the Spirit.

19 Uttering to yourselves Psalms and Hymns and Singing in the Spirit Spiritual Songs, even Singing Melodies in your heart to the Lord.

20 Giving Thanks Always in Behalf of all things to God and Father in the Name of our Lord Jesus Christ.

21 Being made Subject one to another in Fear of God.

Marriage is As Assembly to Christ

22 Wives, you must be for yourselves Continuously Subjecting to your own husbands as to the Lord.

23 For the husband is head of the woman, as also Christ Head of the Assembly, and He is Savior of the Body.

24 But definitely as the Assembly is Subject to Christ, in same manner also, the wife to her own husband in All things.

25 Husbands you must by your choice be Continuously God-Loving your own wife, just as also Christ Loved the Assembly, and Delivered up Himself in Behalf of it,

26 That He might Make Holy Cleansing by the Washing of the Water in the Word.

27 That He might Present it to Himself, an Assembly of Spiritual Perfection, not having a dirty spot, nor wrinkle, or any of such, but definitely in order that it should be Holy and Faultless.

28 In same manner ought the husbands to be Loving their wives, as their own bodies. He that is Loving his own wife is Loving by his Deliberate Choice.

29 Because as in time past, definitely no man has hated his own flesh nature, but definitely nurtures and cherishes it, just as also the Lord the Assembly.

30 For we are being Members of His Body, out from Within His (Sinless) Flesh Nature and out from Within His Bones.

31 For this, a man shall leave his father and mother and he shall certainly cling to his wife, and they, the two, for the purpose of sinful flesh nature, shall be one.

32 This is a great Mystery, but I say for the Purpose of Christ and for the Assembly.

33 But also yourselves according to this One, every man by himself must in same manner God-Love his wife as Himself, so that the wife should be Fearing her husband.

Children and Dads

6 Children, you Must Obey your parents wherein the Lord, because this is Righteous.

2 You must Honor your dad (Matt 23:9) and mother, which is the first in sequence

Commandment with Promise,
(Mark 12:29-30)
3   In order that it might be well with you,
and you shall Live a long time upon the earth.
4   And the dads, you must not provoke
your children to anger, but definitely you
must nurture them in Discipline and
Warning of the Lord. (Col 3:21)

Slaves, be obedient to your lords
5   Bondslaves, you must obey the masters
in sinful flesh nature with fear and trembling, in a Simplicity of God-Good Intentions of your heart as for Christ,
6   Not with pleasing to sight as men pleasers, but definitely as Bondslaves of Christ,
doing the Will of God out from the soul.
7   With Kind acts bondserving as to the
Lord and definitely not man.
8   Spiritually Discerning that if any
whatever God-Good every person should
do, this you shall earn from the Lord,
whether slave or free.
9   And, you lords, do the same to them
yourselves, refraining from threatening,
Spiritually Discerning also that the Master
of you Himself is in the Heavenlies, and definitely has no respect of persons with Him.

Be Strong in God's Armor
10 And now, my Brethren, you Must be
More Strengthened in the Lord, and in His
Dominion, and Strength.
11 You Must Put On All the Armor of
God, for you to be Able to Stand Against
the methods of the devil.
12 For it is not for us, wrestling against
blood and sinful flesh nature, but definitely Against the rulers, Against the authorities, Against the world rulers of darkness
of this age, Against the spiritual evil action
in the heavenlies of earth.
13 Because of this, you Must Receive Up
All the Armor of God, that you should be
Made Able to Stand Against in the day of
evil, yet Having Produced All, To Stand.
14 You Must Stand by your choice,

therefore, Clothed for yourself about your
waist in Truth, and Having Put On for
yourself the Breastplate of Righteousness,
15 And your feet being Covered with the
Instruction of the Gospel of Peace.
16 Above All, Receive Up the Shield of
Faith (Christ inside you), with Whom you
shall be Able to Extinguish All the burning
arrows of evil.
17 And you Must Receive the Helmet of
Salvation, and the Sword of the Spirit, that
is the Word of God.

Praying Always in the Spirit for All
18 By Praying Always with all Prayer and
Supplication in the Spirit, and Being Alert
in this Special Time for yourself, in all
Perseverance and Supplication For All the
Saints.

Paul to Make Known the Mystery
19 And for me, that Spiritual Communication has been Made Given to me, that by
opening my mouth in Boldness, to Make
Known Supernaturally the Mystery of the
Gospel,
20 For which I am an Ambassador in
chain, that therein I myself should Speak
Boldly, as I ought to Utter.

Paul's Farewell
21 But that yourselves also should be now
Spiritually Discerning All things about me,
that I am practicing, Tychicus, my Beloved
Brother and Faithful servant in the Lord,
shall Make All things Known to you,
22 Whom I have sent to you for this same
thing, that you might know the things
about us, and he might encourage your
hearts.
23 Peace to the Brethren, and God-Love
with Faith, from God the Father and the
Lord Jesus Christ.
24 Grace with All them that God-Love
our Lord Jesus Christ in Incorruption.

[*To Ephesians written from Rome*]

The Epistle of Paul the Apostle to the

Philippians

Paul and Timothy to the Saints

1 Paul and Timothy, Bondslaves of Jesus Christ, to all the Saints in Christ Jesus who are in Philippi, with Overseers and Servants.

2 Grace to you and Peace from God our Father and the Lord Jesus Christ.

I thank God for you

3 I Give Thanks to my God upon every mention of you.

4 Always in every Supplication of mine for you all, making Supplication with Joy.

5 For your Fellowship in the Gospel, from the first day until now.

6 Having this confidence yourself, that He starting a God-Good Work by God in you, He shall perform it until the Day of Jesus Christ.

7 Just as it is Righteous for me to regard of value this in behalf of all of you, because I have you in my heart, mutually in my bonds, and for the Defense and Establishment of the Gospel. You are all being Partakers of my Grace.

8 Because God is my witness, as I greatly desire you all alike, in Compassion of Jesus Christ,

Love in Full Knowledge and Seeing

9 And this I am Praying, that your God-Love further much more, and should be continuously much more Abounding in amount in Full Knowledge and with All Perception.

Prove in Truth what is Excellent

10 That you Prove in Truth, those things being excellent in value, that you should be sincere and without offense until the Day of Christ.

11 Being now made Fully Filled with Fruits of Righteousness by Jesus Christ, for the Glory and Full Praise of God.

My bonds encourage Preaching

12 I am Knowing that you, Oh Brethren, are Intending this much more upon me for the advancement of the Gospel now Coming.

13 So that my bonds in Christ have become Openly Manifest in all of the Judgment Hall, and in all remaining places.

14 And many more of the Brethren in the Lord are now being Reassured in my bonds, Earnestly daring Without Fear to be Uttering the Word.

15 Some indeed, also through envy and contention, and some then by God-Good Intentions, preaching Christ.

16 Some are actually much proclaiming Christ out from strife, definitely not sincerely, assuming to introduce affliction to my bonds.

17 But the other out from God-Love, Spiritually Discerning that I am being Positioned for the Defense of the Gospel.

18 What yet? But in all manner, whether in pretense or Truth, Christ is now made proclaimed much, and in this I am rejoicing, but definitely also I will be made rejoicing.

19 Because, I am now discerning through your Supplications and Supply of the Spirit of Jesus Christ, that this shall turn out to my Salvation.

20 According to my earnest Expectation and my prospect, that in nothing I will definitely not be made disgraced, but definitely in All Boldness as always. Also now, I magnify Christ in my body whether through Life, or through death.

Living to Christ, to die is Gain

21   Because to me to Live, (is) Christ, and to die, (is) Gain.

22   But if I live in sinful flesh nature, this fruit of man work to me. But I am making known Supernaturally what I will for myself personally Choose.

23   Because I am made constrained by the two, having by choice a Desire to be Removed, then United with Christ to be very much more the Best.

24   Nevertheless, necessary to Continue with Intent in the sinful flesh nature because of yourselves.

25   And I am now having confidence of this, I am now Discerning why I will Abide, and will Continue with you, for the Advancement of yourselves with Joy and Faith,

26   That your happiness should be Abounding in amount in Christ Jesus with me through my Coming again to you,

Not only to Commit, but to suffer

27   Only, you must be Prevailing Worthily of the Gospel of Christ, that whether I am Coming and Discerning you or being absent, I should Hear this about you, that you are Standing Fast in one Spirit, one soul, Striving Together in the Faith of the Gospel.

28   And in nothing, no more being made terrified by those being adverse, which to them is actually a declaration of damnation, but of Salvation to you and This from God.

29   For to you it has been Made Freely Given in Behalf of Christ, not only to be Continuously Committing to Him, but definitely also to be Continuously suffering in Behalf of Him.

30   Having the same conflict such as you have Spiritually Discerned in me, and now are Hearing by me.

Lowliness of mind, esteem each more

2   Therefore, if any Encouragement in Christ, if any Comfort of God-Love, if any Fellowship of the Spirit, if any Compassion and Sympathy,

2   You must Fulfill my Joy, that you should regard Him of Value, Continuously having His God-Love, United as One, regarding of Value the One.

3   Nothing according to strife or self conceit, but definitely with humility, esteeming one another being superior to yourselves.

4   You must not look every man to himself, but definitely everyone also to the things of others of a different kind.

5   For this among yourselves, you must be Made Regarding of Value These also in Christ Jesus.

Himself came in form of a slave

6   Who, existing in the Spiritual form of God, Esteemed it not robbery to be Equal with God,

7   But definitely He Himself made empty, having taken in Likeness for the form of a slave, He became a Man.

8   And being made found in fashion as a man, He Humbled Himself becoming for Himself Obedient as far as to Death, even Death of a cross.

Confess Jesus Christ is Lord

9   And for this reason, God has Elevated Him to the Highest, and Freely Gave to Him, the Name more Above every Name,

10   That by the Name of Jesus, every knee should Bow in the Heavenlies, and of the earthly, and (those) under the earth.

11   And every tongue should Acknowledge this Jesus Christ, Lord, for the Glory of God, the Father.

Produce your Salvation with Fear

12   So that, Oh my Beloved, just as you have Always Obeyed, as not in my Coming Only, but definitely instead now very much More in My Absence, you Must be Continuously by your choice Producing your own Salvation, with Fear and Trembling.

13   Because it is God Himself Accomplishing

Inside you, both to Will and to Accomplish, in behalf of His God-Good Intentions.

Blameless, Harmless Sons of God

14　You must be Doing All Things, continuously by your choice, without murmurings and doubtings.

15　In order that you should become by your choice Blameless and Harmless, Children of God Without Fault, in the midst of a crooked and made perverted generation, you are among those Continuously Made Appearing as Lights of God in the satan's world.

16　Giving Heed continuously to the Spiritual Word of Life, for Happiness to me in the Day of Christ, that I have not run by my choice, neither labored in empty delusion.

17　But definitely, if also I be Made Offering in Sacrifice and Service to God, for your Faith, I am Glad and Rejoicing together with you.

18　For the same, even yourselves must be Rejoicing, and you must Rejoice Together with me.

All seek their own, not of Christ

19　Now, I am Expecting in the Lord Jesus to rapidly send Timothy to you, that I also should be Comforted to know about you.

20　Because I have no man having of same Mind who genuinely shall Take Thought concerning you.

21　For all are seeking their own, definitely not the Things of Christ Jesus.

22　But you are Knowing the Proof of him, that as a child with a father, he has Bondserved with me in the Gospel.

23　Him, therefore, I am certainly expecting to send, as I should speedily Attentively look about me.

24　But I have Confidence in the Lord, that yet I myself shall Come rapidly.

25　Yet I have esteemed necessary to send to you Epaphroditus, my Brother and Fellow Laborer, and my Fellow Soldier, and your Apostle, and God's Servant of my need.

26　For after that he was greatly desiring after you all, and being very sad since you heard that he has been sick.

27　For he was sick even near death, but definitely God Gave Mercy to him, and not to him only, but definitely also to me, that I might not possibly have grief upon grief.

28　I, therefore, sent him more diligently, that Spiritually Discerning him again, you should have been Made Glad. Also I should be without grief.

29　Therefore, you must be looking for him in the Lord with all Joy, that you should have such More Honorable.

30　Because for the Work by God of Christ, as far as he was approaching near death, disregarding his soul, in order that he might occupy your lacking of Service to God for me.

See the unholy and evil workers

3　And now, Oh Brethren, I must rejoice in the Lord. To write these same things to you, to me actually not lazy, but to you safe.

2　You must Spiritually See the dogs (unholy people). You must Spiritually See the evil works workers. You must Spiritually See the legal circumcision.

3　Because we are Being the Circumcision, Devoting to the Spirit of God, and being Joyful in Christ Jesus, and definitely not having confidence in sinful flesh nature.

4　Even though I have confidence also by sinful flesh nature, if any man other of same kind thinks to be having confidence in sinful flesh nature, I much more.

5　Circumcised eighth day, of kindred of Israel, to tribe of Benjamin, an Hebrew of Hebrews, according to the Law, a Pharisee.

6　According to evil zeal, persecuting the Assembly, according to righteousness which is in the Law, am blameless.

I count all loss for Knowing Christ

7　But what things were gain to me, these things I am now esteeming being damaged loss for Christ.

8　But definitely rather I esteemed

all things being damaged loss, for the Knowledge of Christ Jesus my Lord being Supreme, for Whom I have suffered loss of all things, Esteeming them a dunghill, in order that I may Gain Christ.

Not own righteousness of Law

9   That I should be Made Found with Him not having my righteousness from the Law, but definitely through Christ's Faith, the Righteousness of God in The Way of His Faith (Mind of Christ in you, 1 Cor 2:16).

10 That to Know Him, and the Miracle Power of His Resurrection, and the Fellowship of His suffering, being Made Conformable to His Death,

11 If how in the event I might Achieve to the Resurrection out from the dead.

Not already Received but I Follow

12 Not that I have already Received, nor am now Made Perfect already, but I Follow closely, if that I should Apprehend to that, which also I have been Made Apprehended by Jesus Christ.

13 Oh Brethren, I am definitely not accounting myself to be Now Apprehending. But one thing, forgetting the things back, I am Reaching Out to that before.

I Follow the High Calling of Christ

14 I Follow Closely after the Goal for the Prize of the Above Service of Calling of God within Christ Jesus.

15 Therefore, as many as (are) Perfect, we should be by our choice continuously Regarding of value This, and if anybody regards of value differently, God shall Reveal even This to you.

16 But we have already Attained to This, to be Continuously Walking Orderly by the same Rule of Conduct, to be Regarding of Value the same thing.

Be Followers of me

17 Brethren, you must be Imitators Together of me, and mark them who are Walking in such a manner, just as you are Having us for a Model.

18 Because many walk, whom I was saying to you often, even now I am saying weeping, that they are enemies of the cross of Christ.

19 Whose End damnation, whose god their belly, and they who regard of value earthly things, who glory in their shame,

Our Citizenship is in Heaven!

20 Because our True Citizenship is Existing in the Heavenlies, from which also, we are Waiting for the Savior, the Lord Jesus Christ.

21 Who shall Transform the Body of our lowliness for the result to become ourselves Conformed to the Body of His Glory, according to the Effectual Working of Him to be Able Himself also to Subject All Things to Himself.

Stand Fast in the Lord, Yoke-fellows

4 So that, Oh Brethren, my Beloved and Longed for, my Joy and Crown, in this manner you must Stand Fast in the Lord, Oh Beloved.

2   I encourage Euodias and I encourage Syntyche, that they be Regarding of value themselves in the Lord.

3   And I am earnestly requesting of you also, Oh Truthful Yoke-fellow, you must physically help those women that Strive Together in the Gospel with me, also Clement and the remaining Fellow Laborers of mine, those Named in the Book of Life.

4   Rejoice in the Lord Always, again I Spirit Say Rejoice.

5   Your Kindness must be Made Known to all men. The Lord is near.

6   You must take no thought, but definitely in everything by Prayer and Supplication with Thankfulness, He must be making known Supernaturally your requests to God.

7   And the Peace of God is Being Supreme in every Understanding of mind. He shall

Protect your Hearts and your Comprehension in Christ Jesus. [Heart is your soul (mind, emotion, and will) and your spirit combined with the Holy Spirit (1 Cor 6:17)]

Think on these things

8 And now Brethren, whatever is True, whatever Honest, whatever Righteous, whatever Pure, whatever Lovely, whatever of God-Good Report, if any Virtue and if any Full Praise, you must be accounting these things.
9 Whatever you have both Learned and Received Along, and Heard and have Spiritually Discerned these things Of Mine you are Practicing, and the God of His Peace Will Be With You.

Thank you for Regarding

10 So I was Made to Rejoice in the Lord greatly, for already as in time past, you have Flourished in behalf of Regarding me of value, to those also you were Regarding of value, but you were lacking opportunity.
11 Not that I am saying about my poverty, because I have Learned in whatever I am to be Satisfied.
12 I Spiritually Discern both to be made Humble, and to now Discern to Abound in amount in every way and in all things. I am now Being Made Instructed both to be made filled, and to be hungry, and to be abounding in amount, and to be made lacking.

Capable every way through Christ

13 I am continuously Capable Every Way through Christ, Who is Continuously More Strengthening me.

14 But you have done God-Working, participating of my same affliction.
15 And now yourselves, Philippians, are now Spiritually Discerning also that in beginning of the Gospel, when I departed away from Macedonia, no Assembly shared to me in the Word of giving and receiving, except yourselves alone.
16 For even in Thessalonica you sent both once, and twice to me for what was needful.
17 Not that I am seeking after the physical gift, but definitely I am seeking after the Fruit, that is exceeding in quantity in the Spiritual Communication of you.
18 And I am having already all, and abounding in amount fully filled having received from Epaphroditus the things from yourselves, an odor of a sweet savor, a Sacrifice Accepted, Well Pleasing to God.
19 And my God shall Fulfill all your need, according to His Riches in Glory by Christ Jesus.
20 For now to God and our Father be the Glory Forever and Ever. Amen.

Greetings

21 You must Greet every Saint in Christ Jesus. The Brethren with me are Greeting you.
22 All the Saints are Greeting you, and specifically those from the house of Caesar.
23 The Grace of the Lord Jesus Christ with you all. Amen.

[*To Philippians written from Rome through Epaphroditus*]

The Epistle of Paul the Apostle to the

Colossians

Grace and Peace to you

1 Paul, an Apostle of Jesus Christ by the Will of God, and Timothy, his Brother.
2 To the Saints in Colosse and Faithful Brethren in Christ, Grace to you and Peace, from God our Father and the Lord Jesus Christ.

Your Love in the Spirit is Apparent

3 We are Giving Thanks to God and the Father of our Lord Jesus Christ, always Continuously Praying for you,
4 Having Heard of your Faith of Christ Jesus and the God-Love that is for all the Saints,
5 For the Expectation which is Reserved for you in Heaven, which you Heard before in the Word of Truth of the Gospel,
6 Which is Being Present among you, just as also among all the satan's world, and is Bearing Fruit for Itself, just as also In yourselves since That Day you have Heard, and Fully Knew the Grace of God, in Truth,
7 And just as you have learned from Epaphras, our Beloved Fellow Bondslave, who is in Behalf of you a Faithful Servant of Christ,
8 Who also Made Evident to us your God-Love in the Spirit.

We Pray for you to Walk Worthy

9 Because of this also we, since that day we Heard, are not ceasing Praying for you and asking that you might be made Fully Filled with the Full Knowledge of His Will, in all Wisdom and Spiritual Understanding,
10 To Walk yourselves Worthily of the Lord, to all well Pleasing in every God-Good Work by God, bearing Fruit and Growing to the Full Knowledge of God,

11 Made Empowered in all Miracle Power, according to the Dominion of His Glory, in all Endurance and Long-Suffering with Joy,
12 Giving Thanks to the Father, Who having Made us Able for the portion of the Heritage of the Saints of the Light,
13 Who has Rescued us from the authority of the darkness, and has by His Choice Completely Removed us to the Kingdom Rule of the Son of His God-Love,

Christ Restores us and Creator of all

14 In Whom we are Continuously Having by our choice the Separation Removal through His Blood, the Removal of sin natures and sins,
15 Who is the Image of the Invisible God, the Firstborn of every Creation,
16 For by Him all things have been made Created that are in the heavens, and on earth, both visible and invisible, whether thrones or lordships or rulers or authorities; all things are now made Created by Him, and for Him.

Christ Holds all things together

17 And He is Before all things, and By Him all things (are) now Holding Together,
18 And He is the Head of the Body, the Assembly, Who is the Beginning, the First-born out from the Dead, that in all things He is having the Preeminence,
19 For the Father has been Pleased that Inside Him all the Fullness to Dwell.

Reconciliation Possible by His Death

20 And Through Him to Fully Reconcile All things to Himself, having Made Peace by the Blood of His cross, whether by Him upon the earth, or in the Heavenlies,
21 And you, sometime were made aliens

and enemies in the intellect by evil man works. Nevertheless, just now He has Fully Reconciled,

22 In the Body of His (Sinless) Flesh Nature by His Death, to Present you Holy and Faultless and Unaccused Before His Presence,

23 If you are Continuously Continuing by your choice with Intent in Faith, being Made a Grounded Foundation, and Steadfast, and not being made moved away from the Expectation of the Gospel, which you have Heard and having been Made Preached to every creature which is under Heaven, whereof I Paul have been Made a Servant.

I, Servant to you of Stewardship

24 Who am now Rejoicing in my sufferings in Behalf of you, and supplementing those things lacking in my sinful flesh nature of the afflictions of Christ, in behalf of His Body, which is the Assembly,

25 Whereof I have been Made a Servant to the Stewardship of God, which has been Made Given to me to Fulfill the Word of God.

26 Even the Mystery which is now Made Concealed from the ages, and from generations, but just now Made Manifest to His Saints,

Mystery: Christ in you, the Glory

27 To whom God would Make Known Supernaturally what the Riches of the Glory of this Mystery among the Gentiles, which is Christ Within you (Born from Above; Heb 11:1), the Expectation of Glory,

28 Whom we Proclaim much, warning every man and Teaching every man in all Wisdom, that we might Present every man Perfect with Christ Jesus,

29 Whereto I also Labor, Striving according to His Effectual Working, Who Accomplishes for Himself Inside me by Miracle Power.

All Treasures, Wisdom and Knowledge

2 For I would have you to be Discerning, how great a conflict I have concerning you, and those in Laodicea, also as many as are not now beholding attentively my face, in sinful flesh nature,

2 That their hearts should have been Made Encouraged, having been Made United Together in God-Love, and in All Riches of the Full Persuasion of Understanding, toward Full Knowledge of the Mystery of God from the Father and Christ,

3 In Whom are Kept Secret all the Treasures of Wisdom and Knowledge,

4 This I say then, in order that anyone might not misguide you with an enticing word,

5 For although I am absent in Flesh Nature, but definitely I am United with you in the Spirit, Rejoicing and Spiritually Seeing your Priestly Order, and Steadfastness of your Faith of Christ.

As Received the Lord, so Walk in Him

6 Therefore, as you have Each Received Christ Jesus the Lord, you must by your choice be Continuously Walking with Him,

7 Now being Made Rooted, and are being Made Built Up with Him, and being Made Established in the Faith, just as you have been Made Taught, Abounding in amount in Him in Thankfulness,

8 You must Continuously by your choice be Seeing, that not anyone shall be spoiling you through philosophy and delusional deceitfulness, according to the tradition of men, according to the basic elements of the satan's world and definitely not According to Christ,

9 For in Him is Dwelling all the Fullness of the Godhead Bodily,

10 And you are now being made Fulfilled in Him, Who is the Head of all rulers and Authority,

Circumcision Without Hand

11 In Whom also you have been Made Circumcised, with a Circumcision Made Without Hand, in the Putting Off of the body of sins of the sinful flesh nature, in the Circumcision of Christ,

12 Made Buried with Him, in the Immersion, in which also you have also been Made Raised Up Together with Faith, by the Effectual Working of God, having Raised Him Up out from the Dead,

13 And you, being dead in the spiritual death offenses, and in the uncircumcision of your sinful flesh nature, has He Quickened Together, United With Him, having Freely Forgiven you all spiritual death offenses.

Removing all Ordinances of the Law

14 Blotting Out the Handwriting with the Ordinances against us, that were opponent to us, and it is Now Taking Away, out from the midst, Nailing it to His cross,

15 And Annulling the rulers and the authorities, He made a Show of them in Boldness, causing ourselves to Triumph over them,

16 Anybody must not judge you, therefore, in meat, or drink, or in respect of Feasts, or new moons, or Sabbaths,

17 Which are a shadow of things expecting, but the Body of Christ.

Dead with Christ, are no Ordinances

18 No man by his choice must divert yourselves, volunteering in humility and intruding without reason into a religion of angels which he is not beholding attentively, being made arrogant by his understanding of mind of his sinful flesh nature,

19 And definitely not Holding to Retain the Head, from which All the Body by ligaments and Uniting Bonds is being Made Fully Furnished, and made United Together, increasing in Growth by God,

20 Therefore, if you have Died United with Christ, away from the basic elements of the satan's world why, as living in the satan's world are you made acting out ordinances?

21 Not touch, nor taste, nor approach,

22 Which are all for Eternal death with the using, according to the precepts and doctrines of men,

23 Which is certainly a spiritual communication, having of wisdom in self choosing worship, and in humility, and in neglecting of the body, definitely not in any honor to the satisfying of the sinful flesh nature.

God-Life with Christ

3 If you then be Made Raised Up Together with Christ, you must seek those things Above, where Christ is Sitting by the Right Side of God,

2 You must Regard of Value the things Above, not upon the things of earth,

3 Because you have Died, and your Life is now Made Hid United With Christ Inside God,

4 When Christ, Who is our Life, should be Made Manifest, then also you yourselves shall be Made Manifest, United With Him In Glory.

Mortify your sinful flesh natures

5 Therefore, you Must Mortify your members which are upon the earth: fornication, moral impurity, evil affections, evil desires, evil work, and greediness which is idolatry,

6 Because of these the Wrath for Justice of God is coming upon the sons of disobedience,

7 In which also yourselves have walked as in time past, when you were living in them,

8 But just now yourselves must Put Away also all these: evil wrath, anger, malicious desire for evil work, blasphemy, filthy conversation out from your mouth.

Put off the old man with deeds

9 You must not be lying one to another, Having Annulled the old man with his deeds,

10 And Having Put On for yourself the New man which is being by your choice Made Becoming New into Full Knowledge according to the Image of Him that Created Him,

11 Whereto there is definitely not Jew or Gentile, circumcision or uncircumcision, barbarian, Scythian, slave, free, but definitely Christ All and among all.

Elect Saints of God, Made Loving

12 Put on, therefore, as the Elect Saints of God, and are now being Made Loving, Compassion of Sympathy, Gentleness, Humility, Meekness, Longsuffering,

13 Continue Enduring one another, and Freely Forgiving yourselves. If any should be having a quarrel with somebody, just as also Christ has Freely Forgiven you, in such a manner also yourselves,

14 And God-Love in The Way of all things, Which is the Uniting Bond of Spiritual Perfection. (1 John 4:7)

Then Peace, Word, and Actions

15 And the Peace of God you must Arbitrate among your hearts, for which also you have been Made Outwardly Called (Gospel) in One Body, and you must Become Thankful.

16 The Spiritual Word of Christ must be continuously by your choice Indwelling within yourselves abundantly, in all Wisdom, Teaching and Warning yourselves in Psalms, and hymns, and Spiritual songs, Singing in the Spirit every Grace in the heart of yourselves to the Lord,

17 And everything in whatever kind you should continuously be Doing in the Spiritual Word, or by any Work by God in the Name of Lord Jesus, Give Thanks to God and the Father through Him.

Home Life Instructions

18 Wives, you must be for yourselves Continuously Subjecting to your own husbands as appropriate in the Lord.

19 Husbands, you must by your choice be Continuously God-Loving your wives, and you must not be made bitter against them.

20 Children, you must Obey your parents in all things; because this is well pleasing in the Lord.

21 Dads, you Must Not provoke your children, that they should not be emotionally fixated. (Eph 6:4)

22 The Bondslaves, you must obey in everything from a master according to sinful flesh nature, but not by pleasing to sight as men pleasers, but definitely by Simplicity of God-Good Intentions of heart, Fearing God.

23 And whatever anybody should be doing, when doing from the soul, you must be Working as to the Lord, and definitely not to man.

24 Spiritually Discerning that from the Lord you shall Fully Receive the Restoring of the Inheritance, because you are Bondserving to the Lord Christ.

25 Because he that is being wrong, shall earn from that he has wronged, and there is definitely no respect of persons.

More Personal Instructions

4 Lords, you must offer concern to the Righteous, also equality to the slaves, Spiritually Discerning that yourselves also are having a Lord in Heaven.

2 You must be Continuing in Prayer, Watching in the same with Thanksgiving,

3 Also Together Praying for us, that God might Open a Door to us of Spiritual Communication, to Utter the Mystery of Christ, for which I am also now Made Bound,

4 That I should have Manifested Him, as He is Being Required of me to Utter.

5 You must be Walking in Wisdom to them outside, Purchasing Out from the satan's world in this Special Time.

6 Let the Spiritual Communication of you always (be) with Grace, being now Made Seasoned with Salt Flavoring, Spiritually Discerning how you Must to be Answering every man.

Closing Salutations

7   All about me, Tychicus, the Beloved Brother, and Faithful Servant, and Fellow Bondslave in the Lord, shall make Known to you,

8   Whom I have sent to you for this, that he should Know concerning you, and Encourage your hearts,

9   United with Onesimus. the Faithful and Beloved Brother, who is from you. They shall Make Known to you all things which are here,

10   Aristarchus my fellow prisoner greets you, and Mark the nephew of Barnabas, about whom you have received Commandments. If he might come to you, you must receive him,

11   And Jesus, who is made called Justus, who is out from the circumcision. Fellow Laborers for the Kingdom Rule of God, who have become Support to me.

12   Epaphras greets you, a Slave of Christ from you, always striving for you in Prayers that you should Stand Perfect and now being Made Fully Filled in all the Will of God,

13   Because I bear record to him that He has very much God-Good Zeal for you, and those in Laodicea, and them in Hierapolis,

14   Luke, the Beloved physician, and Demas, greet you.

15   Greet the Brethren in Laodicea, and Nymphas, and the Assembly at his home.

16   And when you should be Made to Read among you this epistle, you must see that also it should be Made Read to the Assembly of Laodiceans, and that you yourselves should Read that also from Laodicea.

17   And you must Speak to Archippus, you must Look to the Service (of Calling) that you have Each Received in the Lord, that you should Fulfill It.

18   The Salutation by my hand, Paul. You must Remember my bonds. Grace with you. Amen.

[Written to Colossians from Rome through Tychicus and Onesimus]

The First Epistle of Paul the Apostle to the

Thessalonians

Paul's Greeting

1 Paul and Silvanus, and Timothy, to the Assembly of Thessalonians inside God the Father and the Lord Jesus Christ. Grace to you and Peace from God our Father and the Lord Jesus Christ,

2   We Give Thanks to God always for you all, making mention of you in our Prayers,

3   Remembering without ceasing your Work by God by Faith, and Labor of God-Love, and Endurance of the Expectation of our Lord Jesus Christ before God and our Father,

4   Knowing, Brethren, being now Made Loved, your Election by God.

Gospel to you in Word and Power

5   For our Gospel became not to you in Spiritual Communication only, but definitely also in the Miracle Power, and in the Holy Spirit, and in very much Full Persuasion, just as you are Now Spiritually Discerning such as occurred among you, for you,

6   And yourselves became close Followers of us and of the Lord, having Received the Word in very much affliction with Joy of the Holy Spirit,

7   So that you became Models to all that are Committing in Macedonia and Achaia,

From you, all Macedonia Heard

8   Because from you is Now Made Sounded Out the Word of the Lord, not only in Macedonia and Achaia, but definitely also in every place. Your Faith, within God, is Now Coming Out, so that not needful for us to have to Utter anything,

9   Because they themselves tell to us what manner of Entrance we had to you, and how you Turned Back to God from idols, to Bondserve the Living and True God,

10 And to await His Son from Heaven, Whom He Raised Up Out From the dead, Jesus Who is Rescuing us from the Coming Wrath for Justice.

Paul's suffering

2 Because yourselves are Now Discerning, Oh Brethren, our Entrance to you, how it is definitely not being empty delusion,

2   But definitely even suffering before, even violently treated, just as you Have Known in Philippi, Speaking Boldly by our God, Uttering to you the Gospel of God in very much conflict,

3   Because our Encouragement was not from deception, neither from moral impurity, neither in subtle half-truth (deceit),

4   But definitely just as we are Now Made Proven in Truth by God, Made to be Committing to the Gospel, so as not Uttering as pleasing to men, but definitely to God, Proving in Truth our hearts.

5   Because as in time past, neither occurred in a Word of flattering, just as now you are discerning, neither in pretense of greediness, God Witness,

6   Nor from man were we seeking Glory, nor from you, nor from others of same kind with a heavy burden, we are Being Able as Apostles of Christ,

7   But definitely we have been Made Gentle among the midst of you, as though a nursing mother should be cherishing her children.

Paul's desires for them

8   So being affectionately desirous of you, we were pleased to have imparted to you, definitely not only the Gospel of God, but definitely also our own souls, since you are Made Beloved to us,

9   Because you remember, Oh Brethren, our Labor and Grieving for night and day, working for not having to owe any of you, we have preached to you the Gospel of God,

10 God and Yourselves Witnesses, we Have Been to you who are Committing, as Holy and Righteously and Blamelessly,

11 Even as you are now Spiritually Discerning, as we Encouraged everyone of you as a father to his children, and Comforted, and Witnessed to you,

12 That you to be Walking Worthily of God. Who Himself is Outwardly Calling (Gospel) you for His Kingdom Rule and Glory.

Thank God for their being Steadfast

13 For this also, we are Giving Thanks to God without ceasing, because you have been each Receiving the Word of Hearing from us. You Received of God, not the word of men, but definitely just as is Of Truth, the Word (Christ Himself) of God, which also is Accomplishing Inside yourselves, who are Committing,

14 For yourselves, Oh Brethren, became close followers of the Assemblies of God, being in Judaea in Christ Jesus. Then you yourselves also have suffered like manner by your own countrymen, just as also ourselves by the Jews,

15 Who both killed the Lord Jesus and their own Prophets, and also have persecuted you. And they are not pleasing to God, and contrary to all men,

16 Forbidding us to Utter to the Gentiles, that they should be Made Saved, thereby to Destroy by bondage to death their sin natures and sins Always. They have at-· tained then with their intent, the Wrath for Justice in the End.

Paul's concern for them

17 But we, Oh Brethren, have been Made Taken from you for a short time, in presence, not in heart. We have been earnestly diligent with very much desire to see your face,

18 For this reason we strongly desired to come to you, indeed I Paul, so once or twice, but the satan has hindered us,

19 For what our Expectation, or Joy, or crown of Rejoicing? Or not also yourselves before our Lord Jesus Christ with His Coming?

20 For you, yourselves, are our Glory and Joy.

Timothy's Report of his visit

3 For this reason, we are no longer refraining; I have been pleased to be made left in Athens alone,

2 And sent Timothy, our Brother, and servant of God, and our Fellow Laborer in the Gospel of Christ, to firmly Establish you, and to Encourage you about your Faith,

3 That no man is to be made affected by these afflictions, because yourselves are Now Spiritually Discerning that for this we are Set,

4 Because also, when we were with you, we were Telling you before that we are expecting tribulation, just as also has come to pass, and you are now Discerning,

5 Because of this, I also was no longer refraining I sent to Know your Faith, fearing that the tempting one was tempting you, and our labor already should become a delusion,

6 But for now, Timothy coming to us from you, and proclaimed to us the Faith and the God-Love of you, and that you are having always God-Good mention of us, greatly desiring to see us, even as we also you,

7 Brethren, because of this we have been made encouraged by you through your Faith in all our affliction and necessity,

8 For now we are Living, if you are yourselves Standing Fast in the Lord,

9 Because what Thanksgiving are we Able to Repay to God over you? For all the Joy, the Rejoicing because of you, before the Presence of our God.

10 Night and day Praying earnestly, excessively, in behalf of you, that we might See your face and Make Complete that lacking of your Faith.

To be Established in Holiness

11 Now God Himself and our Father, and our Lord Jesus Christ Direct our way to you.

12 And the Lord in His God-Love to yourselves has Exceeded in Quantity beyond your dreams and has Abounded in Amount beyond your dreams, to one another and to all, even as also we to you,

13 To firmly Establish your hearts Blameless, in Holiness, before the Presence of God and our Father, in the Coming of our Lord Jesus Christ with all His Saints.

God has Called us to Holiness

4 Therefore finally, Brethren, we are earnestly requesting of you, and are Encouraging in the Lord Jesus, just as you have each Received from us, how He Required you to Walk, and be well Pleasing to God, in order that you should be much more Abounding in amount,

2 Because you Spiritually Discern that I gave a Command to you through the Lord Jesus,

3 Because this is the Will of God, your Personal Holiness, to Abstain yourselves from fornication,

4 To Spiritually Discern everyone of you, to possess his vessel in Personal Holiness and Honor,

5 Not in evil affection of evil desire, even as also the Gentiles, who are not Spiritually Discerning God,

6 That no one is to overstep and to make a gain in a matter to his Brother, since the Lord, an Avenger of evil doing, in regard to all these things, just as we also have forewarned to you and testified,

7   Because God has not Outwardly Called (Gospel) us in the way of moral impurity, but definitely within Personal Holiness,

8   Consequently, he that is rejecting, rejects not man, but definitely God, Who also has Given to us His Holy Spirit.

We are Taught to Love each other

9   But in regard to Brotherly Affection, you are having no need to be writing to you, for you yourselves are taught of God, you are to God-Love one another,

10   Because you also do this to all the Brethren in the whole of Macedonia, but we, Brethren, are encouraging you to much more abound in amount,

11   And to Endeavor to remain quiet and to practice one's own, and to work with your own hands, just as we have Given Command to you,

12   That you should Walk Honestly to them outside, and should not have need of anything.

Lord's Second Coming for the Saints

13   But I would not prefer you to be ignorant, Brethren, concerning those that Rest Asleep, that you should not sorrow, just as also others who have no expectation,

14   Because if we are Committing that Jesus Died and Arose also in such a manner, so those who Rest Asleep in Jesus, God shall Lead United with Him,

15   Because this we are Saying to you by the Word of the Lord, that we who are Living and are surviving for the Coming of the Lord, should never ever prevent those that Rest Asleep.

16   For the Lord Himself shall Come Down, with a Shout, by the Voice of an Archangel, and of a Trumpet by God Coming Down from Heaven, and the dead in Christ shall Arise First of All, (Matt 24:31; 1 Cor 15:52; Zech 9:14-16)

17   After that We who are Living, Who are Made Surviving, shall be Made Caught Up Together United with Them, in the Clouds for Meeting with the Lord in the air, and so We will Always be United With the Lord,

18   So that you must Encourage one another with these Spiritual Words.

About the times and seasons

5 But about the Times and Special Seasons I am Made to Write to you, Brethren, you are having no need,

2   Because yourselves Discern exactly that the Day of the Lord is Coming, in such a manner, as a thief in the night,

3   Because when they should say peace and safety, then Sudden Destruction stands ready upon them, as travail having a womb with child, they should never ever escape.

That Day will not overtake you

4   But yourselves, Brethren, you are definitely not in darkness in order that That Day should apprehend you as a thief,

5   You are all yourselves Sons of Light and the Sons of the Day. We are being definitely not of night neither of darkness,

6   So then, therefore, we should not be sleeping as others, but definitely should also be Watching and should be Serious,

7   Because they that are sleeping, sleep during night, and they that are being made drunken, are being drunk during night,

We are not appointed to His Wrath

8   But we being of the Day should be Serious, putting on a Breastplate of Faith and God-Love, and for a Helmet, an Expectation of Salvation.

9   For God has for Himself definitely not Positioned us to Wrath for Justice, but definitely to Possession of Salvation by our Lord Jesus Christ,

10   Who Died in Behalf of us, in order that whether we should be Watching, or should be Sleeping, we should Have Lived United Together with Him,

11   For this reason you must be Encouraging one another, and you must be Edifying one by one, just as also you are Doing.

Esteem those who Labor with you

12 Now I am earnestly Requesting of you, Brethren, to Spiritually Discern those that Labor among you, and are Standing Before to Maintain you in the Lord, and are Warning you,

13 And them to be Esteemed more Excessively in God-Love for their Work by God (Heb 13:17). You must be in Peace among yourselves.

We are Encouraging you Brethren

14 Now we are Encouraging you, Brethren. You must be Warning the unruly. You must be Comforting the feeble minded. You must be Upholding the weak. You must be Long-suffering within every way,

15 You must behold attentively, No one should pay back evil work for any evil work, but definitely always you must follow closely God-Good, both to one another and in every way,

16 You must be Rejoicing always,

17 You must be Praying without ceasing,

18 You must Give Thanks in all things for this is the Will of God, inside Christ Jesus in yourselves,

19 You must not extinguish the Spirit,

20 You must not be despising Prophecy,

21 You must be Proving in Truth All things. You must Hold Fast that which is God-Work,

22 You must Abstain Away from all appearance of evil.

God Make you Completely Holy

23 And the very God of Peace make you Completely Holy beyond your dreams, and your entire Spirit and Soul and Body made kept blamelessly beyond your dreams within the Coming of our Lord Jesus Christ,

24 Faithful, He that is Outwardly Calling (Gospel) you, Who also shall Accomplish it,

Benediction

25 Brethren, you must Continuously Pray for us,

26 You must Greet all the Brethren with a Holy kiss,

27 I am continuously Urging you, by the Lord, to Make this Epistle Read to all the Holy Brethren,

28 The Grace of our Lord Jesus Christ with you. Amen.

[First written to Thessalonians from Athens]

The Second Epistle of Paul the Apostle to the

Thessalonians

Greetings

1 Paul and Silvanus and Timothy to the Assembly of Thessalonians, in God our Father and the Lord Jesus Christ.

2 Grace to you and Peace from God our Father and the Lord Jesus Christ.

We Thank God for your Faith

3 We are indebted to Give Thanks to God always about you, Brethren, just as it is Worthy that your Faith is Continuously Growing greatly, and your God-Love to everyone is Exceeding in Quantity above all to one another,

4 So that we ourselves boast in you in the Assemblies of God, for your Endurance and Faith in all your persecutions and afflictions, that you Continuously Continue Enduring,

5   Which is a Manifest token of the Righteous Final Judgment of God, that you are Made Counted Worthy of the Kingdom Rule of God, for which you also are also suffering.

God Righteous, troubles enemies

6   If it be so, Righteous with God to repay affliction to those that are troubling you,

7   And to you, who are being made troubled, rest with us when the Revelation of the Lord Jesus from Heaven with His Angels by Miracle power,

8   In Flaming Fire giving Vengeance to those that are not now Discerning God, and are not obeying the Gospel of our Lord Jesus Christ,

9   Who shall pay justice by Just Punishment with Eternal Destruction from the Presence of the Lord, and away from the Glory of His Strength.

God Glorified in His saints

10 When He should Come to be Made Glorified (attributed Spiritual Perfection) by His Saints, and to be Made Admired in all those who are Committing, because our Testimony to you has been Made Committed by you within That Day.

11 For this also we are Praying always about you, that our God should think Worthy of you in His Service of Calling, and it should Have Fulfilled all God-Good Intentions of Goodness, and Work by God through Faith with Miracle Power.

12 So that the Name of our Lord Jesus Christ should have been Made Glorified (attributed Spiritual Perfection) in yourselves, and yourselves in Him, according to the Grace of our God and the Lord Jesus Christ.

The Day of Christ is considered

2 We earnestly Request of you, Brethren, in Behalf of the Coming of our Lord Jesus Christ, and our Assembling Together with Him,

2   That you be not made rapidly shaken, neither of mind, nor frightened, nor by Spirit, nor by Word, nor through Epistle as by us, as that The Day of Christ is now present.

Falling away first, then antichrist

3   No man should have deceived you by any means, because except there should Have Come the apostasy first of all, and that man of sin nature and sin should have been Made Revealed, the son of damnation,

4   Who is being adverse and is made exalting himself over all that is Made Called God, or Worshiped, so that to sit down as god himself in the Temple of God, proving himself that he is god.

Remember what Holds him Back

5   Are you definitely not remembering when I was yet with you, I was Saying these things to you?

6   And now you are Spiritually Discerning what is Holding Back, to Make him Revealed in his own Special Time (by God),

7   Because the Mystery of this lawlessness is already Accomplishing, only is Holding Back for now, until after he occurs out from the midst.

His coming, all power of the satan

8   And then shall the lawless one be Made Revealed, whom the Lord Jesus Christ shall Consume with the Spirit of His Mouth and shall Destroy with the Appearing of His Own Coming,

9   The coming of him (the lawless one) is according to the effectual working of the satan with every miracle power (dunamis) and miracle signs (semeion) and lying wonders,

10 And with every deceitfulness of unrighteousness, inside those that are perishing, for whoever have definitely not Received the God-Love of the Truth, for them to be Made Saved themselves.

God Sends them a strong delusion
11 And because of this, God shall send to them effectual working of deception to commit themselves for purpose and result to the lie,

12 That they all should be made Judged, who not Committing themselves to the Truth, but definitely they have for themselves pleasing in the unrighteousness.

We can Give Thanks Always
13 But we are continuously, ourselves Indebted (Rom 4:4), Giving Thanks to God Always in regard to you, Brethren. You are now Made Continuously Loving by the Lord, because God has by His Choice Personally Chosen you from the Beginning for Salvation, by Personal Holiness of Spirit, and by Faith of Truth,

14 For this Purpose and Result, He Outwardly Called you by our Gospel, for Possession of the Glory (Spiritual Perfection) of our Lord Jesus Christ.

15 So then, therefore, Brethren, you must be continuously Standing Fast, and you must be Holding to Retain the Traditions that you have been made Taught, whether by Word or by our Epistle.

God Comfort your hearts
16 And now, our Lord Jesus Christ Himself, and God also our Father, Who has been Loving us by His choice, also has been Giving Eternal Consolation, and Expectation to God-Good through Grace,

17 Having Comforted your hearts, beyond our dreams, and firmly establishing you, by His choice, in every Spiritual Word and in God-Good Work by God.

From evil men; not all have Faith
3 Finally, you must be Praying continuously, Brethren, for us, that the Word of the Lord should be run, and should be made Attributing Glory, just as also to yourselves.

2 And that we should be Made Rescued from the wrong and evil men, because Faith is definitely not in all men,

3 But the Lord is Continuously Faithful, Who shall Firmly Establish and Maintain you for Himself, away from the evil,

4 And we are Now Persuaded by the Lord in regard to you, because this you are Doing and you shall Do by your choice even as we are Giving Command to you,

5 And, the Lord has Directed by His choice, your Hearts into the God-Love of God, and into the Endurance of Christ beyond your dreams.

Command to withdraw from evil
6 And now we are Giving Command to you, Brethren, in the Name of our Lord Jesus Christ, to Stand Removing yourselves for yourselves, away from every brother continuously walking disorderly by his choice, and not according to the Tradition that he has received along with us,

7 Because yourselves, you are now Spiritually Discerning how by your choice you ought to be Closely Following us. For we definitely have not been disorderly among you.

We ate no man's bread for free
8 Neither have we eaten from any man's bread without pay (freely). But definitely in labor, and grieving night and day, we Continuously Worked, that we have not owed to any of you,

9 Definitely not because we are definitely not having by our choice authority, but definitely in order that ourselves should Have Given a Model to you, for to be Closely Following us,

10 Because even when we were with you, this we were giving Command to you, that if any man would by his choice not work, neither must he be eating,

11 Because we are hearing certain ones among you are walking disorderly, not Continuously Working, but definitely being busybodies,

Avoid any who do not Obey us

12 Now to them that are such, we are Giving Command, and are encouraging through our Lord Jesus Christ, that with silence, they be Continuously Working. They should be eating their own bread.

13 But yourselves, Brethren, you should not by own choice be weary, Continuously Doing God-Good Works,

14 And if any man is not by his own choice Continuously Obeying to our Spiritual Words through this Epistle, you must for yourselves continuously note him, and you must continuously for yourselves no more associate with him, in order that he should be made disrespected,

15 Yet you must be esteeming not as an enemy, but definitely you must be Warning as a Brother.

Benediction

16 Now the Lord of Peace Himself Give you Peace with All, by All Means. The Lord with you All,

17 The Salutation by my hand, Paul, which is a Miracle Sign in every Epistle, so I Write,

18 The Grace of our Lord Jesus Christ with you all. Amen.

[Second written to Thessalonians from Athens]

The First Epistle of Paul the Apostle to

Timothy

Paul Greets Timothy

1 Paul, an Apostle of Jesus Christ by the Commandment of God our Savior, and the Lord Jesus Christ, Who is our Expectation.

2 To Timothy, Truthful child in Faith, Grace, Mercy, Peace from God the Father and Jesus Christ, our Lord.

Teach Love and Faith with Purity

3 Just as I have encouraged you in Ephesus to remain Steadfast when I went into Macedonia, that you should give Command to Teach no other different doctrine,

4 Neither take heed to fables and endless genealogies, which are offering continuous questioning concerns, than instead the Stewardship of God by Faith,

5 Now the End of the Command is God-Love out from a Purified heart, and God-Good conscience, and Faith Unfeigned,

6 Certain ones, who have erred by their choice, have been made turned away to babbling,

7 Desiring to be doctors of the Law, neither comprehending, nor what they are saying, nor about what they are continuously affirming constantly by their choice.

Law for disobedient

8 But we are now Spiritually Discerning that the Law is God-Work, if any man should be using it according to the Commands of Christ,

9 Spiritually Discerning this, that the Law is definitely not being continuously set for the Righteous, but for lawless, unsubmissive, ungodly, for sinners, unholy, profane, for murderers of fathers and murderers of mothers, man slayers,

10 For fornicators, sodomites, enslavers, for liars, for perjured persons, also if anyone other of a different kind that is continuously adverse by his own choice to Sound Doctrine,

11 According to the Gospel of the Glory of the Spiritually Blessed God, to Whom I was Made Committed.

Christ Saves sinners, I am chiefest

12 And I am Continuously Having Grace, which has more Strengthened me with Christ Jesus our Lord, for He has Esteemed me Positioned Faithful for Service (of Calling),
13 Who was before blasphemous, and a persecutor, and injurious, but definitely I have been Made Given Mercy, because I behaved being ignorant with no Commitment,
14 And the Grace of our Lord was Super Abundant with Faith and God-Love inside Christ Jesus,
15 The Faithful Word, and Worthy of all Acceptance, that Christ Jesus came into the satan's world to Save sinners, of whom I am chiefest,
16 But definitely because of this, I have earlier been Given Mercy, that in me Jesus Christ should have for Himself Exhibited All Long-suffering, for a pattern of them Expecting to be Committing in The Way of Him for Life Eternal,
17 Now to the King of the Ages, Incorruptible, Invisible, Alone Wise God; Honor and Glory Forever and Ever. Amen.

I Command: Hold Faith, be Sinless

18 This Command I am Putting Forth to you, Child Timothy, according to the Prophecies Going Before on you, in order that you are for yourself Warring to be in His God-Work Warfare,
19 Having Faith and also a God-Good Conscience, Which some have by their own choice casted away. They have by their choice shipwrecked concerning their Faith,
20 Of whom is Hymenaeus and Alexander, whom I have by my choice Delivered up to the satan, in order that they should be made Disciplined, not to blaspheme.

Encourages Prayer for all

2 I am Encouraging therefore, first of all by all means continuously to be Made Making Supplications, Prayers, Intercessions, Thanksgiving, in behalf of all men,
2 For kings, and all that are in superiority, in order that we might be Living Quiet and Peaceable natural life in all Godliness and Integrity,
3 Because this (is) God-Work and Acceptable in the Presence of God our Savior.

All to be Saved and Know Truth

4 Who is Willing to Make all men Saved, and to Come to a Full Knowledge of the Truth,
5 Because One God and One Reconciler of God and men, the Man Christ Jesus,
6 Who Gave Himself, a Removal Provided By Another in behalf of all men, this Testimony Itself in your own Private Special Time,
7 Thereto I have been Made Positioned a Preacher and an Apostle, that I say by my choice Truth in Christ, I definitely by my choice lie not; A teacher of the Gentiles in Faith and Truth,
8 I Intend, therefore, that men in every place be Praying, lifting up Personally Holy hands, without wrath for justice or of doubting.

Women to be modest and silent

9 In like manner also, that women are adorning themselves in modest women's apparel, with Reverence and Seriousness; not in braided hair or gold or pearls or very valuable raiment,
10 But definitely appropriate by own choice for women Promising Devotion to God with God-Good Works by God,
11 A woman must by her choice be Learning in silence with all subjection,

Women not be in authority over man

12 For I am definitely not permitting a woman to Teach, nor to assert oneself over a man, but definitely to be in silence,
13 Because Adam was Made Formed First, following that, Eve,

14 And Adam was Definitely not made deceivingly seduced, but the woman was made deceivingly seduced, now occurring in a broken Commandment, (Gen 3:3)

15 But she shall be Made Healthy through the childbearing, if they might Continue by their choice in Faith and God-Love, and Personal Holiness with Seriousness.

If a man Seeks to be an overseer

3 If any one man longs after Oversight for himself, the Faithful Spiritual Word, he is desiring by his choice a God-Work Work by God.

2 An overseer must be, therefore, not chargeable, being a husband of one woman, sober, logical, modest, hospitable, willing to Teach,

3 Not liking wine, no striker, not for filthy gain, but definitely Kindness, not quarrelsome, not covetous,

4 God-Working Stands Before to maintain his own home, having children in subjection with all Integrity,

5 And then if any man definitely not Standing Before to Maintain his own home, how shall he be Spiritually Discerning to take care of an Assembly of God?

6 Not a novice, that has not to be made self directed pride, he might by his choice fall into the condemnation of the devil,

7 Moreover, then he must also be himself Having a God-Work Testimony from those outward that he might not fall into reproach, and a snare of the devil.

Servants must be Honest

8 In like manner Servants honest, not double tongued, not with very much wine, take heed, nothing for filthy gain,

9 Having the Mystery of the Faith in a Purified conscience, (Col 1:26-27)

10 And they also, must first of all be made Proved in Truth. They must be Serving, being unaccused.

11 In like manner wives honest, not false accusers (slanderers), sober, Faithful in all things,

12 Servants, you must be husbands of one wife, God-Working Standing Before to Maintain for yourselves children and your own homes,

13 Because having by his choice Served God-Working, he is Purchasing for himself a God-Work Degree, and very much Boldness in Faith which is in Christ Jesus.

House of God is the Assembly

14 These things I am Writing you, Expecting to Come to you more hastily,

15 But If I should continue longer that you should by your choice Spiritually Discern how you are Required to Behave in the Dwelling of God, which is the Assembly of God, a Living Pillar and Unmovable Ground of the Truth,

16 And without controversy, Great is the Mystery of Godliness. God Made Manifested in (Sinless) Flesh Nature, Made Righteous in the Spirit, Made Spiritually Seen among Angels, Made Preached among the Gentiles, made Committed to within the satan's world, made Received Up inside Glory.

Apostasy in the Last Days

4 Now the Spirit especially is Saying, that in the Later Special Times some shall, by their choice, depart away from the Faith, giving attention by their choice, to spirit deceivings and doctrines of demons,

2 In role playing hypocrisy of deliberate lies, making one's own conscience now made insensitive as with a hot iron,

3 Forbidding to marry, to be abstaining from foods that God created to be received with Thankfulness from the Faithful even Now Fully Knowing the Truth,

4 Since every creature of God, a God-Work and Made Receiving with Thanksgiving, definitely nothing unacceptable,

5 Because it is Made Holy by the Word of God and Intercessions,

Be God-Work Bondslave of Christ

6   These things be putting in Remembrance to the Brethren, you shall be a God-Work Servant of Jesus Christ, being Made Respected for the Spiritual Communications of Faith, and The God-Work Doctrine to which you are Now Following Along,

7   But you Must Be Refusing profane and old wives fables, and you must be Exercising yourself to Godliness,

8   Because bodily exercise is for little, but Godliness is Profitable for Everyone, Being Profitable Having by your choice Promise of Life Now, and also of That Expected,

9   This is a Faithful Spiritual Communication and Worthy of All Acceptance,

10   Therein for This we are both Laboring by our choice and Made Scolded Sharply, because we Expect in the Living God, Who is the Savior of all men, Specifically the Faithful,

11   These things you Must Be Giving Command by your choice, and you Must Be Teaching.

Be a Model to Faithful in Word

12   They must not despise your youth, but definitely you Must Become a Model to the Faithful in the Word, in Behavior, in God-Love, in the Spirit, in Faith, in Purity,

13   Until after I come you Must by your choice Continuously Give Attention to Reading, to Encouragement, to Doctrine,

14   You must not neglect in you the Spirit Gift that was Made Given to you by Prophecy with Laying on of hands by the group of Elders,

15   You must be Continuously Meditating These Things. You Must Be with These Things, in order that your Advancement should be Openly Manifest with everyone.

Take Heed to self and Doctrine

16   You must be Continuously Giving Heed to yourself and to the Doctrine; you Must by your choice be Continuously Continuing in Them, because Doing This Continuously you shall both Save yourself and them that are Continuously by their choice Hearing you.

Entreat Elders as Dads

5   You should not be severely critical to an Elder, but you must encourage as (being) a dad, younger (men) as Brethren,

Elder women and widows

2   Elder women as mothers, younger women as Sisters with all purity,

3   You must Honor widows that in fact are widows,

4   But if any widow having children or grandchildren, they must be Learning, first of all showing Reverence to one's own home, and to be paying back Recompense to their parents; because this is God-Work and Acceptable in the Presence of God,

5   Now she that is in fact a widow now made destitute, is now Expecting with Intent to God, and remains Steadfast longer in Supplications and Prayers night and day,

6   But she that is living by her choice in immoral pleasures, is a living now rotting dead body by her choice,

7   And you Must Give Command to These Things that they should not be Chargeable.

Must provide for own vs infidel

8   But if any are not providing for one's own, and specifically not for his own household members, he is now for himself disclaiming the Faith and worse, he is faithless.

Widows over 60 may be Accepted

9   You must not be Making Acceptable a widow to be younger aged than sixty years, being a wife to one husband,

10   Whereby Made Bearing Record with God-Works, Works by God: if she has raised children, if she has lodged strangers, if she has washed Saints feet, if she has

relieved afflicted, if she has Followed After the God-Good Work by God,

11 But you must refuse younger widows, because when they might have lived lustfully against Christ, they are desiring to be marrying,

12 Having condemnation that they have rejected their first Faith,

13 And with all this, they are idle learning, wondering about houses, and definitely not only idle but definitely also babblers of trifles and curious works, uttering things they ought not.

Young women marry, guide house

14 I intend, therefore, younger to marry, bear children, guide the household, be giving no occasion to be adverse, reviling for what cause,

15 Because already some have been made turned away after the satan.

Relatives of younger widows

16 If any Faithful man or Faithful woman is having widows, let them be Relieving them, so must not let the Assembly be Burdened, in order that they should Have Relieved widows in fact.

Elders must Stand Worthy

17 The Elders Standing Before to Maintain God-Working are Made Think Worthy of double Honor, specifically they that Labor in the Word and Doctrine,

18 Because the Scripture Says, you shall not muzzle an ox that treads out the harvest. Also Worthy the Worker of his Reward, (Deut 25:4)

19 You must not be accepting an outside accusation against an elder, except in the place of two or three witnesses.

Anyone that sins must be Exposed

20 You must be Exposing as sin in the Presence of all, in order that also others should be Having Fear of sinning,

21 I am Emphasizing in the Presence of God and the Lord Jesus Christ and the Elect Angels, in order that These Things you should Maintain without prejudging, not anything being Finalized by partiality,

22 You must not rapidly Lay Hands on anyone, neither must you be partakers in other men's sin natures and sins. You Must Keep yourself Pure,

23 You must drink water no longer, but definitely you must be using a little wine, because of your stomach and your more often infirmities,

24 Some men's sin natures and sins are evident beforehand, they are going before into Final Judgment. And then some are following after,

25 Also, in like manner, the God-Works by God is Evident Beforehand, and having different of Same Kind are not able to be Made Hid.

Slaves must honor their masters

6 As many as there are Bondslaves under a yoke, they must be esteeming their own masters worthy of honor in all things, that the Name of God and the Doctrine should not be made blasphemed,

2 Moreover they that are having Faithful masters, they must not be despising, because they are Brethren, you must definitely be much More Bondserving, because they are Faithful and Beloved, Supporters of the Benefit. These things you must Teach and Encourage.

Teaching another doctrine

3 If any man is teaching a different doctrine and is not coming near to being sound in the Word of our Lord Jesus Christ, and according to Godliness in Doctrine;

4 He is made self directed pride not in anything being aware, but definitely picky fondness about questionings, and out from disputing trifles is becoming envy, contention, blasphemies, evil surmisings,

5 Perverse disputings are now made materially destroying the understanding

of mind of men, while now made defrauding (lying) about the Truth, supposing that being a value gain is Godliness. You must Continuously by your choice Depart Away from such,

6   But Godliness with Contentment is Great Value Gain,

7   Because we have brought nothing into this the satan's world, even evident we are not able to bring out anything,

8   And having foodstuffs and raiment, these things shall be Made Sufficient.

Money affection is, a root of all evil

9   But they that are intending to be rich are thereby therein falling into temptation, and a snare, and many uncomprehending and hurtful evil desires, even which are sinking men into destruction and damnation,

10   Because the affection for money is a root of all the evil works, which some longing after have been made seduced by deception away from the Faith, and have pierced themselves through with many sorrows.

You must Follow after Godliness

11   But you, Oh man of God, you Must Flee these things. Also, you Must Follow Closely Righteousness, Godliness, Faith, God-Love, Endurance, Meekness,

12   You must fight the God-Work Conflict of the Faith. You must Take Hold of Eternal Life, for the Purpose and Result of you that has also been Made Outwardly Called (Gospel), and has Confessed the God-Work Profession in the presence of many witnesses,

13   I am Giving Command to you in the Presence of God Who is Offering Spiritual Life to all, and of Christ Jesus who Gave the God-Work Profession Witness to Pontius Pilate,

14   To you to keep this Commandment Without Spot, not chargeable, as far as the Appearing of our Lord Jesus Christ,

15   Who in His Special Times, He will Show Who is Spiritually Blessed, and Alone Potentate, and King of Reignings and Lord of Having Dominions,

16   Who alone is having Immortality, Dwelling in the Light Unapproachable, Whom no man has by his choice Spiritually Seen, neither can see, to Whom Honor and Dominion Eternal. Amen.

The rich are to be rich in God-Works

17   You must be giving Command to the rich, now in this Age, to be not high minded, nor to be by their choice expecting in insecure riches, but definitely in the Living God, Offering Concern to us Abundantly For All Enjoyment,

18   To be rich to be Working God-Good by Works by God, God-Works, Being Willing to Distribute, Willing to Share,

19   Treasuring, by their choice, for themselves a God-Work Foundation, for the Expecting Continuously by their choice, in order that they should Take Hold of Eternal Life.

Maintain that Committed to you

20   Oh Timothy, you Must Maintain by your choice that Committed to you; Turn Away the profane worthless babblings, and disagreements of falsely named knowledge,

21   Which some professing, have erred concerning the Faith. Grace with you. Amen.

[To Timothy, first was written from Laodicea, which is chief city of Phrygia Pacatiana]

The Second Epistle of Paul the Apostle to

Timothy

Greeting to Timothy

1 Paul an Apostle of Jesus Christ through the Will of God, according to the Promise of the Life in Christ Jesus,

2 To Timothy, Beloved child, Grace, Mercy, Peace, from Father God and Christ Jesus our Lord.

Think of you always in Prayers

3 I am by my choice having Grace of God, to Whom I am Devoted from parents, in a Purified conscience, as I am having a Continuous Mention of you, in my Supplications night and day,

4 Greatly desiring to see you, made remembering your tears, that I may be made fully filled with Joy,

5 I am receiving remembrance of Unfeigned Faith in you, Who Indwelt first of all in your grandmother Lois and in your mother Eunice; and I am Now Made Persuaded even In you also.

God not Given us terror but Power

6 Because of this reason in remembrance, I am to Utilize you for the Spirit Gift of God, Who is in you through the Laying On of my hands,

7 For God has not Given to us the Spirit of terror, but definitely of Miracle Power and of God-Love, and of a Logical mind,

8 Therefore, you should not be made ashamed of the Testimony of our Lord, nor of me His prisoner, but definitely you must by your choice suffer affliction together for the Gospel with the Miracle Power of God.

Called with a Service of Calling

9 Who has Saved us and Outwardly Called (Gospel) us with a Holy Service of Calling, definitely not according to our man works, but definitely according His Own Purpose and Grace, which was made Given to us in Christ Jesus before time Eternal,

10 But is now made Manifest by the appearing of our Savior Jesus Christ, Who actually Destroyed death, and brought to Light Life and Incorruption through the Gospel.

I am a Preacher, Apostle, Teacher

11 For this I have been Made Positioned a Preacher, and an Apostle, and a Teacher of Gentiles,

12 Because of that reason, I then suffer continuously by my choice these things, but definitely I am not ashamed, because I Spiritually Know to Whom I am now Continuously Committing by my choice, and I am Now Made Persuaded that He is Exceedingly Able to Maintain my Deposit for His Day,

13 You must Continuously Have the Pattern of Healthy Words, which you have Heard from me, in Faith and God-Love in Christ Jesus,

14 You must Maintain by your choice that God-Work Committed through the Holy Spirit Indwelling in us.

Lord give mercy to Onesiphorus

15 You are now by your choice Spiritually Discerning this, that all in Asia have been made turned away from me, of whom are Phygellus and Hemogenes,

16 The Lord Gave Mercy by His choice beyond dreams to the home of Onesiphorus, for often he has Renewed me, and was not made ashamed of my chain,

17 But definitely, being in Rome, he sought very diligently and found me,

18 The Lord Give beyond dreams to him, to Find Mercy from the Lord in That Day. Also in Ephesus you Know that he so Fully Served.

Suffer as God-Work Soldier

2 You, therefore, my child, you must be more Strengthened by the Grace in Christ Jesus,

2   And the things you have Heard coming from me through many witnesses, these things put forth for yourself to Faithful men, who shall be Sufficient to Teach other ones of a different kind also,

3   Therefore, you must suffer evil as a God-Work Soldier of Jesus Christ,

4   Definitely not warring continuously for himself being made entangling in the transactions of livelihood, in order that he should well please Him that Called him to be a Soldier,

5   And if any man also should be struggling, he is definitely not being made Crowned with a Victor's Wreath, unless he should struggle according to the Commands of Christ,

6   The husbandman that is by his choice Laboring must first of all be Partaker of the Fruits,

7   You Must Comprehend what I am Saying, because the Lord Gave beyond dreams to you Understanding in all things,

8   You must Remember Jesus Christ from Seed of David Raised Up Out from the Dead According to my Gospel,

9   Wherein that I am suffering evil as a criminal as far as bonds, but definitely the Word of God is definitely not now being made bound,

10 Because of this I am Continuously Enduring all things for the Elect, that they should also Acquire by their choice their Salvation by Christ Jesus with Eternal Glory.

Faithful Sayings

11 Faithful the Word, because if by our choice we Have Died Together, we also Will Live Together,

12 If we are Enduring by our choice, we also will Reign Together. If we will disclaim Him, He also shall Disclaim us,

13 If we are by our choice uncommitted, He Continues by His choice Faithful, He is definitely not able to disclaim Himself.

Remember these things

14 You must Remind these things, Testifying in the Presence of the Lord, to not quarrel trifles of no value, to the casting down of those hearing,

15 You must be Diligent by your choice, to Stand before God yourself Approved, a worker not ashamed, Straight Cutting the Word of Truth,

16 But you for yourself must Shun the profane worthless babblings, for they shall develop yet much more ungodliness,

17 And their spiritual communication shall have pasture as a canker sore, of whom is Hymenaeus and Philetus,

18 Who concerning the Truth have erred for themselves, saying the Resurrection is now ending already, and is subverting for themselves the Faith of some.

19 However, the Sure Foundation of God is now Standing, having this Seal, the Lord has Known them that are Being His. (Num 16:5) And you all that are naming the Name of Christ, now must by your choice Depart Away from unrighteousness,

20 But in a great house are not only golden and silver vessels, but definitely also wood and earthen, and some certainly to Honor and some to dishonor,

21 If therefore a man should have Spiritually Cleansed Out himself from these, he shall be a vessel for Honor, and is now being Made Holy and useful to the Master is now being Made Prepared for every God-Good Work by God,

22 Then you must flee also the youthful evil desires; and you must be following closely Righteousness, Faith, God-Love, Peace with them that call upon the Lord out from a Purified heart,

23 But foolish and frivolous questioning refuse, Spiritually Discerning that they are spiritually born to quarrels,

24 And a Bondslave of the Lord definitely ought not to quarrel, but definitely to be Gentle to all, Willing to Teach, Enduring evil work,

25 In Meekness Disciplining those in Fear who are for themselves Opposing themselves; God should Give to them Repentance to Full Knowledge of the Truth, (1 Cor 11:32)

26 That they might by their choice Recover themselves, out from the devil's snare, being made pulled in by him at his will.

Apostasy in the Last Days

3 This you must be Now for yourself Knowing, that in the Last Day violent Special Times will be present,

2   For men shall be loving themselves, covetous, boasters, proud, blasphemous, disobedience to parents, unthankful, unholy,

3   Without natural affection, unalterable, false accusers (slanderers), no self control, fierce, despisers of God-Good,

4   Traitors, reactionary, are made self directed pride, lovers of pleasure much more than lovers of God,

5   Having a form of Godliness, but accepting no responsibility to His Miracle Power, so then also, from these Stay Away,

6   Because out from these are they who creeping into houses and capturing foolish women, continuously now made loaded with sin natures and sins, being made led into many diverse evil desires,

7   Always learning and never ever are being able to come into Full Knowledge of the Truth,

8   In manner as Jannes and Jambres have stood against Moses, in same manner also these are for themselves standing against the Truth; men who are made totally corrupt, in their understanding of mind, reprobates concerning Faith,

9   But they shall definitely not develop by their choice to greater, because their irrationality shall be apparent to all, as theirs also was.

10 But you are now by your choice Following along with my Doctrine, Rearing, Purpose, Faith, Long-suffering, God-Love, Endurance.

11 Persecutions, sufferings such as occurred to me in Antioch, in Iconium, in Lystra, persecutions such as I have undergone, and out from all things the Lord has Rescued me.

12 So also all those who shall by their choice be Living God Fearing in Christ Jesus, they shall be made persecuted.

13 But evil men and seducers shall develop by their choice with intent to worse, deceiving by their choice and being made deceived.

Continue in the things Learned

14 But you must Continue in the things you have Learned, and have been Made Assured, now Spiritually Knowing from Whom you have Learned,

15 And that from a babe you are Spiritually Discerning the Sacred writings, which are being Able to Make you Wise for Salvation through Faith inside of Christ Jesus.

All Scripture is God Breathed

16 All Scripture God Breathed, and Profitable for Doctrine, for Convincing, for Correction, for Discipline in Righteousness,

17 That the man of God should be Lifted Up, being Made Fully Complete to All God-Good Work by God.

Preach the Word

4 I testify therefore, I, in the Presence of God and the Lord Jesus Christ, Who is Expected to Judge the Living and the dead at His Appearing with His Kingdom Rule,

2   You Must Preach the Word, you Must be Standing Ready, in Season, out of Season; Convince of sin, Rebuke, Encourage with all Long-suffering and Teaching.

They shall turn from the Truth

3   For a Special Season shall be when

they shall definitely not Continue Enduring Sound Doctrine, but definitely having made itching hearing, they shall heap teachers upon themselves, after their own evil desires,

4   And they shall actually turn away their hearing from the Truth, but with intent, they shall be made turned away to fables,

5   But you must be Serious in all things. You must suffer evil. You must do the Work by God in your Service (of Calling) of an Evangelist. You Must Fully Persuade.

Paul's Final Farewell

6   Because I, already am Made Offered, and the Special Time of my Departure is Now Continuously by my choice Standing Ready,

7   I have Continuously by my choice Fought the God-Work conflict. I am by my choice Finally Finishing my Course. I am Now by my choice Keeping Faith,

8   Finally, there is Reserved for me the Victor's Wreath of Righteousness, which the Lord, the Righteous Judge, shall Yield to me in that The Day, and not to me only, but definitely also to everyone that is by their choice Loving His Appearing.

Personal Circumstances

9   You must have Diligence to Come to me rapidly,

10 Yet Demas has forsaken me, loving this current age and went to Thessalonica; Crescens to Galatia; Titus to Dalmatia,

11 Luke alone is with me. You must move along, receiving up Mark with yourself, because he is useful to me for Service (of Calling),

12 And Tychicus I have sent out to Ephesus,

13 Coming, you must bring the mantle which I left behind in Troas with Carpus,

and the scrolls specifically of sheep skin parchment.

14 Alexander the coppersmith exhibited many evil works toward me. The Lord Repays beyond dreams to him, according to his man works,

15 So then, you must Maintain yourselves, because by his own choice, he is now extremely standing against our Spiritual Words,

16 In my first defense, no one stood together with me, but definitely everyone forsook me. Has nothing been accounted to them? Not ever possible.

Lord Stood Beside me

17 Nevertheless, the Lord Stood Beside me, and more Strengthened me, that through me the Preaching should be Made Fully Persuaded, and all the Gentiles by their choice should Hear, and be Made Rescued from out of the lion's mouth,

18 And the Lord shall Rescue and shall Save me Away from all evil man work for His Heavenly Kingdom Rule, to whom Glory Forever. Amen.

Final Greetings

19 Greet Prisca and Aquila and the home of Onesiphorus,

20 Erastus continued in Corinth, but Trophimus I left behind in Miletus being sick,

21 You must have diligence to come before winter. Eubulus and Pudens and Linus and Claudia and all the Brethren are Greeting you,

22 The Lord Jesus Christ with your Spirit. Grace with you. Amen.

[The second to Timothy, the first overseer hand chosen of the Ephesians, was written from Rome, when Paul stood the second time before Caesar Nero]

The Epistle of Paul the Apostle to

Titus

Greetings

1 Paul, a Bondslave of God, and Apostle of Jesus Christ, according to Faith of God's Elect, and Full Knowledge of the Truth according to Godliness,

2 In Expectation of Life Eternal, Which God Who cannot lie Promised before time Eternal,

3 But has Manifested in His Own Special Time His Spiritual Word in preaching, to which I have been Made Committed, according to the Commandment of God our Savior,

4 To Titus, Truthful child, according to the common Faith, Grace, Mercy, Peace, from Father God and Lord Jesus Christ our Savior.

Appoint Elders and Overseers

5 For this one cause, I left you in Crete, that you should for yourself Organize what is needing, and you should Make by your choice Elders in every city, as I have Appointed to you,

6 If any man is unaccused, husband of one woman, having Faithful children, not with accusation of partying, or with unsubmissives,

7 Because an overseer must be unaccused as a Steward of God, not self-willed, not soon angry, not liking wine, not a striker, not for filthy gain,

8 But definitely hospitable, a friend of the God-Good, logical, Righteous, Personally Holy, Self-Controlled,

9 Upholding every Teaching of the Faithful Spiritual Word, in order that He should be Exceedingly Able, also to Encourage by Sound Doctrine, and to Expose as sin those contradicting.

Unruly vain teachers for money

10 Because there are many unsubmissives, and trivial talkers, and mental frauds, specifically those of the circumcision,

11 Whose mouths must be covered for this cause, who are subverting whole dwellings, teaching the things they ought not for filthy gain,

12 One of themselves, a Cretian Prophet, spoke of their own: Continuously liars, evil works, wild beasts, idle gluttons,

13 This Testimony is True. Because of this reason, you Must Convince them as sin Sharply, that they should be Sound in the Faith,

14 No more giving attention to Jewish fables and commandments of men, turning away from the Truth,

15 To the Purified, all things actually Purified, but being made defiled and faithless nothing purified, but definitely even their mind and conscience is made defiled.

They profess, but works disclaim

16 They confess to Spiritually Know God, but in man works they are disclaiming, being abominable, and disobedient, and to every God-Good Work by God reprobate.

Home Commands

2 But you must Utter what is appropriate for Sound Doctrine,

2 Old men to be sober, honest, logical, being Sound in Faith, in God-Love, in Endurance,

3 In like manner, aged women in quietness becoming Holiness, not false accusers (slanderers), not become a slave to very much wine, Teachers of God-Works,

4 That they should Teach the younger women to be Right Thinking, to be affectionate to their husbands, affectionately Loving Offspring,

5 Logical, Pure, keepers at home,

God-Good, made Subjecting themselves to their own husbands, that the Word of God should not be made blasphemed,

6 You must Encourage the younger men in like manner to be Logically Minded.

7 For yourself Offering Concern about all things, a Model of God-Works by God, in the Doctrine: Inerrancy, Integrity, Incorruption,

8 Healthy Spiritual Communication that cannot be condemned, in order that they out from contrary disrespect have no foul evil to say of you,

9 Bondslaves to be subject to their own masters, well pleasing in every way, being not contradicting,

10 Not keeping back for yourselves, but definitely exhibiting all God-Good Faith, that they should be Adorning in every way the Doctrine of God our Savior.

The Grace of God Teaches us

11 Because the Grace of God, the Salvation has been Made to Fully Appear to every man,

12 That Disciplining us to Disclaim the ungodliness and worldly evil desires, we should by our choice Live in this current Age, Rationally, and Righteously, and God Fearing,

13 Looking for that Spiritually Blessed Expectation and Appearing of the Glory of the Great God and our Savior Jesus Christ,

14 Who Gave Himself in Behalf of us, in order that He should Remove us away from all lawlessness, so He might Cleanse to Himself a Peculiar People, Zealous of God-Works by God,

15 Also these things you must Utter, Encourage, and Convince of sin with every Commandment of God. Not any man must depreciate value to you.

Citizenship

3 You must Remind them to be for themselves Subject to rulers and authorities, to Listen to be Ready for every God-Good Work by God,

2 To blaspheme no man, to be not quarrelsome, exhibiting All Kindness, Meekness to every man.

Saved by His Mercy and Love

3 Because we were in time past, even we, uncomprehending, disobedient, being made deceived, bondserving to evil desires by our choice, and many diverse sensual desires in malicious desire for evil work, and living by our choice in envy, hatefulness, hating one another,

4 But when the Gentleness and the Affection to mankind of our Savior God was Made to Fully Appear,

5 Definitely not from works in righteousness which we did, but definitely by His Mercy He Saved us, through the Washing of Regeneration and Renewing to a New Kind by the Holy Spirit,

6 Which He has Poured out in us Abundantly through Jesus Christ our Savior,

7 That being Made Righteous by His Grace, we should have been Made Heirs, with Expectation of Eternal Life,

8 Faithful the Spiritual Word, and for these things I am Intending you to Affirm constantly, in order that they are being careful to Stand Before to Maintain Committing to God for God-Works, Works by God, These things are God-Works and Profitable to Men.

Reject heretics after second Warning

9 But you must be Shunning for yourself foolish questionings, and genealogies, and contentions, and Law quarrels because they are useless and self-worship,

10 You must Refuse a heretic man after one and second Warning,

11 Spiritually Discerning that such, he is now made perverted, and he by his choice is sinning being self-condemned.

Paul's Instructions for travel

12 When I shall send Artemas to you or

Tychicus, you must have Diligence to come to me in Nicopolis, for I am now judging to winter there,

13 You must journey with Zenas, the lawyer, and Apollos promptly, that nothing should be needing to them,

14 And you must Learn also to Stand Before to Maintain ours for the Necessary Needs of God-Works by God, in order that they should not be unfruitful,

15 All that are with me are Greeting you. You must Greet those that are Affectionately Loving us in the Faith. Grace with you all. Amen.

[To Titus, hand-chosen (by man) as the first overseer of the Cretians, from Nicopolis of Macedonia]

The Epistle of Paul the Apostle to

Philemon

Thankfulness

1 Paul a Prisoner of Christ Jesus and Timothy our Brother, to Philemon our Beloved and our Fellow Laborer,

2 And to our Beloved Apphia, and to Archippus our fellow soldier, and to them in your home Assembly,

3 Grace to you, and Peace, from God our Father and Lord Jesus Christ, (Ps 110:1)

4 I am Giving Thanks to my God always making Mention of you in my Prayers,

5 Hearing of your God-Love and Faith, Whom you Have with the Lord Jesus, also in all Saints,

6 So that the Fellowship of your Faith should become Powerful in Full Knowledge of all God-Good among yourselves, for the Purpose and Result of Christ Jesus,

7 For we are having very much Thankfulness for Grace and Encouragement in your God-Love, because the Compassions of the Saints are made Refreshed through you, Brother.

Paul Pleads for Onesimus

8 For this reason, I am having very much Boldness in Christ, to instantly Command to you what is Appropriate,

9 Because of God-Love, instead I Beseech, being such as old man Paul, moreover just now also a Prisoner of Jesus Christ,

10 I Beseech you for my child, Onesimus, whom I have Born from Above in my bonds,

11 Who as in time past not useful to you, but just now useful to me and you,

12 Whom I have sent again, so you must Receive him to self. This is my Compassion,

13 Whom I was myself intending to hold back, in order that in behalf of you, he might serve me in the bonds of the Gospel,

14 But without your advice, I have willed definitely to not do anything that as not by necessity, but definitely by volunteering that the God-Good of you might be,

15 Because perhaps through this, he had been made separated for a short time, in order that you have him for Eternity,

16 No more as a slave, but definitely more above; a Bondslave, a Brother Beloved, specifically much to me, and much more to you in sinful flesh nature and in the Lord.

17 Then if you have me, a companion, you must Receive him to self-same as me,

18 And moreover if he has wronged you anything before, you must be accounting responsible to me owing this,

19 I, Paul have written with my hand. I will compensate. But that not I should say to you, how yourself is owing more to me,

20 Yes, my Brother, I have Joy of you in the

Lord beyond dreams. You must refresh my compassion in the Lord,

21 Being Persuaded with your Obedience, I have written to you, Spiritually Discerning that also you shall do above whatever I am saying.

Instruction and Greetings
22 And with all this also you must prepare a lodging for me. I am Expecting, because that through your Prayers, I will be Made freely Given to yourselves.

23 Epaphras, my fellow prisoner, is greeting you in Christ Jesus.

24 Mark, Aristarchus, Demas, Luke, my Fellow Laborers.

25 The Grace of our Lord Jesus Christ with your spirit. Amen.

[To Philemon, written from Rome through Paul's house servant Onesimus]

The Epistle to the

Hebrews

Father has Spoken to us by His Son
1 God, Who in Many Times and Many Manners long ago, Uttered to the fathers by the Prophets;

2 In regard of these last days, He has Uttered to us By the Son, Whom He has Positioned Heir of All things, and Through Whom He has Finalized the Ages,

3 Who, being the Perfect Brilliant Radiance of Glory, and an Exact Image of His Spiritual Being, and is also Bringing All things by the Word of His Miracle Power, when He by Himself Finalized Purification of our sin natures and sins, Sat Down by the Right Side of the Majesty on High, (Ps 110:1)

Father Says His Son is Above the Angels
4 Being so Much Better than the Angels, as now Inheriting a different Name, Above Them.

5 For to which of the Angels as in past, Spoke He, You are My Son, I have Now Born You this Day, and again, I will be to Him for a Father, and He shall be to Me for a Son, (Ps 2:7; 2 Sam 7:16)

6 And again, when He Conducted in the Firstborn into the inhabited earth, He Said, And all the Angels of God Must Worship Him, (Deut 32:43)

7 And actually to the Angels He Said, Who Makes His Angels Spirits, and His Servants a Fiery Flame? (Ps 104:4)

8 But to the Son, Your Throne, God, Forever and Ever, a Scepter of Righteousness, the Scepter of Your Kingdom Rule,

9 You have Loved Righteousness and Hated lawlessness, because of this, God, Your God, has Spirit Anointed You with Oil of Exceeding Joy, above your Partners, (Ps 45:6-7)

10 And You have been a Grounded Foundation, Oh Lord, in the Beginning the Earth, and the Heavenlies are the Works by God of Your Hands,

11 They shall perish but You Continue Constantly, and they shall All be Made Old as a garment,

12 And like as a Covering, You shall Fold them up and they shall be made Changed, but You are the Same, and Your Years shall not Fail, (Ps 102:25-27)

13 But to which of the Angels is He Now Spirit Saying at any time, You must Sit at My Right Side until after I should Position Your enemies a Footstool for Your Feet?

Angel Spirits are Serving to the Saints

14 Are They definitely not All Ministering Spirits, being Made Sent Out for Serving to them Expecting to Inherit Salvation?

Great Salvation, why neglect?

2 Because of this, he must earnestly Give Attention, for Fear that what we have been Hearing, we might let slip,

2 For if That Word Made Uttered through Angels became Permanent, and every broken Commandment and disobeying received Just Recompense (pay back),

3 How shall we escape having neglected so Great of Salvation, which from the Beginning was Received, being Made Uttered by the Lord? It was Made Established for us by them that Heard.

God Bearing Witness

4 God Bears Witness with Miracle Signs, and also Wonders, and many Diverse Miracle Powers, and with Dividings of the Holy Spirit, According to His Own Will.

Christ Salvation of His Brethren

5 Because He has not Subjected the Expected inhabited earth to Angels, about which we are Uttering,

6 But a certain One Testified, Saying in a certain place, What is man that You are Mindful of Him, or the SON of MAN that You are Visiting to him?

7 You Made HIM (SON OF MAN) a certain little lower than Angels. You Crowned HIM with a Victor's Wreath with Glory and Honor; and You Made HIM Ruler over the Works by God of Your Hands,

8 You Have Subjected All things under His Feet. Yet to be Subjected to Him, all have definitely not been Removed from Memory (forgiven) by Him currently unsubmissive to Him. And, Behold attentively, All things are not yet Made Subject to Him, (Ps 8:4-6)

9 But we are Spiritually Seeing Jesus, Made a certain little lower than Angels for the suffering of Death, being now Crowned with a Victor's Wreath with Glory and Honor, so that He for the Grace of God By His Choice has Tasted Death in Behalf of everyone!

10 For it was Appropriate for Him, because For Whom All things and By Whom All things, for Leading many Sons to Glory (Spiritual Perfection), to be Making Perfect the Lord Author of their Salvation through sufferings,

11 For both He that is Making Holy, and they Who are Being Made Holy, All From One, for that reason He is definitely not ashamed to Call Them Brethren,

12 Saying, I will tell Your Name to My Brethren, in the midst of the Assembly. I will sing Praise to You. (Ps 22:22)

He Partook Sinless flesh to Save us

13 And again, I will Have Confidence in Him. And again, Behold, I and the little Children Whom God has Given to Me,

14 Therefore, in fact the little children are now partakers of sinful flesh nature and blood, He also similarly Partook of His (sinless flesh nature), that through Death, He should by His choice Destroy him that is having dominion of death, that is the devil,

15 And should by His choice Deliver them, those through being guilty of bondage of evil through all fear of death, to be Living by their choice,

16 Yet He took definitely not hold of Angels, but definitely, verily He Took Hold of Seed of Abraham.

Merciful and Faithful High Priest

17 From where in Every Way He ought by his choice to be Made Likened to His Brethren, in order that He should Become a Merciful and Faithful High Priest before God, to being Made Merciful for the sin natures and sins of the people,

18 For in that He Himself by His choice suffered, having been made tempted, He is Able to Help those being made tempted.

Christ as a Son over His House

3 Where from, Holy Brethren, Partners of Heavenly Service of Calling, you Must Consider the Apostle and High Priest of our Profession, Christ Jesus,

2   Who is Faithful to Him that Appointed Him, as also Moses in all of his House of Israel, (Num 12:7)

3   For this Man is Thought Worthy of much More Glory than Moses, as Who Built the House of God Himself is having More Excellent Honor,

4   Because every home is built by somebody, but God Built All things.

Moses and Christ, different Houses

5   And Moses, indeed, Faithful in all of his House of Israel, as an Attendant, for a Testimony of that which shall be Made Uttered,

6   Instead Christ, as the Son over His House of God, Whose Home we are Being, if we should Hold Fast the Boldness, and the Happiness of the Expectation Permanent until the End.

Israel Proved God in the wilderness

7   For this reason, just as the Holy Spirit is Saying, This day, if you should by your choice have Heard My Voice,

8   You should not by your choice be hardening your hearts as in the bitter disappointment, according to the day of the temptation in the desolate wilderness, (Ps 95:8-9)

9   When your fathers tempted Me, Proved Me in Truth, and saw My Works by God forty years,

10   For this reason, I was Indignant with that generation and Spoke, They are made to continuously be deceiving in their heart, and they have definitely by their choice not known My Ways,

11   As I Swear in My Wrath for Justice, whether they shall enter into My Spiritual Heavenly Rest? (Ps 95:11)

A heart of no Commitment

12   You must Spiritually be Seeing, Oh Brethren, for Fear that there shall be in any of you an evil heart of no Commitment, by your choice to depart away from the Living God,

13   But definitely, you must encourage yourselves with every person daily, until when it is made called This Day, in order that not anyone of you should be made hardened by deceitfulness of sin nature and sin,

14   Because we are made Partners of Christ, if we should by our choice Hold Permanent the beginning of our Spiritual Being until the End,

15   In this day, if you are made to Say you should by your choice Hear from His Voice, you should not by your choice harden your hearts, as in the bitter disappointment, (Ps 95:7-8)

16   Because some having Heard, rebelled, but definitely not all them that came out from Egypt by Moses.

God Gave Israelites no Heavenly Rest

17   But with whom He was Indignant forty years, Was it definitely not with them who having by their choice sinned, whose carcasses fell down by their choice in the desolate wilderness?

18   And to whom swore He that they shall not be entering into His Spiritual Heavenly Rest, except to the disobedient?

19   So we are Spiritually Seeing that they have not been made able to Enter because of no Commitment.

Fear that we will not enter also

4 We should be afraid. Therefore, for fear that being made left a Promise to enter into His Spiritual Heavenly Rest, some might seem of yourselves to now be lacking,

2   Because also we are now Made preaching the Gospel, even as they also, but definitely the Spiritual Word has definitely not profited them hearing the same, not being made mixed together with Faith in them having heard by their choice.

Only by Committing will we Enter

3   For we are Entering into the Spiritually Heavenly Rest Committing by our choice just as the Spirit Says, As I have Sworn in My Wrath for Justice, whether they shall enter into My Spiritual Heavenly Rest? Although the Works by God have been Made Ended from Conception of the satan's world, (Ps 95:11)

4   For He now Spirit Says, regarding a certain place of the Seventh in such a manner. And God Rested in the Seventh Day from All His Works by God, (Gen 2:2)

5   And in this again, If they shall Enter into My Spiritual Heavenly Rest? (Ps 95:11)

6   In fact then, it is made left behind to certain ones, to Enter for themselves, and those first Having the Gospel made Proclaimed, Entered not in by their own choice because of disobedience,

7   Again, He Determines a Certain Day, saying in David, This Day, after so long a time, just as is now made Spirit Saying, This Day if you should have by your choice Heard His Voice, harden not your hearts, (Ps 95:7,8)

8   For if Jesus had Given them Rest, He would definitely not ever have Uttered of another of the same kind in regard to these things following another Day,

9   So then a Sabbath Rest is made left behind for the People of God,

10 For He having Entered into His Spiritual Heavenly Rest, he is also Resting from his Works by God, as God from His Own,

11 We should be Diligent, therefore, to Enter into that Spiritual Heavenly Rest, that any should not fall down by his choice in the same example of disobedience.

God's Word, Living and Powerful

12 For the Word of God is Continuously Living and Powerful and Sharper more than any two edged Sword; and Continuously Piercing as far as Dividing of soul and of spirit and of joints and of marrows; and a Discerner of the inner thoughts and of intents of heart.

13 So also there is definitely not a creature not Manifest Every Way in the Presence of Him, and naked and exposed to the Eyes of Him, The Spiritual Word then Within us.

Touched with our infirmities

14 Having then, the Great High Priest, Who is now Passed into the Heavenlies, Jesus, the Son of God, we should be Holding to Retain for our Profession,

15 For we definitely have not a High Priest Who is not able to have Sympathy for our infirmities, but now being made tempted by similitude in All things without sin nature and sin,

16 We should come near, therefore, with Boldness to the Throne of Grace, that we might Receive Mercy and might Find Grace for Help in time of need.

A High Priest Called of God

5   For every High Priest for men is being made taking to receive in behalf of men, being made Ruler before God, in order that he also should Offer both Gifts and Sacrifices in behalf of sin natures and sins,

2   Who is able to have feelings on the ignorant by their choice and then made deceived, in fact even he is encompassed with infirmity,

3   And because of this, he ought just as for the people, in such a manner also for himself, Offer in behalf of sin natures and sins,

4   And definitely no one takes this Honor to himself, but definitely he that is Made Called by God, even as also Aaron,

5   In such a manner, also Christ has definitely not Attributed Glory to Himself to become a High Priest, but definitely He that Uttered to Him, You, You are My Son, this Day, I have Born You from Above. [Ps 2:7, Acts 13:33, when He Rose from the Grave]

6   Just as also in Another of a different

kind, He Says, You a Priest Forever, according to the Priestly Order of Melchisedec, (Ps 110:4)

Perfect Author of our Salvation

7   Who in the Days of His (Sinless) Flesh Nature and with both Supplications and Requests with Mighty Strong Crying and Tears, to Who is being able to Save Him from Death, and was made Spiritually Heard for His God Fearing,

8   Even though He is the Son, He Learned Obedience from the things suffered by His Choice,

9   And Being Made Perfect, He Became the Author of Eternal Salvation to All that Obey Him,

10 Made Honor Called by God, a High Priest according to the Priestly Order of Melchisedec.

To Discern God-Work and evil work

11 Of Whom a very much Spiritual Account for us, also impractical to be Saying. In fact, you be now mentally slow in Hearing,

12 Because of the time for when you ought to be teachers, you are having a need to be Taught yourselves again what the Basic Elements of the Beginning of the Oracles of God. And you are now becoming needful to have Milk, and definitely not strong nourishment,

13 Because everyone that Partakes of Milk, unskillful of the Spiritual Word of Righteousness, because he is an Infant,

14 But Strong Nourishment is Perfect through the use of Having Faculties being Made Exercised, Distinguishing Differences between both God-Work and also evil work.

Dismissing Essential Foundation

6 For this reason, dismissing the Beginning of the Spiritual Communication of Christ for Spiritual Perfection, we should not be bringing again the Foundation, laying an Essential Foundation of Repentance away from the dead man works, and of Faith with Intent for God,

2   Of teaching of Washing Baptisms, and also Laying On of Hands, and also of Resurrection of the dead, and Eternal Judgment,

3   And this we will by our choice Do, if it should be God Permitting. (1 Cor 11:23-32)

Impossible through 5 steps

4   Because, impossible to them that have (1) Once been Made Enlightened, and also (2) Tasted the God-Gift of the Heavenly, and (3) Becoming Partners of the Holy Spirit,

5   And (4) Having Tasted God-Work of God, and (5) Miracle Powers of Individual Specific Words also of the Expecting Age,

To Renew them to Repentance

6   And then (6) falling away by their choice to Renew them again in Repentance, crucifying again to themselves the Son of God, and putting to public shame, (Heb 10:26-30; 1 Cor 9:27; 2 Pet 2:20-22)

Thorns and briers rejected

7   For the earth which has often drank the rain showers coming upon it, and delivers herbs fit for them who (plural) is (individually) made Tending also is (individually) Partaking by his choice of the Blessing from God,

8   But (7) bringing out thorns and briars by its choice reprobate (rejected) and near self-cursing, whose End for Burning.

Persuaded better things of you

9   But Beloved, although even as we are Uttering so, we are now Made Persuaded if also better things about you Having Salvation,

10 Because God is definitely not unrighteous to forget your Work by God and Labor of God-Love, that you must Exhibit for yourselves in His Name, Serving by your

choice to the Saints, and are Continuously Serving by your choice,

11 And we are Desiring, every person of you to Exhibit his Diligence, to the Full Persuasion of the Expectation until the End,

12 That not mentally slow, you should by your choice become close Followers of those who through Faith and Longsuffering, are Inheriting by their choice the Promises.

Impossible for God to lie

13 Because God Promised to Abraham, in fact that He was Having no greater to Swear, He Swore by Himself,

14 Saying Assuredly, Blessing, I will Bless you, and Multiplying, I will Multiply you, (Gen 22:16-17)

15 Also, Longsuffering in same manner, he Obtained by his choice the Promise,

16 Because men actually Promise by the Greater, and that Oath for Establishment of Everything to them, an End of contradiction,

17 Wherein God more Abundantly Intends to Show as Example to them, the Heirs of the Promise, the Immutability of His Counsel, He Ensured by an Oath,

18 In order that through Two Immutable Things, in which Impossible for God to lie, we who have Fled for Refuge should have a Stronger Encouragement to Retain that Expectation being Set Before,

19 Which we Have as an Anchor of the soul, and also Safe and Permanent, also Entering into the Innermost of the Veil,

20 Whereto a Forerunner, Jesus has Entered in Behalf of us, made a High Priest Forever, according to the Priestly Order of Melchisedec.

Melchizedek Theophany

7 Because this Melchisedec, King of Salem, Priest of the Most High God, encountering Abraham returning from the defeat of the kings, and Blessed him,

2 Also Abraham fully divided a tenth of all to Whom, first of all actually by interpretation King of Righteousness, and after that also King of Salem, Who is King of Peace, (Gen 14:17-20)

3 Without father, without mother, without descent, having neither beginning of days, nor End of Life, now Made Being Like to the Son of God, Continuing a Priest Forever,

4 Now Perceive how Important this Man to Whom even the patriarch Abraham gave even a tenth of the spoils.

Take tithes for the Greater

5 And actually they of the sons of Levi, the Levitical priesthood, received a Commandment having to tithe the people according to the Law, that is from their Brethren, even though they came out from the loins of Abraham,

6 But He whose descent is not counted from them, is now receiving tithes from Abraham, also is now Blessing him who is having the Promises,

7 And without all contradiction, the younger aged is made Blessed by the Better,

8 And here actually dying men receive tithes there, and these Bear Record that He is Living,

9 And as to say Levi also, who receives tithes, is now made paying tithes through Abraham.

10 Because he was yet in the loins of his father, when Melchisedec Encountered him.

Priesthood changed, so Law also

11 If indeed therefore, Perfection was by the Levitical priesthood, yet a person among them had been made established, what further need for another of a different kind to arise after the Priestly Order of Melchisedec? Then a Priest (needs) to arise definitely not after the priestly order to be made called of Aaron?

12 Because the Priesthood is being transferred from necessity. Removing the Law is occurring,

13 For in regard to This it is being Said,

These things of another of a different tribe is now being by their choice Partakers, for This no one gave attention at the Altar,

14 Because Evident Beforehand, our Lord Rose out from Judah, wherein that Moses Uttered was not a tribe of Priesthood,

15 And further, it is more Abundantly Evident, allowing that after the similitude of Melchisedec, there is Arising Another Priest of a different kind,

16 Who definitely (is) not according to a Law of carnal sinful flesh nature Commandment, but definitely is Occurring According to Miracle Power of Infinite Life,

17 Because He Bears Record, You (are) a Priest Forever, according to the Priestly Order of Melchisedec, (Ps 110:4)

18 Because there is actually occurring a Putting Away of the Commandment going before, because of itself weak and useless,

19 Because the Law Made nothing Perfect, but the Bringing in a Better Expectation, through which we Approach Near to God,

20 And not according to those without an Oath Statement,

21 Because they actually became priests without an oath statement, but Him with an Oath Statement by His Saying to Him, The Lord Swore and shall not Regret, You (are) a Priest Forever, according to the Priestly Order of Melchisedec. (Ps 110:4)

22 By So Much, Jesus Became a Guarantee of a Better Covenant,

23 And they indeed many more priests, being made forbidden to continue along because they are now ending in death,

24 But this Man because He Continues Forever, therein has an Unchangeable Priesthood,

25 Where He Now is able to Save in the Extreme, those who are Coming near to God Through Him, always Living to Make Intercession in Behalf of them,

26 Because He was Being such an Appropriate High Priest to us, Personally Holy, Without evil work, Undefiled, being made Separate from sinners, and made High in the Heavenlies,

27 Who has definitely no necessity daily, as High Priests, first a Sacrifice for their own sin natures and sins, after that Bearing Up for This the people, because this He Finalized One Time, Bearing Up Himself in an Offering,

28 Because the Law makes men High Priests having infirmity, but the Spiritual Word of the Oath Statement, which followed after the Law, the Son Forever Made Perfect.

Christ is now High Priest Forever

8 Now the Above Sum is being Made Saying, We have such a High Priest Who has Sat Down by the Right Side of the Throne of Majesty in the Heavenlies,

2 A Servant of the Holy Place and of the True Tabernacle, which the Lord Pitched and not man,

3 For every High Priest is made to offer both gifts and sacrifices, where from He is making necessary to have something from Him that He should offer,

4 Yet indeed if He were upon the earth, He was not ever a priest. Those being priests are offering gifts according to the Law,

5 Who are devoted as example and shadow of the Heavenlies, just as Moses was Warned as expecting to Complete the Tabernacle, for He Stated, Behold Attentively, Finalize All Things according to the Model made Shown to you in the mountain. (Ex 25:40)

New Covenant replaced Old Covenant

6 Moreover, just now He is Acquiring a different Service to God, by which also He is the Reconciler of a Better Covenant, which is now being made Established on Better Promises,

7 For if that First then was blameless, no place ever was ever Made Sought for a Second,

8 For finding fault in them Saying,

Behold, the Day is Coming Says the Lord, that I will Finish upon the House of Israel, and upon the House of Judah, a New of a different kind Covenant,

9 Not according to the Covenant that I made with your fathers in the day, taking hold by My Hand to Lead Out them Myself from the area of Egypt. Because they persevered not in My Covenant, I also neglected them, Says the Lord,

10 For this, the Covenant that I will Grant to the House of Israel following those days, Says the Lord. I am Giving My Laws into their intellect, and in their hearts I will Inscribe Them, and I will be to them God Already, and they shall be to Me for a People,

11 And they should never ever teach every man his neighbor, and every man his brother, saying you must Know the Lord; for everyone shall Spiritually Know Me from the least of them up to their great,

12 For I will be by Grace to their unrighteousness, and their sin natures and sins, and their lawlessnesses, I Myself have definitely not Remembered further.
(Jer 31:31-34)

13 In that He Says, A New of a different kind, the First is now Made Old, and that Made Old is also Aged Old near Disappearance.

The Old Covenant

9 Therefore, the first was actually having both Righteous Action Worship, and also a worldly Sanctuary,

2 For a Tabernacle was made Built first with both the Candlestick and the Table with the Bread of Purpose, that is made called the Holy Place,

3 And the Tabernacle after the Second Veil, is called the Holiest of Holy Places,

4 Having a golden censer of Incense, and the Ark of the Covenant overlaid all around with gold, the golden jar having the Manna, and the Staff of Aaron which was Budding Forth, and the Tablets of the Covenant,

5 And far above it, the Cherubim of Glory is shadowing the Mercy Seat, about which there is not now about a particular to say,

6 When these are now actually made ready in this manner into the first Tabernacle, the priests went in unceasingly performing the worships,

7 But into the second, the High Priest once a year alone, offered not without blood, in behalf of himself and of the errors of the people.

8 This the Holy Spirit made evident, that The Sanctuary was not at all made Manifest, while the way of the first Tabernacle is yet having standing,

9 Which figure was present at a Special Time, to be offering mutually gifts and sacrifices, that are not able to Make Perfect them devoting according to conscience,

10 Only in foods, and drinkings, and different washings baptisms, and for rules of practice of sinful flesh nature, laying upon until the Special Time of Rectification.

Christ's New Covenant

11 So Christ came up The High Priest, expecting by God-Goods the Greatest now Perfect Tabernacle definitely not made by hand, that is not of this Creation,

12 Neither through blood of he-goats or through calves, but by His Own Blood, He entered One Time into the Holiest, guaranteeing Removal to Heaven,

13 Because if the blood of bulls and of he-goats, and the ashes of an heifer sprinkling, making unholy Holy to the purifying of the sinful flesh nature,

14 How much more the Blood of Christ, Who through the Eternal Spirit Himself offered Faultless to God, shall Cleanse the conscience of you from the dead man works, for Living Continuously by your choice to be Devoted Continuously by your choice to God?

15 And for this Covenant, New of a

different kind, He is the Reconciler. So that by Becoming Death for Separation Removal of us, after the first Covenant of broken Commandments, those now being Made Outwardly Called (Gospel), should Receive the Promise of Eternal Inheritance.

The Death of the Testator

16 Because whereto a Covenant, necessity is Made Bringing the Death of the Testator,

17 Because a Covenant (is) after the dead, otherwise for fear that permanence is prevailing when the Testator is Living,

18 Where from neither the First was made consecrated without blood,

19 For every Commandment had been Made Uttered at all times by Moses according to the Law. Taking the blood of calves and he-goats, with water and scarlet wool and hyssop to the people, he Sprinkled both the Book and all the people,

20 Saying, This the Blood of the Covenant that God has God Commanded to you, (Ex 24:8)

21 Also likewise, he Sprinkled with the Blood the Tabernacle and even all the Vessels of the Service to God,

22 And almost All things by the Law are Made Cleansed by Blood, and without Shedding of Blood no Removal of sins Occurs.

New Covenant made in Heaven

23 Then indeed a necessity for an example of the Things in the Heavenlies to be Made Cleansed Themselves, but the Heavenly things with Better Sacrifices than these,

24 Because Christ did not Enter into the Holy Places made with hands, like figures of the True, but definitely into the Heaven Itself, now Made Known Plainly, in Behalf of us, Before the Presence of God,

25 Neither in order that He might Offer Himself often, as the High Priest enters into the Holiest each year with Blood of another,

26 Then He Himself must often to suffer since Conception of the satan's world, but now for once in the Final End of the satan's world of the Age, He is Now made Manifest for Putting Away of the sin nature and sin, through His Sacrifice of Himself,

27 So as there is Appointed to man once to die, and after that this, Final Judgment,

28 So Christ was once Made Offered to Bear Up as in an Offering for the sin natures and sins of many. A Second Time He shall Spiritually Appear to those without sin nature and sin Waiting for Salvation.

Old Covenant was a shadow of New

10 Because the Law having a shadow of the expected God-Goods, not itself the image of those things for every year with the same sacrifices which they are ever offering, never are able to be coming near to Making Perfect,

2 Otherwise, Would they not have ceased to be offering once Spiritually Cleansed? Because even yet, any man Devoting is having a conscience of sin natures and sins,

3 But definitely by them in remembrance of sin natures and sins every year,

4 (It is) impossible for blood of bulls and he-goats to take away sin natures and sins,

5 For this reason, Entering into the satan's world, He Said, Sacrifice and offering You would not, but a Body You Made Complete for Me.

6 So in burnt offerings for sin nature and sin, I am not pleased.

7 Then I Spoke, Behold, I Now Come in the volume of the Book, Made Written about Me. I Do the Will of You, My God, (Ps 40:6-7)

8 When Higher, He Said, Sacrifice and offering and burnt offerings then for sin nature and sin, You definitely will not, neither have You been Pleased when according to the Law, they are made offered,

Old was Removed to Establish New

9   Then He Spirit Said, Behold, I Now Come to do Your Will, My God, Intentionally Killing the first, that the Second should Stand,

10   By Whose Will, we are being Made Holy through the Offering of the Body of Jesus Christ, One Time.

Priesthood Changed, so Law also

11   And actually every priest was standing by daily to ministering, and offering often the same sacrifices which never are able to Remove Away sin natures and sins.

12   But He, after offering One Sacrifice in Behalf of sin natures and sins Forever, Sat Down by the Right Side of God,

13   And Now is Waiting for, until after His enemies should have been Made Laid Down at the Footstool under His Feet,

14   Yet for by One Offering, He Made Perfect Forever Those being Made Holy.

15   And the Holy Spirit also Witnesses to us, for after that He has Said Before,

16   This is the Covenant I will Grant to them after those days, when Says the Lord, I Give My Law (fixed nature) in your hearts, and in your intellects I will Inscribe them,

17   And their sin natures and sins and their lawlessnesses, I Myself should never ever remember further, (Jer 31:31-34)

18   Now whereto Removal of these, not anymore an Offering for the sin nature and sin.

By His Flesh, New and Living Way

19   Having, therefore, Brethren, Boldness for Entrance into the Holiest by the Blood of Jesus,

20   Who, Once Slain and Now Living, Consecrated for us a Way through the Veil, that is His (Sinless) Flesh Nature,

21   And Now a Great Priest over the House of God,

22   We should Come Near with a True heart with Full Persuasion of Faith, being Now Made Sprinkled upon our hearts Away From an evil conscience, and our Body is Now being Made Washed with Purified water,

23   We should be Continuously Holding the Profession of our Expectation not wavering, because Faithful, He that Promised,

24   And we should be considering one another for Provocation of God-Love, and of God-Works by God,

25   Not forsaking the Assembling Together of ourselves, just as a custom for some, but definitely we are by our choice Encouraging, and so much more when we are Spiritually Seeing The Day Approaching near.

If we sin willfully after Knowing

26   Because our sinning voluntarily, after we have Received the Full Knowledge of the Truth, not anymore is made leaving behind a sacrifice for sin natures and sins, (Heb 6:6)

27   But a certain fearful anticipation of Final Judgment, and fiery zeal to eat expected opponents,

28   He that rejected a certain Law of Moses, died without sympathy, after two or three witnesses, (Deut 17:6)

29   How much seems of worse severe punishment shall He definitely Make Think Worthy, who has trampled down the Son of God, and esteemed the Blood of the Covenant unclean, and insulted the Spirit of Grace, whereby Whom He had been Made Holy?

30   For we Spiritually Discern that He Spoke, Vengeance is Mine, I will Repay, Says the Lord. And again, The Lord shall Judge His people.

Cast not away your Confidence

31   It is a fearful thing to fall into the Hands of the Living God, (Deut 32:35-36)

32   But you must be in Remembrance of the first days wherein yourselves had been Made Enlightened. You Endured a long struggle of sufferings,

33 This actually, when you were made a theater both with afflictions and with reproach, and this when Companions Occurred, each Behaved in the same manner,
34 But because you had Sympathy for my bonds, and have Looked with Joy for the extortion (stealing) of your material goods, you are Knowing to Have Inside yourselves a Better and Continuing Substance in the Heavenlies,
35 Therefore, you should not cast aside your Boldness which has Great Recompense (pay back),
36 Because you have need of Endurance, that having Done the Will of God, you should for yourselves Earn the Promise,
37 For even yet a little while, that which is Coming shall Now Come, and definitely not delay. (Hab 2:3)

The Righteous shall Live by Faith
38 Now the Righteous shall for himself Live Out From Faith, and if any might for himself draw back, My Living Soul is definitely not Pleased with him, (Hab 2:4)
39 But we are definitely not being drawing back into damnation, but definitely of Faith for Possession of the soul.

Faith Defined
11 Now Faith is Spiritual Being (a person who has Christ Within himself, Born from Above; Col 1:27) Continuously Making Expectings: the Convincing of Things not made physically seen,
2 For by This the Elders have been Made Witnesses,
3 By Faith we are Comprehending to be Now Being Made Complete for the Ages by the Word from God, in that out from not appearing, we are Now to become Made Spiritually Seeing.

Without Faith Impossible to Please God
4 By Faith Abel Offered to God a Sacrifice more excellent than Cain, by which he has Made Witness to being Righteous,

God Witnessing of His Gifts, and by them, having died even yet is Uttering,
5 By Faith Enoch has been made Translated, not Spiritually Discerning death, and was not made found, since He has Translated him. Because God after the Removing of him is now Made Witnessing to be Acceptably Pleasing to God, (Gen 5:24)
6 But without Faith, Impossible to Acceptably Please (God), because he that comes near to God must have Committed that He is, and is Being a Rewarder to them Diligently, Continuously Seeking after Him by their choice,
7 By Faith Noah, being Made Warned about that not as yet being made physically seen, was Made Fearing with sincere apprehension, built an Ark for the Salvation of his home, by which he condemned to death the satan's world, and became Heir of Righteousness by Faith,
8 By Faith being made Called, Abraham Obeyed, to depart to the place that he was Expecting to receive for an Inheritance, and he Departed not being aware wherein he is coming,
9 By Faith, he Sojourned upon the earth for the Promise, as in a strange country, dwelling in Tabernacles with Isaac and Jacob, Fellow Heirs of the same Promise,
10 For he Waited for having a City with Foundations, Whose Craftsman and Maker, God,
11 By Faith, also Sarah herself Received Miracle Power for Conception of Seed, and by Special Time of stature of age she Gave Birth, in fact Esteemed Him Faithful having Promised,
12 And for this reason, from One having Made Born, also now made dying, just as these things, the stars of the heaven in their multitudes of different stars, and like as the sand on the seashore of the sea innumerable, (Gen 22:17)
13 These all died, but not having received the Promises according to Faith, but definitely afar off they Spiritually Discerned,

and having been Persuaded, both Greeting and Confessing that they are upon the earth, Strangers and Chosen Foreigners.

14 Because they that are saying such make Known plainly, they are seeking after That Country,

15 Actually, if while away from that (country), they were remembering what they have departed from, whenever Time to return again,

16 But just Now, they are Longing after a better, that is a Heavenly; God for this Reason is definitely not ashamed to be Made Called by them their God, for He has Prepared for them a City.

17 By Faith, Abraham being made Tried, offered Isaac, also He Welcoming for himself the Promises, Offered his Only Born,

18 To whom it was made Uttered, That in Isaac shall your Seed be Made Outwardly Called (Gospel), (Gen 21:12)

19 Accounting how that God, Exceedingly Able to Raise up from the dead, from where He earned for himself yet in a figure.

20 By Faith, Isaac Blessed Jacob and Esau, concerning things Expecting.

21 By Faith Jacob dying, Blessed every son of Joseph, and Worshiped upon the top of his staff.

22 In Faith Joseph deceased. He Remembered concerning the leaving of the sons of Israel, and God Commanded concerning his bones.

23 By Faith, Moses being born, was Made Hid for three months by his father, since he Spiritually Saw a handsome little child, and Feared Not the proclamation of the king,

24 By Faith, Moses became Great, Disclaimed being made called the son of Pharaoh's daughter,

25 Instead, personally Choosing to suffer hardship Together with the people of God, than for a time to have enjoyment of sin nature and sin,

26 Esteeming the Reproach of Christ of greater Riches than treasures inside of Egypt, because he was Concerned for the Recompense (pay back),

27 By Faith, he Left Egypt, Not Made Fearing the anger of the king, because as Seeing Attentively the Invisible. He has been Steadfast by his choice,

28 By Faith, he Kept the Passover and the Sprinkling of the Blood, that He that Annihilated the firstborns should Not Approach Them,

29 By Faith, they Came Through the Red Sea as through Dry Land. The Egyptians, who Receiving a Trial, were Made Completely Swallowed,

30 By Faith, the walls of Jericho, for seven days being Made Surrounded, Fell Down.

31 By Faith, Rahab the harlot Receiving the spies with Peace, Perished Not with those being disobedient,

32 And what further should I say, for it shall be insufficient for me to be reciting concerning the Time of Gideon, and also Barak, and Samson, and Jephthae, and also David, and Samuel, and of the Prophets,

33 Who by Faith Subdued Kingdoms, Worked Righteousness, Obtained Promises, Stopped the Mouths of lions,

34 Extinguished by Miracle Power fire, Fled the mouths of the sword, increased Strong from infirmity, became Mighty in war, turned to Flight camps of aliens,

35 Women received from Resurrection their dead, and others of same kind were made tortured not looking for Separation Removal, that they might Acquire a Better Resurrection,

36 And other ones of a different kind Took Trial of cruel mockings and severe suffering, and further, of bonds and prison,

37 They were made stoned, made sawed apart, made tempted with murder by sword they died, wandered about in sheepskins, in goatskin hides, being made destitute, afflicted, suffering torments,

38 Whom the satan's world was Not Worthy; they Wandered in wildernesses, and mountains, and caves, and in holes of the earth,

All a Good Report, Received not

39 And these all have Born Record by the Faith, and not Earned for themselves the Promise.

40 God Concerning us, Foreseeing a Better Thing, that they without us should not be Made Perfect.

Author and Finisher of our Faith

12 Consequently, we Now Have so great a Large Cloud of Witnesses Encompassing us, Laying Aside every weight and the impeding sin nature and sin. Through Endurance we should Be Running the Race Set Before us.

2 Looking Attentively for Jesus, the Lord Author and Doctrinal Perfection of our Faith, Who for the Joy Set Before Him, Endured the cross, Despising the shame, and also has Sat Down by the Right Side of the Throne of God.

Disciplined by God

3 Because you must Contemplate Him, that Endured such contradiction by sinners toward Himself, in order that you should Not Be exhausted and made discouraged in your souls,

4 You have not yet Withstood until blood, Agonizing against sin nature and sin,

5 Also, you have overlooked the Encouragement which is Preaching Giving Reasonings to you as to Sons. My Son, you must not dislike the Discipline of the Lord, neither must you be made discouraged by His Convincing of sin,

6 Because whom the Lord Loves, He is Disciplining and Scourging every Son whom he is Accepting, (Prov 3:11-12)

7 If you are Enduring discipline that God is Offering to you as Sons, because what Son is he whom the Father is not Disciplining?

8 But if you are without Discipline whereof all are now Becoming Partners, so then you are bastards and definitely not Sons,

9 Furthermore, we were actually having our fathers of sinful flesh nature Instructors we Respected, and Very Much More we shall be Made Subject to the Father of Spirits and Live,

10 Because, indeed, for a few days they were Disciplining according to their thinking, but He Being with Intent for Being Essential for the Result and Purpose of us to be Partakers of His Holy Separated State,

11 And now All Discipline at present certainly seems not Joy, but definitely grief, then afterward yields back the Peaceable Fruit of Righteousness, through them being made Exercised.

Follow Holiness to See the Lord

12 For this reason, make Upright the hands made hanging down, and the palsied knees.

13 And you must make your tracks Upright for your feet, that the crippled should not be made turned away, but instead should be Made Cured. ·(Isa 35:3; Prov 4:26)

14 You must Follow Closely Peace with all, and Now Personal Holiness definitely without Which not one shall Spiritually See the Lord,

15 Looking Diligently that no one be lacking of the Grace of God; that not any root of bitterness springing Up Above should by your choice trouble, for through this many might be made defiled,

16 That not any fornicator or profane as Esau, who for one meal yielded back by himself his Birthright,

17 For you must Recall how then, thereafter, he would have Inherited the Blessing, he was Disapproved, because no place of Repentance was found, even though with tears he diligently sought after it, (Gen 27:36-39)

18 Because you are not coming near to the Mount to be made handling, but is Made Burning Fire, and Gloom, and Darkness, and Tempest,

19 And to the roaring sound of a Trumpet and the Voice of Words that they refused Hearing Spiritual Communication, no more to be made added to them,

20 They were not progressing because they were made ordered. If a wild beast might approach the Mount it shall be made stoned, or a javelin shall be made thrust through, (Ex 19:12-13)

21 And so Fearful was the scene, Moses Spoke, I am very fearful and trembled. (Deut 9:19)

Assembly of Firstborn in Heaven

22 But definitely you are Now Coming near Mount Sion, and to the City of The Living God, to the Heavenly Jerusalem, and to thousands of Angels,

23 To the General Assembly, so also the Assembly of the Firstborn, Now Made Recorded in Heaven, and to God the Judge of All, and to the Spirits of the Righteous Made Perfect,

24 And to Jesus, Reconciler of the New Covenant, and to the Blood of Sprinkling, that is Uttering Better than that of Abel,

25 You must See that you should not refuse Him that Utters. Because if the Same fled not, Whom they were refusing upon the earth, we being Warned as to Very Much More, are turning away for ourselves from the Heavenlies,

26 Whose Voice then Shook the earth, but Now He is Promising, Saying once further, I, I will Shake definitely not only the earth, but definitely also the Heaven, (Hag 2:6)

27 And even further, Once it is Made Evident, that Shaking, Removing as I am now Made Finalizing, in order that those things not Made Shaken should Continue,

28 For this reason, we should be Receiving an Unmovable Kingdom Rule, having Grace by which we should be Devoting Acceptably to God with Reverence and God Fearing, (Heb 13:17)

29 Because also, our God is a Consuming Fire. (Deut 4:24)

Pleasing to God

13 Brotherly Affection must Continue, Continuously by our choice,

2 You must not be forgetful of being Hospitable, for Unknowing some have Guest Lodged Angels,

3 You must be Mindful of the prisoners, as Bound Together with them made suffering torments, as also ourselves being in body,

4 Marriage is Honorable in every way, and the bed Undefiled, but fornicators and adulterers God will Judge,

5 The Manner not covetous, being made Content for the present, because He is Spirit Saying, You should never ever be abandoned, neither should you never ever be forsaken, (Deut 31:6)

6 So that we being Confident are Saying, Lord, Helper to me, and I shall definitely not fear what man shall by his choice do to me. (Ps 118:6)

Follow Example of those Esteemed

7 You must Remember them Esteemed by you, who Utter to you Spiritual Communications of God; his Faith you must Closely Follow, considering the Basic Understanding of his behavior,

8 Jesus Christ, the same yesterday, and today, and Forever.

Different and strange doctrines

9 And you Must Not be made carried about with many diverse strange teachings, because your heart is to be Made God-Work, established in Grace, not in food, in which your walk is definitely not made profitable,

We Have an Altar they have no Right

10 We are Having an Altar, of which they definitely have no Authority to Eat, they are devoting to the tabernacle,

11 Because of those beasts, whose blood is made brought into the Sanctuary by the High Priest for sin nature and sin, the

bodies of these were made fully burned outside the camp,

12 Also Jesus, for this reason, in order that He might Make Holy the people by His Own Blood, suffered outside the Gateway,

13 Accordingly, we might Come Out to Him, outside the camp, Bringing His reproach,

14 Because here we have no Continuing City, but definitely we are Expecting what we are Seeking After,

15 Through Him, therefore, we should be Bearing Up as in an Offering a Sacrifice of Giving Praise to God unceasingly, that Confessing to His Name is a Fruit of lips,

16 But Do Well while in Fellowship, you must not be forgetting, because God is made acceptably Pleased with such Sacrifices.

Persuaded by those Esteemed

17 You must be for yourselves Persuaded, by those Esteemed among yourselves, and you must by your choice be Continuously Submitting, because they are being by their choice Alerting in Behalf of your souls, as yielding back that Spiritual Communication with Joy. Doing this and not groaning, because this (is) gainless to yourselves, (1 Thess 5:12-13; Heb 12:28)

18 Pray for us, for we are Persuaded that we are Having a God-Work Conscience in all things, Willing to Behave God-Working,

19 But I earnestly Encourage this, to Finalize that I should more hastily be Made Restored to you,

20 Now the God of Peace, that Lead Up Out from the Dead, our Great Shepherd of the Sheep, by the Blood of the Eternal Covenant of our Lord Jesus,

You Made Complete beyond dreams

21 Make you Complete beyond dreams in every God-Good Work by God at All times, for doing His Will is being Finalized in you, that is in the Presence of Him Well Pleasing through Christ Jesus to Whom be the Glory Forever and Ever. Amen.

22 And I encourage you to Continue Enduring, Brethren, by Encouragement of that Spiritual Word, even because of a little measure Exhortation Written to you.

23 You are Knowing that Brother Timothy is now made set at liberty with whom, if more hastily he should Come, I will Spiritually See you.

Greet all them Esteemed of you

24 Greet all them of you being Esteemed, and All the Saints. They of Italy Greet you.

25 Grace with you All. Amen.

[*Written to Hebrews from Italy, through Timothy*]

The Epistle of

James

To the scattered Twelve Tribes

1 James, a Bondslave of God and the Lord Jesus Christ, to the Twelve Tribes of those scattered widely, Rejoice.

Trying your Faith gives Endurance

2 Oh, my Brethren, you must esteem with Joy when you might have by your choice fallen among many diverse temptations,

3 Knowing that the Proving by trial of your Faith produces Endurance,

4 But you must be having Continuously by your choice Perfect Work by God Endurance, that you should be Perfect and Entire, therein needing nothing.

5 And if then any of you are made

needing of Wisdom, you must be Asking from God, Who is Giving to All liberally, and not scolding sharply, and it shall be Made Given to him,

6   But he must be Asking in Faith, nothing wavering for himself, because he for himself wavering is like to a wave of the sea made driven by the wind and made tossed,

7   Because that man must not assume that he shall receive even anything from the Lord,

Double-minded man is ever changing

8   A double-minded man (is) ever changing in all his ways.

9   Every Humble Brother must be Joyful and Exalted in himself,

10   But the rich in lowliness himself, because as the flower of grass, he shall pass away,

11   Because the sun has risen with burning heat, and the grass has dried up, and the flower itself has fallen away, and the beauty of the presence of it has for itself perished, and the rich in his journeying shall be made to fade away.

Blessed is man that Endures temptation

12   Spiritually Blessed that man Enduring temptation, for he becomes Approved to Receive the Crown of Life, that the Lord has Promised to them that God-Love Him,

13   No man must say when he is made tempted, I am made tempted of God, because God is not tempted, and He is definitely not tempting anyone with evil work.

All tempting is through your own lusts

14   But every person is made tempted, made pulled away and made enticed, by one's own evil desire,

15   Then the evil desire having conceived, it is being delivered by sin nature, and when sin nature and sin has been made fully finished, it begets death,

16   Oh my Brethren Beloved, you must not be made deceived.

Every Good and Perfect Gift is from God

17   Every God-Good Giving and every Perfect Gift Given by God from Above is coming down from the Father of Lights, with Whom there is definitely no Variableness or shade of Turning,

18   Having been Made Intending, He begat us by the Spiritual Communication of Truth, for the Purpose and Result that we be the Firstfruit, a Kind of His Creatures.

Wrath works are not Righteousness

19   So that, my Beloved Brethren, it must be every man swift to Hear, slow to Utter, slow to Wrath for Justice,

20   Because the evil wrath of man definitely produces not the Righteousness of God,

21   For this reason, put away all moral dirtiness, and overflowing of malicious desire for evil work. In Meekness you must by your choice Receive the Engrafted Word, which is able to Save your souls.

Not Hearers only of the Word, but Doers

22   And you must become Effectual Doers of the Word, and not hearers only, misguiding yourselves,

23   Because if anyone is a Hearer of the Word and definitely not an Effectual Doer, he is like a man considering his (Sinless) Flesh Nature face in a mirror,

24   For he Considered himself, and goes, then immediately has forgotten what Kind he used to be.

A Doer of the Perfect Law of Liberty

25   But who Looks into the Perfect Law of Liberty and Continues along, he not being a forgetful Hearer but definitely has become an Effectual Doer of the Work by God. He shall be Spiritually Blessed in his Final Product,

26   If anyone seems to be religious among you, but bridles not his tongue, but definitely is deceivingly seducing his heart by this self-worship religion,

27 Purified religion and undefiled with God and the Father is this, To visit orphans and widows in their affliction, to be Keeping himself Without Spot from the satan's world.

Do not respect men's persons

2 My Brethren, you must not be having some respect of persons with the Faith of our Lord Jesus Christ of Glory,
2   Because if there might enter into your synagogue a man in bright apparel, a gold ring, and then also might enter in a beggar in dirty apparel,
3   And you might have regard to the wearer of bright apparel, and might have spoken to him, You Sit here God-Working, and to the poor you might speak, You stand there or sit here under my footstool,
4   Have you definitely not been made to judge differences also within yourselves, and become judges with evil thoughts?
5   You must have heard, my Beloved Brethren, has not God Chosen for Himself the poor of this the satan's world, rich in Faith, and Heirs of the Kingdom Rule which He has Promised to them, that are Continuously by their choice Loving Him?
6   But you yourselves have by your choice dishonored the poor. Are not the rich oppressing you by their choice, and themselves draw you out by their choice for judging by laws for judging?
7   Are they themselves not blaspheming by their choice the God-Work Name, made called upon yourselves?

God-Love your neighbor as yourself
8   However, If you are finally fulfilling the Royal Law according to the Scripture, You shall God-Love your neighbor as yourself, doing God-Working, (Lev 19:18)
9   But if you are having respect of persons, you are working sin nature and sin, exposed as sin by the Law as transgressors,
10 Because whoever shall keep the whole Law, but shall offend by his own choice by one sin, he becomes guilty of all,
11 Because He that Spoke, You should not commit adultery, Spoke also, You should not murder. If then you shall not commit adultery, but you shall murder; you are now being a transgressor of the Law, (Ex 20:13-14)
12 So you must Utter, and so you must Do, as by the Law of Liberty, Expecting to be Made Judged,
13 Because Final Judgment without Mercy to him that has shown no Mercy, while Mercy boasts against Final Judgment.

Faith without Works is dead
14 What profit, my Brother, If any man might say he is Having Faith, and might not be Having Works by God? That Faith cannot Save him,
15 And if a brother or a sister might be existing naked, and might be made needing of today's nourishment,
16 And any of you might speak to them, You must go away in Peace, and you must warm yourself, and you must be made filled. But might not by your choice have given to them what is deficient for the body, what is the profit?
17 And in such a manner Faith, if It might not be having Works by God, It is dead, as itself (alone),
18 But definitely a certain one shall Spirit Say, you are having Faith, also I am having Works by God, you must show me your Faith without your Works by God, also I will show you my Faith by my Works by God,
19 You are Committing by your choice that there is One God, you are doing God-Working, but the demons also are committing by their own choice and shudder with fear,
20 But will you know, Oh delusional man, that Faith without Works by God is dead?
21 Was not our father Abraham Made Righteous by Works by God, having Borne up as in an Offering of Isaac, his son, upon the altar? (Gen 22:9)

22 You Spiritually Seeing how Faith was Working together with his Works by God, and by Works by God is Faith Made Perfect,

23 And the Scripture has been made Fulfilled, Saying that Abraham Committed to God, and it was made Accounted to him for Righteousness, and he was Made Called a Friend of God,

24 You are Beholding attentively, accordingly of how Works by God are Making a man Righteous, and definitely not by Faith only (exclusively),

25 And likewise also was not Rahab the harlot Made Righteous by Works by God, humbly Receiving for herself the messengers, and Sent Away by another of a different kind way?

26 Because as the body without the Spirit is dead, in such a manner, Faith without Works by God is dead also.

Perfect man offends not in words

3 Oh, my Brethren, be not many Teachers, Spiritually Knowing that we shall Receive Greater Judgment,

2 Because we are all offending by very much sin. If any certain man offends not by sin in word, he a Perfect man, and exceedingly able to bridle all of the body,

3 Behold, we put bridles in the mouths of the horses to be persuading them for us, and all of the body of them we turn wherever by our choice,

4 Behold, and the ships being so great are made driven by hard winds, also are being made turned wherever by a small rudder, whereto wherever the aim of the steering intending by his choice,

5 Even so the tongue is a little member, and Behold a great thing, how great an issue, a little fire starts a fire by our choice,

6 And the tongue (is) a fire, the satan's world of unrighteousness. In such a manner, the tongue is made ruler among our members, making dirty all of the Body, and sets on fire the course of effects of the (Sinless) Flesh Nature, also is made set on fire by hell,

7 Because every nature of wild beasts, and also of birds, and of creeping things, and also of sea creatures, and those made tamed, and is now made tamed by the fallen nature of man,

8 But the tongue definitely no man is able to tame, unrestrainable evil work, full of deadly poison,

9 By this we are Blessing God, even the Father, and with this, we are cursing men, made according to the similitude of God,

10 Out from the same mouth comes out Blessing and self-cursing. Oh my Brethren, these things should not be so!

11 Does a fountain possibly spring out from the same spring, sweet and bitter?

12 Oh my Brother, a fig tree is not able to bear olives, or a vine, figs. In the same manner no fountain gives forth briny and sweet water.

Wisdom Above, not envy and strife

13 Who is Wise and Endued with Knowledge among you? He must show out from God-Work Behavior, his Work by God in Meekness of Wisdom,

14 But if you have bitter evil envy and strife in your heart, you must not boast against, or lie against, the Truth,

15 This wisdom is descending not from Above, but definitely is earthly, natural sensual soulish, devilish,

16 Because whereto evil zeal and strife, there disorder and every foul evil thing,

17 But actually the Wisdom from Above, is first of all Pure, after that Peaceable, Kindness, being Easily Entreated, full of Mercy, and God-Good Fruits, Impartial and Unfeigned,

18 And Fruit of the Righteousness is made Sown in Peace, by them Making Peace.

Wars and fights come from evil

4 From where wars and quarrels among you? Are they not definitely warring

out from your sensual desires in your members?

2   You are evilly desiring and have not, you are murdering and are fervently desiring, and not able to obtain, you are quarreling and making war, but definitely you have not because you are not to be asking for yourselves,

3   You ask and you receive not, since you ask evil work afflicted for yourselves, in order that in your sensual desires you might have spent.

Friendship with world is enmity to God

4   Adulterers and adulteresses, are you definitely by your choice not seeing that the friendship of the satan's world social system is the hatred of God? Therefore, whoever might intend to be a friend of the satan's world social system is making an enemy of God,

5   Are you thinking that the Scripture Says in delusion, that the spirit that has dwelt inside us greatly desires to envy?

6   But He for this reason is Giving Greater Grace. He is Saying that God is Resisting the proud, and Giving Grace to the Humble. (Prov 3:34)

Submit to God, Resist the devil

7   You must have made yourselves Subject, therefore, to God. You must by your choice Stand against the devil, and he will flee away from you,

8   You must by your choice Approach near to God, and He shall by His choice Approach near to you. Sinners, you must have by your choice Cleansed hands, and double-minded you must have by your choice Purified hearts,

9   You must by your choice have broken hearts and mourn and weep by your choice. Your laughter must be made replaced by mourning, and joy by depression,

10 You must be Made Humble in the Presence of the Lord, and He shall Exalt you.

Slander not a Brother

11 You must not slander one to another, Brethren. He that slanders a Brother, and judges his Brother, is slandering the Law and judging the Law. But if you judge the Law, you are definitely not an Effectual Doer of the Law, but definitely a judge,

12 There is One Lawgiver who is able to Save and destroy. Who are you that judges another by a different kind (lawgiver)?

Boast not in what you will or will not do

13 Come on now, you that say, This day or tomorrow we go into this city, and will continue there a specific one year, and make usable merchandise and will gain,

14 When you are not aware of what there is tomorrow, yet what is your life? A vapor, yet is for a little appearing, and after that is made vanishing away,

15 In place of that, say, If the Lord might have Willed, then we will live and do this or that,

16 But now you boast in your pride; all such rejoicing is evil.

Knowing to Do, but not Doing it, is sin

17 Therefore, to him Spiritually Discerning to Do a God-Work, and is not Doing it, to him it is sin nature and sin.

Rich living in pleasure is evil

5 Come on now, the rich, you must weep, howling in miseries coming upon you,

2   Your riches are now by your choice putrefying, and your clothes are now by your choice becoming moth-eaten,

3   Your gold and silver are now made exuding poison, and the poison of them shall be for a testimony to you, and shall eat your sinful flesh nature as fire stored up within the Last Days,

4   Behold the reward of the workers that gleaned your land, that are now made defrauded by you, are crying out, and the cries in beseeching of them who have been reaping, are now entering into the ears of

the Lord of Hosts,

5   You have by your choice lived in pleasure upon the earth, and you have lived in
immoral pleasures. You have nourished
your hearts, as in a Day of slaughter,

6   You have by your choice been Finally
Judged Condemned. You have murdered
by your choice the Righteous. He for himself is definitely not resisting you.

Patience for the Coming of the Lord

7   Therefore, Oh Brethren, you must be
Longsuffering by your choice, until after
the Coming of the Lord. Behold the Husbandman is waiting patiently for it, for the
most precious Fruit of the earth, until after
whenever He should receive a rain showers by the early rain and the latter rain,

8   Also you must be Longsuffering yourselves. You must Firmly Establish your
hearts, because the Coming of the Lord is
now approaching near,

9   You by your choice must not be groaning against another. Oh Brothern, that you
should not be made condemned to death.
Behold, the Judge was standing before the
Door,

10 Oh My Brethren, you must take an
example of those suffering evil and the
Prophets of Longsuffering who Uttered by
the Name of the Lord,

11 Behold, We Call Blessed those that are
Enduring. You have heard the Endurance
of Job, and have Spiritually Seen the End
of the Lord, that the Lord is very Compas-
sionate and Merciful.

Swear not, let yes be yes, and no be no

12 Oh my Brother, but before all, you must
not swear, neither by Heaven, nor by earth,
nor by any other oath of same kind. But
you must emphatically let your Yes be Yes,
and definitely your No, No, that you should

not fall down in Final Judgment.

13 Is any among you suffering evil? He
must Pray. Is any cheerful? He must sing
melody.

Prayer of Elders through Faith

14 Is any sick among you? You must invite
the Elders of the Assembly, and they must
Pray for him, Anointing him with oil in the
Name of the Lord,

15 And the Vow by God (solemn assertion
by God) through Faith shall make Healthy
the exhausted, and the Lord shall Raise
him up. If sins might be done, they shall be
made Removed from Memory (forgiven)
for him.

Pray for one another

16 You must acknowledge for yourselves
to one another your spiritual death offenses, and you must be wishing in behalf
of one another, A Righteous Supplication is accomplishing very much, so that
you may be Healed by many prevailing
Supplications,

17 The man Elias was similar passions as
us, he Prayed in Prayer that it not rain, and
it rained not upon the earth three years
and six months,

18 And again, he Prayed and the heaven
gave rain showers, and the earth budded
forth its fruit.

If any deceived away from Truth

19 Oh Brethren, if anyone of you among
yourselves has been made deceived away
from the Truth, and anyone Turns him
Back,

20 You must be Knowing, that he who
Turns About a sinner out from the way of
his deception, shall Save a soul out from
death, and shall Cover a multitude of different sins.

The First Epistle of

Peter

In Holiness and Obedience

1 Peter, Apostle of Jesus Christ, to the Elect Chosen Foreigners, of those scattered widely, of Pontus, Galatia, Cappadocia, Asia, and Bithynia,

2 According to Foreknowledge of God the Father in Personal Holiness of the Spirit for Obedience and Sprinkling of Blood of Jesus Christ, Grace to you and Peace be made Multiplied beyond your dreams.

By the Power of God through Faith

3 Most Blessed Worthy of all Spiritual Perfection, God and Father of our Lord Jesus Christ, according to His Large Mercy, having us being Born from Above for a Living Expectation by the Resurrection of Jesus Christ out from the Dead,

4 For an Inheritance Incorruptible and Undefiled, and is being Made Kept Perpetual in the Heavenlies for us,

5 Who, by the Miracle Power of God, is being Made Protected through Faith for Salvation, ready to be Made Revealed in the Last Special Time,

6 In this you exceedingly Rejoice, if for now a little, you must be Made Grieved by many diverse temptations,

7 That the Proving of your Faith by trial being very much more Precious than gold that perishes by fire, and should be Made Found Proven in Truth for Full Praise, and Honor, and Glory with the Revelation of Jesus Christ,

8 Whom having not seen you are Loving, in Whom for now you are not Seeing Attentively you are Committing, and Exceedingly Rejoicing with Joy Unspeakable, even now being Made Attributing Glory,

9 Earning the End of Faith for yourselves, the Salvation of your souls.

Of which the Prophets inquired

10 Of which Salvation the Prophets have inquired and searched diligently, who Prophesied about the Grace for the Purpose and Result of you,

11 Searching for what, or what Special Time was made evident, that the Spirit of Christ Inside them is Testifying before to Christ's sufferings, and the Glories (Spiritual Perfections) that follow these things,

12 To whom it was Made Revealed that definitely not to themselves, but to us they were Serving these things Now Made Declared to you, having Proclaimed the Gospel to you by the Holy Spirit Made Sent Out from Heaven, which the Angels are Desiring to look into. (John 14:26; 15:26; 16:7)

Be Serious to be Perfect

13 For this reason, tighten up the reigns of your intellect, being Serious to be Perfect, you must Expect with Intent to be Bringing to yourselves Grace within the Revelation of Jesus Christ,

14 As Obeying Children, not conforming to the former ignorance in your evil desires,

15 But definitely as He Who Outwardly Called (Gospel) you is the Holy One, so then be yourselves Saints (Holies) in every Behavior,

16 Since it is Written, You must be Holies, Saints, for I am Holy, (Lev 19:2)

17 And If you, for yourselves, Call upon the Father, Who without respect of persons is Judging according to every person's Work by God, you must Behave in Fear, during your time traveling as strangers.

Released from sin by His Blood

18 Since you Spiritually Know, you were definitely not made Removed (from sin) by corruptible pieces of silver or gold, out

from your self-worship behavior received from tradition of your fathers,

19 But definitely by the Most Precious Blood of Christ, as a Sacrificial Lamb, Faultless and Without spot,

20 Actually is being Made Foreknown before Conception of the satan's world, but having Made Manifest in these last times, last times for you,

21 Who through Means of Him are Committing for the Result and Purpose of God, that Raised Him Up out from the Dead and Gave Him Glory, so that your Faith and Expectation is to be for Purpose and Result of God.

Obeying Truth Through the Spirit

22 You Have by your choice Purified your souls, by Obeying the Truth Through the Spirit, in Unfeigned Brotherly Affection from a Purified heart. You must intently God-Love one another,

23 Being made Born from Above, not from corruptible parentage, but definitely Incorruptible through the Word of God, Living and Continuing Forever,

24 Since all sinful flesh nature as grass and all the glory of man as flower of grass made dried up. The grass and the flower thereof fail away,

25 But the Word of the Lord Continues Forever. And this is the Word, the Gospel made Proclaimed to you.

Laying aside all evil

2 Therefore, put away all malicious desire for evil work, and every subtle half-truth (deceit), and role playing hypocrisy, and envy, and all slandering,

2 As newborn babes, you must greatly desire the Reasonable Word, Undeceptive Milk, in order that you should be Made to Grow with it,

3 If it be so, you have Tasted that the Lord is Kind. (Ps 34:8)

Living Stones as Spiritual House

4 To Whom coming near to the Living Stone, by man actually disapproved, but with God, Elect, Most Honorable,

5 And yourselves, as Living Stones, are Made Built a Spiritual Home, a Holy Spiritual Priesthood, Bearing Up as in an Offering Spiritual Sacrifices, well Accepted by God through Jesus Christ,

6 For this reason also, fully behold in the Scripture, Behold, I Lay Down in Sion the Chief Corner Stone, Elect, Precious Stone, Most Honorable, and He that is Continuously by his own choice Committing to Him, should never ever be made shamed, (Isa 28:16)

7 To you, therefore, the Honor to those Committing, but to disobedient the same Stone Whom the builders disapproved, was Made into the Head of the Corner.

8 And a Stumbling Stone, and a Huge Rock of Offense to them stumbling at the Word, being disobedient, wherein also they were made positioned. (Ps 118:22; Isa 8:14)

Holy Nation, a Royal Priesthood

9 But yourselves, Elect Kindred, a Royal Spiritual Priesthood, a Holy Nation, a people for Possession, so that you should Show Forth His Virtues out from darkness, to be Outwardly Called (Gospel) into His Marvelous Light,

10 Who in time past not a people, but now a people of God, who had not been given mercy. but Now are Made Receiving Mercy. (Ex 23:22; Isa 43:20-21; Hos 1:6-9)

Free as Bondslaves of God

11 Beloved, I encourage as foreigners and Chosen Foreigners to Abstain from the carnal sinful flesh nature evil desires, which are warring against the soul,

12 Having your behavior God-Work among the Gentiles, in order that when they slander you as evil doers by the God-Works, Works by God, Behold, they

should Attribute Glory to God in the Day of Oversight,

13 You must be made subject yourselves, therefore, to every governing of man because of the Lord, whether to the king being superior,

14 Or to governors, indeed, as through them made sent for vengeance of evil doers, and Full Praise of God-Good doers,

15 For so is the Will of God doing God-Good by our choice, to Silence the lack of knowledge of mentally unwise men,

16 As Free, and not as having a cloak for malicious desire for evil work, but definitely Liberty as Becomes Bondslaves of God,

17 You must honor all men. You must God-Love the brotherhood. You must Fear God. You must honor the king.

As servants of Christ's sufferings

18 The household servants are made subject in fear to the master, not only to everyone with Kindness and God-Goods, but also to the crooked,

19 Thankful for Grace for this, if because of conscience with God, a man undergoes grief, suffering wrongfully,

20 Because what renown if sinning by your choice, so then you shall endure being made beaten? But if doing God-Good and you are suffering by your choice, this Grace with God shall be Enduring by your choice,

21 For to this you were Made Outwardly Called (Gospel), because Christ also suffered by His choice in Behalf of us, Setting Forth an Ideal Example for us, that we should Follow After in His Steps,

22 Who definitely did no sin, neither subtle half-truth (deceit) found in His Mouth, (Isa 53:9)

23 Who being made reviled was not reviling. Suffering, He was definitely not threatening. He was delivered up in betrayal, after that to Him Who is Judging Righteously,

24 Who Himself Bore Up as in an Offering for our sin natures and sins in His Own Body upon the Tree, in order that we Having Death in Christ's Grave to sin nature and sin, we should by our choice Live in Righteousness, while by His stripes you are Actually Made Cured,

25 For you were as sheep made wandering, but Made Converted, now with Intent to the Shepherd and Overseer of your souls.

Wives and husbands in marriage

3 Likewise, the wives are made Subjected to one's own husbands, that even if any apart from the Word are disobedient to the Word, they should be Made Gained through the Behavior of the wives,

2 While they note your Pure Behavior in fear,

3 Of which it must not be the outward braiding of hair, and wearing gold, or putting on of the satan's world clothes,

4 But the secret Man of the heart, in that Incorruptible and Meek and Peaceable Spirit, which is very valuable in the Presence of God,

5 For in such a manner, as in time past, the Holy women also, who Expected in God, adorned themselves, being made Subjected to their own husbands,

6 Even as Sarah obeyed Abraham, calling him lord; wherein becoming children doing God-Good, and not afraid to any alarm, (Gen 18:12)

7 Likewise, the husbands dwell with, according to Knowledge as to the feminine weak vessels, bestowing Honor as also Fellow Heirs of Grace of Life, that your Prayers be not made cut down,

8 And then all the habit of custom, same persuasion, same feelings, with Brotherly Affection, tenderhearted, very Humble.

9 Not repaying evil work for evil work, or reviling for reviling. But on the contrary, Blessing, Spiritually Discerning that for this you have been made Outwardly Called (Gospel), in order that you should by your choice Inherit a Blessing,

10 Because he that will God-Love Life and Spiritually See God-Good days, must cease his tongue from evil work, and his lips that they utter no subtle half-truth (deceit),

11 He must have avoided from evil work, and he must do God-Good. He must have sought Peace, and he must have Followed it closely,

12 For the Eyes of the Lord upon the Righteous and His Ears toward their Supplication. But the Presence of the Lord is against them doing evil works. (Ps 34:12-16)

Better suffer for Good than evil

13 And who shall evil harm you, if you should by your choice be close Followers of God-Good?

14 But definitely, Spiritually Blessed, if by your choice you are suffering beyond dreams because of your Righteousness, then you might be afraid? Fear them not, neither should you be made troubled. (Isa 8:12-13)

15 But you must Make Holy the Lord God in your hearts, and Continuously Ready with a Defense to everyone that asks you about the Word that is within you, with Expectation, Meekness, and Fear,

16 Having a God-Good conscience; that wherein they might be slandering you as evil doers, they should be Made Shamed, despitefully insulting to you, the God-Good Behavior of Christ,

17 Because Better Doing God-Good, allowing that the Will of God is Willing to suffer, than doing evil,

18 For Christ once also suffered by His choice for sin natures and sins, the Righteous in Behalf of unrighteous, that He might Draw us Near to God, being actually put to Death in Body in (Sinless) Flesh Nature, but made Offering Spiritual Life by the Spirit,

19 By Whom also He Went to Preach to spirits in prison.

20 Being disobedient in time past, when once waited for the Longsuffering of God, made building of an Ark in the days of Noah for that few, that is eight souls, Made Physically Saved through water.

Baptism, Putting Away the flesh

21 Which like figure Immersion so now Saves us, also Putting Off of the filth of sinful flesh nature, but definitely a Response of a God-Good conscience toward God through the Resurrection of Jesus Christ,

22 Who is Made Gone into Heaven by the Right Side of God. And Angels, Authorities, and Miracle Powers have been Made Subject to Him.

In flesh, now Made Ceasing from sin

4 Therefore, Christ in (Sinless) Flesh Nature suffered in Behalf of us, also yourselves must arm for yourselves with His Intent, because he that has been suffering in the sinful flesh nature and sin is now Made Ceasing from sin nature and sin,

2 Thereby no longer for the purpose and result of the evil desires of men, but definitely to the Will of God, Remaining Alive a little time Against the sinful flesh nature of desire.

Live from God in His Spirit

3 Because adequate to us is the time now by your choice Passing Away, of the natural life to the will of the Gentiles to produce going in extreme irregular immorality evil desires, excessive wines, revellings, banquetings, and unlawful idolatries,

4 In this it is made a strange thing, you are not running together among them to the same license of partying, speaking blasphemings,

5 Who shall yield an account to Him, having ready to Judge the Living and the dead,

6 Because for this, was the Gospel Made Preached also to the dead, that they might be Made Judged actually according to men with sinful flesh nature, but should be Living by their choice according to God in the Spirit.

7 But of all things, the End is now

approaching near, therefore, you must be Logically Minded, and you must be serious in Prayers,

8   And before all things, have Fervent God-Love among yourselves, for God-Love shall cover a multitude of different sins, (Prov 10:12)

9   Hospitable for one to another apart from murmuring.

10 Just as every person has Received a Spirit Gift for themselves to be Serving Him as of many diverse God-Work Stewards of the Grace of God,

11 If any Utters as Oracles of God, if any Serve as from Strength which God is Furnishing, that God be Made Attributed Glory in all things through Jesus Christ, to Whom is the Glory and Dominion Forever and Ever. Amen.

As Partakers of Christ's suffering

12 Beloved, you must not be made strange by that burning temptation in you, happening within yourselves, becoming as from a stranger within you,

13 But you must be Rejoicing in as much as you are Being Partakers in the sufferings of Christ, that also in the Revelation of His Glory, you should be Made Glad, being exceedingly Rejoicing,

14 If you be made scolded to shame for the Name of Christ, Spiritually Blessed, because those of the Glory and those of the Spirit of God are Made Refreshed in you. By them He is actually blasphemed, but by yourselves He is Made Attributed Glory,

15 Because any of you must not suffer as a deliberate murderer, or thief, or evil doer, or as a busybody,

16 But if as a Christian, he must not be made disgraced, for in this particular he must Attribute Glory to God.

Judgment begins in Christ's House

17 Because the Special Time for the Judgment to begin with the House of God, though if first of all for us, what (is) the End of those disobeying to the Gospel of God?

18 And if the Righteous hardly be Made Saved, wherein shall the sinner and ungodly for themselves appear? (Prov 11:31)

19 So that also them that are suffering according to the Will of God, they must be putting forth their souls in Doing God-Good, as for a Faithful Creator.

Elders Shepherd Flock not for money

5   The Elders among yourselves, I am Encouraging who am also an Elder, and Witness of the suffering of Christ, also a Companion of the Glory Expecting to be Revealed,

2   You must Shepherd the Flock of God among you, looking Diligently, not by constraint but definitely voluntarily, neither for filthy money, but definitely a Ready Mind. (Titus 1:11)

Neither as lords over God's Flock

3   Neither as being lords over the Allotments, but definitely being Made a Model of the Flock,

4   And when has been Made Manifest the Chief Shepherd, you shall Earn a Crown of Glory that fades not away,

5   Likewise, younger, you must have been Made Subject to the elder, all likewise then being Made Subject one to another. You must be clothed with Humility, for the God of Humility is for Himself Resisting the proud, and is by His choice Giving Grace to the Humble, (Prov 3:34; James 4:6)

6   Therefore, you must have been Made Humbled under the Magnificent Hand of God, that in a Special Time He might by His choice Exalt yourselves,

7   Tossing all your care Upon Him, for He is Caring For yourselves.

Resist the devil Steadfastly by Faith

8   You must be serious. You must be Watching, because the adversary of yourselves, the devil, as a roaring lion is walking, seeking whom he might by his choice

completely swallow,

9   Whom you must Stand Against Strong in the Faith, Spiritually Knowing that the same of the sufferings in the satan's world, is being performed in your Brotherhood.

God Completes beyond your dreams

10 But the God of all Grace, Who Outwardly Called (Gospel) us into the Eternal of His Glory in Christ Jesus, having suffered a little yourself, by your choice He Made Complete yourselves beyond dreams, Firmly Established beyond dreams, Enabled beyond dreams, a Grounded Foundation beyond your dreams.

11 The Glory through Him, and the Dominion Forever and ever. Amen.

Greetings

12 By Silvanus, the Faithful Brother to yourselves, as I Account through a little I have Written, Encouraging and Attesting this is True Grace of God, for Whom you are now by your choice Standing,

13 Those Elect Together in Babylon are Greeting you, also Mark, my Son,

14 You must Greet one another with a Kiss of God-Love. Peace to you, All those in Christ Jesus. Amen.

The Second Epistle of

Peter

Life and Godliness by Full Knowledge

1 Simon Peter, Bondslave and Apostle of Jesus Christ, to them that have Secured Like Precious Faith with us in Righteousness of our God and our Savior Jesus Christ,

2   Grace and Peace be made Multiplied beyond dreams to you by Full Knowledge of God and Jesus our Lord,

3   As all things to us of His Divine Godhead Miracle Power to Life and Godliness, has now been Made Bestowed through the Full Knowledge of our Outward Calling (Gospel), through Glory and Virtue.

Partakers of the Divine Nature

4   Through These, the Exceeding Great the most Precious Promises, are now being Made Bestowed upon us, that through These you should have Become Companions of the Divine Godhead Nature, having Fled from that Eternal death in the satan's world with evil desire.

By all Diligence add to your Faith

5   And beside this, also having Brought along all Diligence, you must have Fully Furnished by your Faith, Virtue, and by the Virtue, Knowledge,

6   And by Knowledge, Self-Control, and by Self Control, Endurance, and by Endurance, Godliness,

7   And by Godliness, Brotherly Affection, and by Brotherly Affection, God-Love,

8   Because these things Existing In you and Exceeding in Quantity, is not making idle neither unfruitful, in the Full Knowledge of our Lord Jesus Christ,

9   Because whoever is not being Present with these things is blind, not Perceiving the Unseen long ago forgotten, having Received the Purification of his sins.

Diligence to Service of Calling

10 Much more, for this Reason, Brethren, you must by your choice be Having Diligence, to make the Service of Calling and

Election of yourselves Permanent, because Doing These Things you should never ever offend by sin, as in times past,

11 Because In Such A Manner, the Entrance into the Eternal Kingdom Rule of our Lord and Savior Jesus Christ shall be Made Abundantly Fully Furnished for you.

We have not followed fables

12 For this reason, I will definitely not neglect to Continuously Remind you concerning these things, even though you are now Spiritually Knowing and are now being Made Firmly Established in the present Truth.

13 For now, I Esteem to be Righteous, among whom I am in this earthly Tabernacle, to Arouse you in Remembrance.

14 Spiritually Knowing that soon I am Putting Off this, my earthly Tabernacle, just as also our Lord Jesus Christ Made Evident to me.

15 Moreover, I will be Diligent to have you constantly also after my leaving, to Keep the Memory of these things,

16 Because we have definitely not followed out devised fables, I have Made Known Supernaturally to you that Miracle Power and Coming of our Lord Jesus Christ, also definitely we Became Eyewitnesses of that same Mighty Power,

17 Because Having Received from God the Father Honor and Glory, a Voice was Made Brought to Him of such a Kind from the Excellent Glory, This is My Beloved Son in Whom I Have Been Pleased,

18 And Being United with Him in the Holy Mountain, we Heard this Voice Brought Out from Heaven.

Also a Permanent Word of Prophecy

19 We have also the Permanent Word of Prophetic Writings, to which you are Doing God-Working, Taking Heed as to a Spiritual Lamp, Shining in a dry dirty dark place, when until after the Day might by our choice Dawn and the Light Bearer should by your choice Have Risen in your hearts,

20 Knowing This First of All, that All Prophecy of Scripture is definitely not Coming to Pass by one's own explanation,

21 Because as in time past, Prophecy was definitely not Made Brought by the will of man, but definitely men by the Holy Spirit, Holy Ones of God Made Driven Have Uttered.

False prophets and teachers

2 But also false prophets occurred among the people, as even false teachers shall be among you, who shall secretly bring damnable heresies, even disclaiming Jesus Master called Lord having Bought them, inflicting soon damnation to themselves,

2 And many shall follow out to the damnation of themselves, because of whom The Way of Truth shall be made blasphemed,

3 And by greediness with crafted spiritual communications they, whose judgment from a long time is definitely not lingering, and their damnation is definitely not slumbering, shall by their choice make usable merchandise of you,

4 For if God definitely Spared not Angels having sinned, but definitely Cast into tartarus with chains into blackness, Delivered Up for now being Made Kept for Final Judgment,

5 And Spared not the satan's world of old times, but definitely Maintained Noah the eighth, a Preacher of Righteousness, Inflicting the flood of Noah upon the satan's ungodly world,

6 And Turning the cities of Sodom and Gomorrah to ashes, Condemned to death with the Casting Down; Now Settling Out an Example for those expecting to be doing ungodly acts.

Lord Knows How to Deliver Godly

7 And Rescued Righteous Lot, made oppressed by those godless, in extreme

irregular immorality of behavior,

8 Because that Righteous soul, inhabiting among them from day to day was tormented by sights and hearings with lawless man works,

9 The Lord Knows to Rescue the Devout out from temptation, and is Keeping the unrighteous for being Made Punished in the Day of Final Judgment.

They that walk after flesh are dead

10 Specifically, them that go after sinful flesh nature in evil desire of uncleanness, and despising Lordship, presumptuous, self-willed, blaspheming, not trembling at Glory,

11 Whereto Angels being Greater in Strength and Miracle Power, are not bringing against them blasphemous Final Judgment from the Lord,

12 But these, as unreasonable natural beasts, are now being made born for taking Eternal death, even blaspheming while they are by their choice being ignorant themselves, shall be made totally corrupt in their Eternal death,

13 Are earning a reward of unrighteousness, indulgently esteeming of value sensual desires in the day, dirty spots and blemishes, feasting together among yourselves, amusing themselves in their deceitfulness,

14 Having eyes full of an adulterous, and cannot cease from sin nature and sin, enticing unstable souls, a heart now made exercising with greediness, having self-cursing children,

15 Who have been made deceived, leaving the Straight Way, following out into the way of Balaam of Beor, who loved by his choice his reward of unrighteousness,

16 But having been Reproved for his own lawless state, a dumb female donkey with a man's voice Spoke Intelligibly, Forbid the madness of the prophet,

17 These are dry wells, clouds being made driven by a storm, to whom the blackness of darkness is now made kept Forever,

18 Yet of great swelling self-importance speaking intelligibly, they are enticing by evil desires of sinful flesh nature in extreme irregular immorality. Those in fact having fled from them therein are made each returning by deception,

19 They are promising liberty to them. Themselves are made existing as slaves in Eternal death, because to what any man is being overcome, then by this he is made a slave.

If after you Flee the dirt of the world

20 Because if Fleeing from the pollution of the satan's world in Full Knowledge of their Lord and Savior Jesus Christ, and then again have been made entangled being overcome by these things, it is now ending for them. The last worse than first,

Better for them not to have Known

21 Because it was better for them not to be Fully Knowing The Way of Righteousness, than Fully Knowing, to turn back from the Holy Commandment Made Delivered Up to them,

22 But it is now by choice happened to them that of the True Proverb, A dog has turned back to his own vomit, and a sow having washed into wallowing of mud. (Prov 26:11)

Remember the Coming Judgment

3 This second epistle, Beloved, I am already Writing to you in which I am Arousing of you your sincere Intellect in Remembrance,

2 To be Made yourself to Remember of the Collection of Specific Words Made Said before by the Holy Prophets and by His Apostles, the Commandment by our Lord and Savior,

3 Knowing This First of All, that there shall come in the last days mockers, going after their own evil desires,

4 And saying, Wherein is the Promise

of His Coming? Because that since the fathers have been made sleeping, all things in same manner are continuing constantly, from the Beginning of Creation,

5   Because this they are willingly unknowing, that the Heavenlies were from a long time, also the earth out from water and by water, are Now Held Together by the Word of God,

6   The satan's world that then through this had been made totally flooded by water, was destroyed,

7   But the Heavenlies and the earth now, by the Same Word, are now Made Stored Up to Fire, Made Keeping for The Day of Final Judgment and damnation of ungodly men.

Not Willing that any might perish

8   But this one, you must not be unknowing yourselves, Beloved, that one day with the Lord as a thousand years and a thousand years as one day,

9   The Lord is definitely Not Slow in His Promise as some esteem tardiness, but definitely is by His choice Longsuffering toward us, not Intending any to be lost, but definitely to find a Place for everyone to Repentance.

Removal of earth and heavens

10 But The Day of the Lord shall definitely Now Come as a thief in the night, that wherein the Heavenlies shall pass away with a great noise and the basic elements shall be Made Removed with fervent heat, and the earth also with the man works therein, shall be Made Fully Burned,

11 Therefore, of all these things being Made Removed, of what manner ought you to Exist in Holy Behavior and Godliness?

12 Watching for and Hurrying the Coming of The Day of God, because of this the Heavens are Made Burning and the basic elements shall be Made Removed, being Made Melted with Fervent Heat,

13 Nevertheless, we are Watching for a New of a Different Kind Heavens and a New of a Different Kind Earth, according to His Promise, wherein He, Righteousness, is Dwelling.

Be Diligent with no spot or fault

14 For this reason, Beloved, Watching for these things. You must be Diligent, Without spots and Without faults with Him to find therein Peace.

The Lord and Paul also Spoke this

15 And you must be Esteeming the Longsuffering of our Salvation Lord, just as also our Beloved Brother, Paul, has Written to you according to the Wisdom Made Given to him,

16 As also in All his Epistles, Uttering in them about these things, in which are certain things hard to be understood, which ignorant and unstable are twisting, as also the remaining Scriptures to their own damnation of themselves.

Knowing This, be Steadfast

17 Yourselves, therefore, Beloved, Foreknowing you Must Maintain that you should not by your choice fall from your own Steadfastness, not being made misguided by the deception of the godless,

18 But you must Grow in Grace and Knowledge of the Lord our Savior Jesus Christ, To Whom the Glory both Now and Forever. Amen.

The First Epistle of

John

We have Heard, Seen, and Handled

1 That which was from the Beginning, which we are Now Hearing, which we are Now Seeing Attentively with our eyes, which we Have Seen, and our hands Have Handled of the Spiritual Word of Life,

2 And the Life has been Made Manifested, and we are Now Seeing Attentively by our choice, and Witnessing by our choice, and Telling to you the Life Eternal, Who was With the Father and was Made Manifested to us.

We may Fellowship with God

3 Whom we have Beheld Attentively and Heard, we are Telling you, that yourselves also should Have Fellowship with us, and moreover our Fellowship with the Father and with His Son Jesus Christ,

4 And these things we are Writing to you, that your Joy may be Now Made Fulfilled.

The Promise that God is Light

5 This then is the Promise which we are Now Hearing from Him, and we are Declaring to you, that God is Light, and definitely is not any darkness in Him,

6 If we might speak that we are having fellowship with Him and we might be walking in darkness, we are lying, and we are definitely not Living the Truth,

7 But if we should Walk in the Light as He is in the Light, we are Having Fellowship with one to another, and the Blood of Jesus Christ, His Son, is Cleansing us from all sin nature and sin.

If we Say we have no sin, we lie

8 If we might speak that we are having no sin nature and sin, we are deceiving ourselves, and the Truth is definitely not in us,

9 If we should Continuously Confess our sin natures and sins, He is Faithful and Righteous to Remove from Memory (forgive) for us the sin natures and sins, that He might Cleanse us from all unrighteousness,

10 If ever we might have spoken that we have not sinned, we are finalizing Him a liar, and His Word is definitely not in us.

I Write that you sin not

2 My little children these things I am Writing to you that you might not sin, and if any might have sinned, we have an Advocate with the Father, Jesus Christ the Righteous,

2 And He is the Atonement Restoration from our sin natures and sins, definitely not for ours only, but definitely for all of the satan's world.

We may Know that we Know Him

3 And in this, we are Knowing that we are Now Knowing Him, if we should be Keeping His Commandments,

4 He that says I am now knowing Him, also is (intentionally) not keeping His Commandments, is a liar, and the Truth is definitely not in this one,

5 But whoever is Keeping His Word Of Truth, in this one the God-Love of God is now being Made Perfect, in this we are Knowing that we are Being in Him,

6 He that is saying to be Abiding in Him, he ought by his choice to have Walked just as He, so also to be by his choice Continuously Walking in that manner as He.

Love your Brother: in the Light

7 Brethren, I am Writing no New of a different kind Commandment to you, but definitely an Old Commandment, which

you were having from the Beginning. The Old Commandment is the Word which you have heard from the Beginning.

8 Again, a New of a different kind Commandment I am writing to you, Which is True and in Him and in you, because the great darkness is made for itself passing on, and the True Light already is Shining,

9 He that is saying he is in the Light, and is hating his Brother, he is being up to now in the great darkness,

10 He that is Loving his Brother is Abiding in the Light, and there is no offense in him.

11 But he that hates his Brother is in great darkness, and is walking in the dark, and definitely not Spiritually Seeing wherein he is moving, for the dark has blinded his eyes.

12 I am Writing to you, Oh little children, because your sin natures and sins are Made Removed from Memory (forgiven) through His Name,

13 I Write to you, Oh fathers, because you are now Knowing from the beginning. I am Writing to you, Oh young men, because you are now Overcoming the evil. I am Writing to you, Oh little children, because you are Now Knowing the Father,

14 I have Written to you, Oh fathers, because you are Now Knowing from the beginning. I have Written to you, Oh young men, because you are Stronger and the Word of God (Christ Himself) is Abiding in you, and you are Now Overcoming the evil.

God-Love not the world nor things in it

15 You must not God-Love the world, neither the things in the satan's world. If anybody might be loving the satan's world, definitely the God-Love of the Father is not Inside him,

16 For all that is in the satan's world, the evil desire of the sinful flesh nature, and the evil desire of the eyes, and the pride of natural life, is definitely not of the Father, but is definitely continuously of the satan's world,

17 And the satan's world is continuously passing on for itself, and the evil desire of it, but he that is Continuously Doing by his choice the Will of God is Continuously Continuing Forever.

Many antichrists are coming

18 Oh little children, it is the Last Short Time, and just as you have Heard that the antichrist is coming, even now many antichrists are occurring, where from we are knowing that it is being the Last Short Time,

19 They departed out from us, but definitely were not of us, because if they were of us they had continued with us, but definitely in order that it should have been Made Manifest that they are definitely not all of us.

20 But yourselves are by your choice Having an Anointing from the Holy One, and you are Now Spiritually Knowing All things,

21 I have not written to you, because you are not now Spiritually Knowing Truth, but definitely because you are Now Spiritually Knowing Him, and that every lie is definitely not out from Truth.

A liar denies Jesus is Christ

22 Who is the liar, except the one disclaiming that Jesus is definitely not the Christ? He is antichrist, that disclaims the Father and the Son,

23 Whoever is continuously disclaiming any responsibility to the Son, is not having the Father. He that is Continuously Admitting Truth of the Son is also Having the Father.

24 Yourselves, therefore, have Heard this from the beginning. He must be Continuously Abiding in you, if Whom from the beginning by your choice you Heard, then He Abided in you, and yourselves shall by your choice Continue with the Son and with the Father,

25 And this is the Promise that He has Promised to us, the Life Eternal.

Written about them who deceives you

26 These things I have written to you, about them that are deceiving you by their choice,
27 But the Anointing Whom yourselves have by your choice Received from Him is by your choice Continuing in you, so also you are definitely not having a need that any man might be teaching you, but definitely as His Anointing is by His choice Teaching you about All things, and is True, and is Definitely Not Lying. Also, just as He has Taught you, you shall by your choice Continue with Him.

He Doing Righteous is Born from Above

28 Even now, Oh little children, you must by your choice be Continuously Abiding with Him, that when He should be Made Manifested, we should Continuously by our choice Have Boldness, and should not be made disgraced by Him in His Coming,
29 If you should be now by your choice Spiritual Discerning that He is Righteous, you are by your choice Continuously Knowing that anyone that is Doing Righteousness By Him has been made Born from Above.

We should be Called Children of God

3 You must Spiritually Know by your choice, what manner of God-Love the Father is now Giving to us, that we should be made Outwardly Called (Gospel) the Children of God. Because of this, the satan's world is definitely not recognizing us, because it has definitely not Known Him,
2 Beloved, now we are Continuously Children of God, and it has not yet been Made Manifested what we will be, but we are being now by our choice Continuously Spiritually Knowing that when He should be Made Manifested, we will be Like Him, when we will Spiritually Look Upon Him just as He Is,
3 And everyone who is Having this Expectation in The Way of Him is Continuously by his choice Purifying himself, just as He is Pure.

4 Everyone doing the sin nature and sin, also is continuously doing by his choice the lawlessness, so then sin nature and sin is the lawlessness,

Took Away our sins and devil's work

5 And you are now Spiritually Knowing that He has made Manifested in order that He might Take Away our sin natures and sins, while in Him is Definitely No sin nature and sin,
6 Whoever is Continuously Abiding in Him, is definitely Not continuously sinning by his choice. Whoever is continuously sinning, is Not Beholding Him Attentively, Neither is now by his choice Knowing Him,
7 Oh little children, nothing must be deceiving you. He that is Doing Continuously Righteousness is Righteous, just as He is Continuously Righteous.
8 He that is continuously by his choice doing sin is of the devil, because the devil is sinning continuously by his choice from the beginning. For this Purpose the Son of God has been Made Manifested, that He should Remove the man works of the devil,

Whoever Born of God, is not sinning

9 Whoever is now Continuously Made Born out from God, is by his choice Not Doing sin nature and sin, because His Seed in him is by his choice Abiding Inside him, and he is definitely not able to continue to be sinning, because out from God he is Now Continuously Being Made Born from Above,
10 In this the Children of God are Openly Manifest, and the children of the devil. Whoever not doing Righteousness Continuously by their choice is definitely not of God, also he that is not continuously by his choice Loving his Brother.

Cain, as also world, hates Righteous

11 For this is the Message which you have Heard from the Beginning, that we should God-Love one another,

12 Not just as Cain, who was of that one of evil, and slew his brother. So why for what cause he slew him? Because the man works of him were evil, and his brother's Righteous.

13 Marvel not, Oh my Brother, if the satan's world is hating you,

14 We are now Spiritually Knowing that we are Now Departed from death into Life, because we are Loving of the Brethren. He that is not Loving the Brethren, is abiding in death, (Rom 6:1-12; Eph 2:5-6)

15 Whoever is hating his Brother is a murderer, and you Spiritually Know that every murderer is definitely not having Life Eternal continuing in him.

Not God-Love in word only

16 In this, we Recognize the God-Love of God, because He Laid Down His (Sinless) Flesh Nature by His choice in Behalf of us, and we are Indebted to Lay Down our lives by our choice in Behalf of the Brethren,

17 But whoever might have the livelihood of the satan's world and might be Seeing his Brother having need, and might shut his compassion from him, how Abides by his choice the God-Love of God in him?

18 My little Children, we must not God-Love in word, nor tongue, but definitely in Work by God and in Truth,

19 And in This we are Knowing that we are Being of the Truth, and we will Reassure our hearts before Him.

Can have Confidence in Prayers

20 For if our heart might Blame us, God is Greater than our heart, and is Knowing All things,

21 Beloved, if our heart might not Blame us, we are Having Boldness with God,

22 And whatever we might Ask, we are Receiving Alongside of Him, because we are Keeping His Commandments, and are doing those things Pleasing in the Presence of Him.

Abide in Him by the Spirit He Gave us

23 And this is His Commandment, that we should by our choice Commit to the Name of His Son Jesus Christ, and should by our choice God-Love one another just as He Gave Commandment to us,

24 And he that is keeping His Commandments is Abiding in Him, and He in him. And in this, we are Knowing that He is Abiding in us by the Spirit Whom He has Given to us.

Test spirits by Doctrine of Christ

4 Beloved, you must not Commit to every spirit, but Prove in Truth the spirits [through the Word; John 17:17], whether they are out from God, because many false prophets are now coming out in the satan's world,

Whether He Came in flesh or not

2 In this you recognize the Spirit of God. Every Spirit that is Confessing Jesus Christ came Inside (Sinless) Flesh Nature is from God,

3 And every spirit that is not Confessing Jesus Christ came inside (Sinless) Flesh Nature is definitely not from God, and this is of the antichrist, that you are now Hearing that is coming, and already is in the satan's world.

Greater He In you than he in the world

4 Yourselves are of God, little children, and you are now Overcoming them, because Greater is He that is Inside you, than he in the satan's world,

5 They are of the satan's world, because of this they are uttering of the satan's world, and the satan's world is hearing them,

6 We are being Continuously of God: He that is Knowing God is Continuously Hearing us. He that is definitely not out from God is definitely not Hearing us. From this, we are even Knowing the Spirit of Truth from the spirit of deception.

God is God-Loving

7 Beloved, we should God-Love one another, because God-Love is of God, and everyone that is God-Loving is now being Made Born from Above and is Continuously by his choice Knowing God, (Col 3:14)

8 He that is not by his choice God-Loving has not Known God, because God is God-Love. [We as True Christians must God-Love by His Spirit Inside us. Lost man of only sinful flesh nature cannot God-Love.]

9 In this was Made Manifest, the God-Love of God Inside us, because God is now Sending Out His Son the Only Begotten Risen Christ into the satan's world that we should Live By Means of Him,

10 In this is God-Love, not that we loved God, but that He God-Loved us, and Sent Out His Son for Atonement Restoration from our sin-natures and sins,

11 Beloved, if God Loved us In Such a Manner, we also Ought to God-Love one another,

12 No man has seen God at any time. If we might be God-Loving one another, God is Continuing Inside us, and His God-Love is being Now Made Perfect Inside us.

He In us because we Having His Spirit

13 In this we are Recognizing that we are Continuing In Him, and He In us, because He is Now Giving to us of His Spirit,

14 And we are Seeing and are Witnessing that the Father Sent Out His Son, Savior of the satan's world,

15 That whoever should have Confessed that Jesus is the Son of God, God is Abiding in him, and he in God.

16 And we now Continuously Recognizing and are now Continuously Committing to the God-Love that God is Having Inside us. The God is God-Love, and he that is Continuously Abiding in God-Love is Continuously Abiding in God, and God in him,

As He Is, So are we in the world

17 In this, our God-Love is Continuously being Made Perfect, with that Boldness we should be Having in that Day of Final Judgment, because just as He Is also we are Being in this the satan's world,

18 There is no fear in God-Love, but definitely Perfect God-Love is Casting fear outside, because fear is having torment, and fearing is not Continuously being Made Perfect in God-Love,

19 We are Continuously Loving Him, because He First Loved us.

He who Loves God Loves his Brother

20 If a man might speak that, I God Love God, and might be hating his Brother, he is being a liar because he is not God Loving his Brother, whom he is now Seeing Attentively. How is he being able to be God Loving Whom he is not now seeing?

21 And this Commandment we are Having from Him, he that is God Loving God also should be Continuously by his choice being God Love to his Brother.

Commit to Jesus as the Christ

5 Whoever is Continuously Committing by his choice that Jesus is the Christ is Now Continuously being Made Born-from-above by God, and everyone that is Loving those Born-from-Above is God-Loving also those Now being Made Born-from-Above by Him,

2 By this we are knowing that we are Loving the Children of God, when we are Loving God and should be Keeping His Commandments,

Love of God is to Keep His Orders

3 Because this is the God-Love of God, that we should be Keeping His Commandments, and His Commandments are definitely not burdensome.

Our Faith Overcomes the world

4 For whoever is now made Born-from-Above out from God is Continuously Overcoming the satan's world, and He, the Faith Inside us, is the Conquest that Overcame

the satan's world,

5   Who is he that is Continuously Overcoming the satan's world, except he that is Continuously Committing by his choice that Jesus is the Son of God.

Three Witnessing, Spirit is Truth

6   This is He that Came Through Water and Blood, Jesus Christ, not by Water only, but definitely by the Water and the Blood. And the Spirit is the Witness because the Spirit is the Truth, (John 17:17)

7   Because there are Three Witnessing Inside of Heaven: the Father, the Word, and the Holy Spirit, and these Three are One,

8   And they are Three Witnessing in the earth, the Spirit, and the Water, and the Blood; and these Three are in One,

9   If we are receiving the testimony of men, the Testimony of God is Greatest, because this is the Testimony of God that He is Now Continuously Bearing Record for His Son.

God's Life Given to us In the Son

10 He that is Continuously Committing by his own choice for the Purpose and Result of the Son of God is Having His Testimony Inside himself. He that is not Continuously Committing by his own choice to God is now by his own choice making Him a liar, because he is definitely now by his own choice not Committing to the testimony, that God is Now Bearing Record for His Son,

11 And this is the Testimony, that God has Given to us Life Eternal, and His Life is In His Son,

12 He that is Having the Son is Having Life, but he that is not Having the Son of God is definitely by his choice not Having Life,

13 These things I have Written to you that are Committing by your choice to the Name of the Son of God, that you should Spiritually Discern that you are Having by your choice Life Eternal, and that you

should be Committing Continuously by your choice to the Name of the Son of God.

We Know our Prayers are Answered

14 And this is the Boldness that we are Having Continuously by our choice to Him, that if we should for ourselves Ask According to His Will, He is Hearing us,

15 And if we are now Spiritually Discerning that He is Hearing us, whatever we should Ask for ourselves, we are Now Spiritually Discerning that we are Having the Requests that we are Now Asking from Him.

If Sin is not to death, Ask in Prayer

16 If any man Spiritually Discerns his Brother is sinning by his choice a sin not to death, he shall Ask and He shall Give to him Life, to not be sinning to death. A sin (that) is to death: I am definitely not saying that he should have earnestly requested in regard to the same, (Mark 3:28-29)

17 All unrighteousness is sin, and there is sin not to death.

18 We are Discerning that whoever is Now Made Born of God is definitely not sinning by his choice, but definitely he that is Made Born from Above by God is Keeping by his choice himself, and the evil one is definitely not touching him,

19 We Spiritually Know that we are Being of God, and all of the satan's world is lying in evil.

Know True God and Eternal Life

20 And we are now Spiritually Discerning by our choice that the Son of God has Now Come, and is Now Giving to us an Intellect that we should be Knowing the True and we are being Continuously in The True in His Son Jesus Christ, Who is The True God and The Life Eternal.

21 Little children you must Maintain yourselves away from idols. Amen.

The Second Epistle of

John

Greeting, elder to the Elect lady

1 The Elder to the Elect lady, and her children, whom I God-Love in Truth, and not I alone, but also All that are Knowing the Truth,

2 For the Truth is Continuing by our choice Inside us, and also shall Be With us Forever,

3 Grace, Mercy, and Peace shall Be With you from Father God and the Lord Jesus Christ, of the Son of the Father, in Truth and God-Love.

Walking In Truth and Love

4 I rejoiced extremely that I am Continuously Finding from your children Walking in Truth, just as we Have Received a Commandment from the Father,

5 And now I am Earnestly Requesting of you, lady, not as Writing a New of a different kind Commandment to you, but what I Have from the Beginning, that we should be God-Loving by our choice one another,

6 And this is God-Love, that we should Walk According to His Commandments. This is the Commandment of God, just as you Have Heard from the Beginning, that you should Walk by your choice In It.

Deceivers say Christ Came not In flesh

7 For many deceivers have entered into the satan's world, who are not confessing Jesus Christ Coming in (Sinless) Flesh Nature. This is the deceiver and the antichrist,

Lose not what you Have Worked

8 You must be Seeing yourselves in order that we should not have lost the things we Have Worked, but definitely should Fully Receive a Full Reward.

Accept only Teachings of Christ

9 Whoever is violating by their choice and are not Continuing in the Teaching of Christ, has not God. He that is Continuing by his choice in the Teaching of Christ, he is Having Both the Father and the Son,

10 If any man is coming to you, and is not Bringing This Teaching, you must not be receiving him into the House, also you must not be saying to him to be rejoicing,

11 For he that is saying to him, To be rejoicing, is being a partaker by his choice of his evil man works.

Greetings

12 Having many things to write to you, I do not Intend through paper and ink, but I expect to Come to you, and Utter to you face to face, that our Joy is Now Made Fulfilled.

13 The Children of you, Elect Sister, are Greeting you. Amen.

The Third Epistle of

John

To Gaius Walking in Truth and Faith

1 The Elder to the Beloved, Gaius, whom I God-Love in the Truth.

2 Beloved, I am wishing you to Always Prosper, and be Healthy just as your soul is Made Continuously Prospering.

3 Because I extremely Rejoiced from the coming of Brethren Witnessing about you in the Truth, just as you are Walking Continuously in Truth,

4 I am having no more Important Joy than to be Hearing, that my children are Walking in the Truth,

5 Beloved, you are Faithful if Doing whatever you Should Work among the Brethren and to the strangers,

6 Who have Born Record of your God-Love in the Presence of the Assembly, that you shall do God-Working with journeying Worthily of God,

7 Because in Behalf of His Name, they came out taking nothing from the Gentiles,

8 We, therefore, ought to be Fully Receiving such, that we should become Fellow Laborers to the Truth.

Diotrephes, prideful and malicious

9 I have written to the Assembly, but Diotrephes who definitely is loving his preeminence, is definitely not showing hospitality to us,

10 Because of this, if I might come, I will remind of his man works that he is continuously doing, berating us with evil spiritual words, and not being content in the way of these things, neither is he showing hospitality to the Brethren, and intending to forbid, casting out from the Assembly.

Follow not evil, but God-Good

11 Beloved, You must not closely follow the evil work, but definitely the God-Good. He that is doing God-Good is of God, but he that is doing evil, is not Now Continuously Seeing Attentively God by his own choice,

12 Demetrius is Made Witnessed by all means, and by the Truth itself, and we also are Now Bearing Record, and now Spiritually Discerning that our Testimony is True,

13 I am having many things to write, but definitely not willing through ink and reed to write to you.

Expecting to See you soon

14 But Expecting to immediately See you, and Utter face to face. Peace to you. The friends Greet you. You Must Greet the friends by name.

The Epistle of

Jude

Jude, brother of James

1 Jude, the Bondslave of Jesus Christ, and Brother of James, to them Now Made Holy in God the Father, and Now Made Kept Inwardly Called (Born Again) in Jesus Christ.

2 Mercy to you, and Peace, and God-Love, Made Multiplied beyond dreams.

Earnestly Contend for Saints' Faith

3 Beloved, I gave all Diligence to Write to you about the Common Salvation. I have of necessity Written to you to Encourage, to Earnestly Contend for the Once Delivered Up Faith of Saints.

Evil men turning Grace into evil

4 For certain men long ago Wrote before about this condemnation. The ungodly have a purpose to deprave others, transferred the Grace of our God into extreme irregular immorality, and disclaiming the Alone Lord God, even our Lord Jesus Christ.

Uncommitted are destroyed

5 I remind you, I am Intending that you yourselves are Now Spiritually Knowing this, that the Lord once Saved the people out from the area of Egypt. The second time (after Kadesh Barnea), He Destroyed them (with 40 years) that had not Committed,

6 And also the Angels that kept not the Beginning of themselves, but definitely left behind their own body habitation, are now kept in bonds under Everlasting blackness for Final Judgment in that Great Day,

7 Same as Sodom and Gomorrah, and the cities about them have devoted to fornication in like manner, and also gone by their choice after sinful flesh nature of another of a different kind, being Set Before, a sample for Fire, experiencing Just Punishment for Eternity,

8 Likewise, however also, these dreamers certainly defile the (Sinless) Flesh Nature, and reject Lordship and blaspheme Glory,

9 Yet Michael the Archangel, when disputing with the devil, Judging differences about the body of Moses, definitely dared not to induce Final Judgment of blasphemy, Spoke, But definitely, The Lord Rebuke you. (Zech 3:2)

10 But these blasphemed what they certainly Know not, but naturally these were aware as unreasonable beasts, among those they made spiritually corrupt.

Woe to them, men twice dead

11 Woe to them, for they have gone the way of Cain, also to the deception of reward by Balaam, also destroyed in the poured out contradiction of Core,

12 These are they within the God-Love of you, hidden reefs feasting together among you without fear, themselves dry clouds shepherded by winds carried about, unfruitful trees with withered fruit, having twice died, made rooted up,

13 Wild great violent waves of the sea foaming out their own shame, wandering stars to whom the blackness of darkness is made kept Forever.

14 And Enoch also, seventh from Adam, Prophesied to these things Saying, Behold, the Lord Came with thousands of His Saints,

15 To execute Final Judgment against all, and Convict all among their ungodly about all of the man works of their ungodliness, that they have done ungodly acts, and of all their sinful ungodly uttered hard against Him,

16 These are murmurers, complainers, going according to their evil desires, and their mouth uttering great swelling admirations to persons for this cause of advantage.

In Last time, mockers after lusting

17 But, Beloved, yourselves must Remember in yourselves the Specific Words by the Apostles, Said before by our Lord Jesus Christ, 18 How they were Saying to you that in the Last Time there shall be mockers, going according to their own evil desires of ungodliness,
19 These are they who distinguish themselves, natural sensual soulish, having not the Spirit.

Building Up your Holy Faith

20 But yourselves, Beloved, Building Up your Holy Faith, Praying Yourselves in the Holy Spirit.
21 You must Keep yourselves in God-Love, Looking for the Mercy of our Lord Jesus Christ for Life Eternal,
22 And to some indeed, you must Give Mercy, Judging Differences for yourselves,
23 And others you must Save with Fear Catching Up out from fire, Hating even a coat made dirty by the sinful flesh nature.

He is Able to Keep you Faultless

24 Now to Him Able to Maintain you without falling, and to Stand Faultless Before the Presence of His Glory with Exceeding Joy,
25 To the Alone Wise God our Savior, Glory and Majesty, Dominion and Authority, both Now and Forever. Amen.

The Revelation

of God the Father through Jesus Christ to His Bondslaves

Revelation of Jesus Christ

1 The Revelation of Jesus Christ, which God Gave to Him to Show His Bondslaves, what must come to pass therein (once started) in rapid succession, and Sent Out to signify through His Angel to His Bondslave, John.
2 Who Bore Record to the Spiritual Communication of God, and the Testimony of Jesus Christ, and also to what He Spiritually Discerned.

Blessed who Reads, Hears, and Keeps

3 Spiritually Blessed, he that Reads and they that Hear the Spiritual Words of this Prophecy, and Keeps those things therein being Made Written to him, because the Appointed Time is near.

John to the Seven Assemblies

4 John, to the Seven Assemblies in Asia, Grace to you and Peace from Him WHO Is, and WHO Was, and WHO Is to Come, and from the Seven Spirits Who are in the Presence of His Throne.

From Jesus Christ the Faithful Witness

5 And from Jesus Christ, the Faithful Witness, the Firstborn from the Dead, and the Ruler of the kings of the earth. To Him that has been Loving us, also Washed us Away from our sin natures and sins in His Own Blood.
6 And has Made us Kings and Priests to God and His Father, to Him the Glory and the Dominion Forever and ever. Amen.

He Comes, every eye seeing Him

7 Behold, He is Coming with the Clouds, and every eye shall see the Spiritual Appearance of Him, and they who pierced Him, and they shall bewail over Him, all the tribes of the earth, emphatically Yes. Amen.

8 I AM, Alpha and Omega, the Beginning and the End, Says the Lord, WHO Is, and WHO Was, and WHO Is to Come, the Almighty.

A Vision of Alpha and Omega

9 I, John, who am also your Brother, also Partaker in the affliction, and in the Kingdom Rule and Endurance of Jesus Christ, am upon the island that is called Patmos, for the Spiritual Communication of God, and with the Testimony of Jesus Christ.

10 I was in the Spirit in the Lord's day, and Heard back of me a Great Voice as a Trumpet.

11 Saying, I AM, the Alpha and the Omega, the First and the Last: and What you See Write in a Book, and you must Send to the Seven Assemblies which are in Asia: to Ephesus, and to Smyrna, and to Pergamos, and to Thyatira, and to Sardis, and to Philadelphia, and to Laodicea.

12 And I turned back to see the Voice who Uttered with me, and being turned back, I saw Seven Golden Candlesticks.

13 And in the midst of the Seven Candlesticks like to the Son of Man, dressed with a Robe down to Feet, and being Clothed About at the Breasts with a Golden Girdle.

14 Also His Head and His Hair like as White Wool, White as Snow, and His Eyes as a Flame of Fire.

15 And His Feet like Fine Brass, as in a Furnace Made Burning, and His Voice as sound of Many Waters.

16 And having in His Right Hand Seven Stars, and Going Out from His Mouth a long broad Two-Edged Sword, and His Outward Appearance as the Sun Shining in His Miracle Power.

17 And when I Spiritually Saw Him I fell down at His Feet as dead, and He Laid On me His Right Hand Saying to me, Be not afraid, I AM, the First and the Last.

18 And I am Living and Became Dead, and Spiritually you Must Behold, I am Living Forever and Ever. Truly. And I am having the Keys of Hades and of death.

Saying, Write These Things

19 You must Write the things you have Spiritually Seen, both the things there Are, then the things which He is by His choice Expecting to Come to Pass after These Things.

Mystery of the Seven Assemblies

20 The Mystery of the Seven Stars which you Spiritually Saw in My Right Hand, and the Seven Golden Candlesticks: The Seven Stars are Angels of the Seven Assemblies, and the Seven Candlesticks which you Spiritually Saw are the Seven Assemblies.

Assembly in Ephesus

2 To the Angel of the Assembly of Ephesus [First Apostolic church], Write, These things Says He that Holds to Retain the Seven Stars in His right Hand, Who Walks in the midst of the Seven Golden Candlesticks,

2 I Spiritually Know your Works by God, and your Labor, and your Endurance, and why you are not able to bear evil work, and have Tried them who are affirming to being Apostles, and they are not, and you Found them false.

3 And Have Borne, and Have Endurance, and for My Name you have Labored and are not now exhausted.

4 But definitely I Have Against you, because you have parted from your First God-Love.

5 You Must Remember, therefore, from where you are now falling away by your choice, and you Must Repent by your choice, and you Must Do the First Works

by God by your choice, otherwise then, I am Coming to you swiftly and I will be Moving your Candlestick from its place, except you should by your choice Repent.

Hate the deeds of the Nicolaitans

6 But definitely This you are Having, that you are Hating the man works of the Nicolaitans, which I also Hate.

7 He that is Having an Ear, you Must Hear by your choice what the Spirit is Saying to the Assemblies, To him Overcoming I shall Give to Him to Eat from the Tree of Life, which is in the Midst of Paradise of God.

Assembly in Smyrna

8 And to the Angel of the Assembly of Smyrna [Second Apostolic church, and suffering through 10 Emperors' persecutions], you Must Write, The First and the Last Who was Dead and now Living is Saying these Things:

Your Works, affliction, poverty

9 I Spiritually Know your Works by God, and the affliction, and the poverty, and you are Rich. Also, the blasphemy of those saying to be Jews themselves, and they are definitely not at all, but definitely, the synagogue of the satan.

10 You must fear nothing that you are Expecting to suffer. Behold, Expect the devil to cast yourselves into prison, that you might be made tempted, and you shall have affliction Ten Days. You Must Be Faithful until death, and I will Give to you the Crown of Life.

11 He Having an Ear, you must have Heard what the Spirit is Saying to the Assembly. He that is Overcoming by his choice should Never Ever be Made Hurt at the second death.

Assembly in Pergamos

12 And to the Angel of the Assembly in Pergamos [Roman Imperial church], you Must Write, The One Having the long broad Two Edged-Sword, He is Saying these things.

The satan's seat, and Nicolaitan

13 I am Now Spiritually Discerning your man works and wherein you are dwelling whereto the throne of the satan (rebeller), and you are Retaining My Name and you have definitely not disclaimed any responsibility to My Faith, and in the Day in which Antipas My Faithful Witness who was killed among you, whereto is dwelling the satan.

14 But definitely I Have a few things against you, because you have there retaining the teaching of Balaam, who taught Balac to cast an offense in the presence of the sons of Israel, to eat meat offered to idols, and to sexually sin.

15 So you have by your choice them also holding to retain the teaching of the Nicolaitans [rulers over people], which I Hate.

16 And you Must Repent, except I Come to you quickly, and I will Make War against them with the Long Broad Two-Edged Sword of My Mouth.

17 He Having an Ear, you Must Hear what the Spirit is Saying to the Assemblies. To him Overcoming, I will Give him to Eat from the Hidden Manna, and I will Give to him a White Voting Stone, and on the Voting Stone a New of a different kind name Made Written, that no man has known, except he that Receives It.

Assembly at Thyatira

18 And to the Angel of the Assembly in Thyatira [Roman Catholic church], you Must Write, These things, are Saying the Son of God, Who is Having His Eyes as a Flame of Fire, and His Feet like Fine Brass.

19 I Spiritually Know your Works by God, and God-Love, and Serving, and Faith, and your Endurance, and your man works and the last more than the First.

Jezebel: fornication, and idols

20 But definitely, I have a few things against you, because you allow the woman Jezebel, who is calling herself a prophetess, teaching and deceiving my Bondslaves to sexually sin, and to eat meat offered to idols.
21 And I Gave her Time in order she should Repent of her own choice Out From her fornication and she definitely has not Repented.
22 Behold, I am Casting her into a bed and them that are continuously committing adultery by their choice with her to great affliction, except that they should Repent by their choice from their man works.
23 And I will Kill her children with death. And all the Assemblies will know that, I AM, Searches the inmost minds and hearts. Also I will Give to you everyone According to your Works by God.
24 But to yourselves I say, and to the remaining in Thyatira, as many as, have not this teaching, and which have not known, as they are saying, the depths of the satan, I will not cast to you another heavy burden of same kind.
25 But what you are having, you must retain by your choice, until when I should now come.
26 And he that Overcomes, and he that Keeps My Works by God until the End, I will Give to him Authority upon the nations.
27 And He shall Shepherd them with a Rod of Iron, as the vessels of a potter are broken into pieces, as also I, I am now Receiving from My Father.
28 And I will Give to him the early Morning Star.
29 He that has an Ear, he must be Hearing, what the Spirit is Saying to the Assemblies.

Assembly in Sardis

3 And to the Angel of the Assembly in Sardis [Reformation church], Write these things Saying, He that is having the Seven Spirits of God and the Seven Stars, I Spiritually Discern your man works, how you have a name that you are Living, and you are continuously dead.

A name you live by, but are dead

2 You must be Watchful, and you must firmly establish those things remaining, expecting to die, because I am now continuously not finding your man works fulfilling, in the Presence of God.
3 You must remember, therefore, how you are continuously by your choice now taking to receive, and have by your choice heard, and you must by your choice be keeping, and you must have by your choice Repented. If, therefore, you should have by your choice not Watched. I will Come Against even as a thief, and you shall never ever recognize what hour I will Come Against you.
4 You have a few names also in Sardis, who have by their choice definitely not made their clothes unclean, and they shall Walk with Me in White, for they are Worthy.
5 He that is by his choice Overcoming, he shall for himself be Clothed in White Garments, and I shall definitely not Blot Out his name from the Book of Life, and I will Acknowledge His Name in the Presence of My Father and in the Presence of His Angels.
6 He that is having an Ear, you must Hear by your choice what the Spirit Says to the Assemblies.

Assembly in Philadelphia

7 And to the Angel of the Assembly in Philadelphia [The Missionary church], You must write these things. He is Saying, Holy and True, having the Key of David, He that Opens, and no man shuts, and Shuts and no man opens.
8 I Spiritually Discern your Works by God. Behold I am now Giving by your choice, in the presence of you, an Open Door. Also, no man can continuously shut it, for you are Continuously Having by

your choice a little Miracle Power, and you have by your choice Continuously Kept My Word, and have not disclaimed My Name.

9   Behold, I am attributing out from the synagogue of the satan, who say themselves to be Jews and they are definitely not, but definitely lie. Behold, they shall make themselves that they might now come, and Worship in the Presence of your Footstool, and should have Recognized that I Loved You,

Kept My Word, I will Keep you

10 Because you have kept the Word of My Endurance, I also, will Keep You out from within the hour of the temptation, expecting to come upon all the inhabited earth, to try them dwelling upon the earth.

11 Behold, I am Coming quickly. You must be Holding to retain what you have, in order that no man might take your Crown.

12 He that Overcomes I will Make Him a Pillar in the Temple of My God, and he should depart outside never ever further. And I Will Write upon Him the Name of My God and the Name of the City of My God, the New of a different kind Jerusalem that Came Down out from Heaven from My God, and My New of a different kind Name.

13 He that has an ear, he must hear what the Spirit is Saying to the Assemblies.

Assembly at Laodicea

14 And to the Angel of the Assembly of Laodiceans [Last day apostate churches] you must Write these things, He Who, The Truly, the Faithful Witness and True, the Beginning of the Creation of God, is Saying:

15 I Spiritually Discern your man works, that you are neither cold nor hot. I would you should beyond your dreams, be cold or hot.

16 So because you are lukewarm and neither cold nor hot, I expect to spit you out from My mouth.

I Know you not, blind and naked

17 Because you are saying, I am rich, and now being rich I have no need, and I am now not Spiritually Knowing you. For you are wretched, and miserable, and poor, and blind, and naked.

18 I Counsel you to Buy from Me gold Made Burning out from fire, that you might be rich, and White Garments, that you might be Clothed, and that your shame and nakedness might not be made Manifest, and you must rub eye salve to your eyes that you might Spiritually See.

19 As many as I might Affectionately God-Love, though I am Convincing of sin and Disciplining, you must earnestly Desire, and therefore you Must Repent.

20 Behold, I am now Standing at the door and Knocking. If anybody might Hear My Voice and Open the door, I will Enter to him, and Dine with him, and he with Me.

21 Him that Overcomes, I will Give to him to Sit Down with Me by My Throne, as I also Overcame and Sat Down with My Father by His Throne.

22 He that is Having an Ear, you Must Hear what the Spirit Says to the Assemblies.

Heaven, God's Throne

4 After these things I Spiritually Saw, and Behold an Opened Door in Heaven, and the First Voice that I heard as a Trumpet Uttering with me, Saying, You Must Ascend Here and I will Show to you the things that Must Occur after these things.

2   And immediately, I was in the Spirit. Behold, a Throne was Set in Heaven, and upon the Throne One is Sitting.

3   And He that is Sitting was like to a vision appearance in jasper and sardine stone, and a Rainbow round about the Throne like an emerald to vision appearance.

Twenty Four Elders Sitting

4   And round about the Throne Twenty

and Four Thrones, and upon the Thrones I Spiritually Saw the Twenty and Four Elders, Sitting, Clothed in White Garments, and They have upon Their Heads Golden Crowns.

5   And out from the Throne goes out Lightning and Thunder and Voices, and Seven Lamps of Fire burning in the Presence of the Throne, Who are the Seven Spirits of God.

Four Beasts: Lion, Calf, Man, Eagle

6   And in the Presence of the Throne a Glass Sea like crystal, and in the midst of the Throne, and around the Throne Four Beasts full of Eyes, before and behind.

7   And the First Beast like a Lion, and the Second Beast like a Calf, and the Third Beast having a Face as a Man, and the Fourth Beast like an Eagle Flying.

8   And Four Beasts, each One having to themselves six wings round itself, and are full of eyes inside, and having no resting place day and night Saying, Holy, Holy, Holy, Lord God Almighty, WHO Was, WHO Is, and WHO Is to Come.

9   And when those Beasts shall Give Glory, and Honor, and Thanksgiving to Him Sitting upon the Throne, Who is Living Forever and Ever,

10 The Twenty and Four Elders shall Fall Down in the Presence of Him that is Sitting upon the Throne, and they are Worshiping Him that is Living Forever and Ever, and are Casting their Crowns in the Presence of His Throne Saying,

Saying, You are Worthy, O Lord

11 You are Worthy, Lord, to Receive the Glory, and the Honor, and the Miracle Power, for You have Created All Things, and because of Your Will they Are, and have been Made Created.

Sealed Book in His Right Hand

5 And I Spiritually Saw in the Right Hand of Him, that is Sitting upon the Throne, a Scroll made Written inside and backside, Stamped with Seven Seals.

2   And I Spiritually Saw a Mighty Angel Extolling with a Great Voice, Who is Worthy to Open the Scroll, and Remove the Seals of it?

3   And definitely no man in Heaven, neither on the earth, nor under the earth, was able to Open the Scroll neither See it.

I wept as no man able to open it

4   And I was very much weeping because definitely no one has been made found Worthy to Open, and to Read the Scroll, neither to See it.

A Lamb as Slain is Able to Open it

5   And one of the Elders Says to me, You must not be weeping, Behold, the Lion Being of the Tribe of Judah, the Root of David, has Overcome to Open the Scroll, and Remove the Seven Seals thereof.

6   And I Spiritually Beheld, and you Must Behold in the Midst of the Throne, and of the Four Beasts, and in the Midst of the Elders, a Lamb now Standing, as now made Slain, having Seven Horns and Seven Eyes, Who are the Seven Spirits of God, now made Sent Out upon all the earth.

And He Took the Scroll

7   And He Came and Now Took the Scroll from the Right Hand of Him Sitting upon the Throne.

Four Beasts & 24 Elders Sang New Song

8   And when He Took the Scroll, the Four Beasts and the Twenty Four Elders Fell Down in the Presence of the Lamb, having every man Harps, also Golden Vials being full of Incense which are the Prayers of the Saints.

9   And they Sang in the Spirit a New of a different kind Song, Saying, You are Worthy to Take the Scroll, and Open the Seals thereof, because You have been Made Slain and actually Bought us for God in

Your Own Blood, out from every tribe and tongue and people and nation.

10 And You have Finalized us for Our God, Kings also Priests, and we will Reign on the earth.

All Heavens' Hosts Sang Praises

11 And I Spiritually Discerned and Heard a Sound of many Angels round about the Throne and the Beasts and the Elders, and the number of them was ten thousands of ten thousands and thousands thousands.

12 Saying with a Great Voice, Worthy is the Lamb Who is now Made Slain to Receive Miracle Power, and Riches, and Wisdom, and Strength, and Honor, and Glory, and Blessing.

Every Creature Sang Praises

13 And every Creature that is in Heaven, and upon the earth, and under the earth, and in the sea, and all things that are also in them, I Heard Saying to Him Sitting upon the Throne, and to the Lamb, Blessing, and Honor, and Glory, and Dominion Forever and Ever.

Four Beasts Say Amen & 24 Elders Worship

14 And the Four Beasts were Saying, Amen. And the Twenty Four Elders Fell Down and Worshiped Him that is Living Forever and Ever.

Lamb Opens the Seven Seals

6 And I Spiritually Saw when the Lamb Opened One of the Seals [Seven seals restoring ownership to Kinsman Redeemer], and I Heard one of the Four Beasts Saying, as a Voice of Thunder. You must Come and Spiritually See.

1st Seal-White Horse, conquers

2 And I Saw and Behold a white Horse, and he that sat on him had a bow, and a crown was given to him. He came out conquering also in order that he might overcome.

2nd Seal-Red Horse, Wars on earth

3 And when He Opened the Second Seal, I Heard the Second Beast Saying, You must Come and you must See.

4 And there came out another of same kind Horse, red flame colored, and he that sat upon him has been made given to him to take peace from the earth, and that they might slay one another, and a great sword made given to him.

3rd Seal-Black Horse, day's wage

5 And when He Opened the Third Seal, I heard the Third Beast Say, You must Come and Spiritually See, and behold, a black Horse, and he that is sitting upon him is having a yoke (balance) in his hand.

6 And I Heard a Voice in the midst of the Four Beasts Saying, A dry grain measure of wheat a penny, and three dry grain measure of barley (for) a penny [represents a days wage or excessive inflation] and do not hurt the oil and the wine.

4th Seal-Pale Horse, disease/war

7 And when He Opened the Fourth Seal, I Heard a Voice of the Fourth Beast Saying, You must Come and See.

Killing 1/4th of earth

8 And I Spiritually Saw, and Behold, a green Horse, and he that sat upon him, the name of him, death and hell, and hades followed with him, and authority was made given to them to kill over a fourth of the earth with a long broad two-edged sword, and in famine, and in death, and by wild beasts of the earth.

5th Seal-Killed for Word of God

9 And when He Opened the Fifth Seal, I Spiritually Saw under the Alter, the Living Souls of them made slayed for the Word of God, and for the Testimony they were Having.

10 And They were Crying Out in a Great Voice Saying, Up to how long a time, O

Lord, Holy and True, shall You not Judge and Avenge our blood from those dwelling upon the earth?

White Robes, Wait For Brethren

11 And White Long Robes were made Given to every person, and Made Spirit Spoken to Them that, They for themselves should be Made Refreshed a little time further, until when they should be Finalized, and their Fellow Bondslaves, also their Brethren, that are Expecting to be killed, as also Themselves. (Matt 24:21-24; Rev 7:14)

6th Seal, Signs in the Heavens

12 And I Spiritually Saw when He Opened the Sixth Seal, and Behold, a great earthquake occurred, and the sun became black as sackcloth of hair, and the moon became as blood.

13 And the stars of heaven fell down to the earth, as a fig tree casts her green figs by a great shaking wind.

14 And the heaven separated away as a scroll rolling together, and every mountain and island have been made moved from their place.

15 And the kings of the earth, and the great men, and the rich, and the chief captains, and the exceedingly able, and the slaves, and every free have hid themselves in the caves, and in the huge rocks of the mountains.

16 And said to the mountains and huge rocks, You must fall down upon us, and hide us from the Face of Him Sitting upon the Throne, and from the Wrath for Justice of the Lamb,

17 Because The Great Day of His Wrath for Justice has come and who is able to stand?

Angels at four corners of the earth

7 And after these things, I Spiritually Saw Four Angels now Standing at the four corners of the earth, Holding to Retain the four winds of the earth, that it might not blow wind upon the earth, nor upon the sea, nor upon any tree.

2 And I Spiritually Saw another Angel of same kind, Ascending from the rising sun, Having a Seal of the Living God, Crying Out a Great Voice to the Four Angels, to Whom it was made Given to Them to Hurt the earth and the sea.

First must Seal Bondslaves of Our God

3 Saying, You should not Hurt the earth, nor the sea, nor the trees, until when we should Seal the Bondslaves of Our God upon their foreheads.

Number Sealed: 144,000

4 And I Heard the number of them Made Sealed, hundred forty four thousand made Sealed, out from every tribe of the sons of Israel.

Seals 12,000 from each of 12 tribes

5 Out from the tribe of Judah twelve thousand are being Sealed, out from the tribe of Reuben twelve thousand are being Sealed, out from the tribe of Gad twelve thousand are being Sealed,

6 Out from the tribe of Aser twelve thousand are being Sealed, out from the tribe of Nephthali twelve thousand are being Sealed, out from the tribe of Manasses twelve thousand are being Sealed,

7 Out from the tribe of Simeon twelve thousand are being Sealed, out from the tribe of Levi twelve thousand are being Sealed, out from the tribe of Issachar twelve thousand are being Sealed,

8 Out from the tribe of Zabulon twelve thousand are being Sealed, out from the tribe of Joseph twelve thousand are being Sealed, out from the tribe of Benjamin twelve thousand are being Sealed.

After this, a Multitude Innumerable

9 After these things, I Spiritually Saw, and Behold, a large Multitude of People that no man was able to number himself

from all nations and tribes and peoples and tongues, Standing in the Presence of the Throne, and in the Presence of the Lamb, Clothed in White Long Robes, and Palms in their Hands.

In White Robes, Praising God
10 And Cried Out with a Great Voice Saying, Salvation to Our God Sitting upon the Throne, and to the Lamb.

All Angels and Elders Praised God
11 And all the Angels Standing around the Throne, and the Elders, and the Four Beasts, and they Fell Down upon their Faces in the Presence of the Throne, and Worshiped God.
12 Saying, Truly, Blessing, and Glory, and Wisdom, and Thanksgiving, and Honor, and Miracle Power, and Strength to our God Forever and Ever. Amen.

An Elder Said: Who are These?
13 And one of the Elders Answered, Saying to me, Who are These that are Clothed in White Long Robes, and from where have They Come?

Came Out From the Great Tribulation
14 And I Spirit Said to Him, Sir, You Spiritually Know, And He Spoke to me, These are They Coming Out From Within the Great Tribulation (Matt 24:21), and Scrubbed their Long Robes and have Whitened Them by their choice in the Blood of the Lamb.
15 Because of this, they are in the Presence of the Throne of God, and are by their choice Being Devoting to Him day and night in His Temple, and He that is Sitting on the Throne shall Dwell among Them.
16 They no more shall hunger by their choice, neither further thirst by their choice, neither should possibly the sun fall down on them, neither any heat.
17 For the Lamb Who is in the Midst of the Throne, shall Shepherd Them, and Guide

Them to Living Fountains of Water, and God shall Blot Out all Tears from their Eyes.

Opened the 7th Seal, Silence half hour
8 And when He Opened the Seventh Seal, there was Stillness in the Heaven as half an hour.

Seven Angels with Seven Trumpets
2 And I Spiritually Saw Seven Angels that were Standing in the Presence of God, and Seven Trumpets were made Given to Them.

The Prayers of All Saints Offered
3 And another Angel of same kind Came and Stood in the place of the Altar, having a Golden Censor of Frankincense, and there was Given to Him very much Incense, that He should Give with the Prayers of the Saints, all upon the Golden Altar in the Presence of the Throne.
4 And the Smoke of the Incense, out from the Hand of the Angel, with the Prayers of the Saints Ascended in the Presence of God.
5 And the Angel Took the Censer of Frankincense, and Made It Full from the Fire of the Altar, and Cast upon the earth, and then were Voices and Thunders and Lightnings and an Earthquake.

1st T: 1/3rd of trees and grass burnt
6 And the Seven Angels that have the Seven Trumpets Prepared themselves to Sound.
7 And the First Angel Sounded and then occurred hail and fire mixed with blood, and cast upon the earth, and the third of the trees made fully burned, and all green grass made fully burned.

2nd T: 1/3rd of sea life, ships perish
8 And the Second Angel Sounded, and same as a great mountain burning with fire was put in the sea, and the third of the sea became blood,

9   And the third of the creatures, which had souls, died in the sea, and the third of the ships materially destroyed.

3rd T: 1/3rd of fresh water made bitter
10 And the Third Angel Sounded, and a great burning star as a lamp fell down from Heaven, and fell down upon the third of the rivers, and upon the fountains of waters.
11 And the name of the star is called wormwood, and the third of the waters became wormwood, and many men died from the waters because it was made bitter.

4th T: 1/3rd sun, moon, stars darkened
12 And the Fourth Angel Sounded and effected the third of the sun, and the third of the moon, and the third of the stars, in order that the third of them should be made darkened, and the one third of them the day and the night likewise, should not appear.

Three Woes of next three Trumpets
13 And I Spiritually Saw and heard One Angel Flying in the midst of Heaven Saying with a Great Voice, Woe, Woe, Woe, to them dwelling upon the earth, by the remaining Sounds of the Trumpet of the Three Angels, expecting to be Sounding.

5th T (1st Woe): 5 months locust stings
9   And the Fifth Angel Sounded and I Spiritually Saw a Star falling down from the Heaven to the earth, and to Him was made given the Key to the deep pit of the bottomless pit.
2   And He Opened the deep pit, the bottomless pit, and smoke ascended out from the deep pit, as smoke of a great furnace, and the sun and the air was made darkened from the smoke of the deep pit.
3   And from the smoke came out locusts upon the earth, and authority was made given to them, as scorpions of the earth have authority.

4   And it was made Spirit Spoken to them that they should not hurt the grass of the earth, neither any green thing, nor any tree, except those men alone who definitely have not the Seal of God upon their foreheads.
5   And it was given to them that they should not kill them, but definitely that they should be made tormented five months, and their state of torment as the state of torment of a scorpion when it might strike harmfully to a man.

Men will seek death but not die
6   And in those days the same men shall seek death, and not find it, and shall desire to die, and death flees from them.
7   And the likenesses of the locusts like horses preparing for war, and on their heads as crowns like gold, and their faces as faces of men.
8   And they were having hairs as hair of women, and their teeth were as lions.
9   And they were having breastplates as breastplates of iron, and the sound of their wings as the sound of many horses of chariots running for war.
10 And they have tails like scorpions, and stings were in their tails with their authority to hurt the men five months.

With angel king called Apollyon
11 And they are having a king over them, the Angel of the bottomless pit, whose Hebrew script name, Abaddon, and in the Greek language, having the name, Apollyon.
12 One Woe has gone, Behold, there is coming yet two Woes further after these things.

6th T (2nd Woe): 200 Million army kills
13 And the Sixth Angel Sounded, and I heard a Voice out from One of the Four Horns of the Golden Altar, which is in the Presence of God.
14 Saying to the Sixth Angel that was

having the Trumpet, You must Remove the Four Angels that are now made bound in the great river Euphrates.

15 And the Four Angels were made Removed, which are made prepared for the hour, and the day, and month, and a year, in order that they should kill the third of men.

16 And the number of the army of the cavalry two thousands of thousands, and I heard the number of them.

17 And in such a manner I Spiritually Saw the horses in the Vision Appearance, and them that are sitting upon them, having flaming breastplates, and jacinth, and burning sulfur. And the heads of the horses, as heads of lions, and from their mouths is going out fire, and smoke, and brimstone.

1/3rd of men of earth killed

18 By these three were the third of men made killed: from the fire, and from the smoke, and from the brimstone going out from their mouths.

19 For their authority is in their mouths, and in their tails, because their tails like serpents having heads with them they hurt.

Yet men still do not repent

20 And the remaining of the men that have not been killed by these plagues, have definitely not repented from the man works of their hands, in order that they should not worship by their choice the demons and idols of gold, and silver, and brass, and carved stone, and wood, which neither are able to see, not hear, nor walk.

21 So they definitely have not by their choice repented from their murders, neither from their assistance by evil spirits (via any method including drugs), nor from their fornication, nor from their stealings.

Mighty Angel comes down from Heaven

10 And I Spiritually Saw another Mighty Angel of same kind come down from Heaven Clothed with a Cloud and a Rainbow upon his Head and his Face as the sun, and his Feet as Pillars of Fire.

Little book, Rt foot on sea/Lt foot on earth

2 And He was having in his Hand a Little Book Opened, and He Positioned his Right Foot upon the sea, and the Left Foot upon the earth.

3 And Cried Out with a Great Voice as a lion roaring, and when he Cried Out Seven Thunders Uttered their Voices.

4 And when the Seven Thunders Uttered their Voices, I was expecting to Write, and I Heard a Voice from the Heaven Saying to me, You must Seal those things the Seven Thunders Uttered, and not write these things.

5 And the Angel which I Spiritually Saw Standing upon the sea, and upon the earth, took up His Hand to the Heaven.

Time shall be no more

6 And swore by Him that is Living Forever and Ever, Who created the Heaven, and the things in it, and the earth and the things in it, and the sea and the things in it, that time shall be no more.

The Mystery of God is finished

7 Definitely in the days of the Voice of the Seventh Angel, when he should be expected to Sound, and the Mystery of God should be made Finally Finished as Proclaimed to His Bondslaves, the Prophets.

8 And the Voice that I Heard out from Heaven, is Uttering with me again, and is Saying, You must Go Away, you must Take the Little Book that is made Opened in the Angel's Hand that Stands upon the sea and upon the earth.

9 And I went to the Angel, saying to him, You must give to me the Little Book, and He Said to me, You must Take and you must Devour it, and it shall be bitter to your belly, but definitely in your mouth it shall be sweet as honey.

10 And I took the Little Book from the Angel's Hand and devoured it, and then it was in my mouth as sweet honey, and when I ate, it was bitter to my belly.

11 Then He Said to me, You must Prophecy again to people, and nations, and tongues, and many kings.

Measure the Temple Sanctuary

11 Then there was made Given to me a reed like a staff, and the Angel had Stood Saying, You must raise up and measure the Temple Sanctuary of God and the Altar, and where Them that are therein Worshiping Him.

Holy City is tread down for 3 1/2 yrs

2 But the Court outside the Temple you must leave out, and you should not measure it, for it has been made given to the nations, even as they shall actually tread down the Holy City forty two months.

Two Witnesses Prophecy for 3 1/2 yrs

3 "And I (God) will Give to My Two Witnesses, and they shall Prophecy a thousand two hundred sixty days in sackcloth."

4 These are the Two Olive Trees, and the Two Candlesticks, Standing in the Presence of the God of the earth.

5 And if any man might be willing to hurt them, Fire goes out from their Mouth, and Devours their enemies, and if any man might be willing to hurt them, he in such a manner must be Killed.

6 These have Authority to Shut the Heaven, that it should not rain showers in the days of their Prophecy, and having Authority over the waters, turning them into blood, and to strike mortally to the earth with every plague, as often if They should Will.

Beast of pit shall kill the 2 Witnesses

7 And when they should have Finally Finished their Testimony, the wild beast that is ascending out from the bottomless pit shall make war against Them, and shall overcome Them, and shall kill Them.

8 And their dead bodies upon the street of the Great City, whereto also Our Lord was Made Crucified, which Spiritually is made called Sodom and Egypt.

9 And they of the people; and tribes, and tongues, and nations shall physically see their dead bodies three days and half, and they shall definitely not be concerned for putting Their dead bodies into the place of the dead.

10 And they that dwell upon the earth shall rejoice over them, and shall be made merry, and shall send gifts to one another, because these Two Prophets Tormented them that dwell upon the earth.

After 3 1/2 days the Witnesses Arise

11 And after three and a half days, the Spirit of Life from God Entered in Them, and They Stood upon their feet, and great fear fell down upon them that saw Them.

12 And They Heard a Great Voice from Heaven Saying to Them, You must Ascend Here. And they Ascended into Heaven in a Cloud, and their enemies saw Them.

Same hour a quake 7,000 men slain

13 And in the same hour a great earthquake occurred, and a tenth of the city fell down and seven thousands names of men killed in the earthquake, and the remaining became afraid, and attributed Glory to God of Heaven.

2nd Woe past, now 3rd Woe

14 And the Second Woe has gone, and Behold, the Third Woe is Coming quickly.

7th T (3rd Woe): World kingdoms fall and become God's to Reign Forever

15 And the Seventh Angel Sounded, and there was a Great Voice in Heaven Saying, The kingdoms of the satan's world have become of Our Lord and of His Christ, and He shall Reign Forever and Ever.

16 And the Twenty and Four Elders, who

are Sitting in the Presence of God upon His Throne, Fell Down upon their Faces and Worshiped God.

17 Saying, We are Giving Thanks to You, LORD GOD ALMIGHTY, WHO Is, and WHO Was, and WHO is Coming, because You are NOW Taking Your Great Miracle Power, and You Have Reigned.

Wrath for Justice, dead to be Judged, Reward Given, Destroy destroyers

18 And the nations have been made angry, and Your Wrath for Justice Has Come, and the Appointed Time of the dead to be Judged, and to Give the Reward to Your Bondslaves the Prophets, and to the Saints, and to those that are Fearing Your Name, the small and the great, also to Materially Destroy those that are materially destroying the earth.

Temple of God opened in Heaven

19 And the Temple of God has been Made Opened in Heaven, and the Ark of His Covenant was Made Seen in His Temple Sanctuary, and there were Lightnings, and Voices, and Thunderings, and Earthquake, and a Great Hail.

Woman in Heaven, twelve stars

12 And he saw the Spiritual Appearance, a great Miracle Sign in the Heaven, a Woman clothed with the sun and the moon under her feet, and upon her head a Crown of Twelve Stars,

2 And while having travailing in birth with a child made tormented, cries out and gave birth.

Red dragon in Heaven, 1/3 stars

3 And he saw the Spiritual Appearance, another of same kind Miracle Sign in the Heaven, and Behold, a great red flame colored dragon having seven heads and ten horns, and upon their heads seven crowns.

4 And his tail drew the third of the stars of Heaven, and cast them to earth, and the dragon was standing before the presence of the woman expecting to give birth, in order that when the Child was born, he might devour her Child.

She birthed a man child

5 And She delivered a Male Son, Who is Expected to Shepherd all the nations with a Scepter rod of iron, and Her Child was Made Caught Up to God, and to His Throne.

She fled into wilderness 3 1/2 yrs

6 And the Woman Fled into the desolate wilderness whereto She has a Place Prepared by God, in order that there She should be Nourished a thousand, two hundred, sixty days.

War in Heaven, Dragon cast out

7 And War occurred in Heaven. Michael and His Angels made War against the dragon, and the dragon and his angels made war,

8 And prevailed not, neither was made found their place further in Heaven.

9 And the great dragon was cast out, that old time serpent, called the devil and the satan, which is deceiving all of the inhabited earth, also his angels with him have been cast out.

10 So I heard a Great Voice, Saying in the Heaven, For now has become the Salvation, and Miracle Power, and Kingdom Rule of Our God, and the Authority of His Christ, because the accuser of our Brethren has been made Finally Cast Down, who accused in the Presence of Our God day and night,

11 And they Overcame him by the Blood of the Lamb, and by the Word of their Testimony, and they Loved not their souls until death.

12 Because of this, the Heavenlies must be Merry, and You that are Dwelling in Them. Woe to those dwelling on the earth, and on the sea, because the devil has come down to you, having great anger for he spiritually knows he is having little time.

Dragon persecuted the woman

13 And when the dragon spiritually saw that he was cast to the earth, he persecuted the Woman who Gave Birth to the Male.

Fled to wilderness for 3 1/2 yrs

14 And to the Woman has been made given two wings of a great eagle, that She might Fly into the desolate wilderness, into Her Place whereto she is Made Nourished there, a Time, and Times and half of a Time, away from the presence of the serpent.

15 And the serpent cast water out from his mouth as a flood after this Woman, in order that he might cause Her carried away by the flood.

16 And the earth helped the Woman, and the earth Opened its mouth, and completely swallowed the flood, that the dragon had been cast out from its mouth.

Dragon makes war with woman's Seed having the Testimony of Jesus

17 And the dragon was made angry by the Woman, and went to make war with the remaining Seed of Her, Who are by their choice Keeping the Commandments of God, and have the Testimony of Jesus Christ.

First beast out of sea

13 And I was made to stand upon the sand of the sea, and I Spiritually Saw a wild beast ascending out from the sea, having seven heads and ten horns, and upon his horns ten crowns, and upon his heads the name of blasphemy.

2 And the wild beast that I Spiritually Saw was like to a leopard, and his feet as a bear, and his mouth as the mouth of a lion, and the dragon gave to him his miracle power, and his throne, and his great authority.

3 And I Spiritually Saw one of his heads as now made slain to death, and the wound of his death made healed and all of the earth marveled after the wild beast.

All world worshiped dragon and beast

4 And they worshiped the dragon that gave authority to the wild beast, and worshiped the wild beast saying, Who is like the wild beast, who is able to make war with him?

Given power to continue 3 1/2 yrs

5 And there was given to him a mouth uttering also great blasphemy, also authority was made given to him to finalize forty two months.

Beast blasphemed God and His

6 And he opened his mouth in blasphemy against God, to blaspheme His Name, and His Tabernacle, and Those Dwelling in Heaven.

Power over Saints and to overcome them

7 And it was given to him to make war with the Saints and overcome them, and authority has been made given to him over every tribe and tongue and nation.

All on earth worship him (but Saints)

8 And all that dwell upon the earth shall worship him, whose names are definitely not made Written in the Book of Life of the Lamb Slain from Conception of the satan's world.

Here is patience, Faith of the Saints

9 If any man has an Ear, you must Hear.

10 If any man is accepting to be gathering together in captivity, he is going away into captivity, if anyone is accepting to killing by a sword, he must himself to be made killed by a sword. Here is the Endurance and the Faith of the Saints.

Another beast out of the earth

11 And I Spiritually Saw another of same kind wild beast ascending out from the earth, and having two horns like a lamb, and uttering as a dragon.

False prophet, authority of 1st beast

12 And he is exercising all the authority of the first wild beast in the presence of him, and causes the earth and they who dwell in it, that they worship the first wild beast, whose wound of death was made healed.

Causes all to worship image of 1st beast

13 And he does great miracle signs, so that he might call fire to come down from heaven to the earth in the presence of men. 14 So he deceives them that dwell upon the earth, through the miracle signs, that he has given to him to do in the presence of the wild beast, saying to them that dwell upon the earth to make an image to the wild beast, who is having the wound of the sword and lived.

15 And it was made given to him to give a spirit to the image of the wild beast, that then the image might utter, and might cause those whoever might not have worshiped the image of the wild beast, that they should be killed.

Causes all to receive the mark

16 And he causes all great and small, and rich and poor, and free and slaves, that they might be given a mark upon their right hand or upon their foreheads.

17 And that no man might be able to buy or sell anything except he is having the mark, or the name of the wild beast, or the number of his name.

18 Here is Wisdom. He that is having Understanding of mind, you must count the number of the wild beast, a number is for the man, and his number, 666.

Lamb and 144,000 on Mt. Sion

14 And I Spiritually Saw, also Behold a Lamb now Standing upon Mount Sion, and with Him hundred forty four thousands having the Name of their Father written upon their foreheads.

2 And I heard a Voice from Heaven, as a Voice of many waters, and as a Voice of great thunder, and a Voice heard of harpers harping on their harps.

3 And they Singing in the Spirit as a Song New of a different kind in the Presence of the Throne, and in the Presence of the Four Beasts and the Elders, and definitely no one able to learn the Song except the hundred forty four thousand, Who are now being made Bought from the earth.

4 These are they Who were not defiled with women, definitely not made unclean, for they are virgins. These are they Who follow the Lamb whereto He might move. These are those made Bought away from (among) men, the Firstfruit of God and the Lamb.

5 And in their mouth has been made found no subtle half-truth (deceit), for they are Faultless, in the Presence of the Throne of God.

Everlasting Gospel on earth

6 And I Spiritually Saw another of same kind Angel, Flying in the midst of Heaven, having the Eternal Gospel to proclaim to those dwelling upon the earth, and every nation, and tribe, and tongue, and people.

7 Saying with a Great Voice, You must be made to Fear God, and you must by your choice Attribute Glory to Him, for the hour of His Final Judgment has Come, and you must by your choice Worship Him that Created the Heaven, and the earth, and the sea, and fountains of waters.

Babylon fallen, that great city

8 And another of same kind Angel followed Saying, Fallen down, fallen down, Babylon, the great city, because she is now giving all nations to drink of the wine, of the Anger, for her fornication.

If anyone worship the beast

9 So then a Third Angel followed them Saying with a Great Voice, If any man worship the wild beast, and his image, and receives a mark upon his forehead or upon

his hand,

10 Also, the same shall drink of the wine of the Anger of God Made Poured out without constraint in the Cup or His Wrath for Justice, Then Tormented in fire and brimstone in the Presence of the Holy Angels, and in the Presence of the Lamb.

11 And the smoke of their state of Torment Ascends Forever and Ever. And If anyone receives the mark of his name, then they have no resting place day or night, who worship the wild beast and the image of him.

Here is the Endurance of Saints

12 Here is the Endurance of the Saints. Here are they that are continuously Keeping by their choice the Commandments of God, and the Faith of Jesus.

13 And I heard a Voice from Heaven Saying to me, You Must Write. Spiritually Blessed, the dead in the Lord dying from henceforth. Emphatically Yes, Says the Spirit, in order that they should be Refreshed from their Labors, and their Works by God are Following with them.

The Harvest of the Age

14 And I Spiritually Saw, then Behold, A White Cloud, and upon the Cloud Sitting like the Son of Man having on His Head a Golden Crown, and in His Hand a Sharp Sickle.

15 And another Angel of same kind Came Out from the Temple Sanctuary, Crying Out with a Great Voice to Him Sitting in the Cloud, You must Thrust Your Sickle, and You must Reap, because the Hour to Reap has Come to You, because the Harvest of the earth has withered.

16 And He that is Sitting on the Cloud, Put in His Sickle to the earth, and Reaped the earth.

17 And another of same kind Angel Came Out from the Temple Sanctuary which is in Heaven, Having also His Sharp Sickle.

18 And another Angel of same kind Came Out from the altar, having Authority over burning fire, and Called for with a Great Screaming to Him having a Sharp Sickle Saying, You must Thrust your Sharp Sickle, and gather the Clusters of the Vine of the earth, since the Grapes have been Fully Ripe.

19 And the Angel put in His Sickle into the earth, and Gathered the Vine of the earth and Cast into the great Winepress of the Anger of God.

20 And the Winepress was Tread Down outside the City, and blood came out from the Winepress as far as the bridles of the horses, for a thousand six hundred furlongs.

Seven Last Plagues from Wrath of God

15 And I Spiritually Saw another of same kind Miracle Sign in the Heaven, Great and Marvelous, Seven Angels having the Seven Last Plagues, because in Them have been made Finally Fulfilled the Anger of God.

2 And I Spiritually Saw as a Glass Sea mixed with Fire, and the Overcomers of the wild beast and of his image and of his mark of the number of his name, Standing on the Glass Sea having Harps of God.

3 And they Sang in the Spirit the Song of Moses, the Bondslave of God, and the Song of the Lamb, Saying, Great and Marvelous Your Works by God, Oh Lord God Almighty, Righteous and True The Ways of You, the King of Saints.

4 Who should never ever fear You, Lord, and should Attribute Glory to Your Name? Now Alone Personally Holy, all nations shall Now Come and shall Worship in the Presence of You, because Your Righteous Actions have been Made Manifest.

5 And after these things, I Spiritually Saw and Behold, the Temple Sanctuary of the Tabernacle of the Testimony in Heaven has been Made Opened.

6 And the Seven Angels Came Out from the Temple Sanctuary, Having the Seven

Plagues, Dressed with Purified and Bright Linen, and Clothed About with Golden Chest Girdles.

Seven Vials given to Seven Angels
7   And One of the Four Beasts Gave to the Seven Angels Seven Golden Vials Full of the Anger of God, Who Lives Forever and Ever.

8   And the Temple Sanctuary was Made Full of Smoke of the Glory of God and of His Miracle Power, so then no man was able to enter into the Temple, until the Seven Plagues of the Seven Angels should be Made Finally Finished.

Pour out the 7 Vials upon the earth
16 And I Heard a Great Voice out from the Temple Sanctuary Saying to the Seven Angels, You must be Going Away and Pouring Out the Vials of the Anger of God upon the earth.

1st Vial: Sores on those with beast's mark
2   And the First Went and Poured Out His Vial upon the earth, and it became a sore evil work and evil upon men, who are having the mark of the wild beast, and worshiping to his image.

2nd Vial: All sea life dies
3   And the Second Angel Poured Out His Vial upon the sea, and it became as blood of the dead, and every living soul died in the sea.

3rd Vial: All fresh water became as blood
4   And the Third Angel Poured Out His Vial upon the rivers and upon the fountains of waters, and they became blood.

5   And I heard the Angel of the waters Saying, You are Righteous, Lord, WHO Is, and WHO Was, and WHO is Personally Holy, because You have Judged these things.

6   For they have shed the Holy Blood of the Prophets, and you have given them blood to drink, because they are worthy.

7   And I Heard another of same kind out from the altar, Saying, Emphatically Yes, Lord God Almighty, True and Righteous, Your Final Judgments.

4th Vial: Sun scorched the earth
8   And the Fourth Angel Poured Out His Vial upon the sun, and it was Made Given to Him to scorch men with fire.

9   And the men were Made Scorched with great heat, and they blasphemed the Name of God, Who is having Authority over these Plagues, but these repented not to Attribute to Him the Glory.

5th Vial: Darkness
10   And the Fifth Angel Poured Out His Vial upon the throne of the wild beast, and his kingdom rule became darkened, and they were chewing their tongues from the pain.

11   And blasphemed the God of Heaven from their pain and from their sores, and definitely repented not of their man works.

6th Vial: Euphrates dried up
12   And the Sixth Angel Poured Out His Vial upon the Great Euphrates river, and dried up the water of it, in order that the way of the kings of the rising sun should be made prepared.

Evil spirits gather kings to Armageddon
13   And I Spiritually Saw three morally impure spirits like frogs: out from the mouth of the dragon, and out from the mouth of the wild beast, and out from the mouth of the false prophet.

14   For they are spirits of demons working miracle signs, which go out to the kings of the earth, and all of the inhabited earth, to gather together themselves for the war of that Great Day of God Almighty.

15   Behold, I am Coming as a thief. Spiritual Blessed is He Watching and Keeping His Garments, that He is not

walking naked, and they might be seeing his indecency.

16 And He Gathered Together them into the place, being Hebrew script, called Armageddon.

7th Vial: Earthquake, all islands and mountains worldwide disappear

17 And the Seventh Angel Poured Out His Vial, into the air, and came out a Great Voice from the Temple Sanctuary of Heaven, from the Throne, Saying, It is Now Ended.

18 And there Became Voices and Thunders and Lightnings, and there Become a great Earthquake, such as not occurred since whereon men were upon the earth, so Great an Earthquake, so Great.

19 And the Great City became into three parts, and the cities, and nations have fallen down, and the great Babylon has been itself Remembered before the Presence of God, to Give to her the Cup of the wine of the Anger of His Wrath for Justice.

20 And every island has fled, and mountains have not definitely been made found.

Great hail falls on men

21 And Great Hail as weight of a talent (75+ lbs) came down out from heaven upon men, and men blasphemed God, from the plague of the Hail, for their plague is Exceedingly Great.

Religious Babylon is woman on beast

17 And there came one of the Seven Angels, having the Seven Vials, and Uttered with me, Saying to me, You must Come Forward, I will Show you the Judgment of the great whore that is sitting upon the many waters,

2 With whom the kings of the earth have sexually sinned, and the dwellers of the earth have been made drunk from the wine of her fornication.

3 So He Carried me Away into a desolate wilderness in the Spirit, and I Spiritually Saw a woman sitting upon a scarlet wild beast, full of names of blasphemy, having seven heads and ten horns.

4 And the woman was clothed in purple clothes and scarlet and gilded with gold and most precious stones and with pearls, having a golden cup in her hand, full of abominations and filthiness of her fornication.

5 And upon her forehead a name is written, MYSTERY BABYLON the GREAT, THE MOTHER OF HARLOTS, AND THE ABOMINATION of the EARTH.

6 And I Spiritually Saw the woman drunken from the blood of the Saints, and from the blood of the Martyrs for Jesus, and I marveled Spiritually Seeing her with great awe.

7 And the Angel Spoke to me, Why then have you marveled? I Spirit Say to you the Mystery of the woman, and the wild beast that is bearing her, having the seven heads and the ten horns.

8 The wild beast that you Spiritually Saw was, and is not, and is expected to ascend from the bottomless pit, and to go away into damnation. And they that are dwelling on the earth shall be made to marvel, their names being definitely not written in the Scroll of Life since Conception of the satan's world. These specifically are physically seeing the wild beast, who then was, and is definitely not, even though is.

9 Here the Understanding of mind that is having Wisdom. The seven heads are seven mountains, whereto the woman herself is sitting upon.

10 And there are seven kings, five have fallen down, and one is, the other of same kind not yet come. And when he should come, he must be continuing himself a little.

11 And the wild beast that was lifted up, and is definitely not, then he is eighth, and is from the seven, and is going away into damnation.

12 And the ten horns which you Spiritually Saw are ten kingdoms, which have not

received the kingdom rule of satan yet, but definitely receive authority as kings one hour with the wild beast.

13 These have one advice, and distribute their miracle power and authority to the wild beast.

14 These make war with the Lamb, and the Lamb shall Overcome them, because the Lord of Lords is also the King of Kings, and those with Him, Inwardly Called (Born Again) and Elect and Faithful.

15 And He Says to me, The waters which you Spiritually Saw, where the whore is sitting, they are peoples, and multitudes of peoples, and nations, and tongues.

Religious Babylon is destroyed

16 And the ten horns which you Spiritually Saw on the wild beast, these shall hate the whore, and shall finalize her bringing to desolation and naked, even shall eat her sinful flesh natures, and shall fully burn her with fire.

God fulfills His Will in their heart

17 Because God Gave into their hearts to do His Advice, and to Finalize Advice as one, to give their kingdom rule to the wild beast, until the Words of God should have been made Finally Fulfilled.

The woman is the great city

18 And the woman that you Spiritually Saw is that great city having kingdom rule over the kings of the earth.

Commercial Babylon is destroyed

18 And after these things, I Spiritually Saw another Angel of same kind coming down from Heaven having Great Authority, and the earth has been Enlightened from His Glory.

2 And He Cried Out in a Great Strength Voice Saying, Fallen down, fallen down, Babylon the great also has become a habitation of demons, and prison of every morally impure spirit, and prison of every morally impure fowl, and are now made continuously hated,

3 Because all the nations are now continuously drinking of the wine of the Anger against her fornication, and the kings of the earth have sexually sinned with her, and the merchants of the earth from the miracle power of her self-serving strength, have by their choice been rich.

4 And I heard another of same kind Voice from Heaven Saying, You must come away from her, My people, that you might not by your choice have participated in her sins, so also that you might not by your choice have received from the plagues of her.

5 For her sins have been made to follow as far as to Heaven, and God remembered her hurtful wrongs.

6 You must pay her as she has paid you and you must double her double according to her man works. Every cup which she has poured out, you must pour out to her double.

7 How much she has glorified herself, and lived lustfully so much. You must give to her a state of torment and mourning: for in her heart she says, I am sitting a queen, and I am definitely not a widow, and I definitely am not and should never ever have known mourning.

8 Because of this, the plagues of her death shall now come in one day, and she shall fully burn with fire, then mourning and famine. For the Stronger Lord God is Judging her.

9 And when seeing the smoke and burning of her the kings of the earth shall bewail over her. They shall weep for her with whom they have sexually sinned and lived lustfully.

10 Standing at a distance away for the fear of her state of torment saying, Woe, Woe, that great city Babylon, that mighty city, for in one hour Your Final Judgment has come.

11 And the merchants of the earth weep and mourn over her, because she is

definitely not buying their merchandise anymore.

12 The merchandise of gold, and silver, and most precious stone, and pearl, and wearing fine linen, and purple clothing, and silk, and scarlet, and all thyme wood, and every ivory vessel, and all most precious belonging of a wooden item, and brass coin, and iron, and marble,

13 And cinnamon, and incense, and ointment, and frankincense, and wine, and oil, and fine flour, and wheat, and animals, and sheep, and horses, and carriages, and bodies and souls of men.

14 And the harvest fruit of evil desire of your soul is gone from you. And all things that are dainty and bright have gone from you, and you should no more never ever find them anymore.

15 The merchants of these things, that have been rich from her, shall stand away at a distance through fear of her state of torment weeping and mourning.

16 And saying, Woe, Woe, that great city, clothed in fine linen, and purple, and scarlet, and gilded in gold, and most precious stone, and pearls,

17 For in one hour so many riches has been brought to desolation, and every ship master and everyone upon the ships, and fellow traveler and sailors and those who are working in the sea, stood away from at a distance.

18 Yet cried out, Behold Attentively, the smoke and burning of her, saying, What is like this great city?

19 And casting dirt upon their heads, and crying out, Weep and mourn, saying, Woe, Woe, that great city, whereby all have been rich that are having ships in the sea from her costliness, but in one hour they have been made brought to desolation.

20 Be Merry over her, Heaven and the Holy Apostles and Prophets, because God has Judged with Your condemnation on her.

21 And one Mighty Angel took up a stone as a great grinding millstone and cast into the sea, Saying, In such a manner with suddenness shall the great city Babylon be put away, and never ever be found further.

22 And the voice of harpers, and minstrels, and pipers, and trumpeters should never ever be heard among you further, and every craftsman, and all crafts should never ever be found among you further, and the sound of the grinding millstone should never ever be heard among you further.

23 And light of a candle should never ever appear in you further, and a voice of a bridegroom and a bride should never ever be heard among you any longer. The merchants of you were the great men of the earth, because by assistance by evil spirits (via any method including drugs), all the nations have been made deceived.

By her all Prophets and Saints slain

24 And by her, the blood of Prophets and Saints, has been made found also of everyone of them made slain upon the earth.

Babylon gone, Praise in Heaven

19 And after these things, I heard a Great Voice of a large multitude of people in Heaven Saying, Alleluia, Salvation, and Glory, and Honor, and Miracle Power to the Lord our God.

2 Because True and Righteous, His Final Judgments, for He has Judged the great whore, who spiritually corrupted the earth with her fornication, and He has Avenged the blood of His Bondslaves at her hand.

3 And second, Spirit is now Saying continuously, Alleluia, and the smoke of her ascends Forever and Ever.

4 And the Twenty and Four Elders, even the Four Beasts, fall down, and Worship God Sitting on the Throne Saying, Amen. Alleluia!

5 And a Voice came out from the Throne Saying, You Must Praise our God, All His Bondslaves, and You that are Fearing Him, both the great and small.

Marriage Supper of the Lamb

6   And I heard as a voice of a large multitude of people, and as a voice of many waters, and as a voice of mighty thunders Saying, Alleluia, for the Lord God Almighty has Reigned.

7   We should be Glad and exceedingly Rejoicing, and should Attribute Him Glory (Spiritual Perfection) for the Marriage of the Lamb has Come, and His Wife has Prepared Herself.

8   And to Her was given, that She should be Clothed in Fine Linen Purified and Bright, for the Fine Linen is the Righteous Actions of the Saints.

9   And He Says to me, Write Spiritually Blessed, They that are being made called to the Marriage Supper of the Lamb. And He Said to me, These are the True Spiritual Words of God.

10   And I fell down before His feet to worship Him, and He Said to me, You must Behold Attentively, Am I not your Fellow Bondslave and your Brother, having the Testimony of Jesus? You must Worship to God, for the Testimony of Jesus Is the Spirit of Prophecy.

Word of God on White Horse

11   And I saw Heaven made Opened, and Behold a White Horse, and Sitting upon him is being called Faithful and True. And in Righteousness He is Judging and Making War.

12   And His Eyes as a Fiery Flame, and upon His Head having many Crowns is now Made Written a Name that no one is now Spiritually Discerning except Him.

13   And He is now made Clothed with Garments dipped in blood, and His Name is made called, The Word of God.

Heaven's Armies on White Horses

14   And the Armies in Heaven followed Him upon White Horses being Dressed with Fine Linen, White and Purified.

15   And from His Mouth is Going Out a Sharp Long Broad Two-Edged Sword, that with It He should Strike mortally the nations, and He will Shepherd them with a Staff of Iron, and He is Treading Down the Winepress of the Wine of His Anger, and the Wrath for Justice of God Almighty.

16   And He has on His Garments and upon His Thigh a Name Written, KING OF KINGS, AND LORD OF LORDS.

17   And I Spiritually Saw one Angel standing in the sun, and Crying Out in a Great Voice Saying, to all the fowls flying in the midst of heaven, Come now and gather together for the Supper of the Great God.

18   In order that you should eat the sinful flesh natures of kings, and sinful flesh natures of chief captains, and sinful flesh natures of the mighty, and flesh natures of horses, and of them sitting upon them, and sinful flesh natures both of every free and also slave, and both least and great.

19   Also, I Spiritually Saw the wild beast, and the kings of the earth and their armies, now made gathering together to do war against Him Sitting Upon a Horse and against His Army.

Beast and false prophet cast into hell

20   And the wild beast has been made caught and with that one false prophet, that did the miracle signs in the presence of him, with which he deceived those that by their choice received the mark of the wild beast, and by their choice are worshiping the image of him. These two were Made Cast living into the Lake of Fire Made Burning with Brimstone.

21   And the remaining have been Made Killed by the Long Broad Two-Edged Sword Going Out from the Mouth of Him Sitting on the Horse. And then all the fowls have been made filled from the sinful flesh natures of them.

Satan in bottomless pit for 1,000 years

20   So then I Spiritually Saw an Angel coming down out from Heaven having the Key of the bottomless pit, and a Great Chain in His Hand.

2   And He Retained the dragon, the old time serpent, which is the devil and satan (rebeller), then Bound him a Thousand Years.

3   Then Cast him into the bottomless pit, and Shut him and sealed over him that he should not deceive the nations further until the Thousand Years should be made Finally Fulfilled. When following these things, He Must Remove him for a little time.

Faithful Saints Reign 1,000 years

4   Then, I Spiritually Saw Thrones and They Sitting Down upon them, and Judgment has been Made Given to them, also the souls of them beheaded because of their Testimony of Jesus and even because of the Word of their God, and who worshiped not by their choice the wild beast neither the image of him, and took not by their choice the mark upon their forehead, nor upon their hand, so they have Lived by their choice and have Reigned by their choice with Christ a Thousand Years.

This is First Resurrection

5   This is the First Resurrection. But the remaining of the dead lived by their choice definitely not again until after a Thousand Years is finally Made Fulfilled.

2nd death has no power on them

6   Spiritually Blessed and Holy, he that is having by his choice part in the First Resurrection. On these the second death is definitely having no authority, but definitely they shall be Priests of God and His Christ and shall Reign with Him a Thousand Years.

Satan released for short while

7   And when the Thousand should have been made Finally Fulfilled, the satan (rebeller) shall be made Removed Out from his prison.

8   And shall come out to deceive the nations within the four corners of the earth. Gog and Magog gathered together them for war, that number as the sand of the sea.

9   And they ascended upon the width of the earth, and surrounded the camp of the Saints and the Loved City. Then Fire Came Down from God out from Heaven and Devoured them.

Devil cast into Lake of Fire

10 And the devil, which by his choice is deceiving them, has been Made Cast into the Lake of Fire and Brimstone, whereto shall be the wild beast and the false prophet, while made tormented day and night Forever and Ever.

Great White Throne Judgment

11 And I Spiritually Saw a Great White Throne, and He that is sitting upon It from Whose Presence the earth and the heaven fled, and no place was made found for them.

12 And I Spiritually Saw the dead, great and small, now Standing in the Presence of God, and Scrolls were made Opened, and another Scroll of the same kind has been made Opened which is that of Life, and out from the dead they have been made Judged by those Writings made upon the Scrolls according to their man works.

13 And the sea gave from within her dead, and death and Hades gave those within their dead, and every person has been made Judged according to their man works.

This is the second death

14 And death and Hades have been made cast into the lake of fire. This is the second death.

15 And if any person, any one, is definitely not made found, now made Written, in the Book of Life, he has been Made Cast into the Lake of Fire.

New Heaven and New Earth

21 And I Spiritually Saw a New of a Different Kind Heaven, and a New of a Different Kind Earth, because the first Heaven and the first Earth have passed away, and the sea is Definitely No More.

2   And I, John, Spiritually Saw the City, Holy Jerusalem New of a Different Kind, coming down from God, out from Heaven, prepared as a Bride Adorned for Her Husband.

Tabernacle of God with Men

3   And I Heard a Great Voice from Heaven Saying, Behold, the Tabernacle of God With Men, and He shall be Dwelling With Them, and They shall be His People, and God Himself, shall be With Them, Their God.

4   And God shall Blot Out the tears away from their eyes, and death shall Definitely Be No More, Neither mourning, Nor strong crying, Nor pain. They shall Definitely Be No More, for those earlier things Have Gone.

I Make ALL New, of a Different Kind

5   And He That Is Sitting upon His Throne Spoke, Behold, I am Finalizing All Things New of a Different Kind. And He Says to me, You Must Write, because these Spiritual Words are True and Faithful.

6   And He Spoke to me. It has Come to Pass, I AM, the Alpha and the Omega, the Beginning and the End. I will Give to him Thirsting Continuously by his choice from the Fountain of Water of Life Freely.

Overcomers Inherit All things

7   He that is Overcoming Continuously by his choice shall Inherit All Things, and I will Be His God and he shall Be to Me a Son.

8   But the terrified, and faithless, and made abhorring, and deliberate murderers, and fornicators, and those assisted by evil spirits (via any method including drugs), and idolaters, and all false, their part (is) in the Lake with Burning Fire and Brimstone, which is the second death.

New Jerusalem, the Lamb's Wife

9   And one of the Seven Angels Came to me, which had the Seven Vials being Full of the Seven Last Plagues, and Uttered with me Saying, You must Come Forward, I will Show you the Bride, the Lamb's Wife.

10 And me He Carried Away in the Spirit to a great and high mountain, then He Showed to me the city of the Great Holy Jerusalem Coming Down from Heaven from God.

11 Having the Glory of God and Her Light of God, like a most precious stone, as a jasper stone being crystal clear.

12 And also having a great high Wall, having twelve Gates and at the Gates twelve Angels, and names inscribed which are the Twelve Tribes of Sons of Israel.

13 For the east Three Gates, for the north Three Gates, for the south Three Gates, and for the west Three Gates.

14 And the Wall of the City having Twelve Foundations, and upon them the names of the Twelve Apostles of the Lamb.

15 And He that Uttered with me was Having a Golden Reed that measured the City, and the Gates thereof, and the Wall thereof.

16 And the City is laid Four Corners Squared, and the Length of it is so as also the Width, and he Measured the City with the Reed in the place of Twelve Thousands Furlongs, the Length and the Width and the Height of it are Equal.

17 And he Measured the wall of it, Hundred Forty Four Cubits, by a measure of man, which is by an Angel.

18 And the Construction of the Wall was of itself jasper, and the City Pure gold, like in appearance as glass Purified.

19 And the Foundations of the Wall of the City is made adorned with every most precious stone. The first a jasper Foundation,

the second sapphire, the third chalcedony, the fourth emerald,

20 The fifth sardonyx, the sixth sardius, the seventh chrysolite, the eighth beryl, the ninth topaz, the tenth chrysoprasus, the eleventh jacinth gem, the twelfth amethyst.

21 And the Twelve Gates twelve pearls, to each one, every Gate was from one pearl, and the Street of the City Purified gold, as appearance as transparent glass.

22 And I Spiritually Saw no Temple in it, because the Lord God Almighty and the Lamb, He is the Temple.

23 And the City has no need of the sun, neither the moon in order that to shine in it, because the Glory of God gave Light to it, and the Lamb the Spiritual Light of it.

24 And the nations which are made Saved shall Walk in the Light of it, and the kings of the earth are bringing their Glory and Honor into it.

25 And the Gates of it should never ever be made Shut by day, because there shall definitely not be night there.

26 And they shall bring the Glory and Honor of the nations into it.

27 And except those Now Made Written in the Lamb's Book of Life, there should never ever enter into it any being made unholy or doing abomination and lying.

Pure River of Water and Tree of Life

22 And He Showed me a Pure River of Water of Life, Bright as Crystal, going out from the Throne of God and of the Lamb.

2 In the Middle of its Street, and on either Side of the River, from there on either Side a Tree of Life, yielding twelve Fruits according to each month, yielding its Fruit one to every person, and the Leafs of the Tree for household Health of the Nations.

Throne of God and the Lamb

3 There shall not be any curse there further, but the Throne of God and the Lamb shall be in it, and His Bondslaves shall be Devoted to Him.

4 And they shall see the Spiritual Appearance of His Face, and His Name upon their foreheads.

5 And there will be no night there, and they are having no need of lamps or light of sun, for the Lord God Gives Light to Them, and They shall Reign Forever and Ever.

Prophets and Saying are True

6 And He Spoke to me, These Spiritual Words Faithful and True, and the Lord God of the Holy Prophets Sent Out His Angel to Show to His Bondslaves what must Occur therein Swiftly.

7 Behold, I am Coming Quickly. Spiritually Blessed is he that is Holding as Sacred My Spiritual Words of the Prophecy of this Book.

8 And I, John, am Spiritually Seeing and Hearing these things, and when I Heard and Saw, I fell down to Worship before the feet of the Angel, who is Showing me these things.

9 Then He Says to me, You must Behold Attentively, because I am your Fellow Bondslave, and of your Brethren, the Prophets, and those who are Keeping the Words of This One Book, Worship God.

Seal not the Prophecies of this Book

10 And Says to me, You should not Seal the Words of the Prophecy of this Book, because the Appointed Time is near.

Pay every man his Works-by-God

11 He that is unjust must be unjust still, and he that is filthy must be filthy still, and he that Righteous must be Made Righteous still, and he that is Holy must be Made Holy still.

12 And, Behold, I am Coming Quickly, and My Reward with Me, to Pay every man as his Work by God shall be.

13 I AM, the Alpha and the Omega, the Beginning and the End, the First and the Last.

Requirements to Access the Tree of Life
14 Spiritually Blessed, they that are Doing His Commandments, in order that He shall have Authority to the Tree of Life, and They should have Entered through the Gates into the City.

15 For outside the dogs (unholy people), and those assisted by evil spirits (via any method including drugs), and fornicators, and the deliberate murderers, and the idolaters, and whoever is affectionately loving and making a lie.

16 I, Jesus have Sent My Angel to Bear Record of These Things to you in the Assemblies. I AM, the Root and the Kindred of David, the Bright and Morning Star.

17 And the Spirit and the Bride Continuously Say "You Must Come by your choice, and He Continuously Hearing, you Must Speak and (say) you Must Come by your choice. And Those that are Continuously Thirsting, you Must Come by your choice. And Whoever is Continuously Willing, you Must be Continuously Taking to Receive by your choice the Water of Life Freely".

18 Because I also Give Witness to everyone Hearing the Spiritual Words of this Prophecy of this Book, if anyone adds to These Things, God shall Add to him the Plagues now Made Written in this Book.

19 And If any man might Take Away from the Spiritual Words of the Book of this Prophecy, God shall Take Away his part from the Book of Life and from the Holy City, and that Now Made Written in This Book.

20 He Who is Testifying to These Things is Saying, Emphatically Yes, I am Coming Quickly. Truly. Emphatically Yes, You Must be Coming, Lord Jesus!

21 The Grace of our Lord Jesus Christ, with you all. Amen.

Notes

Notes

Notes

Notes